A SHIP OF THE AIR

DRIVING TO THE FUTURE

STILL FROM *When the Wind Blows*

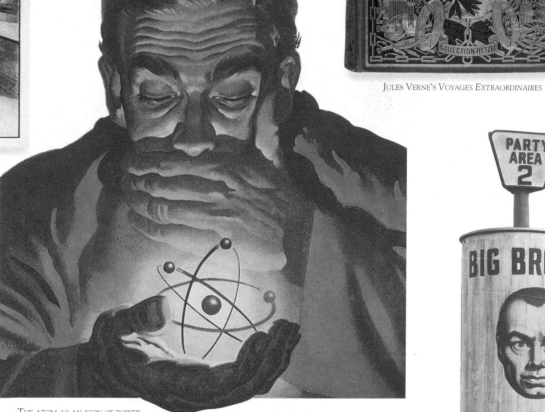
THE ATOM AS AN ICON OF POWER

Jules Verne's *Voyages Extraordinaires*

JAPANESE COMIC
Appleseed

STILL FROM *1984*

19TH-CENTURY "BUILDING MACHINE"

THE ILLUSTRATED ENCYCLOPEDIA

JOHN CLUTE

DORLING KINDERSLEY

LONDON • NEW YORK • STUTTGART

A DORLING KINDERSLEY BOOK

PROJECT EDITORS
CANDIDA FRITH-MACDONALD
TRACIE LEE

SENIOR ART EDITOR
LEE GRIFFITHS

DESIGNER
WENDY BARTLET

MANAGING EDITOR
KRYSTYNA MAYER

MANAGING ART EDITOR
DEREK COOMBES

PICTURE RESEARCHER
JOHN URLING-CLARK

DTP DESIGNER
CRESSIDA JOYCE

PRODUCTION CONTROLLER
RUTH CHARLTON

First published in Great Britain in 1995 by Dorling Kindersley Limited,
9 Henrietta Street, London WC2 8PS

Copyright © 1995 Dorling Kindersley Limited, London
Text copyright © 1995 John Clute

A CIP catalogue record for this book is available
from the British Library

ISBN 0 7513 0202 3

Colour reproduced by Colourscan, Singapore
Printed and bound in Italy by A. Mondadori, Verona

CONTENTS

EARLY SF SPACESHIP

ROBBY THE
ROBOT

*STAR TREK: THE
NEXT GENERATION*

INTRODUCTION

IT HAS BEEN A BIG HUNDRED years in every sense, a great, bucking bronco of a century, and here we are at the end of it. But where is here? And who are we? And where are we going at such a rate?

Over the long decades of the 20th century, millions of words have been expended by thousands of scholars, and others, in attempts to answer questions like these, and there are times when the solutions seem more confused than the problems. The planet is buzzing with human activity, and with stress. The human race itself is more active than ever before, more numerous, more powerful, more dangerous, more happy, more desolate, more alive, more dead. A vast array of futures beguiles and torments us all, and there are thousands of choices that we – as a race – must make about who we are, where we intend to end up, and how many worlds we are going to need in order to house our rocketing populations, and to keep our children from starvation.

WHEN WORLDS COLLIDE

The literature of power

Everything we do now has a direct and massive effect on the years to come. No wonder SF is – according to some – the literature of the century. It is, after all, the only genre of fiction that directly addresses the true nature of the times we live in, and describes the powers we now wield. More than in any previous era, every single thing we do counts. Because we are now so powerful, and numerous, and because we now have the knowledge to transform both our world and ourselves utterly, for good or for ill, each choice we make today has a previously unprecedented, whiplash effect on tomorrow. We do have that much power, all of us.

BATMAN

SF has given joy to millions, and this book tells the story of those stories; but it is also the genre of literature that focuses on that terrible, exciting, alluring, dangerous power we all share.

SF is an acronym for at least three terms used to describe stories usually set in the future. It designates Science Fiction, and that is what I almost always mean in this book when I say SF. But to some, it also means Science Fantasy, which I do not pay much attention to; and it can refer to Speculative Fiction, a phrase that some critics prefer to Science Fiction, for reasons of accuracy and in the hope of imparting greater dignity to their studies. Anyone who wishes to substitute Speculative Fiction for Science Fiction, anywhere in this book, can do so without misunderstanding a word of what is being said.

Defining the terms

What I mean by SF – whether I use the term for Science Fiction or for Speculative Fiction – is simple. Any story that argues the case for a changed world that has not yet come into being is an SF story. But two of these terms need a bit of comment.

A "world" is just that: SF is about worlds, not scenes. It may be a big change for Dickens's Oliver Twist to find his own true home, but his discovery does not change the nature of the laws that govern the world. But if Oliver were an alien – like the lost child in Steven Spielberg's *E.T.* – the entire world could be transformed when he found his home ship, because we would know that our world was not alone, and this knowledge would alter the future for us all.

The other word is "argue". SF is a literature of possible world-changes, however unlikely they may appear;

WHO GOES THERE?

possible continuations of history over the sand-reefs of the Millennium, into brave new centuries. If it had turned out that the vast ring around the sun in Larry Niven's *Ringworld* had been set in place by the wicked Norse god Loki, his book would have been fantasy, and not SF at all, no matter how realistically he had described the ring as it spun. SF writers present us with their changed worlds in terms that are consistent with the language, the assumptions, and the arguments of contemporary science, or in terms that are consistent with our profound sense that human history is a continuous reality, and that changes flow from what we know of that reality. Good SF says:

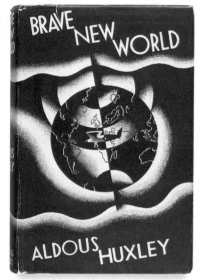

BRAVE NEW WORLD

if A is the case, it follows that B can happen. If physics say black holes exist, it follows that wormholes can happen. If human history does breed dictators, *Nineteen Eighty-Four* can happen.

Good SF – which is what this book is all about – can be enormously entertaining, or direly admonitory; it can provide us with fascinating thought experiments to while away the hours, or extrapolate future dystopias from the politics of the present; it can generate visions of tomorrow's world, or of worlds aeons hence; it can warn, or it can soothe. Because it faces into the wind of the future, it can accustom us to the underlying great fact that shapes our lives at the end of this extraordinary century. That great fact, as I have already said, is change.

The life-story of a genre

SF: The Illustrated Encyclopedia is a guided tour of stories about a million tomorrows. It talks about "Proto SF" stories from earlier centuries, and then goes on to the 19th century, when the genre began to take shape in the works of Mary Shelley, Jules Verne and H.G. Wells; but mostly it looks at the 20th century. We see how the genre took formal shape in the United States,

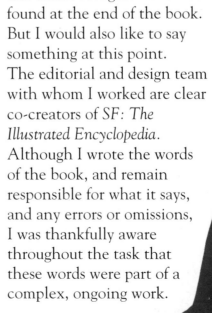

FANTASY AND SCIENCE FICTION
MAGAZINE SPACE STATION

and how American SF spread over the world; we see how SF in other countries also developed, and how very different the different kinds of SF can be.

We look at the guesses earlier SF writers made about the future; but always remembering that the important thing was not to guess right, because SF writers are not futurologists, and never pretend to be – the important thing is the worthy excitement and raw thrill of making any guess at all.

The modern mature genre, and some of the hundreds of active writers, film-makers, editors, and publishers who all keep it so abundantly lively, are examined at length. There are many brilliant stories, and some clunkers; some prescient guesses about the feel of tomorrow, and some clear misses. But again and again, one is reminded of the fact that SF accustoms us to looking; it does not, in the end, tell us what we are going to have to see. SF is the window, not the view.

The making of the book

Like any book that marries together pictures and words, *SF: The Illustrated Encyclopedia* has been a collaborative enterprise. A long list of sincere and necessary thanks and acknowledgments can be found at the end of the book. But I would also like to say something at this point. The editorial and design team with whom I worked are clear co-creators of *SF: The Illustrated Encyclopedia.* Although I wrote the words of the book, and remain responsible for what it says, and any errors or omissions, I was thankfully aware throughout the task that these words were part of a complex, ongoing work.

FLASH GORDON

JOHN CLUTE

future VISIONS

SCIENCE FICTION HAS BEEN praised and criticized as a predictor of the future, both perhaps unfairly. SF has never really aimed to tell us when we might reach other planets, or develop new technologies, or meet aliens: SF speculates about why we might want to do these things, and how their consequences might affect our lives and our planet. Decade-by-decade, this chapter looks at the hopes and fears of this century through the eyes of SF, of politicians, and of the news and current events of the day. Some of them are so wildly off the mark that they look laughable now; others look surprisingly close to home.

ABOVE: 1920s CIGARETTE CARD
LEFT: STILL FROM THE FILM *JUST IMAGINE*

THE 19TH CENTURY: MIGHTY MACHINES

Taxi of the future
Need a cab? Nothing simpler. Just go to your window and wave at an aerial seashell.

THE 19TH CENTURY DAWNED with the world looking very much as it had always looked. Populations were growing, but had not begun to explode noticeably. Steam engines had been invented, but the locomotive and the iron railways that would cross shire and vale had not. The Battle of Trafalgar was fought in sailing ships. But beneath the surface sameness, great engines of change were beginning to turn over the soil of the world. As the century progressed, it began to seem that – sooner or later – somebody would invent something to deal with every challenge, and that they would do so soon.

The last half of the century did indeed experience a tidal wave of innovations – it was the heyday, after all, of geniuses like Thomas Alva Edison. But for every real invention, there were a hundred speculative dreams. Never before – or since – has there ever been such a huge and exuberant expression of joy at the way things might work, and carry us all away.

Fantastical flight
Here the old world and the new meet, in a chimerical cargo ship straight out of a Bestiary of Ideas that Never Flew. Note the Latin tags, the anchors, the huts hanging below the keel – and the wings.

Rote learning
One of the central obsessions of thinkers as the 19th century drew to a close was regularity. It had become obvious that machines worked well because they did exactly the same thing – spun, chugged, turned, wove – again and again. Exactly the same principle is applied here to the education of children. The fact that the illustration – from a French series of collectors' cards – is a joke should not hide the fact that a serious dream is here revealed: education by rote.

Machines for building with

This is the same dream as the teaching machine, from the same series of cards, but this time it is all the more open. The vision here may seem both primitive and over-elaborate – and visions like this were soon being mocked by illustrators like W. Heath Robinson and Rube Goldberg – but the underlying principle is deadly serious. One architect, pushing buttons, can erect a building that is identical to the plan.

Seeing is believing

Here is a vision of our own future, now that videophones are being test-marketed everywhere. The apparatus may be complex, and the image unrealistically large, but the cartoonist has latched onto a real issue: in the privacy of home, what is proper behaviour in front of an invading screen?

Mechanical farming

Old habits take a long while to die. Here we see a steam-driven robot hauling a plough – the tractor had not yet been conceived. This plough-robot is a close cousin to the Steam Man of the Prairie, who rampaged through many late-19th-century dime novels.

THE 1900S: THE FUTURE OF THE CITY

AS THE 20TH CENTURY clocked in, and SF writers and illustrators began to respond to the vast changes that loomed ahead, it began more and more to seem that the great cities of the Western world would be the place – for good or for ill – where the greatest transformations of the world would be witnessed. If millions of folk can live together, millions can die together, too. If huge towers of steel and stone can shoot upwards, then those towers can also tumble. If the great urban conglomerations – like London, or Paris, or New York – represent humanity's hopes for the new century, then they are also symbols of the fear that it may all end. Within a decade, it almost did.

Rude awakening
After his centuries of drugged sleep, the hero of H.G.Wells's When the Sleeper Wakes *is finally roused, and gets his first view of the world-city: huge, multi-layered, roofed, and dense with moving walkways, a cave of steel.*

Lost Liberty
When John Ames Mitchell wrote The Last American *in 1889, the Statue of Liberty had been standing in the New York city harbour for just three years. In the year 2951, an Arab expedition visits historic, ruined America, finds fabled Nu-Yok, and climbs up the hollow interior of the shattered statue. In the deluxe 1902 edition of the book, the illustrator F.W. Read saw Liberty as a mourning figure, staring Ozymandias-like across the liquid desert that shrouds the dead city.*

Cities in the sky
In the powerful imagination of Winsor McCay – he was the creator of Little Nemo in Slumberland, which carries the dreaming Nemo through many vivid and surrealistic landscapes – the city of the future could only go on growing up, until, in the end, "Men Will Live on Mountain Tops". His model here is clearly the southern tip of Manhattan, which even then seemed like the prow of a great mountain.

The urban jungle
Rats, lizards, and Homo sapiens – naked tribes of survivors foraging for food – occupy Winsor McCay's vision of what urban life will be "When Cities Go Back to Ruins". His shattered office blocks, mired in drifts of sand and rubble, resemble the Soviet tenement blocks of a later generation.

The new explorers
One of Mitchell's explorers of ruined New York records: "The extent of the city is astounding … All about us in every direction as far as sight can reach are ruins, and ruins, and ruins. Never was a more melancholy sight … I can write no more."

THE 1910S: AERIAL EMPIRES

FOR THE WESTERN CIVILIZATIONS, the dream of flight began with Icarus; it was subsequently expounded by visionaries like Roger Bacon and Leonardo da Vinci; and it took off in reality in France around 1783, when the Montgolfier brothers began to send balloons into the air, first with animals, and finally, in October 1783, conveying two men across Paris. By the time that the Wright brothers flew the first heavier-than-air machine, thousands of strange flying devices had been invented, many of them almost plausible. Over the next decades, the visions continued. But strangely, it was almost as though the Wright brothers had never existed, because the dreamers paid vanishingly little attention to aeronautical realities. The airships they fancied were vast, unwieldy, and exorbitant. Even more extravagantly than early motorcars – which notoriously still had fixings to which whips could be attached – the early 20th century imagined flight in terms of the immediate past. What really happened, we now realize, was nothing like their hotels, dreadnoughts, and homes in the air; it was a shrinking world.

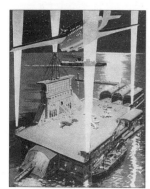

Ocean stopover
Mid-ocean stations were a popular image: no one imagined Concorde.

Ship of the air
This is a bit of fun from a French collectors' card. Forget the Wright brothers, and their aeroplane that flies. Think of an aeroplane as an air ship, and give it a helm, with a helmsman, and a binnacle. Think of it as a bird, and give it flapping wings. Add propellers at the front and on top, a large stateroom in the middle for the passengers, and take off.

The dream comes true
Here, romance triumphs over reality. Although the aeroplane so eloquently figured by the artist does resemble the machine that the Wright brothers flew on 17 December 1903, the landscape is nothing like the bleak, but safely unprecipitous, field at Kitty Hawk where they flew it. Two central facts, however, do come across: the plane is not a balloon or glider; and it is powered. There is another fact, which visionaries took a while to notice: the aeroplane is a quite extraordinarily elegant design. It is a machine for flying.

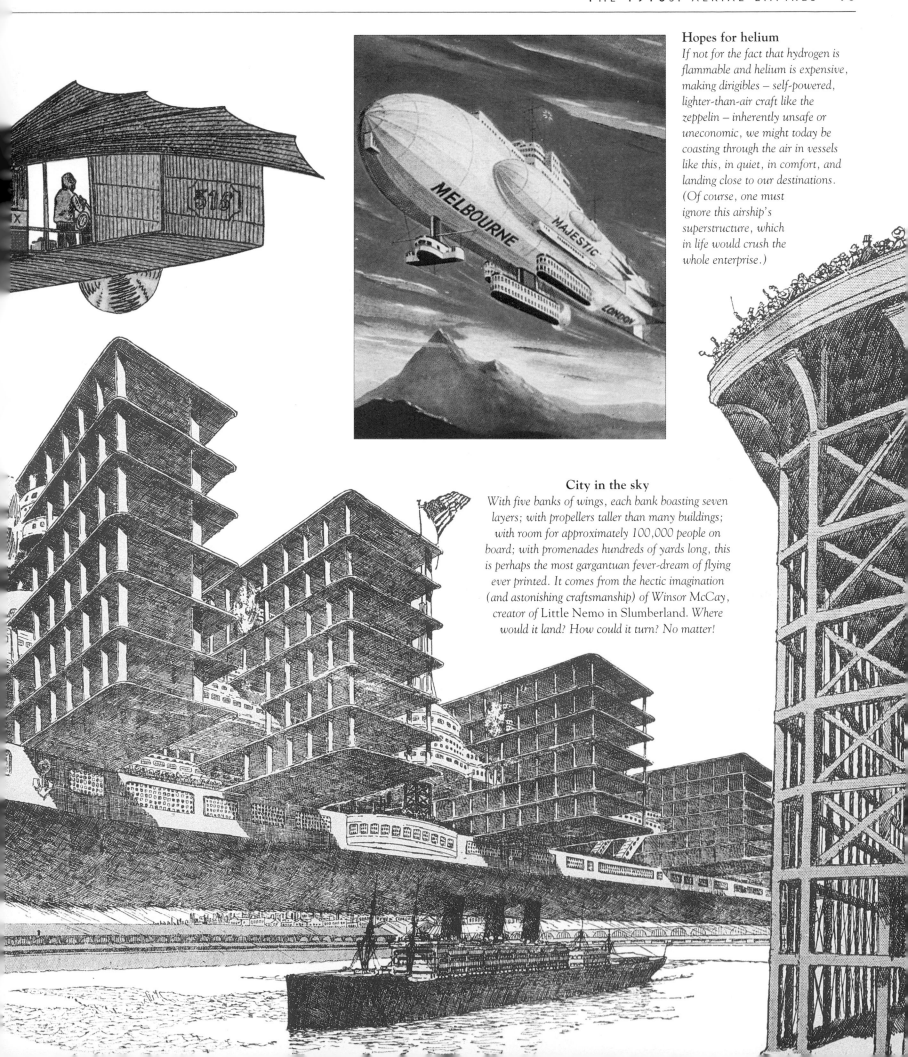

Hopes for helium

If not for the fact that hydrogen is flammable and helium is expensive, making dirigibles – self-powered, lighter-than-air craft like the zeppelin – inherently unsafe or uneconomic, we might today be coasting through the air in vessels like this, in quiet, in comfort, and landing close to our destinations. (Of course, one must ignore this airship's superstructure, which in life would crush the whole enterprise.)

City in the sky

With five banks of wings, each bank boasting seven layers; with propellers taller than many buildings; with room for approximately 100,000 people on board; with promenades hundreds of yards long, this is perhaps the most gargantuan fever-dream of flying ever printed. It comes from the hectic imagination (and astonishing craftsmanship) of Winsor McCay, creator of Little Nemo in Slumberland. Where would it land? How could it turn? No matter!

THE 1920s: MASS TRANSPORT

Aiming for the stars
For some, Earth's bounds were too narrow, and rocketry enjoyed a renaissance.

THERE IS A LOT MORE TO SEE in transportation than there is to make stories about, so it is not surprising that over the years some of the most outrageous devices to carry folk around the globe and off it into space have been described by writers with astonishingly off-hand brevity. Illustrators, on the other hand, revel in speculative images, and it was in the new SF pulp magazines that appeared from 1926 on, all of them heavily illustrated, that the most elaborate visions of future travel were given leg room. If we put space travel to one side, by the 1920s it has become clear to illustrators that transportation is going to have to be about getting people – in large numbers – from one well-known place to another well-known place. Most 1920s images of future travel feature urban backdrops. Transportation is no longer, in other words, a matter of solitary exploration. Now that the world has been effectively traversed, dug into, flown above, and ploughed over, new forms of transporting people around the Earth can be defined as, in reality, new forms of commuting.

Rotor boat
Several ideas are joined in this ocean wheel. There is a nostalgic reminder of the Mississippi paddlewheels; there is the concept of gyroscopic stability; and there is a sense that a lighter-than-air balloon is needed, to keep the great wheel high in the water. Beyond all this, there is the unspoken knowledge that such a precarious construction will need very elaborate docking facilities.

Steel highways
By 1920, in several American cities, this future had already happened. Elevated railways laced through their centres like steel spiderwebs – but none of them were monorails.

A new Atlantis

This is a complex vision of things to come, made instantly nostalgic by Lindbergh's solo non-stop flight across the Atlantic in 1927. But the dream is glorious: a great hotel, balanced on many-fathom-deep pontoons, called Atlantis, after the sunken continent. Biplanes land on the roof, and guests promenade upon five floors (or decks) of the enormous edifice.

Driving to the future

There is something odd about this imagined future: right-hand drive cars (as in England) hurtling down highways where you must drive on the right (as elsewhere in the world). And the illustrator was pretty hopeful about the date of a Channel Tunnel. But, except for the visible rivets, the car itself looks rather like a giant Buick.

Flight of imagination

Clearly, the illustrator saw aeroplanes as flying boats – and indeed the clippers of the 1930s looked a little like this guess. But no one has yet managed to work out how to put windows along the front edges of wings – even fat wings.

THE 1930s: BRIGHT DREAMS

Power from the sky
This is how Amazing magazine saw wind turbines: an extremely complex system involving a whole new element, giving clean, free power for all.

VISIONS OF THE FUTURE are always combinations of prediction and dream, although it can sometimes be hard to tell which is which when it is our own vision that is being examined. But maybe we are far enough now from the 1930s to make a start. What SF writers and illustrators predicted during this decade has, more or less, happened. There has been a huge amount of technological advance. We have new elements, new machines, and new modes of transportation: all of them, more or less, as guessed. It is a different picture, though, when we look at what they dreamed. In the 1930s – a decade of depression and impending world war – the great dream was of a clean future. The world would be a garden, laced together by great, sparkling arterial roads that would somehow leave no grime behind. The finest expression of this was the 1939 New York World's Fair, dominated by huge sculptures and General Motors's spanking-clean, car-driven Futurama.

Confused future
Half a century on, the incongruities seem glaring in this image of a future city from Amazing magazine. The figures in the foreground are dressed in togas, but the architecture is reminiscent of schemes from 1910, and there are vehicles powered by anti-gravity.

A new order

It is night in the great city in this gleaming future from Hollywood. An immaculately clad aviatrix is having an intimate conversation with a young gentleman, who is also conspicuously impeccable. Her personal aeroplane – which she clearly does not need to pilot – navigates itself, at a level lower than the highest buildings, through the heart of the metropolis. To the left, a vast, many-pillared suspension bridge dives down through the buildings, while at ground level, a great multi-lane superhighway carries thousands of cars in the same direction. Our vision of the city is too exalted to permit us a glimpse of any lowly pedestrians. The 1930s were a time of great unemployment and social unrest in America, as elsewhere in the world: it was the job of the future to control the chaos that seemed ready to explode.

Highways to the future

It is typical of this decade's visions of a high-powered future that the city is so often seen in terms of transportation. In this one small illustration, from a set of cigarette cards, we can see a distant ship; an aeroplane about to land at the downtown aerodrome; an expressway diving into a tunnel under a vast river; an urban train at its terminus; and express trains running through a tunnel parallel to the highway. We see no smoke, no traffic congestion, and no crowds. This is the dream: the dream that where transportation existed, life would sanely and surely follow; SF writers carried that dream into space. The impatience of this vision seems, perhaps, touching nowadays.

Ever faster

Here the theme of a clean, transportation-dominated future is both utterly clear, and intriguing to the imagination. We may scoff today at the silver towers separated by sweeping woods and meadows, because the habitable world is much too crowded for this sort of thing. But the vision that dominates the foreground is true SF. It is a swift and silent, mass-transport train, constructed on its own right-of-way, and powered by great magnets, an efficient driving force.

THE 1940s: THE ATOMIC AGE

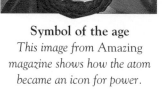

Symbol of the age
This image from Amazing magazine shows how the atom became an icon for power.

SF ATTITUDES TOWARDS THE ATOM, and the exploitation of atomic energy, range from exultation down to despair. There is joy that humanity is close to harnessing the forces that turn the wheels of the universe, anguish that so frail a race as we are will, almost certainly, fail to handle its newly found powers responsibly. Each reaction is both just and partial. Given the huge complexity of the challenges before us, this is only natural. SF writers do know – and constantly dramatize – some home truths. They know that we cannot reject the knowledge we have once gained, that the stars are open only to races that grasp the nettle of near-omnipotence. They also know that nuclear bombs may finish us off quickly, or that industrial pollution may do the same job piecemeal. SF's most important lesson may be that nuclear power does not belong on the surface of the planet. The atom's home is space.

Harnessing power
It is ugly. It is dangerous. It is inefficient. It pollutes the planet. Its waste products poison the surface and the deeps of our world. If it were in high orbit, lasering its energy downwards for use on Earth, while dumping its waste into the voracious Sun, it could make a paradise on our planet. It is a nuclear power plant.

The nuclear family
Why are these folk smiling? Are they going down, or coming up? If they are coming up, they are dead. If they are going down, they will be. In the 1940s and 1950s, throughout the developed world, nuclear shelters like this silly-looking hole proliferated; in some middle-class American communities, most families had one. They were dug into cellars, or in back yards, and were stocked with cans of food, water, bedding, batteries, Geiger counters, and a radio. We are all very, very lucky that they were never needed – because these shelters were almost totally useless.

Poison mushrooms
Two nuclear bombs have been dropped in anger, on Hiroshima and on Nagasaki. A few more mushroom clouds have littered our skies because some nations continued to test their bombs in the open air. But at the end of the 20th century, only fanatics or fundamentalists still dream of setting off a nuclear weapon.

THE 1950s: FLYING SAUCERS

Impish alien
Kelly Freas's little green man, from the cover of Astounding magazine, gives humanity a lot of trouble in Fredric Brown's comic tale Martians Go Home!

ALTHOUGH UNIDENTIFIED FLYING OBJECTS (UFOs) were seen in the 19th century – when they were shaped like airships – the first real craze came in the 1950s, with the addition of alien pilots, and it came to stay. Huge numbers of people believe that Earth has been visited by aliens piloting some sort of UFO, and almost as many people think that that they have observed a flyover or a landing. Perhaps because they are in the business of writing plausible fictions about similar matters, SF writers are very cautious where UFOs are concerned. SF writers and their readers tend to be vividly aware that being plausible and being true are not the same thing at all. Even so, aliens created by some SF writers are, in fact, far more plausible than the aliens that are said to be inhabiting most flying saucers. There is an old saying, that no SF writer would lightly dispute: that truth is stranger than fiction. The most disappointing thing about the UFOs that people believe they have observed is that they are far less strange than fiction.

Mercy mission
Unusually for a film made before the 1970s, the alien in the 1951 film The Man from Planet X is visibly pathetic. His pleas for help for his freezing planet are doomed to fall on deaf ears and, in the end, the army destroys both the lone traveller and his ship.

Familiar strangers

H.G. Wells's 1898 novel, *War of the Worlds, was the first SF novel to make aliens seem plausible, and to give them a reasonable motive for leaving their planet: they need the green fields of Earth, and will wipe us out to gain them. The difference between a UFO and a Wellsian Martian is that the UFO is unknown (but probably uninteresting), and that the Martian is all too familiar. We know its planet, we know its lust for territory, and we recognize its methods.*

Like the British that Wells knew, his Martians are born imperialists. It is appropriate that Wells's Martians landed in Britain, but those in the 1953 film take on America.

The camera lies

Because UFOs are essentially unknowable, and because the people who believe in their reality can be described as believers in search of a belief, hoaxes are very common. There are two signs that identify the dedicated fans of UFOlogy: they are easily duped, because their need to believe is so strong; and they are often duped – it is immaterial to them how often, because the next picture will almost certainly be the real thing. This dramatic photograph, taken in Peru in 1952, undoubtedly reveals its falseness to any analysis: a ship this big, leaving a wake this huge, would be obvious to a whole county. But people believed it.

Stranger ships

To look alien, SF illustrations, like UFOs, have to look beyond what is humanly achievable. This New Worlds magazine cover, whose modified Zeppelin ship probably runs on anti-gravity, looks suitably impossible.

THE 1960s: DREAMS AND IDEALS

Lunar footprint
The dream made manifest: a human footprint on the Moon. Next step, the stars.

IN RECENT YEARS THE 1960s have been targeted by the nostalgia industry, with new films (and old rock music releases) sentimentalizing the hippy generation. This may now be a good time to take a hard look at the dreams and the delusions of that era: it was perhaps the last decade of this century to retain something of those high hopes for the future. There was a general sense of optimism, a belief that things could only get better. This optimism has shaped Western culture in general, and SF in particular, for much of the 20th century, for good and for ill. From bearded rebels to think-tank gurus, the activists of the 1960s believed that the world truly could – and truly would – be improved for everyone, through moral acts taken by individuals. It was a worthy dream.

Festival feeling
No one who is old enough to have attended the great rock concert held at Woodstock, in New York State, in 1969, can be immune from wishing they had actually been there. In the event, thousands did attend, listened to revolutionary music, drank, smoked dope, made love, got wet, got naked, got inspired. The shackles of the dead past were broken, forever. Sure they were.

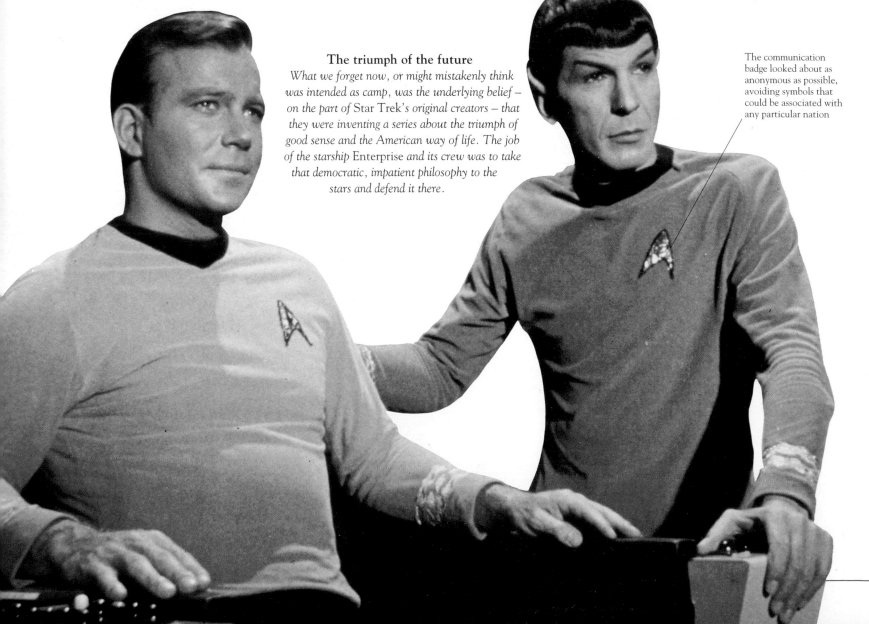

The triumph of the future
What we forget now, or might mistakenly think was intended as camp, was the underlying belief – on the part of Star Trek's original creators – that they were inventing a series about the triumph of good sense and the American way of life. The job of the starship Enterprise and its crew was to take that democratic, impatient philosophy to the stars and defend it there.

The communication badge looked about as anonymous as possible, avoiding symbols that could be associated with any particular nation

International rescue
Today, we have become so accustomed to shots of our own Earth from space that we tend to forget that only a few years ago the very idea of photographing the round, sea-girt planet from above was mocked as just another foolish SF dream. In Marooned, which was made in 1969, such shots still had a powerful effect (even though the film itself was pretty wooden). Shots like this opened our eyes to the magnificence, and fragility, of the planet that gave us birth, and the Russian rescue of American astronauts helped to inspire the Soyuz-Apollo link-up of 1975. The excitement generated by this image should never fade.

The look of Concorde, with its drop nose and delta wings, captured the imagination as much as its speed

Breaking the barriers
In the 1990s, the plans for Concorde would never even stand a chance of getting past the drawing board. The conception, the design, and the actual construction of the aircraft was an act of implicit faith in the road to the technological future. In the final analysis, the supersonic aeroplane may have been a cul-de-sac in technological terms – in the future sub-orbital passenger carriers will be faster and less noisy – but it was an ambitious dream that saw reality, and sang of hope.

THE 1980s: LIFE UNDER GLASS

The original design
Buckminster Fuller's geodesic dome can be built in any size: a house, an exhibition hall, or a city. It is the pattern that was used for enclosed environments for decades.

THE DIFFERENCE BETWEEN ARCOLOGIES and cities is that cities are not developed to the same extent. An arcology – even the primitive versions that we have been building this century – is not merely an innovative home, nor simply a waterproof stadium. It is a structure ideally designed so that whole lives can be led within it: properly integrated, homes, offices, *all* buildings are modules within a complete arcology. In SF, arcologies are generally of two sorts. The first is the extension of the apartment building, as found in Robert Silverberg's *The World Inside*, from 1971, or Larry Niven and Jerry Pournelle's *Oath of Fealty*, from 1981: the former is dystopian, the latter, controversially utopian. The second type of arcology is the space habitat, as found in Michael Swanwick's *Vacuum Flowers*, from 1987. Here – partly because gravity is no object – simple machines-for-living flower into intricate labyrinths, where reality and virtual realities mix indiscriminately. In this environment, SF argues, humans could live truly free lives.

Modern pyramids
There is something profoundly powerful about the triangle. This may be because it symbolizes, for most human beings, our first more or less permanent attempts to prove we were immortal – the great Pyramids of Egypt. Although it is highly likely that in the future we will see more rounded – and thus more efficient – sunshades than this pyramid, an ancient shape holds some symbolism in our next bid for immortality.

Oasis in the desert

Biosphere II, in Arizona, was designed as a self-sustaining habitat for human beings, built on principles derived from Buckminster Fuller's geodesic dome – which itself goes back as far as 1946, when he designed his first "Dymaxion House". Several people lived inside for two years. There was, apparently, a bit of cheating, but the experiment was fundamentally successful. It demonstrated that, in the future, human designers could fabricate structures that would sustain us indefinitely, supplying all our needs for energy, food, water, air, light, and freedom of movement. As the Earth strains more and more at the seams, because the human race proliferates, the knowledge that ultimately we can construct arcologies out in space, and live in them indefinitely, is also good news for expanding humankind.

Recycling plant

The essence of a self-contained arcology, like Biosphere II, is that it is so designed that nothing is wasted, that everything that can be reused is properly cycled, again and again, through the system.
Here we see various forms of plant life, photosynthesizing light into energy and translating waste products back into food and water. The balance is hard to attain – the surface of the planet on which we live is, after all, almost infinitely complex, and its workings are as yet little understood – but Biosphere II marks a beginning. Here, the human race is beginning to learn the kinds of skills necessary if we are to survive as a species.

THE 1990S: EVERLASTING ENERGY

THE STRANGE THING ABOUT clean technology is the fact that we have had it for decades, in SF films, and never wanted it. There is nothing we find more tiresome than toga-clad characters waddling gingerly through a cardboard city that looks like the inside of a washing machine. The real triumph of recent SF cinema has been the introduction of dirt and, with the dirt, an impression of authenticity. The spaceships and stations in the *Alien* films, for example, are utterly filthy – and we loved them. But SF cinema never did have much to do with the real world. Planet Earth is not a set. The dirt is killing us.

Catching rays
A very tiny fraction of the Sun's free energy reaches Earth. A curved surface is able to focus some of that fraction of energy into a receiving tower – but why not do this above the atmosphere, where we could get more energy for less?

Free as the wind
The great advantage of the wind turbine is, of course, its utilization of a renewable resource – because we are swiftly exhausting this planet of its oil and other energy sources. The downside of turbines is that we need so many of them to generate any significant amount of energy.

Geothermal plant

Our home planet is hotter inside than it is out: the Earth's crust is nothing more than a thin layer over the furnace within, as we discover to our cost when volcanoes erupt. The geothermal plant is designed to take advantage of this furnace that lies under our feet, tapping the abundant energy below. In 1960, near San Francisco, a pilot enterprise was begun: it was designed to tap a series of geysers – which are what one might call small liquid volcanoes – and to translate their volatile heat into energy. Since then, working schemes have sprung up in many countries. This at least looks like the free-energy dreams that SF dreamed in the early 20th century – but much more is needed.

The future home?

The energy-sufficient house is a great ecological dream, and it is technologically possible now. But the costs are quite heavy, in two senses: it is still very expensive to build a dwelling to the standards required, and the resulting structure often lacks both appeal and practicality for urban purposes. Although the high-tech house undoubtedly has practical advantages, it will be a long while before a building like this looks anything but alien to most of us.

Highroad to the 21st century

The most efficient, and cleanest, form of transport is, of course, public transport. The problem is that most governments are too cowardly to act on that truth – because to do so means some curtailment of impulse travel, and hence of individual freedom. We continue, instead, to build more and more roads, and to use filth-emitting road transport. A monorail like this one is cheap, clean, and swift. It is also very unpopular.

historical CONTEXT

SCIENCE FICTION TAKES PLACE in the future and in the past, in familiar settings and in distant galaxies, in worlds that might be and worlds that might have been. More than any other genre, it is influenced by the age in which it is written: in times of trouble, it speculates on war, and in times of progress it looks to our destination. The time charts in this chapter put works of SF into historical context, comparing them with the backdrop against which they were created. Individual spreads also examine the themes that have endured from early Proto SF, and those that had their heyday and are now faded memories.

ABOVE: NAZIS IN PARIS
LEFT: JULES VERNE'S *DE LA TERRE À LA LUNE*

PROTO SF

BEGINNINGS ARE ALWAYS EASIER to recognize after they have happened. Over the centuries, a great amount of Proto SF was written, but nobody knew they were doing it; we must keep in mind the fact that the term Science Fiction was not properly invented until 1930.

The beginning of the novel
Before the 18th century, when the realistic novel began to take shape with tales like Fielding's *Tom Jones*, it was all much simpler. There was the drama, there was poetry, and there was prose. Prose was made up of undiscriminated stories, tales, novellas, romances, histories, disquisitions, satires, and eventually what came to be called novels. Science Fiction did not exist, and the various kinds of tale we now describe as Proto SF were not set aside from all the kinds of texts that we would not dream of calling Proto SF. The world of literature before around 1800 is a vast grab-bag, and the texts that we call Proto SF will have to be selected from that grab-bag.

Monkey men
Restif de la Bretonne's La Decouverte d'Australe *(1781) was full of drawings of strange half-human races.*

The start of SF
The way we make that selection is to decide when SF began and what SF is, and then to cherry-pick the texts that justify these decisions. It sounds simple, but turns out to be pretty complex, because the consequences of choosing between the different beginning dates and different definitions are profound. If we decide that SF began when it was named as such, nothing written up to the end of World War I could be called Proto SF: clearly this is silly, and clearly many writers of SF before 1930 knew they were creating something that differed from the realistic novel. If we decide that H.G. Wells began SF with *The Time Machine* in 1895, every SF-like text before that date – including most of Jules Verne's most famous tales – must be called

Othello described "men whose heads do grow beneath their shoulders"

Adventurers often reported seeing cyclops

A sciopode used its single foot for shade

Strange stories from the 17th century
Shakespeare's Othello impressed Desdemona with fantastic descriptions of strange creatures; adventurers to new-found lands told tales for much the same reason.

Proto SF: and this does not work very well, either, for similar reasons. But if we decide that Mary Shelley's *Frankenstein* began SF in 1818, we have fewer problems. Almost any romance (or history, or satire, or narrative of travel to unknown territory) that looks like an ancestor of SF from the perspective of *Frankenstein* comes out of a time in history before prose had been divided into genres. This seems to be a good place to look for Proto SF. At first, it looks as if a great many pre-1800 texts are eligible. It is not as simple as that, however, because what we are after is Proto SF, not simply narratives with fantastic creatures, impossible voyages, ideal cities, political upheavals, or supermen.

Defining Proto SF
What we need to discern – generations of critics have tried to define this, and it is almost certain that there will *never* be a full consensus on the issue – is that element which tells us that one fantastic voyage to the Moon is not Proto SF, while another one, written maybe only a few years later, is. We need a touchstone that defines a text as Proto SF.

Before that date, the stories people wrote were called a variety of things: Fantastic Voyages, Utopias, Future Wars, Gothic Romances, Scientific Romances, Lost World Tales, and so on. After 1930 or so, all of these began to look like the roots of something we now recognize.

That touchstone is not plausibility, or accuracy about the future, or quality of writing. Our touchstone (as far as this book goes) is this: a text is Proto SF when its fantastic and realistic elements are described as though they are part of the same overall reality.

In other words, if the author knows that horses cannot pull a chariot to the Moon, but still writes a tale in which they do so, then we know that this is not Proto SF but something else: an allegory, a political fantasy, a dream.

The Kraken: danger of the deep
One of the dangers of the unknown, the Kraken made it into SF in John Wyndham's The Kraken Wakes.

Early hot-air balloons were unstable and dangerous, but caught people's imagination

Free of Earth
For a century after balloon flight was first achieved, writers sent their heroes off to other planets in hot-air balloons.

This balloon carried two men, Blanchard and Jefferies, across the English Channel

The wings were for steering, not flapping

We know that for this author the real world and the trip to the Moon are entirely different kinds of reality. But if the text is written as though the author believes that horse-drawn moonships *might* be part of a real world, then it is Proto SF. In other words, Proto SF has to embody a sense – not necessarily articulated at length – that the marvels it depicts can be argued for, if necessary by example and analogy from the existing world.

The Age of Reason
Because this kind of argument from nature only took hold around the turn of the 17th century – when Western civilization began to forge ahead in science and technology – we are unlikely to find Proto SF texts before this time. Sir Francis Bacon's *The New Atlantis*, from 1629, is a perfect

example of an argued world. In contrast, Shakespeare's *The Tempest*, circa 1611, is a perfect example of a text whose marvels we now perceive as fantastic, other-worldly; not Proto SF at all.

Given this touchstone, we must exclude from the pantheon of Proto SF such texts as *Other Worlds* (1657–72) by Cyrano de Bergerac, or *Pilgrim's Progress* (1678–84) by John Bunyan, even though many SF critics have given them space. But *Gulliver's Travels*, written in 1626 by Jonathan Swift, is Proto SF, although perhaps only by a whisker, because there are points when it rather feels as though its author's satirical needs overwhelmed the requirements of an argued tale.

But in the end, partly because it is appealing to think that islands in the ocean may contain strange creatures like those Gulliver reports, we believe in the tale as we read it. And that, in the century of Enlightenment, is enough.

Voyages and explorations
The Fantastic Voyage is probably the early tale most visibly influential upon SF. During the two centuries of Proto SF, the Moon became an ever more common destination. The pseudonymous Murtagh McDermot's *A Trip to the Moon*, from 1728, is typical; dozens of others are described in Marjorie Hope Nicolson's *Voyages to the Moon*, from 1948. Also common was the journey within the Earth, into the vast hollows that many thinkers argued – with some plausibility at the time – must exist. The best known of these is the *Journey of Niels Klim to the World Underground*, from 1741, by the Danish Baron Ludvig Holberg. By the 19th century, when a United States army captain urged that an expedition inside be mounted, the notion had become fantasy. By then, *Frankenstein* and the future had arrived.

The original Utopia, nowhere to be found
More's Utopia christened a concept in 1516. His idyllic island was a satire: the name was intended to mean "nowhere", implying the impossibility of the perfect state.

1800-1899: THE INDUSTRIAL AGE

THIS IS THE CENTURY WHEN the gears really begin to mesh. For hundreds of years, Western science and technology have slowly been gathering momentum, and now it is time. Like some vast machine, the world begins to turn, and we begin to realize it is truly round, finite, and *understandable*. The Industrial Revolution is in full swing by 1800, and by 1900 the West bears very little resemblance to the land of Jane Austen. As the engines of change begin to transform

	1800s	1810s	1820s	1830s	1840s
SF EVENTS	Right at the verge of true SF, "Le dernier homme", a poem by Jean-Baptiste Xavier Cousin de Grainville, is published in France, and is then translated into English as a novel, *The Last Man*. Everything is in embryo here: the end of time; the exhaustion of Earth; ruined cities; and the last man and woman, who long to breed but who are persuaded not to by Adam. They are sent back from eternity by a God who despairs, and wishes it all to end. He gets His way.	In 1816, Mary Shelley, Percy Shelley, Lord Byron, and Doctor John Polidori exchange ghost stories at **La Spezia**, the Shelleys' coastal villa in Italy. This – together with nightmares in which her dead infant son is reborn – is enough to make Mary begin to write *Frankenstein*, which is published in 1818. SF is born.	SF is still sleepwalking backwards into the future. Mary Shelley's *The Last Man* (1826) takes the form of manuscripts discovered aeons hence, describing the 19th and 20th centuries in archaic 18th-century terms. The novel's apocalyptic plague has nothing of SF in it: it is just another plague. Jules Verne is born in 1828.	With terrifying speed, the world is being boxed and compassed, but Edgar Allan Poe manages to discover, in "The Hollow Earth" described in *The Narrative of Arthur Gordon Pym* (1838), a venue for something like SF. All the same, it is hardly a tale of expansive spirit. SF is still, almost entirely, a genre for the expression of fears about the future. Its protagonists still shy away from the glare of tomorrow.	The Western imagination is still dominated by a sense that the future bodes ill, a suspicion that science and technology are both savagely undermining the very civilization that made them. Eugene Sue's *Mysteries of Paris* (1844), although not SF, does, all the same, posit an urban world whose labyrinthine intricacies influenced 20th-century SF views of satanic world cities, like that featured in Fritz Lang's *Metropolis* (1926). Dickens darkens in the 1840s; Bulwer Lytton has occult nightmares. The future is beginning to be everywhere.
CINEMA, RADIO, AND TELEVISION			Numerous "moving-picture" devices appear from the 1820s on, including the **Praxinoscope**, the Zoescope, the Thaumatrope, and the Stroboscope. All work by moving a series of static images fast enough to fool the eye.		Louis Jacques Daguerre announces the new world in a new way: his daguerrotype does not allow people to see the future, but it fixes history into frozen images. It is a convention to say that photographs make things seem real: but they also make them seem irretrievably *past*. Very swiftly now, the world is transforming itself. The past is fixed, and the future is unhinged.
MAGAZINES					G.W.M. Reynolds, like Dickens, specializes in serial stories, but his make Dickens look positively genteel. In journals such as his own *Miscellany*, he issues nightmares like "Mysteries of London" (1845), and "Wagner, the Wehr-Wolf" (1847).
WORLD EVENTS	**Napoleon** bestrides the decade. He is First Consul of France in 1800, Emperor in 1804, and virtual ruler of continental Europe only a few years later. Robert Fulton builds a paddle steamer.	In 1813, Verdi and Wagner are born. In 1815, Napoleon is defeated at **Waterloo**, and Bismarck is born. In 1817, Jane Austen dies. In 1819, the United States buys Florida from Spain.	In 1822, **Babbage** conceives the Difference Engine, which is the first computer. However, he cannot fabricate the components to the fine tolerance that his design requires, and it never works.		The conservative regimes of Europe attempt to stall the march of Time; but in the **revolutions** of 1848 we have a glimpse of the next century.

every aspect of individual lives, two important genres of fiction writing are founded: the historical novel, which is created by Sir Walter Scott, attempts to give its readers some imaginative handholds on the world that has passed, before Progress turned everything inside out; and SF, as imagined by Mary Shelley, attempts to get a fix on the Promethean gifts – and possible curses – that have begun to descend upon us from the future.

1850s

In 1851, Jules Verne publishes his first SF story, *"Un voyage en ballon"* [A voyage in a balloon]. Although the story cannot be considered nearly as important as Mary Shelley's *Frankenstein*, it is significant because from this point SF begins to transform into stories of adventure and discovery.

In 1851, Louis Napoleon takes over France, stifling the abortive revolution. In this decade, too, Britain is flexing her imperial muscles in the Crimea and in the Far East. Europeans are leading the way in industry and they are now beginning to rule the world.

1860s

Jules Verne's career takes off like a rocket, with numerous classic novels including **De la terre à la lune** (*From the Earth to the Moon*). SF is no longer a genre for the display of nightmares, but rather a vehicle for portraying future possibilites. H. G. Wells is born in 1866 – his beady eyes are soon to be turned on the world.

In the United States, Edward Everett Hale publishes "The Brick Moon", which describes with great élan the first orbital satellite.

In 1868, Edward S. Ellis writes the first SF dime novel, *The Steam Man of the Prairies*. During the next decade, in this semi-magazine format, hundreds of other stories follow. Most are lost.

The **American Civil War** of 1861–65 brings new technology into the fray, and subsequently to the doorsteps of civilians. Darwin and his theories of evolution fret conservative minds.

1870s

The beginning of this decade sees, in Colonel Sir George Chesney's *The Battle of Dorking*, written in 1871, the first of a huge flood of Dreadful Warning novels, which portray terrifying wars set in the future. The nightmare in this novel does not concern the satanic awfulness of science, but rather our failure to use scientific knowledge to build the best weaponry possible. Bulwer Lytton's *The Coming Race* (1871) gives the world the superhuman Vril race, and so christens the drink Bovril. In 1872, Samuel Butler writes the novel *Erewhon*, which is a mockery of the application of science to people.

The dignified proprietors of *Blackwood's* magazine may have been shocked at the success of **The Battle of Dorking**. But they swallow their dismay, and immediately release the tale in book form.

1880s

By now, SF is familiar to large audiences. Verne has published his best-known tales, and his work begins to darken. In 1888, *Looking Backward 2000–1887*, by Edward Bellamy, counters this pessimism with a vision of middle-class order. In 1886, Robert Louis Stevenson writes his **Strange Case of Dr. Jekyll and Mr. Hyde**, destined to become a much-filmed classic.

Early cinema has a contentious history. In 1888, E.J. Marey nearly invents it, and **Friese-Greene** uses film stock that has holes punched along the edges, which is later to be reinvented by Edison.

In 1882, Frank Reade Jr. takes over from his father, and the **Frank Reade Library** takes off: half magazine, half book. Frank himself covers the planet, and escapes scraps with his inventions.

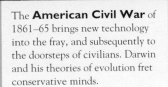

1890s

The central event is the explosion of **H.G. Wells** onto the world scene with *The Time Machine* (1895), and the great, enormously influential SF novels that follow in short succession.

The **Lumière brothers** – Louis and Auguste – inaugurate the showing of films in 1895. They show them in the dark, for money. They think it is a form of education. Wrong.

Konstantin Tsiolkovsky, a scientist, thinks about space ships. They are not guns. They cannot glide. Propellers will not work. Ah! They must be rockets!

LOST WORLDS

UNTIL THE 19TH CENTURY, the idea of Lost Worlds existing was unheard of. And now, at the end of the 20th century, there are really none left. Before 1800, the world had not yet been properly traversed by explorers. Writers who wished to deposit their heroes in strange cultures simply sent them off to unknown regions of the planet, usually to areas that had not yet been fully explored and to islands that had not yet been mapped. After 1950 or so, it became difficult to find niches where Lost Worlds might nestle, and writers were forced to send their heroes, almost invariably, to other planets.

Places or people?

There has never been a solid consensus among SF critics over what to call this subgenre. "Lost World" has long been the most popular term to designate stories whose hero adventurers stumble into previously unknown territories, and almost always find civilizations of great antiquity living there; but some critics prefer to call these tales "Lost Race" stories, on the grounds that what is discovered in the forbidden valley is more important than the valley itself, or the journey undertaken to get there.

In a sense the latter critics are right, because (one might think) there is not much point in travelling if the destination is not worth the trip. But in another sense, they are quite wrong,

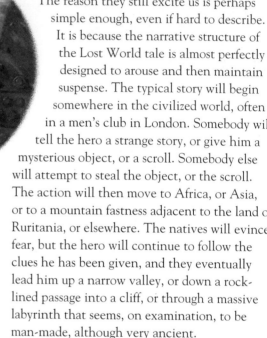

Island hideaway
As late as 1875, Jules Verne could still set a Lost World romance on a mysterious island, hidden in the mist; soon there would be no more islands left.

because (as we all know in our hearts) it is sometimes far better to travel than it is to arrive. It is certainly the case that some of the finest passages in most Lost World novels tend to be those concerned with the perils and mysteries of the long journey into the interior of the island, or the mountain, or the defile, or the continent, or the submarine or subterranean world – for many Lost Worlds are located in the ocean depths, or deep within the hollows of the planet.

Into the unknown

Many of the stories were written by hack writers, or by amateurs who wished to argue that Atlantis still flourished in the Atlantic Ocean, or that the Lost Tribes of Israel had found a home in the desert, or that an élite corps of ancient Greeks (or Egyptians, or Sumerians, or Persians: take your pick of them) had secreted their most occult lore in a hidden place, which they guarded against the infidels, for ever. But even the worst of these stories can still thrill the modern reader, a century after they were written.

The reason they still excite us is perhaps simple enough, even if hard to describe. It is because the narrative structure of the Lost World tale is almost perfectly designed to arouse and then maintain suspense. The typical story will begin somewhere in the civilized world, often in a men's club in London. Somebody will tell the hero a strange story, or give him a mysterious object, or a scroll. Somebody else will attempt to steal the object, or the scroll. The action will then move to Africa, or Asia, or to a mountain fastness adjacent to the land of Ruritania, or elsewhere. The natives will evince fear, but the hero will continue to follow the clues he has been given, and they eventually lead him up a narrow valley, or down a rock-lined passage into a cliff, or through a massive labyrinth that seems, on examination, to be man-made, although very ancient.

This process of discovery may take hundreds of pages. Afterwards, when the Lost World has been penetrated, we come to the dangerous

Step back in time
Edgar Rice Burroughs was a romantic, and The Land That Time Forgot *is full of truculent dinosaurs and other fossils caught in time.*

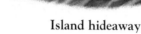

Dated descriptions
A. Hyatt Verrill wrote Boy Adventurers in the Land of the Monkey Men *in the 1920s: it was still widely assumed that blacks and monkeys were closely related.*

Worlds within worlds
Etidorhpa – Aphrodite backwards – is a guided tour of an underground world, and is exceedingly richly illustrated. The guide is eyeless, but the readers feast.

moment when the author must justify the suspense that we have enjoyably endured, but which can readily turn to anticlimax if what we discover – hidden away from the world for all these aeons – is yet another white woman whom superstitious natives worship as a deity because she resembles the statue of their first goddess; or a race of stiff-necked patriarchs who have preserved, for all these years, an ancient scroll that makes it clear that they are the foredoomed rulers of the Earth.

Survivors from the past

The best Lost World writers were men such as the most famous of them, H. Rider Haggard, who in the 1880s wrote *King Solomon's Mines*, *She* – the famous "She Who Must Be Obeyed" – *Allan Quatermain*, and over following decades about a dozen more. The most successful of these books utilize the basic suspense and revelation structure of the genre, but enrich the mix with potently romantic descriptions of the geography of Africa, and with speculations about civilization and race that are dated now, but which eloquently express the uneasiness that white Europeans were beginning to feel as their empires grew to unmanageable proportions in the closing years of the century. Lost World tales allowed Haggard and others to dramatize face-saving assumptions about the nature of evolution: many of their hidden realms contain evolutionary fossils like the dinosaurs that obsessed Edgar Rice Burroughs and his ilk, or Neanderthals, or other less-than-white races.

The world within

The more SF-like Lost World tales – like Verne's *Voyage au centre de la terre (Voyage to the Centre of the Earth)*, from 1863, or Bulwer Lytton's *The Coming Race*, from 1871 – avoided the ever-shrinking geography of the surface of the planet by featuring worlds or societies hidden deep in the Earth. Other SF-like Lost World authors assumed that their Lost Races had retained superpowers and advanced scientific knowledge from antiquity. Later Lost World tales, like Joseph O'Neill's *Land Under England*, from 1935, deepened the sense of threat and conspiracy embodied in the concept; in O'Neill's savage underground dystopia, for instance, a figure much like Hitler is preparing to dominate the world. Another example, Douglas V. Duff's *Jack Harding's Quest*, from 1939, has English explorers finding a hidden valley inhabited by a Lost Tribe of Israel, who have carefully preserved for aeons the horn that once blew down the walls of Jericho, which is analyzed by acoustic experts.

Vision of doom
This image from a 1911 novel perfectly captures H. Rider Haggard's strong attachment to the gold-and-jewel-encrusted settings of his novels, to scenes dominated by men or women who maintain a mesmeric control over their world's hierarchy. In the daylight, Haggard would have none of it, but at night, it haunts.

It proves essential in the coming conflict with the Nazis. After they have noted the harmonies it emits, the experts then destroy the horn, so that nobody else can use it.

But these late novels are written against the grain of history and against the evolutionary flow of SF. James Hilton's *Lost Horizon*, written in 1933, reverses the moral triumphalism of the typical early examples. Here, the Westerners in their aeroplane are the savages, the ignorant ones, and the quasi-immortal inhabitants of the lost Shangri-La are the bearers of true wisdom. After World War II, SF writers keep their eyes pinned firmly to the stars.

EVOLUTION IN SF

BEFORE THE 19TH CENTURY, Europeans saw themselves as central players on a stage that had been created for the great drama scant days before Adam woke. Everything was designed for man; man was essentially different from everything. Other species were food, other races were servants, and the female came from the master's rib. It could not last forever. The 19th century dawned, and a vast time-abyss opened. Geologists began to speculate that the fossil record only made sense if the Earth was at least a million years old, which meant that the stage was there aeons before the play began. Then – with great reluctance, because he understood his theory's implications – Darwin published *The Origin of Species* in 1859, and the house of cards began to collapse. Like birds, and beasts, and women, men were creatures, too.

First fire
Few 19th-century novels on evolution left out the discovery of fire.

Evolution

SF writers do not much like Charles Darwin, not because they think he is wrong (they would be deeply foolish to discount his dauntingly meticulous observations), but because Darwinian theory is profoundly unspectacular.

The survival of the fittest has little to do with gladiatorial combat, and everything to do with breeding success: the more offspring, the better chance your genes have to survive. There are few stories here. But in the 19th century, another theory of evolution was popular: the Chevalier de Lamarck argued that children could directly inherit their parents' accomplishments. SF writers loved this – hence the innumerable prehistoric romances in which Ook discovers fire and his children grow up smoking pipes. H.G. Wells would have no truck with this: it is one reason why he is more revered than imitated.

Teamwork
Part of humankind's climb to dominance, it was speculated, was our ability to act together against a stronger foe.

The use of weapons
This illustration, from Stanley Waterloo's A Tale from the Time of the Cavemen, *shows the use of tools and weapons, which many 19th-century novels saw as vital in our development. Like much later SF, these romances could be called tales of technology, after their own fashion.*

DARWIN AT WORK

It did not look like much: young Charles Darwin, naturalist on HMS *Beagle*, taking a stroll on one of the Galapagos Islands. But in his head a revolution was brewing. How, he mused, can it be that every one of these Islands sports a distinctive version of the regional flora and fauna? All these subspecies! Could they have existed from the dawn of time? One word: no. Twenty years before *The Origin of Species* was published, Darwin knew that the subspecies had diverged from some common ancestor. And if they had come from a single source, then species also evolved from earlier species. *Homo sapiens* is a species: *Homo sapiens* evolved from the mud.

Unique fauna
The unique tortoises of the Galapagos Islands were a clue that told Darwin life forms there had evolved to suit the environmental niche.

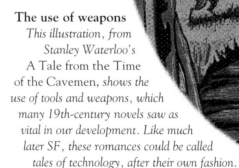

The flipside of evolution

A responsible SF writer like Wells, when he speculates about the fate of *Homo sapiens* in a book like *The Time Machine*, will take care to make his readers understand that there is no going back on evolution. It simply does not have a reverse gear. But to say that is not to say that evolution is a synonym for Progress. Evolution is a process of adaptive change. If the world becomes an unpleasant place to live in, a species may well adapt to the new circumstances by shedding excess size, or even intelligence if the world punishes curiosity with death.

The kind of "devolution" SF pulp writers and film-makers love comes in two forms. First, the throwback to an earlier form of humanity: it says little for our vanity that these throwbacks are almost invariably sex-crazed brutes. Second, the mutation, very popular after the A-bomb; mutant creatures with swollen heads, or tentacles, or scales, or almost anything a makeup artist might dream up, are generally described in terms that make it seem that they have devolved from normal stock. And true to Hollywood, eggheads are always seen as devolved mutants.

Man meets Martian

The interesting point about this illustration from Fantastic Adventures magazine is how it contrasts two evolutionary strategies. The secret of human domination and progress does not lie in specialization, but in its opposite: humans are the least specialized of all advanced mammals. The Martian's big, suckered feet are great for Mars, but would be useless on Earth. We adapt to new environments (even alien ones) by changing our tools, not our foot size.

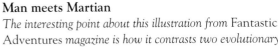

Antennae for telepathic communication

Huge ears, for amplifying sound in a thin atmosphere

Protective helmet, incorporating sound amplifiers

Oxygen tank to supplement supply in air

Huge lungs to gather oxygen from the thin atmosphere

Hand rockets for moving around in space or on ship

Feet with suckers for walking on a low-gravity surface

Hollywood's viewpoint

The makers of One Million Years BC cannot have intended the message, but it comes across clear. Long before the Neanderthals gave in to the tide of Homo sapiens, long before the earliest hominid bounded through the African savannah, a race of crypto-proto-pre-Stone-Age humans boasted hairdoes, beauticians, and bras. Downhill ever since. Bras were only reinvented yesterday.

Evolutionary losers

The astronauts of Planet of the Apes believe that they have come to an alien planet; only at the end of the film does the lone survivor realize that he is on a far-future Earth long after the evolutionary tables have been turned on humanity. He makes some rapprochement with the ruling apes before his terrible discovery of the ruined Statue of Liberty on the shoreline.

1900-1909: A GLOWING FUTURE

IF THE 19TH CENTURY HAD BEEN like some great engine of Progress just beginning to warm up, then the 20th century is inevitably going to experience an inexorable speeding up of the wheels of that engine. This is what is predicted.

And it is all – so runs the flood of expectations – going to be for the best, because the world is surely going to continue to improve. It will become a healthier place to live, a happier place to raise children, a planet of marvels.

1900	1901	1902	1903	1904

SF EVENTS

1901: In *The First Men in the Moon*, the last of his SF masterpieces, H.G. Wells speculates, more daringly than anyone before him, on the wide variations in species that evolution might require across the universe.

1902: Joseph Conrad's enduring classic *The Heart of Darkness*, which has, perhaps, inspired more SF stories than any other work of fiction, is published. Its gruelling odyssey into the unknown, and its vision of the Otherness of alien life, has captured the imaginations of SF writers ever since.

1903: Louis Pope Gratacap's first novel, *The Certainty of a Future Life on Mars*, is published. It features radio communication between Mars and Earth, and an elderly spirit, now resident on Mars, who inspires his Earth-bound son with occultism and electricity.

1904: Hugo Gernsback leaves Europe for America, where his dreams will come true. H.G. Wells publishes, in *The Food of the Gods*, a book whose bullying good cheer about fixing the future is belied by "The Country of the Blind", which also comes out this year. Novels like *The Panchronicon*, by Harold Steel MacKaye – in which a time machine is lost in the 19th century – demonstrate how soon Wells's models are being used in tales edging slowly, but surely, towards genre SF.

1900: While it cannot really be called SF, L. Frank Baum's classic tale of **The Wonderful Wizard of Oz** shines like a bright new day upon the bright new century, and tells us it will work like a song.

CINEMA, RADIO, AND TELEVISION

1900: Ideally, there should be newsreels at the turn of the century, and we should be able to hear the great figures of the time lay down their hopes and fears. But the cinema is lagging behind, even if only by a few years, and a film like George Méliès's *Le voyage dans la lune* (A Trip to the Moon) is little more than a series of jokes. *The X-Ray Mirror* (now lost) is simply two minutes of tomfoolery.

THE MAGIC OF MÉLIÈS

GEORGE MÉLIÈS

200,000 LEAGUES UNDER THE SEA

Méliès comes into his own in these years, making the first real SF film, *Le voyage dans la lune* (A Trip to the Moon) in 1903; and *Deux cent mille lieues sous les mers* (200,000 Leagues under the Sea) in 1907. Although not the first version this is the most famous.

1904: Méliès is still the dominant figure in cinema. His *Voyage à travers l'impossible* (Whirling the Worlds) weds Verne to farce in a wild and weird 30-minute epic, featuring an impossibly fast automobile, a funicular railway that becomes a spaceship, and many other comical visions of futuristic transportation. The jokes do not detract from the visions: rather, they tell us that Méliès and his contemporaries feel cheerful about the prospects in store.

MAGAZINES

1902: British magazines such as *Strand* and *Pearson's* have become home to much SF, which nests quite comfortably beside P.G. Wodehouse's first frolics and Conan Doyle's stories of Sherlock Holmes. Many of H.G. Wells's early novels are first published in magazines like these, and they are often heavily illustrated.

WORLD EVENTS

1900: The Boer War embarrasses the British Empire, but in Paris, the **16th World Exhibition**, which has 100,000 exhibitors, loudly proclaims the new century; Art Nouveau vies with Jugendstil.

1903: The **Wright brothers** inaugurate the age of air at Kitty Hawk. Evelyn Waugh is born, scowling. In Russia, the Mensheviks split from the Bolsheviks, who are led by Lenin.

Men and women are – after all – not only taller, cleaner, healthier, and longer lived than their ancestors; they are more rational, too. The future is anticipated with a huge optimism. For a decade or so, it really does seem that the good times have arrived. Despite the gnawing fears of the few wise men and women who are concerned about the precariousness of the new developments, it looks, for a while, as though there might be peace in the world.

1905

Jules Verne dies. His later works were threaded through with hints of a bleak, pessimistic foreboding about the impersonal hugeness of the world to come, and of the unfettered power-madness of its potential rulers. Gabriel Tarde's novel, *Fragment d'histoire future* (*Underground Man*), foresees a time when humanity, having survived into an epoch when the Solar System's resources have been exhausted, sinks below ground into a Utopia that may – or may not – be simply too sterile for human beings to survive.

Einstein postulates the light quantum, proves the existence of atoms, and writes two papers on the Special Theory of Relativity. His revelations will change the world.

1906

The flood of Future War novels continues. William Le Queux's **The Invasion of 1910**, with its maps and arguments about military strategy, may be hard to read today, but in 1906, it made thousands quake in their beds.

Comic and outrageous special effects continue. Cars are clearly seen to be the way to the future: in **The ? Motorist**, they are driven into space.

1907

The most vivid and important SF novel of the year is Jack London's *The Iron Heel*, one of the many early-20th-century SF novels about conflict between Capital and Labour, but the only one that still lives. In 1912 (the story goes) the Socialists win the American election, but are not allowed to take office. Revolution, chaos, and war ensue. Also in this year, Robert A. Heinlein is born.

Paul Cornu's helicopter flies for 20 seconds. Bakelite is invented by Leo Bäkeland. The *Lusitania* is launched. William James's *Pragmatism* is published.

1908

H.G. Wells, in a late flicker of pure storytelling *joie de vivre*, shows the world how to write a convincing Future War novel in **The War in the Air**. Here is the true bite of war.

The **Pathé brothers** are one of the dominant forces in film-making of the time: their studio includes directors like Segundo de Chomon and Ferdinand Zecca.

A LA CONQUÊTE DU MONDE
PATHÉ FRÈRES   1894-19...

1909

Garrett P. Serviss's third SF novel, *A Columbus in Space*, is published in *All-Story*, and lauds yet another explorer hero: his first novel, *Edison's Conquest of Mars*, which had been published in an 1898 newspaper, was the first Edisonade for adults, making Thomas Alva Edison into an Earth-saving inventor-genius and conqueror of alien races. The characteristic heroes of American SF are beginning to appear.

Here are the makers and shakers of the film industry of 1909 in one photograph. The circled figures are, from left to right, **D.W. Griffith**, **George Méliès**, and the **Pathé brothers**.

Both *Argosy* and *All-Story* are published by the large and aggressive Munsey publishing empire, and they are the most important pulps of their era. SF adventures predominate.

Ezra Pound publishes *Exultations*. Richard Strauss premières *Elektra*. The Girl Guides are founded, two years after the Boy Scouts. Selfridge's department store opens in London. In America, Henry Ford develops the Model T.

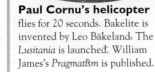

1910-1919: THE WORLD AT WAR

IT IS THE WORST OF TIMES, it is the best of times for the writers of the kind of story that will, eventually, come to be called Science Fiction. World War I is simply too terrible, too searing a fulfilment of idle prophecies of doom, to be assimilated easily into story form. There are many more great poems written during the conflict than there are novels, and the greatest prose responses to the Great War do not begin to appear until some years afterwards.

1 9 1 0 | 1 9 1 1 | 1 9 1 2 | 1 9 1 3 | 1 9 1 4

SF EVENTS

1910: Finally, the spate of Future War novels begins to diminish – perhaps because the real thing is beginning to look all too likely. P.G. Wodehouse's *The Swoop!*, published the previous year, had also had an effect, by exposing some of the more boring scenarios to ridicule. But books like the anonymous *The German Invasion of England* still yawningly appear; even C.J. Cutcliffe-Hyne's effort, *The Empire of the World*, is tedious. H.G. Wells sharpens up *When the Sleeper Wakes*, published in 1899 as *The Sleeper Awakes*; but mostly it is fearfully quiet.

1911: F.W. Mader's **Wunderwelten** (*Distant Worlds*) takes its young crew at faster-than-light speed to Alpha Centauri: the SF universe is growing. An early superman tale, J.D. Beresford's *The Hampdenshire Wonder*, ends in tears.

1912: It is almost the end of the line for the Lost World novel before **The Lost World**, by Arthur Conan Doyle, establishes a name for the subgenre. But there are no more worlds left to find.

1913: It is almost the exact opposite of a Lost World, although it is set, like many Lost Worlds, underground: Bernhard Kellermann's novel **Der Tunnel** (*The Tunnel*) is a paean to the lacing together of the world through a transatlantic tunnel. World War I intervenes.

1914: An anonymous anti-German parody of Lewis Carroll's **Alice** books, **Malice in Kulturland**, prefigures the tone of wartime propaganda; at the same time, H.G. Wells's *The World Set Free* (published at the same time as *The War That Will End War*, which popularizes a good phrase but fails as prediction) argues that war gives birth to utopia.

CINEMA, RADIO, AND TELEVISION

1910: Thomas Alva Edison's film company makes the first film version of **Frankenstein**. It will not be the last. It is just 16 minutes long, full of violence and mysticism, and is more the parent of horror than it is of SF.

THE EDISON KINETOGRAM
VOL. 1   LONDON, APRIL 15, 1910   No. 1

SCENE FROM FRANKENSTEIN
FILM No. 6604

EDISON FILMS TO BE RELEASED FROM MAY 11 TO 18 INCLUSIVE

1913: The image of a Martian exiled to Earth, and not recognizable as an alien, probably originates in George du Maurier's *The Martian* (1897); Robert Ganthony's 1899 stage play, *A Message from Mars*, features a similarly subdued presentation of the visitor who, angel-like, reforms a needy Earthling. The 1913 film tamely, but successfully (it was remade at least twice), repeats the formula.

MAGAZINES

1911: The first fruit of Gernsback's competence as a generator of magazines, and of his didactic impulse, appears in *Modern Electrics*, with the magazine form of *Ralph 124C 41+*.

1912: Edgar Rice Burroughs, writing as Norman Bean, publishes "Under the Moons of Mars" in *All-Story*. Later, in book form, it would be known as *A Princess of Mars*.

1913: Hugo Gernsback stops publishing *Modern Electrics* and founds *Electrical Experimenter*.

1914: Arthur Machen publishes, in the *London Evening News*, the story **"The Bowmen"**, in which a corps of ghostly bowmen from the Battle of Agincourt comes to the aid of the British forces.

WORLD EVENTS

1910: Marie Curie publishes her *Treatise on Radiography*. Professor Evans excavates Knossos. Mark Twain and Florence Nightingale die. Alban Berg's String Quartet and Igor Stravinsky's *Firebird* are premiered. The Post-Impressionist Exhibition opens in London. The Futurist Manifesto is published.

1912: Three SF writers – John Jacob Astor, Jacques Futrelle, and W.T. Stead – go down on the **Titanic**. None of them had predicted the event.

1914: The Indian summer of high civilization in Europe ends in June, with the **assassination** of Archduke Ferdinand and the outbreak of World War I that follows.

Little SF is written during the war that is not escapist. Afterwards, slowly, the conflict begins to take on a quite different coloration. It has undoubtedly been traumatic for the whole of the European world; but at the same time, its huge deadliness must surely mean that there could be no more wars. At last the world is free of the dead weight of the past, and at last SF writers can begin to create the great bandwagon of the future.

1 9 1 5

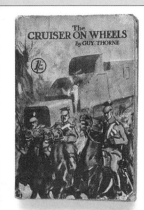

Guy Thorne was not much of a prophet, but for once he is right. In **The Cruiser on Wheels**, tanks appear in the war, just a couple of years early.

Arthur Machen's tale of the previous year, with the **bowmen** translated into angels, becomes a classic piece of war mythology: soldiers claim to have seen angels, and newspapers report the sightings. Songs, and even a waltz, are written in honour of the "event".

The *Lusitania* is sunk, making American entry into the war inevitable. Einstein's General Theory of Relativity is revealed. The Germans introduce poison gas as a weapon of war, and **Zeppelins** appear in the skies.

1 9 1 6

In Austria, Gustav Meyrink publishes *Das grüne Gesicht* (*The Green Face*), surprisingly without interference from the censors. It depicts a post-War apocalypse, a great wind that wipes Europe clean of its years of obscene strife.

After *Der Golem*, based on Gustav Meyrink's novel, **Homunculus** carries on the artificial-person theme, in the tale of a perfect, but soulless, android.

In Sweden, Otto Witt launches what many critics think of as the first genuine SF magazine, *Hugin*. The name is the Old Norse word for "thought": it was the name of one of Odin's ravens. The journal lasts for 85 issues, folding in 1920.

Tanks are used on battlefields. The United States enters the war, effectively ending it. Lenin leads a revolution in Russia. In Britain, T.S. Eliot publishes *Prufrock and Other Observations*.

1 9 1 7

In *The Messiah of the Cylinder*, by Victor Rousseau, a sleeper wakes in a socialist dystopia of the future, a state of affairs for which he demonstrates a hearty contempt. By novel's end, he has wiped the new world off the map. The book is regarded as a riposte to H.G. Wells's much superior (and profoundly less didactic) *When the Sleeper Wakes*.

In the middle of the Great War, **Himmelskibet** (*The Airship*) is made in Denmark. Akin to a Space Opera, it features a Martian high priest's daughter who brings peace to this warring planet.

1 9 1 8

Look closely at these pages of text, and you will see pencil markings. They show the libellous parts of Rose Macaulay's **What Not?**, satirizing a British press baron. They are cut, and the book is republished the following year.

Hans Heinz Ewers's **Alraune** was filmed several times. Two versions are made this year. One of them is made by Michael Curtiz, who later makes *Casablanca*.

The War That Will End War goes into recess until 1939. British women get the vote. Lytton Strachey publishes *Eminent Victorians*. Airmail service begins between New York and Washington, and Daylight Saving Time is introduced across the United States.

1 9 1 9

The first version of Milo Hastings's *City of Endless Night* appears in Bernarr Macfadden's *True Story* magazine, under the title "Children of 'Kultur'". Centuries hence, in bunkers buried deep in the Earth, a proto-Nazi dystopia practises eugenics and thought control, and prepares to conquer the world. Fritz Lang might never have conceived the edifice of *Metropolis* without this model to learn from.

Craig Kennedy, the scientific detective figure who was created by Arthur B. Reeve, featured, off and on, in several films of the late 1910s. Some of the published books were, in fact, novelizations of these films, in which Kennedy invented and discovered his way to the denouement. Typically, *The Carter Case* involves a master criminal who dabbles in science, the threatened daughter of an industrial magnate, and a posse of the usual suspects.

Rutherford splits the atom and a young unknown named Adolf Hitler joins the German Workers' Party as a spy for the authorities.

THE DARKENING WORLD

ANYONE WHO STUCK TO reading just classic Golden Age American genre SF would be hard put to find very much pessimism, or very many dystopias, in the thousands of stories and novels available. Feelings of pessimism are what *losers* feel: they are not feelings fit for the heroes of the spaceways in a new age.

But writers and illustrators at the turn of the century were not so sure that all the changes the world was experiencing would be happy changes; many of them were bought only at great cost. In this, the writers at the beginning of our century share many concerns with the SF writers who are now active, at its end.

A double edge

Right at the start of SF stands Mary Shelley's *Frankenstein* (see page 212). This is, in one way, a tale of hope. Its subtitle, *The Modern Prometheus*, tells us that the "monster" is an emblem of the new: he is a Prometheus figure who steals the secret of fire – or knowledge – from the gods or from nature, and bequeaths that knowledge to the human race. The cost to him of this gift is high, and humanity is ungrateful, but the deed is done. The dark side of the tale is that this Prometheus that Frankenstein creates is also a misshapen figure out of our worst nightmares. There are some things, Shelley tells us, that we are not meant to know. There are some forms of knowledge that may make monsters out of us.

Freezing up

Once the engines of natural change have been unleashed, anything can happen. The recently discovered Ice Age, for instance, may return, or the Sun may cool, and our Earth may die.

Who will inherit the Earth?
Here is the way the world might end, after Darwin. If evolution works, it is only natural that the sea will disgorge brand-new monsters.

The changing world

As the 19th century passed and the 20th arrived, material advances seemed at times to dominate everyone's minds; but in truth the split never quite healed. The image of Progress was a Janus-faced figure, looking forwards and looking back: Prometheus faces the marvel-filled future, and gives us the tools to earn our way forwards, while the monster faces backwards into the abyss, into the depths of time, into a great darkness that smothers all our concerns. Industrialization, urbanization, the explosive development of railways, and the sudden binding of the world into one communications unit through the invention of telegraphs and telephones,

all of these things began to teach us how fragile and insignificant our human concerns and conceits were, when understood in terms of what science had begun to discover about our planet and ourselves.

At the beginning of the 19th century, it was generally believed that the Universe had been created by God, specifically for us, no more than ten thousand years ago – a period of time that could be measured and comprehended. By the beginning of the 20th century, however, geologists like Sir Charles Lyell had aged the Earth to millions upon millions of years: an immeasurable span of time, and a period most demeaning to humanity. And Charles Darwin had likewise demonstrated that we were not by any means the foreordained protagonists of the world story, but simply a prominent part of the furniture of evolution.

Man or ape?
As a political cartoon, this Will Dyson work is highly effective. But it also says something more general: beneath our human skin there lurks bestiality.

SF responses

Given the turmoil of the 19th century, it is not so surprising that most early SF writers saw the future in terms of risk and loss, and that the recent applications of the laws of nature to human history made them feel profoundly vulnerable. Even Jules Verne, apparently such an advocate of material progress, is now known to have written a pessimistic novel, *Paris au XXme siècle* [Paris in the 20th century] (see page 112), set in an invention-choked, crowded, damaged world, rejected by his publisher as too extreme. H.G. Wells is more widely known for creating a *fin de siècle* sense that the world was due for a catastrophe. Wells was not only a student of evolutionary theory, but also a sharp observer, and he felt, like many of his contemporaries, that humanity was on thin ice. Most works of the time contain Dreadful Warnings about a cultural and natural world come unhinged, without stability, values, or calm. And of course, in a way, they were all absolutely right.

Politics personified
Circe is a figure who entraps men, who lures them into a beast state, forever. Dyson's bestial horde is German, but the message is universal.

The future arrives

Then, little more than a decade into the new century, the ice broke under us. Out of Serbia's strike for independence grew a huge political crisis that began a Europe-wide war. The Great War, as it was known at the time, was the greatest catastrophe the Western world had ever experienced: it destroyed a century of uneasy peace and wiped out half a generation. It really destroyed far more than that: it called into question the balance of power, those intricate and delicate political arrangements that had proved inadequate to contain human passions. It showed that the people in charge were woefully unready for challenges to the established order of the world, and it forced change: Germany abandoned its royalty, women in Britain and America got the vote, the Czar was deposed, and nowhere was the political order the same. As SF reflects the world, so within a few years, and as a direct consequence of World War I, the world's greatest dystopias were being written. The works of writers such as Kafka, Čapek, Zamiatin, and Huxley were all products of this war. And, despite the popular view that he became a braying optimist, none of H.G.Wells's novels written after the Great War expresses anything but the most guarded hope of our survival – in some of them his disgust with the human species is Swiftian.

The cost of the war
Once again, images from World War I from Will Dyson's Kultur Cartoons, which appeared in 1915. At one level, this is a stinging attack on the cynical ruthlessness of statesmen. But beneath lies the pit.

WORLD WAR I

The American Civil War was the world's first SF conflict, with its futuristic submarines and weaponry – but it was a local spat compared to World War I. In the aftermath of the war that was supposed to end war, nothing would ever be the same again. Even early magazine SF, with its rigid optimism, seems to be a reaction to the horrors – as though Space Operas might lift us from the trenches forever.

Unburied dead
Between the trenches, in No Man's Land, ghouls lived underground – so the legend went. Those who lived brought back images too harsh to be ignored.

1920-1929: THE AFTERMATH OF WAR

THERE HAD BEEN DOZENS of Future War novels, but nobody guessed. Even H.G. Wells, in the year war broke out, wrote *The War That Will End War*, as though warfare on a large enough scale would teach people some interesting lessons.

By 1920, in the aftermath of a conflict that has effectively destroyed a whole generation, and poisoned belief in the old system of hierarchical and deference-based world-order, everyone, SF writers included, knows better, in their hearts.

1920	1921	1922	1923	1924

SF EVENTS

KarelČapek gives us the word robot, from the Czech language, and **R.U.R.**, his feverish play about a robot revolt, draws huge crowds all over the world.

Not many SF novels of note are published this year. Homer Eon Flint and Austin Hall's *The Blind Spot* appears in *Argosy All-Story* magazine. J.D. Beresford has plucky thoughts about the future in *Evolution*, and there are lots of ghost stories. Parents are busier, however: 1921 sees the birth of dozens of future writers, including James Blish, Ken Bulmer, F.M. Busby, Alfred Coppel, Carol Emshwiller, Stanisław Lem, Charles Eric Maine, Brian Moore, and Mordecai Roshwald. Not forgetting Richard M. Powers, the most innovative cover artist of the 1950s.

It is still good to live in the Soviet Union, and **Alexei Tolstoy**'s *Aelita*, a sweeping Space Opera, argues for the triumph of socialist principles on Mars.

It is a year of settling in to the rapid new world, and of attempts to begin to take stock. Novels like P. Anderson Graham's *The Collapse of Homo Sapiens*, Ronald Knox's *Memories of the Future*, E.V. Odle's *The Clockwork Man* and H.G. Wells's *Men Like Gods* all begin to explore the future – not previously a significant area for British SF writers – in order to get a sense of the present. Elmer Rice's play *The Adding Machine* is a Čapek-like satire.

In Central Europe, there still seems hope for the future, although it is feared that Germany – embittered by the Treaty of Versailles – might rise again. Indeed, a novel like Karel Čapek's remarkably intense *Krakatit* describes this world in vivid metaphors: by unleashing the atom, a scientist unleashes the the Id within.

CINEMA, RADIO, AND TELEVISION

One of the first great films, **Der Golem** (*The Golem*) retells one of the legends of Central Europe: in the 16th century, Rabbi Loew activates a figure of clay to save the Jews in the Prague ghetto, and in 1920, the golem breathes again.

Dr. Mabuse, der Spieler, (*Dr. Mabuse, the Gambler*) is Fritz Lang's hypnotic, labyrinthine vision of the underside of Progress. Mabuse, hypnotist and criminal, drives Germany to the brink.

René Clair makes his experimental masterpiece, the low-budget *Paris qui dort* (*The Crazy Ray*). Paris is sent to sleep, with only a few wakeful ones left in a world where time seems to have stopped.

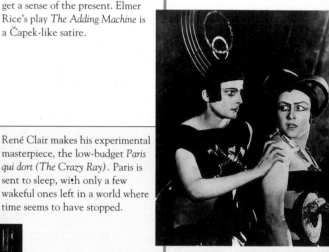

Tolstoy's 1922 novel **Aelita** becomes a smashing film, filled with comic asides about life in the Soviet Union, and fantastic Art Deco sets. Within a few short years, such fun will be forbidden.

MAGAZINES

Argosy and *All-Story Weekly* join as **Argosy All-Story Weekly**. SF contents include work by Murray Leinster, Ray Cummings, Abraham Merritt, Otis Adelbert Kline, and Robert E. Howard.

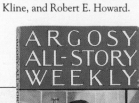

Bernarr Macfadden published a lot of SF over a long career, in many of his magazines, including *Brain Power*, which is launched this year and edited by F. Orlin Tremaine, who will eventually edit *Astounding*. Later (rumour has it) Macfadden bankrupts Hugo Gernsback.

For years, Hugo Gernsback had been publishing magazines extolling science and technology. This year, he devotes an entire issue of his *Science and Invention* to SF. In retrospect, the consequence – the founding of *Amazing Stories* – seems inevitable.

WORLD EVENTS

Gandhi goes to jail for 6 years and in Rome, **Mussolini** marches into power for 22. T.S. Eliot publishes *The Waste Land*, Sinclair Lewis publishes *Babbitt*.

The United States moves further into isolation, not joining the International Court of Justice. **Inflation soars in Germany**, making banknotes worthless. Mustafah Kemal is elected President of Turkey.

We have an extraordinary new universe to grapple with, but the same old *Homo sapiens* at the wheel. Old verities are being challenged: the World State is a shambles, despite the League of Nations, and the *pax aeronautica* is a farce; but scientific achievements of the previous century – such as electricity, telephony, the internal combustion engine, the theory of flight – are all now being developed at an unprecedented rate. So what next? Space!

1925

Hugo Gernsback publishes *Ralph 124C 41+*, and the executors of Kafka's will publish – against his instructions – *Der Prozess (The Trial)*. The first was written in 1912, and the second in 1915, but only now do they appear in book form. It is hard to imagine two more different worlds. One is a future full of technological answers to life's dilemmas; the other a vision of a world defined by those dilemmas, with only one ultimate answer: death.

Electrical recordings are released, and talking pictures are forecast by A.O. Rankine. Kodak produces 16mm film stock, and Scottish inventor **John Logie Baird** develops the technology to transmit pictures by television.

Hitler publishes *Mein Kampf*. Unemployment insurance is introduced in Great Britain. Sergei Eisenstein's *Battleship Potemkin* is released. The *New Yorker* magazine is founded. The civil war in Ireland ends. Peter Sellers is born.

1926

Suddenly the range widens. From Robert M. Coates's surreal *The Eater of Darkness* to Guy Dent's *Emperor of the If*, the gates are opening wide again, for the first time since the Great War. Thea von Harbou novelizes her screenplay for her husband's epic film *Metropolis*, and Edgar Rice Burroughs continues to plough through space with *The Moon Maid*. Charlotte Haldane's *Man's World* is an early feminist dystopia. Atomic power and alchemy are brought together in Reginald Glossop's *The Orphan of Space*.

Fritz Lang's **Metropolis** has mad scientists, robots disguised as maidens, slaves, assembly lines from Hell, huge dials, and rebellion. The greatest image of the film is the underground city itself, from which the masses spew forth.

In this year, Hugo Gernsback founds **Amazing Stories**, and the literature we recognize as SF is finally born.

Robert A. Goddard launches a successful liquid-fuel rocket in the United States. In England, a General Strike is called and is defeated. Trotsky is evicted from the Politburo. Rudolph Valentino dies. A.A. Milne publishes *Winnie the Pooh*.

1927

There are two novels by John Taine – *Quayle's Invention* and *The Gold Tooth* – the best of a quiet year.

1928

In Great Britain, the publisher **Victor Gollancz** founds the firm that still bears his name, and immediately – with E.H. Visiak's *Medusa* – begins to publish writers at the cutting edge of various genres, including SF: Franz Kafka, M.P. Shiel, Murray Constantine, and Charles Williams.

The third remake of *Alraune* stars Brigitte Helm, who played Maria in *Metropolis*, playing a darkly erotic version of the woman who is a scientist's soulless creation.

Joseph Stalin takes over the Soviet Union, and shuts down the arts as fast as he can. In America, Walt Disney makes the first Mickey Mouse cartoon.

1929

Buck Rogers in the 25th Century begins life as a comic strip. Hugo Gernsback uses the term "science fiction" for the first time, although it had been invented elsewhere. Kay Burdekin, who later writes as Murray Constantine, publishes *The Rebel Passion*, Jack Williamson publishes *The Girl from Mars*, and S. Fowler Wright publishes *The World Below*.

Fritz Lang's **Die Frau im Mond** (*The Woman in the Moon*) looks astonishingly real, thanks to Willy Ley, and invents the countdown.

The **Wall Street Crash** deflates the belief that Progress is inevitable. Faulkner publishes *The Sound and the Fury*. The Graf Zeppelin flies around the world.

SCIENCE AND INVENTIONS

WE ARE THE TOOLMAKERS of this planet. We are the creatures that have the opposing thumbs, the bump of curiosity, the ravenous appetite, the territorial aggression that foments the need in us to fight others of our kind, and the deep memory capacity that allows us to keep in our minds whatever we fabricated yesterday. We are the species, above all, that tinkers with things.

The roots of technology

In the 16th century, Sir Francis Bacon almost single-handedly invented the modern world through his development of the concept of inductive reasoning, his insistence that things caused things to happen, and his belief that human beings could make things that make other things happen. For quite a few years after, all seemed well in the Western World. Progress and technology – which, after all, can be defined as things making things happen – seemed to be indissolubly linked. It was not until the end of the 18th century that contradictory voices began to make themselves heard.

Electric defence
In early American magazine SF, technology was seen as being there to help and defend humanity, although things did have a tendency to go awry at times. Military machines designed to repel strange attacks from outer space featured largely both on and between the covers of the lurid early pulps.

And it is all very well for us to believe that some new invention will be of benefit to all, or that it is perfectly obvious that the world is a better place to live in because of (for example) the development of a vaccine, but good stories are not made of things working out for the best – at least they are not made from things working out at first. Even happy endings need fraught beginnings.

It was only with Mary Shelley's *Frankenstein* (see page 212) that a full imaginative response to the double-edged sword of technology finally appeared. It is fitting that *Frankenstein* is often thought to be the first SF novel, because it encapsulates the hopes and the fears that drive SF even today. SF has always been inextricably involved with technology, praising new inventions, taking the human race into new places, and arguing for world upon world where human beings have made things that have made other things happen. But at the same time, SF writers have also always been deeply dubious about all this technology, just as Mary Shelley was. There was so much to admire in the clanging new worlds of the 19th century, but there were also things to fear. This double-edged quality of SF technology has not changed from then until now.

Goggles, helmets, and ear protectors all show – this stuff can be dangerous, and is only for the intrepid

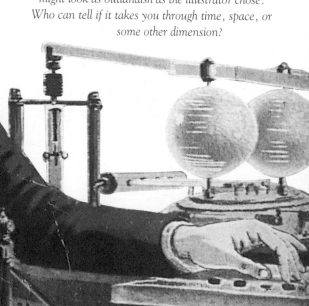

Unimpaired vision
Realism had no place in the pulp world: a machine might look as outlandish as the illustrator chose. Who can tell if it takes you through time, space, or some other dimension?

The human angle
Metropolis *is full of technology, but it enslaves rather than frees the workers. In the end, a saintly woman and an idealistic man must save them.*

The pursuit of knowledge

Technology is not only things, but knowledge of things. Western civilization has for centuries felt that the pursuit of knowledge is profoundly necessary, almost holy. Some say that knowledge for its own sake (pure science) and knowledge to make things move (technology) are two different things. They are wrong: the two are different stages on the same road, and the inventions of SF are visions of the road ahead.

Where that road will lead, only we can say. Hugo Gernsback's wide-eyed-wonder tale of future technology, *Ralph 124C 41+* (see page 214) was published as a book in 1925, the year before he kickstarted the magazine SF market in the United States with *Amazing Stories*, trumpeting itself as "the magazine of scientifiction" and full of wonderful inventions and passion for the new, for the future. For Hugo Gernsback, and later for John W. Campbell Jr. and pretty much the whole of American genre SF, that road to the future led, without any question, ever upwards. But, as one might put it, while technology is about spokes, stories are about folks. So, despite the fact that many SF writers have always equated technology and progress, it is not surprising that, for the sake of the story, even the most optimistic SF tales do tend to get the world into some pretty bad trouble before the dark clouds are lifted by dint of a great new invention.

Tidy solution
The inventor Rotwang believes that he has created the worker of the future for Metropolis, but what is to become of the workers of the present? His "mechanical man" is first put to devious use, to destroy them.

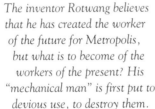

The darker side

Technology carries two main risks, and, because they are in the business of stories, even the most optimistic SF writers were quick to see them. The first is the fact that tools cause other tools, weapons cause other weapons: every action has a reaction, every defence, a new offence. SF has concentrated upon inventions of war perhaps because it is in the theatre of combat that this law is written most clearly. If we invent an electro-magnetic vortex-defender, to see off an invasion, the next installment will see a hyper-vortex spinning down on our helpless planet – until the brand-new hyper-vortex defender comes on stream.

The other thing to fear is local autonomy – machines that run themselves. Once things make things happen, then the logic of technology is that the process must continue. The berserk robots of the Golden Age were tamed by Asimov, but they have become today's Artificial Intelligences who think they are God.

1930-1939: THE DEPRESSION DECADE

ROUSING, GALAXY-SPANNING adventure stories, or Space Operas, feature strongly in these years. But Space Opera does not spring fully fledged out of the minds and hearts of pulp writers searching for new territories for their heroes to conquer, and having nothing to do with the mundane world. Space Opera, in fact, represents for many of its fans a necessary escape from a world engulfed in a Great Depression, and visibly descending, unbelievably, once

1930 · 1931 · 1932 · 1933 · 1934

SF EVENTS

In Britain, Olaf Stapledon's *Last and First Men* is published to critical acclaim. Stapledon and the critics think of this not as a work of SF, but as a piece of philosophical writing. On a smaller scale, **The World in 2030**, by the Earl of Birkenhead, is published, full of speculation on the shape of the next century and futuristic illustrations of how it might look.

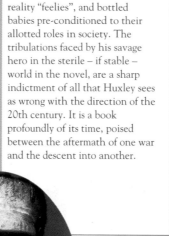

Aldous Huxley's *Brave New World* is published, giving us the social-control "soma" drug, the virtual-reality "feelies", and bottled babies pre-conditioned to their allotted roles in society. The tribulations faced by his savage hero in the sterile – if stable – world in the novel, are a sharp indictment of all that Huxley sees as wrong with the direction of the 20th century. It is a book profoundly of its time, poised between the aftermath of one war and the descent into another.

John Collier's **Tom's A-Cold** (published in the United States as *Full Circle*) takes a contemplative and almost wishful look at a post-holocaust world some 60 years into the future.

Space Opera is well established in the magazine markets of the United States by now, although earlier stars of the form, such as Ray Cummings and Neil R. Jones, are already on the wane. E.E. Smith's **Skylark** series reaches its culmination in *Skylark of Valeron*, and his **Lensmen** series begins with *Triplanetary*, which is serialized in *Amazing* magazine. Jack Williamson's *Legion of Space* begins what is his best series from this time, and Flash Gordon makes his first appearance in the newspapers.

CINEMA, RADIO, AND TELEVISION

In America, *Just Imagine* appears, and nearly puts an end to SF cinema. It is a strange musical set in a future where names have become numbers and people take food pills: it flops.

The classic James Whale version of **Frankenstein** appears. A decision to cast Boris Karloff rather than the originally intended Bela Lugosi in the title role leads the film to lean to horror, which sets the pattern for Hollywood "SF" films for decades to come.

19th-century novels continue to come to the screen: *Dr. Jekyll and Mr. Hyde* is the most sexually suggestive of the screen versions of the book.

James Whale builds from the success of *Frankenstein* with his classic screen version of H.G. Wells's **The Invisible Man**. The film makes a star of Claude Rains, whose voice has to carry most of the film, and does so with style. It is best to forget the misbegotten brood of sequels.

MAGAZINES

Science Wonder Stories and Air Wonder Stories merge to become **Wonder Stories**. *Astounding Stories of Super Science*, a pulp-adventure magazine, appears.

Science and Invention, the last incarnation of Gernsback's *Electrical Experimenter*, folds. *Astounding Stories of Super Science* changes its name to *Astounding Stories*.

Astounding Stories is bought by Street and Smith, who change the editorial policy and raise it to a new position of prominence in the field.

WORLD EVENTS

Hitler's National Socialist Party comes to prominence in the German elections. An English edition of **Mein Kampf** is published. Gandhi marches across India in protest against the salt tax.

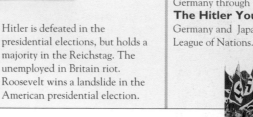

Hitler is defeated in the presidential elections, but holds a majority in the Reichstag. The unemployed in Britain riot. Roosevelt wins a landslide in the American presidential election.

Hitler becomes Chancellor in Germany through intrigues. **The Hitler Youth** is formed. Germany and Japan leave the League of Nations.

again, into the shattering disaster of another World War. In Europe, writers like Aldous Huxley and Olaf Stapledon are responding more directly to the spirit of the age. By the end of the decade, however, in the United States,

John W. Campbell's new generation of SF writers is also beginning to use the conceptual potentials of the genre to come to grips with famine, war, and pestilence. For SF, out of the surrounding destruction, the great years have begun.

1 9 3 5

For Europeans, the threat of war is close and political satires and dystopias dominate. Irish author Joseph O'Neill uses a Lost World setting for his powerful satire, *Land under England*. An attack on the fascism developing under Hitler, it is set in a totalitarian state controlled by telepathy that does away with free will.

Maurice Renard's novel *Le mains d'Orlac (The Hands of Orlac)* makes its second screen appearance as **Mad Love**. This version concentrates on the doctor who performs the hand transplant and his obsession with his patient's wife. Peter Lorre's performance is far from the standard mad scientist fare.

In Germany, Jews are deprived of their citizenship. **Dust storms** across the United States wipe out crops and displace farming communities. Gershwin's *Porgy and Bess* premieres.

1 9 3 6

In mainland Europe, novels that tell of some impending doom are less circumspect than those written in Britain. In 1935, mainstream German writer Paul Gurk had written *Tuzub 37*, in which a ravaged world rebels against humanity; this year, Czech author Karel Čapek publishes his classic novel *Vàlka s Mloky* (*War with the Newts*), in which the exploited and oppressed Newts exact their revenge on humanity by drowning the world in an expansionist flood.

Flash Gordon makes it onto the cinema screen in a weekly serial. Each episode begins with a recap of the story with comic-strip illustrations, displayed on a screen. And each episode ends with some awful fate about to happen to our heroes.

As Gernsback's empire continues to decline, *Wonder Stories* is sold and becomes *Thrilling Wonder Stories*. More garish than it had been under Gernsback, it features lots of monsters and adventures, and has considerable success.

1 9 3 7

The first Flash Gordon in book form, **Flash Gordon in the Caverns of Mongo**, is published. It hints at the transfer of Hard SF from the magazine market to the book market following the approaching war.

John W. Campbell Jr. becomes editor of *Astounding Stories* magazine. He changes the title to *Astounding Science Fiction*, which the much-named magazine will keep until 1960.

Orwell publishes *The Road to Wigan Pier*, a portrait of depression Britain. Europeans flock to fight in the Spanish Civil War. With Germany allied to Mussolini's Italy and occupying the Rhineland, war looms closer.

1 9 3 8

The biggest media event of the year is the radio dramatization of H.G. Wells's *War of the Worlds* by **Orson Welles**. The broadcast is mistaken for a real newscast and causes widespread panic. This seems implausible today, but broadcast radio had been around less than 20 years, and the times were right for panic.

Germany annexes Austria and occupies the Sudetenland.

1 9 3 9

Lewis Caroll's **Alice** books are parodied again in the run-up to World War II. **Adolf in Blunderland** casts Hitler into a surreapolitik landscape of incompetence and insanity.

Startling Stories magazine starts as a companion to *Thrilling Wonder Stories*. Campbell's *Astounding* publishes debuts from Heinlein, Sturgeon, and van Vogt, and an Asimov story.

After annexing the remains of Czechoslovakia, **Hitler invades Poland**. Britain and France enter the war.

TIME TRAVEL

WE ARE ALL TIME TRAVELLERS. We do not stop travelling forwards in time until we die, and even then our bodies continue to forge onwards. By the end of the 19th century, SF stories of time travel had done little more than speed up the process slightly. In literary terms, there is very little difference between a sleeper awakening after several centuries of coma, and a young man leaping through a portal into futurity. So time travel forwards was not, in truth, very remarkable – until 1895, when H.G. Wells wrote *The Time Machine* (see page 213), taking his time traveller so far into the future that everything changes. But in 1889, Mark Twain popularized travel into the past in *A Yankee at the Court of King Arthur* (see page 213), and he opened a Pandora's Box. Almost all the time travel in modern SF has, since then, been in a backwards direction.

The long sleep
In 19th-century Valdar the Oft-Born, *the hero wakes in different ages.*

To the end of time
The narrator of Wells's The Time Machine *tells a tale of time travel hundreds of centuries into the future, of narrow escapes, and of cosmic awe. The film version is good on escapes, but short on awe.*

Living in a box
It may have been born out of budgetary requirements – after all, a time machine that looks like a police call box was hardly going to bankrupt the BBC – but it proved to be an inspiration of genius. Like portals in fantasy tales, the TARDIS in Doctor Who is a door into a world bigger inside than outside; not only that, it takes the Doctor anywhen, whenever he wants.

Son of the TARDIS
In the anarchic 1989 film Bill and Ted's Excellent Adventure, which is spoof SF, it is not surprising to find a spoof TARDIS. Unlike the real thing, Bill and Ted's phone box is smaller inside than out, and is soon uncomfortably crammed with people and relics collected from all over time for a school history report.

Which way to go?

There are two kinds of time travel, one simple, one almost infinitely complex. The simple kind is travel into the future, and it is simple for a simple reason: a character who travels into the future cannot affect the present. His main function will almost certainly be to serve as a point-of-view from which to describe the new world into which he has come. It is for this reason that many of the classic 19th-century utopias and dystopias – if set in the future, which they often were – use protagonists who have slipped through time, or awoken from a century or so of slumber (which is the same as travelling through time for a century or so). For modern readers, most 19th-century novels of time travel are, frankly, boring. Wells's great tale is an exception to the rules and it is enormously exciting: by casting its protagonist into a setting hundreds of thousands of years hence, it is able to present an Earth whose alienness is terrifying, but at the same time a consequence of the forces of biological and social evolution. But Wells's tale stands alone; it has almost never been imitated.

One reason for this is obvious: most modern SF tales are already set in the future, and there is little reason for SF writers to convey future protagonists into worlds that are yet more remote. More interesting by far to the 20th-century SF writer has been the example of Mark Twain. When Twain's Connecticut Yankee takes a trip back to Arthurian England, the plot thickens immediately, and the implications of the story become both fascinating and dangerous. At its heart, time travel back into the past is a highly subversive literary device. When Twain's Boss beards the Knights of the Round Table and sparks off an industrial revolution, he is threatening to undermine the whole course of history that Twain's readers understand to be true; and although Twain is only writing a fiction, his story is still capable of making readers uneasy.

Escape to the past

There is, apart from these two, a third kind of time travel, which also used to be fairly popular in SF, but is less commonly found today. In this type of story, a time traveller from some era in the future arrives in the present-day world.

At 88 mph ...
The film Back to the Future *has excitements, paradoxes, and problems galore. And all in a De Lorean.*

Sometimes the visitor brings scientific marvels, or is escaping future horrors, as in some tales by Simak, who used the device more than any other writer; sometimes the protagonist simply arrives by accident, as in E.V. Odle's 1923 novel *The Clockwork Man*. But the device is not very popular, perhaps because it is hard to identify with characters who may be superior to us.

With the rise of SF magazines in the United States came the rise of time travel into the past. Hundreds of stories in which young men travelled backwards to kill their grandfathers, marry their grandmothers, and so forth, were published in quick succession. Dozens of novels were written in which a man (rarely, in those early days, a woman – SF still scrupulously adhered to the sexist distinction between adventurer and adventuress) travelled in a time machine, opened his eyes in the time of the dinosaurs, or Napoleon, or Abraham Lincoln,

and tied history into a near-infinite complexity of knots. But the creation of new timelines is very similar to the creation of Alternate Worlds (see page 62). The two themes very often come together at the point when the time traveller is about to change things forever – deliberately or accidentally – quite possibly, in the process, changing the future so that he could never have been born. At this moment, often enough, the Time Police show up to knit everything back together, so that history can follow its proper and pre-ordained, or at any rate *preferred*, course. And everything is returned to its "normal" state. Well, sometimes, anyway.

Time vortex
The man caught in the coils of this time machine from Wonder Stories *magazine probably invented it (because he looks old), and it will probably kill him.*

No bikers here
One thrill of a time-travel tale is confrontation between technologies of different eras. Here, in a story from Aboriginal SF *magazine, Redcoats fighting the American Revolution have to deal with a Harley Davidson.*

ALTERNATE WORLDS

The Jurassic world
A world dominated by smart dinosaurs is a world in which tiny mammals still skulk in holes, dodging the rulers.

IT SOUNDS SO SIMPLE. Take some event in world history – the asteroid hit that may have ended the dinosaurs' reign millions of years ago, or the defeat of Napoleon at Waterloo – and imagine what the consequences might be if that event had never happened. What if the dinosaurs had survived, and become smart? What if Napoleon had triumphed, and Britain failed to build an empire? It sounds simple, but the beginning is the only simple thing there is about an Alternate World. Take, for example, a world in which Wolfgang Amadeus Mozart does not die aged 36, of diseases now curable – a simple change – and continues to compose for another 30 years. His next opera would probably have been a version of Shakespeare's *The Tempest*, and might have jump-started Romanticism, 20 years early. Which would have left Beethoven high and dry. And would Wagner have composed his *Ring* cycle if Mozart had jumped the gun? And with no *Ring*, what would there have been for Hitler to hum?

The sign of the cross
If Jesus had not been crucified, thus changing the world utterly for Christians, His followers could not have conquered the Roman Empire in His name, and a Mithraic Rome might have dominated Europe for centuries more.

Without Waterloo
Napoleon was a world hero to his contemporaries, who believed he was both a military genius and a brilliant reformer of the antiquated legal system. What if he had never been born? Or had won at the Battle of Waterloo?

In the beginning

In the very first Alternate World of all, Eve spurns the apple of knowledge, and history never even happens: without sin, nothing starts. Declining to sin in Eden is not, therefore, the kind of Alternate World beginning point that makes for a good plot – because stories only work if there is something wrong, something that needs to be changed. The difference between most stories and Alternate World stories is that the latter focus almost exclusively on the moment of some change, and upon its immediate consequences, rather than on the long-term developments that result from it. Moreover, Alternate World stories depend on the basic assumption that one small differing outcome, at one point in time, will change the entire world. SF writers sometimes call this a Jonbar Point (or Hinge), after a Jack Williamson character from the 1930s, who creates one world if he picks up a pebble and another if he picks up a magnet and becomes a great scientist.

The American Civil War
There are a dozen Jonbar Points, each lovingly examined by phalanxes of dreamers, at which the South might have won. So say the dreamers.

What Alternate World stories tend to claim, therefore, is that individual human actions count; that it is not the vast momentum of world history that shapes our very lives, but some individual action – Abraham Lincoln forgets to go to the theatre – that has made our world what it is. And this means that the world we live in is not, therefore, a trap from which there is no escape. We can get out; we can find an alternative.

One particular set of Alternate World stories assumes that when a Jonbar Point is reached, every choice that can be made at that point is made, and that each of those choices generates a different parallel world. Some – like Leinster's *Sidewise in Time*, written in 1950, or Simak's 1953 tale, *Ring Around the Sun*, or Heinlein's *Job*, written in 1984 – assume that a huge number of these parallel universes can exist,

Decline and fall
If the British Empire had lasted, would it be a superpower today?

just sufficiently out of synch that they do not collide. Satirical lessons are often conveyed through comparisons of such worlds.

What if...?

The more traditional Alternate World tale tends to focus on the intellectual pleasures to be had unpacking the full range of consequences that are possible from one change. History is full of favourite What Ifs: the survival of the dinosaurs; Alexander the Great's formidable old age; the Roman victory at Carthage; the escape of Jesus; the sinking of Japan; Columbus failing to find America; the victory of the Spanish Armada over Queen Elizabeth's England; Newton brained by a falling apple; Napoleon gaining the day at Waterloo; Babbage inventing a working computer in 1820; the South winning the American Civil War; the assassination attempt failing at Sarajevo; Lenin dying in Berlin; Franklin Delano Roosevelt dying immediately after his election; Hitler winning; the A-bomb not working; de Gaulle staying in office and fighting for a post-empire France; Stalin dying of tetanus in 1948; General MacArthur becoming President of the United States; JFK avoiding Dallas;

the successful revolution begun at Tiannamen Square signalling a new way of life for China.

A world of choice

The possibilities, in other words, are endless. The only requirement is the belief that actions count. The SF stories that act out that belief tend to come in two categories. There are those stories – such as Philip K. Dick's *The Man in the High Castle* (see page 223), a Hitler Wins scenario, or Keith Roberts's *Pavane*, written in 1968, where the Spanish Armada has conquered – that examine the implications of a changed event, whether or not one, or many, Alternate Worlds are assumed. And there are those stories – such as Isaac Asimov's 1955 tale, *The End of Eternity*, or Keith Laumer's intricate *Worlds of the Imperium*, written in 1962, or Barrington J. Bayley's novel *The Fall of Chronopolis* from 1974 – that concentrate on Jonbar Points, and generally involve time travel in plots that pit differing Alternate Worlds against each other, each defending its own reality from others' attempts to jig the Jonbar Point decision so history will flow their way.

In the end, however, the central theme of the Alternate World tale is the belief that the world is up to us.

New world order
Hitler provides dozens of Jonbar Points. The main one is that he does not invade Russia, and wins the war. The outcome? Horror, in almost every case.

1940-1949: GLOBAL CONFLICT

THE WAR SPREADS OUT from Europe to engulf all the globe. Novels speculating on the outcome and consequences of the war are published while it is in progress, but once it is all over, British and American SF seem to lose interest, although the first Alternate World in which Hitler wins is published in Hungary just a few months after he has lost. The war makes the 1940s a mixed decade for SF. It removes many writers from the field, temporarily or permanently.

1 9 4 0	1 9 4 1	1 9 4 2	1 9 4 3	1 9 4 4

SF EVENTS

1940 — SF writers like weapons and high drama; but most of them are sane people, strongly anti-Nazi, and democratic at root. This makes World War II hard to write about, as the Nazis display a great knack at the aesthetics of modern warfare. One good Dreadful Warning SF novel about what might happen if Hitler gained the upper hand is *Lightning in the Night* by Fred Allhoff. It appears in *Liberty* magazine, and only reaches book form in 1979.

1941 — SF almost disappears from Great Britain, due to military service and **paper shortages**. Phil Stong edits the first major SF anthology, *Of Other Worlds*.

1942 — Heinlein climaxes a stunning series of novels and short stories with a magazine version of what would become *Beyond this Horizon*, then – like many other dominant SF writers – does war work until the end of hostilities. Fantasies like *Land of Unreason* by L. Sprague de Camp and Fletcher Pratt rewrite history so that reason might triumph. The most important books are by non-genre writers. Vita Sackville-West's *Grand Canyon* predicts a Nazi victory, while Austin Tappan Wright's *Islandia* creates a vast Pacific utopia and Peter Vansittart's *I Am the World* satirizes totalitarianism.

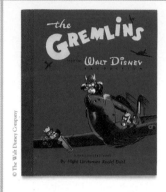

1943 — Walt Disney plans a naughty but nice **Gremlins** tale as a wartime pick-me-up. The result is Roald Dahl's first book, but no film appears. Hermann Hesse writes *Das Glasperlenspiel (Magister Ludi)*.

© The Walt Disney Company

1944 — Clifford Simak, one of the few writers of modern SF too old for active duty, begins to publish in *Astounding* magazine the tales that make up *City*, for which he is best remembered. Aldous Huxley publishes *Time Must Have a Stop*, Olaf Stapledon produces his last great SF novel, *Sirius*, and Philip Wylie publishes *Night Unto Night*. But in general, this is a year of quiet anticipation.

CINEMA, RADIO, AND TELEVISION

Yellow Peril meets the future. Long before Pearl Harbor was bombed, **Dr. Cyclops** much resembles the kind of "Jap" who later featured in propaganda films.

Batman is the tragedy of *Metropolis* replayed as farce. As an escapist urban fantasy, whose ambivalent, masked hero-villain turns out all good, it hits the spot in a war year.

MAGAZINES

From 1939, John W. Campbell Jr.'s *Unknown* has specialized in rationalized magic and fantasy nearly indistinguishable from SF proper. Campbell finally kills *Unknown* in order to save precious paper for *Astounding*.

Nothing daunted by the war, **The Shadow** continues to prowl the world in search of criminals, including Genghis Khan's super-powered descendant.

A few years earlier, dozens of SF magazines came and went. By 1944, only the big pre-war names are left on the stands.

WORLD EVENTS

Paris falls: the fake war is over. Trotsky is assassinated. Walt Disney makes *Fantasia*.

Japan bombs **Pearl Harbor**, and Germany invades Russia, forcing the world's two largest powers into the war. Allied victory is now inevitable.

Heavily armed occupying forces attack the **Warsaw ghetto**. Some of the Jews presume to defend themselves. They die, but take some Nazis with them.

The "V" of the **V-2** flying bomb is the vengeance that Hitler begins wreaking in September.

It sends SF cinema into a tail-spin of fear and escapism from which it does not begin to recover until the 1950s. And the wartime paper shortages kill off any magazine on either side of the Atlantic that looks less than healthy.

After the war, as if in recognition of the needs of the new age, or as a response to the growing maturity of SF writers, book publication of SF begins to burgeon, until by the late 1940s specialist SF houses are starting up.

1945	1946	1947	1948	1949

1945

In *Astounding* magazine, A.E. van Vogt climaxes five years of ferocious production with *The World of A*, which Simon and Schuster publishes as a book in 1948. In Great Britain, C.S. Lewis publishes *That Hideous Strength*, and George Orwell publishes *Animal Farm*.

The Purple Monster Strikes, a low-budget serial, introduces two themes to American cinema: alien invasions, and possession of humans by shape-changing aliens.

In August, the dropping of the first **atomic bombs** ends World War II, and begins the first chapter of global history.

1946

Tentatively at first, the floodgates begin to open. Van Vogt's **Slan** appears in book form, as does E.E. Smith's **The Skylark of Space**, McComas and Healy's essential anthology, *Adventures in Time and Space*, and Pat Frank's *Mr. Adam*.

New Worlds is founded, after a false start in fanzine form before the war set in. It is the central British SF magazine for three decades, and anthologies still appear today.

The lights in a neighbouring town dim every time it is used; it is **ENIAC**, the first real computer.

1947

Gnome Press is not the first, but it is the most successful small press to concentrate on SF. Edd Cartier's logo for the company says it all.

J.O. Bailey's **Pilgrims Through Space and Time** is the first academic attempt to understand SF. It remains useful.

Irregular and badly distributed, *Fantasy Book* is founded. In only eight issues over four years, it publishes Asimov, van Vogt, Leinster, and Cordwainer Smith's stunning first story, "Scanners Live in Vain", which had been rejected by all of the established SF magazines.

1948

By now, major SF writers like Heinlein are beginning to get their early work published by the specialty houses, whose ranks are augmented this year by **Shasta**, founded by T.E. Dikty, soon to become Julian May's husband. Shasta's taste is impeccable: de Camp, Heinlein, and Alfred Bester. They turn down L. Ron Hubbard's first book on Dianetics.

Nobody has ever really understood why it was **Superman**, rather than any of the other superheroes, who became world-famous; but the mystique was even strong enough to make this terrible cheapy into a money-spinner.

The image of the Competent Man, earlier espoused by Heinlein in *Astounding*, has gradually been transformed, in John W Campbell's mind, into a license for unfettered "unorthodoxy". By the late 1940s, long after Heinlein had stopped contributing to it, *Astounding* is preparing itself to embrace the tenets of Dianetics.

1949

It is a year of taking stock of the unparalleled changes the century has witnessed. George Orwell publishes *Nineteen Eighty-Four*, and George R. Stewart publishes *Earth Abides*. But young writers, having recuperated from military service, are beginning to feel their oats. The first magazine designed to cater to them, *The Magazine of Fantasy and Science Fiction*, is founded. There is a scent of spring in the SF air.

The Magazine of Fantasy and Science Fiction appears, and is still going strong over 40 years on. The lurid **A. Merritt's Fantasy Magazine** dies in five issues.

Mao takes over China. NATO is founded. Apartheid begins in South Africa. Einstein publishes his **Generalized Theory of Gravitation**. Carol Reed makes *The Third Man*.

$$g_{i\,hse}=0;\ \Gamma_{\underline{\iota}}=0;\ R_{\iota k}=0;\ g_{,6}^{43}=0$$

1950-1959: A SILVER AGE

THERE IS A JOKE that the Golden Age of SF is about 12. This is true in that what happens at that age is what you remember as golden, and it does not only apply to SF. Every genre, or interest, or focus of organized passion has its own Golden Age, just like SF. But there are real and absolute Golden Ages, too: it is fair to say that some times are more focused, more heightened, and more gladdened by good spirits and a sense of newness, than are others.

	1950	**1951**	**1952**	**1953**	**1954**
SF EVENTS	For a few years, the small presses have had the field to themselves. Now it is the turn of Doubleday, which features writers such as Isaac Asimov and Ray Bradbury. Doubleday publishes SF as SF: it is proud of it.	**Rayon fantastique**, one of the lists that come to dominate French SF publishing, is launched, with *Genus Homo* as an early title, translated as *Le regne du gorille*.	Although **Ballantine Books** does not release an SF title until the sixteenth book it publishes – Frederik Pohl's *Star Science Fiction Stories* anthology in 1953 – the founding of this list turns out to be significant for writers and readers alike: Ballantine provides affordable paperback originals from the best writers in the field.	The 1953 World SF Convention gives the first **Hugo Award** – named after Hugo Gernsback. In Germany, the Utopia imprint popularizes the term "SF".	SF begins to reflect on itself in Donald Tuck's *Handbook of Science Fiction and Fantasy*. The **Présence du futur** imprint is launched in France.

CINEMA, RADIO, AND TELEVISION

Destination Moon arrives with the new decade, heralding a new maturity. Sober, serious, brightly lit, it is almost the first SF film made in the United States. Up to now, it had all been horror.

One of the last interesting SF serials, **Mysterious Island** conveys Verne's plot, and adds an alien from Mercury.

Destination Moon was a film crying in the wilderness. By 1952, with nonsense like *The Beast from 20,000 Fathoms*, Hollywood is back on form with horror.

Tame, twee, and truly terrible, **Project Moonbase** is as good as SF gets in the 1950s. It is Heinlein's last Hollywood effort.

One of the very few successful combinations of the horror/monster film and SF film, *Them!* gives a pre-*Gunsmoke* James Arness a chance to fight giant ants. The film has wonderful desert scenes and a great climax in the sewers of Los Angeles.

MAGAZINES

Fifteen SF magazines are launched this year. The most important is *Galaxy*. But *Worlds Beyond* and *Science Fantasy* hit the stands as well. **Astounding** publishes the first Dianetics article.

In France, *Fiction* and the first incarnation of **Galaxie** are published. *Galaxie* merely reprints abridged translations of American originals, and founders.

WORLD EVENTS

George Bernard Shaw dies at the grand age of 94. The Korean War begins. Kon-Tiki is launched.

Some of the buildings look more like beehive hairdos than expressions of the future, but the **Festival of Britain** does, all the same, finally brush aside the austerities of war.

The United States explodes its first hydrogen bomb in the South Pacific at **Eniwetok Atoll** – a safe distance from home, but not from the observing ships.

Dien Bien Phu falls. Bikini Island is demolished by the H-bomb. **Robert Oppenheimer** is declared a "security risk", and Senator McCarthy witch-hunts "Commies" on television.

In SF – one supposes – the immediate pre-war period was the real, right-stuff Golden Age, although it was hardly a halcyon period for the world. And, while the 1950s are a time of prosperity and hope, for SF it would be better to call them the Age of Silver. They are a period of more assurance and maturity, more suave and profitable than the years that preceded them; but they are also a time for some reflection. SF has grown up – and perhaps it has already begun to age.

1955	1956	1957	1958	1959

SF's Age of Silver is flourishing, and more writers than ever before are making reasonable incomes from their work. Good novels by Asimov, Knight, and others continue to appear. Some genre magazines are prosperous, but the pulps have seen the last of the glory days. Greg Benford starts a fanzine with his twin brother.

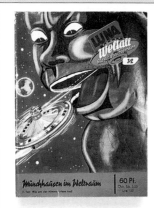

The **Luna** pulp series begins in Germany: reprints of circulating library titles dominate the list.

In Germany, the **Terra** series joins the SF publishing fray: all three publishing houses that will be dominant in Germany now have an SF imprint.

C.M. Kornbluth dies. In Germany, the **Terra-Sonderband** list is edited by Walter Ernsting, who began the Utopia imprint in 1953.

With *Starship Troopers*, Heinlein starts a revolution: SF books will no longer avoid issues eschewed by the prim magazines. In France, **Fiction** publish the first French SF anthology.

Another rare genuine SF film appears. **This Island Earth** duly climaxes – after the old fashion – in the aliens' death, but it boasts an exciting plot.

The robot in **Forbidden Planet**, bound by Asimov's Three Laws of Robotics, has become a cliché. But in 1956, such sophistication was revolutionary in the cinema, and Robbie still delights.

The Fly continues the silliness of the decade. A scientist experiments with a matter transmitter and somehow gets mixed up with a fly. The fly gets his head and arm, and the scientist gets the fly's head and wing, but strangely there is enough brain for both of them. The scientist tries to reverse the process but fails and eventually pleads for death. For such a ridiculous idea, the film was a surprising success.

On one side, there is silliness with monsters in *The Giant Behemoth*; on the other, gloom as the world is devastated by atomic aftermath in *On the Beach*: but they are both called SF.

The first real SF magazine in Germany, **Utopia Magazin**, makes a promising start, but ends after 26 issues.

Astounding serializes Asimov's *The Naked Sun*. *Galaxy* has Bester's *The Stars My Destination*, and *Fantasy and Science Fiction* runs Heinlein's *The Door into Summer*.

The German **Galaxis** is founded. Well produced, but crippled by the fact that its writers are not yet familiar, it folds after 15 issues.

A down-market version of *Fiction*, **Satellite** publishes good material, most of it translated, in its early years; then it declines into shoddiness, and folds in 1962.

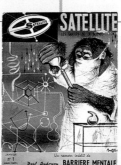

The Suez crisis ends Anthony Eden's career. Sputnik I orbits the world, and shocks the West. A dog named Laika orbits in **Sputnik II**.

Wernher von Braun, the former German V-2 scientist, helps America fight back against Sputnik with Explorer.

The Russian probe **Lunik I** reaches the Moon, and then Lunik III takes photographs of it. No longer is the Solar System just a playground for Space Opera. It is history.

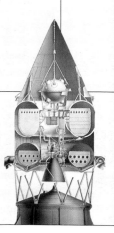

1960-1969: FICTION IS FACT

AS THE DECADE OPENS, no human has yet broken the bonds of Earth; as it closes, men are standing on the Moon. The impact of this change is enormous, but our reaction to the achievement is mixed. After the initial euphoria we begin to understand the limitations of what we have gained, and how far we still have to go. The great adventure is not as dramatic as SF writers would have wished; it is not quite as glorious as the scientists expected;

	1960	**1961**	**1962**	**1963**	**1964**
SF EVENTS	 THE BOOK THAT MADE SCIENCE FICTION GROW UP — KINGSLEY AMIS — NEW MAPS OF HELL Kingsley Amis's series of lectures on SF, delivered at Princeton University in 1959, is published as **New Maps of Hell**.	Robert A. Heinlein follows up the Hugo he won for *Starship Troopers* in 1960 with another for *Stranger in a Strange Land*. This is the beginning of what might be called the Heinlein Unbound period: radical heroes, father-figures, and messiahs, spouting a didacticism that brooks no argument. *Stranger in a Strange Land* is the best of the books from this phase.	Having spent the latter years of the 1950s trying unsuccessfully to break into the mainstream fiction market, Philip K. Dick publishes the Hugo-winning *The Man in the High Castle*. This is arguably the best of the Alternate World scenarios in which Hitler won World War II, and certainly Dick's best-known novel – if one discounts the recognition that *Blade Runner* brought to *Do Androids Dream of Electric Sheep?*.	 LA PLANÈTE DES SINGES Pierre Boulle's **La planète des singes**, translated as *Planet of the Apes*, is published.	 WILLIAM ATHELING, JR. — the issue at hand A collection of James Blish's SF criticism, written under the name of William Atheling, is published, called **The Issue at Hand**.
CINEMA, RADIO, AND TELEVISION	 H.G. WELLS' THE TIME MACHINE Cinema's ransacking of SF authors continues, with George Pal's adventure-romance version of **The Time Machine**.	It is not a good year for films. Be it new scripts like *The Day the Earth Caught Fire* or adaptations like *Master of the World* and *Mysterious Island*, all of them think rather more about sets than scripts.	Last year we had *A Voyage to the Bottom of the Sea*, featuring a futuristic atomic submarine – entertaining in a childish sort of way. *The Manchurian Candidate* appears this year. Brilliant, satirical, political, and superbly written, it features a war "hero" returning from Korea, who has been programmed to kill a liberal politician. SF has found a home outside of fantasy or horror – a trend that will grow.	 **Doctor Who** begins its 26-season marathon. The *TARDIS* is there from the start, the Daleks arrive in the second story.	
MAGAZINES	*Astounding Science Fiction* gradually changes its name to *Analog Science Fact ∧ Science Fiction*. Campbell had always wanted to change the title, disliking the word "astounding", but he has had to wait over 20 years to do it.	Frederik Pohl, taking up another strand of his career, becomes editor of *Galaxy* and *If*, widening their range of content and contributors. Brian W. Aldiss's *Hothouse* is published in *The Magazine of Fantasy and Science Fiction*.	*The Magazine of Fantasy and Science Fiction* begins its special anniversary issues with an issue devoted to Theodore Sturgeon. 	 quarber merkur 23 *Analog* moves to a glossy, new format, similar to a mass-market magazine. In Austria, the literary **Quarber Merkur** is founded.	Galaxie — L'AVENTURE DANS L'ANTICIPATION — MAI 1964 N° 1 2 F 50 — AU CARREFOUR DES ÉTOILES par CLIFFORD SIMAK — LES SACRIFIÉS par A.E. VAN VOGT — VOIR L'HOMME INVISIBLE par ROBERT SILVERBERG The second incarnation of **Galaxie**, published by OPTA, begins in France. In Britain, Michael Moorcock becomes editor of *New Worlds*.
WORLD EVENTS	The first weather satellite is launched. Concorde is planned. Albert Camus and Boris Pasternak die.	**Yuri Gagarin** becomes the first man in space in April. Rudolf Nureyev defects. The Berlin Wall goes up.	**Telstar** relays the first live transatlantic pictures, including a test card from Britain, and Yves Montand singing from France.	In the United States, **President Kennedy** is shot. In Britain, John Profumo resigns from the cabinet in a sex scandal. Russia puts the first woman into space. 	In South Africa Nelson Mandela goes to prison. The Soviet Zond 2 and the American Mariner 4 both take off for Mars.

In SF – one supposes – the immediate pre-war period was the real, right-stuff Golden Age, although it was hardly a halcyon period for the world. And, while the 1950s are a time of prosperity and hope, for SF it would be better to call them the Age of Silver. They are a period of more assurance and maturity, more suave and profitable than the years that preceded them; but they are also a time for some reflection. SF has grown up – and perhaps it has already begun to age.

1 9 5 5

SF's Age of Silver is flourishing, and more writers than ever before are making reasonable incomes from their work. Good novels by Asimov, Knight, and others continue to appear. Some genre magazines are prosperous, but the pulps have seen the last of the glory days. Greg Benford starts a fanzine with his twin brother.

Another rare genuine SF film appears. **This Island Earth** duly climaxes – after the old fashion – in the aliens' death, but it boasts an exciting plot.

The first real SF magazine in Germany, **Utopia Magazin**, makes a promising start, but ends after 26 issues.

1 9 5 6

The **Luna** pulp series begins in Germany: reprints of circulating library titles dominate the list.

The robot in **Forbidden Planet**, bound by Asimov's Three Laws of Robotics, has become a cliché. But in 1956, such sophistication was revolutionary in the cinema, and Robbie still delights.

Astounding serializes Asimov's *The Naked Sun*. *Galaxy* has Bester's *The Stars My Destination*, and *Fantasy and Science Fiction* runs Heinlein's *The Door into Summer*.

1 9 5 7

In Germany, the **Terra** series joins the SF publishing fray: all three publishing houses that will be dominant in Germany now have an SF imprint.

The German **Galaxis** is founded. Well produced, but crippled by the fact that its writers are not yet familiar, it folds after 15 issues.

The Suez crisis ends Anthony Eden's career. Sputnik I orbits the world, and shocks the West. A dog named Laika orbits in **Sputnik II**.

1 9 5 8

C.M. Kornbluth dies. In Germany, the **Terra-Sonderband** list is edited by Walter Ernsting, who began the Utopia imprint in 1953.

The Fly continues the silliness of the decade. A scientist experiments with a matter transmitter and somehow gets mixed up with a fly. The fly gets his head and arm, and the scientist gets the fly's head and wing, but strangely there is enough brain for both of them. The scientist tries to reverse the process but fails and eventually pleads for death. For such a ridiculous idea, the film was a surprising success.

A down-market version of *Fiction*, **Satellite** publishes good material, most of it translated, in its early years; then it declines into shoddiness, and folds in 1962.

Wernher von Braun, the former German V-2 scientist, helps America fight back against Sputnik with Explorer.

1 9 5 9

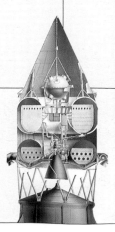

With *Starship Troopers*, Heinlein starts a revolution: SF books will no longer avoid issues eschewed by the prim magazines. In France, **Fiction** publish the first French SF anthology.

On one side, there is silliness with monsters in *The Giant Behemoth*; on the other, gloom as the world is devastated by atomic aftermath in *On the Beach*: but they are both called SF.

The Russian probe **Lunik I** reaches the Moon, and then Lunik III takes photographs of it. No longer is the Solar System just a playground for Space Opera. It is history.

AFTER THE APOCALYPSE

THE CATASTROPHES IN 1950s SF really began in 1945. Many novels had been published depicting the fall of civilization before this date, in the United States, in Europe, and elsewhere; but they had rarely specified very clearly just what it was that caused the collapse. If they ever did make things clear, they tended to seem pretty foolish: sometimes it was socialism that stultified the course of world history, and brought humanity back into a state of barbarism; sometimes it was the vote for women; sometimes it was a cosmic catastrophe, like a change in the Moon's orbit – scientifically loony – that crashes it into the ocean, and makes waves. Only after 1945, after two atomic bombs had been dropped on Japan to bring to an end World War II, did SF writers have a real-life event available to them that was of an order of magnitude sufficient to justify a radical change in humanity's fortunes upon this planet. By the time 1950 came around, ending civilization was as easy as falling off a log.

Inheriting the Earth
The image of a world devoid of humans and populated only by the creations – the robots – that they leave behind was a popular one.

The beginning of the end

As the 1950s progressed, SF writers – and their readers – settled right into the end of things. The dominant underlying message of American SF remained positive: it still seemed possible, and important, to describe Competent Men (and, increasingly, Women) domesticating the ravaged future by learning how to operate it. But increasingly, SF magazines began to follow the lead of the book publishers – who had tended to treat post-catastrophe tales with less apprehension over the previous years – and to begin to create detailed visions of life after the end of high technology, progress, and growth.

The first great post-catastrophe novel was written by a man who had no direct connection with the SF genre itself. But George R. Stewart's *Earth Abides* (see page 217) was competent in non-genre terms, and at the same time created a model of life after the collapse that SF writers soon assimilated. Stewart neatly modernized the kind of catastrophe that European writers, such as J. Leslie Mitchell and John Collier, had tended to imagine, the sort of catastrophe that, without being too clear about exactly how it all happens, manages to wipe out most of humanity while leaving the landscape relatively intact.

Statue of Liberty
This Fantasy and Science Fiction *magazine illustration is not the first use of the Statue of Liberty as a symbol for the collapse of America. As early as the turn of the century, illustrations feature a shattered Liberty. As an icon, she is both profoundly irresistible and profoundly fragile.*

The wilder west
Western films had always used the image of a pioneer coming across bones left by an earlier, failed trek as a signal for the giving up of hope. SF illustrators used the same image with a technological twist.

Stewart's plague has the same "cleansing" effect, but his depiction of its onslaught is clearly post-nuclear in feel. It could, in other words, as easily have been a bomb rather than a virus.

The wheel of time

SF writers after Stewart also made liberal use of his assumption – narrated through a story that is, at times, deeply moving – that, regardless of the efforts of any individual survivors, a profound interregnum will inevitably separate the fall of a civilization and the renewal of a literate and technological humanity. The assumption that some sort of an interregnum is inevitable – both the assumption and the term were probably derived from Arnold J. Toynbee's *A Study of History*, a multi-part work whose successive volumes appeared throughout this decade – ran gravely counter to the dominant SF assumption that the building blocks of knowledge and technology would hoist us over any abyss.

There is something else new here, too. Until the 1950s, most American genre SF – with the possible exception of Isaac Asimov's **Foundation** series (see page 231) – was written in the assumption that history either was or could be linear, a story that did not repeat itself. Post-catastrophe stories usually assume – although they do not always make the assumption explicit – that history is cyclical. It is a wheel on which progress will be followed by catastrophe,

which will be followed by interregnum, which will be followed by the rise of a new civilization. The most famous genre example of this, and the most explicit, is Walter M. Miller's *A Canticle for Liebowitz* (see page 222), which was published in three parts right through the middle of the 1950s, and which made it almost impossible for any SF writer to escape the juggernaut-wheel of the cycle.

Post-catastrophe pastorals

It is not comforting to think that our greatest achievements may dissolve in an instant, and that some new civilization, perhaps aeons hence, will repeat our triumphs and re-enact our calamitous fall all over again. SF writers who concentrated on the first days after the collapse – like Wilson Tucker in *The Long Loud Silence*, written in 1952, or Mordecai Roshwald in *Level Seven*, from 1959 – wrote necessarily grim, comfortless tales.

It is not surprising, therefore, that many SF writers of the 1950s tended to concentrate on the subsequent period of interregnum, which they often treated as a kind of pastoral escape from the higher ordeals of world history. By transforming The World After the Bomb into a Ruritanian network of tiny principalities, each with its own way of life, SF writers managed to romanticize humanity's dread nightmare of universal desolation.

Ecological disaster
Civilization need not end with a bang: changes in the environment could begin a decline into desert.

The popularity of post-catastrophe tales is in part due to this romanticizing of life after collapse, as though the 20th century had never happened. It represents a slowly growing feeling on the part of many SF writers that it was permissible to think that maybe the 20th century should not have happened. Perhaps Western civilization had lost its balance somewhere, and perhaps the termination would come as a direct consequence of that. Perhaps the task of survivors, like the monks in *A Canticle for Liebowitz*, was to preserve what was worthwhile in the old world, and at the same time to shape a new world that would not just re-enact the old tragedy.

New apparitions
Early SF illustration had generally tended to be representational, but more symbolic images appeared after the war. Death might now appear directly as an icon of inescapable doom, in the same way that the outline of a mushroom cloud or an illustration of an atom might. SF was no longer all bright adventure.

Always within Death's grasp, humanity moves in doomed circles

1960-1969: FICTION IS FACT

AS THE DECADE OPENS, no human has yet broken the bonds of Earth; as it closes, men are standing on the Moon. The impact of this change is enormous, but our reaction to the achievement is mixed. After the initial euphoria we begin to understand the limitations of what we have gained, and how far we still have to go. The great adventure is not as dramatic as SF writers would have wished; it is not quite as glorious as the scientists expected;

1960 | 1961 | 1962 | 1963 | 1964

SF EVENTS

1960

Kingsley Amis's series of lectures on SF, delivered at Princeton University in 1959, is published as **New Maps of Hell**.

1961

Robert A. Heinlein follows up the Hugo he won for *Starship Troopers* in 1960 with another for *Stranger in a Strange Land*. This is the beginning of what might be called the Heinlein Unbound period: radical heroes, father-figures, and messiahs, spouting a didacticism that brooks no argument. *Stranger in a Strange Land* is the best of the books from this phase.

1962

Having spent the latter years of the 1950s trying unsuccessfully to break into the mainstream fiction market, Philip K. Dick publishes the Hugo-winning *The Man in the High Castle*. This is arguably the best of the Alternate World scenarios in which Hitler won World War II, and certainly Dick's best-known novel – if one discounts the recognition that *Blade Runner* brought to *Do Androids Dream of Electric Sheep?*.

1963

Pierre Boulle's **La planète des singes**, translated as *Planet of the Apes*, is published.

1964

A collection of James Blish's SF criticism, written under the name of William Atheling, is published, called **The Issue at Hand.**

CINEMA, RADIO, AND TELEVISION

Cinema's ransacking of SF authors continues, with George Pal's adventure-romance version of **The Time Machine**.

It is not a good year for films. Be it new scripts like *The Day the Earth Caught Fire* or adaptations like *Master of the World* and *Mysterious Island*, all of them think rather more about sets than scripts.

Last year we had *A Voyage to the Bottom of the Sea*, featuring a futuristic atomic submarine – entertaining in a childish sort of way. *The Manchurian Candidate* appears this year. Brilliant, satirical, political, and superbly written, it features a war "hero" returning from Korea, who has been programmed to kill a liberal politician. SF has found a home outside of fantasy or horror – a trend that will grow.

Doctor Who begins its 26-season marathon. The *TARDIS* is there from the start, the Daleks arrive in the second story.

MAGAZINES

Astounding Science Fiction gradually changes its name to *Analog Science Fact ⊕ Science Fiction*. Campbell had always wanted to change the title, disliking the word "astounding", but he has had to wait over 20 years to do it.

Frederik Pohl, taking up another strand of his career, becomes editor of *Galaxy* and *If*, widening their range of content and contributors. Brian W. Aldiss's *Hothouse* is published in *The Magazine of Fantasy and Science Fiction*.

The Magazine of Fantasy and Science Fiction begins its special anniversary issues with an issue devoted to Theodore Sturgeon.

Analog moves to a glossy, new format, similar to a mass-market magazine. In Austria, the literary **Quarber Merkur** is founded.

The second incarnation of **Galaxie**, published by OPTA, begins in France. In Britain, Michael Moorcock becomes editor of *New Worlds*.

WORLD EVENTS

The first weather satellite is launched. Concorde is planned. Albert Camus and Boris Pasternak die.

Yuri Gagarin becomes the first man in space in April. Rudolf Nureyev defects. The Berlin Wall goes up.

Telstar relays the first live transatlantic pictures, including a test card from Britain, and Yves Montand singing from France.

In the United States, **President Kennedy** is shot. In Britain, John Profumo resigns from the cabinet in a sex scandal. Russia puts the first woman into space.

In South Africa Nelson Mandela goes to prison. The Soviet Zond 2 and the American Mariner 4 both take off for Mars.

it is not as revolutionary as politicians might have hoped. The technological advances of the space race soon become part of the everyday fabric of our world and its industry, and are quickly taken for granted. These advances contrast with political troubles which make it clear that technology does not automatically bring peace and prosperity, and that no part of the globe can exist any longer in isolation. In response, SF begins to find new goals, and new futures.

1 9 6 5

Dune, first published in *Analog* magazine in 1963, makes it into book form. It wins both a Hugo and the first Nebula for best novel, confirming Herbert as an author of major stature. *Dune* is not only the most outstanding achievement of Herbert's writing career, it is a groundbreaking achievement in the field. Never before has a planet, with all its conditions, its ecology, and its culture, been so carefully thought out and presented: Arrakis appears as the most real of SF's fictional worlds.

Cele Goldsmith's editorship of *Amazing Stories* and *Fantastic* magazines comes to an end. Under Pohl, *Galaxy* and *If* are doing well, publishing material as varied as E.E. Smith's *Skylark DuQuesne*, through Heinlein's *The Moon is a Harsh Mistress*, to Harlan Ellison's "*Repent, Harlequin!" Said the Ticktockman*.

The United States sends troops into **Vietnam**. Martin Luther King is awarded the Nobel Peace Prize.

1 9 6 6

The **Nebulas** are first awarded. Unlike the Hugos, the Nebulas are named for the year of publication of the works considered, so the awards given in 1966 are called the 1965 awards.

The crew of **Star Trek** take to the skies for the first time. Although the series is destined to achieve cult status, it is not markedly successful in the ratings at first.

The first of Damon Knight's *Orbit* anthologies is published. Although not the first anthology series, it comes at an important time: essentially a magazine in book format, with elements such as letters pages stripped out, *Orbit* can achieve a distribution wider than many magazines, which are facing increased competition from books and television.

In China the Cultural Revolution begins. Soviet and American probes land on the Moon.

1 9 6 7

Harlan Ellison's anthology *Dangerous Visions* is published, gathering together works from the best of the New Wave writers, with abundant commentary from Ellison himself.

In Britain, *The Prisoner* begins. Like other series that later become cult viewing, it is not outstandingly successful on this first showing on television.

One of the more successful small French magazines, **Horizons du Fantastique**, is launched this year.

Israel fights the Six Day War against the neighbouring Arab states. Concorde, the first supersonic aircraft, is unveiled.

1 9 6 8

Arkady and Boris Strugatski are the most notable postwar Russian SF authors, writing many of their best-known works in the 1960s. In 1968 **The Molecular Café**, an anthology of Soviet SF for publication in the West, is published, edited by the brothers. Their editorship is, however, kept anonymous.

2001: A Space Odyssey shows how visually splendid SF can look on the big screen and paves the way for a new generation of SF films.

In Spain, **Nueva Dimension**, the most influential Spanish SF magazine, is founded. In America, the trade journal *Locus* is founded.

Martin Luther King is shot. Russia sends in tanks to crush the Prague Spring in Czechoslovakia. Students riot in Paris.

1 9 6 9

Vision of Tomorrow is the first English-language magazine to publish a Stanisław Lem story, but it only lasts a year.

The **Apollo 11** mission finally puts two men on the Moon. Hippies flock to Woodstock, but the Manson murders sound a death knell.

THINKING MACHINES

KNOWLEDGE FROM THE FUTURE, or a more advanced intelligence, might have been able to help us, back in the Dark Ages before the microchip, before the desktop or laptop computer had entered the home and begun to show its stuff – to show us how good it is at some things, and how stupid it is at others. Some outside hint might have been able to tell us how radically dissimilar are the human mind and the computer. What the human mind can do, the computer cannot compute, while what the computer dazzles us with, through its ability to replicate stacked series of operations at tens of millions of instructions per second, the human brain fizzles at the thought of. In the 1960s, however, the bent of cybernetics study was to demonstrate parallels, not the yawning gaps.

Man or mouse
Pscyhology in the 1960s was still in the grip of the behaviourists, who held the dangerous beliefs that human consciousness could be measured, that what could not be measured did not exist, and that what could be measured could be controlled. Humans were like rats in a maze to them.

Programming pioneers

The first software manual for programming was written by Ada Lovelace in 1842. She was the daughter of Lord Byron, whose poetry bridged the Classical tradition and the Romantic mode, and she was also halfway across the stream. She had a mathematical mind of considerable acuity, and was deeply interested in Charles Babbage's Difference Engine and Analytical Engine, devices that it is fair to describe as the first computers. But Babbage's – and Ada's – problem lay not in the power of the mind but in the coarse inefficacy of the tools: knobs and gears, and all the gross, inefficent hugeness of First Industrial Age technology.

A century later, the situation had hardly changed. Although it was possible, in the late 1940s, to build computers, these were great, clumsy giants, and hardly more powerful than a wristwatch is today.

The mechanical mind
If the human mind were nothing but an inefficient computer, then it might look something like this inside, divided into partitions, like a laboratory.

The basic technology available still functioned, very crudely, through enormous and unreliable gadgets like vacuum tubes, programmed via hand-punched punch cards. It was a nightmare in the real world, but it was not a nightmare in the world of SF. As a whole, the SF genre paid almost no attention at all to the computer.

Invisible to SF

At first glance, this is strange. How could SF – much of it written by men and women who are very alert to the movements and anticipations of science – have missed out on the central technological revolution of the last half of the 20th century? There are three answers to this.

The first is the least plausible: that hundreds of SF writers simply missed the boat, failed to remember Babbage and Ada Lovelace, and did not even notice the invention of the first genuine electronic brain in 1942.

Power failure
A computer might become a government or a God, but could it ever be relied on? Or would we all be stranded helplessly when it failed?

The second is more interesting. From the early days, SF writers had an understandable interest in the description of scientific marvels that could be visualized in the mind's eyes of their readers: hence the huge dynamos, the flaring ray-guns, and the "thinking machines" with thousands of toggles. Hence (perhaps) Asimov's wrong turning into robots, at a time when he should have been focusing his incisive mind on problems of circuitry, rather than the moral behaviour of boxes that clanked as they walked.

Computer as prison
An image that repeats the idea that minds and computers are alike.

Hence the genre's almost complete failure to anticipate the revolutions of miniaturization that began with the advent of the microchip, and made the modern computer possible. Perhaps, because they could not be seen with the naked eye, they could be held in the *mind's* eye of the fiction writer. The third answer may explain the other two: the computer appeared to present a challenge to *Homo sapiens*. The small amount of speculation about computers that appeared before the 1960s failed to see them as almost infinitely adaptable tools, concentrating instead on visions in which computers replaced humanity, or took over from humanity, or became God. The computer was not imagined simply because to do so was to welcome into our bosoms the ultimate enemy.

Of course, once its profound limitations are properly understood, the computer loses this threatening aspect: a large number of Computer-is-God stories appeared during the post-war years, but few appear in the 1990s.

The human computer

In an age that saw computers as parallels of the human mind, it is not surprising to discover that stories in which computers figure tend to occupy the same genre niches, and to address the same fears and anticipations, as the "soft" science of psychology. In the 1960s, these sciences are most often seen to be in the service of advertising agencies and the like, being used to imprison humans in behavioural traps for the profit of others. The thought that to study the human mind is to entrap it is perhaps naïve, and the prevalence of the notion – even when not explicitly argued – does not make us feel that this whole vast region of speculation was very adequately examined by SF. But we do know why it was not: the mind is a spooky place.

There were exceptions: Mark Clifton, in the ***Ralph Kennedy*** stories, uses a cybernetic expert to cope positively with psi phenomena, which can be seen as an attempt to neutralize fears about any intimate connection between the science of the computer and the sciences of the mind.

Programmed people
One of the great 1960s nightmares was the control of human behaviour, as though they were punchcards in a vast computer. In the 1990s, we guess this would not work, or would create lame puppets.

In Britain, J.G. Ballard – a man whose scientific numeracy was used to propound lessons radically at odds with the bent of most American SF – welcomed the marriage of science and mind hinted at by the coming of the computer. Transforming a term used earlier by Robert Bloch and J.B. Priestley, Ballard claimed that the subject of SF was Inner Space: the surreal, convoluted, passion-ridden, and death-haunted interior of the human mind. Some of his darker fictions read like nightmares of a vast computer failing to understand the mammals that dance like mayflies around its immortal sensors.

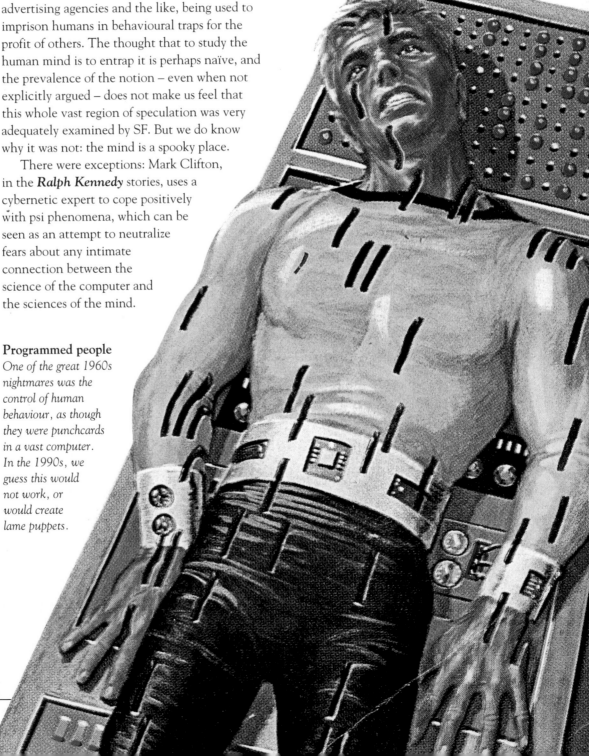

SPACE FLIGHT

BEFORE 1600, HORSEDRAWN CHARIOTS, harnessed birds, and whirlwinds carried voyagers on their travels above. Then we found that there was a vast vacuum out there. True space flight is first hinted at in Johannes Kepler's *Somnium* from 1634, but Kepler, fearing religious censorship, used demons to propel his craft. With Jules Verne's *De la terre à la lune* (see page 212), spaceships began to look like rockets; from 1945 on, the German V-2 rocket was the dominant image. Sleek rockets tore across SF magazine covers, and we went to the Moon in a descendant of this World War II weapon; for a while it looked as if a tool of death had become a slingshot to the future. The dream has foundered in reality, but rockets and generation starships still sail the SF galaxy, although other, more down-to-Earth visions have joined them. SF gathers energy from out in space, where the Sun burns free, and sends it downwards to the Earth. It puts industry where the gravity is minimal, and keeps pollution far away. It lets us eat, and breathe, and grow.

Spherical ship
Mark Twain liked gadgets, but he never really cottoned on to rockets, as demonstrated by Captain Stormfield's Visit to Heaven, from 1909.

Cinema launch
Méliès's Le voyage dans la lune (A Trip to the Moon) *packs both Verne and Wells into its 21 minutes, during which a vast projectile is made, sent into space with passengers, hits the Moon, and returns.*

Bulbous portholes and rivetted plates, inspired by submarine design, were common before the V-2-rocket look

In a real rocket, everything but this nose cone would be the engine and a huge fuel tank

Amazing design
Some early SF spaceships looked like rockets; others, like this 1920s model from Amazing magazine, closely resembled armoured squid. We can guess its mission: to cruise the starways, and to conquer them.

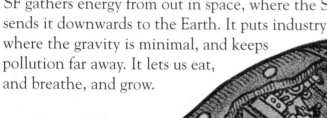

Passengers would have cabin-like accommodation

With all this luggage, the illustrator must have envisioned interplanetary holidays

Spaceships of this time were often rather like luxury liners, complete with four-star restaurants

Somehow, the problem of zero gravity would be solved to allow for a ballroom

Strange omission
This rocketship, which illustrated a late-1930s French educational magazine for children, fascinatingly combines old thought and new science. On one hand, the ship looks like a bullet; on the other, its portholes protrude in a very un-aerodynamic fashion. On one hand, it is a rocket, because exhaust flames are visible; on the other, there is no room for an engine. Where the motor would be is nothing but some exceedingly ill-stacked luggage, which would be crushed within seconds of takeoff.

Too close for comfort
Rocket scientists Ley and Oberth advised Fritz Lang on Die Frau im Mond (The Woman in the Moon): *the ship was so like the V-2 that the Nazis withdrew the film.*

Roller-coaster takeoff

When Worlds Collide was written in 1931, long before nuclear war was the usual way to end the world. So its planetary collision seemed a bit archaic when George Pal made the film in 1951. It cannot be denied that the spaceship wobbles visibly as it scoots along its bizarre takeoff ramp, but it does glitter impressively, and artist Chesley Bonestell's visions of Earth from space are truly awe-inspiring.

THE SF SPACE RACE

The early 1960s, and the space race is on: this magazine cover illustration looks like the Moon, and it certainly looks like Russians. But it also looks like yet another V-2 rocket, when what is needed is a realistic moon-lander.

Poetic licence
With no air to make it flap, the Russian flag must be thoroughly starched.

Neighbourhood NASA

After World War II, American SF often depicted space rockets built by inventive Yanks working in their back yards. In the dream, all it takes is this handful of people: a genius with his hands, a test pilot, a brilliant scientist, and a man with money and guts. It was not a dream to be despised – as children, NASA scientists dreamed that dream. But in the end, space was just too expensive for SF's back-yard dreamers.

THE REAL SPACE RACE

The Soviets had a lot of firsts in the space race: first into space, with Sputnik; first probe past the Moon; first man and woman in space; and first manmade object on another planet. But the Americans put the first man on the Moon in 1969, the symbol that endured beyond all.

The next generation

By the late 1970s, space reality seemed drab. The hugely detailed and staggeringly sized space dreadnoughts of Star Wars were a new answer to the old need for romance, and the fictional spaceships of today are freckled with mysterious knobs and turrets. And even though they cruise through soundless vacuum, these spaceships sure do hum.

This unaerodynamic ship would be built in space and never enter a planet's atmosphere

A.S.S. TOCUMWAL

Apollo mission craft
Reality shrank SF rockets to tiny landing modules. But men lived in these, and stepped from them onto the Moon.

1970-1979: LOOKING INWARDS

THE STORY OF THE WORLD and the story of SF in the 1970s are very closely linked. In reality, we made it to the Moon and looked back at an Earth made new. We have come so far, and what we see most clearly is how far we have still to go. Standing on the Earth, one cannot see it. Standing on the Moon, one can see the Earth whole, and blot it out with one hand. We have to learn to look at the Earth, and ourselves, from a new perspective. In SF, we have made a

	1970	1971	1972	1973	1974
SF EVENTS	Marge Piercy's first SF novel, **Dance the Eagle to Sleep**, comes at the beginning of a decade that sees more women writing SF, and feminist writers exploring SF as a didactic genre.	Donald A. Wollheim leaves Ace and sets up DAW Books. No longer restrained by corporate caution, he gives his paperback writers as much freedom to deal with taboo subjects (like sex) as their hardback "betters" had long enjoyed. Several authors who primarily concentrate on Science Fantasy and the Planetary Romance move to the new house; and Wollheim continues to introduce new talent, like C.J. Cherryh, into the field.	Harry Harrison and Brian Aldiss institute the **John W. Campbell Memorial Award** for the best SF novel published in English during the previous year. Voted by a panel, the award is a prestigious one, quite different in flavour from the Hugos or Nebulas. Brian Aldiss's **Billion Year Spree** is published. Probably the the best-known, and also one of the best, critical works on SF, this is more than a simple history: it is an argument for SF's origins and heritage.		Ursula Le Guin's *The Dispossessed* is published, and wins both Hugo and Nebula awards. This is a mark of how far SF has come: subtitled *An Ambiguous Utopia*, this is a book that the Gernsbacks and the Campbells of the early days might have dreamed of, but could find no one to write. It is contemplative, doubting, questioning, and quite lacking in any kind of conventional adventure.
CINEMA, RADIO, AND TELEVISION	A young unknown by the name of George Lucas makes a surreal SF film called *THX 1138*. It is essentially a new telling of an old story, that of a subterranean, computer-run dystopia and the final escape to the surface. The film is not a commercial hit, but it is re-released at the end of the decade with more success.	Kubrick's screen adaptation of Burgess's **A Clockwork Orange** is released. It wins the Hugo for Best Dramatic Presentation, but Kubrick, alarmed at the reaction in Britain, withdraws the film there, assuring it of a cult following, with semi-clandestine screenings for ever after.	Stanisław Lem's highly intelligent novel **Solaris** is made into an equally intelligent film.	**Moonbase 3** is set in a turn-of-the-century research establishment on the Moon. The new director (Donald Houston) faces stress and staff hostility but, sadly, no aliens.	
MAGAZINES			Ben Bova, who has been editing *Analog* since John W. Campbell Jr.'s death in July 1971, is officially credited as the editor. The stagnation and slow decline of the title are reversed by the fresh approach.		In Japan, **SF Magazine**, begun in 1960 with translations from *Fantasy and Science Fiction*, becomes a forum for Japanese work.
WORLD EVENTS	Sir Allen Lane, the man who founded Penguin Books and essentially began mass-market paperback publishing, dies. In France, President Charles de Gaulle dies. In Japan, the author Yukio Mishima tries to start an army rebellion; failing, he commits suicide.	Britain goes decimal. **Soyuz** docks with the Salyut space station, but the cosmonauts do not make it back alive.	 The Vietnam War finally ends. **Skylab**'s first crew goes up. Oil prices rise 70 per cent as a result of tension in the Middle East.		In the United States, **President Nixon** is forced to resign over the Watergate scandal.

Billion Year Spree — The history of science fiction — Brian W. Aldiss

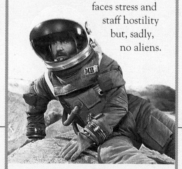

similar journey. After creating monsters and giving them life, we journeyed out to the stars, and had a Golden Age of adventure. After World War II, a different kind of age called for new maturity and scope, and SF changed again.

Now there comes a period of reappraisal. After rapid technological developments culminated in the conquest of space in the 1960s, a certain navel-gazing quality is discernible in this decade – perhaps it is inevitable.

1975   1976   1977   1978   1979

1975

In France, the first titles in the **Anthologie de la Science-Fiction**, edited by Gérard Klein, are published. Curiously, there are no French works in the 36 core titles of the series.

Harlan Ellison's bleak *A Boy and His Dog* hits the cinema screen. Dog lovers hate it.

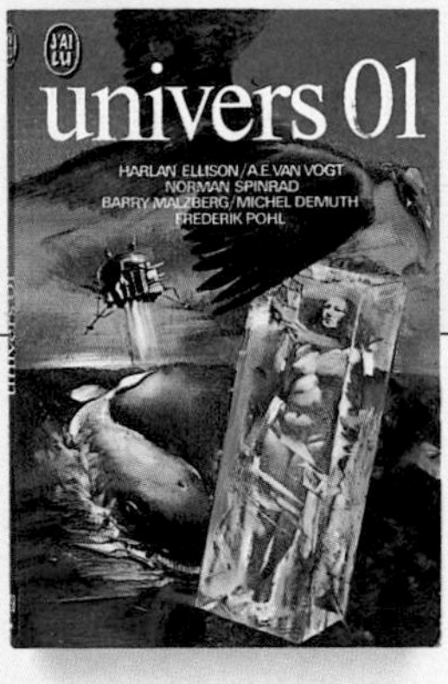

In France, the mass-market house J'ai lu begins publishing its SF anthology series **Univers**.

Soyuz and **Apollo** craft and crews meet up in a moment of *détente* far above the Iron Curtain. Margaret Thatcher becomes leader of the Conservative Party.

1976

Rumours of remarkable new SF films in the making begin to surface, and publishers see a manuscript entitled *Star Wars*, novelizing an unseen film that purports to star Alec Guinness. The "wiser" editors pooh-pooh the possibility, and the book takes some time to sell. And what was that about Steven Spielberg? Some kind of conference of the third sort?

It is a good time for SF as a whole, commercially speaking – but *Odyssey Science Fiction* is founded, and lasts only two issues; *SF Digest* lasts only one. *Science Fiction Monthly* shuts down. And the intelligent *Galileo* begins its rocky 15-issue course to 1980 oblivion.

Chairman Mao dies and the backlash begins in China.

1977

Kesselring publish the **Collectif** anthologies, heavily politicized SF that some say puts the last nail in the coffin of genre SF in French.

Star Wars, a Space Opera about an Empire, a Resistance, a Princess, Knights, and cute robots, revitalizes SF cinema.

Isaac Asimov's *Science Fiction Magazine* is founded.

Refugees flee from Vietnam, the first wave of **boat people** but not the last.

1978

The **Saga de Los Aznar** [Aznar Saga] series, by George H. White, published in Spain in the 1950s, receives a European Science Fiction Award.

BBC radio broadcasts Douglas Adams's **The Hitchhiker's Guide to the Galaxy**. It will later be a publishing success.

Bob Guccione founds *Omni*, a lavishly illustrated science magazine. With a budget to support high payment rates, it quickly establishes a reputation for the quality of the fiction included in its pages.

1979

Darko Suvin's *Pour une poétique de la science-fiction*, written in 1977, is translated as **Metamorphoses of Science Fiction**, and he is given the Pilgrim Award.

Ridley Scott (helped by G.R. Giger's designs) makes *Alien*, and demolishes the Hollywood cliché that the future is lifelessly clean. A spaceship is invaded by an alien who picks off the inhabitants one by one. The film is a breakthrough on all counts. It is scary and suspenseful as a story, and the special effects and set designs are a huge leap forwards for SF cinema.

Three Mile Island leaks radioactive gas. Margaret Thatcher comes to power.

CITY LIFE

SAMUEL JOHNSON ONCE SAID "when a man is tired of London, he is tired of life." This may be so, but the garden-suburbs of Sir Thomas More's *Utopia* make it clear that he was sick and tired of 16th-century London and, on the whole, SF writers have not done terribly well with the challenge of the city, despite their liking for modernistic towers. When space heroes came to town it was to get drunk, to beard the tyrant, to enjoy a tickertape parade, or to report home. They did not plunge into the life of a great city, because to do so is to become anonymous, and the heroes of SF are anything but anonymous. Recently, SF has entered the city, and found it claustrophobic. Are SF writers tired of life?

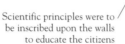

In the Renaissance, the human-centred, embracing circle had come to be a dominant symbol

The ideal city of the Renaissance

The utopian mind, according to opponents, is arithmetic. The scholar Campanella's vision of the City of the Sun from 1623, with its central temple staring like Big Brother down upon the poor inhabitants, has a very limited appeal today. Campanella never expected to live in his city, but his image of absolute control has haunted dictators ever since.

Scientific principles were to be inscribed upon the walls to educate the citizens

The city was arranged in concentric circles, mimicking astronomy's heavenly spheres

Early origins

SF writers know that the great urban centres of the world will draw together the best that humans can do; but also that they attract the worst. This double-edged quality is found on Swift's flying island of Laputa, encountered by Gulliver on his travels in the 17th century: it is peopled by scientists, all engaged in extraordinary research, and all half mad. This is possibly the first flying city in SF – both flying cities and crazed scientists have, of course, put in many appearances since. The city has also remained a venue for the more satirical or dystopian brands of SF.

Metropolis

Fritz Lang's 1926 vision is one of the cinema's most memorable cities. Skyscrapers, elevated trains, and streets crowded with cars and teeming humanity, all these have been seen elsewhere: in books, in films, and in real life. But seldom have they been endowed with such an overpowering sense of threat.

Free of Earth

Maybe it is because New York is already an island that there is a temptation to free it entirely from its surroundings. 1930s pulp illustrators found it irresistible, and the neatest thing many writers can think of to do with a messy city is to hoist it into the sky, shake it down, clean it out, and send it on its way.

But the greatest tales of travelling cities – James Blish's **Cities in Flight** stories – were written by a New Yorker who died in London. And the heroes of his series, who are city men and women, must deal with the cowboys of the space lanes, who disparage the great spaceship that Manhattan has become as nothing but a tramp: an Okie.

Served by aeroplanes, a flying city needs a beacon to guide them

Air travel must become the standard way of travel for a flying city

All kinds of fanciful antigravity devices have been imagined for keeping cities aloft

Machines for living in

Utopian thinkers have always been tantalized by the challenge presented by the city: how to organize it so that it benefits all its inhabitants, without sacrificing the special flavour that makes it nectar for some of them. Postwar planners thought that they had found the answer: if buildings could be regarded as efficient machines, then so could cities. Instead of sprawling organic growth, we could have planned and designed cities, and SF writers, as much as anyone, promulgated this gleaming future dream. But these cities of avenues, parks, and clean, open spaces instead became, within a few short decades, the nightmare of crumbling high-rise slums, and a venue for overpopulation tales.

Hothouse city

Civilizations under glass have been popular in post-holocaust scenarios. By the time the 1970s and Logan's Run came around, the sanitized, carefully controlled city was a sinister place, and abandoned, unpredictable nature was the preferred path.

The mean streets

It may not be a very realistic vision of the future in Los Angeles, but the makers of Blade Runner knew exactly what they were doing. They wanted to generate a sense of urban fantasy, to recreate for a 1980s audience the sense of the dark labyrinth of the city that inspired writers like Charles Dickens. The smoke, the rain, the steam, the grotesques, the disorientation, and the overdecorated cop cars: all of this is Dickens all the way home. After this, the christening of Cyberpunk was only a year away.

OTHER WORLDS

THERE ARE TWO SOLAR SYSTEMS. There is the simple one: the one that has real planets, real moons, real asteroids, real comets, a real Sun. And there is the complicated one: the one that has evolved through the imaginations of alchemists, astrologers, philosophers, utopists, dreamers, and poets. SF writers have, over the years, slowly and sometimes not very surely, made the two systems into one. In retrospect it seems inevitable. After the 17th century, educated people knew that other worlds orbited the Sun; today we know what most of these worlds actually look like, close up. But there were some strange detours: the astronomer Schiaparelli saw channels on Mars in 1877, and everyone thought he meant canals, and Edgar Rice Burroughs created an ancient Martian culture. Kim Stanley Robinson's **Mars** trilogy is the end of a long road, and marks the true marriage of the dream and the reality.

Another Earth
Cyrano de Bergerac shows us how the educated man imagined other planets in 1657.

New perspectives
Long before we made it to the Moon, writers were there, looking back. When John Ames Mitchell's Drowsy appeared in 1917, these views of our planet were still the stuff of fiction. Over four decades later we saw it for real; and seeing our home as just a fragile island in space has changed our perspective forever.

Under the moons of Mars
By 1930 or so, SF writers knew that there was no liveable atmosphere on Mars, but those with wilder imaginations were still able to speculate on the possibility that the "canals" were relics of ancient Martian civilizations that died aeons ago. Explorers from Earth might even find huge, complex metropolises and wondrous technology. The Martians themselves might be long dead; or they might not.

Brave new worlds
If there are no Lunarians, or Venusians, or Martians, these places are up for grabs. This territorial dispute, imagined in the 1950s, is between two groups of spacesuited humans, the representatives of two vast and opposing superpowers from Earth, alas. The spaceships themselves are conspicuously modern lunar modules: the irony, of course, is that they are identical in design.

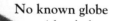

No known globe
After the home planets, the universe lies before us, and Hard SF writers of the 1950s, basing their speculations on what had been learned from our system, envisaged some remarkable environments. Here is Hal Clement's high-gravity planet of Mesklin: so intense is Mesklin's spin that the planet is flattened, giving gravity that varies from the equator to the poles.

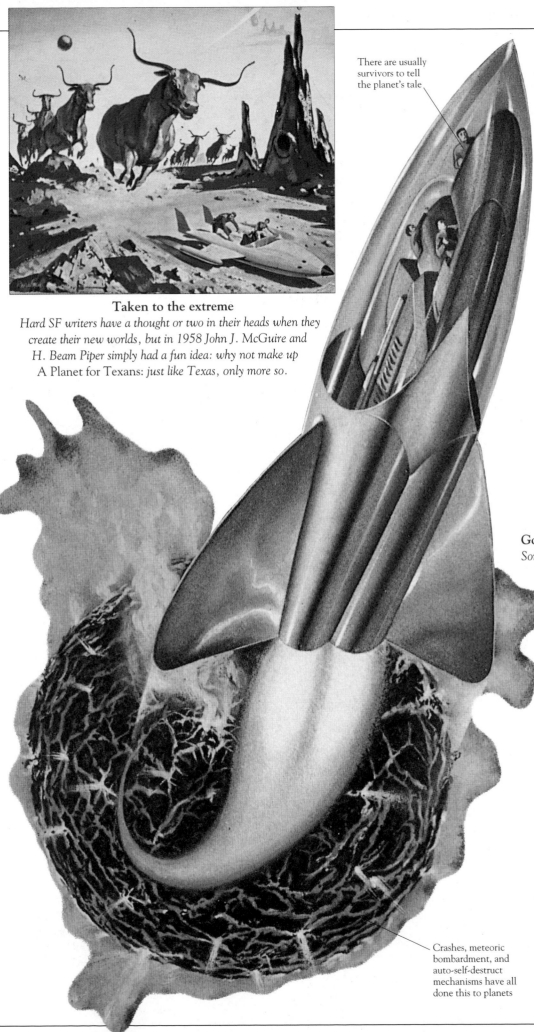

Taken to the extreme
Hard SF writers have a thought or two in their heads when they create their new worlds, but in 1958 John J. McGuire and H. Beam Piper simply had a fun idea: why not make up A Planet for Texans: *just like Texas, only more so.*

There are usually survivors to tell the planet's tale

Crashes, meteoric bombardment, and auto-self-destruct mechanisms have all done this to planets

WORLD BUILDING

As we learn more about the planets in our own Solar System, it becomes more intriguing to play intellectual games with the scientific principles that gave rise to their various environments, hot or cold, dense or low-gravity, firm or liquid. Now that we know more about what is, we can do a better job of asking what if. Some SF writers now specialize in generating scientifically plausible models for the creation of a wide range of worlds. Sometimes these worlds are so intriguing that other writers settle on them too, giving rise to shared-world texts.

Working model
When writing his **Helliconia** *trilogy, set on a planet with century-long seasons, Brian Aldiss overpainted a standard globe with his world, as an aide-mémoire.*

Going out with a bang
Some writers might crease their brows about plausible worlds, but others had stories to tell, and what could be more visual and visceral simultaneously than an exploding planet? The fact that planets do not tend to explode may have baulked some writers, but in the 1950s Superman's Krypton, the Forbidden Planet, and This Island Earth's Metaluna duly fume and boom.

The red planet
In his trilogy of Red Mars *(see page 235),* Green Mars, *and* Blue Mars, *Kim Stanley Robinson creates a vision of our neighbouring planet that not only makes one wish to live there, but also shows us how to go out there and do it.*

GENDER ROLES

THE FIRST SF NOVEL MAY have been written by Mary Shelley, who so happened to be a woman, but her *Frankenstein* was a male scientist, and his monster was likewise a man. And as SF began, so it continued for a long time to come. This is not surprising. During the 19th century, Western Civilization believed that it understood about women: they were essentially emotional creatures, vulnerable, passive, revered, and hearth-bound. By definition, SF occupied other realms: it was all about adventure, exploration and penetration of the unknown, warfare, combat, hard science, and the end of the world in tracts of ice or fire. It was only *natural*, it was assumed, that the protagonists who acted out the leading roles in these scenarios were most likely to be male. But such assumptions have taken a beating over the course of the 20th century, and gender is now understood to be controlled by nurture as well as nature. Since World War II, SF has increasingly, if reluctantly, recognized the fact.

Early adventurers
Adventure, exploration, guns, threats, science, and men rule the roost.

All change or no change?
In The Last Man on Earth, *a film from 1924, all males over 14, with one exception, have died. In this still, two women box for him. Even with no men around, they still wear elaborate makeup.*

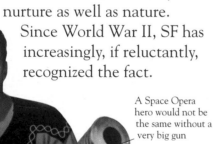

A Space Opera hero would not be the same without a very big gun

Fashion victim
In a scene that is absolutely typical of the great 1930s serials, a heroic Flash Gordon protects a shrinking Dale Arden from the minions of Ming the Merciless, or some other foe. He did this several times each episode. Note that, although Dale's short skirt is in fact reasonably practical, her glossy boots boast high heels, and her feathered cap is extremely fashionable. Also, she does not carry a gun. Flash, on the other hand, is all combat boots and business. War, clearly, is man's work.

When on Venus ...
Edgar Rice Burroughs wrote feverish tales of derring-do on Mars and Venus, specializing in scenes where erotic women stride about (usually naked), and fight by the sides of their men.

Strategic bits of machinery preserved modesty

Message in a bottle
By 1951, when World of If *by Rog Phillips appeared with this image on the cover, American SF publishers were beginning, quite reluctantly, to admit that their readership was growing up, and that quite a few SF readers were actually women. But the old habits died hard. Blasé, drugged, and dangerous, the undressed lady is, of course, clearly just about to escape her bonds.*

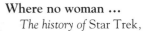

Taking a stand

This does not happen very often in the 1920s. The woman on the left is actually defending herself against the assault of a robot with rivets all over, a lustful scowl, and an upright tendril. But look: there are spaceships and tentacles. Some man is going to have to rescue her from this!

Where no woman ...

The history of Star Trek, from the 1960s to the Millennium, is also a history of the rapid emancipation of women in popular adventure-tale venues. Here is the first step, and it is a very neat one indeed. Because she is both female and black, Lieutenant Uhura represents two denigrated communities in the shape of one actress. She may not be the captain yet, but she is on the bridge.

Some superheroine

By the 1980s, it was clearly time for a change. Helen Slater, as Supergirl, stars in one of several films of the time with out-front heroines, although she never makes it as big as her older, male cousin. But the real star of the film is Faye Dunaway, who has a fine, if very politically incorrect, time playing a late-20th-century version of H. Rider Haggard's 19th-century creation, the immortal She.

The new generation

SF never had much time for children, unless they were examples of Homo superior *hiding until adulthood, but by 1990, Dan Simmons could, in* The Fall of Hyperion, *weave a complex plot involving care and sacrifice around one infant in swaddling clothes.*

One mean mother

Ah Flash! If you could be alive today! Half a century after Dale Arden clung to a man's arm for protection, Sigourney Weaver, in Aliens, *wields a heavy rifle, rescues a child, and sports neat boots with nary a high heel in sight. She is a genuine protagonist.*

1980-1989: NEW BEGINNINGS

AFTER THE INTROSPECTION OF the 1970s, the world begins to forge forwards into change again. These are the Thatcher years in Europe, the Reagan years in the United States, and the years of *glasnost* and *perestroika* in the Soviet Union.

A decade of rapid change over the world, by the end of it the Berlin Wall and several East European regimes have been torn down. Affordable information technology in the shape of computers, video equipment, and satellites has

	1 9 8 0	1 9 8 1	1 9 8 2	1 9 8 3	1 9 8 4

SF EVENTS

1980

Tom Doherty leaves Ace Books and founds **Tor Books** in conjunction with Pinnacle Books. The new house quickly establishes a name for publishing good SF by both new and established authors.

1981

Serge Brussolo, one of the major French SF authors of the 1980s, publishes **Sommeil de sang** [Blood sleep] one of the titles that assures his stature.

1982

Probably the greatest event of the year is not the publication of a new book, but the film version of an old one. Ridley Scott's *Blade Runner*, based on Philip K. Dick's *Do Androids Dream of Electric Sheep?*, makes Dick into a household name and shows people that as well as being big and bold, SF can be bleak and stylish. It also sets the scene for Cyberpunk to become the media obsession of the decade.

1983

Bluejay Books is set up, its books being distributed through St. Martin's Press. Despite a strong list of authors, the imprint is not successful, and survives for only three years.

1984

William Gibson's *Neuromancer* is published, winning Hugo, Nebula, and Philip K. Dick awards, and putting Cyberpunk very firmly on the map. The technology may be dubious, and the politics vague, but the gritty texture and the impotence of the protagonists are what this is really all about.

CINEMA, RADIO, AND TELEVISION

1980

The second part of George Lucas's *Star Wars* trilogy, *The Empire Strikes Back*, is released. The film suffers a little from the usual problems associated with being the second in a trilogy, having to continue the previous storyline while keeping enough back for the grand finale. It combats this by being more serious and philosophical than its predecessor, but it is the stunning special effects and exhilarating action that win the day.

1981

What is going to be the decade of cinematic sequels continues with *Mad Max 2*. In Great Britain, *The Hitchhiker's Guide to the Galaxy* moves from radio to television and immediately reaches a much wider audience.

1982

Spielberg's *E.T.* breaks all the records at the cinema. John Carpenter remakes **The Thing**. Although far from subtle, this version is in fact closer to John W. Campbell Jr.'s original story than the 1951 film.

1983

The *Star Wars* trilogy reaches its conclusion in *Return of the Jedi*. The unfortunate legacy of this last film are the Ewoks, who have two rather saccharine spin-off films of their own.

On television, the American series "V" starts well, but gradually deteriorates in quality as commercial interest demands greater simplicity.

1984

David Lynch brings Frank Herbert's **Dune** to the cinema screen. Unfortunately, not much of the original story remains. James Cameron's *Terminator* is more successful.

MAGAZINES

1980

In France, the first edition of **SF et Quotidien**, one of the few successful French magazines of the 1980s, is published.

1981

In Britain, the editorial board of *Interzone* magazine is beginning to put together the first issue, dated Spring 1982. After a downbeat start, it becomes one of the survival stories of the 1980s magazine market, and a catalyst in the revival of British SF writing.

1983

Proving that it is still right in the flow of SF, *Analog* serializes Greg Bear's *Blood Music*. Frank Miller makes a splash in the comics market with *Ronin*, the drawings executed in a trademark style that is to become famous.

WORLD EVENTS

1980

Ronald Reagan becomes President of the United States. The Solidarność trade union is set up in Poland. John Lennon is shot.

1981

The space shuttle **Columbia** is the first reusable spacecraft. The Prince of Wales gets married, watched by 700 million people.

1982

Britain goes to war in the Falklands. Israel takes on the Lebanese on the streets of **Beirut**.

1983

Reagan touts "Star Wars" missile shields for defence against the Soviet Union.

1984

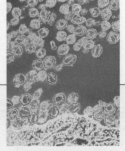

The immune disorder that appeared in the early 1980s is named the **Human Immunodeficiency Virus**, or HIV.

brought a new information revolution. SF, too, takes new strength, and looks to new skies. In some ways, SF becomes less distinct, more assimilated, in this decade. Free-market economics have their effect: SF series, television and film ties-ins, and game spin-offs all abound. Cyberpunk becomes the media's favourite buzz word, and something of a bane to its creators. Amidst it all, authors are writing genre material in great quantity, and of great quality.

Good guys look

In the 1950s, aliens came in all v *still roughly divided into anthropo* *shape-changers. On this cover* *magazine, a reassuring message* *universality of some kinds*

The alien sage

Here, thanks to the masterful *puppetry that came to cinema in* *the 1980s, we are witness to a* *superb matching of SF and* *fantasy icons. Yoda, who is* *Luke's mentor in The Empire* *Strikes Back, reminds us of one* *of the innumerable variety of* *sages from the land of Faerie;* *but he is also part of the SF* *universe, a strange, irascible,* *but deeply wise creature who* *serves as a teacher to erratic* *young humans. He has the gaze* *of a wise reptile, and he* *imparts wisdom.*

1 9 8 5	1 9 8 6	1 9 8 7	1 9 8 8	1 9 8 9
This is a year of arrivals, rather than debuts. Writers who are not quite new to the scene begin to hit their stride. Orson Scott Card arrives on the scene properly with *Ender's Game*, the first of the **Ender** books, winning Hugo and Nebula awards. Greg Bear writes *Blood Music* and *Eon*. Iain Banks, after *The Wasp Factory* the previous year, shows his wider genre interest in *Walking on Glass*.	 The **Arthur C. Clarke Award** for SF novels is first given. Margaret Atwood's *The Handmaid's Tale* wins.	With the relaxation of the political situation in the Soviet Union, Arkady and Boris Strugatski are allowed abroad, and are the guests of honour at the WorldCon in Great Britain.	Robert A. Heinlein dies. Although he has not written anything for some years that has not aroused mixed response, his death is a blow.	At the close of the decade, *Locus* magazine is recording a rise of over 50 per cent in the number of SF titles published each year, as compared to figures for 1980.

NOTABLE FIGURE

Wolfgang Jeschke is one of the most prominent people in German SF writing and publishing. He has a string of novels to his name, starting with *Der Letzte Tag der Schöpfung* (*The Last Day of Creation*), and has frequently been translated in a market that is often hostile to authors not writing in English. He is a distinguished editor of over a hundred anthologies of German and translated SF, and for 20 years he has been in charge of Heyne Verlag's SF line, introducing a wide variety of foreign SF into the German market. In 1987, he received international recognition when he was granted the Harrison Award for achievements in international SF.

WOLFGANG JESCHKE

The **Back to the Future** trilogy begins at the cinema. The first film is hugely popular, and the majority of people who go to see it do not think of it as even remotely SF.

Aliens, an unusually strong sequel, is directed by James Cameron rather than Ridley Scott, and introduces more aliens, more light, and heavy artillery. Sigourney Weaver returns to the mystery planet to help a space patrol combat another outbreak of aliens. The sets may not be as impressive, but the film beats its predecessor on characterization, dialogue, and tension.

Star Trek: The Next Generation takes off in the United States. It is a great deal more sophisticated than its forerunner.

In Britain, *Red Dwarf* begins its run, spoofing SF conventions with a cast of antiheroes. It soon becomes a cult series.

Doctor Who, having stumbled through numerous actors and plots for a few years, is finally pulled off the screen.

In America, a new magazine, *Aboriginal SF*, is founded, edited by Charles C. Ryan. This is to be one of the most successful semi-professional magazines to enter the field in the 1980s. *Batman* comes into the age of Cyberpunk with Frank Miller's graphic novel *Batman: The Dark Knight Returns*, which is hugely popular, and nominated for a Hugo award.

Alan Moore's *Watchmen* confirms his success in the American comics market and takes the concept of superheroes into whole new areas.

In America, *Journal Wired* has a brief life. It is notable for the involvement of Mark Ziesing, who runs the successful book publishing company, Mark V. Ziesing, or MVZ.

Gorbachev comes to power in the Soviet Union. French secret service agents sink the *Rainbow Warrior*, a Greenpeace ship.

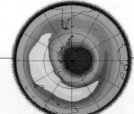

The space shuttle **Challenger** explodes on take off in the United States, killing the crew of seven. In the Soviet Union, Chernobyl power station blows up.

At a conference in Montreal, 70 nations finally agree to act to save the **ozone layer** by reducing the use of chloro-fluorocarbons.

Ronald Reagan visits Russia and seals the treaty to reduce the superpowers' nuclear arsenals.

The **Berlin Wall**, last relic of the disappearing borders between East and West, comes down. Bits are sold as souvenirs of the 1980s.

THEY C

A Botuan
This 18th-century tree-person is far from credible as a life form: he simply looks, and acts, like a man dressed up as a tree.

always, therefore, t
necessary so that w
different environm
of being. Since the
aliens, and more ali

Angelic a
*Old habits die hard. Fenton
published in a magazine in 1
identical to humans, although
wings are artificial, but the h
allegorical function: the M*

1990-1994: FACING A NEW CENTURY

THE FAST-APPROACHING END OF this century is also the end of the Millennium. The year 2000 is looked forward to with an almost childish anticipation. The new Millennium brings expectations of cataclysmic change, of the dawning of a new period of enlightenment, and of a global understanding of what is needed to ensure our survival on the planet. Compared to the dawning of the previous Millennium, the cataclysms that face us now are more

1990 · 1991 · 19

SF EVENTS

Brian Stableford begins his ***Werewolves of London*** series with the title volume. Set in the 19th century, it revolves around a set of "angels" who have the power to affect quantum events or, to put it another way, who can perform miracles. Our world is as incomprehensible to them as theirs is to us, and the differing world-views of science and the occult are examined at length as they try to make sense of it. Not high on events, the trilogy is a metaphysical trip through the nature of reality.

The Turner Tomorrow Award is founded by **Ted Turner**, head of the huge Turner Corporation. A novel alternative to paying authors huge advances, it offers a huge prize – $500,000 – to the best book published by Turner Publishing containing practical solutions to world problems. This is the largest financial award in the SF market, but it has not yet managed to establish itself as a prestigious prize.

Isaac Asimov dies. His later works had included two volumes of autobiography, and a collection of anecdotes, *Asimov Laughs Again*, is published this year. He leaves 50 years of SF titles, science articles, columns, and books, and an SF magazine that was launched into a falling market and became one of the most successful titles in the field.

CINEMA, RADIO, AND TELEVISION

There is a lot of muscle in the SF cinema of the 1990s. This year sees Arnold Schwarzenegger in **Total Recall**, an "adaptation" of a Philip K. Dick short story. Although the story is largely the scriptwriter's, the paranoia is straight out of Dick.

James Cameron repeats his early success with **Terminator 2: Judgment Day**. We have a leaner, meaner heroine, and a more humane, more human Terminator. The basic premise of action, action, and more action that made the first film so successful is slightly modified, but this is the same old Cameron.

More and more, it is becoming apparent that there is good money to be made in the SF cinema market. This encourages some mainstream actors who might not have been interested in the genre

MAGAZINES

In Australia, *Eidolon* is founded. It is a subscription-only magazine that survives well by publishing a rich mixture of fiction, articles, and reviews. It is to win a 1991 Ditmar Award.

While things are quieter on the magazine front these days, comics have taken new fire. In the comic *Judgment On Gotham* we see the linking of two rather different heroes, the anguished Batman and the gung-ho Judge Dredd. It is not a meeting of minds, but it is noisy.

WORLD EVENTS

In South Africa, **Nelson Mandela** is freed from prison after 27 years. Yeltsin is elected President of the Republic of Russia. Iraq invades Kuwait. Germany is reunified. The Channel Tunnel workers meet in the middle.

Operation "Desert Storm" starts the **Gulf War**. A high-tech war, it is waged against the Iraqi lines of communication as much as against the troops, and is all over in a matter of months.

subtle than the divine retribution expected before; now we know our destruction lies in our own hands, and that man is his own, and the planet's, worst enemy. The extent of our responsibility is awe-inspiring; what comes next is, to a great extent, our choice. We look to the future with both hope and apprehension. SF, as a medium for our dreams and nightmares is like Janus, the god of doors, looking forwards and back. This seems fitting at the threshold of a new age.

9 2   1 9 9 3   1 9 9 4

Orbit publish the one-and-a-half-million-word **Encyclopedia of Science Fiction**, edited by John Clute and Peter Nicholls. Weighing in impressively, it is a hugely expanded follow up to the 1979 title. It wins Hugo, Locus, and Eaton Grand Master awards, and a special award from the British Science Fiction Association. It also proves to be a quite unexpected success commercially.

Dan Dare, who first appeared in the pages of the *Eagle* in 1950, is no more. The magazine had folded before, in 1969, but was revived in 1982 with a Dan Dare directly descended from the original hero. But, sadly, the markets of the present are no longer there for the pilot of the future.

to look it over. This year, Chevy Chase and Darryl Hannah are tempted into the fold, and star in **Memoirs of an Invisible Man**. Although it is watchable, it does not really set the cinema audiences on fire.

Sylvester Stallone follows his friend and business partner Schwarzenegger into the SF ring with **Demolition Man**. A frozen cop is thawed out in the future to chase an escaped criminal whom this politically correct new world cannot cope with. The film is a romp, not a serious SF offering, and Wesley Snipes as the criminal is the blond bombshell to put all others in the shade.

This year sees the first version of *Frankenstein* for many decades in Kenneth Branagh's lavish and very Gothic production. At the other end of the scale, with futurist visions, come films like

Stargate, perhaps hoping to find a spark of millennial fever for their mystical escapades through the pyramids. And action-man Van Damme joins the explosive need of the market with *Timecop*.

The seemingly endless crisis of SF magazines in Great Britain continues with the incorporation of Paul Brazier's *Nexus* into *Interzone*, which is in its twelfth year under David Pringle. But even *Interzone* hovers close to the brink.

Yugoslavia ceases to exist, dissolving into separate states, and into war. Reforms in South Africa press ahead. In America, there are race riots in Los Angeles after police, caught on home video beating a black suspect with batons, are acquitted of any crime. The case goes to appeal court.

British Prime Minister **John Major** and Irish Taoiseach **Albert Reynolds** sign the

Downing Street Declaration in an attempt to bring to an end the terrorism in Northern Ireland. In the United States, a huge arsenal of weapons is found after the seige at a religious cult's headquarters at Waco ends in a blaze. Some 95 cult members die, either by fire or from gunshot wounds.

There are free **multiracial elections** in South Africa, resulting in Nelson Mandela being elected president. In Great Britain there is new hope for peace as terrorists declare a ceasefire in Northern Ireland. Elsewhere, things are not so harmonious: in Rwanda, a bloody civil war sees thousands massacred.

THE RED PLANET

MARS HAS GLOWED DOWN upon us since before we had voices to name it. It is part of the structure of the human animal, the animal who looks up and gives names to the distant lights it sees in the night sky. It has been home to lost civilizations, and a venue for high adventures.

In the age that achieved space travel, it was and remains the next step out from the Moon. In the closing years of the 20th century, Mars is not so much a planet – although we now know more clearly than ever before what kind of a planet it is – as a portal to beyond.

The myth of Mars

In the myth-making minds of human beings, the tide-turning Moon has always been seen as a woman, and Mars, named after an ancient god of war, has always been a man. Since we have endowed both bodies with personalities and even gender, it seems natural, somehow, that they should both show us faces: we have always seen a visage on the Moon, and science more recently found a face on Mars. But the face that we see in the Moon is that of a man, and the face that was photographed by the Viking orbiter on the surface of Mars – a pattern made up of the shadows of hills and valleys, that seems to resolve itself into a human face gazing directly up (or down) at us – looks female. The Mars

The myth-maker
Schiaparelli did not think Mars was full of canals; it was perhaps inevitable that others believed that it was.

woman's eyes are shadowed and there is a curtain of hair down one side of the head. Her mouth is half-open. She was carved there aeons ago (at least, so the popular mythology would have it) to invite us up, or warn us away, or to hitch a lift, or ask us for help. Very, very clearly, she is nothing but a natural, chance formation; but the potency of Mars as both an emblem of human passions in past centuries, and a target for human colonization in the next, makes it almost irresistible for us to speculate upon what "she" might mean by residing there, with her unreadable message to humanity from the far depths of time and space.

The canals of Mars

We have, after all, as readers of SF, never been shy about populating our neighbouring planet with all sorts of creatures; nor have we ever been reticent about expressing our profound need to make the planet mean something to us.

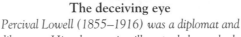

The deceiving eye
Percival Lowell (1855–1916) was a diplomat and dilettante. His telescope is still around, but nobody now can see what he saw through it.

It is a fact that the planet is clearly visible to the naked eye, and that with a cheap telescope it is possible to think that we can detect meaningful features on its surface. The strength of our need to make those vague features reflect our beliefs can be seen in the famous story of the *canali* discovered in 1877 by the astronomer Giovanni Schiaparelli (1835–1910).

All that Schiaparelli ever saw was a pattern of irregular narrow lines or streaks of some darker substance on the surface of the planet.

This is all that he meant to claim he saw when he used the Italian word for channels to describe his observations. Given the human need to make a sensible story of the Solar System, it was perhaps inevitable that *canali* would be translated into English as "canals", and that someone would argue that the features Schiaparelli had described were created works. Someone turned out to be a rich young American named Percival Lowell, who turned to astronomy in his middle years. He had the money to buy a fairly powerful telescope, which showed him what he wanted to see. In 1896, in the book he called simply *Mars*, Lowell argued strenuously for the existence of a schematic pattern of canals that crisscrossed the planet, met at various "oases", and in general very closely resembled an irrigation network. He never gave up his belief in hydraulic societies on the "desert" planet.

The first invasion from Mars

It was from a Mars like this that H.G. Wells's invaders travelled to Earth in his 1898 novel *The War of the Worlds* (see page 213). The scientifically grounded Wells was quite sceptical about the presence of real life on the real Mars.

Martian invaders
"Across the gulf of space," H.G. Wells's The War of the Worlds *begins, "minds that are to our minds as ours are to the beasts that perish, intellects vast and cool and unsympathetic, regarded this earth with envious eyes…" Wells was too sharp to believe Lowell, but Mars was ideal as an invasion launch-pad.*

Edgar Rice Burroughs, the next writer to use Mars extensively in his work, never cared. It was enough for him, and for dozens of other writers, that Mars could plausibly be imagined to contain life, and he transported his hero John Carter there with the greatest of aplomb to dominate the Martians. This is what Earthmen did so well, in so many tales, partly just because they were human, and partly because Mars (being smaller) has a lower gravity than Earth and so would have weaker inhabitants.

Burroughs never worried about whether or not the Mars of his dreams – a paradise straight out of *Arabian Nights*, full of naked (but safely non-human) women – could ever possibly exist, in either past or present. Later writers of Martian Planetary Romances, like the formidable Leigh Brackett, tended to set their tales in the deep past, before the waters had vanished beneath the surface of the planet.

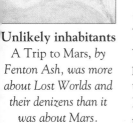

Unlikely inhabitants
A Trip to Mars, by Fenton Ash, was more about Lost Worlds and their denizens than it was about Mars.

The reason behind this overwhelming preference for the past as a setting is almost certainly because authors could in this fashion get around the present-day hostility of the real planet. The result of it has been that Mars, at least in the popular SF imagination, has almost always been described as ancient. It is ancient in Ray Bradbury's *The Martian Chronicles*, written in 1950, and it is positively worn out by the time that it appears in Philip K. Dick's dark 1964 novel *Martian Time-Slip* (see page 223). But Mars is, of course, no older than the planet Earth, and for the SF writers of recent years, it is brand new.

Fact meets fiction

Recent probes have generated huge amounts of information about Mars. They have mapped, contoured, and geologized it, named the bits that had not been given soubriquets, and confirmed its almost certain lifelessness. They have confirmed the sense that serious SF writers always had: that Mars was not at all a friendly place for human beings, but was our best bet for a serious attempt to colonize another world.

Perhaps because it is now feasible to imagine Mars as a venue for credible tales, SF writers have issued a slew of novels about Mars in the last years of the century. Some of them – like Jack Williamson's *Beachhead*, from 1992 – are Space Operas at heart; but most of them show that their authors have been paying very close heed to advances made by recent science and technology.

Tomorrow's venue
Finally, we begin to see just what it is that we have been dreaming about for all these centuries. And it starts us dreaming again, now that we know the universe is real and tangible.

The Martian volcanoes dwarf the Earth's highest peaks

Moving to Mars
By mid-century, Mars was suburbanized, home for ordinary folk in novels like Judith Merril's The Tomorrow People. *Great glass domes were established as a feature of the Martian landscape.*

In various ways, the novels being written by writers like Bear, Bisson, Bova, McAuley, Kim Stanley Robinson, and many others admit that Mars may be the next venue, after suborbital space and the Moon, to become no longer an exclusive SF terrain.

The most ambitious of these stories – Kim Stanley Robinson's triptych made up of *Red Mars* (see page 235), *Green Mars*, and the projected *Blue Mars* – comes close to being a manifesto, although it never stops being a story. Through its sustained internal debate on the practicalities and ethics of terraforming Mars into a planet capable of bearing human life, it familiarizes us not only with the hugeness of the task but also with the huge number of practical steps that we could be taking to realize it. The portal of Mars, in this tale and its cousins, stands open for us.

UNIVERSE OF FUTURE

REVOLT IN THE
ICE EMPIRE
by
RAY CUMMINGS

influential MAGAZINES

MAGAZINES HAVE ALWAYS BEEN central to Science Fiction writing. The early pulp magazines christened the genre, and almost every writer in the history of SF has debuted through a story published in one magazine or another. In the course of their professional lives, writers might edit the very magazines that had carried their debuts, bringing their own vision to the genre and shaping its future. Even today, when the classic SF titles are fighting for their shares of a diminished market, numerous semi-professional magazines, with far smaller circulations, are still a proving ground for up-and-coming authors.

ABOVE: HUGO GERNSBACK'S COLOPHON
LEFT: *PLANET STORIES* MAGAZINE COVER ART

EARLY PULP MAGAZINES

WHEN WE SAY PULP, we may be describing a category of magazine, smaller than most of today's glossy magazines, printed on cheap, wood-pulp paper, and generally devoted to fiction. We may also be describing the fiction published in these "pulps" – popular action stories in various genres.

These are the magazines and the stories that gave SF its start as a genre, first through including it among other adventure stories, then by promoting it specifically in dedicated titles, after the lead given by *Amazing Stories*. The format is now history, but pulp stories are still written.

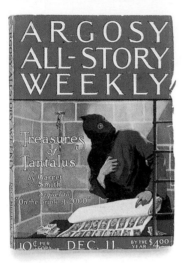

Argosy All-Story Weekly

Dates 1920–29 **Editor** Matthew White Jr.

The Argosy became a pulp magazine in 1896, when its content turned exclusively to fiction. It published SF stories regularly for over 1,000 issues, until 1943 – although it was never considered to be an SF magazine. In 1920, it was merged with its stable companion, *All-Story Weekly*.

Weird Tales

Dates 1923–54 **Editors** Edwin Baird, Otis Adelbert Kline, Farnsworth Wright, Dorothy McIlwraith

Fundamentally important to supernatural fiction and fantasy, *Weird Tales* was also significant for SF, especially in its prime, 1923–40, when it published works by H.P. Lovecraft, Robert E. Howard, Robert Bloch, Jack Williamson, Ray Bradbury, and others.

Amazing Stories

Dates 1926– **Editors** Hugo Gernsback, T. O'Conor Sloane, Raymond A. Palmer, Cele Goldsmith, Ted White, Elinor Mavor, George Scithers, Patrick Lucien Price, Kim Mohan

Magazines had, of course, been publishing SF before *Amazing Stories* appeared: both *Hugin* in Sweden and *Der Orchideengarten* in Germany published enough to be thought of as specialist journals. But it was in 1926, when Hugo Gernsback started up *Amazing Stories*, "the magazine of scientifiction", that everything came together: the time, the culture, and the magazine.

Not that it was much of a success at first. Gernsback was interested in science and in stories reflecting his technological utopianism. That, and an urge towards respectability, led him towards reprinting prestigious authors like Wells and Verne. But Leinster and Williamson, as well as *Buck Rogers* and Doc Smith's *Skylark* series, debuted here. The spark had been lit.

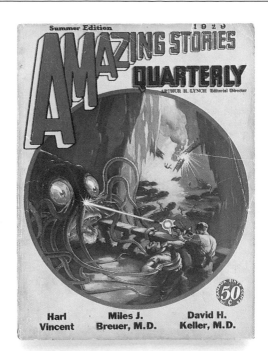

Amazing Stories Quarterly

Dates 1928–34 **Editors** Hugo Gernsback,
T. O'Conor Sloane

Amazing Stories' unsober sister magazine from 1928
soon became familiar for a cosmos-shaking kind of
Space Opera, the sort of tale pioneered by Edmond
Hamilton and John W. Campbell Jr. (as a writer),
with suns and planets shooting about like pinballs.

Astounding Stories

Dates 1930–38
Editors Harry Bates,
F. Orlin Tremaine

It is here that we have to
think about the two meanings
of pulp. In physical terms,
Amazing Stories was pulp; but
its original stories tended to
the stiff-necked and didactic.
It was with the appearance of
Astounding Stories that SF
truly embraced pulp style.
The first issues concentrated
on competently told
adventure tales, heavy on
action, low on science.
Eventually, with writers like
Stanley Weinbaum, and new
editors, and the inception of
E.E. Smith's *Lensmen* series,
SF and pulp were truly wed.
Then John W. Campbell Jr.
came along (see page 101).

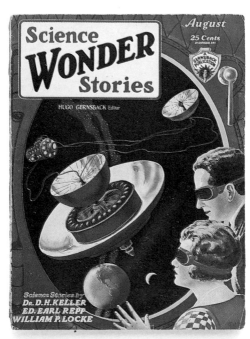

Science Wonder Stories

Dates 1929–30 **Editor** Hugo Gernsback

All sorts of conditions contributed to the growth of
SF as a genre, and of these fandom is one of the most
important. Hugo Gernsback, after losing control of
Amazing Stories in 1929, immediately founded
Science Wonder Stories, which included letter
columns and competitions, and loudly espoused
Gernsback's evangelical sense that SF was vital.

Air Wonder Stories

Dates 1929–30 **Editor** Hugo Gernsback

The problem with *Air Wonder Stories* is that there
are only so many SF tales to be told about futuristic
aircraft, air bandits, air Robin Hoods, floating cities,
and floating airports. After less than a year, the title
was merged with *Science Wonder Stories,* its sister
title, and became the rousing *Wonder Stories,* soon
to become *Thrilling Wonder Stories* (see page 100).

Scientific Detective Monthly

Date 1930 **Editor** Hugo Gernsback

Founded only three years after *Amazing Stories,*
Gernsback's *Scientific Detective Monthly* is an example
of the pulp-magazine breeding pool from which SF
was eventually to emerge as a distinct genre. Here,
detectives use obscure bits of scientific knowledge to
trap criminals. While it is not strictly speaking SF,
the ambience is certainly SF-like.

THE GOLDEN AGE OF PULPS

REALITY IS ALWAYS MORE complex than the labels that we use to describe it. But the years of the 1930s, the Golden Age of the SF pulp magazines, were a vibrant time to write stories in, to edit magazines in, and to read your dreams writ large. Gernsback had broken the ground, and a slew of others now followed him towards a bright new future. The United States led in this new magazine field. Open any page of any American pulp up until the bombing of Pearl Harbor, and you breathe the air of freedom. It was all new. It was in our hands. It was straight on from Now.

G-8 and his Battle Aces

Dates 1933–44
Editors Rogers Terrill, Alden H. Norton

Today, G-8 would inhabit an alternate history of World War I, with anything possible. In the 1930s, they just made believe that the Germans had an astonishing array of SF menaces, from rockets to genetically engineered giant bats. G-8 was an ace pilot and master spy, and saved us 110 times, all of them full-length tales written by Robert J. Hogan, a hero of the pulps.

Dusty Ayres and his Battle Birds

Dates 1934–35
Editor Rogers Terrill

Like Hogan, Robert Sidney Bowen had the habit of writing entire magazines solo. When *Battle Birds*, an aviation pulp, began to fail, Bowen was asked to create a storyline for the retitled *Dusty Ayres and his Battle Birds*. His epic is set in a near future, with all but America conquered by a villainous Asiatic empire. In the nick of time, just as the magazine folded, Dusty Ayres and America were victorious.

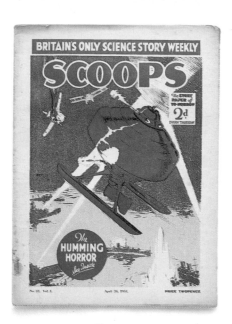

Scoops

Date 1934 **Editor** Hadyn Dimmock

What a mistake to make. To launch the very first – and very nearly the last – British SF magazine on a weekly schedule; to deny that it was SF; to publish its juvenile stories anonymously; and to ignore (until it was too late) every SF writer in the world: bad mistake, bad mistake. Just a short 20 weeks after it had started, *Scoops* rested in peace.

Tales of Wonder

Dates 1937–42 **Editor** Walter Gillings

A much better try than *Scoops*, *Tales of Wonder* published real SF stories by real SF writers, including early work by John Wyndham (writing then as John Beynon), and Arthur C. Clarke's first professional piece. But World War II took it down – took its writers, took the paper it was printed on, and in the end, took Walter Gillings, its editor.

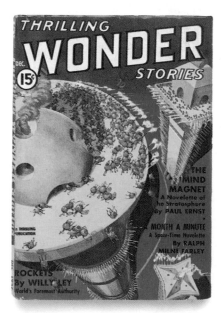

Thrilling Wonder Stories

Dates 1936–55 **Editors** Mort Weisinger, Oscar J. Friend, Sam Merwin Jr., Samuel Mines, Alexander Samalman

Hugo Gernsback's *Wonder Stories* (see page 99) was the best SF magazine of the early 1930s. Then it was sold in 1936, and became *Thrilling Wonder Stories*, publishing reams of glorious escapist adventure and Planetary Romance. It was fabulous fun.

Astounding Science Fiction

Dates 1938–60
Editor John W. Campbell Jr.

A decade after its launch (see page 99), *Astounding Stories* became *Astounding Science Fiction* and took off. The reason was simple: John W. Campbell Jr., who edited the journal from a year before the name change through its 1960 change to *Analog* (see page 103), up to his death in 1971. Pulp SF was fun, but it was time to do better. Campbell insisted on realistic speculation, clean writing, and heroes with moderately plausible virtues. *Astounding* under him brought into the field – or gave their first real chance to – most of the writers who dominated our sense of what mature SF was like: Asimov, van Vogt, Heinlein, de Camp, Simak, and Sturgeon. And he was wise enough to keep the greatest Space Opera writer of all: E.E. Smith.

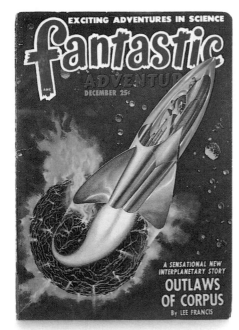

Fantastic Adventures

Dates 1939–53 **Editors** Raymond A. Palmer, Howard V. Browne

Not all magazines could be winners all the time. *Fantastic Adventures* always seemed to be falling between stools – it was neither SF nor fantasy; it was inconsistent in quality; it was erratic in targeting an audience. But there were some terrific tales in it. Not enough, but some.

Captain Future

Dates 1940–44 **Editors** Leo Margulies, Mort Wiesinger, Oscar J. Friend

His real name is Curt Newton, but everyone knows him as Captain Future; his Space Opera adventures dominate *Captain Future*. Most of the tales were by Edmond Hamilton, who also wrote comics. After the war, when the pulp market shrank, comic-book superheroes began to resemble Captain Future.

Planet Stories

Dates 1939–55 **Editors** Malcolm Reiss, Jerome Bixby

True to its name, *Planet Stories* concentrated on Planetary Romances, SF fairy tales set on verdant Venus and martial Mars. With writers like Ray Bradbury and Leigh Brackett – who introduced her famous adventurer, Erik John Stark, here – the content was far more sophisticated than the covers.

Startling Stories

Dates 1939–55 **Editors** Mort Weisinger, Oscar J. Friend, Sam Merwin Jr., Samuel Mines, Alexander Samalman

When *Startling Stories* was born into the *Thrilling Wonder Stories* stable, no one expected that it would take over. But from 1945, with Kuttner and Moore supplying hundreds of thousands of words of their best copy, it was to become a treasure trove.

THE POSTWAR BOOM

THE PULP SF EXTRAVAGANCES and dreams of technological triumph that characterized the Golden Age carried SF through the vast turmoil of World War II, but by the late 1940s a new generation of writers, some of them veterans, began to challenge the old certainties. The West was more prosperous than ever before, and it looked as though its citizenry might be able to support many more magazines than publishers had ever dreamed. By 1950, the best of the new journals were already active; the next ten years or so see-sawed between flood and drought.

New Worlds

Dates 1946–70 **Editors** John Carnell, Michael Moorcock, David S. Garnett

Fanzine issues of *New Worlds* predate World War II, but the greatest British SF magazine properly began in 1946. Carnell's issues emphasized traditional fare; the more radical content of Moorcock's New Wave issues in the 1960s shocked the SF world.

Science Fantasy

Dates 1950–67 **Editors** Walter Gillings, John Carnell, Harry Harrison, Keith Roberts

This companion of *New Worlds* published, for many years, some of the best SF from British writers, including Ballard, Brunner, Bulmer, and Moorcock. In its last years, the content was dominated by Thomas Burnett Swann, who – fittingly – restricted himself solely to Science Fantasy.

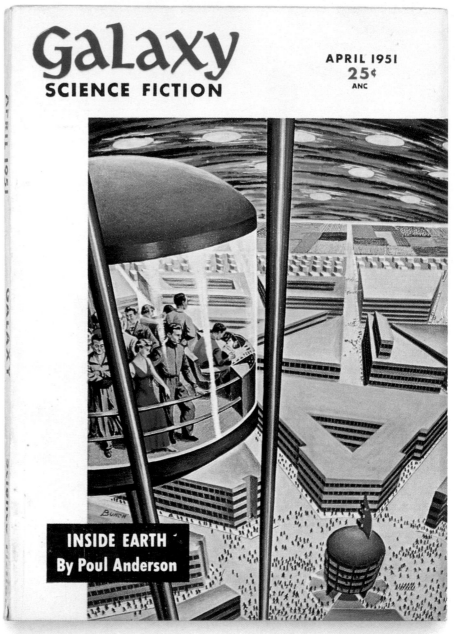

Galaxy Science Fiction

Dates 1950–80 **Editors** H.L. Gold, Frederik Pohl, James Baen, Eljer Jakobssen

Under its first two editors – Horace Gold from 1950 to 1961 and Frederik Pohl from then until 1969 – *Galaxy* supplanted *Astounding/Analog* as the default "voice" of American SF at its best. At the latter magazine, John W. Campbell had become difficult to deal with, and Gold's new-broom appeal is clearly evident in the very first issue of *Galaxy* in 1950, which included stories from *Astounding* stalwarts like Asimov and Simak. More significantly, this first issue also featured fine stories from Richard Matheson and Sturgeon, writers who now had two homes in the world of SF magazines (*The Magazine of Fantasy and Science Fiction* being the other). Bradbury and Heinlein soon came on board, and Bester published *The Demolished Man* here. For 20 years, *Galaxy* remained the first and last word.

The Pedestrian · RAY BRADBURY · One in a Thousand · J. T. McINTOSH
Axolotl · ROBERT ABERNATHY · First Strike · JAMES BLISH
The Star Ducks · BILL BROWN · Mission · KRIS NEVILLE

The Magazine of Fantasy and Science Fiction

Dates 1949–
Editors Anthony Boucher, J. Francis McComas, Avram Davidson, Edward L. Ferman, Kristine Kathryn Rusch

FSF, as it is usually called, and *Galaxy* are always seen as complementary twins. While *Galaxy* took over from *Astounding*, *FSF* explored territory hitherto neglected: SF and fantasy selected primarily for their literary quality. To show that fantastic fiction had a long literary pedigree, *FSF* editors – Anthony Boucher being the most important – published many reprints. New work came from Knight, Leiber, Matheson, Sturgeon, Keyes, and Zelazny. If critics did not ringfence SF and fantasy from "real" literature, *FSF* would be recognized as the home, for half a century, of many of America's best short stories.

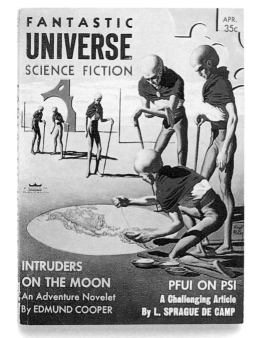

Fantastic Universe

Dates 1953–60 **Editors** Sam Merwin Jr., Hans Stefan Santesson

Some magazines never seem to establish much of an identity, or publish much worthwhile material, but still they rest fondly in their readers' memories. *Fantastic Universe*, which published second-rank work by many well-known writers, is one of these.

Analog

Dates 1960– **Editors** John W. Campbell Jr., Ben Bova, Stanley Schmidt

After about 1950, *Astounding* began to seem like a fossil. In 1960, responding to the new world, it was redubbed *Analog*; thus it has remained. With Bova taking over in 1971 there was a broadening of scope, and the magazine continues publishing estimable (though sometimes predictable) Hard SF.

Nebula Science Fiction

Dates 1952–59 **Editor** Peter Hamilton

SF in the UK was dominated for decades by John Carnell, but the small, still Scottish voice of *Nebula* should not be forgotten. Editor Peter Hamilton had a remarkable eye for talent, buying the first stories of Brian W. Aldiss, Barrington Bayley, and Robert Silverberg. He was about to serialize a Robert Heinlein novel when his finances collapsed.

If

Dates 1952–74 **Editors** James L. Quinn, Damon Knight, H.L. Gold, Frederik Pohl, Ejler Jakobssen

As a bridesmaid, *If* was a natural Hugo winner, and did win the award for best magazine three times. But nobody ever seemed to think of *If* as first choice. For a while, under Damon Knight, the magazine was prominent, but sales were unhealthy, and *If* was eventually merged with *Galaxy*.

CONTEMPORARY PUBLICATIONS

BY 1970 OR SO, THE CHALLENGE of the book had been met by some SF magazines, although many had died. But SF in book form now dominated the field. Of the old guard, *Astounding* and *Fantasy and Science Fiction* magazines continued to maintain their circulations, and some new journals were quite successful, but we had entered the era of the SF bestseller: when authors could dream of million-copy novels, it is understandable that some of them forgot all about the journals. But the journals still remained the best place to find and nurture new talent.

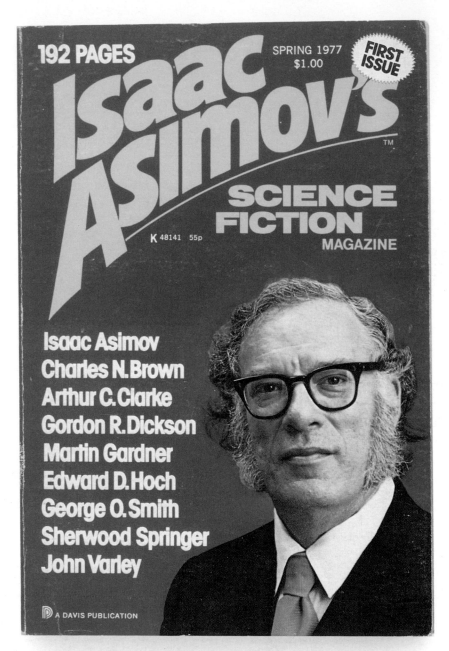

Isaac Asimov's Science Fiction Magazine

Dates 1977– **Editors** George H. Scithers, Shawna McCarthy, Gardner Dozois

It was Isaac Asimov's magazine in the same loose sense that *Alfred Hitchcock's Mystery Magazine* was Hitchcock's, although Asimov did write a regular editorial column for the journal until shortly before his death in 1992. The tone of the contents during the first years was conspicuously amiable, but after Gardner Dozois became editor in 1986, the magazine came to be recognized as the most prestigious of all SF journals, with both Dozois and the stories that he published winning many prizes, and the range of subject matter inexorably broadening year by year. The magazine's contributors are a pantheon lot; in recent years they have included Octavia Butler, Orson Scott Card, Nancy Kress, Lucius Shepard, Robert Silverberg, Michael Swanwick, Kate Wilhelm, Connie Willis, and Roger Zelazny.

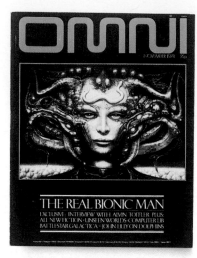

Omni

Dates 1978– **Editors** Ben Bova, Robert Sheckley, Ellen Datlow

Omni does not publish a huge amount of fiction, but what appears in its glossy pages has huge distribution, with circulation often over a million. Ellen Datlow, fiction editor from 1981, has kept the quality extremely high, the content occasionally daring.

Aboriginal Science Fiction

Dates 1986–91 (publication became erratic after this date) **Editor** Charles C. Ryan

As SF magazines lost their place in readers' hearts, fringe journals began to fill niches in the complex field that had developed. *Aboriginal* has been one of the most successful, making most of its sales through subscription, publishing obscure and well-known writers, juxtaposing the familiar and the unknown.

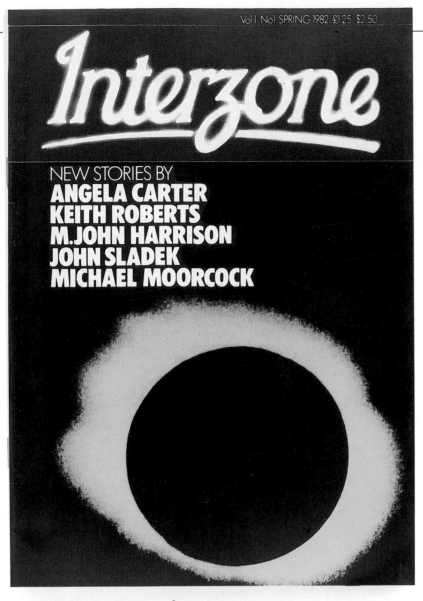

Vol 1 No 1 SPRING 1982 £1·25 $2·50

Interzone

NEW STORIES BY
ANGELA CARTER
KEITH ROBERTS
M. JOHN HARRISON
JOHN SLADEK
MICHAEL MOORCOCK

Interzone

Dates 1982– **Editors** John Clute, Colin Greenland, Roz Kaveney, Simon Ounsley, David Pringle

Begun in 1982 as an attempt – largely successful – to fill the vacuum left in British SF publishing by *New Worlds*, *Interzone* was originally edited and published by a collective, which gradually shrank to David Pringle by 1988. The magazine became a breeding pool for many of the younger writers now becoming prominent: Stephen Baxter, Richard Calder, Greg Egan, Ian MacDonald, Paul J. McCauley, Kim Newman, and Geoff Ryman. In 1994, *Nexus* magazine merged with *Interzone*.

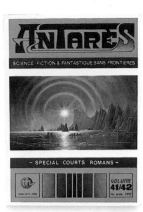

Antares

Dates 1981– **Editor** Jean-Pierre Moumon

This highly professional French journal publishes a mix of original works by French writers, stories in translation (mostly from English), interviews, and a substantial section of *bandes dessinées* (comic strips, a favourite literary form in France).

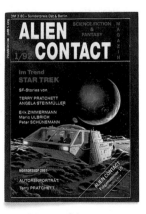

Alien Contact

Dates 1990– **Editors** Hardy Kettlitz, Gerd Frey, Hans-Peter Neumann

Published from Berlin, this journal began life under the Communist regime. It gives an effective, glossy impression, and publishes work both in German and in translation, the latter mostly from English.

SF MAGAZINES FROM EASTERN EUROPE

Ikarie
Dates 1990–

Fantastyka
Dates 1982–

Anticipatia
Dates 1982–

String
Dates 1988–

Under the rule of the Communists, Eastern Europe's SF magazines were often beacons of coded hope, in which freer, richer, or more exciting futures could be secretly dreamed of. The Romanian *Anticipatia*, more than 500 issues old, has survived the vast turmoils of the 1980s, and continues to publish both original native works and translations of foreign material, as does the much younger *String*, also published from Bucharest. *Ikarie* serves the readers of the Czech Republic, and *Fantastyka* has long provided a similar mix in Poland.

CHAPTER FOUR

major AUTHORS

ALTHOUGH SCIENCE FICTION HAS been a distinct genre for most of this century, it has changed and developed considerably over the decades. In this chapter, time charts list major literary works of each era, the themes and icons that were important to each generation, and the authors who made their debuts in each year. The charts give an overview of what was happening in any given year and trace the changing influences. Author profiles, with bibliographies, follow the charts. They are grouped decade-by-decade, linking authors to the period in which they came to prominence or were most prolific or influential.

ABOVE: JULES VERNE

LEFT: A SELECTION OF PROFILED AUTHORS

1800-1899: THE BIRTH OF THE BOOK

IN 1800, IN BRITAIN, THREE decades before the invention of cheap paper to print books on, the dissemination of novels was heavily restricted by the high cost of producing them. By the end of the 19th century, this had changed utterly: large numbers of writers earned their livings in Grub Street, publishing's spiritual home, churning out huge amounts of literature and sub-literature, much of it printed on paper so cheap that no copies at all of some early SF texts survive.

1800s	1810s	1820s	1830s	1840s

NOTABLE WORKS

1800s

The Temple of Nature
ERASMUS DARWIN, 1803

The Last Man
JEAN-BAPTISTE DE GRAINVILLE, 1805

The Armed Briton
WILLIAM BURKE, 1806

1810s

Armata: A Fragment
THOMAS ERSKINE, 1817

Frankenstein, or The Modern Prometheus
MARY SHELLEY, 1818

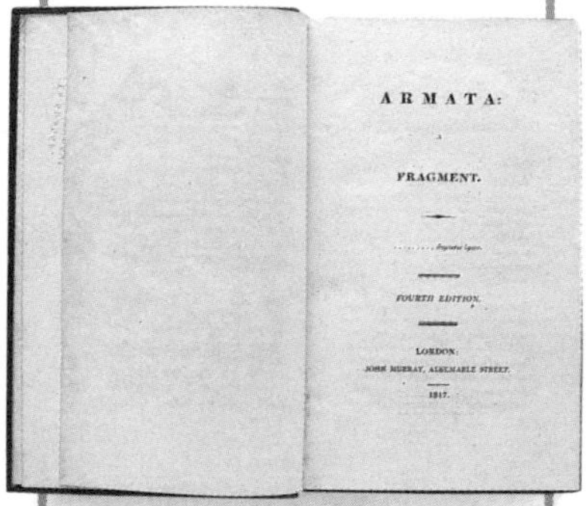

ARMATA

1820s

Melmoth the Wanderer
CHARLES MATURIN, 1820

Symzonia
CAPTAIN ADAM SEABORN, 1820

The Rebellion of the Beasts
ANONYMOUS, 1825

The Last Man
MARY SHELLEY, 1826

A Voyage to the Moon
GEORGE TUCKER AS JOSEPH ATTERLEY, 1827

The Mummy!
JANE LOUDON, 1827

Salathiel
GEORGE CROLY, 1828

1830s

Ahasvérus
EDGAR QUINET, 1833

The Narrative of Arthur Gordon Pym
EDGAR ALLAN POE, 1837

1840s

Eureka
EDGAR ALLAN POE, 1848

The Triumph of Woman: A Christmas Story
CHARLES ROWCROFT, 1848

A Voyage from Utopia
JOHN FRANCIS BRAY, 1842
(PUBLISHED 1957)

The Wandering Jew
EUGENE SUE, 1844–45

ICONS

1800s
With the turn of the century, suddenly the future becomes imaginable as something that will be profoundly different from all our yesterdays. The wheel of time begins to turn.

1810s
Mary Shelley's *Frankenstein* bequeaths the monster to the whole of SF that is to follow, for better or – too often – for worse. It also provides a pattern for asking questions about the new future, for expressing hopes, fears, and speculations in fictional form.

1820s
In 1826, John Symmes inspires Symmes's Theory of Concentric Spheres, which argues that the Earth is hollow, is habitable within, and can be entered from the North and South Poles. Dozens of tales plunge right in.

1840s 
SF still sports with images of apocalypse and horror. The various **maelstroms** that feature in Edgar Allan Poe's stories can stand for the decade.

DEBUTS

1810s 
As there is no SF profession, no career structure to be initiated into, an early-19th-century debut may represent a simple one-off. Thomas Erskine's *Armata* is all that he writes. But **Mary Shelley**, who debuts with *Frankenstein* in 1818, continues with *The Last Man* in 1826.

1830s 
Because he used fantastic imagery in his poetry and prose, and wrote hoax tales, it is difficult to say which is the first SF to come from **Edgar Allan Poe**. But "Hans Phaal" (1835) is a good bet.

1840s
It is hard to identify the first SF or SF-like work by 19th-century authors. *Zanoni* (1842) is Bulwer Lytton's first significant effort, and the story "The Birthmark" (1843) is a good guess for Nathaniel Hawthorne.

At the beginning of the century, writers like Mary Shelley and Thomas Erskine – whose *Armata* appeared in 1817 – were writing for a limited, upper-class audience. In 1899, George Griffith and H.G. Wells were writing for everyone.

At the beginning of the century, speculative fiction was written for the owners of society; come the century's end, SF is also being written for those who wished to change the world. The transformation is immense.

1850s

Phantastes
GEORGE MACDONALD, 1858

Poems and Stories
FITZ-JAMES O'BRIEN, 1855–62

The Air Battle
HERMANN LANG, 1859

In 1850, the world is still too big to grasp whole in the imagination, still holds mysteries in its deep valleys, somewhere east of Samarkand. It is still an SF adventure to traverse the globe.

Although **Jules Verne** published some SF-like stories in the 1850s, it is only in the 1860s that he explodes into the public view, and founds SF as a genre.

1860s

Journey to the Centre of the Earth
JULES VERNE, 1863

A Voyage to the Moon
CHRYSOSTOM TRUEMAN, 1864

Captain Hatteras
JULES VERNE, 1864–66

The Cloud King
WILLIAM HAYWARD, 1865

From the Earth to the Moon
JULES VERNE, 1865

The Steam Man of the Prairies
EDWARD S. ELLIS, 1868

After several hundred fictional journeys to the **Moon**, in 1865, at last, in Jules Verne's hands, it becomes a real destination.

1870s

THE BRICK MOON

from the papers of Captain Frederic Ingham, by

EDWARD EVERETT HALE

THE BRICK MOON

The Brick Moon
EDWARD EVERETT HALE, 1870

The Coming Race
EDWARD BULWER-LYTTON, 1871

The Battle of Dorking
GEORGE CHESNEY, 1871

With *The Invasion of England* and **The Battle of Dorking**, Future Wars begin to loom over SF's horizons in this decade.

NOTABLE AUTHOR

Camille Flammarion (1842–1925) typifies the intellectual stew that generated SF. Astronomer, mystic, and storyteller, he was obsessed by life after death, and on other worlds, and seemed to see no real distinction between the two. His *Lumen* (1872) recounts the travels of an occult spirit through realistically described space.

CAMILLE FLAMMARION

1880s

LOOKING BACKWARD 2000–1887

After London
RICHARD JEFFERIES, 1885

Looking Backward, 2000–1887
EDWARD BELLAMY, 1888

Dr. Jekyll and Mr. Hyde
ROBERT LOUIS STEVENSON, 1888

A Connecticut Yankee in King Arthur's Court
MARK TWAIN, 1889

Between 1877, when Giovanni Schiaparelli reports *canali* on Mars, and 1896, when Lowell publishes *Mars*, disseminating his mistranslation of *canali* as canals, the budding SF genre suddenly discovers the planet as a real place, a landscape full of genuine alien beings. Wells is just around the corner.

1890s

News from Nowhere
WILLIAM MORRIS, 1890

The Time Machine
H.G. WELLS, 1895

Two Planets
KURD LASSWITZ, 1897

Edison's Conquest of Mars
GARRETT P. SERVISS, 1898

NEWS FROM NOWHERE

In 1893, H.G. Wells publishes "The Advent of the Flying Man", followed by novels too numerous to list, George Griffith publishes *The Angel of the Revolution*, and Konstantin Tsiolkovsky publishes *On the Moon*. Other writers new to SF this decade include William Dean Howells, John Jacob Astor, and M.P. Shiel.

MARY SHELLEY

BORN / DIED **1797-1851**

NATIONALITY **English**

KEY WORKS ***Frankenstein, or the Modern Prometheus, The Last Man***

I T is well nigh impossible to track the first 25 years of Mary Wollstonecraft Shelley's life, unless one has a good flowchart or a photographic memory. She was the daughter of William Godwin, the author of *Caleb Williams*, and of Mary Wollstonecraft, the author of *A Vindication of the Rights of Woman*, who had already borne an illegitimate child by another man and died of puerperal fever shortly after Mary's birth. Godwin married a widow with two children, and had a son with her. Mary grew up in an insecure, hectic household.

Then, aged 16, she met Percy Shelley, fell in love, and eloped from the frying pan into the fire. They ended up at La Spezia, on the Italian coast, where everything became even more complicated: Shelley's pregnant wife followed them and lived in; Byron arrived, and slept with one of Mary's sisters; another sister killed herself a few months later; Shelley's wife also committed suicide; and finally Mary married Shelley. Meanwhile, still in her teens, she had written the world's first full-blown SF novel.

Frankenstein (see page 210), which was eventually published two years after it was written, seems to reflect something of the high emotional chaos

that had marked its author's early life. It bears a clear formal resemblance to many of the Gothic novels that had been so astonishingly popular over the previous decades (estimates of the number published run as high as 5,000 titles). The frame story that enfolds the main tale, itself told by the protagonist to a bemused listener, is typical of the Gothic mode. Classic Gothic themes – constraint, threatened identity, pursuit, arcane experimentation in matters not meant for human consumption, parody, an aura of evil – pervade the whole text, and both Victor Frankenstein and the "monster" that he creates have become Gothic archetypes.

The full title of the book is *Frankenstein, or The Modern Prometheus*: Victor, the overreaching scientist who attempts to re-create the work of God, fabricates nothing but a shambles, a vicious parody of creation, unlike the original Prometheus, who moulded humans out of mud; and his monster, terribly alone, exiled by his artificial nature from any rapport with humanity, is in turn a Prometheus whose gift of fire must gutter in the black night.

Frankenstein is a great Gothic tale, a re-enactment in highly melodramatic terms of Mary Shelley's own sense of isolation from normal human society. But it is also far more than that. The monster is, at one and the same time, both an utterly unnatural creation and the perfect model of the *tabula rasa*: the unspoilt natural man, the Noble Savage who needs only to open a book in order to become fully human.

Created by the use of electricity, galvanized into animate life, Shelley's monster is – or might be, given the opportunity – fully open to the new world of the 19th century, a time when any experiment might well bear fruit, any dream might become reality. It was a time of revolution, of urgent striving for a better world; and the monster's fiery longing for that better world can be seen as a profoundly unsettling signal that the established order may be turning upside-down. But *Frankenstein* stops short of total upheaval.

> ❝ *Mary Shelley's novel reflects the high emotional chaos that marked her early life* ❞

Perhaps because the monster represents an abomination against nature, and certainly because he is thwarted by the benighted folk who surround him, he is ultimately doomed to live a life of murderous frustration. At tale's end he disappears, alone, into the Arctic ice.

In 1822, Percy Shelley drowned while sailing in the bay at La Spezia, and Mary's life finally settled down. She worked hard and wrote stories and other novels, including one other work that could be called SF: *The Last Man*, a post-holocaust tale set about AD 2090.

The original monster
Unlike the many subsequent cinematic interpretations of the monster, Mary Shelley's creation relied on more than simple appearance for its effect.

Most of the tale is sentimental romance, but eventually a plague, which begins in Constantinople, wipes out all of humanity. One man survives, and he is last seen drifting south in a boat, just as alone as the monster Frankenstein had created. Mary Shelley herself died at the age of 53, after nearly three decades of solitary widowhood.

Mary W. Shelley

BIBLIOGRAPHY

NOVELS
1818 ***Frankenstein, or the Modern Prometheus*** Larkington, Hughes, Harding, Mavor and Jones
1826 ***The Last Man*** Henry Colburn

SHORT STORY COLLECTIONS
1891 ***Tales & Stories by Mary Wollstonecraft Shelley*** William Patterson
1976 ***Collected Tales and Stories*** Johns Hopkins University Press

LORD LYTTON

BORN / DIED
1803-73

NATIONALITY
English

OTHER NAMES
Bulwer Lytton, Sir Edward Bulwer-Lytton

KEY WORK
The Coming Race

NOBODY seems to know what to call the man. His name at birth was Edward George Earle Lytton Bulwer; after 1843, having inherited his mother's estate, he became Edward George Earle Lytton Bulwer-Lytton; and on being elevated to the peerage in 1866, he made a final up-market move to Edward George Earle Lytton Bulwer-Lytton, Lord Lytton. Only his friends (we may assume) called him Bul. We shall stick to Lytton.

He was an important writer, less for style than because of his exuberant energy and his uncanny ability to anticipate trends – *Pelham* is the first novel with a dandy hero, and *The Last Days of Pompeii* revolutionized historical fiction. His supernatural tales, like *Zanoni*, are fascinating and ornate. And in *The Coming Race*, Lytton wrote a seminal SF novel. The story itself is not remarkable: exploring a mineshaft, a young man stumbles across the underground civilization of the Vril-ya, a ruthless, scientifically advanced matriarchy. He lives there for a while, and is helped to escape by a Vril lady who loves him. But as a satire on both Darwinism and eugenical utopianism, and as an inspired tour of a high-tech world, the tale shows some very sharp teeth.

Occult tales
A Strange Story *involves the search for the elixir of life, a theme that recurs in* The Coming Race.

BIBLIOGRAPHY

NOVELS AND NOVELLAS
1833 **Asmodeus at Large** Carey, Lea and Blanchard
1834 **The Pilgrims of the Rhine** Saunders and Otley
1835 **The Student** Saunders and Otley
1842 **Zanoni** Saunders and Otley
1861 **A Strange Story** Tauchnitz
1871 **The Coming Race** Blackwood
1905 **The Haunted and the Haunters, or The House and the Brain** Gowan's

EDGAR ALLAN POE

BORN / DIED **1809-49**

NATIONALITY **American**

KEY WORKS **The Narrative of Arthur Gordon Pym of Nantucket, The Science Fiction of Edgar Allan Poe**

POE is of endless interest. He was a terrible man – an alcoholic and a paedophile, who lived in self-induced, depressive squalor – and, many think, a pretty bad writer. There is a noisy, posturing inflatedness about even his best work, as though one were being orated to by a confidence-man whose tricks have long passed their sell-by date. But at the same time, he is deeply original: he virtually invented the short story as an art form, he created the detective tale, and he mixed together supernatural and scientific elements with considerable sophistication in stories that continue to mesmerize.

Poe's short stories read uneasily as SF, usually taking the form of abstract dialogues or discussions, or being told as hoaxes. But *The Narrative of Arthur Gordon Pym of Nantucket* carries its stowaway hero, after adventures in the South Seas, into a tropical Lost World at the heart of Antarctica. The tale ends enigmatically when Pym comes across a horrific white monster, but its dreamlike intensity has haunted SF writers ever since. Jules Verne was only the first to write a continuation of it; perhaps the most famous is Lovecraft's *At the Mountains of Madness*.

BIBLIOGRAPHY

NOVELS AND NOVELLAS
1838 **The Narrative of Arthur Gordon Pym of Nantucket** Harper
1846 **Mesmerism "In Articulo Mortis"** Short

SHORT STORY COLLECTIONS
1840 **Tales of the Grotesque and Arabesque** Lea and Blanchard
1845 **Tales of Edgar A. Poe** Wiley and Putnam
1850 **The Works of the Late Edgar Allan Poe** John Redfield, four volumes to 1856
1976 **The Science Fiction of Edgar Allan Poe** Penguin

Death masque
Much of Poe's work is Gothic horror with a speculative slant. In "The Masque of the Red Death", a plague sweeps the land, and decay finds the aristocracy at the height of their decadence.

JULES VERNE

BORN / DIED **1828-1905**

NATIONALITY **French**

KEY WORKS *Voyage au centre de la terre, De la terre à la lune, Autour de la lune, Vingt milles lieues sous les mers, L'île mystérieuse, Paris au XXe siècle*

EVEN as late as 1828, the year in which Francisco Goya died and Jules Verne was born, the shadow of one dead man continued to haunt the crowned heads of Europe. Napoleon had died in exile seven years before, but the revolutionary principles that he espoused (although he had later betrayed them) still challenged any complacent sense that hierarchical order, old religion, safe science, and the *Ancien Régime* still held unanswerable sway over the hearts and minds of the citizens of Europe. So the lid was resolutely clamped down, while hierarchy

was mocked by pen and by paintbrush, religion stumbled over the discoveries of geology and the theories of Darwin, science generated technologies far more revolutionary than most political manifestoes, and the kings and queens gritted their teeth against the storms to come. It is against this backdrop that the long and strange career of Jules Verne – the bourgeois Catholic lawyer's son from the French provinces who revolutionized popular fiction – must be understood.

From his very first works, published in the 1850s, Verne tried ferociously to keep to the surface of events. He busily extolled anything and everything that spelled Progress, but without ever stopping to examine the dynamics of 19th-century progress, even as it was transforming the world about him.

National status
Verne's success made him a hero of the French public. This cartoon by Gill shows the world at the tip of his pen; another showed the planet on stage in a puppet theatre operated by Verne. The Prix Jules Verne *was given annually in France for the best novel in the spirit of his work: sadly, the award was discontinued in 1980.*

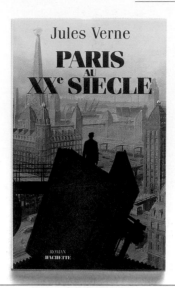

NOTABLE WORK

Published for the first time ninety years after its author died, *Paris au XXe siècle* [Paris in the 20th century] is an early and unusual Verne novel. It is set in a Paris where life revolves around the pursuit of wealth. People crowd onto an overburdened Metro system each day, communicate with each other by machines that closely resemble fax machines, and live impoverished lives. Hetzel rejected the novel, saying that it was too extreme and depressing, which may explain the optimistic tone of Verne's other work.

PARIS IN THE 20TH CENTURY

He defended the political *status quo*, all the while turning his face from the fact that sooner or later the pressure of progress would grow too great, and the world explode into war.

Because Verne's translators into English and other languages have treated him as a mere garrulous spinner of tales for children, and cut out any material that failed to fit this preconception, his non-French readers have not generally noticed, for nearly a century, how deeply stress-ridden and conservative his SF was from its earliest days. They have missed the chance to confront a phenomenon: Jules Verne, one of the two founding fathers of modern SF, did not want the future.

But modern SF – which treats the future as a rich tapestry to examine and inhabit for its own sake – did not exist in 1863, when Verne published the first of his 60 *Voyages Extraordinaires* (Extraordinary Voyages), *Cinq semaines en ballon* (Five Weeks in a Balloon). As with almost all of his SF, the story is set at a time more or less contemporary with its publication. Some of Verne's Extraordinary Voyages are of little or no SF interest, being essentially adventure tales set in various exotic and picturesque locales. They allow Verne to make political speculations, sometimes deeply tedious, about a world justly – he felt – dominated by Europe. The only one of these non-SF novels that has remained famous is

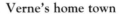

Verne's home town
Jules Verne came from a wealthy middle-class family, and was born and brought up in Nantes. The port's busy atmosphere and the apparent romance of ocean life must have had some effect on the young Verne. He ran away to sea at a young age, switching places with a cabin boy, and escaped discovery until after the ship had left port. Later, he sent his heroes adventuring abroad instead.

Le tour du monde en 80 jours (*Around the World in Eighty Days*), a tale that does verge on the fantastic. In Verne's SF, we find less travelogue and fewer politicians. Novels like *Voyage au centre de la terre* (*Journey to the Centre of the Earth*), *De la terre à la lune* (*From the Earth to the Moon*) (see page 212), *Autour de la lune* (*Around the Moon*), *Vingt milles lieues sous les mers* (*Twenty Thousand Leagues under the Sea*), and *L'île mystérieuse* (*The Mysterious Island*) are perhaps both the safest, and most exhilarating, SF books ever to be written.

They are safe because Verne regarded science and inventions as machines to tame the unknown. His heroes illuminate and domesticate that world with the aid of their almost magical devices. There may be darknesses that the explorers turn their faces from, in a half-acknowledged fear that the electric lights of science are insufficient to penetrate all mysteries, and Captain Nemo, the Byronic owner and absolute commander of the submarine *Nautilus*, may demonstrate that the world is not being conquered painlessly, nor without injustices being committed against those who oppose European Progress; but these recessional notes are minor. For two decades and more, the novels of Jules Verne represented the triumph of the machine, taking the whole world in stride.

Fantastic creations
Early editions of Verne are illustrated with dramatic scenes. This encounter with a squid comes from the first edition of Twenty Thousand Leagues under the Sea.

Cinema adaptations
When Verne's novels came out of copyright in the 1950s, film studios flocked to adapt them. The Mysterious Island casts prisoners escaping the American Civil War in a balloon as the heroes who are washed up on the shore.

In his later years, however, this bright picture darkens considerably. From about 1886, when *Robur le conquérant* (*Robur the Conqueror*) appeared, Verne's work shows an ever-increasing distrust of science and technology, of the politicians whose task it is to manage the vast compact of European empires, and of the heroes that his imagination brings forth. The great airship with which Robur intends to dominate the world is called the *Albatross*; and there are moments when the ill-balanced

thrust of 19th-century progress does seem to lie heavy on Verne's spirit. He never stopped writing: there are dozens of tales between *Robur the Conqueror* and his last novel. That final book, *L'étonnante aventure de la mission Barsac* (*The Barsac Mission*), is a savage assault on the pretension of Western Progress to construct anything resembling an ideal society; it serves as an epitaph to an author whose vision carried readers and inspired writers, but ultimately could not convince its own creator.

BIBLIOGRAPHY

NOVELS AND NOVELLAS
1863 **Cinq semaines en ballon** Hetzel, translated as **Five Weeks in a Balloon; or, Journeys and Discoveries in Africa**
1864 **Voyage au centre de la terre** Hetzel, translated as **A Journey to the Centre of the Earth**
1865 **De la terre à la lune** Hetzel, translated as **From the Earth to the Moon**
1866 **Voyages et adventures du Capitaine Hatteras** Hetzel, translated as **The Adventures of Captain Hatteras**
1867 **Les enfants du Capitaine Grant** Hetzel, translated as **In Search of the Castaways**
1869 **Autour de la lune** Hetzel, translated as **Around the Moon**
1870 **Vingt milles lieues sous les mers** Hetzel, translated as **Twenty Thousand Leagues under the Sea**

1872 **Aventures de trois russes et de trois anglais dans l'Afrique australe** Hetzel, translated as **Meridiana**
1873 **Le tour du monde en 80 jours** Hetzel, translated as **Around the World in Eighty Days**
1874 **Le Docteur Ox** Hetzel, translated as **Dr. Ox's Experiment and Other Stories**
L'île mystérieuse Hetzel, translated as **The Mysterious Island**
1875 **Le "Chancellor": journal du passager J.-R. Kazallon; Martin Paz** Hetzel, translated as **The Wreck of the Chancellor**
1876 **Michel Strogoff, Mscou-Irkoutsk** Hetzel, translated as **Michael Strogoff, the Courier of the Czar**
Les indes-noires Hetzel, translated as **The Child of the Cavern**

1879 **Les cinq cents millions de la bégum** Hetzel, with Paschal Grousset, translated as **The Begum's Fortune**
1880 **La maison à vapeur** Hetzel, translated as **The Steam House**
1881 **La Jangada** Hetzel, translated as **The Giant Raft**
1882 **Le rayon vert** Hetzel, translated as **The Green Ray**
L'école des Robinsons Hetzel, translated as **School for Crusoes**
1884 **L'Archipel en feu** Hetzel, translated as **The Archipelago on Fire**
1886 **Robur le conquérant** Hetzel, translated as **The Clipper of the Clouds**, retitled **Robur the Conqueror**
1889 **Sans dessus dessous** Hetzel, translated as **Topsy-Turvy**, retitled **The Purchase of the North Pole; a Sequel to "From the Earth to the Moon"**

1892 **Le Château des Carpathes** Hetzel, translated as **The Castle of the Carpathians**
1895 **L'île à hélice** Hetzel, translated as **The Floating Island**
1896 **Face au drapeau** Hetzel, translated as **For the Flag**
1897 **Le Sphinx des glaces** Hetzel, translated as **An Antarctic Mystery**
1901 **La grande forêt, le village aérien** Hetzel, translated as **The Village in the Treetops**
1901 **Les histoirs de Jean-Marie Cabidoulin** Hetzel, translated as **The Sea-Serpent: the Yarns of Jean Marie Cabidoulin**
1904 **Maître du monde** Hetzel, translated as **The Master of the World**
1905 **Le phare du bout du monde** Hetzel, translated as **The Lighthouse at the End of the World**

1908 **La Chasse au météore** Hetzel, translated as **The Chase of the Golden Meteor**
1909 **Les naufragés du Jonathan** Hetzel, translated as **The Survivors of the "Jonathan"**
1910 **Le secret de Wilhelm Storitz** Hetzel, translated as **The Secret of William Storitz**
1919 **L'étonnante aventure de la mission Barsac** Hachette, translated as **The Barsac Mission**
1994 **Paris au XXe siècle** Hachette **[Paris in the 20th century]**

SHORT STORY COLLECTIONS
1871 **Une ville flottante** Hetzel, translated as **A Floating City**
1910 **Hier et demain** Editions Hetzel, translated as **Yesterday and Tomorrow**

H.G. WELLS

BORN / DIED **1866-1946**

NATIONALITY **English**

OTHER NAME **Reginald Bliss**

KEY WORKS **The Time Machine, The Island of Doctor Moreau, The Invisible Man, The War of the Worlds**

H E had a high, squeaky voice, and his skin smelled like honey. He loved his wives, but he slept with any woman who – intoxicated by the smell of honey – would let him into her bed. He was a tubercular, working-class lad in a world that killed his sort young, but he lived to the age of 80, in sunlight and in shadow. He pretended to disdain the difficult art of fiction, but he could not stop writing novels, and a full dozen of them still jolt us with their brilliance, their clarity of mind, their prescience. He invented the British Scientific Romance, although he did not invent the term, and he was the most important SF writer the genre has yet seen, although he never called his work Science Fiction. He was a man of the future, but in his last book, *Mind at the End of its Tether*, he predicted doom in the shape of things to come.

The first, and perhaps the most important, influence upon H.G. Wells was his university tutor, T.H. Huxley, dean of the Huxley clan and Charles Darwin's most formidable proponent and popularizer. And if there is one single principle that can be seen to inform Wells's work from beginning to end, it is the conviction that the human species, along with all other species, can be defined as an outcome of the process of evolution – that we are bound to time's arrow. This acute awareness of the profound engine of nature, working in obedience to laws and rhythms beyond our immediate apprehension or control, defines the Scientific Romance, and it is not remarkable that Wells has always been central to that mode. But the hugeness of his influence upon America is perhaps more surprising. Almost all of his works were reprinted in the early editions of *Amazing Stories* magazine during the 1920s by Hugo Gernsback, who clearly believed that they were texts of central importance to the self-conscious new genre.

They remain central to this day. *The Time Machine* and *The War of the Worlds* (see page 213) are perhaps the best-known Wells works, but to single these two out above the rest is to miss both the consistent high quality of his output and the enduring questions that he examines. His fascination with evolution (see page 40) comes out in *The Island of Doctor Moreau*, which continues to haunt us even today, with its scathing indictment of any forced manipulation of species as a kind of vivisection. Wells was also a highly innovative writer: *The Invisible Man* applies scientific method to subject matter that had previously been dealt with only in supernatural fiction, and *The First Men in the Moon* represents very nearly the first – and certainly one of the most realistic – attempts in literature to envision a genuine alien creature in its own environment.

Alien colonists
The invading Martians of The War of the Worlds *were intended to parallel human empire-builders here on Earth. The oldest version of the alien invasion story, it has been used ever since.*

New audiences
Hugo Gernsback reprinted many of H.G. Wells's novels in the pages of his magazines, introducing them to a new generation and a new nation. Some of the illustrative interpretations must have given Wells pause for thought.

BIBLIOGRAPHY

NOVELS AND NOVELLAS
1895 **The Time Machine** Heinemann
     The Wonderful Visit Dent
1896 **The Island of Doctor Moreau** Heinemann
1897 **The Invisible Man: A Grotesque Romance** Pearson
1898 **The War of the Worlds** Heinemann
1899 **When the Sleeper Wakes** Harper, revised as **The Sleeper Awakes**
1901 **The First Men in the Moon** Newnes
1902 **The Sea Lady: A Tissue of Moonshine** Methuen
1904 **The Food of the Gods, and How it Came to Earth** Macmillan
1905 **A Modern Utopia** Chapman and Hall
1906 **In the Days of the Comet** Macmillan
1908 **The War in the Air, and Particularly How Mr. Bert Smallways Fared While it Lasted** George Bell
1914 **The World Set Free: A Story of Mankind** Macmillan
1923 **Men Like Gods** Cassell
1924 **The Dream** Cape
1928 **Mr. Blettsworthy on Rampole Island** Benn
1930 **The Autocracy of Mr. Parham** Heinemann
1933 **The Shape of Things to Come** Hutchinson
1936 **The Croquet Player** Chatto and Windus
1937 **The Camford Visitation** Methuen

1937 **Star Begotten: A Biological Fantasia** Chatto and Windus
1939 **The Holy Terror** Michael Joseph
1940 **All Aboard for Ararat** Secker and Warburg
1941 **You Can't Be Too Careful: A Sample of Life, 1901–1951** Secker and Warburg

SHORT STORY COLLECTIONS
1895 **The Stolen Bacillus** Methuen
1897 **The Plattner Story** Methuen
     Thirty Strange Stories Arnold
1899 **Tales of Space and Time** Harper
1903 **Twelve Stories and a Dream** Macmillan
1911 **The Country of the Blind** Nelson
     The Door in the Wall Mitchell Kennerly
1915 **Boon** Unwin, as Reginald Bliss
1927 **The Short Stories of H.G. Wells** Benn
1984 **The Man With the Nose** Athlone Press
1987 **The Complete Short Stories of H.G. Wells** St. Martin's Press

SELECTED NON-FICTION
1897 **Certain Personal Matters** Lawrence and Bullen
1901 **Anticipations of the Reaction of Mechanical and Scientific Progress Upon Human Life and Thought** Chapman and Hall

1901 **The Discovery of the Future** Unwin
1903 **Mankind in the Making** Chapman and Hall
1906 **The Future in America** Chapman and Hall
1908 **New Worlds for Old** Constable
     First and Last Things Constable
1914 **The War That Will End War** Palmer
1916 **What Is Coming** Cassell
1920 **The Outline of History** Newnes, in two volumes
1928 **The Open Conspiracy** Gollancz, retitled **What Are We to Do with our Lives?**
1930 **The Science of Life** Amalgamated Press, in three volumes
1931 **The Work, Wealth, and Happiness of Mankind** Doubleday, in two volumes
1934 **Experiment in Autobiography** Gollancz-Cresset, in two volumes
1938 **World Brain** Methuen
1939 **The Fate of Homo Sapiens** Secker and Warburg
1942 **Phoenix** Secker and Warburg
     The Conquest of Time Watts
1945 **The Happy Turning: A Dream of Life** Heinemann
     Mind at the End of its Tether Heinemann

As a prophet, Wells was not sanguine: *When the Sleeper Wakes*, one of his rare tales actually set in the future, foresees the exhilaration and nightmare of the megalopolis, and *The War in the Air* is one of the best dreadful-warning tales ever, showing how appalling aerial war might become. *The World Set Free* describes, very clearly, an atomic bomb.

Wells's later novels have survived less well, and deserve better. They share an impatience with humanity, society, politics: *Mr. Blettsworthy on Rampole Island* is an incandescent satire, reminiscent of Jonathan Swift's *Gulliver's Travels*; *The Shape of Things to Come* predicts World War II, and offers hundreds of pages of suggestions about how we might recover from it; and *The Holy Terror* hints at an age of charismatic dictators. Like the man himself, these later books are both wise and foolish. Their foolishness is of a time long past; their wisdom has no date.

The sceptical socialist
Wells always tried to deal with contemporary social issues. From 1903 to 1908 he was a member of the Fabians, a society dedicated to the gradual introduction of socialism in Britain. Many intellectuals of the day were members of the society, including the playwright George Bernard Shaw, caricatured above on the cover of Boon: *he and Wells did not concur on much.*

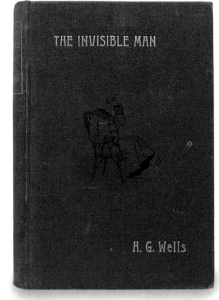

THE INVISIBLE MAN

A classic tale of the overreaching scientist hoist on his own petard, *The Invisible Man* suffers from both the effects and the side effects of his discovery. The 1933 film adaptation (see page 254) has justly become a classic. Unfortunately, it led to a series of sequels that owed nothing to the novel except an abject apology.

CLAUDE RAINS IN THE 1933 FILM

The twisted idealist
In The Island of Doctor Moreau, *Wells wrote a new, post-Darwin take on the Frankenstein story: Doctor Moreau seeks to make surgical shortcuts through evolution, populating his island with bizarre beasts. Although their appearance is modified through surgery, and they are "civilized" through chanted laws, they inevitably return to their old behaviour. The doctor himself was a complex character: in this 1932 film adaptation,* The Island of Lost Souls, *he was inaccurately – if compellingly – rewritten as a sadistic tyrant, which displeased Wells.*

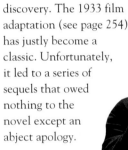

1925-1949: SF IS CHRISTENED

FOR MANY YEARS, FOR HISTORIANS OF SF, the choice of writers has seemed simple, and fairly limited. First came Jules Verne, H.G. Wells, Edgar Rice Burroughs, and Abraham Merritt. Then *Amazing* magazine starts in 1926, and the world of SF blossoms and becomes established in that magazine and in its subsequent rivals. A genre is born. Of course, the magazines are not wholly responsible for the creation of SF. In Europe between the wars, authors like

1925-1929

NOTABLE WORKS

The Moon Maid
EDGAR RICE BURROUGHS, 1926

The Eater of Darkness
ROBERT M. COATES, 1926

Emperor of the If
GUY DENT, 1926

Metropolis
THEA VON HARBOU, 1926

The Short Stories of H.G. Wells
H.G. WELLS, 1927

THE AMPHIBIAN

The Skylark of Space
E.E. SMITH, 1928 MAGAZINE

The Amphibian
ALEXANDER BELAYEV, 1928

By Rocket to the Moon
OTTO WILLI GAIL, 1928

Orlando
VIRGINIA WOOLF, 1928

The World Below
S. FOWLER WRIGHT, 1929

BY ROCKET TO THE MOON

ICONS

Hugo Gernsback reprints almost all of H.G. Wells's works in the early issues of his new *Amazing* magazine, in a doomed attempt to ensure that the new genre of SF will be written mainly to teach. But he has no real chance against the thrust of the new century. In America, as early as 1925 or so, space has become the New Frontier, and it takes **heroes**, gun-toting inventors, warriors, and cowboys in space to ride their shining new spaceships out into the realms of the unknown.

DEBUTS

Edmond Hamilton publishes "The Monster-God of Mamurth" in *Weird Tales* magazine in 1926. In *Amazing* magazine, during 1928, Kurt Siodmak publishes his first story in English, "The Eggs from Lake Tanganyika"; **E.E. Smith** publishes a magazine version of *The Skylark of Space*; Jack Williamson publishes "The Metal Man"; and Philip Nowlan publishes the first Buck Rogers story, "Armageddon – 2419 AD".

1930-1934

NOTABLE WORKS

The Black Star Passes
JOHN W. CAMPBELL JR., 1930
MAGAZINE

Last and First Men
OLAF STAPLEDON, 1930

Tomorrow's Yesterday
JOHN GLOAG, 1932

Brave New World
ALDOUS HUXLEY, 1932

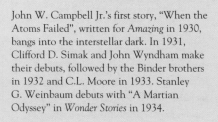
WHEN WORLDS COLLIDE

Tom's A-Cold
JOHN COLLIER, 1933

Lost Horizon
JAMES HILTON, 1933

The Shape of Things to Come
H.G. WELLS, 1933

When Worlds Collide
PHILIP WYLIE AND EDWIN BALMER, 1933

The Strange Invaders
ALUN LLEWELLYN, 1934

The Legion of Space
JACK WILLIAMSON, 1934
MAGAZINE

ICONS

Space heroes get restless if peace clogs up the dark between the stars. By 1930, writers like John W. Campbell Jr., Edmond Hamilton, and Doc Smith begin to organize the galaxies into great **warring camps**. The resulting battles between great armies of massive, invincible dreadnoughts – especially in Smith's hands – still seem astonishingly vast, noisy, and chaotic, and the scale on which they are set is mind-boggling.

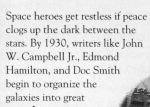

DEBUTS

John W. Campbell Jr.'s first story, "When the Atoms Failed", written for *Amazing* in 1930, bangs into the interstellar dark. In 1931, Clifford D. Simak and John Wyndham make their debuts, followed by the Binder brothers in 1932 and C.L. Moore in 1933. Stanley G. Weinbaum debuts with "A Martian Odyssey" in *Wonder Stories* in 1934.

1935

NOTABLE WORKS

Land Under England
JOSEPH O'NEILL, 1935

Tuzub 37
PAUL GURK, 1935

Odd John
OLAF STAPLEDON, 1935

War With the Newts
KAREL ČAPEK, 1936

WAR WITH THE NEWTS

ICONS

After the unregulated combat of the various warring camps of the galaxy in the early 1930s, it is time to narrow the field. The biggest wars of the decade are the escalating conflict between

DEBUTS

Debuts come thick and fast now. In 1935, Ross Rocklynne; in 1936, Henry Kuttner; in 1937, Nelson Bond, L. Sprague de Camp, Willy Ley, Eric Frank Russell, and Frederik Pohl with a poem; in 1938, Arthur C. Clarke debuts with an article, and Lester del Rey, L. Ron Hubbard, and William F. Temple also debut. But 1939 is the real beginning of modern SF: there are several debuts – Alfred Bester, and Fritz Leiber with "Two

Olaf Stapledon, Maurice Renard, and Karel Čapek are all writing what we now class as highly sophisticated SF – although they themselves never know it by that name – before the term has ever been coined across the Atlantic.

Towards the end of his life, when he was visiting America, Stapledon was bemused to learn that he had "fans". But the heart of genre SF of this time is unquestionably American, based on fans and magazines, and still speaks to us directly.

1939

TUZUB 37

Swastika Night
KATHARINE BURDEKIN AS MURRAY CONSTANTINE, 1937

Star Maker
OLAF STAPLEDON, 1937

Out of the Silent Planet
C.S. LEWIS, 1938

The New Adam
STANLEY WEINBAUM, 1939

1940-1944

Slan
A.E. VAN VOGT, 1940 MAGAZINE

Methuselah's Children
ROBERT A. HEINLEIN, 1941
MAGAZINE

Sixth Column
ROBERT A. HEINLEIN, 1941
MAGAZINE

Lest Darkness Fall
L. SPRAGUE DE CAMP, 1941

Beyond This Horizon
ROBERT A. HEINLEIN, 1942
MAGAZINE

The Weapon Shops of Isher
A.E. VAN VOGT, 1941–2
MAGAZINE

MAGISTER LUDI

Magister Ludi
HERMANN HESSE, 1943

Gather, Darkness!
FRITZ LEIBER, 1943
MAGAZINE

Perelandra
C.S. LEWIS, 1943

Sirius
OLAF STAPLEDON, 1944

1945-1949

That Hideous Strength
C.S. LEWIS, 1945

The World of Ā
A.E. VAN VOGT, 1945 MAGAZINE

Star of the Unborn
FRANZ WERFEL, 1946

Doppelgangers
GERALD HEARD, 1947

Against the Fall of Night
ARTHUR C. CLARKE, 1948 MAGAZINE

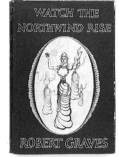

WATCH THE NORTHWIND RISE

STAR OF THE UNBORN

Watch the Northwind Rise
ROBERT GRAVES, 1949

The Star Kings
EDMOND HAMILTON, 1949

Red Planet
ROBERT A. HEINLEIN, 1949

Nineteen Eighty-Four
GEORGE ORWELL, 1949

Earth Abides
GEORGE R. STEWART, 1949

Civilization and Boskone in Doc Smith's *Lensmen* sequence, which explodes onto the scene in *Astounding* magazine in 1937.

There have always been **supermen** in SF. Although H.G. Wells never actually created them, the heroes of *The Food of the Gods* (1904) are superior beings by virtue of their size. J.D. Beresford in *The Hampdenshire Wonder* (1911), and Philip Wylie in *Gladiator* (1931), which inspired the creation of the *Superman* comic strip, and even Olaf Stapledon in *Odd John* (1935), are all

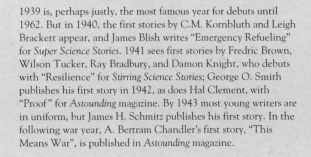

writing about doomed superbeings. The first supermen to enjoy successful careers appear in A.E. van Vogt's *Slan*, serialized in *Astounding* magazine in 1940, and Jack Williamson's *Darker Than You Think*, published in *Unknown* magazine in the same year. Ever since, few authors have not included multi-powered superbeings somewhere in their writings.

The most famous example of SF as a predictive medium is Cleve Cartmill's "Deadline", which John W. Campbell publishes in *Astounding* magazine in 1944, and which describes the forthcoming atomic bomb in scary detail. But in general, the post-war SF writers treat the **nuclear age**, and its risks, with hope. On one side waits the abyss: but on the other, infinite power and travelling.

Sought Adventure" for *Unknown*, Robert A. Heinlein with "Lifeline" for *Astounding*, **Isaac Asimov** with a bad story, and A.E. van Vogt with "Black Destroyer" in *Astounding*. Ray Bradbury and Theodore Sturgeon also debut.

1939 is, perhaps justly, the most famous year for debuts until 1962. But in 1940, the first stories by C.M. Kornbluth and Leigh Brackett appear, and James Blish writes "Emergency Refueling" for *Super Science Stories*. 1941 sees first stories by Fredric Brown, Wilson Tucker, Ray Bradbury, and Damon Knight, who debuts with "Resilience" for *Stirring Science Stories*; George O. Smith publishes his first story in 1942, as does Hal Clement, with "Proof" for *Astounding* magazine. By 1943 most young writers are in uniform, but James H. Schmitz publishes his first story. In the following war year, A. Bertram Chandler's first story, "This Means War", is published in *Astounding* magazine.

Jack Vance writes "The World-Thinker" for *Thrilling Wonder Stories* in 1945; the following year, Margaret St. Clair arrives on the scene, as do William Tenn with "Alexander the Bait", and Arthur C. Clarke with his first fiction, "Loophole", both in *Astounding*; 1947 sees debuts by Poul Anderson and H. Beam Piper; and in 1948, Charles Harness and Judith Merril write their first stories. The most famous debut of 1949 is also a farewell: **George Orwell**'s first SF publication, *Nineteen Eighty-Four*, is his last, and he dies soon after finishing the book.

OLAF STAPLEDON

BORN / DIED **1886-1950**

NATIONALITY **English**

OTHER NAME **born William Olaf Stapledon**

KEY WORKS **Last and First Men, Star Maker, Odd John, Sirius**

MOST SF has a human dimension, even when galaxies are tumbling. There is some sort of protagonist, some sort of story in which the protagonist is involved: if the theme is the death and rebirth of the universe, even then there will be somebody there experiencing the wonderful sight, someone we can recognize and identify with. For most readers, the problem with Stapledon is that his conceptual grasp is so large, his perspectives so daunting, that mere mortal point-of-view characters are swept aside.

It is because his conception is so vast that the Future History (see page 66) constructed by Stapledon over several books failed to hook large numbers of readers in the manner that was perfected by Heinlein. The first title in the Stapledon history, in terms of internal chronology, is *Last Men in London*. The protagonist is one of the Last Men – an immensely evolved being from two billion years hence – who has sacrificially bonded himself into a symbiotic relationship with a young human, one of the First Men – who are us, of course – at the time of World War I. His attempts to rouse the consciousness of the race are doomed to near failure, as First Men continue to revel in the murk of prehistory.

The Future History takes off properly with *Last and First Men*, which encompasses all 18 races of humanity, from *Homo sapiens* on up until the Last Men are encountered, almost unimaginably distant from the mire and mud of 20th-century existence. Over the two billion intervening years, almost anything that has ever been

dreamed of in Space Opera or in cosmological SF occurs, recurs, dies, is examined, and is transcended.

But we are only just beginning. *Star Maker* (see page 215) takes the story onwards for another hundred billion years. Races and galaxies spiral upwards through the aeons until, at the end of the race, the disembodied consciousness that has been privy to the great, hugely expansive story is brought face to face with the Star Maker himself, a being rapt with a cold ecstasy of awareness of the evolved universe.

"Stapledon's grasp is so large that mere mortal characters are swept aside"

This rapture at the excellence of beingness has nothing pious about it, because for Olaf Stapledon, that which was excellent in the cold, long dark of existence was hard-earned, and it paid no recompense in any earthly coin. What it bestowed instead was an ecstasy of contemplation.

Such thoughts – which permeate Stapledon's attempts to limn cosmic awe – are perhaps a little daunting for readers looking for a simple sense of wonder, and Stapledon has always been more revered than read, although many SF writers still continue to think of him as the central SF imagination of the

BIBLIOGRAPHY

NOVELS AND NOVELLAS
1930 **Last and First Men: A Story of the Near and Far Future** Methuen
1932 **Last Men in London** Methuen
1935 **Odd John: A Story Between Jest and Earnest** Methuen
1937 **Star Maker** Methuen
1942 **Darkness and the Light** Methuen
1944 **Sirius: A Fantasy of Love and Discord** Secker and Warburg
1946 **Death into Life** Methuen
1947 **The Flames** Secker and Warburg
1950 **A Man Divided** Methuen
1976 **Nebula Maker** Bran's Head

SHORT STORY COLLECTIONS
1944 **Old Man in New World** Allen and Unwin
1976 **Four Encounters** Bran's Head
1980 **Far Future Calling: Uncollected Science Fiction and Fantasies** Trainer

NON-FICTION
1934 **Waking World** Methuen
1939 **Philosophy and Living** Penguin
1954 **The Opening of the Eyes** Methuen

century. In any case, Stapledon also wrote novels whose grasp – although intellectually formidable – is not so inhumanly grand.

Odd John is an extremely eloquent, and extremely ironic, tale of a man who represents a positive mutation, an evolutionary leap forwards through the ranks from First to Second Man, and even further; he telepathically gathers his peers together on an isolated island, but when the normals invade this insular stronghold, he discovers that he has evolved too far to fight back. The island is destroyed, and we remain First Men, in the mire.

Sirius, very movingly, presents the life story of a dog whose large brain – the result of a breeding experiment – leads him into an ultimately tragic relationship with a human woman; in the end, as Stapledon renders the ecstasy felt by the dog at the vast, thrumming intricacy of the world, a kind of terminal peace descends. For Stapledon, the peace of understanding was God.

W.O.S.

Cosmopolitan background
Stapledon spent part of his youth in Port Said, Egypt, a bustling and sophisticated cultural melting-pot that gave him a broad view of the world.

E.E. SMITH

BORN / DIED 1890-1965

NATIONALITY American

KEY WORKS *The Skylark of Space* series, the *Lensmen* series

SMITH'S advanced degree was in food chemistry, and he ended his professional career as a manager of the General Mix Division of J.W. Allen and Company, but no one really cared what he did to make a living; in his real life he was Doc Smith, the man who created Space Opera.

This view of things is not perhaps quite true. It is not entirely fair to suggest that nobody had ever written an SF story set in space and with plenty of action before 1928, when Smith's *The Skylark of Space* (see page 216) first appeared in *Amazing* magazine, or even before 1917 or so, when Smith actually drafted this first novel: several space adventures had been published before World War I broke out. Garret P. Serviss published *Edison's Conquest of Mars* in a New York newspaper as early as 1898, for example, so it cannot even be claimed that Smith wrote the first significant Edisonade.

But Doc Smith did, all the same, create Space Opera, because the secret of Space Opera is not that its hero is a brave inventor-adventurer, who comes up with devastating new gadgets whenever an enemy shows up coming over the horizon; nor is it the fact that a tale is being set in space. The secret – it is a simple one – is scale.

Smith's first series was the *Skylark of Space* sequence, which he continued, intermittently, to write for most of his life, the last of them, *Skylark DuQuesne,* being published posthumously. Richard Seaton begins as a young inventor genius, but within a few pages his home-made spaceship has o'erleapt the Solar System, and he and his friends have begun their real travels into the galaxy, being chased all the while by the villainous Blackie DuQuesne. Their story is really very simple: each time Blackie comes up with a new weapon, or conquers a new planet to build a huge new spaceship for his further conquests, Seaton simply builds something bigger and faster and more deadly, and both sides get down to pummelling one another. It is all great fun, and the scale becomes very large: but it is a bit difficult to pay attention at times, because the perspective needed to give life to scale begins to fade when everything becomes gigantic.

It was with his second series, the *Lensmen* books, that Doc Smith proved how revolutionary his creative instincts actually were. Like a veritable pulp Stapledon, he created a history for our local group of galaxies that extended back in time for a couple of billion years, and forwards indefinitely. Two billion years ago, the good Arisians became conscious of the unutterably evil Eddorians, and decided to create – over the next few thousand aeons – a civilization capable of fighting back against the inevitable onslaught from the minions of Eddore, the vast swirling hordes of Boskone. And so it all begins. One of the species that the Arisians have nurtured from algae is, of course, *Homo sapiens,* and the heroes of the six *Lensmen* sagas are all humans. As each volume progresses, the hero fights and defeats a vast galactic organization of evildoers, but at the start of each subsequent volume, he discovers that this organization was only part of a larger, more secret, more deadly galaxy-spanning organization. The hero of the central volumes, Kim Kinnison, never finds out that behind this vile hierarchy reside the Eddorians. They are too immensely powerful for him to cope with, and it is only his children, the Children of the Lens, who will be capable of carrying out the final steps of the Arisian campaign in the final volume of the series. By the time the end was reached, Smith had shot us beyond the furthest star.

> **"** *By the end of the* **Lensmen** *series, Doc Smith had shot us beyond the furthest star* **"**

Edward E. Smith, Ph.D.

BIBLIOGRAPHY

NOVELS AND NOVELLAS

1946 ***The Skylark of Space*** Buffalo Book Co.
1947 ***Spacehounds of IPC*** Fantasy Press
1948 ***Skylark Three*** Fantasy Press
    Triplanetary Fantasy Press
1949 ***Skylark of Valeron*** Fantasy Press
1950 ***First Lensman*** Fantasy Press
    Galactic Patrol Fantasy Press
1951 ***Gray Lensman*** Fantasy Press
1953 ***Second Stage Lensmen*** Fantasy Press
1954 ***Children of the Lens*** Fantasy Press
1960 ***The Vortex Blaster*** Gnome Press, retitled
    Masters of the Vortex
1965 ***The Galaxy Primes*** Ace
    Subspace Explorers Canaveral Press

1966 ***Skylark DuQuesne*** Pyramid
1976 ***Masters of Space*** Futura, with E. Everett
    Evans
    The Imperial Stars Pyramid, with Stephen
    Goldin (further ***Family D'Alembert***
    novels by Goldin alone, writing as Smith)
1978 ***Lord Tedric*** Baronet, with Gordon Eklund
    (further ***Tedric*** stories by Eklund alone,
    writing as Smith)
1983 ***Subspace Encounter*** Berkley

SHORT STORY COLLECTIONS

1975 ***The Best of E. E. "Doc" Smith*** Futura
1979 ***Masters of Space*** Jove

NOTABLE WORK

TRIPLANETARY

FIRST LENSMAN

GALACTIC PATROL

GREY LENSMAN

SECOND STAGE LENSMEN

CHILDREN OF THE LENS

Triplanetary introduces us to the great scheme. *First Lensman* introduces the Lens, a lenticular mind- and body-enhancing device made by the Arisians to strengthen their human allies.

Galactic Patrol, Gray Lensman, and *Second Stage Lensmen* feature Kinnison, the big, tough, clever top dog in the Galactic Patrol, who careens about the galaxy with his friends, his weapons, and his Lens, fighting Boskone. At the end of his story, he begins to take it easy, but *Children of the Lens* reveals what we already know: Eddore itself must be conquered, or the galaxies will never be safe.

JACK WILLIAMSON

BORN **1908**

NATIONALITY **American**

OTHER NAME **Will Stewart**

KEY WORKS **Darker Than You Think, The Humanoids**

H IS first story, "The Metal Man", was published in 1928, before Science Fiction had been named, and his latest novel, *Demon Moon*, in 1994. Sixty-eight years of publication is not record-breaking, but the life and career of Jack Williamson almost perfectly encompass the life of SF itself, and for that reason those decades of activity seem particularly significant.

He started where the genre started, with large amounts of adventure fiction for the pulps, some of it published much later in book form in titles such as *The Legion of Space*. He grew as the genre grew, and by the late 1940s was producing his best work: *Darker Than You Think*, an SF tale that suggests that

werewolves may be genetic throwbacks to an Ice Age race of shapechangers; and *The Humanoids*, which envisions a future when robots will coddle humans into a state of drug-induced passivity.

Later years saw some incisive collaborations with Frederik Pohl, and several 1980s novels devoted to genetic

speculations about our species. By this point, Williamson was beginning to differ from younger writers: he still continued to think the world would all work out for the best.

Jack Williamson

BIBLIOGRAPHY

NOVELS AND NOVELLAS
1929 **The Girl from Mars** Stellar, with Miles J. Breuer
1947 **The Legion of Space** Fantasy Press
1948 **Darker Than You Think** Fantasy Press
1949 **The Humanoids** Simon and Schuster
1950 **The Green Girl** Avon
The Cometeers Fantasy Press
Seetee Shock Simon and Schuster, as Will Stewart
1951 **Seetee Ship** Gnome Press, as Will Stewart
Dragon's Island Simon and Schuster, retitled **The Not-Men**
1954 **Undersea Quest** Gnome Press, with Frederik Pohl
1955 **Dome Around America** Ace
Star Bridge Gnome Press, with James Gunn
1956 **Undersea Fleet** Gnome Press, with Frederik Pohl
1962 **The Trial of Terra** Ace
1964 **The Reefs of Space** Ballantine, with Frederik Pohl

1964 **Golden Blood** Lancer
The Reign of Wizardry Lancer
1965 **Starchild** Ballantine, with Frederik Pohl
1967 **Bright New Universe** Ace
1968 **Trapped in Space** Doubleday
1969 **Rogue Star** Ballantine, with Frederik Pohl
1972 **The Moon Children** Putnam
1975 **Farthest Star** Ballantine, with Frederik Pohl
1976 **The Power of Blackness** Berkley
1977 **Dreadful Sleep** Robert Weinberg
1979 **Brother to Demons, Brother to Gods** Bobbs Merrill
1980 **The Humanoid Touch** Holt Rinehart
1981 **The Birth of a New Republic** P.D.A., with Miles J. Breuer
1982 **Manseed** Ballantine
1983 **The Queen of the Legion** Pocket Books
Wall Around a Star Ballantine, with Frederik Pohl
1984 **Lifeburst** Ballantine
1986 **Firechild** Bluejay
1988 **Land's End** Tor

1990 **Mazeway** Ballantine
The Singers of Time Doubleday, with Frederik Pohl
1992 **Beachhead** Tor
1994 **Demon Moon** Tor

SHORT STORY COLLECTIONS
1952 **The Legion of Time** Fantasy Press, retitled in two volumes **The Legion of Time** and **After World's End**
1969 **The Pandora Effect** Ace
1971 **People Machines** Ace
1975 **The Early Williamson** Doubleday
1978 **The Best of Jack Williamson** Ballantine
1980 **The Alien Intelligence** P.D.A.
1990 **Into the Eighth Decade** Pulphouse Press

NON-FICTION
1972 **Teaching Science Fiction** privately
1973 **H.G. Wells: Critic of Progress** Mirage Press
1984 **Wonder's Child: My Life in Science Fiction** Bluejay

HENRY KUTTNER AND C.L. MOORE

BORN / DIED **Kuttner 1914-58, Moore 1911-87**

NATIONALITY **American**

OTHER NAMES **Paul Edmonds, Noel Gardner, James Hall, Keith Hammond, Hudson Hastings, C.H. Liddell, K.H. Maepen, Scott Morgan, Lawrence O'Donnell, Robert O'Kenyon, Lewis Padgett, Woodrow Wilson Smith**

KEY WORKS **Robots Have No Tails, Judgment Night, Doomsday Morning, Fury**

T HE story goes that when Henry Kuttner and Catherine Moore were collaborating, which was usually, they would work alternately on one typewriter. When one was finished, the other would take over. If there was a

difference, nobody could say for sure what it was; certainly neither of the authors could. When a collaborative story was published, it could appear as by both authors, or one of them, or under any of several pseudonyms, the best known of these being Lewis Padgett and Lawrence O'Donnell.

Still, there are differences. Before they married in 1940, Henry Kuttner specialized in quick, witty, slick SF, sword-and-sorcery pastiches, and comic

stories, often featuring lunatics and mechanical creatures who drop in from the future; many are collected in *Robots Have No Tails*. His only successor in this field is Ron Goulart. Moore began earlier but developed more slowly, and became known for her Science Fantasy tales about a female barbarian on Mars named Shambleau, and for flamboyant but sombre Space Opera. She influenced writers such as Leigh Brackett, Andre Norton, and Marion Zimmer Bradley.

Together, their work ran the gamut from Space Opera through tall tales to genuine epics of speculation, such as *Fury*. It is almost certainly the case, although nobody can really be sure, that Moore had the more powerful imagination; and it has been suggested that her subordination during Kuttner's life reflected mid-century sexual mores in America. Kuttner died before SF began to look in upon itself, but in her last years Moore was widely honoured.

BIBLIOGRAPHY

Almost everything signed Kuttner was probably written with Moore: only those which are certain to be collaborations are listed as such here.

HENRY KUTTNER NOVEL
1968 **The Creature from Beyond Infinity** Popular Library

HENRY KUTTNER COLLECTIONS
1952 **Robots Have No Tails** Simon and Schuster, as Lewis Padgett, retitled **The Proud Robot**
1953 **Ahead of Time** Ballantine
1961 **Bypass to Otherness** Ballantine
1962 **Return to Otherness** Ballantine
1965 **The Best of Kuttner** Mayflower, in two volumes
1975 **The Best of Henry Kuttner** Doubleday
1985 **Elak of Atlantis** Gryphon

C.L. MOORE NOVELS
1952 **Judgment Night** Gnome Press
1957 **Doomsday Morning** Doubleday
1990 **Vintage Season** Tor

C.L. MOORE COLLECTIONS
1953 **Shambleau and Others** Gnome Press
1954 **Northwest of Earth** Gnome Press
1969 **Jirel of Joiry** Paperback Library, retitled **Black God's Shadow**
1975 **The Best of C.L. Moore** Doubleday
1981 **Scarlet Dream** Donald M. Grant, retitled **Northwest Smith**

COLLABORATIVE NOVELS
1950 **Fury** Grosset and Dunlap, retitled **Destination Infinity**
1951 **Tomorrow and Tomorrow, and the Fairy Chessmen** Gnome Press, as Lewis Padgett,

parts published as **Tomorrow and Tomorrow**, and as **The Far Reality** (USA) and **Chessboard Planet** (UK)
1953 **Well of the Worlds** Galaxy, as Lewis Padgett
1954 **Beyond Earth's Gates** Ace, as Lewis Padgett
Mutant Gnome Press, as Lewis Padgett
1964 **Earth's Last Citadel** Ace, as Henry Kuttner
Valley of the Flame Ace, as Henry Kuttner
1965 **The Time Axis** Ace, as Henry Kuttner
The Dark World Ace, as Henry Kuttner
1971 **The Mask of Circe** Ace, as Henry Kuttner

COLLABORATIVE COLLECTIONS
1950 **A Gnome There Was** Duell, as Lewis Padgett
1954 **Line to Tomorrow** Bantam, as Lewis Padgett
1955 **No Boundaries** Ballantine, as Lewis Padgett
1980 **Clash by Night** Hamlyn, as Henry Kuttner
1983 **Chessboard Planet and Other Stories** Hamlyn, as Henry Kuttner

A.E. VAN VOGT

BORN **1912**

NATIONALITY **Canadian**

KEY WORKS **Slan, the Null-A series, the Weapon Shops series**

THERE is always a ghost at the feast. Van Vogt was born in Winnipeg – although, incomprehensibly, he seems to have not been invited to the World Science Fiction Convention held there in 1994 – and lived in Canada almost until the end of World War II. In 1939, after working in other genres, he begun to write SF for John W. Campbell Jr.'s *Astounding* magazine, and within a very short time – along with Asimov, de Camp, Heinlein, and Sturgeon – he had become a central figure of the new Golden Age SF. He was prolific, inventive, and very popular.

But around 1950 he virtually stopped writing, and produced little more than rejigged versions of earlier work for almost 20 years. When he began to produce new stories again, around 1968, his time had passed. He had been gone too long – and maybe his work was always too peculiar – for him to become one of the oldtime writers who, like Asimov, restarted their careers on a wave of nostalgia. Van Vogt is a forgotten giant of the Golden Age, a living ghost. Are there good reasons for this?

There are two. The first is complex: from the start, van Vogt specialized in a kind of dream SF – stories whose logic was hard to pin down; heroes who were both godlike and juvenile; venues as difficult to understand as an Escher drawing. *Slan* (see page 216), which appeared in *Astounding* in 1940, told the story of Jommy Cross, a mutant child, a slan, with two hearts and a huge amount of brainpower. So far so good, and the tale became a model for this kind of wish-fulfilment epic: but Jommy's adult exploits are almost incomprehensible. Different categories of slan proliferate, various planets and weapons and subterfuges clash, and when – at novel's close – it turns out that the ruler of the world is also a slan, we are too dizzied by it to quarrel with the outcome.

This is as nothing compared with *The Weapon Shops of Isher* or *The World of Á* (see page 217), or the sequels of these astonishingly intricate tales. Realities conflict, doppelgangers attack one another, time abysses yawn wide, supermen transform eras, empresses and empires crumble, huge spacefleets flicker across the scene, and arcane philosophizing fills in the cracks. These stories sound too silly for words – until one reads them, when the astonishing dream-like intensity of the early van Vogt's style captures one, and pulls one through harum-scarum events at a pace that leaves no time for questioning.

Magazine start
Van Vogt was one of the stars of Campbell's Astounding "stable".

Such intensity of expression is hard to maintain, and it may be that van Vogt simply became tired after a decade of ceaseless production. Stories told so intensely, with such disregard for common sense, are easy to mock, and it may be that during the years of his inactivity readers got used to thinking of van Vogt as an eccentric. But there is a second reason for his oblivion. In 1950 or so, van Vogt became enthralled by Dianetics, a highly controversial system of mental and spiritual betterment devised by a fellow SF writer, L. Ron Hubbard. Van Vogt became deeply involved in the early years of the enterprise, and although he never became similarly

Discord in Scarlet
Van Vogt won a claim that Ridley Scott's Alien *used this tale from* The Voyage of the Space Beagle.

involved in Scientology, the ominous child of Dianetics, the momentum he lost as a writer was lost for ever.

Almost everything published before 1969 originated in the 1940s: these titles are hauntingly compulsive. Almost everything since is new: complexities remain, but the drive has gone. It is often said that early van Vogt wrote like a man caught in an ornate, unstoppable dream. Late van Vogt writes as though he has awoken into the drabness of the day, and cannot quite remember the glories of the night.

> **"Van Vogt wrote like a man caught in a dream"**

BIBLIOGRAPHY

NOVELS AND NOVELLAS
1946 **Slan** Arkham House
1947 **The Weapon Makers** Hadley, retitled **One Against Eternity**
    The Book of Ptath Fantasy Press, retitled **Two Hundred Million A.D.**
1948 **The World of Á** Simon and Schuster, retitled **The World of Null-A**
1950 **The Voyage of the Space Beagle** Simon and Schuster, retitled **Mission: Interplanetary**
    The House That Stood Still Greenberg, revised as **The Mating Cry**, retitled with original text **Undercover Aliens**
1951 **The Weapon Shops of Isher** Greenberg
1952 **The Mixed Men** Gnome Press, retitled **Mission to the Stars**
1953 **The Universe Maker** Ace
1954 **Planets for Sale** Frederick Fell, with E. Mayne Hull
1956 **The Pawns of Null-A** Ace, retitled **The Players of Null-A**
1957 **Empire of the Atom** Shasta
    The Mind Cage Simon and Schuster
1959 **The War Against the Rull** Simon and Schuster
    Siege of the Unseen Ace, retitled **The Three Eyes of Evil**
1962 **The Wizard of Linn** Ace
    The Violent Man Farrar Straus
1963 **The Beast** Doubleday
1965 **Rogue Ship** Doubleday
1966 **The Winged Man** Doubleday, with E. Mayne Hull
1969 **The Silkie** Ace
1970 **Quest for the Future** Ace
    Children of Tomorrow Ace
1971 **The Battle of Forever** Ace
1972 **The Darkness on Diamondia** Ace
1973 **Future Glitter** Ace, retitled **Tyranopolis**
1974 **The Secret Galactics** Prentice Hall, retitled **Earth Factor X**
    The Man With a Thousand Names DAW Books
1977 **The Anarchistic Colossus** Ace
    Supermind DAW Books, retitled **Supermind: I.Q. 10,000**
1979 **Renaissance** Pocket Books
1980 **Cosmic Encounter** Doubleday
1983 **Computerworld** DAW Books, retitled **Computer Eye**
1984 **Null A3** DAW Books, retitled **Null-A Three**

SHORT STORY COLLECTIONS
1948 **Out of the Unknown** Fantasy Press, with E. Mayne Hull, expanded as **The Sea Thing and Other Stories**
1950 **Masters of Time** Fantasy Press, two novellas separately published as **Earth's Last Fortress** and **The Changeling**
1952 **Away and Beyond** Pellegrini and Cudahy
    Destination: Universe! Pellegrini and Cudahy
1964 **The Twisted Men** Ace
1965 **Monsters** Paperback Library, retitled **The Blal**
1968 **The Far-Out Worlds of A.E. van Vogt** Ace, expanded as **The Worlds of A.E. van Vogt**
1971 **More Than Superhuman** Dell
    The Proxy Intelligence Paperback Library, retitled **The Gryb**
    M33 in Andromeda Paperback Library
1972 **The Book of van Vogt** DAW Books, retitled **Lost: Fifty Suns**
1974 **The Best of A.E. van Vogt** Sphere
1978 **Pendulum** DAW Books

NON-FICTION
1975 **Reflections of A.E. van Vogt** Fictioneer

ROBERT A. HEINLEIN

BORN / DIED **1907-88**

NATIONALITY **American**

OTHER NAMES **Anson MacDonald, Lyle Monroe, John Riverside, Caleb Saunders**

KEY WORKS *Sixth Column, Double Star, Time for the Stars, Have Space Suit – Will Travel, Starship Troopers, Stranger in a Strange Land, The Moon is a Harsh Mistress, Time Enough for Love*

MOST writers are children at heart. Most SF writers, however, seem to have begun their careers as literal children. Certainly the boys who were fans in the 1930s and dreamed of writing about the stars – girl fans were rare for a long while, and few women writers emerged from fandom until the 1950s – saw their names in print by the time they reached puberty, either in fanzines or in the letter columns that magazine publishers created in order to maintain loyalty. Jack Williamson was a published author at the age of 19; Asimov and Pohl were sending letters and stories in before they were shaving.

But not Robert A. Heinlein. The most influential figure in the history of American SF entered the field in 1939, at the age of 32. If he wrote anything that remotely resembled SF before that age, it does not survive; if he sent letters to magazine columns, they were not printed. He began his adult life as as a naval officer, a career that ended prematurely due to ill-health in 1934. He then tried his hand at engineering and politics. It was only after these – and other – experiences in the wider world that he turned to writing.

The speed of his ascent was almost frightening. By 1942, when he went to work as an engineer for the Naval Air Experimental Station, he had already published three novels in *Astounding* magazine – *Sixth Column* (see page 217), *Methuselah's Children*, and *Beyond this Horizon* (see page 217) – and about 30 stories. But it was not the number of pieces, nor their smooth appeal, that was different; it was how they made up a Future History (see page 66), a chart of which was published in *Astounding*. Other authors had written series, and Olaf Stapledon had composed a history of aeons hence, but never before had anything like Heinlein's chart been seen. His Future History started the day after tomorrow (which is how *Sixth Column* was retitled), and it worked: it was more than a chart; it was a ladder.

> *"Heinlein could make the wildest or most personal of visions sound like common sense"*

There are various ways of defining the Golden Age of SF, which ran from about 1938 to about 1945, but one good way of getting at the exhilaration that writers and readers of SF felt during those years is to suggest that they somehow felt that they were indeed constructing a ladder to the future. That SF itself was the chart, and that each new issue of each SF magazine was not only a book full of stories, but a step in the furtherance of the grand plan. And there, at the very heart of it all, was Robert A. Heinlein; he had the capacity to make the wildest, or the most personal, of visions sound like common sense, like the kind of sage but enticing advice that an adolescent might dream of receiving from an adventurous uncle who had travelled a lot. The uncle with a mysterious job in government...

Destination Hollywood
Heinlein scripted a few films in the 1950s, starting with Destination Moon *– a realistic film, apart from the convention that had private enterprise mount the mission, and the studio's feeling that a realistic Moon surface was too dull.*

When he got back to writing after the war, Heinlein did not try to recapture the exhilaration of those first days, perhaps because he was too wise, but also perhaps because his relationship with John W. Campbell Jr., and therefore with Campbell's *Astounding* magazine, had cooled. What he did do was, once again, innovative and clever. He began a series of SF juveniles for Scribners, then a highly prestigious publishing house that had previously shown no interest in mere genre literature, and he began to publish full-grown SF stories in magazines like the *Saturday Evening Post*. Singlehandedly (as it seemed) he punched holes in the assumptions that SF was a ghetto, and that there was no point in trying to escape.

By 1950, magazines were no longer his main market. More visibly than any other SF writer of stature, he had shifted his focus to the hardcover book market, and over the next 10 years published a total of 22 – a steady stream of superbly crafted, cunning, exuberant, optimistic fiction. A handful of them taken together – *Double Star* (see page 220), *Time for the Stars*, *The Door into Summer*, *Citizen of the Galaxy*, *Have Space Suit – Will Travel*, and *Starship Troopers* (see page 221) – constitute a stunning survey of what was best in American SF up to that point.

Pseudonymous work
Works outside the Future History, such as "By His Bootstraps", appeared under other names.

But the last of these titles was the first of the new Heinlein, and his story begins to become rather more complex. *Starship Troopers*, written as a juvenile, advocates a military training so intense that brainwashing pales beside it, and ferociously over-estimates military as opposed to civilian values. It was with this book that many began to find Heinlein an objectionable ideologue of the right. Although it was never precisely true that he was right-wing in any simple sense, it was certainly the case that, from 1960 on, his fiction was increasingly devoted to the promulgation of highly controversial notions about politics, sex, gender, and the military. And it is also true that these notions did tend to extravagantly over-value individual action taken without regard for others. Of course, Heinlein was writing fiction, and in fiction it is always possible to make ideas, however extreme, turn out for the best. But *Stranger in a Strange Land* was read by Charles Manson. *Farnham's Freehold* was read by blacks, who might find its premises distressing. *I Will Fear no Evil* was read by women, who might find its sexual imperialism less than welcome. And it is possible to think that, in *Time Enough for Love*, Lazarus Long gets away with murder, and is pretty smug about it, too.

A real problem with fiction as a forum for debate is that it is very difficult for an author not to deal a crooked deck. It is hard to let the bad guy – the character impertinent enough to disagree with the author – win the argument. Heinlein *never* let the bad guy win. In all of his late novels, liberals, commies, ecologists, government officials, *et al* bit the dust with appalling regularity.

Unfortunately, that is not the whole of this sad story. Heinlein may have begun his career as a dominant man who did not much like competition, but his early works give off a feeling of community, a sense that more than one character in

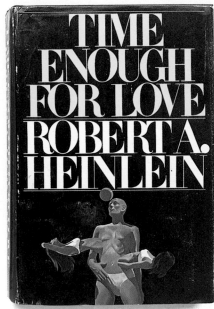

Who could have guessed that *Methuselah's Children* – a neat, tidy tale written in 1941 – was going to lead to this? *Time Enough for Love* tells the further adventures of Lazarus Long, star of the first book, and it is an explosion of story-telling. Lazarus, a Heinlein wish-fulfilment figure, is spunky, spermy, pugnacious, argumentative, immortal, and always right. He time-travels, breeds with his mother, and fills towns with his offspring. He dies, but only to rise again in *To Sail Beyond the Sunset*.

TIME ENOUGH FOR LOVE

each book attracts the attention and love of the author. In the late books, this is no longer the case. A book like *"The Number of the Beast"*, ostensibly chock-full of characters, ends up sounding as if there is only one person in the book: Heinlein himself.

Although he was kindly (but aloof) in his personal dealings, and although after his death it began to be hinted that he had been the anonymous benefactor of more than one fellow writer in financial difficulties, it must be said that Heinlein's late work shows a profound alienation from the genre that he had done so much to establish. The man revealed in *Grumbles from the Grave* was not a happy one. This may have been partly due to age, and to the severe ill health that plagued him in the 1970s – for certainly the last works are more temperate than those written when he was most unwell.

But the main reasons probably lie in SF itself. The kind of Future History that Heinlein had given his heart to in 1940 could no longer, by the 1960s, dazzle his readers and fellow writers, could no longer convince them that the world of the future would somehow resemble the art of the present. In the end, it was not that SF failed Heinlein, but that the world failed SF.

BIBLIOGRAPHY

NOVELS AND NOVELLAS
1947 *Rocket Ship Galileo* Scribners
1948 *Space Cadet* Scribners
Beyond this Horizon Fantasy Press
1949 *Sixth Column* Gnome Press, retitled *The Day After Tomorrow*
Red Planet Scribners
1950 *Farmer in the Sky* Scribners
1951 *The Puppet Masters* Doubleday
Between Planets Scribners
Universe Dell, expanded as *Orphans of the Sky*
1952 *The Rolling Stones* Scribners, retitled *Space Family Stone*
1953 *Starman Jones* Scribners
1954 *The Star Beast* Scribners
1955 *Tunnel in the Sky* Scribners
1956 *Double Star* Doubleday
Time for the Stars Scribners
1957 *The Door into Summer* Doubleday
Citizen of the Galaxy Scribners
1958 *Methuselah's Children* Gnome Press
Have Space Suit – Will Travel Scribners

1959 *Starship Troopers* Putnam
1961 *Stranger in a Strange Land* Putnam
1963 *Podkayne of Mars: Her Life and Times* Putnam
Glory Road Putnam
1964 *Farnham's Freehold* Putnam
1966 *The Moon is a Harsh Mistress* Putnam
1970 *I Will Fear No Evil* Putnam
1973 *Time Enough for Love: The Lives of Lazarus Long* Putnam
1980 *"The Number of the Beast"* New English Library
1982 *Friday* Holt Rinehart
1984 *Job: A Comedy of Justice* Ballantine
1985 *The Cat Who Walks Through Walls: A Comedy of Manners* Putnam
1987 *To Sail Beyond the Sunset: The Life and Loves of Maureen Johnson* Putnam

SHORT STORY COLLECTIONS
1950 *The Man Who Sold the Moon* Shasta
1950 *Waldo and Magic, Inc.* Doubleday
1951 *The Green Hills of Earth* Shasta

1953 *Revolt in 2100* Shasta
Assignment in Eternity Fantasy Press, abridged as *Lost Legacy*
1959 *The Menace from Earth* Gnome Press
The Unpleasant Profession of Jonathan Hoag Gnome Press, retitled *6 x H: Six Stories*
1966 *The Worlds of Robert A. Heinlein* Ace
1967 *The Past Through Tomorrow: Future History Stories* Putnam
1973 *The Best of Robert Heinlein* Sidgwick and Jackson
1979 *Destination Moon* Gregg Press
1980 *Expanded Universe* Grosset and Dunlap
1992 *Requiem: New Collected Works* Tor

NON-FICTION
1989 *Grumbles from the Grave* Ballantine
1992 *Tramp Royale* Ace
1993 *Take Back Your Government* Baen Books

1950-1954: A BRIGHT NEW AGE

THE GOLDEN AGE OF SF ended with the ending of World War II but, after a period of quiet, by 1950 a bright new age is about to begin for everyone, and SF takes on the new mantle of optimism. New magazines are founded, and new publishers begin to produce SF books. Modestly established writers like Frederik Pohl begin to take fire and reach new heights of popularity; and new writers like Philip K. Dick begin to define the new age. It is a time of

1 9 5 0

NOTABLE WORKS

I, Robot
ISAAC ASIMOV

The Martian Chronicles
RAY BRADBURY

Needle
HAL CLEMENT

Galactic Patrol
E.E. SMITH

The Dreaming Jewels
THEODORE STURGEON

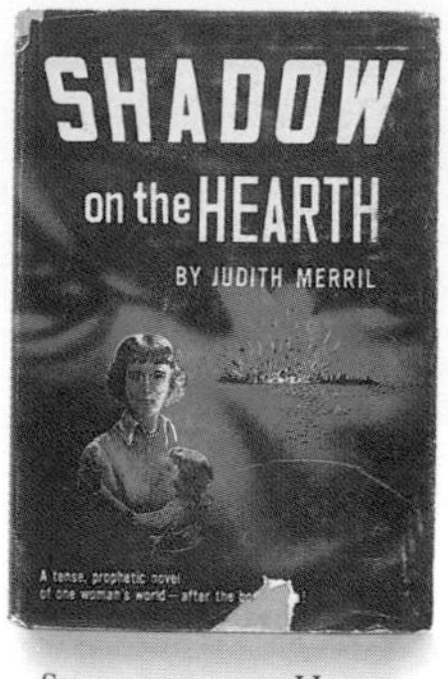

THE VOYAGE OF THE SPACE BEAGLE

SHADOW ON THE HEARTH

The Man Who Sold the Moon
ROBERT A. HEINLEIN

Shadow on the Hearth
JUDITH MERRIL

The Dying Earth
JACK VANCE

The Voyage of the Space Beagle
A.E. VAN VOGT

1 9 5 1

Foundation
ISAAC ASIMOV

The Illustrated Man
RAY BRADBURY

Prelude to Space
ARTHUR C. CLARKE

Rogue Queen
L. SPRAGUE DE CAMP

The Puppet Masters
ROBERT A. HEINLEIN

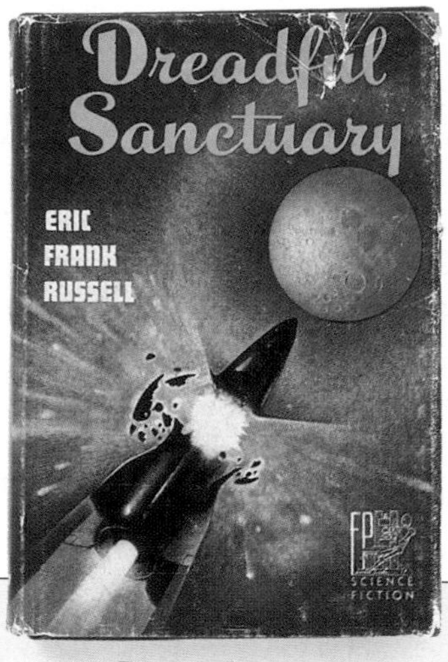

Dreadful Sanctuary
ERIC FRANK RUSSELL

Grey Lensman
E.E. SMITH

The Weapon Shops of Isher
A.E. VAN VOGT

The Disappearance
PHILIP WYLIE

The Day of the Triffids
JOHN WYNDHAM

DREADFUL SANCTUARY

1 9

Foundation and Empire
ISAAC ASIMOV

Jack of Eagles
JAMES BLISH

This Island Earth
RAYMOND F. JONES

Takeoff
C.M. KORNBLUTH

Judgment Night
C.L. MOORE

JUDGMENT NIGHT

ICONS

A whole new generation of postwar SF writers is appearing on the scene and finding markets for its troubled, sophisticated visions. Doubleday and Company begins to publish Isaac Asimov. The fascinaton with space travel dominates, and so do spaceships. Robert A. Heinlein's film script for

Destination Moon memorably captures both the thrill of leaving Earth, and the sleek beauty and power of the rockets that carry us on our journeys to other planets. Once we arrive on the alien worlds, we meet robots, aliens, and also ourselves, in books by Asimov, van Vogt, and Bradbury.

As the Cold War deepens, SF writers respond with images of threat and invasion. Images of mental control abound on the covers of magazines such as **Astounding Science Fiction**. The main icon of the year is probably the alien invader who takes over human minds, the "puppet master" in Heinlein's brilliant, paranoid phrase. Earth becomes a "dreadful sanctuary", and soon enough it will be "the day of the triffids", and surviving humans will be doomed to scrabble blindly for life in the forgotten corners of the invaded world. But E.E. Smith, Arthur C. Clarke, and others are still pressing outwards.

SF satires begin to appear, almost for the first time, in the United States. The central icon of the year is the city, although the theme is treated in various ways. Clifford D. Simak's novel of that name treats cities

DEBUTS

Richard Matheson's famous first story, "Born of Man and Woman", is published in the newly founded *Magazine of Fantasy and Science Fiction*. Gordon R. Dickson's "Trespass", written with Poul Anderson, is published in *Fantastic Story Quarterly*.

Writing as Gill Hunt, **John Brunner** publishes his first novel, *Galactic Storm*. He is 17. Harry Harrison publishes the short story "Rock Diver", Julian May publishes "Dune Roller", and Walter M. Miller publishes "Secret of the Death Dome".

There is a plethora of first publications in short story form. They include Algis Budrys's "The High Purpose" in *Astounding Science Fiction* magazine, and Philip K. Dick's "Beyond Lies the Wub". Frank Herbert's "Looking for Something?" is published in

introspection, wild humour, paranoia, and a newly realistic interest in exploring the Solar System. The Cold War is in full swing, and SF writers glory in portraying the fall of rigid dictatorships across the galaxy. By the middle of the decade, the SF vision of America seems secure, and SF writers can depict a world-wide triumph of the American Dream. In this period, the SF genre comes to belong to America, as much as the new world belongs to SF.

5 2   1 9 5 3   1 9 5 4

PLAYER PIANO

The Sound of His Horn
SARBAN

City
CLIFFORD D. SIMAK

Destination: Universe!
A.E. VAN VOGT

Player Piano
KURT VONNEGUT JR.

Limbo
BERNARD WOLFE

Second Foundation
ISAAC ASIMOV

The Demolished Man
ALFRED BESTER

Fahrenheit 451
RAY BRADBURY

Childhood's End
ARTHUR C. CLARKE

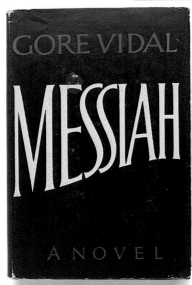

BRING THE JUBILEE

Starman Jones
ROBERT A. HEINLEIN

The Space Merchants
C.M. KORNBLUTH AND FREDERIK POHL

Bring the Jubilee
WARD MOORE

Ring Around the Sun
CLIFFORD D. SIMAK

More Than Human
THEODORE STURGEON

The Kraken Wakes
JOHN WYNDHAM

Brain Wave
POUL ANDERSON

The Caves of Steel
ISAAC ASIMOV

Mission of Gravity
HAL CLEMENT

Lord of the Flies
WILLIAM GOLDING

Shadows in the Sun
CHAD OLIVER

Untouched by Human Hands
ROBERT SHECKLEY

Children of the Lens
E.E. SMITH

Messiah
GORE VIDAL

NOTABLE WORK

MESSIAH

In his capacity as a satirist, Gore Vidal has written several works that are on the fringes of SF. *Messiah*, set in a secular United States, has a new messiah arriving to lead a spiritual renaissance. It is a satire on religion and on America, targets that he returned to in a later novel, *Live From Golgotha*, which has time-travelling television crews present at the crucifixion.

almost with nostalgia. But Kurt Vonnegut Jr. is more savage in his portrayal of the city in *Player Piano*, as are most of the new writers who are waiting in the wings for 1953.

After a few muted years, the fireworks begin. SF writers are publishing stories that grapple with the big issues, from tomorrow's censorship to the destiny of the race. Ace Books, Ballantine Books, and their competitors are defining SF in North America, and authors respond with huge energy. Of the ten best books published in 1953, five remain their author's best ever. Even the ones that are less well remembered, like Cyril Kornbluth's **The Syndic**, take on big ideas.

It is a highly varied year, in which the output of SF writers ranges from the hard science of Hal Clement to the religious satire of Gore Vidal. SF is beginning to mature. The icon this year is the figure of a human being standing upright, or trying to do so. Measuring himself against the aliens in his midst, as in *Shadows in the Sun*; or leaping onto a new world, as in *Children of the Lens*: what is to be remembered from this year is human beings, on their feet.

Startling Stories magazine, Donald Kingsbury's "Ghost Town" in *Astounding Science Fiction* magazine, and Robert Sheckley's "Final Examination" in *Imagination* magazine.

Marion Zimmer Bradley publishes two short stories, "Women Only" and "Keyhole" in *Vortex Science Fiction*, and Anne McCaffrey publishes "Freedom of the Race" for Hugo Gernsback's *Science Fiction Plus*. Evelyn Waugh, previously known for his series of black inter-war satires, makes his SF debut with *Love Among the Ruins: A Romance of the Near Future*.

Brian W. Aldiss publishes "Criminal Record", for *Science Fantasy* magazine, and Avram Davidson publishes "My Boy Friend's Name is Jello", for *Fantasy and Science Fiction* magazine. Robert Silverberg publishes "Gorgon Planet", and will go on to win a Hugo for Most Promising New Author.

1955-1959: THE ESTABLISHED GENRE

BY NOW, SF IS GOING down smooth. Certainly, there have been a few shakeouts in the magazine market – causing all sorts of dire predictions of the end of the genre – and there are more yet to come; and small-press publishing houses, such as Gnome and Shasta, are beginning to find that the competition from larger trade houses, like Ace, Ballantine, and Doubleday, is more than they can handle. But most of the old masters of SF are still in their prime, and the newer

1 9 5 5

NOTABLE WORKS

Earthman, Come Home
JAMES BLISH

The Big Jump
LEIGH BRACKETT

Solar Lottery
PHILIP K. DICK

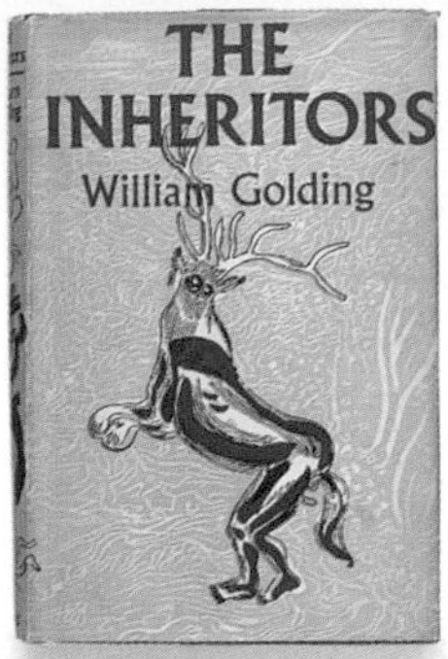

The Inheritors
WILLIAM GOLDING

Hell's Pavement
DAMON KNIGHT

THE INHERITORS

Not This August
C.M. KORNBLUTH

Sargasso of Space
ANDRE NORTON

The Chrysalids
JOHN WYNDHAM

EARTHMAN, COME HOME

ICONS

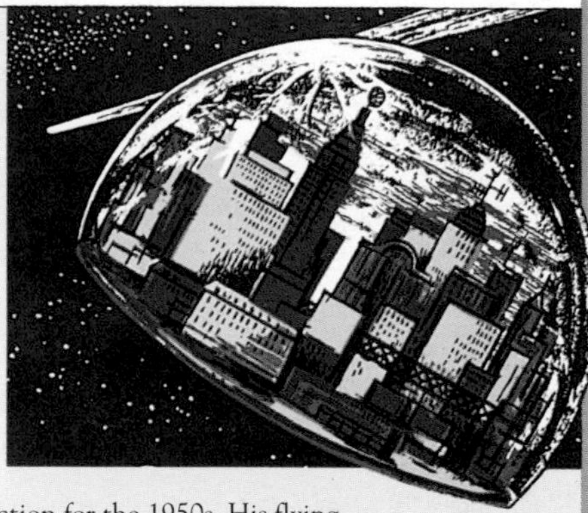

With the publication in book form of the best of the **Cities in Flight** tales as **Earthman, Come Home**, James Blish demonstrates how he has transformed the old concept of the flying city – examples of which extend far back into the realms of Proto SF – into a complex, modern construction for the 1950s. His flying Manhattan combines ship, culture, drama, and a vision of how humans might really live, one day.

DEBUTS

An important year for first books sees Richard Wilson's *The Girls from Planet 5*, **Robert Silverberg**'s *Revolt on Alpha C*, William Tenn's *Of All Possible Worlds*, Frank Herbert's *The Dragon in the Sea*, Damon Knight's *Hell's Pavement*, and Philip K. Dick's *Solar Lottery*.

1 9 5 6

NOTABLE WORKS

Tiger! Tiger!
ALFRED BESTER

The Death of Grass
JOHN CHRISTOPHER

Nerves
LESTER DEL REY

The Man Who Japed
PHILIP K. DICK

Double Star
ROBERT A. HEINLEIN

Time for the Stars
ROBERT A. HEINLEIN

Agent of the Unknown
MARGARET ST. CLAIR

To Live Forever
JACK VANCE

Immortality for a few...
to live
Mature science fiction
forever
Jack Vance
Ballantine Books

TO LIVE FOREVER

ICONS

Paranoia, which has already shown itself to be a motif of prime importance for the cinema of the decade, makes a strong showing in SF books this year: Alfred Bester's outstanding *Tiger! Tiger!* is a classic tale of betrayal and revenge.

DEBUTS

Debuts include Margaret St. Clair's *Agent of the Unknown*, Gordon R. Dickson's *Alien from Arcturus*, and **Jacques Sternberg**'s *Toi, ma nuit (Sexualis '95)*. In magazines, *New Worlds* has "Escapement" and *Science Fantasy* has "Prima Belladonna" both by J.G. Ballard, *Fantastic* has Kate Wilhelm's "The Pint-Sized Genie", and *Infinity Science Fiction* has Harlan Ellison's "Glowworm".

1 9

NOTABLE WORKS

They'd Rather Be Right
MARK CLIFTON AND FRANK RILEY

The Cosmic Puppets
PHILIP K. DICK

The World Jones Made
PHILIP K. DICK

The Green Odyssey
PHILIP JOSÉ FARMER

The Black Cloud
FRED HOYLE

ON THE BEACH

ICONS

SF is beginning to show wide variety in its concerns: the huge, mineral-poor, Balkanized planet so beloved of Planetary Romances has a late showing in Jack Vance's *Big Planet* and Philip José Farmer's *Green Odyssey*; Fred Hoyle's black cloud is a strange alien; Nevil

DEBUTS

In magazines, David R. Bunch makes his debut with "Routine Emergency" in *If*. Philip José Farmer makes an impression with his first novel, *The Green Odyssey*. Other authors who make their debut in book form this year include the Italian author Italo Calvino, with *Baron in the Trees*, Jane Gaskell with *Strange Evil*, Tom Godwin with *The Survivors*, H. Beam Piper with *Crisis in 2140*, written in collaboration with

arrivals – including the veterans of World War II and those who began writing after the war – are writing SF as to the manner born. SF is old enough now to be done properly. When two writers as radically different as Harlan Ellison

and Robert Silverberg, the one as raucous with passion as the other is steely with efficient ambition, can both think of the SF genre as the natural arena for their writing, then surely the form has begun to mature.

5 7   1 9 5 8   1 9 5 9

Non-Stop
BRIAN ALDISS

The Enemy Stars
POUL ANDERSON

A Case of Conscience
JAMES BLISH

Who?
ALGIS BUDRYS

The Spave Willies
ERIC FRANK RUSSELL

NIOURK

Doomsday Morning
C.L. MOORE

Slave Ship
FREDERIK POHL

On the Beach
NEVIL SHUTE

Big Planet
JACK VANCE

Niourk
STEFAN WUL

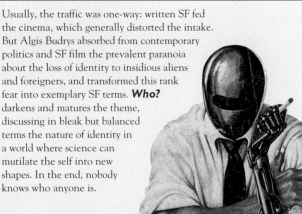
THE COSMIC RAPE

IMMORTALITY DELIVERED

Immortality Delivered
ROBERT SHECKLEY

The Cosmic Rape
THEODORE STURGEON

Andromeda
IVAN YEFREMOV

Inter Ice Age 4
KOBO ABE

The Falling Torch
ALGIS BUDRYS

The Pirates of Zan
MURRAY LEINSTER

Starship Troopers
ROBERT A. HEINLEIN

The Quatermass Experiment
NIGEL KNEALE

The Marching Morons
C.M. KORNBLUTH

Eden
STANISŁAW LEM

A Canticle for Liebowitz
WALTER M. MILLER JR.

Level Seven
MORDECAI ROSHWALD

The Country of Crimson Clouds
ARKADY AND BORIS STRUGATSKI

The Sirens of Titan
KURT VONNEGUT JR.

THE FALLING TORCH

Shute predicts a slow end to the world from the vantage point of Australia; and Stefan Wul looks to the far future.

Usually, the traffic was one-way: written SF fed the cinema, which generally distorted the intake. But Algis Budrys absorbed from contemporary politics and SF film the prevalent paranoia about the loss of identity to insidious aliens and foreigners, and transformed this rank fear into exemplary SF terms. **Who?** darkens and matures the theme, discussing in bleak but balanced terms the nature of identity in a world where science can mutilate the self into new shapes. In the end, nobody knows who anyone is.

Apocalyptic visions of the future dominate books at the end of the decade. Both Walter M. Miller's *A Canticle for Liebowitz* and Kurt Vonnegut's *The Sirens of Titan* have different kinds of cosmic overview of apocalypse: the first has the sense that disaster is cyclical, the second regards it as completely out of our control.

John J. McGuire, and **James White** with *The Secret Visitors*.

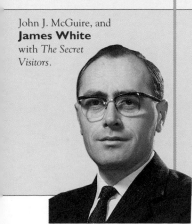

First SF novels include *Non-Stop* by Brian W Aldiss, *After the Rain* by John Bowen, and **Le gambit des étoiles** (*Starmasters' Gambit*) by Gérard Klein. Magazine debuts include Colin Kapp's "Life Plan" in *New Worlds*, Richard McKenna's "Casey Agonistes" in *Fantasy and Science Fiction*, and Thomas Burnett Swann's "Winged Victory" in *Fantastic Universe*.

First SF novels include Mordecai Roshwald's *Level Seven*, John Updike's *The Poorhouse Fair*, and the Strugatskis' *Strana bagrovykh tuch* [The country of crimson clouds]. In magazines, Keith Laumer's "Greylorn" appears in *Amazing*, Joanna Russ's "Nor Custom Stale" appears in *Fantasy and Science Fiction*, and Michael Moorcock's "Peace on Earth", with Barrington Bayley, appears in *New Worlds*.

ISAAC ASIMOV

BORN / DIED **1920-92**

NATIONALITY **American, born in Russia**

OTHER NAME **Paul French**

KEY WORKS **The *Robot* series, the *Foundation* series**

ISAAC Asimov would have been the father of modern Science Fiction, but for Robert A. Heinlein. Asimov had the credentials: he began as a fan in the 1930s; he published his first story before World War II began; he helped define the Golden Age of American SF by creating the **Robot** and **Foundation** series; by the time of his death he had published about 500 books. Hyperactive, amiable, and prolific, he *sounded* like SF. But Heinlein, a more powerful and cunning writer, came just before him, and was a born father figure: suave, demanding, and charismatic.

Asimov was never suave. Instead, he played the younger brother: brash, boastful, workaholic geek, ruthless (but inept) with women, self-assertive (but strangely self-defeating) as a publicist of his own miracles of productivity. While Heinlein remained mysterious, Asimov was a writer of utter clarity. He had no mystery. Because he knew how to explain (it is a rare gift), he became

one of the greatest and most prolific popularizers of science and the arts. But he proved deeply inept at the task of describing human responses to environments or challenges. The heart of an Asimov novel lay in long conversations between the important characters; events were reported from off-stage, and commented upon. Theoretical solutions were established for problems of science, and of plotting. The story ended in a flicker of action. It was like ice water. Readers loved it.

His most famous story came early. "Nightfall" (1941) is the single most popular SF story ever published. It tells of the inhabitants of a planet revolving around a sun that is part of a multiple-sun system. With so many sources of light in the sky, the people experience nightfall only once every 2,000 years, when an eclipse occurs. Once night does fall, they realize that the universe is unimaginably vast: they go mad.

Asimov's famous Three Laws of Robotics (see page 306) also came early. In 1940 he created, with Campbell, these rules for robot intelligences, rules that had little to do with robotics, but a great deal to do with the treatment of the robot theme in the 1930s. Any SF writer who created a robot monster had to argue that Asimov was wrong in his formulation of the laws that guaranteed their safety: few dared.

Asimov himself found the Laws a challenge, and spent much of his time over the next 50 years working out

> **"** *Asimov was never suave. Instead he played the brash, boastful, workaholic younger brother* **"**

fictional responses to them. No matter how daring the premise, the Laws always triumphed. The **Robot** stories began around 1940, and were first collected in his first book, *I, Robot*. Later, in *The Caves of Steel* and *The Naked Sun*, maybe his two best single novels, he created the robot detective R. Daneel Olivaw, who came to seem perhaps the most human (or least inhuman) of his protagonists. But even R. Daneel is, in the end, a servant to humanity. It was not until Asimov returned to the robot theme late in life, in stories like "The Bicentennial Man", that he began to express a somewhat more complex view. In this story, and in the novels

The Robots of Dawn and *Robots and Empire*, he began to take into account speculations on artificial intelligence, and to suggest, cautiously, that perhaps the human species was sufficiently violent and irrational to need wardens, not slaves. In the end, however, his original tactical error – concentrating on robots rather than computers – kept him from fully confronting cyberspace.

> **"** *Foundation's popularity shows how much SF readers love argument* **"**

The **Foundation** stories also began in the early 1940s, and proved even more popular than the robots. The trilogy *Foundation*, *Foundation and Empire*, and *Second Foundation* consistently tops reader polls as the most popular SF series ever. Since much of it is dominated by talk (however intelligent or informed) this shows how much the SF audience loves argument, loves futures it can believe.

NOTABLE WORK

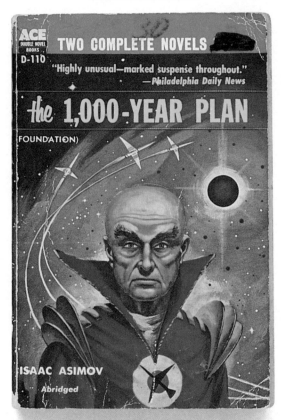

THE 1,000-YEAR PLAN

The stories that made up the **Foundation** had a chequered early history. They were first published as books in the 1950s, and the first of them, *Foundation*, appeared, cut and retitled as *The 1,000-Year Plan*, in 1955. In the same year, the second book, *Foundation and Empire*, appeared retitled as *The Man who Upset the Universe*. Most of the stories were published by John W. Campbell Jr. in *Astounding Science Fiction* magazine. Campbell was important to Asimov as publisher and as mentor: each credited the other with the formulation of the Three Laws of Robotics.

FOUNDATION STORY IN *ASTOUNDING* MAGAZINE

Set thousands of years hence, as a vast interstellar empire crumbles, the series is a clear retelling of the decline and fall of Rome, and suggests a secular alternative to the rise of Christianity. In Asimov's universe, civilization is saved not by a religion but by two Foundations, the second of them secret, whose task it is to ensure that the predictions of psychohistorian Hari Seldon are not disturbed by accidents or unpredictable events. In the end, after long Dark Ages, civilization is restored. The Foundations, resolutely created by Asimov without any touch of religious glamour,

The other Asimov magazine
Isaac Asimov did not always succeed: Asimov's SF Adventure Magazine lasted for just one issue.

may not be entirely convincing as saviours of a truculent, widespread humanity. But the argument is strongly made, and bravely told.

Even during the years of his early success, Asimov had always felt it important to establish a "proper" career. After taking a PhD (delayed by war service) in 1948, he began to teach chemistry at university level. He did not finally abandon teaching until 1958, when he stopped writing fiction (just at the time that Sputnik signalled a change of rules for the writing of SF), and began to publish a stream of popular science texts. By the early 1980s, there were hundreds of them.

During this time, Asimov wrote only one novel, *The Gods Themselves* (see page 227). A singleton, not connected to either of his major series, it won both the Hugo and Nebula awards. It is one of his best stories: a sharp-tongued analysis of the sociology of science, and a very sophisticated presentation of parallel universes.

By the 1980s, Asimov had become extremely famous, and found himself tempted to make a full re-entry into

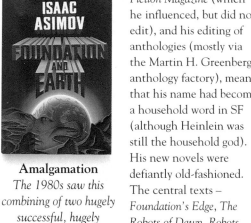

Amalgamation
The 1980s saw this combining of two hugely successful, hugely separate ideas.

SF, his first and last love. It was not, however, as though he had been absent from view. His monthly science column in *The Magazine of Fantasy and Science Fiction* (see page 103), which ran eventually to 399 pieces, his founding of *Isaac Asimov's Science Fiction Magazine* (which he influenced, but did not edit), and his editing of anthologies (mostly via the Martin H. Greenberg anthology factory), meant that his name had become a household word in SF (although Heinlein was still the household god). His new novels were defiantly old-fashioned. The central texts – *Foundation's Edge*, *The Robots of Dawn*, *Robots and Empire*, *Foundation and Earth*, *Prelude to Foundation*, and *Forward the Foundation* – are a massive attempt to weld his two series into one. As robots did not exist in the **Foundation** universe, this proved a heavy task, and one incomplete at his death. The result was a vast, unfinished edifice, extremely popular with readers, but not enormously appealing to critics, who tended to feel that Asimov had lost much of his early intense conciseness.

One odd thing about Asimov is that he was afraid of flying. In his later years, when his health was precarious, he therefore travelled little, staying in New York and writing. He admitted to being happy only in front of his typewriter. Books continued to stream out. Among them – surprisingly, given a considerable reticence about personal matters, and his restricted lifestyle – were four volumes of autobiography. The first are huge. The last, *I. Asimov*, was shorter, but still compendious. Its last pages were the last he was to write. When it came out, it was hard to believe that the flood had ceased. Isaac Asimov, it seemed, would always be there, at the heart of traditional SF, speaking to us in a voice that sounded, with all faults, to be the true voice of the genre. He was the sound of SF.

Omnipresence
So well known was Asimov's name that it was used to sell authors who were themselves often quite accomplished.

BIBLIOGRAPHY

NOVELS AND NOVELLAS
1950 *Pebble in the Sky* Doubleday
1951 *The Stars, Like Dust* Doubleday, abridged as *The Rebellious Stars*
Foundation Gnome Press, abridged as *The 1,000-Year Plan*
1952 *The Currents of Space* Doubleday
Foundation and Empire Gnome Press, retitled *The Man Who Upset the Universe*
1953 *Second Foundaton* Gnome Press
1954 *The Caves of Steel* Doubleday
1955 *The End of Eternity* Doubleday
1957 *The Naked Sun* Doubleday
1966 *Fantastic Voyage* Houghton Mifflin
1972 *The Gods Themselves* Doubleday
1982 *Foundation's Edge* Doubleday
1983 *The Robots of Dawn* Doubleday
1985 *Robots and Empire* Doubleday
1986 *Foundation and Earth* Doubleday
1987 *Fantastic Voyage II* Doubleday
1988 *Prelude to Foundation* Doubleday
Azazel Doubleday
1989 *Nemesis* Doubleday
1990 *Nightfall* Gollancz, with Robert Silverberg
1991 *Child of Time* Gollancz, with Robert Silverberg, retitled *The Ugly Little Boy*

1992 *The Positronic Man* Gollancz, with Robert Silverberg
1993 *Forward the Foundation* Doubleday

SHORT STORY COLLECTIONS
1950 *I, Robot* Gnome Press
1954 *The Martian Way* Doubleday
1957 *Earth is Room Enough* Doubleday
1959 *Nine Tomorrows: Tales of the Near Future* Doubleday
1964 *The Rest of the Robots* Doubleday
1967 *Through a Glass, Clearly* New English Library
1968 *Asimov's Mysteries* Doubleday
1969 *Nightfall and Other Stories* Doubleday
1972 *The Early Asimov: Or Eleven Years of Trying* Doubleday
1974 *Have You Seen These?* NESFA Press
1975 *Buy Jupiter* Doubleday
1976 *The Bicentennial Man* Doubleday
1982 *The Complete Robot* Doubleday
1983 *The Winds of Change* Doubleday
1986 *The Alternate Asimovs* Doubleday
Robot Dreams Doubleday
The Best Science Fiction of Isaac Asimov Doubleday
The Best Mysteries of Isaac Asimov Doubleday

1989 *The Asimov Chronicles* Dark Harvest
1990 *Robot Visions* Roc
1990 *The Complete Stories, Volume One* Doubleday
1992 *The Complete Stories, Volume Two* Doubleday

CHILDREN'S BOOKS
1952 *David Starr, Space Ranger* Doubleday, as Paul French
1953 *Lucky Starr and the Pirates of the Asteroids* Doubleday, as Paul French
1954 *Lucky Starr and the Oceans of Venus* Doubleday, as Paul French
1956 *Lucky Starr and the Big Sun of Mercury* Doubleday, as Paul French
1957 *Lucky Starr and the Moons of Jupiter* Doubleday, as Paul French
1958 *Lucky Starr and the Rings of Saturn* Doubleday, as Paul French
1983 *Norby the Mixed-Up Robot* Walker, with Janet Asimov
1984 *Norby's Other Secret* Walker, with Janet Asimov
1985 *Norby, Robot for Hire* Walker, with Janet Asimov

1985 *Norby and the Invaders* Walker, with Janet Asimov
1986 *Norby and the Queen's Necklace* Walker, with Janet Asimov
1987 *Norby Finds a Villain* Walker, with Janet Asimov
1989 *Norby and Yobo's Great Adventure* Walker, with Janet Asimov
Norby Down to Earth Walker, with Janet Asimov
1990 *Norby and the Oldest Dragon* Walker, with Janet Asimov
1991 *Norby and the Court Jester* Walker, with Janet Asimov

SELECTED NON-FICTION
Asimov wrote over 400 non-fiction titles, many of Science Fiction interest. A few of these are:
1960 *The Intelligent Man's Guide to Science* Basic Books, in two volumes, revised as *The New Intelligent Man's Guide to Science*
1962 *Fact and Fancy* Doubleday (plus many further volumes, collecting hundreds of popular science essays first published in **The Magazine of Fantasy and Science Fiction** and elsewhere)

1964 *Asimov's Biographical Encyclopedia of Science and Technology* Doubleday

AUTOBIOGRAPHIES
1979 *In Memory Yet Green* Doubleday
1980 *In Joy Still Felt* Doubleday
1992 *Asimov Laughs Again* Doubleday
1994 *I. Asimov* Doubleday

SELECTED WORKS AS EDITOR
Asimov edited over 100 anthologies, many with Martin H. Greenberg. Among these, prominent titles include:
1962 *The Hugo Winners* Doubleday (plus several sequels)
1974 *Before the Golden Age* Doubleday
1979 *Isaac Asimov Presents The Great Science Fiction Stories, Volume 1, 1939* DAW Books, with Martin H. Greenberg (plus 24 further volumes, taking the series to 1963)
1982 *Laughing Space* Houghton Mifflin, with J.O. Jeppson (Janet Asimov)
1988 *The Mammoth Book of Classic Science Fiction: Short Novels of the 1930s* Carroll and Graf, with Martin H. Greenberg and Charles G. Waugh (plus various sequels)

HAL CLEMENT

BORN **1922**

NATIONALITY **American**

OTHER NAMES **born Harry Clement Stubbs, George Richard**

KEY WORKS **Mission of Gravity, Close to Critical, Star Light**

THERE is something about Hard SF that almost always seems more attractive in the abstract than when it is encountered on the page. Not even Hal Clement, who is the most likeable of all Hard SF writers, is immune, and some of his later novels give off a kind of weary flatness. Hard SF may be defined as SF in settings that are plausible in terms of what we know or can guess about science, and that makes arguments about the science that underpins those worlds. Usually. Hal Clement obeys the first of these injunctions, but pays little attention to the second. The best of his books, *Mission of Gravity* (see page 220),

therefore reads, at times, like an inspired travelogue: we follow its heavy-planet hero on his long quest as though he were a guide. *Through the Eye of a Needle* is a kind of detective novel, in which an alien cop takes over a human in order to catch an alien fugitive. *The Nitrogen Fix* describes a future Earth where only a few humans have survived ecological devastation. Again, the main effect is of a tour of wonder, because the devastated planet retains a strange beauty. We return to Clement for the sights he affords.

" Hal Clement "

BIBLIOGRAPHY

NOVELS AND NOVELLAS
1950 **Needle** Doubleday, retitled **From Outer Space**
1953 **Iceworld** Gnome Press
1954 **Mission of Gravity** Doubleday
1956 **The Ranger Boys in Space** Boston, Page
1957 **Cycle of Fire** Ballantine
1964 **Close to Critical** Ballantine
1971 **Star Light** Ballantine
1973 **Ocean on Top** DAW Books
1978 **Through the Eye of a Needle** Ballantine
1980 **The Nitrogen Fix** Ace
1987 **Still River** Ballantine
1994 **Isaac's Universe: Fossil** DAW Books

SHORT STORY COLLECTIONS
1965 **Natives of Space** Ballantine
1969 **Small Changes** Doubleday, retitled **Space Lash**
1979 **The Best of Hal Clement** Ballantine
1987 **Intuit** NESFA Press

L. SPRAGUE DE CAMP

BORN **1907**

NATIONALITY **American**

OTHER NAME **Lyman R. Lyon**

KEY WORK **Rogue Queen**

POLYMATH, raconteur, man of the world, L. Sprague de Camp does not much resemble the usual SF writer: he is not a fan turned author; he has never restricted himself to SF or to any other sort of fiction; and he is happy to write in collaboration with others, including his wife, Catherine Crook de Camp, who is pictured with him above.

In the 1930s, before John W. Campbell Jr. had persuaded him to contribute to his *Astounding Science Fiction* and *Unknown* magazines, De Camp had a variety of writing jobs. When he came to SF and fantasy, he was therefore an experienced author, and even his first stories give off a smooth glow, like the fiction found in the slick magazines,

such as *The Saturday Evening Post*, that flourished before World War II began. It may be because of this sophisticated background that from the first he paid little attention to distinctions between SF and fantasy. *Lest Darkness Fall* and *The Incomplete Enchanter* (the latter with Fletcher Pratt) are tales whose inventive heroes, having been thrust into fantasy or archaic environments, transform their new worlds through the power of their pragmatic, inventive, 20th-century minds. De Camp was the first master of this sort of rationalized fantasy, often imitated since.

When he does turn his talents towards SF, de Camp manages to make stories like *Rogue Queen*, or *Cosmic*

Manhunt, or *The Hostage of Zir* read almost like fantasies. Colourful and romantic, these tales give off an almost oriental flavour, but with an added touch of wry. In *Rogue Queen*, for instance, a politically incorrect hive queen on a planet just discovered by humans is persuaded – not terribly plausibly, it must be said – of the benefits of democracy. Like many of de Camp's SF books, *The Hostage of Zir* is set on a flamboyant barbarian planet called Krishna. Fun (as in all his work) is had by all concerned.

L. Sprague de Camp

BIBLIOGRAPHY

NOVELS AND NOVELLAS
1941 **Lest Darkness Fall** Holt
The Incomplete Enchanter Holt, with Fletcher Pratt (final version, including sequels: **The Complete Compleat Enchanter**)
1942 **Land of Unreason** Holt, with Fletcher Pratt
1948 **The Carnelian Cube** Gnome Press, with Fletcher Pratt
1950 **Genus Homo** Fantasy Press, with P. Schuyler Miller
The Castle of Iron Gnome Press, with Fletcher Pratt
1951 **Rogue Queen** Doubleday
The Undesired Princess Fantasy
1954 **Cosmic Manhunt** Ace, retitled **A Planet Called Krishna;** again retitled **The Queen of Zamba**
1957 **Solomon's Stone** Avalon
The Return of Conan Gnome Press, with Björn Nyberg, retitled **Conan the Avenger**

1958 **The Tower of Zanid** Avalon
An Elephant for Aristotle Doubleday
1960 **The Glory That Was** Avalon
Wall of Serpents Avalon, retitled **The Enchanter Compleated**
1962 **The Search for Zei** Avalon, retitled **The Floating Continent**
1963 **The Hand of Zei** Avalon
1968 **Conan of the Isles** Lancer, with Lin Carter
The Goblin Tower Pyramid
1971 **The Clocks of Iraz** Pyramid
Conan the Buccaneer Lancer, with Lin Carter
1973 **The Fallible Fiend** Signet
1976 **The Virgin and the Wheels** Berkley
1977 **The Hostage of Zir** Berkley
1978 **The Great Fetish** Doubleday
1979 **Conan the Liberator** Bantam, with Lin Carter

1980 **Conan and the Spider God** Bantam
The Treasure of Tranicos Ace, with Robert E. Howard
1982 **Conan the Barbarian** Bantam, with Lin Carter
1982 **The Prisoner of Zhamanak** Phantasia Press
1983 **The Unbeheaded King** Ballantine
The Bones of Zora Phantasia Press, with Catherine Crook de Camp
1987 **The Incorporated Knight** Phantasia Press
1988 **The Stones of Nomuru** Donning, with Catherine Crook de Camp
1989 **The Honorable Barbarian** Ballantine
1991 **The Pixillated Peeress** Ballantine
The Swords of Zinjabar Baen Books, with Catherine Crook de Camp

1991 **Sir Harold and the Gnome King** Wildside Press
1992 **The Venom Trees of Sunga** Ballantine

SHORT STORY COLLECTIONS
1948 **Divide and Rule** Fantasy Press
The Wheels of If Shasta
1953 **The Continent Makers and Other Tales of the Viagens** Twayne
Tales from Gavagan's Bar Twayne, with Fletcher Pratt
Sprague de Camp's New Anthology of Science Fiction Panther
1955 **Tales of Conan** Gnome Press, with Robert E. Howard, retitled **Conan: The Flame Knife**
The Tritonian Ring Twayne
1963 **A Gun for Dinosaur** Doubleday
1966 **Conan the Adventurer** Lancer, with Robert E. Howard

1967 **Conan the Usurper** Lancer, with Robert E. Howard
1968 **Conan the Freebooter** Lancer, with Robert E. Howard
Conan the Wanderer Lancer, with Robert E. Howard and Lin Carter
1969 **Conan of Cimmeria** Lancer, with Robert E. Howard and Lin Carter
1970 **The Reluctant Shaman** Pyramid
1971 **Conan of Aquilonia** Lancer, with Lin Carter
1977 **The Best of L. Sprague de Camp** Doubleday
1978 **Conan the Swordsman** Bantam, with Lin Carter and Björn Nyberg
1979 **The Purple Pterodactyls** Phantasia Press
1993 **Rivers of Time** Baen

AS EDITOR:
De Camp has edited several anthologies, the first of which was:
1963 **Swords and Sorcery** Pyramid

JOHN WYNDHAM

BORN / DIED **1903-69**

NATIONALITY **English**

OTHER NAMES **born John Wyndham Parkes Lucas Beynon Harris, John Beynon, John Beynon Harris, Wyndham Parkes, Lucas Parkes, Johnson Harris**

KEY WORKS ***The Day of the Triffids, The Chrysalids***

BEFORE he became famous as John Wyndham, John Beynon Harris was a moderately bad pulp writer in prewar England. He gave no clue of being anything more than a crafter of adventures in any genre (sometimes SF, often not) that his editors needed.

After the war, Harris, having been silent for a few years, suddenly seemed to go through a sea-change. He found a new publisher – Michael Joseph, a firm not known for SF – and began to write as John Wyndham. And in 1951 came *The Day of the Triffids* (see page 218), a tale that captured the insecurities of the middle-class English reader in the austerity years perfectly, and envisioned to a nicety the kinds of self-protective communities that would comfort that readership. With most of humanity blinded by mysterious explosions in space, survivors are hounded by monster plants. All sounds grim, but the protagonists band together, and survive. The comforting implausibility of this outcome, along with the calm, analgesic style of the Wyndham persona, contribute to what Brian Aldiss called the Cosy Catastrophe.

The Kraken Wakes repeats much of the same comforting structure, but it is only these first two books that fully exemplify the kind of tale Aldiss was describing. *The Midwich Cuckoos*, for instance, is much more unsettled and unsettling: aliens impregnate women in the village of Midwich, who give birth to strange, compelling children, the cuckoos of the title. There is no comfort here, in the end, no sense that the almost accidental discovery and elimination of the aliens has anything at all to do with a triumph of middle-class virtues. The heart of the story – and of Wyndham's true art – is unease. It was only occasionally that he could coat it with reassurances.

Later novels, like *Chocky* or *Web*, are significantly less happy as fiction, and even more tellingly insecure. In the end, Wyndham represented what he most fervently hoped to disguise: the loss of Empire, the exposure of his blessed isle to the winds of fate.

BIBLIOGRAPHY

NOVELS AND NOVELLAS
1935 **The Secret People** Newnes, as John Beynon
1936 **Planet Plane** Newnes, as John Beynon, revised as **Stowaway to Mars**
1945 **Love in Time** Utopian Publications, as Johnson Harris
1951 **The Day of the Triffids** Michael Joseph, retitled **Revolt of the Triffids**
1953 **The Kraken Wakes** Michael Joseph, retitled **Out of the Deeps**
1955 **Re-Birth** Ballantine, retitled **The Chrysalids**
1957 **The Midwich Cuckoos** Michael Joseph, retitled **Village of the Damned**
1959 **The Outward Urge** Michael Joseph, as John Wyndham and Lucas Parkes
1960 **Trouble With Lichen** Michael Joseph
1968 **Chocky** Michael Joseph
1979 **Web** Michael Joseph

SHORT STORY COLLECTIONS
1954 **Jizzle** Dobson, revised with several substitutions as **Tales of Gooseflesh and Laughter**
1956 **The Seeds of Time** Michael Joseph
1961 **Consider Her Ways and Others** Michael Joseph, revised with several substitutions as **The Infinite Moment**
1973 **The Best of John Wyndham** Sphere, retitled **The Man from Beyond**
1973 **Sleepers of Mars** Coronet
1973 **Wanderers of Time** Coronet
1979 **Exiles on Asperus** Severn House, as John Beynon

ERIC FRANK RUSSELL

BORN / DIED **1905-78**

NATIONALITY **English**

OTHER NAMES **Duncan H. Munro, Webster Craig, Maurice G. Hugi**

KEY WORKS **Sinister Barrier, Dreadful Sanctuary, "Allamagoosa"**

HE was of the same generation and nationality as Wyndham, but two SF authors could hardly be less alike. Wyndham wrote decorously for the English or for anglophile Yanks, Russell exuberantly for Americans and English readers of American-style SF. Except for Arthur C. Clarke, whom everyone knew was English, Russell was for years the most popular non-American genre SF writer, and many Americans had no idea he was not one of them.

Sinister Barrier is typical. Published in John W. Campbell Jr.'s *Unknown* magazine, it has the United States threatened by aliens who see humans as pets. The hero works out the invasion's nature, and defeats it. *Dreadful Sanctuary* was also serialized by Campbell, in *Astounding* magazine. Russell's best novel, it is told in a sparky style, depicting the possibilities of space with all the optimistic verve that American readers expected of their postwar writers.

BIBLIOGRAPHY

NOVELS AND NOVELLAS
1943 **Sinister Barrier** World's Work
1951 **Dreadful Sanctuary** Fantasy Press
1953 **Sentinels from Space** Bouregy
1956 **Three to Conquer** Avalon
1957 **Wasp** Avalon
1958 **The Space Willies** Ace, revised as **Next of Kin**
1962 **The Great Explosion** Dobson
1964 **With a Strange Device** Dobson, retitled **The Mindwarpers**

SHORT STORY COLLECTIONS
1954 **Deep Space** Fantasy Press
1956 **Men, Martians, and Machines** Dobson
1958 **Six Worlds Yonder** Ace
1961 **Far Stars** Dobson
1962 **Dark Tides** Dobson
1965 **Somewhere a Voice** Dobson
1975 **Like Nothing on Earth** Dobson
1978 **The Best of Eric Frank Russell** Ballantine

Space travel is also achieved by private enterprise against fanatical and conspiratorial opposition, in typically American form.

But Russell's most popular works were short stories, almost all of them published in the United States. Russell found it easy to comply with the Campbell stricture against stories with aliens superior to *Homo sapiens*: tales of bumbling aliens failing to comprehend the swift, private-enterprise canniness of humans on the loose in the galaxy poured from him. They remain enjoyable, evoking nostalgia for long-gone days of such simplicities of optimism; Russell gives us the joys of yesterday's tomorrow.

The Russell hero
The hero of The Space Willies *is a typical Eric Frank Russell creation: laconic, resourceful, and winning a war by his wits alone.*

ARTHUR C. CLARKE

BORN **1917**

NATIONALITY **English, resident in Sri Lanka**

OTHER NAMES **Charles Willis, E.G. O'Brien**

KEY WORKS ***Against the Fall of Night, Childhood's End, 2001: A Space Odyssey, Rendezvous with Rama, The Fountains of Paradise***

OVER a career that began before World War II broke out, and which has extended into the 1990s, Arthur C. Clarke has become a legend. He became famous inside the SF field within a few years, and extended that fame across the world a short decade or so after he began to publish his novels and popular science texts. Without achieving the unassailable stature of Heinlein within the field, but without indulging in the self-publicizing marathons of Asimov, he managed, with seeming serenity, to become the most widely known figure that the SF world has ever generated. This intense fame has never faded.

In retrospect, while it all seems possible, it was hardly inevitable. Clarke began his writing career in England, in the late 1930s, with some inconspicuous non-fiction. Before he was properly launched as a writer, he served in the Royal Air Force

from 1941 to 1946, and gained a science degree in 1948; only when he was almost 30 did he begin to lay down hints of the remarkable fertility of his creative processes. His first fiction sale was to John W. Campbell Jr.'s *Astounding* magazine in 1946; "Rescue Mission" was an absolutely perfect story for Campbell's tastes. A spacefleet, operated by an ancient, wise, but slow-thinking alien race, visits Earth some decades after the Sun has gone nova; the commander mourns the loss of the young human race, then discovers a fleet of sub-light-speed ships plodding away from the hot Sun. Touched by this huge effort, the alien commander orders his fleet to help the humans on their way. Complacently, he ponders the deep awe this young race will feel at the masterful science of the ancients. But – as the last sentence of the story makes clear – 40 years later, after the perky human race has presumably run circles around the old fogeys from the centre of the galaxy, he is beginning to have some very profound misgivings.

It is, perhaps, a silly story, but it remains, half a century on, thoroughly readable. The confidence it displays about our capacity to make sense of the world, and our ability to engineer that sense into great, world-spanning projects, has remained ever since.

It was this confidence that allowed Clarke to predict, in a non-fiction piece written in 1945, the geosynchronous communication satellite.

Because Clarke is so knowledgeable, and so wise to the relationship between science and technology, he has been able to simultaneously both excite and

soothe both his readers and the governments who have come to him for advice. Clarke's best fiction, all the same, inhabits a world of thought and emotion very far distant from the avuncular optimism of his popular science and his works of speculation about future technologies.

BIBLIOGRAPHY

NOVELS AND NOVELLAS

1951 **Prelude to Space** Galaxy, retitled **Master of Space**, again retitled **The Space Dreamers**
The Sands of Mars Sidgwick and Jackson
1952 **Islands in the Sky** Winston
1953 **Against the Fall of Night** Gnome Press, revised as **The City and the Stars**
Childhood's End Ballantine
1955 **Earthlight** Ballantine
1957 **The Deep Range** Harcourt Brace
1963 **Dolphin Island** Holt Rinehart
1968 **2001: A Space Odyssey** New American Library
1973 **Rendezvous with Rama** Gollancz
1975 **Imperial Earth: a Fantasy of Love and Discord** Gollancz
1979 **The Fountains of Paradise** Gollancz
1982 **2010: Odyssey Two** Phantasia Press
1986 **The Songs of Distant Earth** Ballantine
1988 **Cradle** Gollancz, with Gentry Lee
2061: Odyssey Three Grafton
A Meeting With Medusa Tor
1989 **Rama II** Gollancz, with Gentry Lee
1990 **The Ghost from the Grand Banks** Gollancz
1991 **The Garden of Rama** Ballantine, with Gentry Lee
1993 **Rama Revealed** Gollancz, with Gentry Lee
The Hammer of God Gollancz

SHORT STORY COLLECTIONS

1956 **Reach for Tomorrow** Ballantine
1957 **Tales from the White Hart** Ballantine
1958 **The Other Side of the Sky** Harcourt Brace
1961 **A Fall of Moondust** Harcourt Brace
1962 **Tales of Ten Worlds** Harcourt Brace
1967 **The Nine Billion Names of God** Harcourt Brace
1968 **The Lion of Comarre; and Against the Fall of Night** Harcourt Brace
1972 **The Wind from the Sun: Stories of the Space Age** Harcourt Brace
Of Time and Stars Gollancz
1973 **The Best of Arthur C. Clarke 1937–1971** Sidgwick and Jackson
1983 **The Sentinel** Berkley

SELECTED NON-FICTION

1950 **Interplanetary Flight: An Introduction to Astronautics** Temple Press
1951 **The Exploration of Space** Temple Press
1960 **The Challenge of the Sea** Holt Rinehart
1962 **Profiles of the Future** Gollancz
1972 **The Lost Worlds of 2001** New American Library
1984 **1984: Spring: A Choice of Futures** Ballantine
1992 **How the World Was One** Gollancz

AUTOBIOGRAPHIES

1977 **The View from Serendip** Random House
1989 **Astounding Days** Gollancz

To Roger –
little did I
know!
Art C Clarke

Obscure origins
10 Story Fantasy was an undistinguished magazine with a lifespan of just one issue – but that issue included "Sentinel of Eternity", the germ of 2001.

Against the Fall of Night – first written in the 1940s, and reaching definitive form as *The City and the Stars* in 1956 – places humanity in an evolutionary perspective where aeons seem like years. Following on from the examples of Wells and Stapledon, Clarke makes it clear that in terms of a genuinely long-term view, our species is locked into a life cycle like any other species; and although our glories may make the darkness glitter, surely darkness does, in the end, cover all.

This elevation of view is even more sharply evident in Clarke's most famous early novel, *Childhood's End* (see page 219), in the opening pages of which the human race is effortlessly conquered by mentor aliens who resemble demons. As the tale develops, it turns out that the human race is destined to give birth to a successor form of humanity, superior to both us and the mentors. After the new humans form a group mind and go adventuring into the heart of the universe, to meet the

Singleton tale
Ghost from the Grand Banks is a rare solo novel from recent years.

makers of larger things, mortals like us are doomed to be left on the drying shore of time, alone.

There is a poetry about these early works that continues to haunt the imagination, drawing readers back decades after they first encountered Clarke. It may be the combination of technological savvy and love of the twilit end of the universe, because it is rare to find savvy and wisdom on the same page. It may simply be that he seems to be telling the truth. But as the decades passed, some of the poetry faded away, perhaps inevitably, from his fiction, and he turned more and more to popular science, and to works about scuba-diving in his beloved Pacific Ocean. And then it all changed.

The catalyst that turned Clarke into a world-famous figure and symbol to the world of SF's cutting edge was *2001: A Space Odyssey*, film and book. Clarke and Stanley Kubrick worked up a script for the film, and Clarke

NOTABLE WORK

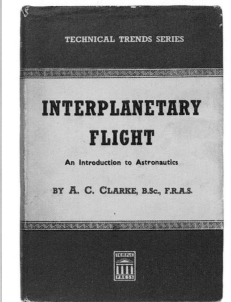

Arthur C. Clarke edited a science magazine briefly before becoming an SF writer, and has always published a great deal of non-fiction and speculative science alongside his SF. *Interplanetary Flight*, published in 1950, was among the first of a long string of titles produced over the decade. This work in non-fiction brought him a UNESCO award in 1962 and a reputation that made him a natural choice as a CBS television commentator for Apollo Moon missions.

INTERPLANETARY FLIGHT

simultaneously translated the original screenplay – which had originated in a short story called "Sentinel of Eternity" (retitled "The Sentinel") from 1951 – into the novel. It may be the case that Kubrick's film sours and disrupts Clarke's vision of evolution constantly at work. But it did not matter. After 1968, the whole world knew Clarke.

Later novels have been mixed. *Rendezvous with Rama* (see page 227) won all the awards it could,

and its description of a vast, empty, totally enigmatic spaceship conveys a powerful sense of wonder; but its collaborative sequels have been comparatively sorry affairs, reducing to genre clichés the magnificent scale of the original. *Imperial Earth* was an inspired travelogue of the Solar System, but not much more; but *The Fountains of Paradise* very excitingly promulgates in fictional form the notion of a space elevator – a metal cable connecting a point on Earth with a terminus in space. By taking an elevator up the gravity well of Earth, Clarke suggests, humans could enter free space with ease, rescuing the Earth from our devouring energy needs. It could almost, he suggests, be done today, if there were the will to accomplish it.

Other late fiction has been less convincing. *The Ghost from the Grand Banks* has enthralling moments, as a 21st-century team attempts to raise the *Titanic,* but the skeleton of the tale lacks flesh; this thinness is even more evident in *The Hammer of God*, which reads like a series of notes for a novel. But the footnotes hardly matter. The smooth, calm voice of Clarke, listing the nature of the world, will be with us as long as there is an SF to remember.

Film fame
A huge production, taking two years and an army of technicians, the film of 2001: A Space Odyssey *won Oscars and a Hugo, and brought lasting fame to its originators.*

RAY BRADBURY

BORN 1920

NATIONALITY American

OTHER NAMES Edward Banks, William Elliott, D.R. Banat, Leonard Douglas, Leonard Spaulding, Brett Sterling

KEY WORKS *Dark Carnival, The Martian Chronicles, Fahrenheit 451*

BRADBURY has spent more than half a century writing stories that are impossible to ignore, but hard to pay proper attention to. It has always been a strange experience to read a Bradbury tale in the expectation – because it was published in an SF magazine, or it is actually set on Mars – that a real future is being delineated, or real arguments being made about how it might be earned, reached, lived through.

Nothing, in fact, could be further from Bradbury's intentions than to write SF, as ordinarily described. He is not interested in the objective world, in science, or space travel, or galaxies, or prognosis, or political systems, or time travel into the future. And when his characters travel backwards, it is not to change the past, but to honour it. In the end, his works amount to quests for the state of enchantment where place and self are one. In the end, he is looking for paradise.

It is not surprising, therefore, that much of his work looks backwards, and that the overwhelming emotional force of his best stories turns, in less inspired tales, to cloying nostalgia. *The Martian Chronicles* hover at the edge of bathos, but they do not fall. We know that his romantic, ancient Mars was a fantasy even in the 1940s, when most of the tales were written; but somehow this

" In the end, Bradbury is looking for paradise "

does not matter, because the vision of twilight and solace is so consummately passed on to us. We know that the shape-changing Martians could never have existed, that human colonization could never have been accomplished in a state of seemingly drugged torpor; but this does not matter either, because it is the dream of a lost Eden that drives us to continue reading. Mars is not terraformed; what is changed, irretrievably, is the human heart.

Bradbury's greatest single tale is almost certainly *Fahrenheit 451* (see page 219), but he wrote dozens of works during the 1940s and 1950s, in which the search for the remembered paradise and a sense of danger are intricately mixed. Towards the end of this period, he wrote a filmscript for John Huston of the 19th-century classic *Moby Dick*, and the whale can stand as a metaphor for Bradbury's longings. For decades, he has been obsessed by this dense, evocative image of nostalgia, quest, and danger, this vision of American Gothic. The great whale encompasses his dreams, the dark and the light.

BIBLIOGRAPHY

NOVELS AND NOVELLAS
1953 *Fahrenheit 451* Ballantine
1957 *Dandelion Wine* Doubleday
1962 *Something Wicked This Way Comes*
      Simon and Schuster

SHORT STORY COLLECTIONS
1947 *Dark Carnival* Arkham House, abridged
      as *The Small Assassin*
1950 *The Martian Chronicles* Doubleday,
      retitled *The Silver Locusts*
1951 *The Illustrated Man* Doubleday
1953 *The Golden Apples of the Sun*
      Doubleday
1955 *The October Country* Ballantine
1959 *A Medicine for Melancholy* Doubleday,
      revised as *The Day it Rained Forever*
1962 *R Is for Rocket* Doubleday
1964 *The Machineries of Joy* Simon and
      Schuster
1965 *The Vintage Bradbury* Random House
1966 *S Is for Space* Doubleday
1969 *I Sing the Body Electric!* Knopf
1976 *Long After Midnight* Knopf
1979 *To Sing Strange Songs* Wheaton
1980 *The Stories of Ray Bradbury* Knopf
1983 *Dinosaur Tales* Bantam
1988 *The Toynbee Convector* Knopf

SELECTED PLAYS AND OTHER WORKS
Bradbury has written numerous plays, poems,
and pamphlets. Larger collections include:
1975 *Pillar of Fire and Other Plays for
      Today, Tomorrow, and Beyond
      Tomorrow* Bantam
1982 *The Complete Poems of Ray Bradbury*
      Ballantine

Ray Bradbury

Fahrenheit filmed
At the end of Fahrenheit 451, *the hero and his lover, played in the Truffaut film by Oscar Werner and Julie Christie, find refuge in a rural, literary Eden.*

FRITZ LEIBER

BORN / DIED **1910-92**

NATIONALITY **American**

KEY WORKS ***Gather, Darkness!,
The Big Time, The Wanderer,
A Specter is Haunting Texas, the
Fafhrd and the Gray Mauser series***

MOST writers are really children at heart, and most of them fade young. Fritz Leiber, on the other hand, was that most unusual of authors: a full-grown person, spattered with flaws, starred with humanity. And unlike most writers – who tend to milk the childhood that governs their talent, and whose work therefore tends to lessen in value as the years pass – Leiber's output only improved with advancing age.

Not that his first story is negligible, because "Two Sought Adventure", published in *Unknown* magazine in 1939, introduces Fafhrd and the Gray Mouser, the most human and likeable of all sword-and-sorcery duos. But by the late 1960s, Leiber had markedly deepened his portrait of the two companions: the Gray Mouser was based on Harry Fischer, the college friend who had initially suggested that Leiber write the stories, while Fafhrd was a self-portrait.

Leiber began his career as a fantasy author, and wrote some horror as well as much SF, but unlike (for example) Ray Bradbury, he always paid strict attention to the genre that he was working within: he won recognition and lifetime-achievement awards in all three of the fields in which he wrote. As a result, his works are extremely varied. *Gather, Darkness!* and *Conjure Wife* are vigorous Science Fantasies; *The Big Time* is a dazzling closet drama of time-paradox; *The Wanderer* is a rollicking and melancholic tale of planetary disaster narrowly averted; *A Specter is Haunting Texas* is a picaresque; *Our Lady of Darkness* is a deeply affecting tale of urban horror.

Leiber was an acknowledged alcoholic, who overcame this affliction (more than once); he was interested in cats, sex, women, men, the occult, the past, and the future. He lived, and he wrote, in the round.

[signature: Fritz Leiber]

BIBLIOGRAPHY

NOVELS AND NOVELLAS

1950 ***Gather, Darkness!*** Pellegrini and Cudahy
1953 ***Conjure Wife*** Twayne
   The Green Millennium Abelard
   The Sinful Ones Universal Giant, retitled
      You're All Alone
1957 ***Destiny Times Three*** Galaxy Novel
1961 ***The Big Time*** Ace
1962 ***The Silver Eggheads*** Ballantine
1964 ***The Wanderer*** Ballantine
1966 ***Tarzan and the Valley of Gold*** Ballantine
1968 ***The Swords of Lankhmar*** Ace
1969 ***A Specter is Haunting Texas*** Walker
1977 ***Our Lady of Darkness*** Berkley
   Rime Isle Whispers Press, retitled ***Swords
      and Ice Magic***
1988 ***The Knight and Knave of Swords*** Morrow

SHORT STORY COLLECTIONS

1947 ***Night's Black Agents*** Arkham House,
   abridged as ***Tales from Night's Black
   Agents***
1957 ***Two Sought Adventure*** Gnome Press
1961 ***The Mind Spider*** Ace

1962 ***Shadows With Eyes*** Ballantine
1964 ***A Pail of Air*** Ballantine
   Ships to the Stars Ace
1966 ***The Night of the Wolf*** Ballantine
1968 ***The Secret Songs*** Hart Davis
   Swords Against Wizardry Ace
   Swords in the Mist Ace
   Swords and Deviltry Ace
1969 ***Night Monsters*** Ace
1970 ***Swords Against Death*** Ace
1974 ***The Best of Fritz Leiber*** Sphere
   The Book of Fritz Leiber DAW Books
1975 ***The Second Book of Fritz Leiber***
   DAW Books
1976 ***The Worlds of Fritz Leiber*** Ace
1978 ***The Change War*** Gregg Press
1978 ***Bazaar of the Bizarre*** Donald
   M. Grant
   Heroes and Horrors Whispers Press
1979 ***Ship of Shadows*** Gollancz
1983 ***Changewar*** Ace
1984 ***The Ghost Light*** Berkley
1990 ***The Leiber Chronicles: Fifty Years of
   Fritz Leiber*** Dark Harvest

THEODORE STURGEON

BORN / DIED **1918-85**

NATIONALITY **American**

OTHER NAMES **born Edward
Hamilton Waldo, E. Hunter
Waldo; E. Waldo Hunter**

KEY WORKS ***The Dreaming Jewels,
More Than Human, Venus Plus X***

STURGEON was not the happiest of writers, but he was more intense in his joys than almost any of his peers. He suffered spasms of overproduction and long periods of writer's block, but his fellow writers admired him above all others for his professionalism, his technique, his adventurousness. He was dismissed and rehabilitated a dozen times, but he was always loved.

Some early stories – "Microcosmic God" (1941), or "Killdozer" (1944) – might have been written by any of a dozen competent contemporaries, but the mature Sturgeon story – "Bianca's Hands" (1947), "Maturity" (1947), "The World Well Lost" (1953), or "The Man Who Lost the Sea" (1959) – is almost impossible to mistake, and often focuses on the traumas of being a lonely child or adolescent in a world of uncaring, or malign, adults. The style is sometimes excessive, trying too hard to convey too great a complexity of emotion for easily approachable language; but more often it is both incandescent and unforgettable. After all is told, love triumphs.

At least three of Sturgeon's longer works will always be remembered. The first, *The Dreaming Jewels*, is one of the best of his wish-fulfilment metaphors. Young Horty, persecuted by a vicious stepfather, runs away to a carnival, where he finds protection and friends, and falls in love with the world.

But Horty is no usual child: he is a telepathic shape-changer, "dreamt" into existence by jewel-like aliens, and at the same time represents the true human spirit. As in all of Sturgeon's finest dreams of freedom, to escape the trammels of our mortal condition is to be fully human at last.

This potent aspiration is even more eloquently expressed in *More Than Human* (see page 219), although again without a realistic world to back it up. Only in *Venus Plus X*, one of the few utopian novels by an American SF author, does Sturgeon try to create a society untrammelled by constraints on sexuality or imagination. Woundingly, it was published only in paperback, and disappeared from view. Sturgeon's last novel, the posthumous *Godbody*, shows the strain of trying to maintain so soaring a vision in a complex and unresponsive world.

[signature: Theodore Sturgeon]

BIBLIOGRAPHY

NOVELS AND NOVELLAS

1950 ***The Dreaming Jewels*** Greenberg, retitled
   The Synthetic Man
1953 ***More Than Human*** Farrar Straus
1958 ***The Cosmic Rape*** Dell, retitled
   To Marry Medusa
1960 ***Venus Plus X*** Pyramid
1961 ***Some of Your Blood*** Ballantine
   Voyage to the Bottom of the Sea
   Pyramid
1986 ***Godbody*** Donald Fine

SHORT STORY COLLECTIONS

1948 ***Without Sorcery*** Prime Press, abridged as
   Not Without Sorcery
1953 ***E Pluribus Unicorn*** Abelard Press
1955 ***Caviar*** Ballantine
   A Way Home Funk and Wagnalls, abridged
   as ***Thunder and Roses***
1958 ***A Touch of Strange*** Doubleday
1959 ***Aliens 4*** Avon
1960 ***Beyond*** Avon
1964 ***Sturgeon in Orbit*** Pyramid
1965 ***The Joyous Invasions*** Gollancz
   And My Fear is Great/Baby is Three
   Galaxy Magabook
1966 ***Starshine*** Pyramid
1971 ***Sturgeon is Alive and Well*** Putnam
1972 ***The Worlds of Theodore Sturgeon*** Ace
1974 ***Case and the Dreamer*** Nelson
   Doubleday
1978 ***Visions and Venturers*** Dell
1979 ***The Golden Helix*** Nelson Doubleday
   The Stars are the Styx Dell
   Maturity: Three Stories Minneapolis
   Science Fiction Society
1984 ***Alien Cargo*** Bluejay
1987 ***A Touch of Sturgeon*** Simon and Schuster
   To Marry Medusa Baen Books
1994 ***The Ultimate Egoist*** North Atlantic Books

WILLIAM TENN

BORN **1920**

NATIONALITY **American**

OTHER NAME **born Philip Klass**

KEY WORKS **Of Men and Monsters, The Seven Sexes, The Square Root of Man, The Wooden Star**

BIBLIOGRAPHY

NOVELS AND NOVELLAS
1968 **Of Men and Monsters** Ballantine
A Lamp for Medusa Belmont

SHORT STORY COLLECTIONS
1955 **Of All Possible Worlds** Ballantine
1956 **The Human Angle** Ballantine
1958 **Time in Advance** Bantam
1968 **The Seven Sexes** Ballantine
The Square Root of Man Ballantine
The Wooden Star Ballantine

AS EDITOR
1953 **Children of Wonder** Simon and Schuster,
retitled **Outsiders**
1968 **Once Against the Law** Macmillan, with
Donald E. Westlake

THE failure of SF to retain the interest of William Tenn is one of the tragedies of the post-war genre. Tenn – who in real life, as Philip Klass, is a university professor – began publishing his witty, ironic, slashing, urbane, compassionate stories in 1946, and had stopped, more or less, by 1970. It was not good for the field that he did. Almost half a century after he started, his tone seems more contemporary than ever, his satires on human pretensions all the more necessary.

That first story – "Alexander the Bait", published in *Astounding* magazine by John W. Campbell Jr. despite its iconoclastic assault on a dearly held SF belief – is typical. It contended that the exploration of space would be accomplished by organized teams of employees rather than – this is where he trampled Golden Age SF dogma – individual entrepreneurs who leapfrog over sclerotic socialist bureaucracies to conquer the stars.

Dozens of fine tales followed, some of them collected in early volumes such as *Of All Possible Worlds*, most of the rest of them assembled in 1968 when Ballantine Books issued a collected William Tenn edition: *The Seven Sexes, The Square Root of Man*, and *The Wooden Star*. These volumes provided a showcase of his work over two decades,

Of All Possible Worlds
Many of Tenn's stories for Galaxy *magazine found their way into this first collection.*

but proved at the same time to mark his farewell as a writer of fiction. Although a few excellent stories have intermittently appeared in recent years, they serve only to intensify the frustration that there have not been many, many more.

In that set of Ballantine books is one novel, the only full-length fiction Tenn has yet written. *Of Men and Monsters* – the magazine title, *The Men in the Walls*, is both more accurate and more memorable – is a brilliant tale, reminiscent in its satirical strategies of Jonathan Swift's *Gulliver's Travels*. In this version, however, it is human beings who are the Lilliputians. A race of giant aliens has settled on Earth. They are scarcely aware of humanity, except as a kind of vermin. (Disch's *The Genocides*, in which similarly indifferent alien settlers exterminate us as if we were worms in an apple, was drafted at about the same time.) The novel is told through the experiences of a young human, who comes into his adulthood through discovering the true position of humanity. This is wryly humiliating, and told with huge narrative zest; but the novel ends on a note of hope. Hidden in the wainscots of the vast alien spaceships, human beings begin to hitch-hike their way to the stars, where they may find a more rewarding niche than Earth now allows them. We need more Tenn.

DAMON KNIGHT

BORN **1922**

NATIONALITY **American**

OTHER NAME **Donald Laverty**

KEY WORKS **"To Serve Man", "The Country of the Kind", *Hell's Pavement, In Search of Wonder***

KNIGHT, like his contemporary, William Tenn, is a sharp satirist, an incisive commentator on human nature whose 1950s stories shocked parts of the SF community; and like Tenn, he found it difficult to keep his attention focused on the job of writing fiction for an audience he was more than likely to miff. But Damon Knight is also a born novelist, critic, editor, and organizer. And he has long been married to Kate Wilhelm, one of the most fluent writers in the modern genre. He has never, therefore, really left the SF field.

It is the case, however, that the 1950s represent Knight's prime years as a writer of fiction. During this decade, he produced short stories like the famous "To Serve Man" from 1950, and "The Country of the Kind" from 1956, which held up acid mirrors to suburban America, and novels like *Hell's Pavement*, which romped at greater length through dystopian scenarios. But American SF is not inherently a self-critical genre, and so Knight was never to become one of its central spokesmen – or at any rate not through his fiction.

But Knight has made his presence felt elsewhere in the genre. The pieces in *In Search of Wonder* represent the first genuinely literate criticism and book reviewing – along with that of James Blish – to which the American SF field had been subjected. And in 1965, he founded the Science Fiction Writers of America, a writers' organization that served to defend their interests in a rapidly growing market. And his **Orbit** series of original anthologies was extremely valuable.

More recently, there have been several enigmatic novels, like riddles to be solved in the next volume – which we can only eagerly await.

BIBLIOGRAPHY

NOVELS AND NOVELLAS
1955 **Hell's Pavement** Lion, retitled **The Analogue
Men**
1959 **The People Maker** Zenith, revised as
A for Anything
Masters of Evolution Ace
1961 **The Sun Saboteurs** Ace
1964 **Beyond the Barrier** Doubleday
1965 **Mind Switch** Berkley, retitled **The Other
Foot**
The Rithian Terror Ace
1980 **The World and Thorinn** Berkley
1984 **The Man in the Tree** Berkley
1985 **CV** Tor
1988 **The Observers** Tor
1991 **A Reasonable World** Tor
1992 **Why Do Birds** Tor

SHORT STORY COLLECTIONS
1961 **Far Out** Simon and Schuster
1963 **In Deep** Berkley
1965 **Off Center** Ace
1966 **Turning On** Doubleday
1967 **Three Novels: Rule Golden, Natural State,
The Dying Man** Doubleday, retitled
**Natural State and Other Short Story
Collections**
1974 **Two Novels: The Earth Quarter, Double
Meaning** Gollancz

1976 **The Best of Damon Knight** Nelson
Doubleday
1979 **Rule Golden and Other Stories** Avon
1980 **Better Than One** NESFA Press, with
Kate Wilhelm
1985 **Late Knight Edition** NESFA Press
1991 **One Side Laughing** St. Martin's Press
God's Nose Pulphouse

NON-FICTION
1956 **In Search of Wonder** Advent
1970 **Charles Fort, Prophet of the Unexplained**
Doubleday
1977 **The Futurians** Day
1981 **Creating Short Fiction** Writer's Digest

SELECTED WORKS AS EDITOR
1962 **A Century of Science Fiction** Simon
and Schuster
1966 **Cities of Wonder** Doubleday
Orbit Putnam, and 20 further volumes
through 1980
1974 **The Golden Road** Simon and Schuster
1977 **Turning Points: Essays on the Art of
Science Fiction** Harper
1984 **The Clarion Awards** Doubleday

C.M. KORNBLUTH

BORN /DIED **1923-58**

NATIONALITY **American**

OTHER NAMES **Arthur Cook, Cecil Corwin, Walter C. Davies, Kenneth Falconer, S.D. Gottesman, Paul Dennis Lavond, Scott Mariner**

KEY WORKS ***The Space Merchants, Wolfbane, The Marching Morons***

BIBLIOGRAPHY

NOVELS AND NOVELLAS
1952 ***Gunner Cade*** Simon and Schuster, with Judith Merril, as Cyril Judd
Outpost Mars Abelard Press, with Judith Merril, as Cyril Judd, revised as ***Sin in Space***
Takeoff Doubleday
1953 ***The Space Merchants*** Ballantine, with Frederik Pohl
The Syndic Doubleday
1954 ***Search the Sky*** Ballantine, with Frederik Pohl
1955 ***Gladiator-at-Law*** Ballantine, with Frederik Pohl
Not This August Doubleday, retitled ***Christmas Eve***
A Town is Drowning Ballantine, with Frederik Pohl
1959 ***Wolfbane*** Ballantine, with Frederik Pohl

SHORT STORY COLLECTIONS
1954 ***The Explorers*** Ballantine
1955 ***The Mindworm*** Michael Joseph
1958 ***A Mile Beyond the Moon*** Doubleday
1959 ***The Marching Morons*** Ballantine
1962 ***The Wonder Effect*** Ballantine, with Frederik Pohl, revised as ***Critical Mass***
1968 ***Best SF Stories*** Faber
1970 ***Thirteen O'Clock and Other Zero Stories*** Dell, edited by James Blish
1976 ***The Best of C.M. Kornbluth*** Doubleday, edited by Frederik Pohl
1980 ***Before the Universe*** Bantam, with Frederik Pohl
1987 ***Our Best*** Baen, with Frederik Pohl

GIVEN the rate at which SF writers of the 1950s faded from view – Budrys, Dick, Knight, Kuttner, Walter M. Miller Jr., Sheckley, Tenn – it is surprising that so many of them simply burned out or left the field, and how few of them departed early for the best of all reasons: Dick died young; Henry Kuttner, who had been active from the 1930s, died in 1958, aged 53; and Cyril Kornbluth died the same year. He too had been active in the field for years, but he had started as a teenager, and when he died, he was just 35 years old.

Into those 35 years he packed a large life: he was an active and controversial fan before World War II, and began a life-long professional association with Frederik Pohl at the same time; he was decorated for bravery in combat; he wrote with Judith Merril – *Gunner Cade* remains highly readable for its satirical view of a military fraternity – and with Pohl; he wrote some scathing, pessimistic stories, and was assaulted by conventional fans and critics – in language that made it sound as though they were accusing him of being unpatriotic – for "nihilism"; he wrote solo novels. Then he died.

Marching Morons
In the title story Kornbluth foresaw a bread-and-circuses world kept placid by game shows.

It is the collaborations with Pohl that, for the moment, keep Kornbluth's name alive. *The Space Merchants,* which was their first novel together, remains a central satirical text of the 1950s, targeting advertising men, corrupt governments, suburbia, and self-delusion. It is now, in a sense, also a historical novel, for the age of conformism that it mocked has passed, and life at the end of the century does not much resemble the grey, suburban desert that was envisioned by SF satirists half a century ago. But *The Space Merchants* deftly brings it all back into focus again. *Wolfbane,* Pohl and Kornbluth's final collaboration, is a *tour de force* in which aliens shift Earth from its orbit and shanghai humanity into becoming units in a vast computer. What would Kornbluth be writing now?

[signature: Cyril Kornbluth]

WALTER M. MILLER JR.

BORN **1922**

NATIONALITY **American**

KEY WORKS **"Crucifixus Etiam", "The Darfsteller", *A Canticle for Leibowitz***

WALTER M. Miller wrote quite a few short stories in the 1950s, and some of them are remembered. But they have nothing to do with his current reputation, which is unfair. Of his 40 or so short stories, several are of real stature. "Crucifixus Etiam", from 1953, can stand here for all of them: a labourer working on the terraforming of Mars learns that he can never return to Earth, and he gives the rest of his life as a kind of religious sacrifice for generations yet to come. Like almost all of Miller's work, the story shows the religious concerns that always preoccupied him: he had converted to Roman Catholicism at the age of 25.

But, more than almost any other SF writer of anything like the first rank, Miller is a one-book figure. That one book is, however, the classic novel *A Canticle for Leibowitz* (see page 222). For years, it has been rumoured that there is a sequel in the works: it has never appeared, and it is hard to see where it would fit.

The story, which is deeply and engagedly religious, is divided into three parts (each part having been published a few years before, in an earlier version, in *Galaxy* magazine). The first section of the story is set six centuries after a nuclear holocaust has driven the world into a new Dark Age. Deep in the American desert lies the Catholic Order of Liebowitz. Named after a Jewish engineer, who memorized forbidden books in the period just after the holocaust, the Order continues its founder's work, and manages to preserve the best of humanity's written knowledge. A Liebowitz blueprint – a holy relic to the order – is rescued, with the aid of the Wandering Jew, whom not even the Bomb can relieve of his eternal penance.

The second part of the story is set another six centuries further on, and sees history beginning to repeat itself. (Throughout the book, Miller contrasts his sense that secular history is circular with the countervailing belief that sacred history is constantly moving forwards into a possible state of grace.) Electricity is reinvented, and the industrial revolution is about to start again: the Abbey is threatened.

The third part of the novel, set another six centuries into the future, depicts in the harshest possible terms the return of the secular awfulness of the 20th century. Euthanasia clinics (abhorrent to Miller's conservative Catholic beliefs) proliferate, and another nuclear war brings a second holocaust. Meanwhile, the members of the Order prepare to escape from Earth in a spaceship, hoping that in Alpha Centauri they can build a new society in which technology does not corrupt the human soul.

> ❝*Almost all of Miller's work shows the religious concerns that so preoccupied him*❞

The complexity of the work as a whole is quite extraordinary. Each section of the book both prefigures and echoes the other sections, giving the effect of a mosaic. There is humour, pathos, tragedy, myth, speculation, irony, and hope. It is one of the two or three finest single achievements of modern SF: there can, really, be no possible sequel to such a book.

BIBLIOGRAPHY

NOVEL
1960 ***A Canticle for Liebowitz*** Lippincott

SHORT STORY COLLECTIONS
1962 ***Conditionally Human*** Ballantine
1965 ***The View from the Stars*** Ballantine
1980 ***The Best of Walter M. Miller, Jr.*** Pocket Books
1982 ***The Darfsteller*** Corgi
1984 ***The Science Fiction Stories of Walter M. Miller, Jr.*** Hall

PHILIP JOSÉ FARMER

BORN **1918**

NATIONALITY **American**

OTHER NAME **Kilgore Trout**

KEY WORKS ***The Lovers*, the *Riverworld* series**

For a genre that sees itself as cutting edge, SF has been more than a trifle timid. Nowhere is this more evident than in the treatment of sex. Early pulp magazines were sometimes extremely lurid; several specialized in graphic sado-masochistic scenarios, with naked women bound and awaiting rescue. But the SF pulps were relatively restrained, their illustrations being restricted to alien monsters' attempts to make hay with gals in bikinis. The only venues to permit nudity were the Mars and Venus of Planetary Romance.

By the 1950s, reticence had become oppression, caution about adolescent readers, priggishness. Enter Philip José Farmer. After a false start in the 1940s, he came to sudden notoriety in 1952 with the "The Lovers" in *Startling Stories* magazine – after both *Astounding* and *Galaxy* had rejected it because of its subject matter. Because Farmer's tale is completely lacking in prurience, and because it speculates incisively and in strict SF terms about the nature of sex, it proved a ground-breaker, and by 1961 (when Heinlein published *Stranger in a Strange Land*) the floodgates were opening.

But in 1952, "The Lovers" was a stunner. A human man is sent to an alien planet to arrange the extermination of its insectoid native species. He finds that the natives are capable of mimicking human shape, and falls in love with the female who has seduced him. Their sex is explicit.

Her pregnancy is fatal to her – this often happens, even in modern SF – and he is left to raise, and to love, his insect children. It is the kind of xenobiological tale oft-told today, but it raised hackles in the year General Eisenhower won the Presidency.

Farmer was given the Best New Writer of the Year Hugo Award in 1953, and it looked as though he would soon become one of the staple writers of the genre. His iconoclasm – which applied to religion and society – was profoundly needed. His skill was unquestionable. But he had several years of bad luck: among other setbacks, a long manuscript was lost. Although *The Green Odyssey* (see page 221), his first novel, superbly married SF and Planetary Romance, he seemed unable to make a living at his craft.

Only with the 1960s did his career really take off. *The Lovers* appeared as a novel. *The Maker of Universes* started a long, rhapsodically complex series about a nest of pocket universes. *A Feast Unknown* scabrously parodied Tarzan. *To Your Scattered Bodies Go*

Things are not what they seem
The human hero of The Lovers *falls in love with an alien in human guise, knowing that it is not her true appearance. The short story won Farmer a Hugo award.*

(see page 227) – and its many sequels set the whole of the reincarnated human race along the banks of a vast river, where pranks and quests weave together intoxicatingly. And *Dayworld, Dayworld Rebel,* and *Dayworld Breakup* grippingly depict a world so crowded that several minds must share the same body, in shifts.

Farmer is always at the edge. He parodies, probes, jokes, comments, and blasphemes. He is rather like Kurt Vonnegut, to whom he paid homage in

Venus on the Half-Shell. His novels are full of action and characters and speculative verve; but they seem, at the same time, strangely solitary. They stand at the borders of conventional SF, and point things out.

Philip José Farmer [signature]

BIBLIOGRAPHY

NOVELS AND NOVELLAS
1957 ***The Green Odyssey*** Ballantine
1960 ***Flesh*** Galaxy
    A Woman a Day Galaxy, retitled ***The Day of Timestop***, again retitled ***Timestop!***
1961 ***The Lovers*** Ballantine
1962 ***Cache from Outer Space*** Ace, expanded as ***The Cache***
1964 ***Inside Outside*** Ballantine
    Tongues of the Moon Pyramid
1965 ***Dare*** Ballantine
    The Maker of Universes Ace
1966 ***The Gate of Time*** Belmont, revised as ***Two Hawks from Earth***
    The Gates of Creation Ace
    Night of Light Berkley
1968 ***The Image of the Beast*** Essex House
    A Private Cosmos Ace
1969 ***Blown: or, Sketches Among the Ruins of my Mind*** Essex House
    A Feast Unknown: Volume IX of the Memoirs of Lord Grandith Essex House
1970 ***Behind the Walls of Terra*** Ace
    Lord Tyger Doubleday
    Lord of the Trees Ace
    The Mad Goblin Ace, retitled ***Keepers of the Secrets***
    The Stone God Awakens Ace
1971 ***To Your Scattered Bodies Go*** Putnam
    The Fabulous Riverboat Putnam
    The Wind Whales of Ishmael Ace

1972 ***Time's Last Gift*** Ballantine
1973 ***The Other Log of Phileas Fogg*** DAW Books
    Traitor to the Living Ballantine
1974 ***The Adventure of the Peerless Peer by John H. Watson, M.D.*** Aspen Press
    Hadon of Ancient Opar DAW Books
1975 ***Venus on the Half-Shell*** Dell, as Kilgore Trout
1976 ***Flight to Opar*** DAW Books
1977 ***The Dark Design*** Berkley
    The Lavalite World Ace
1979 ***Dark is the Sun*** Ballantine
    Jesus on Mars Pinnacle
1980 ***The Magic Labyrinth*** Berkley
1981 ***The Unreasoning Mask*** Putnam
1982 ***A Barnstormer in Oz; or, A Rationalization and Extrapolation of the Split-Level Continuum*** Phantasia Press
    Greatheart Silver Pinnacle (linked stories)
    Stations of the Nightmare Tor (linked stories)
1983 ***Gods of Riverworld*** Putnam
    River of Eternity Phantasia Press
1985 ***Dayworld*** Putnam
1986 ***Dayworld Rebel*** Putnam
1990 ***Dayworld Breakup*** Tor
1991 ***Red Orc's Rage*** Tor
    Doc Savage: Escape from Loki: Doc Savage's First Adventure Bantam
1993 ***More Than Fire*** Tor

SHORT STORY COLLECTIONS
1960 ***Strange Relations*** Ballantine
1962 ***The Alley God*** Ballantine
    The Celestial Blueprint Ace
1971 ***Down in the Black Gang*** Nelson Doubleday
1973 ***The Book of Philip José Farmer; or, the Wares of Simple Simon's Custard Pie and Space Man*** DAW Books
1979 ***Riverworld and Other Stories*** Berkley
1980 ***Riverworld War: The Suppressed Fiction of Philip José Farmer*** Ellis Press
1981 ***Father to the Stars*** Pinnacle
1982 ***Stations of the Nightmare*** Pinnacle
    The Purple Book Berkley
1984 ***The Classic Philip José Farmer*** Crown (two volumes)
    The Grand Adventure Berkley
1992 ***Riders of the Purple Wage*** Tor

FICTIONAL BIOGRAPHIES
1972 ***Tarzan Alive: A Definitive Biography of Lord Greystoke*** Doubleday
1973 ***Doc Savage: His Apocalyptic Life*** Doubleday

AS TRANSLATOR
1976 ***Ironcastle*** DAW Books (adapted from J.H. Rosny aîné's ***L'étonnante aventure de Hareton Ironcastle***)

JACK VANCE

BORN 1916

NATIONALITY American

KEY WORKS *The Dying Earth*, **the Demon Princes series**

H E is a gardener: he gardens worlds and men. Almost every book by Vance is dominated by a landscape, rural or urban. These landscapes are intricately shaped by a leisurely, sure hand. They are exotic, they differ radically from each other, they proliferate and flourish: that is the heart of the vision. Vance's universe, the billions of stars that his rhetoric points to, is a flourishing universe.

It will surely suffer heat death, this universe, but not yet. The societies that breed on the planets circling the galaxy's multifarious suns, however, are not so lucky. Vance has described dozens of separate cultures, sometimes with considerable acumen, sometimes with a sharp sense of how theories

of human behaviour might pan out if taken as true. *The Languages of Pao*, for example, extrapolates upon the hypothesis that the deep structure of a language determines both the nature of the culture in which it exists, and the way humans perceive the world. It does not matter that this Whorf-Sapir hypothesis (named after the linguists who developed it) has been severely challenged since Vance wrote his novel; what matters is that the book gloriously demonstrates what kind of a world might ensue if Whorf-Sapir were right. It is a thought experiment; it is what SF, for some people, is all about.

The Dying Earth, Vance's first book, is justly famous. His first full-length novel, *To Live Forever*, is a harsh dystopia, set on a future Earth riven by the possibility of immortality.

Perhaps oddly for a man absorbed in the variousness and complexity of things, Vance tends to create cold, careful, solitary protagonists, who do not trust their own species, other species, or the environment; even more surprisingly, Vance seems to think they are right.

As a result, he has developed a reputation for somewhat grumpy libertarianism – a reputation hard to deny, given the voluminously intelligent ways in which he makes

Startling story

Like much of Vance's early work, "Big Planet" was first published in Startling Stories magazine.

NOTABLE WORK

From the early years of the century, Science Fantasy tales had been set in a vague far future, but it was only with *The Dying Earth* that anyone managed to pin this venue down into something firm enough to support an SF story. *The Dying Earth* is set so far in the future that history, which has repeated itself dozens of times, is a fairytale. Here, magic and technology are the same thing, and human beings play in the garden of time.

THE DYING EARTH

---

it clear that even his most anti-social heroes know just what they are doing, and to whom. His most famous hero is Kirth Gersen, the avenging figure of the **Demon Princes** series (made up of *The Star King, The Killing Machine, The Palace of Love, The Face,* and *The Book of Dreams*). Each book sees Gersen inflict punishments on his enemies that one might expect in a Western. In the end, though, in *Maske*, and *Wyst*, and *Lyonesse*, and a dozen others, it is the gardener of worlds who triumphs.

BIBLIOGRAPHY

NOVELS AND NOVELLAS
1950 *The Dying Earth* Hillman
  Periodicals (linked stories)
1953 *The Space Pirate* Toby Press, cut
  as *The Five Gold Bands*
  Vandals of the Void Winston
1956 *To Live Forever* Ballantine
1957 *Big Planet* Avalon
1958 *The Languages of Pao*
  Avalon
  Slaves of the Klau Ace, retitled
  *Gold and Iron: (Slaves of
  the Klau)* Ace
1963 *The Dragon Masters* Ace
1964 *The Houses of Iszm* Ace
  Son of the Tree Ace
  The Star King Berkley
  The Killing Machine Berkley
1965 *Monsters in Orbit* Ace
  Space Opera Pyramid
1966 *The Blue World* Ballantine

1966 *The Brains of Earth* Ace
  The Eyes of the Overworld
  Ace
1967 *The Palace of Love* Berkley
  The Last Castle Ace
1968 *City of the Chasch* Ace, retitled
  Chasch
1969 *Emphyrio* Doubleday
  Servants of the Wankh Ace,
  retitled *Wankh*
  The Dirdir Ace
1970 *The Pnume* Ace
1973 *The Anome* Dell, retitled
  The Faceless Man
  The Brave Free Men Dell
  Trullion: Alastor 2262
  Ballantine
1974 *The Asutra* Dell
  The Gray Prince Bobbs Merrill
1975 *Marune: Alastor 933*
  Ballantine

1975 *Showboat World* Pyramid, retitled
  *The Magnificent Showboats
  of the Lower Vissel River,
  Lune XXIII, South, Big Planet:
  Showboat World*
1976 *Maske: Thaery* Berkley
1978 *Wyst: Alastor 1716*
  DAW Books
1979 *The Face* DAW Books
  Morreion Underwood-Miller
1981 *The Book of Dreams*
  Underwood-Miller
1983 *Cugel's Saga* Pocket Books
  Suldrun's Garden Berkley
1984 *Rhialto the Marvellous*
  Brandwyne Books
1985 *Lyonesse: The Green Pearl*
  Underwood-Miller, retitled
  Lyonesse
1987 *Araminta Station*

1989 *Lyonesse: Madouc*
  Underwood-Miller, retitled
  Madouc
1991 *Ecce and Old Earth*
  St. Martin's Press
1992 *Throy* Underwood-Miller

SHORT STORY COLLECTIONS
1964 *Future Tense* Ballantine, retitled
  Dust of Far Suns
1965 *The World Between* Ace, retitled
  The Moon Moth
1966 *The Many Worlds of Magnus
  Ridolph* Ace, expanded as *The
  Complete Magnus Ridolph*
1969 *Eight Fantasms and Magics*
  Macmillan, retitled *Fantasms
  and Magics*
1973 *The Worlds of Jack Vance* Ace
1976 *The Best of Jack Vance*
  Pocket Books

1979 *Green Magic: The Fantasy
  Realms of Jack Vance*
  Underwood-Miller
1979 *The Seventeen Virgins; The
  Bagful of Dreams: The
  Adventures of Cugel
  the Clever* Underwood-Miller
1980 *Galactic Effectuator*
  Underwood-Miller
1982 *The Narrow Land* DAW Books
  Lost Moons Underwood-Miller
1985 *Light from a Lone Star*
  NESFA Press
1986 *The Augmented Agent*
  Underwood-Miller
  The Dark Side of the Moon
  Underwood-Miller
1990 *Chateau d'If* Underwood-Miller
1992 *When the Five Moons Rise*
  Underwood-Miller

JAMES BLISH

BORN / DIED **1921-75**

NATIONALITY **American**

OTHER NAMES **Donald Laverty, John MacDougal, Arthur Merlyn, William Atheling Jr.**

KEY WORKS **"Surface Tension", the Okie series, A Case of Conscience**

IF American SF were interested more in intellectual discourse than in the telling of stories, if it were interested more in thinkers ravaged by heavy thoughts than in heroes, then James Blish might have been the most significant figure in the whole history of the genre. It is not that he could not write stories; "Surface Tension", which is set on a world whose colonizing humans have been bioengineered into creatures that are almost invisibly tiny, is one of the great tales of conceptual breakthrough. What was wrong – or right – with Blish was that he almost always stopped his stories to think.

He came from much the same background as writers like Damon Knight, C.M. Kornbluth, and Frederick Pohl, and did journeyman work for the same editors. He tried for some years to act like a genre writer, and around 1950, with novels like *Jack of Eagles*, gave the inaccurate impression that he wanted to become a great storyteller.

He did not. His SF masterpieces are *A Case of Conscience* (see page 221), a taxing examination of the concept of original sin, and the stories and novels making up *Cities in Flight*, in which the German philosopher Oswald Spengler's theory of history (that civilizations go through cycles of growth and decay) clamps down on the rampageous Space Opera he had begun to tell. But both these works stick in the mind like glue.

The late *Star Trek* books were written for money. The real James Blish is to be found elsewhere, lost in coils of thought.

BIBLIOGRAPHY

NOVELS AND NOVELLAS
1952 **Jack of Eagles** Greenberg, retitled **ESPer**
1953 **The Warriors of Day** Galaxy
1955 **Earthman, Come Home** Putnam
1956 **They Shall Have Stars** Faber, revised as **Year 2018!**
1957 **The Frozen Year** Ballantine, retitled **Fallen Star**
1958 **The Triumph of Time** Avon, retitled **A Clash of Cymbals**
  A Case of Conscience Ballantine
  VOR Avon
1959 **The Duplicated Man** Avalon, with Robert A.W. Lowndes
1961 **The Star Dwellers** Putnam
  Titan's Daughter Berkley
1962 **The Night Shapes** Ballantine
1964 **Doctor Mirabilis** Faber
1965 **Mission to the Heart Stars** Putnam
1967 **A Torrent of Faces** Doubleday, with Norman L. Knight
  Welcome to Mars Faber
1968 **Black Easter, or Faust Aleph-Null** Doubleday
  The Vanished Jet Weybright and Talley
1970 **Spock Must Die!** Bantam
1971 **The Day After Judgment** Doubleday
  . . . And All the Stars a Stage Doubleday
1972 **Midsummer Century** Doubleday
1973 **The Quincunx of Time** Dell
1978 **Mudd's Angels** Bantam, with J.A. Lawrence

SHORT STORY COLLECTIONS
1957 **The Seedling Stars** Gnome Press
1959 **Galactic Cluster** New American Library
1961 **So Close to Home** Ballantine
1965 **Best Science Fiction Stories of James Blish** Faber, revised as **The Testament of Andros**
1967 **Star Trek** Bantam
1968 **Star Trek 2** Bantam
1969 **Star Trek 3** Bantam
1970 **Anywhen** Doubleday
1971 **Star Trek 4** Bantam
1972 **Star Trek 5** Bantam
  Star Trek 6 Bantam
  Star Trek 7 Bantam
  Star Trek 8 Bantam
1973 **Star Trek 9** Bantam
1974 **Star Trek 10** Bantam
1975 **Star Trek 11** Bantam, retitled **Day of the Dove**
1977 **Star Trek 12** Bantam, with J.A. Lawrence
1979 **The Best of James Blish** Ballantine
1980 **Get Out of my Sky, and There Shall be no Darkness** Panther

NON-FICTION
1964 **The Issue at Hand: Studies in Contemporary Magazine Science Fiction** Advent, as William Atheling Jr.
1970 **More Issues at Hand: Critical Studies in Contemporary Science Fiction** Advent, as William Atheling Jr.
1987 **The Tale That Wags the God** Advent

CORDWAINER SMITH

BORN / DIED **1913-66**

NATIONALITY **American**

OTHER NAMES **born Paul Myron Anthony Linebarger; Felix C. Forrest, Carmichael Smith**

KEY WORKS **"Scanners Live in Vain", the Instrumentality series**

CORDWAINER Smith would have been an absolutely central figure had American SF taken an alternative course. In this case, the genre would have had to concentrate on the recovery of humanity's past glories, rather than on the triumphs and tribulations that we might yet experience. His work is all about the huge romantic weight of the past; it has almost nothing to do with the huge romantic thrust of progress into the future.

His first story, the deservedly famous "Scanners Live in Vain" (1950), was rejected by all of the major SF magazines; if this seems incredible to us today, because readers in the 1990s have no difficulty in understanding that this is an astonishingly first-rate story, that may be because the world has changed so radically since World War II. "Scanners Live in Vain", with its dark, savage depiction of the individual human costs of triumphing in space, and its prophetic cynicism about the profound effects of technological change on the "heroes" who make themselves obsolete through their very success, was not a story that the SF world wanted to hear in 1950.

Instrumentality
This collection of short stories was Cordwainer Smith's first SF book.

BIBLIOGRAPHY

NOVELS AND NOVELLAS
1947 **Ria** Duell, as Felix C. Forrest
1948 **Carola** Duell, as Felix C. Forrest
1949 **Atomsk** Duell, as Carmichael Smith
1964 **The Planet Buyer** Pyramid
1968 **The Underpeople** Pyramid
1975 **Norstrilia** Ballantine

SHORT STORY COLLECTIONS
1963 **You Will Never Be the Same** Regency
1965 **Space Lords** Pyramid
1966 **Quest of the Three Worlds** Ace
1970 **Under Old Earth** Panther
1971 **Stardreamer** Beagle
1975 **The Best of Cordwainer Smith** Doubleday, retitled **The Rediscovery of Man** (not the same as the 1993 title)
1979 **The Instrumentality of Mankind** Ballantine
1993 **The Rediscovery of Man: The Complete Short Science Fiction of Cordwainer Smith** NESFA Press

SELECTED NON-FICTION
1937 **The Political Doctrines of Sun Yat-Sen** Johns Hopkins University Press
1948 **Psychological Warfare** Infantry Journal Press

Later, his vision softened, although the implications of that first tale were never contradicted. This may well be because Smith – a political scientist and expert on China – was already a mature man in 1950, and his soaring, romantic pessimism about the old age of the human race was not likely to alter signficantly. Nor did it: almost everything he wrote – even "Scanners Live in Vain" – fits into a consistent universe, extending over several millennia. But although this universe is detailed enough to take a place in SF's Future Histories, the emphasis was not on telling the story but on remembering it.

In the far future, humanity has lost its bite; the ruling Instrumentality decides to reintroduce elements of strife and mortality; the great Smith tales are ballads ambiguously celebrating this return to roots. They are autumnal, wry, poetic, sentimental, and grave. Reading them, we feel like creatures of a golden, gaudy, faintly humorous dawn.

Paul Linebarger

ANDRE NORTON

BORN **1912**

NATIONALITY **American**

OTHER NAMES **born Alice Mary Norton; Andrew North**

KEY WORKS **The *Witch World* series**

I T is not simply that Andre Norton's bibliography is immense, although it certainly is that, and it is still daily growing. What is perhaps most extraordinary about Norton's long array of titles is the steely consistency of production that they reveal: for not a year has passed since 1951 without at least one, and often up to four, new titles to add to the list.

Although she started young, publishing her first novel as early as 1934, she did start slowly. It was not until she was a mature woman, fully in control of her style and fully aware of what it was she wished to convey to her readers, that the flood was unleashed. In the 1950s, she followed the lead that had been given by Heinlein, whose 1940s SF novels for young readers showed the publishers that those readers relished the real thing: real stories that seemed to project real futures. Norton quickly established herself as an author of clean-cut, romantic, optimistic, and vibrantly adventurous SF novels for adolescent readers.

It should be noted, however, that when the publishers reprinted these books in paperback, they did so without any reference to their original juvenile market. From the very first, adults could read Norton without feeling distanced from the quick, clear, alert beat of her mind; she has never written a condescending word. She writes in a speaking voice that does not much vary. Her work – from the early, boyish adventures like *Star Rangers*,

NOTABLE WORK

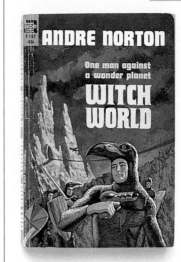

The tale starts in *Horn Crown*, in which humans find a gate into an Alternate Universe, and come to the land of Estcarp in Witch World, and live there. The ensuing tales – *Witch World* itself, the first published, is the second in the internal chronology – gradually paint the complex portrait of a land haunted by sorcery and defined by legends, a matriarchy with plenty of room for sword and sorcery, rites of passage tales, and myths. There is an underlying SF rationale, but the feel is fantasy.

WITCH WORLD

to the complex, plot-filled, and lengthy later works like *Golden Trillium* – is all of one consistent piece.

This is all true, but it is also all not quite true. If Norton has had to fight any battles with the world that reads her, they have to do with her profound distrust for raw science and technology. It is a distrust that she has often seemed to mask in her books, but one that explicitly underpins her greatest overall achievement, the enormous, and enormously successful, series of **Witch World** novels. For Andre Norton is essentially a romancer of worlds, not a smasher of them.

Andre Norton

BIBLIOGRAPHY

NOVELS AND NOVELLAS
1934 **The Prince Commands** Appleton Century
1938 **Ralestone Luck** Appleton Century
1942 **Follow the Drum** Penn
1946 **The Sword is Drawn** Houghton Mifflin
1947 **Rogue Reynard** Houghton Mifflin
1948 **Scarface** Harcourt Brace
1949 **Sword in Sheath** Harcourt Brace, retitled **Island of the Lost**
1951 **Huon of the Horn** Harcourt Brace
1952 **Star Man's Son, 2250 A.D.** Harcourt Brace, retitled **Daybreak, 2250 A.D**
1953 **Star Rangers** Harcourt Brace, retitled **The Last Planet**
1954 **The Stars Are Ours!** World
       At Swords' Point Harcourt Brace
1955 **Star Guard** Harcourt Brace
       Yankee Privateer World
       Sargasso of Space Gnome Press, as Andrew North
1956 **The Crossroads of Time** Ace
       Stand to Horse Harcourt Brace
       Plague Ship Gnome Press, as Andrew North
1957 **Sea Siege** Harcourt Brace
       Star Born World
1958 **Star Gate** Harcourt Brace
       The Time Traders World
1959 **Secret of the Lost Race** Ace, retitled **Wolfshead**
       The Beast Master Harcourt Brace
       Voodoo Planet Ace, as Andrew North
       Galactic Derelict World
1960 **Storm Over Warlock** World

1960 **The Sioux Spaceman** Ace
       Shadow Hawk Harcourt Brace
1961 **Star Hunter** Ace
       Catseye Harcourt Brace
       Ride Proud, Rebel! World
1962 **Eye of the Monster** Ace
       The Defiant Agents World
       Lord of Thunder Harcourt Brace
       Rebel Spurs World
1963 **Witch World** Ace
       Key Out of Time World
       Judgment on Janus Harcourt Brace
1964 **Ordeal in Otherwhere** World
       Night of Masks Harcourt Brace
       Web of the Witch World Ace
1965 **The X Factor** Harcourt Brace
       Quest Crosstime Viking, retitled **Crosstime Agent**
       Steel Magic World
       Three Against the Witch World Ace
       Year of the Unicorn Ace
1966 **Moon of Three Rings** Viking
       Victory on Janus Harcourt Brace
1967 **Operation Time Search** Harcourt Brace
       Octagon Magic World
       Warlock of the Witch World Ace
1968 **Dark Piper** Harcourt Brace
       The Zero Stone Viking
       Fur Magic World
       Sorceress of the Witch World Ace
1969 **Postmarked the Stars** Harcourt Brace
       Uncharted Stars Viking
       Bertie and May World, with Bertha Stenn Norton
1970 **Ice Crown** Viking

1970 **Dread Companion** Harcourt Brace
1971 **Android at Arms** Harcourt Brace
       Exiles of the Stars Viking
1972 **Breed to Come** Viking
       The Crystal Gryphon Atheneum
       Dragon Magic Crowell
       Garan the Eternal Fantasy Publishing Co.
1973 **Here Abide Monsters** Atheneum
       Forerunner Foray Viking
1974 **Iron Cage** Viking
       The Jargoon Pard Atheneum
       Lavender-Green Magic Crowell
       Outside Walker
1975 **The Day of the Ness** Walker, with Michael Gilbert
       Knave of Dreams Viking
       No Night Without Stars Atheneum
       Merlin's Mirror DAW Books
       The White Jade Fox Dutton
1976 **Star Ka'at** Walker, with Dorothy Madlee
       Red Hart Magic Crowell
       Wraiths of Time Atheneum
       Perilous Dreams DAW Books
1977 **The Opal-Eyed Fan** Dutton
       Velvet Shadows Fawcett
1978 **Star Ka'at World** Walker, with Dorothy Madlee
       Quag Keep Atheneum
       Yurth Burden DAW Books
       Zarsthor's Bane Ace
1979 **Star Ka'ats and the Planet People** Walker, with Dorothy Madlee
       Snow Shadow Fawcett
       Seven Spells to Sunday Atheneum, with Phyllis Miller

1981 **Star Ka'ats and the Winge Warriors** Walker, with Dorothy Madlee
       Ten Mile Treasure Pocket Books
       Voorloper Ace
       Forerunner Pinnacle
       Gryphon in Glory Atheneum
       Horn Crown DAW Books
1982 **Moon Called** Simon and Schuster
       Caroline Pinnacle, with Enid Cushing
1983 **Wheel of Stars** Simon and Schuster
       Lavender-Green Magic Crowell
       'Ware Hawk Atheneum
1984 **House of Shadows** Atheneum, with Phyllis Miller
       Stand and Deliver Dell
       Gryphon's Eyrie Tor, with A.C. Crispin
       Were-Wrath Cheap Street
1985 **Forerunner: The Second Venture** Tor
       Ride the Green Dragon Atheneum, with Phyllis Miller
1986 **Flight in Yiktor** Tor
1987 **The Gate of the Cat** Ace
       Serpent's Tooth Andre Norton Ltd.
1989 **Imperial Lady** Tor, with Susan Shwartz
1990 **The Jekyll Legacy** Tor, with Robert Bloch
       Black Trillium Doubleday, with Marion Zimmer Bradley and Julian May
       Dare to Go A-Hunting Tor
1991 **The Elvenbane** Tor, with Mercedes Lackey
       Storms of Victory Tor, with P.M. Griffin

1992 **Flight of Vengeance** Tor, with P.M. Griffin
       Songsmith Tor, with A.C. Crispin
1993 **Empire of the Eagle** Tor, with Susan Shwartz
       Redline the Stars Tor, with P.M. Griffin
       Golden Trillium Bantam
1994 **Firehand** Tor, with P.M. Griffin
       On Wings of Magic Tor, with Patricia Matthews and Sasha Miller
       The Hands of Llyr Morrow

SHORT STORY COLLECTIONS
1970 **High Sorcery** Ace
1972 **Spell of the Witch World** Ace
1974 **The Many Worlds of Andre Norton** Chilton, retitled **The Book of Andre Norton**
1977 **Trey of Swords** Grosset and Dunlap
1980 **Lore of the Witch World** DAW Books
1988 **Moon Mirror** Tor
1989 **Wizards' Worlds** Tor

SELECTED WORKS AS EDITOR
1953 **Space Service** World
1973 **Gates to Tomorrow: An Introduction to Science Fiction** Atheneum
1985 **Magic in Ithkar** Tor, with Robert Adams, with three further volumes to 1987
1987 **Tales of the Witch World** Tor, with two further volumes to 1990

GORDON R. DICKSON

BORN **1923**

NATIONALITY **American, born in Canada**

KEY WORKS **The *Dorsai* series, *Timestorm*, *Wolf and Iron***

THERE is the case of Hilaire Belloc and G.K. Chesterton, known as Chesterbelloc when working together. And there is the case of Poul Anderson and Gordon R. Dickson, who have never been that close, but who have always been thought of in the same breath. It is a mistake to do so; but it is not a big mistake.

There are, after all, similarities between them. They are of an age; they went to the University of Minnesota together; they began to publish within a few years of one another; they have collaborated; they are northern by residence and northern by inclination, both having a strong predilection for tales that are set in a heroic, Nordic, twilit age; they have both been described as right-wing – although that could hardly be called an unusual

political orientation for American SF writers; they both have difficulty writing about believable women; they are both prolific; they both write what are known as filksongs (songs that resemble folksongs, but which are written within and about the SF community), and both of them may even, on occasion, sing them; and they are both romantics.

On the other hand, Poul Anderson has a love of active and complex communities that Dickson simply does not share, with the result that Anderson's long series are populous with folk, and Dickson's long series – there is only one – is a complex tale of solitudes. While Anderson's Hard SF reads with some discomfort as poetry slightly misplaced, even Dickson's fantasy reads like SF in loose clothing. And Poul Anderson is American; Gordon R. Dickson, although he came south by about the age of 12, is still intrinsically Canadian.

Gordon R. Dickson's early books are mostly Space Operas with thought bumps all over them, and they climax with *The Genetic General*, the first of the *Dorsai* series or **Childe Cycle**: later novels include *Necromancer, Soldier, Ask Not, The Tactics of Mistake, The Final Encyclopedia, Chantry Guild, Young Bleys*, and *Other*, and there are short story collections, too. The whole sequence has turned out to be a kind of albatross around the neck of – and a life's work for – its author. The reason is philosophy. Dickson has developed the concept of "conscious evolution":

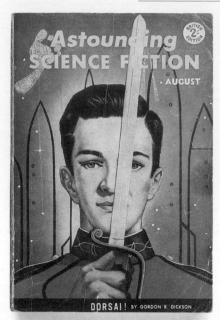

Dorsai! was what Dickson called this adventure when it appeared in magazine form; *The Genetic General* is what Ace Books called their cut version; but *Dorsai!* it became again, and remains. Donal Graeme is the greatest of the Childe figures destined to knit humanity together into one superculture. But *Dorsai!* is a lot more fun than that sounds: it is the classic SF tale of a young man who finds that his powers are greater than anyone dreamed. For humanity's sake, he conquers the world.

DORSAI!

its originality may not be great, but its demands on his creative juices are stupendous, because it demands of him that the *Dorsai* books demonstrate through action plots the slow, conscious coming into being of the complete, ideal human being. This being is a man (Dickson is not much interested in women) who will gather together the different categories of *Homo sapiens*, as they have spread across the planets, and make them into one coordinated species. The hero of the tales is a Dorsai – citizen of a warrior planet – and his task is not made more plausible by the sense

readers sometimes have that his profound intuitions about human nature are essentially strategic. That he makes a good Genetic General, in other words, but not much of a guru.

The rest of Dickson's career – enough books for some writers – has been sidebarred to **Dorsai.** But *Wolf and Iron* may be the best post-catastrophe novel since *Earth Abides* (see page 217) or *A Canticle for Liebowitz* (see page 222).

Gordon R Dickson

BIBLIOGRAPHY

NOVELS AND NOVELLAS
1956 *Alien From Arcturus* Ace, revised as *Arcturus Landing*
1956 *Mankind on the Run* Ace, revised as *On the Run*
1960 *The Genetic General* Ace, revised as *Dorsai!*
 Time to Teleport Ace
 Secret Under the Sea Holt Rinehart
1961 *Naked to the Stars* Pyramid
 Delusion World Ace
 Spacial Delivery Ace
1962 *Necromancer* Doubleday, retitled *No Time for Man*
1963 *Secret Under Antarctica* Holt Rinehart
1964 *Secret Under the Caribbean* Holt Rinehart
1965 *The Alien Way* Bantam
 Mission to Universe Berkley

1967 *The Space Swimmers* Berkley
 Planet Run Doubleday, with Keith Laumer
 Soldier, Ask Not Dell
1969 *None But Man* Doubleday
 Wolfling Dell
 Spacepaw Putnam
1970 *Hour of the Horde* Putnam
1971 *The Tactics of Mistake* Doubleday
 Sleepwalker's World Lippincott
1972 *The Outposter* Lippincott
 The Pritcher Mass Doubleday
1973 *Alien Art* Dutton
 The R-Master Lippincott, revised as *The Last Master*
1974 *Gremlins, Go Home!* St. Martin's Press, with Ben Bova
1975 *Star Prince Charlie* Putnam, with Poul Anderson
1976 *The Dragon and the George* Doubleday

1976 *The Lifeship* Harper, with Harry Harrison, retitled *Lifeboat*
1977 *Timestorm* St. Martin's Press
1978 *The Far Call* Dial Press
 Home from the Shore Sunridge Press
 Pro Ace
1980 *Masters of Everon* Doubleday
1984 *Jamie the Red* Ace, with Roland Green
 The Final Encyclopedia Tor
1986 *The Forever Man* Ace
1987 *Way of the Pilgrim* Ace
1988 *Chantry Guild* Ace
1989 *The Earth Lords* Ace
1990 *The Dragon Knight* Tor
 Wolf and Iron Tor
1991 *Young Bleys* Tor
1992 *The Dragon on the Border* Ace
1993 *The Dragon at War* Ace
1994 *Other* Tor

SHORT STORY COLLECTIONS
1957 *Earthman's Burden* Gnome Press, with Poul Anderson
1970 *Danger – Human* Doubleday, retitled *The Book of Gordon Dickson*
 Mutants Macmillan
1973 *The Star Road* Doubleday
1974 *Ancient, My Enemy* Doubleday
1978 *Gordon R. Dickson's SF Best* Dell, revised as *In the Bone*
1979 *The Spirit of Dorsai* Ace
1980 *Lost Dorsai* Ace
 In Iron Years Doubleday
1981 *Love Not Human* Ace
1983 *Hoka!* Simon and Schuster, with Poul Anderson
 The Man From Earth Baen
1984 *Survival!* Baen
 Dickson! NESFA Press, revised as *Steel Brother*

1985 *Beyond the Dar al-Harb* Tor
 Forward! Baen
 Invaders! Baen
1986 *The Last Dream* Baen
 The Dorsai Companion Ace
 The Man The Worlds Rejected Baen
 Mindspan Baen
1987 *Stranger* Tor
1988 *Beginnings* Baen
 Ends Baen
 Guided Tour Tor

SELECTED WORKS AS EDITOR
1975 *Combat SF* Doubleday
1978 *Nebula Winners Twelve* Harper
1991 *The Harriers* Baen
1993 *The Harriers, Book 2: Blood and Honor* Baen

KURT VONNEGUT

BORN **1922**

NATIONALITY **American**

KEY WORKS **The Sirens of Titan, Canary in a Cat House, Slaughterhouse-Five, Galápagos**

IT is such a famous fact about Kurt Vonnegut, and it is such an extraordinary thing to have happened to a man who had the gift of words to tell us the story afterwards, that it seems almost too neat, too meant, to be true. But it is true: Kurt Vonnegut was an American soldier during World War II, and he was captured by the Germans, and he was being held as a prisoner of war in Dresden when the Allies firebombed it, killing a number of people as yet unknown (120,000 is a guess) and incinerating the city. Vonnegut was one of the very few survivors of the Dresden firestorm.

Ever since, like some Ishmael with St. Vitus's Dance, he has been telling us what the 20th century has come to.

Kurt Vonnegut is also one of the funniest writers in the world, and with the exception of John T. Sladek – who began some time after Vonnegut but then fell silent as a comic writer after only a decade or so – he is the only genuinely and instinctively funny writer to concentrate on SF. But here is a ticklish point. Vonnegut has always been touchy about being associated with the genre, and although he is clearly sympathetic with SF writers' attempts to face the real world, he clearly thinks, at the same time, that much of what appears under the banner of SF is garbage. So it is not necessarily either a favour or a compliment to call him an SF writer.

On the other hand, it is necessary to claim Vonnegut. It is only critics from outside the genre who fail to recognize that a speculative novel that is set in the future and concerned with the fate of the human race is quite clearly and obviously SF, even if it has been written by a funny man who has establishment credentials. Vonnegut's first novel, *Player Piano*, is just one distinguished example in a long line of dystopian visions that were drawn from the new, industrialized, conformist, post-World-War-II world order.

BIBLIOGRAPHY

NOVELS AND NOVELLAS
1952 *Player Piano; or Utopia 14* Scribners
1959 *The Sirens of Titan* Dell
1962 *Mother Night* Fawcett
1963 *Cat's Cradle* Holt Rinehart
1965 *God Bless You, Mr. Rosewater, or Pearls Before Swine* Delacorte Press
1969 *Slaughterhouse-Five, or The Children's Crusade: A Duty-Dance with Death* Delacorte Press
1973 *Breakfast of Champions, or Goodbye, Blue Monday* Delacorte Press
1976 *Slapstick, or Lonesome No More!* Delacorte Press
1979 *Jailbird* Delacorte Press
1982 *Dead-Eye Dick* Delacorte Press
1985 *Galápagos* Delacorte Press

1987 *Bluebeard* Delacorte Press
1990 *Hocus Pocus* Putnam

SHORT STORY COLLECTIONS
1961 *Canary in a Cat House* Fawcett
1968 *Welcome to the Monkey House* Delacorte Press

NON-FICTION
1974 *Wampeters, Foma and Ganfalloons: Opinions* Delacorte Press
1981 *Palm Sunday: An Autobiographical Collage* Delacorte Press
1991 *Fates Worse Than Death: An Autobiographical Collage of the 1980s* Putnam

The target of the novel – automation – precisely prefigures the targets that would be chosen by Sladek, whose exuberantly black and surreal comedies often resemble Vonnegut's. Both authors are typical of a particular brand of humorist, in that they tend to see human beings as intractable, self-fuelled, alien creatures. Robots, and Martians, and folk back home, for Vonnegut, are all equally strange, equally obsessed.

His next novel, which appeared after a gap of some years, was *The Sirens of Titan* (see page 221). It hilariously mocks an old SF plot, the one in which an ancient race (like the Arisians that figure in E.E. Smith's **Lensmen** series) uplifts humanity over the centuries so that we can take on our heavy galactic responsibilities. Unfortunately, the Tralfamadorians have raised humans from the mire in order that we may produce a replacement part for a stranded spaceship on Titan containing a robot courier, whose message has been waiting to be delivered for some fifty thousand years. The message turns out to be "Greetings."

Cat's Cradle and *God Bless You, Mr. Rosewater* both continue the assault, continue to analyze the gap between what humans say they are doing and what, in fact, they actually do with themselves. Wacky gurus and melancholy women proliferate here.

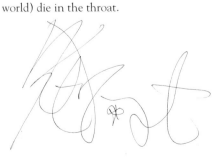

Ruined city
The firebombing of Dresden left it in ruins for years after the war ended.

Mother Night, which is not SF, is a terribly bleak look at a Nazi sympathizer; it is unusual among Vonnegut's novels, not for being downbeat, for Vonnegut's particular brand of cheer has always teetered right at the edge of the abyss, but because it offers us absolutely no disguise for the abyss, no antic posturing, and no jokes to give us any cover.

With his next novel, *Slaughterhouse-Five* (see page 225), Vonnegut faced his Dresden, and brought back the news. His protagonist, Billy Pilgrim, finds it impossible to go on living in the world that gave him the firestorm to remember, and sails off through both space and time with the alien Tralfamadorians.

Galápagos, set long after the holocaust, also plays with time, as though playing with time were a way to dodge the fire. And *Hocus Pocus*, which extrapolates today's America into 2001 and is the saddest of all Vonnegut's works, tells some jokes, but lets them (and the world) die in the throat.

NOTABLE WORK

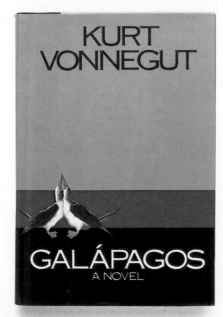

GALÁPAGOS

Kilgore Trout, who is based on Theodore Sturgeon, appears throughout Vonnegut's work. He is a hack writer, but speaks the truth, out of the side of his mouth, when his foot is not in it. Here the ghost of his son looks back over a million years of human life on Galápagos – Darwin's forcing-house of evolution – where survivors settled and evolved after a plague in the 20th century. What they become – flippered seaweed-eaters who have lost most of their marbles – seems better than dying. Maybe.

POUL ANDERSON

BORN 1926

NATIONALITY American

KEY WORKS The Technic History series, Brain Wave, Tau Zero, The Boat of a Million Years

POUL Anderson has written one or two bad books in his time, but then, he can afford to. Since beginning to publish his stories in 1947, he has hardly stopped: almost every year has seen a book or two or more appear, running to a current total of at least 65 novels, and hundreds of short stories – but that is not the real point. Other authors can claim to have been at least as prolific, but there is no other SF author who has produced as much high-quality work, with such variety, and with such continued verve, for anything approaching the half century of constant endeavour that Anderson can boast. He has won all of the major awards, most of them more than once. He is central to the SF field, although sometimes – this is the downside of reliability – he tends to be taken for granted. He should not be.

The majority of Poul Anderson's books make up parts of various series, the most important of these being two nominally separate sequences – the **Psychotechnic League** books and the **Dominic Flandry** books – which when read together comprise a long, loose, remarkably varied Future History (see page 66), whose overall title is the **Technic History**. The best of the **Psychotechnic** books, all of them featuring a fat Rabelaisian trader to the stars called Nicholas van Rijn, include *Mirkheim* and *The Earth Book of Stormgate*. The best **Flandry** books include *Ensign Flandry*, *The Day of Their Return*, and *A Knight of Ghosts and Shadows*. These books are rich, moody, character-filled, action-packed, twilit, and windblown: they are filled with the romance, and the darkness, of our dreams of space.

Among Anderson's many non-series novels, most of his important work has been in the SF field, but he has also written both detective and historical novels, and several significant fantasies, including *The Broken Sword, Three Hearts and Three Lions*, and the sequel, *A Midsummer Tempest*. On the SF side, the high points span all five decades of Anderson's career. One of his first novels, *Brain Wave* (see page 220) is famous, as is *The High Crusade*, in which a troupe of medieval knights, hijacked by aliens, takes over a new world. *Tau Zero* is an enthralling tour to the end of the universe and beyond. Among his later works, *The Boat of a Million Years* takes a long and jaundiced look at Earth's history, as seen through the eyes of a cadre of immortals, and *Harvest of Stars* faces some of the consequences brought to the world as a result of unbridled progress, eventually sending its protagonists elsewhere, to start again. Each of these books is different, but all of them share a sweeping, and sometimes melancholy, intoxication with the future, where the dreams come to rest.

Magazine publications
Anderson's stories appeared in magazines ranging from Astounding to Fantasy and Science Fiction. His novella The Makeshift Rocket *was originally titled "A Bicycle Built for Brew" and an* Astounding *cover story.*

BIBLIOGRAPHY

NOVELS AND NOVELLAS
1952 **Vault of the Ages** Winston
1954 **The Broken Sword** Abelard Schuman, revised 1971
Brain Wave Ballantine
1955 **No World of their Own** Ace, retitled **The Long Way Home**
1956 **Star Ways** Avalon, retitled **The Peregrine**
1957 **Planet of No Return** Ace, retitled **Question and Answer**
1958 **The Snows of Ganymede** Ace
War of the Wing-Men Ace, retitled **The Man Who Counts**
1959 **Virgin Planet** Avalon
The War of Two Worlds Ace
We Claim These Stars Ace
The Enemy Stars Lippincott
1960 **The High Crusade** Doubleday
Earthman, Go Home! Ace
1961 **Twilight World** Torquil
Mayday Orbit Ace
Three Hearts and Three Lions Doubleday
1962 **After Doomsday** Ballantine
The Makeshift Rocket Ace
1963 **Let the Spacemen Beware!** Ace, retitled **The Night Face**
1964 **Three Worlds to Conquer** Pyramid

1965 **Agent of the Terran Empire** Chilton
The Corridors of Time Doubleday
Flandry of Terra Chilton
The Star Fox Doubleday
1966 **Ensign Flandry** Chilton
The Fox, the Dog, and the Griffin Doubleday
World Without Stars Ace
1969 **The Rebel Worlds** NAL, retitled **Commander Flandry**
Satan's World Doubleday
1970 **A Circus of Hells** NAL
Tau Zero Doubleday
1971 **The Byworlder** NAL
The Dancer from Atlantis NAL
Operation Chaos Doubleday
1972 **There Will be Time** Doubleday
1973 **Hrolf Kraki's Saga** Ballantine
The People of the Wind NAL
1974 **The Day of Their Return** Doubleday
Inheritors of Earth Chilton, with Gordon Eklund
Fire Time Doubleday
A Midsummer Tempest Doubleday
A Knight of Ghosts and Shadows Doubleday, retitled **Knight Flandry**

1975 **Star Prince Charlie** Putnam, with Gordon R. Dickson
The Winter of the World Doubleday
1977 **Mirkheim** Berkley
1978 **The Avatar** Berkley
1979 **The Merman's Children** Berkley
A Stone in Heaven Ace
The Demon of Scattery Ace, with Mildred Downey Broxon
1980 **Conan the Rebel** Bantam
The Devil's Game Pocket Books
1983 **Time Patrolman** Tor
1984 **Orion Shall Rise** Phantasia
1985 **The Game of Empire** Tor
1986 **The King of Ys: Roma Mater** Baen, with Karen Anderson
1987 **The King of Ys: Gallicenae** Baen, with Karen Anderson
1988 **The King of Ys: Dahut** Baen, with Karen Anderson
The King of Ys: The Dog and the Wolf Baen, with Karen Anderson
The Year of the Ransom Walker
1989 **The Boat of a Million Years** Tor
The Saturn Game Tor
1991 **The Longest Voyage** Tor
1993 **Harvest of Stars** Tor

SHORT STORY COLLECTIONS
1957 **Earthman's Burden** Gnome Press, with Gordon R. Dickson
1960 **Guardians of Time** Ballantine
1961 **Strangers from Earth** Ballantine
Orbit Unlimited Pyramid
1962 **Un-Man** Ace
1964 **Time and Stars** Doubleday
Trader to the Stars Doubleday
1965 **Agent of the Terran Empire** Chilton
1966 **The Trouble Twisters** Doubleday
1968 **The Horn of Time** NAL
1969 **Beyond the Beyond** NAL
Seven Conquests Macmillan
1970 **Tales of the Flying Mountains** Macmillan
1973 **The Queen of Air and Darkness** Doubleday
1974 **The Many Worlds of Poul Anderson** Chilton, retitled **The Book of Poul Anderson**
1975 **Homeward and Beyond** Doubleday
1976 **Homebrew** NESFA Press
The Best of Poul Anderson Pocket Books
1978 **The Earth Book of Stormgate** Berkley

1979 **The Night Face and Other Stories** Gregg Press
1981 **The Psychotechnic League** Pinnacle
The Dark Between the Stars Berkley
Fantasy Pinnacle
Explorations Pinnacle
Winners Pinnacle
1982 **Cold Victory** Tor
Maurai and Kith Tor
The Gods Laughed Pinnacle
Starship Tor
New America Tor
1983 **Hoka!** Simon and Schuster, with Gordon R. Dickson
The Long Night Tor
Conflict Tor
The Unicorn Trade Baen, with Karen Anderson
1984 **Past Times** Tor
Dialogue With Darkness Tor
1989 **Space Folk** Baen
1991 **Alight in the Void** Tor
Kinship with the Stars Tor
1992 **The Armies of Elfland** Tor

ROBERT SHECKLEY

BORN **1926**

NATIONALITY
American

KEY WORKS
**Untouched by
Human Hands,
The Status
Civilization**

BIBLIOGRAPHY

NOVELS AND NOVELLAS
1958 **Immortality Delivered** Avalon, retitled
　　Immortality Inc.
1960 **The Status Civilization** NAL
1962 **Journey Beyond Tomorrow** NAL, retitled
　　Journey of Joenes
1966 **The 10th Victim** Ballantine
　　Mindswap Delacorte
1968 **Dimension of Miracles** Dell
1975 **Options** Pyramid
1978 **The Alchemical Marriage of Alistair
　　Crompton** Michael Joseph, retitled
　　Crompton Divided
1983 **Dramocles** Holt Rinehart
1987 **Victim Prime** Methuen

1988 **Hunter/Victim** NAL
1990 **Bill, the Galactic Hero On the Planet of
　　Bottled Brains** Avon, with Harry Harrison
　　Alien Starswarm Dime Novels
　　Minotaur Maze Axolotl Press
1991 **Bring Me the Head of Prince Charming**
　　Bantam, with Roger Zelazny
1993 **If at Faust You Don't Succeed** Bantam, with
　　Roger Zelazny

SHORT STORY COLLECTIONS
1954 **Untouched by Human Hands** Ballantine
1955 **Citizen in Space** Ballantine
1957 **Pilgrimage to Earth** Bantam
1960 **Store of Infinity** Bantam

1960 **Notions: Unlimited** Bantam
1962 **Shards of Space** Bantam
1968 **The People Trap** Bantam
1971 **Can You Feel Anything When I Do
　　This?** Doubleday, retitled **The Same
　　to You Doubled**
1973 **The Robert Sheckley Omnibus** Gollancz
1978 **The Robot Who Looked Like Me** Sphere
1979 **The Wonderful World of Robert
　　Sheckley** Bantam
1984 **Is THAT What People Do?** Holt Rinehart
1991 **The Collected Short Stories of Robert
　　Sheckley** Pulphouse, in five volumes

FOR two reasons, Robert Sheckley has been thought of as a writer's writer: he tends to write short stories in preference to novels, which means he has taken the hard, craftsman's course to fame; and he writes funny, which is the hardest, the most dedicated, and sometimes the grimmest task an author can face. He began in the halcyon days of the 1950s, a time in SF when a whole herd of sacred cows had been grazing unmolested for much too long. In collections of stories like *Untouched by Human Hands* (which remains his best-known book) he spoofed the SF versions of the world of tomorrow, their heroes and heroines, their aliens and beasts. In novels like *The Status Civilization* (uneasily rivetted together, but full of verve) he targeted the huge gaps that yawn between our ideals of the good society that we want to see and the realities of hierarchy that we create and live with.

Sheckley's later career has been less happy. With the passing years, his comic satires have come to seem nostalgic rather than attacking, consoling rather than disconcerting.

Robert Sheckley

ALGIS BUDRYS

BORN **1931**

NATIONALITY **American, born
in Lithuania**

KEY WORKS **Who?, The Falling Torch,
Rogue Moon**

BUDRYS is a congenial, sociable man in public; his friends are many. He faintly resembles Michaelmas, the quiet, portly, and deeply intelligent reporter in the novel that takes his name, and who is revealed to be the secret, compassionate ruler of the world. But there is another side to Algis Budrys, which comes out in novels such as *Who?* and *The Falling Torch* and *Rogue Moon*. These are austere, intricate, bleak tales, in which the obsessed, solitary heroes tackle metaphysical and political problems of the darkest hue, and triumph only ambiguously. *Rogue Moon* is the greatest of these: the plot concerns an alien artefact on the Moon, being explored by teleported doppelgangers of the riven and suicidal Al Barker back on Earth; each of the doubles is killed in turn. Finally, Barker himself teleports to the Moon, where he faces inextricable dilemmas as to the nature his own selfhood, and ultimately he commits suicide.

Budrys was at his creative peak in the 1950s, and in recent years has spent some of his considerable energy as an influential SF book reviewer. Controversially, he has also edited a series of original anthologies that was indirectly connected to the Church of Scientology: but many of the stories that he selected for this, all by new authors, were excellent.

BIBLIOGRAPHY

NOVELS AND NOVELLAS
1954 **False Night** Lion,
　　retitled **Some Will Not Die**
1958 **Man of Earth** Ballantine
　　Who? Pyramid
1959 **The Falling Torch** Pyramid
1960 **Rogue Moon** Fawcett
1967 **The Amsirs and the Iron Thorn** Fawcett,
　　retitled **The Iron Thorn**
1977 **Michaelmas** Berkley
1993 **Hard Landing** Bantam

SHORT STORY COLLECTIONS
1960 **The Unexpected Dimension** Ballantine
1963 **Budrys' Inferno** Berkley, retitled
　　The Furious Future
1978 **Blood and Burning** Berkley

NON-FICTION
1983 **Non-Literary Influences on Science Fiction**
　　Borgo Press
1985 **Benchmarks: Galaxy Bookshelf** Southern
　　Illinois University Press

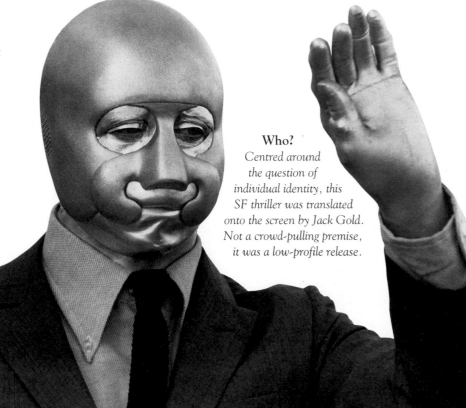

Who?
*Centred around
the question of
individual identity, this
SF thriller was translated
onto the screen by Jack Gold.
Not a crowd-pulling premise,
it was a low-profile release.*

1960-1964: ON THE CUSP

DECADES HAVE A TREMENDOUS significance to the human mind: they are much more than a measure of time, they are an indicator of change. It is certainly true that, as the 1960s dawned, there was, to the minds of SF writers and readers, a sense of change in the air. There was a stretching and shifting of boundaries, and a loosening of ties. Now that Sputnik was beginning to sink in, the consequences could be imagined; at first nobody realized that it was to spell an

1960

NOTABLE WORKS

New Maps of Hell
KINGSLEY AMIS

Rogue Moon
ALGIS BUDRYS

The Genetic General
GORDON R. DICKSON

Flesh
PHILIP JOSÉ FARMER

Facial Justice
L.P. HARTLEY

The Child Buyer
JOHN HERSEY

The Weans
ROBERT NATHAN

Drunkard's Walk
FREDERIK POHL

The Status Civilization
ROBERT SHECKLEY

Venus Plus X
THEODORE STURGEON

VENUS PLUS X

ICONS

Children as *Homo superior* appear again and again in SF, and can be seen in two ways. They may grow up to dominate the world, as in *The Genetic General*, the first book in the *Dorsai* series. This is the more traditional presentation; another, rather more cynical view is that they will be the victims of their own powers, the argument of *The Child Buyer*, in which prodigies are bought and sold.

DEBUTS

Ben Bova makes his debut with "A Long Way Back" in *Astounding* magazine and **R. A. Lafferty** debuts with "Day of the Glacier" in *Science Fiction* magazine. First SF novels include *Les fleurs de Vénus* [Flowers of Venus] by Philippe Curval, *The Man with Nine Lives*, by Harlan Ellison, and *Deathworld* by Harry Harrison.

1961

NOTABLE WORKS

The Lovers
PHILIP JOSÉ FARMER

Dark Universe
DANIEL F. GALOUYE

The Stainless Steel Rat
HARRY HARRISON

Stranger in a Strange Land
ROBERT A. HEINLEIN

The Big Time
FRITZ LEIBER

DARK UNIVERSE

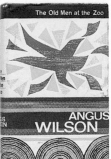

THE OLD MEN AT THE ZOO

Solaris
STANISŁAW LEM

Some of Your Blood
THEODORE STURGEON

The Old Men at the Zoo
ANGUS WILSON

ICONS

It is a sign of the new decade that Philip José Farmer can publish, in **The Lovers**, the expansion of a 1952 story that previously generated much commotion. A human on an alien planet falls in love with a native insectoid female, whose pregnancy causes her death. Intricately plausible aliens are more often found from now on.

DEBUTS

First SF novels of interest include Marion Zimmer Bradley's *The Door Through Space*, A. Bertram Chandler's *The Rim of Space*, Herbert Franke's *Der Orchideenkäfig* (*The Orchid Cage*), and Angus Wilson's *The Old Men at the Zoo*. Fred Saberhagen debuts with "Volume Paa-Pyx" in *Galaxy* magazine.

19

NOTABLE WORKS

Hothouse
BRIAN ALDISS

The Drowned World
J.G. BALLARD

A Clockwork Orange
ANTHONY BURGESS

The Jewels of Aptor
SAMUEL R. DELANY

The Ebb Tide of Space
PHILIPPE CURVAL

THE EBB TIDE OF SPACE

ICONS

Parallel and Alternate Worlds have been around in SF since the 1930s, and this year sees two quite different takes on the theme. *Worlds of the Imperium* begins a trilogy set in Parallel Worlds that must constantly be alert to keep themselves stable, while *The Man in the High Castle* is one of the most celebrated books to look at a Hitler victory.

DEBUTS

Significant debuts include Burgess's *A Clockwork Orange*, Delany's *The Jewels of Aptor*, and Moore and Davidson's collaborative *Joyleg*. Other debuts in this year are J.G. Ballard's *The Wind from Nowhere*, H.B. Fyfe's *D-99*, Arthur Sellings's *The Silent Speakers*, Evelyn E. Smith's *The Perfumed Planet*, Peter van Greenaway's *The Crucified City*, and, in France, *Babel 3805* from **Pierre Barbet**. Writers making

end as well as a beginning. In 1960 it began – although not quite as precipitately as it might have seemed at the time – to look as though SF were at the cusp of becoming the true literature of the late 20th century. The childhood and adolescence of the American genre had passed, and after many squabbles and triumphs, SF appeared, finally, to have grown up. It was the right time to bestow a major literature of change upon the world, and to change that world.

6 2   1 9 6 3   1 9 6 4

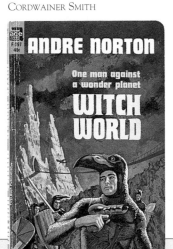

JOYLEG

The Man in the High Castle
PHILIP K. DICK

Worlds of the Imperium
KEITH LAUMER

A Wrinkle in Time
MADELEINE L'ENGLE

Joyleg
WARD MOORE AND
AVRAM DAVIDSON

A Trace of Memory
KEITH LAUMER

Witch World
ANDRE NORTON

Way Station
CLIFFORD D. SIMAK

You Will Never Be the Same
CORDWAINER SMITH

WITCH WORLD

GABRIEL

Gabriel
DOMINGO SANTOS

The Man Who Fell to Earth
WALTER TEVIS

Cat's Cradle
KURT VONNEGUT

The Mile-Long Spaceship
KATE WILHELM

Greybeard
BRIAN ALDISS

The Burning World
J.G. BALLARD

The Whole Man
JOHN BRUNNER

Nova Express
WILLIAM S. BURROUGHS

Martian Time-Slip
PHILIP K. DICK

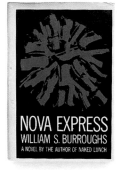

NOVA EXPRESS

The Penultimate Truth
PHILIP K. DICK

Farnham's Freehold
ROBERT A. HEINLEIN

The Wanderer
FRITZ LEIBER

The Invincible
STANISŁAW LEM

Hard to be a God
ARKADY AND BORIS STRUGATSKI

THE WANDERER

From paranoia to alienation is a short trip, but a profound one. The mental state of paranoia – at least in SF films and books – is usually justified by the sight of a real enemy. Alienation has no enemy but the self, because the enemy has triumphed, and is long gone. In Walter Tevis's *The Man Who Fell to Earth*, our planet is the existential abyss for an alien who comes to arrange asylum for his dying race, but finds man's response to him impossible to bear.

SF in Britain changes direction: the principal British magazine, *New Worlds*, reflects the shift, and in *The Burning World*, J.G. Ballard provides the first masterpiece of what could be called British post-genre SF. In this vision, Earth has become an alien planet, and SF has become a form of historical fiction.

debuts in *Fantastic* magazine include Thomas M. Disch with "The Double-Timer" and Ursula K. Le Guin with "April in Paris".

Two first collections from important new short-story writers are published: Cordwainer Smith's *You Will Never Be the Same*, and Kate Wilhelm's **The Mile-Long Spaceship**. Debut SF novels include Dean McLaughlin's *The Fury from Earth*, and Terry Carr's *Warlord of Kor*. Debuts in magazines include Alexei Panshin's "Down to the Worlds of Men" in *If*, and Piers Anthony's short story "Possible to Rue" in *Fantastic*. "Lullaby 1990", a poem by Sheri S. Tepper, appears in *Galaxy*.

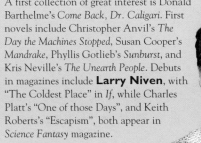

A first collection of great interest is Donald Barthelme's *Come Back, Dr. Caligari*. First novels include Christopher Anvil's *The Day the Machines Stopped*, Susan Cooper's *Mandrake*, Phyllis Gotlieb's *Sunburst*, and Kris Neville's *The Unearth People*. Debuts in magazines include **Larry Niven**, with "The Coldest Place" in *If*, while Charles Platt's "One of those Days", and Keith Roberts's "Escapism", both appear in *Science Fantasy* magazine.

1965-1969: THE FUTURE IS NOW

IT WAS ONLY NOW, in the late 1960s, that the implications of Sputnik and the ensuing space race began to filter through the whole of the SF genre. Only now did writers and readers begin to understand that the future could no longer be imagined as an easy jump away: the future was right here and now, and it was not easy, it was a great deal more difficult than expected. It turned out that near-space was merely a continuation of human history here on Earth,

1 9 6 5

NOTABLE WORKS

Earthworks
BRIAN ALDISS

Masters of the Maze
AVRAM DAVIDSON

Dr. Bloodmoney
PHILIP K. DICK

Elidor
ALAN GARNER

Dune
FRANK HERBERT

MASTERS OF THE MAZE

The Three Stigmata of Palmer Eldritch
PHILIP K. DICK

A Plague of Demons
KEITH LAUMER

Cyberiad
STANISŁAW LEM

CYBERIAD

ICONS

As we begin to understand the huge complexities of Mother Earth more fully, the visualization of other planets becomes correspondingly a more challenging and arduous task. Frank Herbert's dune-planet of **Arrakis** is intricately and massively constructed on an extrapolated model of the desert climates of Earth. Unsurprisingly, the more care it takes to construct a world, the more its creators care for the result: this is a loved planet.

DEBUTS

First SF novels include William R. Burkett's *Sleeping Planet*, Hortense Calisher's *Journel from Ellipsia*, D.G. Compton's *The Quality of Mercy*, Thomas M. Disch's *The Genocides*, G.C. Edmondson's *The Ship That Sailed the Time Stream*, and **Michael Moorcock**'s *The Sundered Worlds*. Magazine debuts include Gregory Benford's "Stand-In" in *Fantasy and Science Fiction*, Brian Stableford's "Beyond Time's Aegis" in *Science Fantasy*, written with Craig A. Mackintosh, Vernor Vinge's "Apartness" in *New Worlds*, and Gene Wolfe's "The Dead Man" in *Sir*.

1 9 6 6

NOTABLE WORKS

The Crystal World
J.G. BALLARD

Giles Goat-Boy
JOHN BARTH

Babel-17
SAMUEL R. DELANY

Make Room! Make Room!
HARRY HARRISON

The Moon is a Harsh Mistress
ROBERT A. HEINLEIN

Flowers for Algernon
DANIEL KEYES

Earthfasts
WILLIAM MAYNE

World of Ptavvs
LARRY NIVEN

The Watch Below
JAMES WHITE

The Dream Master
ROGER ZELAZNY

This Immortal
ROGER ZELAZNY

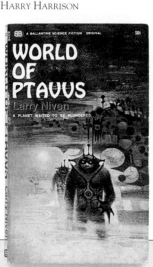

WORLD OF PTAVVS

ICONS

The year is dominated by complex views into the human interior, with Delany's examination of language, Keyes's unflinching take on intelligence, and Zelazny's baroque visualizations of psychology and mortality. Going against this stream, Niven's *World of Ptavvs* posts to the board an exuberant new agenda for humanity.

DEBUTS

John Barth's *Giles Goat-Boy* is among the year's debut novels, as are E.L. Doctorow's *Big as Life*, Ursula K. Le Guin's *Rocannon's World*, Keith Roberts's *The Furies*, Norman Spinrad's *The Solarians*, and Roger Zelazny's *This Immortal*. Magazine debuts include Gardner Dozois with "The Empty Man" in *If*, Doris Piserchia with "Rocket to Gehenna" in *Amazing*, and Christopher Priest with "The Run" in *Impulse*.

1 9

NOTABLE WORKS

Chthon
PIERS ANTHONY

The Einstein Intersection
SAMUEL R. DELANY

Ice
ANNA KAVAN

Berserker
FRED SABERHAGEN

Thorns
ROBERT SILVERBERG

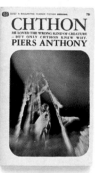

CHTHON

ICONS

Several of this year's major new works – most notably *The Einstein Intersection*, which went on to win a Nebula Award, and *Thorns*, a stylized novel of alienation and psychic vampirism – respond to the new intricacies of the unfolding worlds of SF with plots that see reality as a labyrinth,

DEBUTS

First SF novels include Piers Anthony's *Chthon*, Richard Cowper's *Breakthrough*, Mark Geston's *Lords of the Starship*, Anne McCaffrey's *Restoree*, Mike Resnick's *The Goddess of Ganymede*, and Ian Wallace's *Croyd*. Magazine debuts include Greg Bear with "Destroyers" in

and there were no answers or panaceas up there in orbit, just further opportunities for real men and women to act well and badly, exactly as they had always done below. What SF writers began to sense, too, was that – now that near-space was a part of history – it was going to be a great deal harder to convince the reader that the radiant future could be simply leaped into. It could not, and it cannot, and SF began to feel older for realizing it.

67 · 1968 · 1969

THORNS

Dumarest 1: The Winds of Gath
E.C. TUBB

The Last Castle
JACK VANCE

The Moon is a Harsh Mistress
ROBERT A. HEINLEIN

Lord of Light
ROGER ZELAZNY

Stand on Zanzibar
JOHN BRUNNER

The Weathermonger
PETER DICKINSON

Camp Concentration
THOMAS M. DISCH

The Final Programme
MICHAEL MOORCOCK

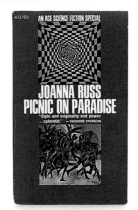

PICNIC ON PARADISE

FAR RAINBOW/THE SECOND INVASION

Rite of Passage
ALEXEI PANSHIN

Pavane
KEITH ROBERTS

Picnic on Paradise
JOANNA RUSS

Hawksbill Station
ROBERT SILVERBERG

Far Rainbow/The Second Invasion from Mars
ARKADY AND BORIS STRUGATSKI

Barefoot in the Head
BRIAN ALDISS

Macroscope
PIERS ANTHONY

The Jagged Orbit
JOHN BRUNNER

Heroes & Villains
ANGELA CARTER

Ubik
PHILIP K. DICK

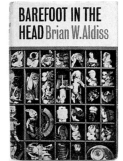

BAREFOOT IN THE HEAD

The War for the Lot
STERLING LANIER

The Left Hand of Darkness
URSULA K. LE GUIN

Nightwings
ROBERT SILVERBERG

Bug Jack Barron
NORMAN SPINRAD

Slaughterhouse-Five
KURT VONNEGUT

THE JAGGED ORBIT

constantly doubling back upon itself. Religion is seen as a twist of this labyrinth of reality. This is reflected in two books in particular: both *The Einstein Intersection,* and *Lord of Light,* which won a Hugo Award, involve humanity's reinvention of itself in the images of gods.

Significant works are written in a number of sub-genres this year. One of the most notable is *Stand on Zanzibar,* which picks up the overpopulation theme of Harry Harrison's *Make Room! Make Room!* from 1966 and takes it to a logical, and terrifying, conclusion.

By the end of the 1960s, the long refusal of American SF to attempt to cope with gender issues – its refusal, in effect, to incorporate half the human race into its model of the human being of the future – had become deeply embarrassing. But Joanna Russ's *Picnic on Paradise* from 1968 had featured a female protagonist whose heroics simply occurred, without any reference to her gender, and this year, Ursula K. Le Guin, in *The Left Hand of Darkness,* calmly rewrites the terms in which gender is understood.

NOTABLE AUTHOR

SF in Britain never lacked toughness but, in 1968, when M. John Harrison published "Baa Baa Blocksheep" in *New Worlds* magazine, a new tone of obduracy could be heard. He was obsessed by entropy, metaphors of empire loss, and other New Wave themes; and he quarried away at these topics until they became chiselled images of the real world.

M. JOHN HARRISON

Famous Science Fiction, Dean R. Koontz with "Soft Come the Dragons" in *Fantasy and Science Fiction,* and Barry N. Malzberg with "We're Coming Through the Window" in *Galaxy.*

Among the notable books Joanna Russ's and Peter Dickinson's are debuts. Others include John Boyd's *The Last Starship from Earth,* Dean R. Koontz's *Star Quest,* Ron Goulart's *The Sword Swallower,* Bob Shaw's *The Two-Timers,* and John T. Sladek's *The Reproductive System.* Magazine debuts include Robert Holdstock's "Pauper's Plot" in *New Worlds,* and James Tiptree Jr.'s "Birth of a Salesman" in *Astounding.*

Wyman Guin's *The Standing Joy,* Angela Carter's *Heroes & Villains,* Brian Stableford's *Cradle of the Sun,* Michael Crichton's *The Andromeda Strain,* Vernor Vinge's **Grimm's World,** and David S. Garnett's *Mirror in the Sky,* are all debut SF novels. Magazine debuts include Joe Haldeman's "Out of Phase" in *Galaxy* and Ian Watson's "Roof Garden under Saturn" in *New Worlds.*

STANISŁAW LEM

BORN **1921**

NATIONALITY **Polish**

KEY WORKS *Solaris, Opowieści o pilocie Pirx, Cyberiada*

Sometimes it seems easy enough to understand SF: there are dreams of the future, and there are adventures to be told there. Simple. But there, over in left field, we notice Stanisław Lem, and he is staring back at us: stumpy, surly, ferociously intelligent, deeply contemptuous of almost any American SF novel ever written, and probably the best (and certainly the most famous) single SF author of the late 20th century not to write in English. You are all talking nonsense, he says (in Polish), let me show you how to do it.

It cannot be denied that he has a point. Much English-language SF is all too closely tied to entertainment values, and is much too obedient to the "laws" of the genre. Lem has been arguing for over four decades, both in his theoretical works and in his own

BIBLIOGRAPHY

NOVELS, NOVELLAS, AND SHORT STORIES

1951 *Astronauci* Czytelnik [The astronauts]
1955 *Obłok Magellana* Iskry [The Magellan nebula]
Sezam Iskry [Sesame]
1957 *Szpital Przemienienia* Wydawnictwo Literackie, translated as **The Hospital of the Transfiguration**
1959 *Śledztwo* Ministerstwo Obrony Narodowej, translated as **The Investigation**
Eden Iskry, translated as **Eden**
Inwazja z Aldebarana Ministerstwo Obrony Narodowej [Invasion from Aldebaran]
1961 *Powrót z gwiazd* Czytelnik, translated as **Return from the Stars**
Pamiętnik znaleziony w wannie Wydawnictwo Literackie, translated as **Memoirs Found in a Bathtub**
Solaris Ministerstwo Obrony Narodowej, translated as **Solaris**
1964 *Niezwyciężony i inne opowiadania* Ministerstwo Obrony Narodowej, translated as **The Invincible**
1965 *Cyberiada* Ministerstwo Obrony Narodowej, translated as **Cyberiad**
1966 *Wysoki Zamek* Ministerstwo Obrony Narodowej [The high castle]
1968 *Opowieści o pilocie Pirxie* Wydawnictwo Literackie, translated as **Tales of Pirx the Pilot** and **More Tales of Pirx the Pilot**

1966 *Głos pana* Czytelnik, translated as **His Master's Voice**
1971 *Doskonała Próżnia* Czytelnik, translated as **A Perfect Vacuum**
"Ze Wspomnień Ijona Tichego: Kongres Futurologiczny" in *Bezsenność* Wydawnictwo Literackie, translated as **The Futurological Congress**
Dzienniki Gwiazdowe Iskry, parts published earlier translated as **The Star Diaries,** full text as **Memoirs of a Space Traveler: The Further Reminiscences of Ijon Tichy**
1973 *Golem XIV* Czytelnik, selections are translated with *Wielkość Urojona*
Wielkość Urojona Czytelnik, translated as **Imaginary Magnitude**
1977 *Katar* Wydawnictwo Literackie, translated as **The Chain of Chance**
1981 *The Cosmic Carnival of Stanisław Lem*
1982 *Wizja Lokalna* Wydawnictwo Literackie [The scene of the crime]
1984 *Prowokacja* Wydawnictwo Literackie [Provocation]
1986 *One Human Minute Fiasko* Wydawnictwo Literackie, translated as **Fiasco**
1987 *Pokój na Ziemi* Wydawnictwo Literackie [Peace on Earth]
1988 *Ciemność i pleśń* Wydawnictwo Literackie [Darkness and mildew]

fiction, that any SF story that comforts lazy readers is an SF story that betrays the very notion of SF. For Lem, SF is not just storytelling: it is above all a mode of *argument*, a means by which to penetrate through the mystifications of bourgeois thought. For Lem, unless an individual SF story is quite clearly and cognitively based on argument and on understanding of the true nature of the universe, then it betrays not only SF as a mode, but also the whole human race, for SF writers are meant to think, to punish, and to heal.

Lem's most famous SF novel is *Solaris* (see page 222). But novels like *Fiasco* repeat and deepen the lessons of this masterpiece: the heroes apply all the tools of thought available to them to the analysis of alien manifestations and artefacts. The result of their unthinking thought is fiasco – Lem's lesson in a nutshell. What can be understood, and what cannot, must be clearly *understood*. All else is merely cheap sleight of hand.

Haunted
Unlike the book, the film of Solaris *is dominated by the relationship between the scientist and her "phantom", created by the impenetrable lake.*

HARRY HARRISON

BORN **1925**

NATIONALITY **American, resident in Ireland**

OTHER NAMES **born Henry Maxwell Dempsey; Felix Boyd, Hank Dempsey**

KEY WORKS **The *Stainless Steel Rat* series, the *Bill, the Galactic Hero* series, *Make Room! Make Room!***

It is not easy to understand at first why humour does not usually work in SF: comedy seems to be an ideal expression of the spirit of freedom that makes art fully human, so it might seem natural to expect that SF, with all the freedom of the yet-untold, should glory in the humour of the stars.

The answer, all the same, is simple: the problem with SF as a comic venue is precisely its freedom. Comedy, after all, glories in the haphazard and the pretentious in real, fixed societies. In SF there is sometimes too little for the joke to attach to, and it falls flat into slapstick. Harrison is a funny SF writer who has not always avoided slapstick – *Star Smashers of the Galaxy Rangers* is too broad and untargeted to do more than make one smile ruefully – but if he has a genuine target to aim at, he is one of the sharpest and funniest authors in the field.

Harrison has two favourite targets. The first of them is bureaucracy, and the *Stainless Steel Rat* series at times comes close to savagery in its attacks on rigidity and thinking by precedent. The second is the military mind, and although later sequels have descended to pun-laden slapstick, *Bill, the Galactic Hero* takes a jaundiced view of heroism and the propaganda generated by defenders of the soldier's art. Anyone who reads Heinlein's *Starship Troopers* should also read *Bill, the Galactic Hero*.

So well known are his comic series that readers easily forget Harrison's other sides. *Make Room! Make Room!*, which is about overpopulation, conveys its lessons about human self-delusion with unanswerable grimness. *Deathworld*, *Deathworld 2*, and *Deathworld 3* are extremely hard-hitting adventure novels; *Homeworld*, *Wheelworld*, and *Starworld* are exuberant Space Operas; and the

Harrison's rat
Harrison's cartoon image of the Stainless Steel Rat, on the first British hardbacks, differs markedly from the usual garish portrayal of the character.

Eden Alternate World trilogy is an impressively ambitious and extended examination of the familiar "what-if" premise of sentient dinosaurs.

Harry Harrison, most often in collaboration with his colleague Brian Aldiss, has also created a number of influential anthologies, most notably the **Best SF** annual series, which ran for a decade from 1968. Like Aldiss, Harrison is a man of letters in the SF world, a figure who carries over into the "outside" world the vivacity of the SF subculture. Politically, unlike many humourists, who tend to mourn the past that they mock, he is a liberal.

BIBLIOGRAPHY

NOVELS AND NOVELLAS
1960 **Deathworld** Bantam
1961 **The Stainless Steel Rat** Pyramid
1962 **Planet of the Damned** Bantam, retitled **Sense of Obligation**
1964 **Deathworld 2** Bantam, retitled **The Ethical Engineer**
1965 **Bill, the Galactic Hero** Doubleday
   Plague from Space Doubleday, retitled **The Jupiter Legacy**
1966 **Make Room! Make Room!** Doubleday, retitled **Soylent Green**
1967 **The Technicolor Time Machine** Doubleday
1968 **Deathworld 3** Dell
   The Man from P.I.G. Avon
1969 **Captive Universe** Putnam
1970 **The Daleth Effect** Putnam, retitled **In Our Hands, the Stars**
   The Stainless Steel Rat's Revenge Walker
   Spaceship Medic Faber
1972 **Tunnel Through the Deeps** Putnam, retitled **A Transatlantic Tunnel, Hurrah!**
   Stonehenge Scribners, with Leon E. Stover, retitled **Stonehenge: Where Atlantis Died**
   The Stainless Steel Rat Saves the World Putnam
1973 **Star Smashers of the Galaxy Rangers** Putnam
1975 **The California Iceberg** Faber
1976 **The Lifeship** Harper, with Gordon R. Dickson, retitled **Lifeboat**
   Skyfall Faber
1978 **The Stainless Steel Rat Wants You!** Michael Joseph
1979 **Planet Story** Pierrot
1980 **Homeworld** Bantam
1981 **Wheelworld** Bantam
   Starworld Bantam
   Planet of No Return Simon and Schuster
1982 **Invasion: Earth** Ace

1982 **The Stainless Steel Rat for President** Bantam
1983 **A Rebel in Time** Granada
1984 **West of Eden** Granada
1985 **A Stainless Steel Rat is Born** Bantam
1986 **Winter in Eden** Grafton
1987 **The Stainless Steel Rat Gets Drafted** Bantam
1988 **Return to Eden** Grafton
1989 **Bill, the Galactic Hero on the Planet of Robot Slaves** Avon
1990 **Bill, the Galactic Hero on the Planet of Bottled Brains** Avon, with Robert Sheckley
1991 **Bill, the Galactic Hero on the Planet of Tasteless Pleasure** Avon, with David Bischoff
   Bill, the Galactic Hero on the Planet of the Zombie Vampires Avon, with Jack C. Haldeman II
   Bill, the Galactic Hero on the Planet of Ten Thousand Bars Avon, with David Bischoff, retitled **Bill, the Galactic Hero on the Planet of the Hippies from Hell**
1992 **Bill, the Galactic Hero: The Final Incoherent Adventure** Avon, with David M. Harris
   The Turing Option Warner, with Marvin Minsky
1993 **The Hammer and the Cross** Tor, with John Holm (Tom Shippey)

SHORT STORY COLLECTIONS
1962 **War with the Robots** Pyramid
1965 **Two Tales and Eight Tomorrows** Gollancz
1970 **Prime Number** Berkley
   One Step from Earth Macmillan
1976 **The Best of Harry Harrison** Pocket Books
1993 **Stainless Steel Visions** Tor
1994 **Galactic Dreams** Tor

CLIFFORD D. SIMAK

BORN / DIED
1904-88
NATIONALITY
American
KEY WORKS
Way Station, City

WHILE SF covers the universe, the universe may also be found in a grain of sand. For Clifford D. Simak, whose writing career lasted well over half a century, the universe was found in one small corner of southwestern Wisconsin, close to the small cities he lived in all his life. For most of that life, he had a second career as a newspaperman who concentrated on his local region. Everything he learned as a reporter and ruminator in public upon rural life went into his fiction.

He is the great pastoral writer of the genre. He treats his region as a paradise whose inhabitants – farmers, visiting professors, young families – almost always live in harmony with their environment. When aliens arrive through space or time, folk who live in harmony respond to the allure of otherness like the hero of *Way Station*. He responds with respect, but with an essential reserve, and serves as a host for travelling aliens. It is only when he understands – as so many characters in

Simak stories come to understand – that the aliens may bring a chance of peace and plenty to the folk that he takes positive action.

In *Way Station*, the world is saved. In *Time and Again*, the outcome is uncertain. In *City* (see page 218), the entire planet becomes an expanded enclave, a worldwide Wisconsin; the dogs who inherit the Earth revere it. Later novels tend to repeat the lessons of earlier work, and at times may seem dilatory. But the acute nerve of the newspaperman never left Simak, whose last works were written when he was in his eighties: novels like *The Visitors* and *Project Pope* retain much of the old, serene love of the human landscape.

What happened to Simak, as the years passed, was neither simple nor very nice: what happened was the 20th century. The small-town verities he so intelligently fostered became less and less easy to advocate to an audience that had left the old civilities for edge city and the culture of the mall. By the time of his death, the rural Wisconsin he honoured had become an SF dream, a past that never made it to the future.

BIBLIOGRAPHY

NOVELS AND NOVELLAS
1946 **The Creator** Crawford
1950 **Cosmic Engineers** Gnome Press
1951 **Time and Again** Simon and Schuster, retitled **First He Died**
   Empire Galaxy Novels
1952 **Ring Around the Sun** Simon and Schuster
   City Gnome Press
1961 **Time Is the Simplest Thing** Doubleday
   The Trouble With Tycho Ace
1962 **They Walked Like Men** Doubleday
1963 **Way Station** Doubleday
1965 **All Flesh Is Grass** Doubleday
1967 **Why Call Them Back from Heaven?** Doubleday
   The Werewolf Principle Putnam
1968 **The Goblin Reservation** Putnam
1970 **Out of their Minds** Putnam
1971 **Destiny Doll** Putnam
1972 **A Choice of Gods** Putnam
1973 **Cemetery World** Putnam
1974 **Our Children's Children** Putnam
1975 **Enchanted Pilgrimage** Berkley
1976 **Shakespear's Planet** Berkley
1977 **A Heritage of Stars** Berkley
1978 **Mastodonia** Ballantine, retitled **Catface**
   The Fellowship of the Talisman Ballantine
1980 **The Visitors** Ballantine
1981 **Project Pope** Ballantine

1982 **Special Deliverance** Ballantine
   Where the Evil Dwells Ballantine
1986 **Highway of Eternity** Ballantine, retitled **Highway to Eternity**

SHORT STORY COLLECTIONS
1956 **Strangers in the Universe** Simon and Schuster
1960 **The Worlds of Clifford Simak** Simon and Schuster, retitled **Aliens for Neighbours,** retitled **Other Worlds of Clifford Simak**
1962 **All the Traps of Earth** Doubleday, retitled, in two volumes **All the Traps of Earth** and **The Night of the Puudly**
1964 **Worlds Without End** Belmont
1967 **Best Science Fiction Stories of Clifford Simak** Faber
1968 **So Bright the Vision** Ace
1975 **The Best of Clifford D. Simak** Sidgwick and Jackson
1977 **Skirmish** Putnam
1986 **The Marathon Photograph** Severn House
   Brothers Severn House
1988 **Off-Planet** Severn House
1990 **The Autumn Land** Mandarin
1991 **Immigrant** Severn House
1993 **The Creator and Other Stories** Severn House

BRIAN W. ALDISS

BORN **1925**

NATIONALITY **English**

OTHER NAMES **Jael Craken, John Runciman, C.C. Shackleton**

KEY WORKS **Non-Stop, Hothouse, Greybeard, Barefoot in the Head, The Saliva Tree, Billion Year Spree, Frankenstein Unbound, The Malacia Tapestry, the Helliconia series**

BRIAN Aldiss has been likened to his friend and colleague J.G. Ballard more often than either could probably care to recall. But Ballard writes dense, monomaniac books, attacking the same themes again and again, and his work cuts deep and narrow, while Aldiss has an exuberant, gregarious, far-seeking imagination, rarely repeats himself, and writes a great deal. He is harder, therefore, to pin down. In the end, however, he is almost certainly a more significant figure than his dark twin.

It is certainly a prolific career and, like anyone who attacks a wide range of topics, Brian Aldiss has written a few clunkers along the way. What is remarkable is that he has also written so many superb and various books. His first novel, *Non-Stop*, remains to this day one of the two or three classic presentations of its subject matter. *Hothouse*, which followed four years later, is also a central text for anyone interested in tales of the dying Earth; decades after reading it, one still feels the humidity, the fecundity, the tropic tensions of his Earth in the days when the Sun grows.

Books of striking immediacy like *The Dark Light Years*, *Earthworks*, and *Greybeard* – about a desolate near-future Earth paralyzed by infertility – follow one another rapidly. The sheer range of Aldiss's novels is notable: *An Age* is a pyrotechnic investigation of time travel; *Report on Probability A* is both a genuine experimental novel and an SF tale, simultaneously;

Barefoot in the Head is a treatment of post-war apocalypse in psychedelically Joycean terms; *Frankenstein Unbound* examines Mary Shelley; *The Malacia Tapestry* is a surreal fantasia; and the **Helliconia** books (see page 232) are a virtuoso exercise in planet-building, with a wise pessimism that distinguishes them from any American models.

Curiosity piece
This award from Eurocon for Billion Year Spree is one of Aldiss's personal favourites.

NOTABLE WORK

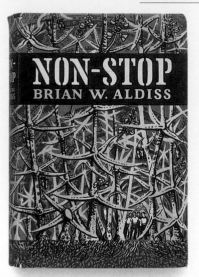

NON-STOP

The generation-starship story is central to SF, and although classic examples depend on readers not initially knowing that the worlds described are actually contained in giant spaceships, it remains an extremely popular plot device. *Non-Stop* tells the central story beautifully: a devolved culture, which has forgotten its origins, finds that it is on a colony ship designed to seed the neighbouring stars. After the heroes break into the control chamber, the sky is the limit.

Most recently, *Somewhere East of Life* is a near-future look at the shattered mosaic of Eastern Europe, written in a complex and elegiac manner that is both world-weary and a rage against the dying of the light.

Aldiss is simultaneously fierce, and sad, and happy, and he has said almost everything that can be said in SF.

BIBLIOGRAPHY

NOVELS AND NOVELLAS
1958 **Non-Stop** Faber, revised as **Starship**
1959 **Vanguard from Alpha** Ace, retitled **Equator**
1960 **Bow Down to Nul** Ace, retitled **The Interpreter**
1961 **The Male Response** Galaxy Books
The Primal Urge Ballantine
1962 **Hothouse** Faber, cut as **The Long Afternoon of Earth**
1964 **The Dark Light Years** Faber
Greybeard Faber
1965 **Earthworks** Faber
1967 **An Age** Faber, retitled **Cryptozoic!**
1968 **Report on Probability A** Faber
1969 **Barefoot in the Head: A European Fantasia** Faber
1970 **The Hand-Reared Boy** Weidenfeld and Nicolson
1971 **A Soldier Erect** Weidenfeld and Nicolson
1973 **Frankenstein Unbound** Cape
1974 **The Eighty-Minute Hour** Doubleday
1976 **The Malacia Tapestry** Cape
1977 **Brothers of the Head** Pierrot
1978 **Enemies of the System** Cape
1980 **Moreau's Other Island** Cape, retitled **An Island Called Moreau**
Life in the West Weidenfeld and Nicolson
1982 **Helliconia Spring** Cape
1983 **Helliconia Summer** Cape
1985 **Helliconia Winter** Cape
1987 **The Year Before Yesterday** Franklin Watts, revised as **Cracken at Critical Ruins** Hutchinson
1988 **Forgotten Life** Gollancz
1991 **Dracula Unbound** Grafton
1993 **Remembrance Day** Gollancz
1994 **Somewhere East of Life** HarperCollins

SHORT STORY COLLECTIONS
1957 **Space, Time, and Nathaniel: Presciences** Faber, cut as **No Time Like Tomorrow**
1959 **The Canopy of Time** Faber, revised as **Galaxies Like Grains of Sand**
1963 **The Airs of Earth** Faber, revised as **Starswarm**
1965 **The Best Science Fiction Stories of Brian Aldiss** Faber, retitled **Who Can Replace a Man?**
1966 **The Saliva Tree and Other Strange Growths** Faber
1969 **Intangibles, Inc** Faber, revised as **Neanderthal Planet**
1970 **The Moment of Eclipse** Faber
1972 **The Book of Brian Aldiss** DAW Books, retitled **The Comic Inferno**
1977 **Last Orders** Cape
1979 **New Arrivals, Old Encounters** Cape
1981 **Foreign Bodies** Chopmen
1984 **Seasons in Flight** Cape
1988 **Best Science Fiction Stories of Brian W. Aldiss** Gollancz, retitled **Man in his Time**
1989 **A Romance of the Equator: Best Fantasy Stories of Brian W. Aldiss** Gollancz
1991 **Bodily Functions** Avernus
1993 **A Tupolev Too Far** Gollancz

NON-FICTION
1955 **The Brightfount Diaries** Faber
1970 **The Shape of Further Things: Speculations on Change** Faber
1973 **Billion Year Spree: A History of Science Fiction** Weidenfeld and Nicolson, much expanded as **Trillion Year Spree: The History of Science Fiction,** with David Wingrove
1975 **Science Fiction Art** New English Library
1978 **Science Fiction as Science Fiction** Bran's Head
1979 **This World and Nearer Ones** Weidenfeld and Nicolson
1983 **Science Fiction Quiz** Weidenfeld and Nicolson
1985 **The Pale Shadow of Science** Serconia Press
1986 **And the Lurid Glare of the Comet** Serconia Press
1990 **Bury My Heart at W.H. Smith's: A Writing Life** Avernus

SELECTED WORKS AS EDITOR
1961 **Penguin Science Fiction** Penguin, with sequels
1962 **Best Fantasy Stories** Faber
1968 **Best SF 1967** Berkley, with Harry Harrison, with eight further volumes through 1976
1974 **Space Opera** Weidenfeld and Nicolson
Space Odysseys Futura
1975 **Hell's Cartographers: Some Personal Histories of Science Fiction Writers** Weidenfeld and Nicolson
Decade: the 1940s Macmillan, with four further volumes through 1978
1976 **Galactic Empires** Weidenfeld and Nicolson, in two volumes

PRIMO LEVI

BORN / DIED **1919-87**

NATIONALITY **Italian**

KEY WORKS ***Il sistema periodica, La Chiave a Stella, Storie naturali***

THE essence of Primo Levi, for readers who are not Italian, or for those only familiar with those works of his that have been translated, is his life. The last 40 or so years of that life were devoted to attempts – some of which were valorous, and others of which led to writing of an extraordinary poignance – to deal with the fact that he was a survivor of Auschwitz. Although Levi made use of his extensive knowledge of science – he was by training an industrial chemist – to write works that could be thought of as SF, both his fiction and his non-fiction, his fabulations and his autobiographies, have to be read as metaphors of the holocaust.

His most famous work of fiction, *Il sistema periodica (The Periodic Table)*, uses the Russian chemist Mendeleyev's periodic table of the elements as the base for a series of 21 reminiscences, suggesting that the profound calm of scientific order can be imposed on, and in itself soothe, the anguish of a life led too close to the furnace.

Transposed into a set of apparently autobiographical encounters with a master mechanic, who proves in the end to be imaginary, *La Chiave a Stella (The Monkey's Wrench)* conveys a similar sense of the miraculous reality of a sane and measurable world. These two texts are both strongly resonant for readers of SF, because, like the best SF, they argue that scientific knowledge of the world can indeed solve some of the world's problems.

For a man like Primo Levi, SF-tinged speculative science – which has an estranging effect on some humanists who prefer to live in ivy-sheltered comfort – was a lifeline.

This ironic, but deeply felt, use of hard sciences as an underpinning for metaphor and autobiography marks out Levi as a highly unusual writer in the context of Italian culture, where the sciences and the humanities are particularly estranged from one another. Recognizable genre SF stories are, all the same, not important to his overall career, although some of the short stories assembled in *Storie naturali (The Sixth Day and Other Tales)* are indeed SF. More often, his work could be said to resemble SF. For example, a tale like "Excellent is the Water" begins with a genuine SF premise – water gradually turns more viscous, a process starting in Italy and slowly becoming a world-wide phenomenon –

> ❝*Both his fiction and his non-fiction have to be read as metaphors of the holocaust*❞

but the metaphorical implications of the tale soon come to dominate the telling, and we soon understand that what Levi is in reality addressing is the depersonalization of modern life. Similarly, in the title tale of the translation *The Mirror Maker*, in which a man constructs mirrors that show how we are seen by others, Levi's concern is more with the moral than the ideological implications.

Not even all this constant and compulsive rationalizing of life's irrationality helped very much – and nor could any other recourse to any other kind of knowledge or human contact save him in the end. As is well-known, Levi lost the struggle, and killed himself in 1987.

BIBLIOGRAPHY

NOVELS AND NOVELLAS
1975 *Il sistema periodica* Einaudi, translated as **The Periodic Table**
1978 *La Chiave a Stella* Einaudi, translated as **The Monkey's Wrench**
1982 *Se non ora, quando?* Einaudi, translated as **If Not Now, When?**

SHORT STORY COLLECTIONS
1966 *Storie naturali* Einaudi, translated as **The Sixth Day**
1986 *Racconti e saggi* La Stampa, translated with added essays as **The Mirror Maker**

ITALO CALVINO

BORN / DIED **1923-85**

NATIONALITY **Italian, born in Cuba**

KEY WORKS ***Il Cavaliere inesistente, Le città invisibili, Se una notte d'inverno un viaggiatore, Ti con zero, Le cosmicomiche***

ITALO Calvino, like Primo Levi, knew a good deal about science; and, as was the case with Levi, an ability to make use of the protocols of scientific discourse marked him off from the central traditions of Italian literature. But Calvino was far more aggressive as a writer than Levi was, and as a result his fiction far more radically challenges his fellow Italians – and the rest of the world, for he has been very widely translated – to understand that the techniques of genres like SF are not only usable, but also necessary if the 20th century is to be understood.

This does not, all the same, make very much of his work read like what we recognize as genre SF. At the heart of all Calvino's work lies a complex, and exceedingly sophisticated,

> ❝*Calvino was a genuinely postmodernist author*❞

set of arguments about the relationship between the story that is being told and the narrator who is telling the story. As something of a literary polymath – as well as writing fiction, Calvino was an editor and an essayist – his approach to the nature of fiction was quite complex. Calvino was, in short, a genuinely postmodernist author, and none of his mature work is simply a story about the world. He is far from being the Isaac Asimov of Italy.

Calvino began his writing career with novels like *Il Visconte dimezzato (The Cloven Viscount)* and *Il Cavaliere inesistente (The Non-Existent Knight)*.

BIBLIOGRAPHY

NOVELS AND NOVELLAS
1952 *Il Visconte dimezzato* Einaudi, translated as **The Cloven Viscount**
1957 *Il Barone rampante* Einaudi, translated as **The Baron in the Trees**
1959 *Il Cavaliere inesistente* Einaudi, translated as **The Non-Existent Knight**
1963 *La giornata d'uno scutatore* Einaudi, translated with other stories as **The Watcher**
1972 *Le città invisibili* Einaudi, translated as **Invisible Cities**
1973 *Marcovaldo ovvero le stagioni in citta* Einaudi, translated as **Marcovaldo, or, the Seasons in the City**
1979 *Se una notte d'inverno un viaggiatore* Einaudi, translated as **If on a Winter's Night a Traveler**
1983 *Palomar* Einaudi, translated as **Mr. Palomar**

SHORT STORY COLLECTIONS
1967 *Ti con zero* Einaudi, translated as **T Zero**
1968 *Le cosmicomiche* Einaudi, translated as **Cosmicomics**, expanded as **Cosmicomiche vecchie e nuove**
1969 *Il Castello dei Destini incrociati* Einaudi, translated as **The Castle of Crossed Destinies**
1984 *Gli, amoir dificile* Einaudi, translated as **Difficult Loves**
1986 *Sotto il sole giaguaro* Garzanti, translated as **Under the Jaguar Sun**

The latter is about an uninhabited suit of armour kept alive by its "passion" for ceremony and story; this is similar to the creatures in L. Frank Baum's various fables about the Land of Oz, in which all manner of mechanical contrivances, which logically ought to be lifeless, turn out to be alive simply because they behave that way. Something closer to conventional SF can be found in the linked stories in *Le cosmicomiche (Cosmicomics)* and *Ti con zero (T Zero)*, both of which star, and are also narrated by, Qfwfq, who is as old as the universe; the tales so told turn out to be moral fables about matters of science, art, evolution, and more profound matters. Calvino's most famous work, *Se una notte d'inverno un viaggiatore (If on a Winter's Night a Traveler)*, in which a reader pursues the texts of books through translations, labyrinthine conspiracies and layers of realities that melt and dissolve as soon as they are grasped, is not truly SF; nor, technically, can *Le città invisibili (Invisible Cities)*, in which Marco Polo rhapsodizes upon a series of surreal cities, be called SF; but the latter of these tales does display a sense of wonder that is pure SF.

AVRAM DAVIDSON

BORN / DIED **1923-93**

NATIONALITY **American**

OTHER NAME **Ellery Queen**

KEY WORKS **"Or All the Seas with Oysters", Clash of Star-Kings, The Enquiries of Doctor Eszterhazy**

AVIDSON was most like himself in the 1970s and 1980s, but his great years were the 1960s. This is not an insult. The problem with Davidson was that his best and most intriguing impulses, insights, and digressions were not the kind easily expressed in novel form. He could never write a novel such as *Tristram Shandy*, or the *Pickwick Papers*.

Davidson was an intellectual packrat, wandering from one subject to another, or approaching single subjects with a bemused and polymathic amplitude, as in the ingratiating essays in *Adventures in Unhistory*. In order to tell a sustained story, he had to mentally become somebody else.

His later novels, from the 1970s and 1980s, such as *Peregrine: Secundus* or *Vergil in Averno*, are (as novels) rather boneless: they are rambles through pastures of eccentric knowledge, with pleasant quiet moments. Those who love Davidson's later work love it deeply. But there have never been enough fans of his books to keep him properly in print.

Another problem is that he found it hard to finish his most personal projects. Earlier, he wrote conventional novels, he finished them, and he will undoubtedly be remembered for *Rogue Dragon*, *Masters of the Maze*, and *Clash of Star-Kings*, all from the mid-1960s.

BIBLIOGRAPHY

NOVELS AND NOVELLAS
1962 **Joyleg** Pyramid, with Ward Moore
1964 **Mutiny in Space** Pyramid
     And on the Eighth Day Random House, as Ellery Queen
1965 **Rogue Dragon** Ace
     Rork! Berkley
     Masters of the Maze Pyramid
1966 **The Enemy of my Enemy** Berkley
     Clash of Star-Kings Ace
     The Kar-Chee Reign Ace
1969 **The Island Under the Earth** Ace
     The Phoenix and the Mirror Doubleday, retitled **The Enigmatic Speculum**
1971 **Peregrine: Primus** Walker
1973 **Ursus of Ultima Thule** Avon
1981 **Peregrine: Secundus** Berkley
1987 **Vergil in Averno** Doubleday
1988 **Marco Polo and the Sleeping Beauty** Baen, with Grania Davis

SHORT STORY COLLECTIONS
1962 **Or All the Seas with Oysters** Berkley
1965 **What Strange Stars and Skies** Ace
1971 **Strange Seas and Shores** Doubleday
1975 **The Enquiries of Doctor Eszterhazy** Warner, expanded as **The Adventures of Doctor Eszterhazy**
1978 **The Redward Edward Papers** Doubleday
1979 **The Best of Avram Davidson** Doubleday
1982 **The Collected Fantasies of Avram Davidson** Berkley

NON-FICTION
1993 **Adventures in Unhistory: Conjectures on the Factual Foundations of Several Ancient Legends** Owlswick Press

The last of these is a good example of his talents: two warring alien races have visited Mexico in ancient times; they now return, in search of weaponry with which to commit devastation upon each other, and embroil contemporary humans in complex, suspenseful doings. Mexico is described with energy and sensitivity, and the story is strong, haunting, mature, and adventurous. Short stories from any time in his career remind one of Robert Burton, who wrote *The Anatomy of Melancholy*, in 1621, and of Chesterton, and maybe of Franz Kafka. They smell of old books, but also convey a sharp, abysmal, contemporary reek of terror: even the stories in *The Enquiries of Doctor Eszterhazy* belie their Ruritanian setting. Davidson may have abandoned big canvases, but he remained a dark magician of lore, and a genuine explorer of this crowded century.

OR ALL THE SEAS WITH OYSTERS

AVRAM DAVIDSON

Award winner
"Or All the Seas with Oysters" won Davidson a Hugo.

Avram Davidson

R.A. LAFFERTY

BORN **1914**

NATIONALITY **American**

KEY WORKS **Past Master, Space Chantey, Fourth Mansions, Nine Hundred Grandmothers, Arrive at Easterwine, Does Anyone Else Have Something Further to Add?**

ELIGION does not much figure in SF: what faith a writer gives credence to does not usually matter. Here, as in much else, Lafferty stands more or less alone. He is a Roman Catholic, and beneath the exorbitant playfulness of his tales works an engine of judgment. Lafferty is a moralist. More than that, his wildest flights not only affirm moral truths that should govern behaviour; they also represent an amibitious attempt to delineate the universe in terms consistent with a sense that the whole of material reality is a kind of divine theatre, that our actions are part of a cosmic drama.

In the 1960s, Lafferty looked for a while as though he was ambitious to become a central figure in SF literature, but he soon took flight – today it can be frustrating work trying to buy Lafferty books. The progression of titles is a map of his course away from the mainstream. In *Past Master*, Sir Thomas More is translated into a future utopia in order to try to save it, but manages mainly to repeat the sins that may have caused his execution. *Space Chantey* is a hilarious rendering of Homer's *Odyssey* as Space Opera, and *Fourth Mansions* paints a violently baroque picture of human history as a drama whose godlike protagonists hide in secret organizations and manipulate humans, for good or for evil, from behind the scenes. *Arrive at Easterwine* is the story of a sentient – and blasphemously soulful – computer.

Lafferty's later works make even *Fourth Mansions* look simple. In series, novels, stories, and sermons that enlist every kind of fable, traditional tale, and live or dead mythology imaginable, Lafferty continues to construct rich, zany, dark parables about our human condition. SF is only one of the tools that he uses to get at the truth, to tell God's great drama.

R.a. Lafferty

BIBLIOGRAPHY

NOVELS AND NOVELLAS
1968 **Past Master** Ace
     The Reefs of Earth Berkley
     Space Chantey Ace
1969 **Fourth Mansions** Ace
1971 **The Flame is Green** Walker
     The Fall of Rome Doubleday
     The Devil is Dead Avon
     Arrive at Easterwine Scribners
1972 **Okla Hannali** Doubleday
1976 **Not to Mention Camels** Bobbs Merrill
1977 **Apocalypses** Pinnacle (two complete novels)
1979 **Archipelago** Manuscript Press
1982 **Aurelia** Donning
1983 **The Annals of Klepsis** Ace
1984 **Half a Sky** Corroboree Press
1987 **Serpent's Egg** Morrigan
     My Heart Leaps Up Drumm Books, in five short volumes
1988 **East of Laughter** Morrigan
1989 **Sindbad: the Thirteenth Voyage** Broken Mirrors Press
     The Elliptical Grave United Mythologies Press
1990 **Dotty** United Mythologies Press
1992 **More Than Melchisedech** United Mythologies Press, in three volumes
     Argo United Mythologies Press

SHORT STORY COLLECTIONS
Much of Lafferty's later work in short form has been published only in booklet form: only some of these are listed here.
1970 **Nine Hundred Grandmothers** Ace
1971 **Strange Doings** Scribners
1974 **Does Anyone Else Have Something Further to Add?** Scribners
1976 **Funnyfingers, and Cabrito** Pendragon Press
     Horns on their Heads Pendragon Press
1983 **Golden Gate** Corroboree Press
     Four Stories Drumm Books
     Through Elegant Eyes Corroboree Press
1984 **Ringing Changes** Ace
1985 **Slippery** Drumm Books
1988 **The Early Lafferty** United Mythologies Press
1990 **The Early Lafferty II** United Mythologies Press
     Episodes of the Argo United Mythologies Press
1991 **Lafferty in Orbit** Broken Mirrors Press
     Mischief Malicious United Mythologies Press
1992 **Iron Tears** Edgewood Press

HERBERT FRANKE

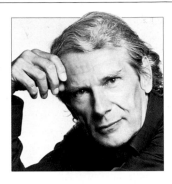

BORN **1927**

NATIONALITY **German**

OTHER NAME **Sergius Both**

KEY WORKS *Der Orchideenkäfig, Ypsilon Minus, Endzeit*

ONE of Germany's most important SF writers, Herbert Franke began his publishing career in the 1950s with non-fiction works on subjects like speleology – he is a devoted spelunker – and computer graphics, a subject he also taught at the University of Munich. He also wrote a number of short stories during these years.

Franke's first two novels, *Das Gedankennetz* (The Mind Net), and *Der Orchideenkäfig* (The Orchid Cage), are typical of his earlier work in their distinctly European depiction of the future as a world under the control of impersonal forces, and of the entrapment of human protagonists in that world. For a while, there seemed no escape from

The Mind Net
Franke was a consulting editor for Goldmann and was published by them.

this world, as the protagonist of *Ypsilon Minus* discovers when computers excise three years of his life, which he can see only as a film, but Franke began to make use of the superman, in novels like *Schule für Übermenschen* [School for supermen], whose internal superiority allows him to baffle an inimical outside world.

Later novels are looser in their construction, and seem to permit a more flexible understanding of the forces that try to control us, although they continue to analyze the distortion of reality engendered by computers and the like. Franke has kept pace with the century: he clearly feels that it is much harder to constrain individual actions today, but that it is correspondingly far easier to shape our perceptions of reality, so that in the end we still behave according to the needs of the world's owners.

Franke's later novels, such as *Endzeit* [The end of time], become increasingly metaphysical in their implications, and contain moments of effective poetry. The protagonists of *Endzeit* – after disillusioning attempts to increase the world's water supply with the aid of computer simulations – have religious experiences as an apocalyptic, cleansing rain miraculously begins to fall. Franke is from a central Europe that saw the future as a prison; it is good that he now sees some exits.

BIBLIOGRAPHY

NOVELS AND NOVELLAS
1961 *Das Gedankennetz* Goldmann, translated as **The Mind Net**
Der Orchideenkäfig Goldmann, translated as **The Orchid Cage**
1962 *Die Glasfalle* Goldmann **[The glass trap]**
Die Stahlwüste Goldmann **[The steel desert]**
1963 *Planet der Verlorenen* Goldmann, as Sergius Both **[Planet of the lost]**
1965 *Der Elfenbeinturm* Goldmann **[The ivory tower]**
1970 *Zone Null* Kindler
1975 *Ypsilon Minus* Suhrkamp
1979 *Sirius Transit* Suhrkamp, as Sergius Both
1980 *Schule für Übermenschen* Suhrkamp **[School for supermen]**
1982 *Tod eines Unsterblichen* Suhrkamp **[Death of an immortal]**
Transpluto Suhrkamp
1984 *Die Kalte des Weltraums* Suhrkamp **[The coldness of space]**

1985 *Endzeit* Suhrkamp **[The end of time]**
1986 *Der Atem der Sonne* Suhrkamp **[The breath of the Sun]**
1990 *Zentrum der Milchstrasse* Suhrkamp **[The middle of the Milky Way]**

SHORT STORY COLLECTIONS
1960 *Der Grüne Komet* Goldmann **[The green comet]**
1963 *Fahrt zum Licht: Utopische Kurzgeschichten* Sansyusya **[Journey to light: Utopian short stories]**
1972 *Einsteins Erben* Insel **[Einstein's heirs]**
1977 *Zarathustra kehrt Zurück* Suhrkamp **[Zarathustra returns]**
1978 *Ein Kybork namens Joe* Kom **[A cyborg named Joe]**
1981 *Paradies 3000* Suhrkamp **[Paradise 3000]**
1982 *Keine Spur von Leben* Suhrkamp (radio plays) **[No sign of life]**
1990 *Spiegel der Gedanken* Suhrkamp **[Mirror of thought]**

GÉRARD KLEIN

BORN **1937**

NATIONALITY **French**

OTHER NAME **Gilles d'Argyre**

KEY WORKS *Les tueurs de temps, Le sceptre du hasard, Les seigneurs de la guerre*

SOME critics regard Gérard Klein as the single most important French SF writer since Jules Verne: he is certainly the most important figure in the field of French SF this century.

His active writing career lasted only 15 years or so, but his works are highly esteemed, and have been deeply influential. The first seven of his eight acknowledged novels were published by a list that usually concentrated on pulp titles, and the fact that they were published pseudonymously might make one suspect that they, too, were pulps.

Titles like *Les tueurs de temps* – which translates as "The Killers of Time", although the American translation is cannily titled *The Mote in Time's Eye* – also seem to give a pretty strong hint that Klein may not have been very ambitious as a writer of fiction.

It would be wrong to take the hint. Klein's last three novels in particular are knowing exercises in philosophy, making sophisticated use of time travel as a device to assess the relationship between mental realities and the world outside. In *Les seigneurs de la guerre* (*The Overlords of War* – the English translation by John Brunner), time travel is used to create an arena where history is played out, like an argument. This is Klein at his best.

Since leaving the field of fiction writing, Klein has been the founding editor of the *Ailleurs et demain* [Elsewhere and Tomorrow] imprint of SF texts for Robert Laffont, responsible for shaping the taste of French SF readers for the last 35 years. As an active critic and scholar, he is a primary theorist of the genre.

BIBLIOGRAPHY

NOVELS AND NOVELLAS
1958 *Le gambit des étoiles* Hachette, translated as **Starmaster's Gambit**
1960 *Chirurgiens d'une planète* Fleuve Noir, as Gilles d'Argyre **[Refitting a planet]** revised as *Le rève des fôrets* **[The dream of the forests]**
1961 *Le Voiliers du soleil* Fleuve noir, as Gilles d'Argyre **[The sailships of the sun]**
Le temps n'a pas d'un odeur Denoël, Présence du futur, translated as **The Day Before Tomorrow**
1964 *Le long voyage* Fleuve noir, as Gilles d'Argyre **[The long journey]**
1965 *Les tueurs de temps* Fleuve noir, as Gilles d'Argyre, translated as **The Mote in Time's Eye**
1968 *Le sceptre du hasard* Fleuve noir, as Gilles d'Argyre **[The sceptre of chance]**
1971 *Les seigneurs de la guerre* Robert Laffont, Ailleurs et demain, translated as **The Overlords of War**

SHORT STORY COLLECTIONS
1958 *Les perles du temps* Denoël, Présence du futur **[The pearls of time]**
1966 *Un chant de pierre* Éric Losfeld **[A song of stone]**
1973 *La loi du talion* Robert Laffont, Ailleurs et demain **[An eye for an eye]**
1975 *Histoires comme si* Union Générale d'Edition **[Stories like if]**

1979 *Le Livre d'or de la Science Fiction: Gérard Klein* Presses Pocket **[The golden book of Science Fiction: Gérard Klein]**

AS EDITOR
As well as editing specific titles, Gérard Klein is also the overall editor of Robert Laffont's Ailleurs et demain SF series, begun in 1960.
1975 *Le Grandiose avenir, anthologie de la Science-Fiction française, tome I* Seghers, with Monique Battestini, two further volumes to 1977 **[The grandiose future, anthology of French Science Fiction, volume I]**
1976 *La Grande Anthologie de la Science-Fiction* Le Livre de Poche, with Jacques Goimard and Demetre Ioakimidis **[The great anthology of Science Fiction]**
1978 *Le Livre d'or de la science fiction: Ursula Le Guin* Presses Pocket **[The golden book of Science Fiction: Ursula Le Guin]**
Le Livre d'or de la science fiction: Frank Herbert Presses Pocket **[The golden book of Science Fiction: Frank Herbert]**

AS TRANSLATOR
1959 *Les mondes divergents* Satellite **[The divergent worlds]** translation of *The Eye in the Sky* by Philip K. Dick, revised as *l'Oeil dans le ciel* **[The eye in the sky]**

PHILIP K. DICK

BORN / DIED **1928–82**

NATIONALITY **American**

KEY WORKS **The Man in the High Castle, The Three Stigmata of Palmer Eldritch, Do Androids Dream of Electric Sheep?, A Maze of Death**

IT is preposterous that Dick is dead. His dark, unsettling imagination lives on in *Blade Runner* (see page 283), the nightmarish *film noir* that Ridley Scott made of his novel, *Do Androids Dream of Electric Sheep?*. He lives on in Cyberpunk, although he died two years before Gibson published *Neuromancer* (see page 232). His 45 novels are alive today: his brushes with insanity are like glimpses of our own future as the century races towards the Millennium. In the year 2000, he would have been just 72 years old – continuing to have bad dreams, and to pass them on to us.

Philip K. Dick was one of the two or three genuinely great writers born and bred in the world of SF, and remains one of the most significant interpreters of America in the latter part of the century. He was not an easy man – erratic, oft-married, half-insane for years, paranoid – and his publishing career was not an easy one. His bibliography is deceptive: many of his early books did not appear until after his death, and he wrote fast and erratically when he was in spate, with the result that masterpieces and clumsy commercial fictions appeared one after another. As the order in which books were published is not the order in which they were written, we will consider the books here with regard to the year of their composition, while the bibliography gives the year of publication.

The latest to reach publication – *Gather Yourselves Together* – is, in fact, almost the first to have been written, sometime around 1950. Like most of the other posthumous titles, it is neither SF nor fantasy. Dick was first, although not foremost, a writer of contemporary novels, most of them set in California, where he was born.

Social disorder
The raffle in Solar Lottery *determines where folk fit into society's hierarchies.*

Books such as *The Broken Bubble*, which Dick wrote in 1956, *In Milton Lumky Territory*, from 1958, *Confessions of a Crap Artist*, written in 1959, and *Humpty Dumpty in Oakland*, written in 1960 are fluid, testy, incisive, and probing examinations of modern life. Not one of them, however, tempted a commercial publisher. While working on these novels (the fame of which is now growing), Dick was also immersing himself deeply in SF. Tales like *The Cosmic Puppets*, or *Dr. Futurity*, both of which were written in 1953, hardly prefigured, however, the incandescent dreamer who burst onto the scene with his fourth-written but first-published novel, *Solar Lottery*, written in 1954, which is one of his ten or so best SF books. It is as complex as a tale by van Vogt in his prime, but far more modern in feel. The world has become seemingly tranquil through the use of lotteries to run it but, in fact, the system is corrupt: harried and neurotic rulers (a Dick speciality) make the wrong decisions; underlings betray leaders; wives dominate humble salesmen; and reality is a sham, a prop that can be whipped from under one's feet.

Thanks for the memories
Total Recall *was expanded from a brief short story, "We Can Remember it for You Wholesale", but the film retained Dick's multilayered paranoia.*

Time Out of Joint, written in 1958, intensifies the message. Its protagonist is duped into thinking he is just an ordinary citizen in an ordinary town; in reality he is a "precog" (extrasensory talents, such as precognition, that do their possessors no good at all, are a further Dick speciality), and his entire universe has been constructed for him by the military in order to create puzzling situations, which he solves by using his talents. These situations mirror strategic problems in an ongoing war, so the protagonist – he is similar to Ender in Orson Scott Card's novel *Ender's Game* (see page 232) – may unknowingly commit genocide by deciding how to navigate a traffic jam.

The Man in the High Castle (see page 223), which Dick wrote in 1961, is his first full masterpiece, the most famous Alternate World novel written about the consequences of a Hitler victory in World War II. Its narrative is complex, flowing, and urgent; its characters are haunted and utterly believable; and its sad resonances are impossible to forget. *Martian Time-Slip* (see page 223), written in 1962, is set on a Mars disastrously unlike Ray Bradbury's sentimentalized planet. Everything goes wrong for the settlers:

BIBLIOGRAPHY

NOVELS AND NOVELLAS
1955 **Solar Lottery** Ace, revised as **World of Chance**
1956 **The World Jones Made** Ace
     The Man Who Japed Ace
1957 **Eye in the Sky** Ace
     The Cosmic Puppets Ace
1959 **Time Out of Joint** Lippincott
1960 **Dr. Futurity** Ace
     Vulcan's Hammer Ace
1962 **The Man in the High Castle** Putnam
1963 **The Game-Players of Titan** Ace
1964 **Martian Time-Slip** Ballantine
     The Simulacra Ace
     The Penultimate Truth Belmont
     Clans of the Alphane Moon Ace
1965 **The Three Stigmata of Palmer Eldritch** Doubleday
     Dr. Bloodmoney, or How We Got Along After the Bomb Ace
1966 **The Crack in Space** Ace
     Now Wait for Last Year Doubleday
     The Unteleported Man Ace, revised as **Lies, Inc.**
1967 **Counter-Clock World** Berkley
     The Zap Gun Pyramid

1967 **The Ganymede Takeover** Ace, with Ray Nelson
1968 **Do Androids Dream of Electric Sheep?** Doubleday, retitled **Blade Runner**
1969 **Ubik** Doubleday
     Galactic Pot-Healer Berkley
1970 **A Maze of Death** Doubleday
     Our Friends from Frolix 8 Ace
1972 **We Can Build You** DAW Books
1974 **Flow my Tears, the Policeman Said** Doubleday
1975 **Confessions of a Crap Artist** Entwhistle
1976 **Dies Irae** Doubleday, with Roger V. Zelazny
1977 **A Scanner Darkly** Doubleday
1981 **VALIS** Bantam
     The Divine Invasion Timescape
1982 **The Transmigration of Timothy Archer** Timescape
1984 **The Man Whose Teeth Were All Exactly Alike** Mark Ziesing
1985 **In Milton Lumky Territory** Dragon Press
     Radio Free Albemuth Arbor House
     Puttering About in a Small Land Academy
1986 **Humpty Dumpty in Oakland** Gollancz
1987 **Mary and the Giant** Arbor House
1988 **Nick and the Glimmung** Gollancz

1988 **The Broken Bubble** Arbor House
1994 **Gather Yourselves Together** WCS Books

SHORT STORY COLLECTIONS
1955 **A Handful of Darkness** Rich and Cowan
1957 **The Variable Man** Ace
1969 **The Preserving Machine** Ace
1973 **The Book of Philip K. Dick** DAW Books, retitled **The Turning Wheel**
1977 **The Best of Philip K. Dick** Ballantine
1980 **The Golden Man** Berkley
1984 **Robots, Androids, and Mechanical Oddities** Southern Illinois University Press
1985 **I Hope I Shall Arrive Soon** Doubleday
1987 **The Collected Stories** Underwood-Miller, in five volumes, separately issued as: **Beyond Lies the Wub**, retitled **The Short Happy Life of the Brown Oxford; Second Variety**, retitled **We Can Remember it for You Wholesale; The Father-Thing**, retitled **Second Variety; The Days of Perky Pat**, retitled **The Minority Report;** and **The Little Black Box**, retitled **We Can Remember it for You Wholesale** (this is not the same as the retitling of **Second Variety**)

reality is a hollowed-out travesty of the truth, and paranoid, paranormal children bedevil harassed dictators, pointed reminders of the frailty of the human will. But the novel is – at the same time that it terrifies and saddens us with its message about the ultimate meaninglessness of life – utterly hilarious in its depiction of the way obsessed people shape their worlds. It is a tall tale about absurdity; it is a great book, quite possibly Dick's best.

Dr. Bloodmoney, or How We Got Along After the Bomb, written in 1963, is even bleaker, and not as funny. The virtuoso element here, over and above its extravagantly cynical depiction of a post-holocaust America, lies in the extraordinary, multilevelled intricacy of the plotting, through which the plight of small, ordinary men and women both mirrors and mocks the pretentions of the great to mould events. After four minor works, all written over a period of just a few months, Dick wrote the fourth volume in this sequence of prime titles. *The Three Stigmata of Palmer Eldritch* (see page 223), written in 1964, engages the world of psychotropic (mind-shaping) drugs through the story of Eldritch, an entrepreneur whose product eats realities,

> **"***Dick was grappling with greater demons than most of us will ever imagine***"**

substituting for the lost, real world a nightmare environment, which is interpenetrated by Eldritch's weird essence. As with Dick's earlier novel *Eye in the Sky*, written in 1955, this can be read as a dire, haunted comment on the nature of God.

The landscape of Dick's novels, wherever they may ostensibly be set, is a Los Angeles bleached into surreal perspectives and populated by driven hordes of Americans who have found that the Pacific Ocean marks the end of their travels in search of paradise. Unlike most American SF writers – even those who came to maturity in the ominously placid 1950s – Dick is a profound pessimist about the human condition, about the triumphs of science and technology, about the honesty of governments, and about inner and outer space. Beneath every smiling face, in a Dick novel, the stigmata of Palmer Eldritch are likely to exist – for the cruelty of the world lurks unseen while, at the same time, it cannot help but reveal itself everywhere.

There were a few more novels to come before Dick finally stepped too close to the edge. Written in 1966,

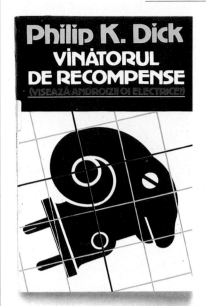

NOTABLE WORK

Do Androids Dream of Electric Sheep? is not famous only because Ridley Scott's *Blade Runner* was based on it, and made it famous. It is famous because it intensifies all of the implications of Dick's earlier masterpieces, and because it reads like a concentrated chamber opera, a précis of entropy. The main protagonist's task is to hunt for illegal androids, but the novel bristles with the presence of legal android animals, which the frail, desolate, remaining humans commune with in order to alleviate their guilt at spoiling the planet.

DO ANDROIDS DREAM OF ELECTRIC SHEEP?

Do Androids Dream of Electric Sheep? has become famous; *Ubik*, written the same year, transforms the Eldritches of the world into corpses who continue to dominate, even though they are technically dead. In 1968, Dick wrote *A Maze of Death* (see page 226), which carries the lesson of death even further. By this point, Dick had written too much, too fast, for too little money, and the pressure mounted. *Flow My Tears, the Policeman Said*, from 1970, is a strained and minor work, although it strives for

significance; and very soon after its composition he began to believe that he was receiving messages from higher beings. He took – it is believed – millions of words of notes, which he called the "Exegesis", and began to construct an extremely elaborate vision of the layers of illusion that he believed prevented us from understanding the truth that lies beneath: that the underlying reality is, in some sense, animate. Dick's beliefs during these years constituted, in other words, a form of latter-day Gnosticism.

None of all this would be more than sad were it not for the eloquence of his case, and were it not for *VALIS*, a stunning tale, written in 1978, that combines mocking self-analysis and convincing fictional depictions of the new world. Dick was grappling with greater demons than most of us will ever imagine. But then he died.

Paranoid visions
There is not a great deal of technological speculation in Dick's novels. Most of the sleek, homicidal machines in his work are unfriendly – such as this police "spinner" from the film Blade Runner, *which is built to kill.*

Philip K. Dick

FRANK HERBERT

BORN / DIED **1920-86**

NATIONALITY **American**

KEY WORK **The Dune series**

HERBERT, like most people with big ideas, sometimes found that words failed him, and so used too many of them. This could make him, at times, something of a windbag. His classic second novel *Dune* (see page 224) was, as most SF readers will know, a vast compendium of lore – from the theological through the sociological and the ecological and beyond – which somehow still managed not to submerge the central story of Paul Atreides. But the several sequels that followed – *Dune Messiah*, *God Emperor of Dune*, *Dune This*, *Dune That*, and *Dune Umpteen et cetera* – were not as rewarding as the original; a couple of them are talkfests, with neither salt nor savour.

Frank Herbert came from the Pacific coast, the remote edge of the United States, and he remained there for all his life. The place is apparent in his work: wherever they may be set, his novels seem to breathe a different air than most other American fiction. There is a certain feeling of impatient brusqueness running through them, even when Herbert is at his most longwinded, and a sense of rapport with the outdoor world that appears, at times, almost uneasy. Given that White civilization began to plunder the far northern reaches of the Pacific coast almost within living memory, this unease is not entirely surprising. Nor is it surprising that so many of Herbert's works – tales like *Soul Catcher*, for example – are attempts to redeem environments that our modern world has, perhaps irredeemably, transformed. Time and again, Herbert's venues are used as tests of humanity's ability to live in harmony with reality; often, we fail them.

His first novel, *The Dragon in the Sea*, treats a 21st-century submarine as a kind of test environment, in which men must learn to live sanely within themselves and in accordance with the rules of reality, or die. *Destination: Void* is set in a similarly constrained test environment: a starship whose guiding computer, once it has been transformed into an artificial intelligence, defines itself as God. The crew must establish a kind of ecological rapport with their new deity, trading their worship for its agreement to continue operating the ship for them. *The Santaroga Barrier* describes the evolution of a higher intelligence within a constrained community, which it tests, and which in turn tests it. *Hellstrom's Hive* – which is set in yet another closed test environment – describes the creation of a human collective based on the model of the social insects.

There is a tirelessness about the man and about his works. Part guru, part Ancient Mariner, Frank Herbert showed us how to make SF think.

BIBLIOGRAPHY

NOVELS AND NOVELLAS

1956 **The Dragon in the Sea** Doubleday, retitled **21st Century Sub**, retitled **Under Pressure**
1965 **Dune** Chilton
1966 **The Green Brain** Ace
     Destination: Void Berkley
     The Eyes of Heisenberg Berkley
1968 **The Santaroga Barrier** Berkley
     The Heaven Makers Avon
1969 **Dune Messiah** Putnam
1970 **Whipping Star** Putnam
1972 **The God Makers** Putnam
     Soul Catcher Putnam
1973 **Hellstrom's Hive** Doubleday, retitled **Project 40**
1976 **Children of Dune** Berkley
1977 **The Dosadi Experiment** Putnam
1979 **The Jesus Incident** Berkley, with Bill Ransom
1980 **Direct Descent** New English Library
1981 **God-Emperor of Dune** Putnam
1982 **The White Plague** Putnam
1983 **The Lazarus Effect** Putnam, with Bill Ransom
1984 **Heretics of Dune** Gollancz
1985 **Chapter House Dune** Gollancz, retitled **Chapterhouse: Dune**
1986 **Man of Two Worlds** Putnam, with Brian Herbert
1988 **The Ascension Factor** Putnam, with Bill Ransom

SHORT STORY COLLECTIONS

1970 **The Worlds of Frank Herbert** New English Library
1973 **The Book of Frank Herbert** DAW
1975 **The Best of Frank Herbert** Sidgwick and Jackson
1980 **The Priests of Psi** Gollancz
1985 **Eye** Berkley

Doomed effort?
Dune reached the cinema screen in the mid-1980s, in a film adaptation that spared nothing to achieve its striking visual effects, but unfortunately – perhaps inevitably – reduced Herbert's dense text to a melodrama.

ARKADY AND BORIS STRUGATSKI

BORN / DIED
Arkady 1925-91
Boris 1931-

NATIONALITY
Russian

KEY WORK
**Trudno byt'
bogom**

THE Strugatski brothers wrote almost everything for which they will be remembered while living as citizens of the Soviet Union. This was in itself something of a tragedy, because Soviet SF was not permitted to posit worlds contradictory to the predictive assumptions of the official Marxist-Leninism, and much of their SF was consequently written in code. The bigger tragedy is that although censorship is now significantly less repressive, there will probably be no more great Strugatski novels. Arkady died in 1991; and there are rumours only of new work from Boris alone.

Censorship is, of course, a blight, and the Strugatskis' coded language – often described as Aesopian, after the slave who told hard truths in the form of animal fables – is sometimes hard going for Western readers used to hearing messages shouted in clear. But even the laziest reader will find a rumbustious tale like *Trudno byt' bogom* (*Hard to be a God*) impossible to resist.

The later *Piknik na obochine* (*Roadside Picnic*), filmed by Andrei Tarkovsky as *Stalker*, is a subtly scathing fable about the rubbish left on Earth by alien picnickers, whose debris proves highly dangerous to us natives. "*Za milliard let do konsta sveta*" (*Definitely Maybe*) and *Ulitka na sklone* (*The Snail on the Slope*) both subversively argue that no form of knowledge can be ultimately secure, not even (by implication) Marxist-Leninist precepts about the course of Progress. *Gadkie lebedi* (*Children of Rain*) has ironic fun with the old SF standby of superchildren raised in secret to rule the world. Neither censorship nor translation problems can stop the Strugatskis in the end: they are writers of genius, and they speak to us.

BIBLIOGRAPHY

NOVELS AND NOVELLAS
1959 **Strana bagrovykh tuch** Detgiz [**The country of crimson clouds**]
1960 **Shest' spichek** USSR [**Six matches**]
Put'na Amal'teiu Molodaia Gvardiia [**Destination: Amaltheia**]
1963 **Dalekaia Raduga** Molodaia Gvardiia, translated as **Far Rainbow**
1964 **Trudno byt' bogom** Molodaia Gvardiia, translated as **Hard to be a God**
1965 **Khishchnye veschchi veka** Molodaia Gvardiia, translated as **The Final Circle of Paradise**
Ponedel'nik nachinaetsia v subbotu Detskaia Literatura, translated as **Monday Begins on Saturday**
1966 **Ulitka na sklone** in Soviet journals, translated as **The Snail on the Slope**
Gadkie lebedi in Soviet journals, translated as **Children of Rain**
1968 **Vtoroe nashestvie marsian** USSR, first part translated as second title in **Far Rainbow: and the Second Invasion from Mars**
1969 **Skazka o troike** USSR, translated as second title in **Roadside Picnic & The Tale of the Troika**

1969 **Obitaemyi ostrov** Detlit, translated as **Prisoners of Power**
1970 **Otel 'U pogibshchego alpinista'** in Soviet journal [**Hotel 'To the Lost Climber'**]
1972 **Piknik na obochine** USSR, translated as first title in **Roadside Picnic & The Tale of the Troika**
1976 **"Za milliard let do konsta sveta"** in Soviet journal, translated as **Definitely Maybe**
1979 **"Zhuk v muraveinike"** in Soviet journal, translated as **Beetle in the Anthill**
1985 **"Volney gasiat veter"** in Soviet journal, translated as **The Time Wanderers**
1989 **Grad obrechennyi** USSR [**The doomed city**]
Otiagoshchennye zlom, ili sorok let spustia Prometei [**Burdened by evil, or 40 years after**]

SHORT STORY COLLECTIONS
1962 **Vozvrashchenie (Polden': XXII vek)** Molodaia Gvardiia, translated as **Noon: 22nd Century**
Stazhery USSR, translated as **Space Apprentice**
1982 **Escape Attempt** USSR

HARLAN ELLISON

BORN **1934**

NATIONALITY **American**

OTHER NAMES **Nalrah Nosrille, Jay Charby, Wallace Edmonson, Ellis Hart, Jay Solo, Cordwainer Bird**

KEY WORKS **"'Repent, Harlequin!' Said the Ticktockman", "I Have No Mouth, and I Must Scream", Dangerous Visions**

ONLY a few writers have ever made their reputations by short stories. Almost always, our awareness of the facility of a V.S. Pritchett or a John O'Hara in shorter literary forms comes after we have read their novels or other work. So Harlan Ellison stands alone, in this as in other matters, because his novels are short, bad, few, forgettable, and forgotten. The best of his tales published as single works are *All the Lies That Are My Life* and *Mephisto in Onyx*: both are of novelette length, and both are pretty fine, although each of them shows the odd moment of strain.

There is something very odd about Ellison as a writer. It helps to explain both his weakness at longer fictional forms and his remarkable strength at the short-story length. Unlike most authors, who tend to do their work in solitary and put together their tales over weeks or months, Ellison is a performance artist. Although most of his fiction is written in normal solitude, he has always been perfectly happy to write in public – even, at times, in shop windows. When he does this, he writes in great, swooping bursts of inspiration, which unsurprisingly do not often take him past the limits of the short story; when the inspiration pays off, we have before us a tale like

"'Repent, Harlequin!' Said the Ticktockman" (1965), or "I Have No Mouth, and I Must Scream" (1967), or "The Prowler in the City at the Edge of the World" (1967), or "Pretty Maggie Moneyeyes" (1967). As their titles hint, these stories display a high rhetorical intensity and a satirical bite.

While Ellison will probably be best remembered for his fiction, he has also been a controversial columnist and essayist for decades, and his anthologies (especially the outstanding *Dangerous Visions*) are like his short stories. They are among the best the field has seen.

At his best, Ellison's work is full of a rage for authenticity, an urgency about being human and real in a world of deranging impersonality and evil. His world is an existential testing ground, and the future is a gauntlet that human beings must run.

BIBLIOGRAPHY

NOVELS AND NOVELLAS
1960 **The Man With Nine Lives** Ace
1967 **Doomsman** Belmont
1975 **Phoenix Without Ashes** Fawcett, with Edward Bryant
1980 **All the Lies That Are My Life** Underwood-Miller
1991 **Run for the Stars** Tor
1993 **Mephisto in Onyx** Ziesing

SHORT STORY COLLECTIONS
1960 **A Touch of Infinity** Ace
1962 **Ellison Wonderland** Paperback Library, retitled **Earthman, Go Home**
1965 **Paingod and Other Delusions** Pyramid
1967 **I Have No Mouth, and I Must Scream** Pyramid
From the Land of Fear Belmont
1968 **Love Ain't Nothing But Sex Misspelled** Trident
1969 **The Beast That Shouted Love at the Heart of the World** Avon
1970 **Over the Edge** Belmont
1971 **Alone Against Tomorrow** Macmillan; retitled in two volumes **All the Sounds of Fear** and **The Time of the Eye**
Partners in Wonder Walker (collaborative)
1974 **Approaching Oblivion** Walker
1975 **Deathbird Stories: A Pantheon of Modern Gods** Harper
No Doors, No Windows Pyramid
1978 **Strange Wine** Harper
1979 **The Fantasies of Harlan Ellison** Gregg Press
1980 **Shatterday** Houghton Mifflin
1982 **Stalking the Nightmare** Phantasia
1987 **The Essential Ellison** Nemo Press
1988 **Angry Candy** Houghton Mifflin
1994 **Mind Fields** Morpheus

AS EDITOR
1967 **Dangerous Visions** Doubleday
1972 **Again, Dangerous Visions** Doubleday

MICHAEL MOORCOCK

BORN **1939**

NATIONALITY **English, resident in the United States**

OTHER NAMES **Michael Barrington, Bill Barclay, Edward P. Bradbury, James Colvin, Desmond Reid**

KEY WORKS **The *Jerry Cornelius* series, the *Elric* series, the *Colonel Pyat* series, *Mother London***

THERE is no good place to start with the phenomenon that is Michael Moorcock. This is no accident. Almost every single book he has ever written (with the exception of a couple of oddities like *Caribbean Crisis*, his first novel, and *Mother London*, his finest single book) has been either designed or retrofitted to take its place in the huge superseries that is now generally called **The Tale of the Eternal Champion**. This champion goes by a number of names – Jerry Cornelius, Elric of Melniboné, Corum, Hawkmoon, Jerek Carnelian, and Von Bek, to list only some of his more familiar embodiments. Each of the Champions seems to have submerged knowledge, or memories, of being each of the others.

In series after series, the Eternal Champion strives, sometimes unwillingly, to balance the forces of Order and Chaos. The various worlds in which these conflicts take place can be described as a multiverse: a vast palimpsest of realities, each of them sharing central characters, and each of them reflecting in various ways the eternal strife between law and the creative mind (which represents chaos, a necessary component in any living system). Over all of this vast array of conflicts reigns the slow increase of entropy.

Some of the worlds are fantasy realms; others, like the 1960s London of Jerry Cornelius, are Science Fictional; still others, like the Edwardian Alternate Future inhabited by Oswald Bastable, combine fantasy and SF.

Some of these many stories are routine, although an air of sly, ironic melancholy suffuses even the silliest moments; others are significant fabulations. In the latter category the most important are *Mother London*, and, of the series, the **Cornelius** books (*The Final Programme*, *A Cure for Cancer*,

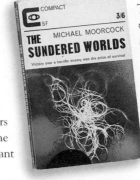

Victorian scraps
The Condition of Musak *used these as a source.*

Multiple worlds
The Sundered Worlds *was the novel that first introduced Moorcock's multiverse, the setting in which the endlessly varying and repeating personas of the Eternal Champion came to be reflected.*

The English Assassin, and *The Condition of Muzak*, plus some later collections), and the **Colonel Pyat** sequence (which has only light touches of the fantastic, although it refers to the rest of the multiverse in passing, and includes *Byzantium Endures*, *The Laughter of Carthage*, and *Jerusalem Commands*). Over the years, as these series have progressively come to dominate Moorcock's creative mind, the fluent fabulist of yore has turned into a deeply meditative creator of myths for the Millennium.

BIBLIOGRAPHY

NOVELS AND NOVELLAS
1962 **Caribbean Crisis** Fleetway, with James Cawthorn, both as Desmond Reid
1965 **Stormbringer** Jenkins
The Sundered Worlds Compact, retitled **The Blood Red Game**
The Fireclown Compact, retitled **The Winds of Limbo**
Warriors of Mars Compact, as Edward P. Bradbury, retitled **The City of the Beast**
Blades of Mars Compact, as Edward P. Bradbury, retitled **The Lord of the Spiders**
The Barbarians of Mars Compact, as Edward P. Bradbury, retitled **The Masters of the Pit**
1966 **The Twilight Man** Compact, retitled **The Shores of Death**
Printer's Devil Compact, as Bill Barclay, revised as **The Russian Intelligence**
The LSD Dossier Compact, ghosted for Roger Harris
Somewhere in the Night Compact, revised as **The Chinese Agent**
1967 **The Jewel in the Skull** Lancer
The Wrecks of Time Ace, revised as **The Rituals of Infinity**
1968 **The Final Programme** Avon
Sorcerer's Amulet Lancer, retitled **The Mad God's Amulet**

1969 **The Secret of the Runestaff** Lancer, retitled **The Runestaff**
The Ice Schooner Sphere
Behold the Man Allison and Busby
The Black Corridor Ace
1970 **The Eternal Champion** Mayflower
Phoenix in Obsidian Mayflower, retitled **The Silver Warriors**
1971 **A Cure for Cancer** Allison and Busby
The Knight of the Swords Mayflower
The Queen of the Swords Mayflower
The King of the Swords Mayflower
The Sleeping Sorceress New English Library, retitled **The Vanishing Tower**
The Warlord of the Air Ace
1972 **An Alien Heat** MacGibbon and Kee
Breakfast in the Ruins New English Library
The English Assassin Allison and Busby
Elric of Melniboné Hutchinson
1973 **The Bull and the Spear** Allison and Busby
Count Brass Mayflower
The Champion of Garathorm Mayflower
The Oak and the Ram Allison and Busby

1973 **The Jade Man's Eyes** Unicorn Bookshop
1974 **The Sword and the Stallion** Allison and Busby
The Land Leviathan Doubleday
The Hollow Lands Harper
1975 **The Distant Suns** Unicorn Bookshop, with James Cawthorn
The Quest for Tanelorn Mayflower
1976 **The Sailor on the Seas of Fate** Quartet
The Adventures of Una Persson and Catherine Cornelius in the Twentieth Century Quartet
The End of All Songs Harper
1977 **The Condition of Muzak** Allison and Busby
The Transformation of Miss Mavis Ming W.H. Allen, retitled **A Messiah at the End of Time**
The Weird of the White Wolf DAW Books
The Bane of the Black Sword DAW Books
1978 **Gloriana, or, The Unfulfill'd Queen** Allison and Busby
1979 **The Real Life Mr. Newman** Allison and Busby
1980 **The Golden Barge** Savoy
The Great Rock'n'Roll Swindle Virgin

1981 **The Entropy Tango** New English Library
The Steel Czar Mayflower
The War Hound and the World's Pain Pocket Books
Byzantium Endures Secker and Warburg
1982 **The Brothel in Rosenstrasse** New English Library
1984 **The Laughter of Carthage** Secker and Warburg
1986 **The City in the Autumn Stars** Grafton
The Dragon in the Sword Ace
1988 **Mother London** Secker and Warburg
1989 **The Fortress of the Pearl** Ace
1991 **The Revenge of the Rose** Grafton
1992 **Jerusalem Commands** Secker and Warburg

SHORT STORY COLLECTIONS
1963 **The Stealer of Souls** Spearman
1966 **The Deep Fix** Compact, as James Colvin
1969 **The Time Dweller** Hart Davis
1970 **The Singing Citadel** Mayflower
1976 **Moorcock's Book of Martyrs** Quartet, retitled **Dying for Tomorrow**
The Lives and Times of Jerry Cornelius Allison and Busby

1976 **Legends from the End of Time** W.H. Allen
1977 **Sojan** Savoy
1980 **My Experiences in the Third World War** Savoy
1984 **The Opium General** Harrap
Elric at the End of Time New English Library
1989 **Casablanca** Gollancz
1993 **Earl Aubec** Millennium

NON-FICTION
1983 **The Retreat from Liberty** Zomba
1986 **Letters from Hollywood** Harrap
1987 **Wizardry and Wild Romance: A Study of Epic Fantasy** Gollancz

SELECTED WORKS AS EDITOR
1965 **The Best of New Worlds** Compact
1967 **Best SF Stories from New Worlds** Panther, eight volumes extending through 1974
1968 **The Traps of Time** Rapp and Whiting
1969 **The Inner Landscape** Allison and Busby
1970 **The Nature of the Catastrophe** Hutchinson, with Langdon Jones, revised as **The New Nature of the Catastrophe**

JOANNA RUSS

BORN **1937**

NATIONALITY **American**

KEY WORKS **Picnic on Paradise, The Female Man**

FOR decades, women writers of SF had either disguised themselves as men, or written "women's" stories, or kept mum. Joanna Russ was one of the first women authors in the field of SF to apply toughly argued feminist viewpoints to the literature of the fantastic. Alyx, the streetwise – but definitely not gamine – protagonist of *Picnic on Paradise* and *Alyx*, was to stand as a model for countless successors:

she had her Space Opera adventures, suffered her defeats, and enjoyed her triumphs, all of it without paying any attention to matters of "femininity" or gender. She was like a huge sigh of relief to thousands of readers, a great many of them male.

But Joanna Russ was not finished with the issue yet. *The Female Man* is the single greatest feminist SF novel written, and one of the most significant books of the last 30 years in any literary genre. With superbly controlled anger, it tells the same woman's story as it would have occurred in several contrasting Alternate Universes, and delineates the fate of women in oppressive cultures, and the joy of women – of all human beings – in cultures not obsessed by the task of trivializing and demonizing all that is

the Other. The task given to anyone reading this novel is to understand that everyone is somehow someone else's Other, everyone is someone else's demon or scapegoat.

Russ's short stories are similarly acute, although relatively few of them have so devastating an effect on our preconceptions as her novels. *Souls* – a novella so fine that it was eventually published as a separate volume – is typical in its attentiveness to character, and to place, and in its evocation of threatened lives. To be a woman, for Russ, is to live under threat.

Joanna Russ

BIBLIOGRAPHY

NOVELS AND NOVELLAS
1968 *Picnic on Paradise* Ace
1970 *And Chaos Died* Ace
1975 *The Female Man* Bantam
1977 *We Who Are About To ...* Dell
1978 *Kittatinny: A Tale of Magic* Daughters
   The Two of Them Berkley
1980 *On Strike Against God* Out and Out
1989 *Souls* Tor

SHORT STORY COLLECTIONS
1976 *Alyx* Gregg Press, retitled **The Adventures of Alyx**
1983 *The Zanzibar Car* Arkham House
1985 *Extra(ordinary) People* St. Martin's Press
1987 *The Hidden Side of the Moon* St. Martin's Press

NON-FICTION
1983 *How to Suppress Women's Writing* University of Texas Press
1985 *Magic Mommas, Trembling Sisters, Puritans and Perverts: Feminist Essays* Crossing Press

LARRY NIVEN

BORN **1938**

NATIONALITY **American**

KEY WORKS **The Tales of Known Space series, The Mote in God's Eye**

NIVEN may be a very private person, but his fiction is enormously and exuberantly extrovert – or it once was. The first joyful stories and novels in

the ***Known Space*** series (see page 66), his huge and ongoing Future History of the next several thousand years, display a prolific inventiveness perhaps never seen in SF before, or since. Wedding an ingenious understanding of the hard sciences to a sportive sense of human behaviour, he created a libertarian future that most of us would give our eye teeth to inhabit. There were vile threats – the alien in *World of Ptavvs* is truly terrifying – and later volumes increasingly felt the burden of adjusting to the precedents set by so many complex preceding stories, but the overall sense was of a universe of open doors. All we needed was the mind, the tools, the will, and a little help from our friends. In *Ringworld* (see page 226), there were almost too many

friends from too many different previous stories, and the tale's great concept – a flat, inhabitable ring around a sun – almost foundered.

At the same time, with Jerry Pournelle, Niven was also writing blockbuster SF tales like *The Mote in God's Eye*, in which his highly fertile imagination (the alien moties are Nivenesque) fuelled Pournelle's epic plots. But the later books, solo and collaborative, seem decreasingly in love with the new. The race is over, and there is no prize.

Larry Niven

BIBLIOGRAPHY

NOVELS AND NOVELLAS
1966 *World of Ptavvs* Ballantine
1968 *A Gift from Earth* Ballantine
1970 *Ringworld* Ballantine
1971 *The Flying Sorcerers* Ballantine, with David Gerrold
1973 *Protector* Ballantine
1974 *The Mote in God's Eye* Simon and Schuster, with Jerry Pournelle
1976 *Inferno* Pocket Books, with Jerry Pournelle
   A World Out of Time Holt Rinehart
1977 *Lucifer's Hammer* Playboy Press, with Jerry Pournelle
1978 *The Magic Goes Away* Ace

1980 *The Ringworld Engineers* Phantasia Press
   The Patchwork Girl Ace
   Mordred Ace, with John Eric Holmes
1981 *Dream Park* Phantasia Press, with Steven Barnes
   Oath of Fealty Phantasia Press
   Warrior's Blood Ace, with Jerry Pournelle and Richard S. McEnroe
   Warrior's World Ace, with Jerry Pournelle and Richard S. McEnroe
1982 *The Descent of Anansi* Tor Books, with Steven Barnes
1983 *Roger's Rangers* Ace, with Jerry Pournelle and John Silbersack

1984 *The Integral Trees* Ballantine
1985 *Footfall* Ballantine, with Jerry Pournelle
1987 *The Legacy of Heorot* Gollancz, with Steven Barnes and Jerry Pournelle
   The Smoke Ring Ballantine
1989 *The Barsoom Project* Ace, with Steven Barnes
1991 *Achilles' Choice* Tor, with Steven Barnes
   Dream Park: The Voodoo Game Pan, with Steven Barnes, retitled **The California Voodoo Game**
   Fallen Angels Baen, with Jerry Pournelle and Michael Flynn

1993 *The Gripping Hand* Pocket Books, with Jerry Pournelle, retitled **The Moat Around Murcheson's Eye**

SHORT STORY COLLECTIONS
1968 *Neutron Star* Ballantine
1969 *The Shape of Space* Ballantine
1971 *All the Myriad Ways* Ballantine
1973 *The Flight of the Horse* Ballantine
   Inconstant Moon Gollancz
1974 *A Hole in Space* Ballantine
1975 *Tales of Known Space* Ballantine
1976 *The Long ARM of Gil Hamilton* Ballantine
1979 *Convergent Series* Ballantine

1984 *The Time of the Warlock* Steel Dragon Press
   Niven's Laws Philadelphia Science Fiction Society
1985 *Limits* Ballantine
1990 *N-Space* Tor
1991 *Playgrounds of the Mind* Tor

AS EDITOR
1981 *The Magic May Return* Ace
1984 *More Magic* Ace
1988 *The Man-Kzin Wars* Baen, with three further volumes extending through 1991

ROGER ZELAZNY

BORN **1937**

NATIONALITY **American**

KEY WORKS **Four for Tomorrow, The Doors of his Face, the Lamps of his Mouth, This Immortal, Lord of Light, the Amber series**

T HE class of 1962 may never be matched. First published that year were Samuel R. Delany, Thomas M. Disch and Ursula K. Le Guin; but the most spectacular was probably Roger Zelazny. Delany was young, and over the top stylistically; Disch began slowly, as did Le Guin. But Zelazny arrived fully fledged, like some god out of the sea, surfing towards us on his shell; and for many he did his best work within a year or so of his debut.

This may be unfair. It is certainly cruel. But there can be no doubt that the early work was spectacular.

His first stories – many of them are collected in *Four for Tomorrow* and *The Doors of his Face, the Lamps of his Mouth* – are dense recreations of mythic material in SF terms, with heroes and villains who are directly descended from the archetypes of the human race. Frequently, these figures suffer profound metamorphoses, giving otherwise orthodox SF storylines a resonance straight out of the darker sort of Celtic fantasy. Indeed, a story like "A Rose for Ecclesiastes" is hard to understand as being either SF or fantasy, because it weds the two genres in its attempt to understand the truths beneath the tale of a failed Earth poet on Mars, who renews not only himself but also the ancient Martian race and the sterile planet itself. The story is a poem about godlike actions, but is told, at one level, in the strictest SF terms.

Zelazny's first novel also triumphed through balancing various kinds of story. The hero of *This Immortal* (see page 224) is indeed undying, but is also hugely exuberant and in love with life. The setting is a future Earth, whose inhabitants have been transfigured into figures who resemble and parody the

ancient gods. When aliens arrive and declare the hero, Conrad, the ruler of Earth, rebirth begins. Other novels of similar complexity, like *Lord of Light* (see page 224), soon followed.

But with *Nine Princes in Amber*, Zelazny began a new phase in his career. He had become a

smoother and more efficient writer, although not necessarily a better one, and this novel began the **Amber** series, which still continues. Amber is a higher, more intense plane than that of Earth, and the actions of its godlike inhabitants constitute the deeper structures of human actions – humans being the apes of gods. The action is constant, sometimes confusing, and the series is enormously popular.

If some readers have been slightly disappointed by some of Zelazny's more recent work, it is perhaps because they sense that a writer of such intense intelligence, a writer whose imagination is fiery and liquid and intoxicating, could have perhaps written the great SF novel of the latter years of the 20th century. Zelazny never did this. What he has done, for many years now, is give us some of the sharpest entertainments the field has ever seen. Perhaps, one day, the great book will come.

BIBLIOGRAPHY

NOVELS AND NOVELLAS
1966 **This Immortal** Ace
 The Dream Master Ace, retitled (original magazine version and title) **He Who Shapes**
1967 **Lord of Light** Doubleday
1969 **Isle of the Dead** Ace
 Creatures of Light and Darkness Doubleday
 Damnation Alley Putnam
1970 **Nine Princes in Amber** Doubleday
1971 **Jack of Shadows** Walker
1972 **The Guns of Avalon** Doubleday
1973 **Today We Choose Faces** New American Library
 To Die in Italbar Doubleday
1975 **Sign of the Unicorn** Doubleday
1976 **Doorways in the Sand** Harper
 The Hand of Oberon Doubleday
 Bridge of Ashes New American Library
 Deus Irae Doubleday, with Philip K. Dick
 My Name is Legion Ballantine
1978 **The Courts of Chaos** Doubleday
1979 **Roadmarks** Ballantine
1980 **Changeling** Ace
1981 **Madwand** Phantasia Press
 The Changing Land Ace
1982 **Coils** Tor, with Fred Saberhagen
 Eye of Cat Underwood-Miller
1985 **Trumps of Doom** Arbor House
1986 **Blood of Amber** Arbor House

1987 **A Dark Traveling** Walker
1987 **Sign of Chaos** Arbor House
1989 **Knight of Shadows** Morrow
1990 **The Black Throne** Baen, with Fred Saberhagen
 The Mask of Loki Baen, with Thomas T. Thomas
 The Graveyard Heart Tor
 Home is the Hangman Tor
1991 **Bring Me the Head of Prince Charming** Bantam, with Robert Sheckley
 Prince of Chaos Morrow
1992 **Flare** Baen, with Thomas T. Thomas
1993 **A Night in the Lonesome October** Morrow
 If at Faust You Don't Succeed Bantam, with Robert Sheckley
1994 **Wilderness** Forge, with Gerald Hausman (semi-autobiographical)

SHORT STORY COLLECTIONS
1967 **Four for Tomorrow** Ace, retitled **A Rose for Ecclesiastes**
1971 **The Doors of his Face, the Lamps of his Mouth** Doubleday
1980 **The Last Defender of Camelot** Pocket Books
1982 **Dilvish, the Damned** Ballantine
1983 **Unicorn Variations** Pocket Books
1989 **Frost and Fire** Morrow

Film failure
Damnation Alley *was substantially unlike the book.*

SAMUEL R. DELANY

BORN **1942**

NATIONALITY **American**

OTHER NAME **K. Leslie Steiner**

KEY WORKS **The Einstein Intersection, "Time Considered as a Helix of Semi-Precious Stones", Dhalgren, the Nevèrÿon series, The American Shore**

DELANY might be called a tearaway, back in 1962. Something of a child prodigy, he rocketed through a high-powered education, and sold his first novel, *The Jewels of Aptor*, before he was 20. He enjoyed a singularly complex life, much of it engagingly exposed in *Heavenly Breakfast: An Essay on the Winter of Love* and *The Motion of Light in Water: Sex and Science Fiction Writing in the East Village 1957–65*, memoirs he published long after the events described in them. He was black, bisexual, intensely social, precocious, and extremely glad to be alive.

For five years his career continued the happy course. His relationship with Marilyn Hacker, now an extremely well-known poet, flourished (they married, had a child, and then divorced after several years), and the novels flooded out. *Babel-17* is the easiest to admire; but all are overflowingly rich.

The climax of Delany's first period, *The Einstein Intersection* (see page 224), was one of the most ambitious novels yet to appear under the label of SF (astonishingly, it was first published by a mass-market house, as a paperback). In a baroque far future, an alien race has taken over the abandoned Earth. The hero's resemblance to the Orpheus of myth is anything but accidental; his quest into a Jungian underworld, where human archetypes roam the labyrinths of the collective unconscious, is to capture a sense of meaning for the new inhabitants of the dying planet.

NOTABLE WORK

BABEL-17

Babel-17 comes from a time when SF writers like Delany felt they could conquer the literary world. It is perhaps the brightest of all Delany's novels, intriguingly examining sex roles (the protagonist is a woman) and language (as the title hints, the tale is about a weapon that works as a language disintegrator). Like all his early work, the tale overflows with mythopoeic vigour and material. There are Space Opera shenanigans, romantic plots, sophisticated debates, and entrancing characters: it is a cornucopia.

Nova was also a climax, but in this case, instead of concentrating on complex interior quests, it focused on a search across a Space Opera universe for a grail-like object. And, for a while, that seemed to be that: Delany had fallen silent. In reality he was very busily at work on two projects: a language, based on modern literary critical theory, with which to describe and to defend SF as a genre of importance; and what was to be his magnum opus to date.

That huge work was *Dhalgren*, and it is perhaps the most difficult SF novel that has still sold in large numbers. It is the circular story of a typical Delany hero – a lone artist named Kidd – who comes to a mysterious city, has complex adventures there, writes a book which is almost certainly called "Dhalgren", and who leaves the way he came (as in James Joyce's *Finnegans Wake*, the last sentence of the book is the beginning of the first sentence of the book). *Dhalgren* became a cult text, and Delany became something of a guru. Ever since, his pronouncements on issues of gender, race, genre, and politics have been given – and have fully deserved – very careful attention.

At the same time, however, his career in fiction faltered somewhat. The knotted intensity of some of his earlier work began to seem clotted and self-consciously insistent in later novels like *Triton* and *Stars in my Pocket like Grains of Sand*, although the **Nevèrÿon** series retained much of the old vigour. Into these stories – ostensibly sword-and-sorcery adventures set in an imaginary land – Delany subversively inserts gender, sex, and race issues. There is a lot of sado-masochism in these stories,

and in *Stars in my Pocket* too, but always designed to shock readers out of their preconceptions, never simply to give a quick vicarious thrill.

Delany's most important work in recent decades may well be pedagogical. He has become an influential professor of English Studies, and has published several intensely demanding works of criticism, whose account of the nature of SF must be grappled with by any critic of the field. The most remarkable of these may be *The American Shore*, a full-length book devoted to the analysis of one short story, "Angouleme", by Thomas M. Disch; in reworked form, the tale forms part of Disch's novel *334* (see page 227). The two collections *Starboard Wine* and *The Straits of Messina* contain most of Delany's most readable essays. He is not an easy read, but he is a necessary one.

Delany has had several careers and addressed many issues. He has energized every role he has taken on. He is a large presence, and seemingly a grave one; but for decades he has guaranteed that those who listen to him will be chaffed, amused, challenged, and understood.

BIBLIOGRAPHY

NOVELS AND NOVELLAS
1962 **The Jewels of Aptor** Ace
1963 **Captives of the Flame** Ace, revised as **Out of the Dead City**
1964 **The Towers of Toron** Ace
1965 **City of a Thousand Suns** Ace
 The Ballad of Beta-2 Ace
1966 **Empire Star** Ace
 Babel-17 Ace
1967 **The Einstein Intersection** Ace
1968 **Nova** Doubleday
1973 **The Tides of Lust** Lancer, retitled **Equinox**
1975 **Dhalgren** Bantam
1976 **Triton** Bantam
1978 **Empire: A Visual Novel** Berkley
1983 **Nevèrÿona, or, The Tale of Signs and Cities** Bantam
1984 **Stars in my Pocket like Grains of Sand** Bantam
1989 **The Star Pit** Tor
1990 **We, in Some Strange Power's Employ, Move on a Rigorous Line** Tor
1993 **They Fly at Çiron** Incunabula
1994 **The Mad Man** Richard Kasak

SHORT STORY COLLECTIONS
1978 **Driftglass** Doubleday, expanded as **Driftglass/Starshards**
1979 **Tales of Nevèrÿon** Bantam

1981 **Distant Stars** Bantam
1985 **Flight from Nevèrÿon** Bantam
1987 **The Bridge of Lost Desire** Arbor House, revised as **Return to Nevèrÿon**

NON-FICTION
1977 **The Jewel-Hinged Jaw: Notes on the Language of Science Fiction** Dragon Press
1978 **The American Shore: Meditations on a Tale of Science Fiction by Thomas M. Disch – "Angouleme"** Dragon Press
1979 **Heavenly Breakfast: An Essay on the Winter of Love** Bantam
1984 **Starboard Wine: More Notes on the Language of Science Fiction** Dragon Press
1988 **The Motion of Light in Water: Sex and Science Fiction Writing in the East Village 1957–65** Arbor House
 Wagner/Artaud: A Play of 19th and 20th Century Critical Fiction Ansatz
1989 **The Straits of Messina** Serconria Press

AS EDITOR
1970 **Quark** Paperback Library, with Marilyn Hacker, four volumes through 1971
1980 **Nebula Award Winners 13** Harper

KATE WILHELM

BORN **1928**

NATIONALITY **American**

KEY WORKS **The Downstairs Room, Where Late the Sweet Birds Sang**

THE regions that Kate Wilhelm's heart answers to have suffered much of the damage the century has inflicted upon rural areas, whose traditions and ecologies are vulnerable. She is a little bit like Simak, but wryer, more sour. He behaved, at times, as if he simply could not credit what was being done to his beloved world. She, coming later, saw it already done.

Nor does Kate Wilhelm restrict herself to the Pacific coast, although some of her tales – like "The Winter Beach", which makes up the extremely moving first half of *Welcome, Chaos* – eloquently delineate the mists, salt harshness, and enclave security of the northern Pacific edge of the United States. Again and again, her work turns to matters of responsibility for the effects of science and the intemperate human (very often male) will on a fragile environment. Early novels, like *Let the Fire Fall*, were flamboyant, but pretty sloppy; later tales are splendidly sombre. *Where Late the Sweet Birds Sang* follows a group that survives ecological catastrophe and bases a new life upon cloning, but examines that life with a sad, wise eye. *Death Qualified: A Mystery of Chaos* infuses similar concerns for the world into a murder mystery and courtroom drama whose SF elements, although omnipresent, never distort the grave portrait of a society recognizably our own, and recognizably adrift.

Her novels, although admirable, do at times stray from their course (*Death Qualified* excepted). Her short fiction – especially her novellas, for she is one of the finest novella writers in the field – makes an extremely impressive body of work. Most of the stories assembled in collections like *The Downstairs Room*, *The Infinity Box*, or *And the Angels Sing* are set in an intimately familiar near future; many of them deal specifically with cloning and other biological manipulations of social life. Wilhelm is particularly strong on families, on the intrusions from within and without that rend (or strengthen) small groups of humans as they live out their lives on the edge of the world to come.

BIBLIOGRAPHY

NOVELS AND NOVELLAS
1965 **The Clone** Berkley, with Theodore L. Thomas
1966 **The Nevermore Affair** Doubleday
1967 **The Killer Thing** Doubleday, revised as **The Killing Thing**
1969 **Let the Fire Fall** Doubleday
1970 **Year of the Cloud** Doubleday, with Theodore L. Thomas
1971 **Margaret and I** Little Brown
1974 **City of Cain** Little Brown
1976 **The Clewiston Test** Farrar Straus
Where Late the Sweet Birds Sang Harper
1977 **Fault Lines** Harper
1979 **Juniper Time** Harper
1981 **A Sense of Shadow** Houghton Mifflin
1982 **Oh, Susannah!** Houghton Mifflin
1983 **Welcome, Chaos** Houghton Mifflin
1986 **Huysman's Pets** Bluejay
1987 **The Hamlet Trap** St. Martin's Press
1988 **The Dark Door** St. Martin's Press
Crazy Time St. Martin's Press
1989 **Smart House** St. Martin's Press
1990 **Cambio Bay** St. Martin's Press
1990 **Sweet, Sweet Poison** St. Martin's Press

1991 **Death Qualified: A Mystery of Chaos** St. Martin's Press
The Girl Who Fell Into the Sky Pulphouse
1992 **Seven Kinds of Death** St. Martin's Press
Naming the Flowers Pulphouse

SHORT STORY COLLECTIONS
1963 **The Mile-Long Spaceship** Berkley, retitled **Andover and the Android**
1968 **The Downstairs Room** Doubleday
1971 **Abyss** Doubleday
1975 **The Infinity Box** Harper
1978 **Somerset Dreams** Harper
1980 **Better Than One** NESFA Press, with Damon Knight
1981 **Listen, Listen** Houghton Mifflin
1989 **Children of the Wind** St. Martin's Press
1991 **State of Grace** Pulphouse
1992 **And the Angels Sing** St. Martin's Press

AS EDITOR
1974 **Nebula Award Stories 9** Gollancz
1977 **Clarion SF** Berkley

MARION ZIMMER BRADLEY

BORN **1930**

NATIONALITY **American**

OTHER NAMES **Marion Bradley, Valerie Graves**

KEY WORKS **The Darkover series, The Mists of Avalon**

SHE began by writing unremarkable SF adventures for Ace Books, and could have been anybody. *Seven from the Stars* was a spiffing tale, written exactly to the cut of cloth required by the publisher, but it did no more than serve its modest purpose. Nobody, it is safe to assume, guessed what would happen when she expanded a 1958 magazine tale into *The Planet Savers*, publishing it with *The Sword of Aldones* in 1962; no one guessed that the novels set on the planet of Darkover would initiate one of the two or three most popular series ever in the SF world.

Part of the secret of *Darkover*'s success is its increasing subtlety and social relevance. Early tales were of the adventures of Darkover's inhabitants, human colonists long separated from the rest of the galaxy, who have in the interim developed psi powers. Later books, like *The Heritage of Hastur* or *The Shattered Chain* or *Sharra's Exile*, both rewrite the earlier stories in more psychologically acute terms, and also introduce female protagonists. Many other writers have contributed tales to anthologies set on Darkover; it now looks as if the series will never stop.

But Marion Zimmer Bradley's most famous book is not set on Darkover. *The Mists of Avalon* is an Arthurian fantasy, told from the viewpoint of Morgan le Fay. The late *Darkover* novels rewrite Darkover. This long tale rewrites the mythic matter of Britain.

BIBLIOGRAPHY

NOVELS AND NOVELLAS
1961 **The Door Through Space** Ace
1962 **Seven From the Stars** Ace
The Planet Savers Ace
The Sword of Aldones Ace
1963 **The Colors of Space** Monarch
1964 **The Bloody Sun** Ace
Falcons of Narabedla Ace
1965 **Star of Danger** Ace
1969 **The Brass Dragon** Ace
1970 **The Winds of Darkover** Ace
1971 **The World Wreckers** Ace
1972 **Darkover Landfall** Ace
Witch Hill Greenleaf, as Valerie Graves
1973 **Hunters of the Red Moon** DAW Books
1974 **Spell Sword** DAW Books
1975 **Endless Voyage** Ace, revised as **Endless Universe**
The Heritage of Hastur DAW Books
1976 **The Shattered Chain** DAW Books
Drums of Darkness Ballantine
1977 **The Forbidden Tower** DAW Books
1978 **Stormqueen** DAW Books
The Ruins of Isis Donning
1979 **The Survivors** DAW Books, with Paul E. Zimmer
1980 **The House Between the Worlds** Doubleday
Two to Conquer DAW Books
Survey Ship Ace
1981 **Sharra's Exile** DAW Books
1982 **Hawkmistress** DAW Books
Web of Light Donning
1983 **The Mists of Avalon** Knopf, as Marion Bradley
Thendara House DAW Books
1984 **Web of Darkness** Pocket Books, retitled **The Fall of Atlantis**

1984 **The Inheritor** Tor
City of Sorcery DAW Books
1985 **Night's Daughter** Ballantine
Warrior Woman DAW Books
1987 **The Firebrand** Simon and Schuster
1989 **The Heirs of Hammerfell** DAW Books
1990 **Black Trillium** Doubleday, with Julian May and Andre Norton
1993 **Rediscovery** DAW Books, with Mercedes Lackey
The Forest House Michael Joseph

SHORT STORY COLLECTIONS
1964 **The Dark Intruder** Ace
1985 **The Best of Marion Zimmer Bradley** Academy, revised as **Jamie and Other Stories**
1986 **Lythande** DAW Books

AS EDITOR
1980 **The Keeper's Price** DAW Books
1982 **Sword of Chaos** DAW Books
1984 **Sword and Sorceress** DAW Books, nine volumes through 1992
1985 **Free Amazons of Darkover** DAW Books
1987 **Red Sun of Darkover** DAW Books
The Other Side of the Mirror DAW Books
1988 **Four Moons of Darkover** DAW Books
1990 **Domain of Darkover** DAW Books
1991 **Leroni of Darkover** DAW Books
Renunciates of Darkover DAW Books
1993 **Towers of Darkover** DAW Books
Marion Zimmer Bradley's Darkover DAW Books

JOHN BRUNNER

BORN **1934**

NATIONALITY **English**

OTHER NAMES **Gill Hunt, John Loxmith, Kilian Houston, Trevor Staines, Keith Woodcott**

KEY WORKS ***Stand on Zanzibar, The Jagged Orbit, The Sheep Look Up, The Shockwave Rider***

Brunner published his first novel before most of his contemporaries had been on their first date, and more than 40 years later, still a relatively young man, he continues to apply his sharp, cynical, very European mind to the most American of literary forms.

Brunner's output for Ace Books in the 1950s and 1960s was, for most of those who read and collected it, the work of an American. The realization that he was, in fact, profoundly English surprised many fans, who may have been young and naive, but did have some reason for their failure to understand the drift of his work. Early novels like *The World Swappers* or *The Atlantic Abomination* feel American:

comfortable with American storylines featuring frontiers in space and aliens without number, swift, easy, and eloquent, these are among the best SF adventures ever. But even an early tale, like *Sanctuary in the Sky*, gives some warning signs for the wary. In this novel, a small masterpiece of dramatic irony, assorted human representatives of complacent, human-settled planets conduct their squabbles in a space artefact that has "always" been there. One of them, whose origins no one knows, disappears, and the artefact begins to emit a profound humming sound. In the end, the humbled cast learn that their companion is from Old Earth; that the artefact is a spaceship, which they had failed to make proper use of; that the sound is that of a vast engine; and that he is taking his ship back. The tone of the tale is deeply recessional; a warning that success is not guaranteed, but must be earned, that every triumph has its cost.

One can regret Brunner's decision to stop writing SF adventures, because they were astonishingly well done, but it was almost certainly inevitable that he would. By the mid-1960s, novels like *The Squares of the City*, whose plot replicates a chess game, began to show his true ambition, and in 1968 he published *Stand on Zanzibar* (see page 225), still his most famous book. This was followed by several more large, intricate, scathing analyses of the consequences of our technological progress. With *Zanzibar*, these novels – *The Jagged Orbit, The Sheep Look Up*, and *The Shockwave Rider* – make up a

NOTABLE WORK

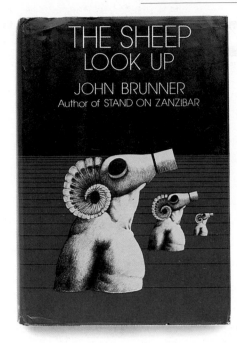

The Sheep Look Up is very possibly the finest of all novels about the pollution of Earth. A multistranded plot follows half a dozen seemingly unconnected characters, whose stories cross and recross in cause or effect of the gradual but remorseless destruction of the basic environmental systems. Two decades on, the forebodings of disaster that is always avoidable but is not avoided, of a world that dies with a whimper, read as prescient.

THE SHEEP LOOK UP

quartet of Dreadful Warnings. Brunner perhaps hoped to accomplish two tasks with these huge accomplishments. First, their messages might be attended to by SF readers, and by readers in the world at large, and people who knew the stakes might actually do something to prevent catastrophe. Second, they might free him economically to write more of the same.

Neither hope was realized. Both population and pollution continue to mount inexorably; political corruption remains endemic; the electronic revolution that Brunner predicted in 1974 seems more than likely to lure its

customers into virtual-reality hidey-holes, allowing them to ignore the decline of the world outside. And Brunner's career came close to foundering. But he has accomplished vastly: some of the 1980s books are of vital interest, and he may have decades left in which to force us to think.

BIBLIOGRAPHY

NOVELS AND NOVELLAS
1951 ***Galactic Storm*** Curtis Warren, as Gill Hunt
1959 ***Threshold of Eternity*** Ace
 The Brink Gollancz
 The World Swappers Ace
 Echo in the Skull Ace, revised as ***Give Warning to the World***
 The Hundredth Millennium Ace, revised as ***Catch a Falling Star***
1960 ***The Atlantic Abomination*** Ace
 Slavers of Space Ace, revised as ***Into the Slave Nebula***
 Sanctuary in the Sky Ace
1961 ***Meeting at Infinity*** Ace
 I Speak for Earth Ace, as Keith Woodcott
1962 ***Secret Agent of Terra*** Ace, revised as ***The Avengers of Carrig***
 The Super Barbarians Ace

1962 ***The Ladder in the Sky*** Ace, as Keith Woodcott
 Times Without Number Ace
1963 ***Space-Time Juggler*** Ace
 The Astronauts Must Not Land Ace, revised as ***More Things in Heaven***
 The Psionic Menace Ace, as Keith Woodcott
 Castaways' World Ace, revised as ***Polymath***
 The Rites of Ohe Ace
 The Dreaming Earth Pyramid
 Listen! The Stars! Ace, revised as ***The Stardroppers***
1964 ***Endless Shadow*** Ace, revised as ***Manshape***
 To Conquer Chaos Ace
 The Whole Man Ballantine, retitled ***Telepathist***

1965 ***The Altar on Asconel*** Ace
 The Day of the Star Cities Ace, revised as ***Age of Miracles***
 Enigma from Tantalus Ace
 The Repairmen of Cyclops Ace
 The Long Result Faber
 The Squares of the City Ballantine
 The Martian Sphinx Ace, as Keith Woodcott
1966 ***A Planet of your Own*** Ace
1967 ***Born Under Mars*** Ace
 The Productions of Time Signet
 Quicksand Doubleday
1968 ***Stand on Zanzibar*** Doubleday
 Bedlam Planet Ace
 Father of Lies Belmont
1969 ***The Jagged Orbit*** Ace
 Double, Double Ballantine
 Timescoop Dell
 The Evil That Men Do Belmont

1971 ***The Dramaturges of Yan*** Ace
1971 ***The Wrong End of Time*** Doubleday
1972 ***The Sheep Look Up*** Harper
1973 ***The Stone That Never Came Down*** Doubleday
1974 ***The Shockwave Rider*** Harper
 Total Eclipse Doubleday
 Web of Everywhere Bantam
1980 ***The Infinitive of Go*** Ballantine
 Players at the Game of People Ballantine
1983 ***The Crucible of Time*** Ballantine
 The Great Steamboat Race Ballantine
1984 ***The Tides of Time*** Ballantine
1987 ***The Shift Key*** Methuen
1989 ***Childen of the Thunder*** Ballantine
1991 ***A Maze of Stars*** Ballantine
1993 ***Muddle Earth*** Ballantine

SHORT STORY COLLECTIONS
1962 ***No Future In It*** Gollancz
1965 ***Now Then*** Mayflower-Dell
1966 ***No Other Gods But Me*** Compact
1967 ***Out of my Mind*** Ballantine
1968 ***Not Before Time*** New English Library
1971 ***The Traveler in Black*** Ace, expanded as ***The Compleat Traveller in Black***
1972 ***From This Day Forward*** Doubleday
 Entry to Elsewhen DAW Books
1973 ***Time-Jump*** Dell
1976 ***The Book of John Brunner*** DAW Books
1980 ***Foreign Constellations*** Everest House
1988 ***The Best of John Brunner*** Ballantine

THOMAS M. DISCH

BORN **1940**

NATIONALITY **American**

OTHER NAMES **Cassandra Knye, Thom Demijohn, Leonie Hargrave**

KEY WORKS ***Camp Concentration, 334, The M.D.: A Horror Story***

O f all living authors of SF, or fantasy, or horror, Disch stands out for the high stature that other writers have always granted him, and – until recently – for the low profile that he has occupied in the minds of readers. Only in the 1990s, with the huge success of *The M.D.*, has he become a bankable writer. There are some reasons for this.

Disch began writing SF in 1962, publishing the first of many books, *The Genocides*, in 1965. A grim tale, it is not much loved by readers for pretty obvious reasons; but *Mankind Under the Leash*, the next book, was comparatively jolly, as its other titles show. In magazine form, it was called "White Fang Goes Dingo",

and it settled down as *The Puppies of Terra*. At first glance, it seems pretty hilarious: humanity is enslaved by aliens, who like our looks and the way we dance; the hero decides to drive away his new masters by annoying them, the way a dog might annoy a busy executive. Eventually, they leave – as the last line puts it, "They couldn't stand the barking." Amusing and slight, one might think: a quick read and a grin. But few remember the tale.

There are reasons. Under its happy-go-lucky surface, *Mankind Under the Leash* presents a searingly dismissive view of humanity's accomplishments; its hero is a wimp with brains, and his victory consists of irritating a superior race until it abandons us. SF readers were not slow to understand that Disch marched to a different drum from the writers they were used to; and they did not much warm to the new realism, nor to the high chill factor of his prose: he wrote as though you had to earn the right to enjoy him.

Camp Concentration (see page 225), one of the peaks of Disch's SF career, deepened and harshened the onslaught. The title is a pun: inmates in a military concentration camp are injected with a deadly wonder drug that vastly increases human intelligence and the capacity to concentrate on tasks, but at the cost of driving its users flamboyantly insane (and very camp) after a short period.

Magazine illustration
An experimental rabbit and an alchemical animal, by Pamela Zoline for Camp Concentration.

NOTABLE WORK

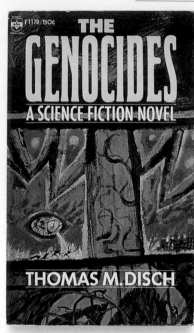

THE GENOCIDES

There is something awe-inspiring about the chutzpah of this dire tale. In traditional SF, most aliens are defeated when they invade Earth, and when they do triumph, they become temporary tyrants, fated to succumb to a brave human underground. In *The Genocides*, Disch's first novel, the aliens take over the surface of the planet without seeming to notice humanity at all. A few humans do survive within the Earth's crust, for a while – but only until the alien arrivals fumigate their new apple.

The analogy with syphilis is explicit – syphilis has very often been (wrongly) treated by writers as a disease that first inspires, then kills. Even grimmer, if possible, was *334* (see page 227), whose title is also playful: it is the address where the action takes place; and it represents – if written 3,3,4 – an arithmetical pattern that governs the characters, sequences, and geography. There is no hero – Disch does not cotton to heroes – and no hope.

Less grim, but lacking any easy enjoyment, *On Wings of Song* returns to Disch's abiding concern with the making of art. Many of his most interesting protagonists are artists –

although most of them are failures – and the hero of this tale, set in a New York city at the brink of disintegration, longs for success in opera. His eventual triumph is deeply ambiguous. In this novel, Disch may have been making a veiled statement about his own SF career; since its publication, he has concentrated in other genres.

Disch has experimented in various modes: *Clara Reeve* is an enormously complicated Gothic tale; *The Brave Little Toaster* (made into an animated film) and its sequel *The Brave Little Toaster Goes to Mars* are tales for wise children; and there are several highly respected volumes of poetry. With *The Businessman: A Tale of Terror*, *The M.D.: A Horror Story*, and *The Priest: A Gothic Romance*, he finally reached a large audience. These horror fantasies unflinchingly plumb the dark underside of the human condition. *The M.D.*, the best known, features a doctor given a magic staff (or caduceus) by the Devil; he makes a terrifying mess of the wishes granted him by this tool. It is a harsh message, but a necessary lesson: Disch's entire career, in a nutshell.

BIBLIOGRAPHY

NOVELS AND NOVELLAS
1965 **The Genocides** Berkley
1966 **Mankind Under the Leash** Ace, retitled **The Puppies of Terra**
The House That Fear Built Paperback Library, with John Sladek, both as Cassandra Knye
1967 **Echo Round His Bones** Berkley
1968 **Camp Concentration** Hart Davis
Black Alice Doubleday, with John Sladek, both as Thom Demijohn
1969 **The Prisoner** Ace, retitled **The Prisoner: I Am not a Number!**
1972 **334** MacGibbon and Kee
1975 **Clara Reeve** Knopf, as Leonie Hargrave
1979 **On Wings of Song** Gollancz
1984 **The Businessman: A Tale of Terror** Harper
1985 **Torturing Mr. Amberwell** Cheap Street
1986 **The Brave Little Toaster** Doubleday
1988 **The Silver Pillow** Mark V. Ziesing
1988 **The Brave Little Toaster Goes to Mars** Doubleday

1989 **The M.D.: A Horror Story** Knopf
1994 **The Priest: A Gothic Romance** Millenium

SHORT STORY COLLECTIONS
1966 **One Hundred and Two H-Bombs** Compact, expanded as **White Fang Goes Dingo and Other Funny SF Stories**
1968 **Under Compulsion** Hart Davis, retitled **Fun With your New Head**
1973 **Getting into Death** Hart Davis MacGibbon
1977 **The Early Science Fiction Stories of Thomas M. Disch** Gregg Press
1980 **Fundamental Disch** Bantam
1982 **The Man Who Had No Idea** Gollancz

POETRY
1970 **Highway Sandwiches** privately printed, with Marilyn Hacker and Charles Platt
1971 **The Right Way to Figure Plumbing** Basilisk Press

1980 **Poems from a Pillow** Anvil Press
1981 **ABCDEFG HIJKLM NPOQRST UVWXYZ** Anvil Press
1982 **Burn This** Hutchinson
1982 **Orders of the Retina** Toothpaste Press
1984 **Here I Am, There You Are, Where Were We** Hutchinson
1986 **The Tale of Dan de Lion: A Fable** Coffee House Press
1989 **Yes, Let's: New and Selected Poems** Johns Hopkins University Press
1991 **Dark Verses and Light** Johns Hopkins University Press

AS EDITOR
1971 **The Ruins of Earth** Putnam
1973 **Bad Moon Rising** Harper
1975 **The New Improved Sun** Harper
1976 **New Constellations** Harper, with Charles Naylor
1977 **Strangeness** Scribners, with Charles Naylor

J.G. BALLARD

BORN **1930**

NATIONALITY **English**

KEY WORKS ***The Wind from Nowhere, The Drowned World, The Burning World, The Crystal World, The Atrocity Exhibition, Crash, Empire of the Sun***

BALLARD is, for some, the most important SF writer of the latter half of the 20th century, and it is easy to see why they think so. Like Disch – both began writing in the early 1960s, and both were involved in *New Worlds* magazine – J.G. Ballard has always cast a very cold eye on the programme of traditional SF. Highly effective in his choice of images, he has created a wide range of metaphors that render his bleak beliefs grippingly unavoidable. He is a shaper of our dreams about the dark side of the century.

From the very first, Ballard felt that traditional SF's vision of the future as a high road we travel in our bright, new gear, with our bright, new tools was an almost completely foolish delusion. For him, the end of the 20th century is the end of the technological dream, not the beginning of the time when the dream will finally triumph. The Space Age ended long ago, Ballard said long ago, presciently; nor was he soon forgiven for understanding that extremely melancholy fact.

His first four novels are a quartet of disasters – death to our planet (and our dreams of daylight mastery) by wind, by water, by fire, and by a transcendental transfiguration into crystal: the classical elements, in other words. Indeed, there is an alchemical intensity to these tales, especially *The Drowned World* and *The Burning World* (see page 223). They feel very dangerous to read, as though to understand what they meant would – as with an alchemical experiment – somehow excite the world into obeying their instructions about ending it all. This feeling of risk becomes all the more intensified when one realizes that the protagonists of all of these four books do themselves actively welcome the catastrophes that they – and the planet – are experiencing.

Wartime childhood

Empire of the Sun showed Ballard's childhood in the destruction and ruination of war.

BIBLIOGRAPHY

NOVELS AND NOVELLAS
1962 ***The Wind from Nowhere*** Berkley
 The Drowned World Berkley
1964 ***The Burning World*** Berkley, revised as ***The Drought***
1966 ***The Crystal World*** Cape
1973 ***Crash*** Cape
1974 ***Concrete Island*** Cape
1975 ***High-Rise*** Cape
1979 ***The Unlimited Dream Company*** Cape
1981 ***Hello America*** Cape
1982 ***News from the Sun*** Interzone
1984 ***Empire of the Sun*** Gollancz (autobiographical)
1987 ***The Day of Creation*** Gollancz
1988 ***Running Wild*** Hutchinson
1991 ***The Kindness of Women*** HarperCollins (autobiographical)
1994 ***Rushing to Paradise*** Flamingo

SHORT STORY COLLECTIONS
1962 ***The Voices of Time*** Berkley
1962 ***Billenium*** Berkley

1963 ***The Four-Dimensional Nightmare*** Gollancz
 Passport to Eternity Berkley
1964 ***The Terminal Beach*** Gollancz, with some stories different retitled ***Terminal Beach***
1966 ***The Impossible Man*** Berkley
1967 ***The Disaster Area*** Cape
 The Day of Forever Panther
 The Overloaded Man Panther
1970 ***The Atrocity Exhibition*** Cape, retitled ***Love and Napalm: Export USA***
1971 ***Chronopolis*** Putnam
 Vermilion Sands Berkley
1976 ***Low-Flying Aircraft*** Cape
1977 ***The Best of J.G. Ballard*** Futura
1978 ***The Best Short Stories of J.G. Ballard*** Holt Rinehart
1980 ***The Venus Hunters*** Granada
1982 ***Myths of the Near Future*** Cape
1988 ***Memories of the Space Age*** Arkham House
1990 ***War Fever*** Collins

For many American SF writers, these novels – and the short stories that Ballard was writing at the same time – are simply unforgivable. These works take the upwardly mobile imagery of SF and transform it into a litany of loss, decline, and death. They are told with absolute conviction, in a metaphor-rich style that unswervingly and unerringly underlines the message. They are like nightmares – nightmares that haunt the waking hours of those writers who wish to go on believing in the virtues of material progress.

Over subsequent years, Ballard gradually moved away from tales that could properly be described as SF at all. *Crash* is a profound metaphorical analysis of the interaction of sex, urban life, and the alluring metal labyrinth of the automobile; but it is not really SF. Neither *Concrete Island* nor *High-Rise* do more than edge into the fuzziest sort of near future. *Hello America*, on the other hand, engages its protagonists in a tour of post-catastrophe America, but is his weakest book. *Empire of the Sun* (filmed by Steven Spielberg) is autobiographical, and shows the roots, in wartime Shanghai, of Ballard's darkest imagery. But SF or not, he is a psychopomp – he is the one who guides us through the dream.

1970-1974: THE NEXT GENERATION

BY NOW, WE ARE REACHING the third and fourth generations of SF authors and readers, and many of the men – and increasingly, women – now entering the SF field might be forgiven for regarding its language, its goals, its readership, and the ghetto closet that it still inhabits in the minds of establishment critics as circumstances written in stone. In truth, the SF subculture has been evolving just as fast as the world outside, and has been grappling just as bravely

1970 | 1971 | 19

NOTABLE WORKS

The Atrocity Exhibition
J.G. Ballard

Being There
JERZY KOSINSKI

This Perfect Day
IRA LEVIN

Bettyann
KRIS NEVILLE

Ringworld
LARRY NIVEN

The City Dwellers
CHARLES PLATT

Downward to the Earth
ROBERT SILVERBERG

Tower of Glass
ROBERT SILVERBERG

The Müller-Fokker Effect
JOHN SLADEK

Nine Princes in Amber
ROGER ZELAZNY

THE ATROCITY EXHIBITION

Half-Past Human
T.J. BASS

A Maze of Death
PHILIP K. DICK

The Tactics of Mistake
GORDON R. DICKSON

To Your Scattered Bodies Go
PHILIP JOSÉ FARMER

The Committed Men
M. JOHN HARRISON

The Futurological Congress
STANISŁAW LEM

A Cure for Cancer
MICHAEL MOORCOCK

A Time of Changes
ROBERT SILVERBERG

The Gods Themselves
ISAAC ASIMOV

The Sheep Look Up
JOHN BRUNNER

Invisible Cities
ITALO CALVINO

334
THOMAS M. DISCH

Beyond Apollo
BARRY N. MALZBERG

THE IRON DREAM

NOTABLE WORK

ROBERT SILVERBERG
THE WORLD INSIDE

In the middle of his decade of consummate fertility, Robert Silverberg, in *The World Inside*, issues a sombre vision of one of the outcomes available to the human race, if the question of overpopulation continues to be seen as an issue of individual ethics, or even aesthetics, rather than a question asked by biology of all of us: do we wish this planet to survive our personal breeding habits? In the book, huge city constructs, or "Urbmons", keep billions of us alive – and imprisoned.

THE WORLD INSIDE

ICONS

In the great days of Space Opera, 30 years earlier, it was more or less de rigueur for writers to create the hugest space dreadnoughts imaginable, and even to activate the occasional planetoid. What these vast dinosaurs of space lacked was any scientific or technological underpinning: they simply did not compute. This is no longer possible in 1970, and truly enormous artefacts, like Larry Niven's sun-encircling ringworld, have to be thought through with care.

Genetic engineering – one of the great themes of modern science – got short shrift from traditional SF writers, except when they wanted to create monsters, or supermen. By now, however, it is becoming clear that much more can be said on the subject, and there are hints at almost infinite malleability of the human vehicle.

There can be no doubt that, for most of this century, American SF failed the city. Very little cogent speculation about the possible development of urban life has appeared within the genre, beyond a trivial and unconsidered assumption that planet-covering "urbs" would be the centres of government.

DEBUTS

First SF novels include Neal Barrett Jr.'s *Kelvin*, Gregory Benford's *Deeper Than the Darkness*, Barrington J. Bayley's *The Star Virus*, **Christopher Priest**'s *Indoctrinaire*, Marge Piercy's *Dance the Eagle to Sleep*, Suzette Haden Elgin's *The Communipaths*, and Gene Wolfe's *Operation ARES*. In magazines, debuts include Michael Bishop's "Piñon Fall" in *Galaxy*, Edward Bryant's "Sending the Very Best" in *New Worlds*, Vonda N. McIntyre's "Breaking Point" in *Venture*, and Pamela Sargent's "Landed Minority" in *Fantasy and Science Fiction*.

Among the year's debut novels, **The Committed Men** and *Half Past Human* are also notable works. Other debuts are *Moderan* by David R. Bunch, *The Flying Sorcerers* by David Gerrold and Larry Niven, *Alice's World* by Sam J. Lundwall, *Sacred Elephant Flies* by Bruce McAllister, and *Humanity Prime* by Richard A. Lupoff. In anthologies, *Clarion I* has Vonda McIntyre's "Only at Night" and Octavia Butler's "Crossover", and in magazines, *Worlds of Fantasy* has Connie Willis's "Santa Titicaca", *Amazing* has George Alec Effinger's "The Eight Thirty to Nine Slot", and *Galaxy* carries George R.R. Martin's "The Hero".

Richard Adams's *Watership Down*, Michael Coney's *Mirror Image*, George Alec Effinger's *What Entropy Means to Me*, Alan Dean Foster's *The Tar-Aiym Krang*, and George Zebrowski's *The Omega Point* are among the SF debut novels this year. Lisa Tuttle's first story, "Stranger in the House", appears in the *Clarion II* anthology.

with the incredible, complex possibilities of the century – perhaps more bravely than the world's politicians have. New and different futures seem to become possible with every passing day, and no two of them are the same.

It is hard for a genre that makes its money primarily from entertainment to cope with a world so infinitely volatile; but that is the task that SF writers have set themselves, and face daily. The genre can only adapt.

7 2   1 9 7 3   1 9 7 4

AN ALIEN HEAT

An Alien Heat
MICHAEL MOORCOCK

Other Days, Other Eyes
BOB SHAW

Dying Inside
ROBERT SILVERBERG

The Iron Dream
NORMAN SPINRAD

The Fifth Head of Cerberus
GENE WOLFE

Frankenstein Unbound
BRIAN ALDISS

Crash
J.G. BALLARD

Rendezvous with Rama
ARTHUR C. CLARKE

Time Enough for Love
ROBERT A. HEINLEIN

Japan Sinks
SAKYO KOMATSU

Hiero's Journey
STERLING E. LANIER

Herovit's World
BARRY N. MALZBERG

Protector
LARRY NIVEN

The Embedding
IAN WATSON

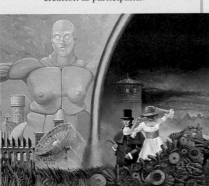

HEROVIT'S WORLD

Fire Time
POUL ANDERSON

The Fall of Chronopolis
BARRINGTON BAYLEY

Walk to the End of the World
SUZY MCKEE CHARNAS

The Twilight of Briareus
RICHARD COWPER

The Dispossessed
URSULA K. LE GUIN

THE FALL OF CHRONOPOLIS

WALK TO THE END OF THE WORLD

Flow My Tears, the Policeman Said
PHILIP K. DICK

The Mote in God's Eye
LARRY NIVEN AND JERRY POURNELLE

Inverted World
CHRISTOPHER PRIEST

A Quest for Simbilis
MICHAEL SHEA

Silverberg's *The World Inside* was about population, and about city-planning. But Thomas M. Disch's *334* lives and breathes its author's love-hate understanding of New York. In Europe, Calvino's *Invisible Cities* bases reflections on life around far-flung cities, and Brunner's cities are a blight on our species and the Earth.

By the middle of the 1970s, SF will be beginning to look into itself, and back into its own history, as if looking into a mirror, through the category of stories and novels that is now usually known as Recursive SF. Ahead of the game, Brian Aldiss applies his theory that SF was begun by Mary Shelley in 1818 to the form itself in his novel **Frankenstein Unbound**.

This novel dramatizes the thesis, featuring both Shelley and her creation as participants.

The bad market odour of utopian and dystopian writing is, perhaps, merited: most examples of this double genre are extremely dull and tendentious essays, slumming it as fiction. It is a mark, therefore, of Ursula K. Le Guin's bravery, and the willingness of matured readers to cope with the didacticism of utopian thinking, that *The Dispossessed* appears to such acclaim this year. Its balanced presentation of utopian-dystopian models perfectly represents the balance characteristic of her strong mind.

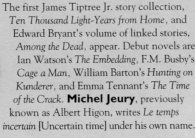

The first James Tiptree Jr. story collection, *Ten Thousand Light-Years from Home*, and Edward Bryant's volume of linked stories, *Among the Dead*, appear. Debut novels are Ian Watson's *The Embedding*, F.M. Busby's *Cage a Man*, William Barton's *Hunting on Kunderer*, and Emma Tennant's *The Time of the Crack*. **Michel Jeury**, previously known as Albert Higon, writes *Le temps incertain* [Uncertain time] under his own name.

Of the notable books of the year, Suzy McKee Charnas's *Walk to the End of the World* is a first novel. Other debut SF novels include *A Quest for Simbilis* by Michael Shea and *The Texas-Israeli War*, by Howard Waldrop and Jake Saunders. Joan Vinge's first published story, "Tin Soldier", appears in the anthology *Orbit 14*.

1975-1979: THE ABSORPTION OF SF

BY NOW, SF'S NEW WAVE is part of history, Sputnik, the space race, and the Moon landing are all parts of history, and the suspicion is beginning to sneak up on some SF writers that the genre of SF itself may be a part of history.

It may be an honoured part, perhaps, but it is no longer the coherent tool for understanding – and popularizing – the future that it once was. The suspicion grows that SF is no longer a beacon to lead to the future, but a monument.

1 9 7 5

NOTABLE WORKS

The Shockwave Rider
JOHN BRUNNER

Imperial Earth
ARTHUR C. CLARKE

The Deep
JOHN CROWLEY

Dhalgren
SAMUEL R. DELANY

The Forever War
JOE HALDEMAN

DHALGREN

THE FEMALE MAN

The Birthgrave
TANITH LEE

Galaxies
BARRY N. MALZBERG

The Female Man
JOANNA RUSS

Orbitsville
BOB SHAW

Man in a Cage
BRIAN STABLEFORD

1 9 7 6

The Malacia Tapestry
BRIAN ALDISS

The Alteration
KINGSLEY AMIS

Patternmaster
OCTAVIA E. BUTLER

Triton
SAMUEL R. DELANY

Arslan
M.J. ENGH

KATE WILHELM

WHERE LATE THE SWEET BIRDS SANG

Doctor Rat
WILLIAM KOTZWINKLE

Man Plus
FREDERIK POHL

Requiem for Tomorrow
DANIEL WALTHER

Where Late the Sweet Birds Sang
KATE WILHELM

REQUIEM FOR TOMORROW

1 9

Mirkheim
POUL ANDERSON

Michaelmas
ALGIS BUDRYS

Starhiker
JACK DANN

A Scanner Darkly
PHILIP K. DICK

JOHN VARLEY
The Ophiuchi Hotline

THE OPHIUCHI HOTLINE

ICONS

Joe Haldeman's *The Forever War* soon becomes an icon of SF's belated attempt to come to terms with the implications of the war in Vietnam, a conflict that put paid to the old genre sense that conquering alien planets was a gas.

The strongest theme in the novels of this year is biology, and the authors' approaches to it are various. William Kotzwinkle has an uprising among laboratory animals, Kate Wilhelm has clones, Frederik Pohl has a cyborg made for Mars, and Octavia Butler has dynastic struggles right at the start of her **Patternist** series.

One of the great virtues of SF has been its openhearted assumption that the Universe is populous, that we are not necessarily the only living things in the trillions of stars that our instruments are just now beginning to count. What Frederik Pohl's *Gateway* does is to describe an imaginatively plausible network of access points

NOTABLE AUTHOR

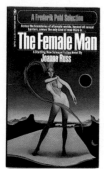

Alan Dean Foster represents something that could not have existed in SF before the 1970s. He is a complete professional, fast and competent, a man who works in SF as happily as a fish swims in water. His independent novels – most notably the **Human Commonwealth** series – are just what they promise to be, and they make compulsive reading. But he is more widely read – although perhaps not known – as by far the most successful producer of film and television novelizations the field has seen.

ALAN DEAN FOSTER

DEBUTS

Of the notable books, *The Forever War*, *The Birthgrave*, and *The Deep* are debuts. Other debuts include Primo Levi's *Il Sistema periodico* (*The Periodic Table*), Felix Gotschalk's *Growing Up in Tier 3000*, and Michael Bishop's *A Funeral for the Eyes of Fire*. *Dead Babies* is Martin Amis's SF debut, *Grimus* is Salman Rushdie's.

Debut novels include Robert Holdstock's *Eye Among the Blind*, Tim Powers's *The Skies Discrowned*, Chelsea Quinn Yarbro's *Time of the Fourth Horseman*, Spider Robinson's *Telempath*, **C.J. Cherryh**'s *Gate of Ivrel*, Octavia Butler's *Patternmaster*, K.W. Jeter's *The Dreamfields*, Jack Chalker's *A Jungle of Stars*, and Pamela Sargent's *Cloned Lives*.

John Varley's *The Ophiuchi Hotline* is a particularly strong debut novel. Others are George R.R. Martin's *Dying of the Light*, Gwyneth Jones's *Water in the Air*, James P. Hogan's *Inherit the Stars*, Mary Gentle's *A Hawk in Silver*, Garry Kilworth's *In Solitary*, and Bruce Sterling's *Involution Ocean*.

Not everyone feels this – even as the end of the century approaches, many SF writers continue to argue about the world, and to entertain an ever-growing readership, with stories that are unashamedly cast in the old genre moulds.

And even those who have doubts do retain one central consolation: that if the world is becoming too conscious of the innumerable possible futures jostling for its attention, SF had a central role in creating that urgent consciousness.

7 7

If the Stars are Gods
GREG BENFORD AND GORDON EKLUND

Midnight at the Well of Souls
JACK CHALKER

Time Storm
GORDON R. DICKSON

The Word for World is Forest
URSULA K. LE GUIN

The Condition of Muzak
MICHAEL MOORCOCK

Gateway
FREDERIK POHL

A Dream of Wessex
CHRISTOPHER PRIEST

The Ophiuchi Hotline
JOHN VARLEY

The Martian Inca
IAN WATSON

1 9 7 8

The Avatar
POUL ANDERSON

Web of the Chozen
JACK L. CHALKER

Motherlines
SUZY MCKEE CHARNAS

The Road to Corlay
RICHARD COWPER

Strangers
GARDNER DOZOIS

MOTHERLINES

The Stand
STEPHEN KING

Dreamsnake
VONDA N. MCINTYRE

The Two of Them
JOANNA RUSS

Up the Walls of the World
JAMES TIPTREE JR.

False Dawn
CHELSEA QUINN YARBRO

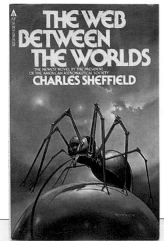

UP THE WALLS OF THE WORLD

1 9 7 9

The Fountains of Paradise
ARTHUR C. CLARKE

Engine Summer
JOHN CROWLEY

On Wings of Song
THOMAS M. DISCH

Jem
FREDERIK POHL

Catacomb Years
MICHAEL BISHOP

Titan
JOHN VARLEY

Transfigurations
MICHAEL BISHOP

Kindred
OCTAVIA E. BUTLER

If On a Winter's Night a Traveller
ITALO CALVINO

The Hitchhiker's Guide to the Galaxy
DOUGLAS ADAMS

The Web Between the Worlds
CHARLES SHEFFIELD

THE WEB BETWEEN THE WORLDS

to the unimaginable riches of the rest of reality. There are other gateways in this year's works: Gordon R. Dickson's *Time Storm* delivers Alternate Worlds by the crate, and Christopher Priest's *A Dream of Wessex*, John Varley's *The Ophiuchi Hotline*, and Ian Watson's *The Martian Inca* can all be regarded as gateway novels.

SF writers are now free to assume competent female protagonists, and in this year Charnas, McIntyre, Russ, Tiptree, and Yarbro all do so. Vonda McIntyre's **Dreamsnake** is perhaps the most interesting: female protagonists who are empowered by their capacity to heal are on delicate ground – it is far too easy (especially for men) to sentimentalize such healing women into walking comfort stations. But the icon of healer is potent, and in a literary sense it has a healing effect on the SF genre as a whole. Partly because of books like *Dreamsnake*, it is no longer possible for SF authors to pretend that a rounded society can be properly described simply in terms of the wars that it wages and the frontiers that it penetrates.

In 1979, Arthur C. Clarke's *The Fountains of Paradise* and Charles Sheffield's *The Web Between the Worlds* simultaneously advance the notion that orbital launching pads, tied to Earth by enormously long, monofilament "beanstalks" or space elevators, might solve the problem of escaping Earth's gravity well without bankrupting whole space programmes with every launch. Now all we have to do is climb the elevator, like Jack, into the big world above.

Orson Scott Card makes his magazine debut with "Ender's Game" in *Analog*, and Charles Sheffield's "What Song the Sirens Sang" appears in *Galaxy*.

First SF debut novels of interest include *Star Rigger's Way* by Jeffrey A. Carver, *The Sword Smith* by Eleanor Arnason, *Sight of Proteus* by Charles Sheffield, *I Am Not the Other Houdini* by Mike Conner, *Blind Voices* by Tom Reamy, and *The Outcasts of Heaven Belt* by Joan Vinge. In France, **Serge Brussolo**'s first story appears in *Futurs au présent* [Present futures], an anthology edited by Philippe Curval.

First SF books of interest include Douglas Adams's novelization of his radio serial *The Hitchhiker's Guide to the Galaxy* (later, the scripts will also be published), Greg Bear's *Psychlone*, Harry Turtledove's *Wereblood*, Orson Scott Card's *Capitol: The Worthing Chronicle*, David Drake's *Hammer's Slammers*, and David Langford's spoof *An Account of a Meeting with Denizens of Another World, 1871*, written as William Robert Loosley edited by David Langford.

URSULA K. LE GUIN

BORN **1929**

NATIONALITY **American**

KEY WORKS **The *Hainish* series, *The Left Hand of Darkness*, the *Earthsea* series, *Always Coming Home***

SOME writers are swollen with hopes of fame, and they will go nameless. Others astonish with their modesty, and Ursula K. Le Guin is pre-eminent among these. Like one or two other SF figures of unassailable stature, Le Guin is deeply courteous. She seems to meet people in the expectation, or maybe simply the hope, that she will learn from the encounter. She is like the novelist Doris Lessing: they do not reflect the world, they absorb it.

From the first, Le Guin was quietly remarkable. An unruffled narrative technique and calm pacing made these first stories like land mines, timed to explode in the mind after being read.

Her first novels, *Rocannon's World* and *Planet of Exile*, were first published as paperbacks, and looked like Space Operas. They were set in what she called the Hainish universe, which – typical of the more ambitious Space Opera – supplies a myth of origin and framework for individual storylines. The Hain are a predecessor race who have seeded the galaxy with human-like stock (including the inhabitants of Earth), and the several novels and stories set in this universe make up a Future History extending from a few hundred years hence up the line for two or three thousand further years. This sort of Future History represents a convention harking back to Asimov and Heinlein, but Le Guin does something rather different with it.

In *Rocannon's World*, a typical situation – stranded human on distant planet learns how to rescue population from alien invaders – is submerged in the tale's real subject: the protagonist's earnest attempts to learn "mindspeech" and so to understand and assimilate the culture. It is an anthropologist's dream, which pervades Le Guin's work – unsurprisingly, given that her father was an eminent anthropologist and her mother wrote at least one intensely intelligent book in the field. *Planet of Exile* is again the story of a protagonist who, on another distant planet, uses her powers – here telepathy – to unify races by understanding both of them.

NOTABLE WORK

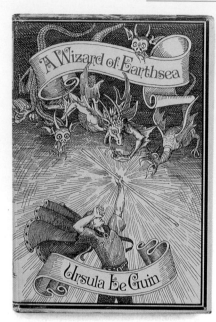

Earthsea is a glorious world of islands set in an enormous, crystal-clear sea. On the Inner Isles, the central archipelago at the heart of the Inmost Sea, a variety of societies exists. Young Ged leaves rocky, rural Gont for the island of Roke. He learns to control magic, to balance good and evil, plus and minus, and becomes a Mage. In the following books he finds the Ring that will reunite all of Earthsea, and defends his world from the fanatics of the Unmaking. And the sun shines.

A WIZARD OF EARTHSEA

BIBLIOGRAPHY

NOVELS AND NOVELLAS
1966 ***Rocannon's World*** Ace
Planet of Exile Ace
1967 ***City of Illusions*** Ace
1968 ***A Wizard of Earthsea***
Parnassus Press
1969 ***The Left Hand of Darkness*** Ace
1971 ***The Lathe of Heaven*** Scribners
The Tombs of Atuan Atheneum
1972 ***The Farthest Shore*** Atheneum
1974 ***The Dispossessed: an Ambiguous Utopia***
Harper
1976 ***The Word for World is Forest*** Putnam
Very Far Away from Anywhere Else
Atheneum, retitled ***A Very Long Way from Anywhere Else***
1979 ***Malafrena*** Putnam
1980 ***The Beginning Place*** Harper, retitled
Threshold
1982 ***The Eye of the Heron*** Gollancz
1985 ***Always Coming Home*** Harper
1990 ***Tehanu: the Last Book of Earthsea***
Atheneum
1991 ***Searoad: Chronicles of Klatsand***
HarperCollins

SHORT STORY COLLECTIONS
1975 ***The Wind's Twelve Quarters*** Harper
1976 ***Orsinian Tales*** Harper
1982 ***The Compass Rose*** Harper
1987 ***Buffalo Gals and Other Animal Presences***
Capra Press

NON-FICTION
1973 ***From Elfland to Poughkeepsie***
Pendragon Press
1975 ***Dreams Must Explain Themselves***
Algol Press
1979 ***The Language of the Night: Essays on Fantasy and Science Fiction*** Putnam
1989 ***Dancing at the Edge of the World: Thoughts on Words, Women, Places***
Grove Press

AS EDITOR
1976 ***Nebula Stories 11*** Gollancz
1980 ***Interface*** Ace, with Virginia Kidd
Edges Pocket Books, with Virginia Kidd
1993 ***The Norton Book of Science Fiction***
Norton, with Brian Attebery

And then, in 1969, Le Guin suddenly became a figure to reckon with, although the novel that began to focus attention on her – *The Left Hand of Darkness* (see page 225) – was also a paperback original. Again, it is told with deceptive smoothness, but this time the drive under the tale comes undodgeably to the surface. The world of SF – along with the academics who uneasily monitor that world – knew at once that a star was born.

Humans live on the planet Winter, and when a galactic envoy pays a visit – it is typical of Le Guin's anthropology-influenced fiction that most of her best stories involve visitors from outside – he little expects to receive any revelations. But he soon discovers that the inhabitants of Winter are technically hermaphroditic, and that they develop either male or female sexual characteristics during – and only during – periods of fertility. The envoy's assumption that he has been dealing with a man is, therefore, culture-bound. In a tone of implacable, calm attentiveness, Le Guin managed, in this one book, to make gender analysis and gender consciousness central and legitimate topics for speculative fiction.

> **"***It is typical of Le Guin that most of her best stories involve visitors from outside***"**

Others – like Delany, Russ, and James Tiptree Jr. – may have since written angrier, or more radical works, but none have quite managed Le Guin's devastating assurance.

In the meantime, ostensibly for children, she began the **Earthsea** quartet of novels, set in an archipelago upon a planet almost entirely covered by water. In *A Wizard of Earthsea*, Ged (the main character of the first three novels) learns some of the powers and the responsibilities of a Mage-in-training; wizardry in Le Guin's universe involves no more – or less – than learning to balance the Yin and Yang of realities, of forces, and of desires. In *The Tombs of Atuan* and *The Farthest Shore* he becomes wiser, helps a young woman to know herself, and finally saves the world from an unbalanced, monotheistic fanaticism, at the cost of great weariness to himself. In *Tehanu*, the final volume, published much later, a woman becomes protagonist, and rewrites the Earthsea story in terms that divest magic of much of its fantasy splendour, simultaneously engendering a powerful sense of the complex grittiness of human life on any planet.

In *The Dispossessed* (see page 228), the last of her Hainish books, Le Guin took American SF about as far as it could go in the direction of utopian discourse. SF has never been entirely comfortable with this form, perhaps because it tends to represent, and argue for, an achieved goal, rather than on the actions that may lead – beyond the last page – to a satisfied world. *The Dispossessed* avoids narrative paralysis by featuring two utopias, one dominating a planet, the other that planet's moon. The first is a complex, humane capitalism, the second a complex anarchism. Neither is markedly evil; neither is perfect. Travelling from one to the other, the protagonist is uncomfortable with both. Throughout, there are hints at consequences of the invention of the "ansible", a device that will allow instant communication throughout the inhabited worlds.

By this time, Le Guin was well on the way to being – along with Dick – the SF writer that academics felt most comfortable discussing. The editor of one academic journal has said, in an unguarded moment, that in the 1970s and 1980s, four out of every five pieces submitted were on Le Guin or Dick. Le Guin has had to cope with astonishing exposure, and because she has always written with an appearance of utmost clarity, she has had to cope with being too easily "understood" by critics.

> *Her work mixes SF, fantasy, and didactic content*

It may be as a reaction to this focus – although it may also result from a sense that she had exhausted the potential of her **Hainish** worlds for a while – that Le Guin has moved away from straight SF. Her **Orsinia** books (*Orsinian Tales* and *Malafrena*) are moral fables set on an Alternate Earth similar to our own. *The Beginning Place* is a fantasy that minutely examines the experiences of an adolescent passing into young adulthood. And, although set in a post-catastrophe future, and technically SF, *Always Coming Home* shows how thoroughly Le Guin has revised old SF, with its narrative drive and its hopeful sense that heroic actions win the day. The book is not even told like a novel: it is a collage of all kinds of material – including songs, fables, artwork, and an audio cassette – making up a portrait of a matriarchal society that does not progress, but is. Utopianism by the back door, this is an astonishingly brave book. It also works.

More and more, her work mixes SF and fantasy with didactic content that goes down easy: her later stories are too multifarious to allow righteousness. Unlike any SF writer before her, she has become a wise Teller of Tales.

Debut work
Ursula Le Guin's first published story was "April in Paris", a tale with a neat twist on selling your soul.

JAMES WHITE

BORN **1928**

NATIONALITY **Northern Irish**

KEY WORKS **The *Sector General Hospital* series, *The Watch Below***

BIBLIOGRAPHY

NOVELS AND NOVELLAS
1957 *The Secret Visitors* Ace
1962 *Second Ending* Ace
1963 *Star Surgeon* Ballantine
1965 *Escape Orbit* Ace, retitled **Open Prison**
1966 *The Watch Below* Ballantine
1969 *All Judgement Fled* Rapp and Whiting
1971 *Tomorrow is Too Far* Ballantine
1972 *Dark Inferno* Michael Joseph, retitled **Lifeboat**
1974 *The Dream Millennium* Michael Joseph
1979 *Underkill* Corgi
Ambulance Ship Ballantine
1985 *Star Healer* Ballantine
1987 *Code Blue – Emergency* Ballantine
1988 *Federation World* Ballantine
1991 *The Silent Stars Go By* Ballantine
1992 *The Genocidal Healer* Ballantine

SHORT STORY COLLECTIONS
1962 *Hospital Station* Ballantine
1964 *Deadly Litter* Ballantine
1969 *The Aliens Among Us* Ballantine
1971 *Major Operation* Ballantine
1977 *Monsters and Medics* Ballantine
1982 *Futures Past* Ballantine
1983 *Sector General* Ballantine

FOR more than half a century now, it has always been the case that one – or two, or three – British writers have written work that might be termed American SF, have published much of their output in the United States, and have done so with both grace and pleasure. John Russell Fearn and Eric Frank Russell were the first of them; for a while, Arthur C. Clarke sounded American, and then sounded just like himself; E.C. Tubb, Ken Bulmer, and John Brunner followed in turn. And then came James White.

White's famous **Sector General** series began with the short stories collected in *Hospital Station* and has continued on in through several volumes of both short stories and novels, including *Ambulance Ship* and *The Genocidal Healer*. The tales are the clearest demonstration there can possibly be of the virtues of writing in the way he does. There is the gargantuan, 384-level hospital and space habitat, set on the Galactic Rim; there is the great Galaxy itself, full of diverse and well-characterized aliens in need of an array of medical treatments; there is a technofix view of medicine, right alongside a sense that inventive and humane doctors still sometimes know better than any gadget how to cure an

Debut appearance
Sector General Hospital first appeared in Hospital Station, *a collection of linked short stories.*

organic being; and above all, there are the smooth, very polished, and seemingly effortless stories themselves. All in all, the **Sector General** series is delightful; caring, and yet poised. But James White has done much more than this series. His individual novels have a momentum that is intoxicating. The best of them all is *The Watch Below*, in which two storylines are brought together. A merchant ship from World War II is sunk, leaving just five survivors to breed in a pocket of trapped air, which keeps them alive for decades. The second, parallel tale is of an alien starship that is engaged on a long search for a planet with large areas of water. In the middle of the 21st century, it arrives on Earth, just in time to save the descendants of the human survivors in the merchant ship. At the story's close, it is difficult not to cheer. James White does that for us.

IAN WATSON

BORN **1943**

NATIONALITY **English**

KEY WORKS **The Embedding, The Jonah Kit, The Flies of Memory**

MANY SF authors have more titles to their credit than Ian Watson, and a writer need not be versatile or have a fast, sharp brain in order to produce a lot of books. But Watson gives an impression of astonishing fertility. His novels are so full of ideas and turns of thought that it is as though he had written hundreds. Instead, it is a mere 26 or so. Mere.

One thing that must haunt Watson is that the praise heaped upon his first novel, *The Embedding,* has obscured for some the incessant inventiveness of the other 25 – not to speak of the eight volumes of short stories, a commendable number to reach publication, especially in the late 20th century, when short stories are generally disparaged.

The Embedding (see page 228) is, of course, memorable. It gives a thorough and sophisticated examination of the Whorf-Sapir hypothesis on the power of language to shape perception. There are three stories: an Amerindian tribe changes its tongue as it changes its drugs; alien visitors try to understand humanity through an analysis of its languages; and children are taught to speak an artificial language. The stories come together in a dazzling climax.

Watson's concern with language continues in *The Jonah Kit,* which imagines the devastation felt by whales when they discover that languages are mere patterns of connected sound, and that the true reality of the universe cannot be apprehended through words.

In *The Martian Inca,* an alien virus transforms human perceptions of the universe. In *The Flies of Memory,* the universe threatens to disintegrate unless continually memorized by its inhabitants. *Lucky's Harvest* and *The Fallen Moon* replay the Finnish epic *Kalevala* as SF; the **Warhammer** books are Space Opera; *The Fire Worm* retells legend; and *Queenmagic, Kingmagic* is a game of chess. Watson is never still. He jostles the worlds of thought.

BIBLIOGRAPHY

NOVELS AND NOVELLAS

1973 **The Embedding** Gollancz
1975 **The Jonah Kit** Gollancz
1977 **The Martian Inca** Gollancz
      Alien Embassy Gollancz
1978 **Miracle Visitors** Gollancz
1979 **God's World** Gollancz
1980 **The Gardens of Delight** Gollancz
1981 **Under Heaven's Bridge** Gollancz, with
      Michael Bishop
      Deathhunter Gollancz
1983 **Chekhov's Journey** Gollancz
1984 **Converts** Granada
      The Book of the River Gollancz
1985 **The Book of the Stars** Gollancz
      The Book of Being Gollancz
1986 **Queenmagic, Kingmagic** Gollancz
1987 **The Power** Headline
1988 **The Fire Worm** Gollancz
      Meat Headline
      Whores of Babylon Paladin
1990 **The Flies of Memory** Gollancz
      Warhammer 40,000: Inquisitor
      Games Workshop

1991 **Nanoware Time** Tor
1993 **Warhammer 40,000: Space Marine**
      Boxtree
      Lucky's Harvest Gollancz
1994 **The Fallen Moon** Gollancz
      Warhammer 40,000: Harlequin
      Boxtree

SHORT STORY COLLECTIONS

1979 **The Very Slow Time Machine**
      Gollancz
1982 **Sunstroke** Gollancz
1985 **Slow Birds** Gollancz
      The Book of Ian Watson Mark V. Ziesing
1987 **Evil Water** Gollancz
1989 **Salvage Rites** Gollancz
1991 **Stalin's Teardrops** Gollancz
1994 **The Coming of Vertumnus** Gollancz

AS EDITOR

1981 **Pictures at an Exhibition**
      Greystoke Mobray
1983 **Changes** Ace, with Michael Bishop
1986 **Afterlives** Vintage, with Pamela Sargent

CHRISTOPHER PRIEST

BORN **1943**

NATIONALITY **English**

OTHER NAMES **John Luther Novak, Colin Wedgelock**

KEY WORKS **Inverted World, The Space Machine,** the **Dream Archipelago** series

HE is certainly a turbulent Priest. For 15 years he has rocked boats with well-judged, negative assessments of SF's literary qualities, its pretensions to offer guidelines for conduct to the human race, and its subject matter in general. He claims to write no more SF, although *The Quiet Woman* is in fact a neat, dour, swift, scouring Near Future morality tale of a bleak, flattened England.

Christopher Priest comes out of the British New Wave, that sudden, brief explosion of what seemed genius then, and even in retrospect seems to have inspired some of the very best work of half a dozen or so significant writers: Aldiss, Ballard, Moorcock, Disch, and Sladek. Priest was a slow learner: his first stories are wooden and derivative; his first novels, *Indoctrinaire* and *Fugue for a Darkening Island,* move stiffly through not unpredictable storylines. But the writer who evolved from these experiences carried on into the 1970s a New Wave impatience with established forms, convenient truths, and old SF verities.

His masterpiece is *Inverted World,* a novel that haunts readers years after they have put it away. It is a parable of perception, like many of Ian Watson's books, but is more gut-wrenching than anything by Priest's contemporary.

Literary gimmick
A dictionary definition of glamour, on a card signed by Priest was the publicity for The Glamour.

A great city moves across what seems from the outside to be a kind of post-catastrophe Europe. From inside, it seems that the city's inhabitants are forced to shift it ever onwards along a hyperbolic surface that distorts time, and that they must do so because they will literally lose themselves if they do not keep up. As a metaphor for the human condition at a point of extremis, it is as vivid as a dream.

The Space Machine, on the other hand, seems to work its effects solely on the surface. Making the assumption that H.G. Wells's *The Time Machine* and *The War of the Worlds* describe the same fictional environment, it knits them together with an effect of ironic nostalgia. The **Dream Archipelago** of *A Dream of Wessex* and the tales in *An Infinite Summer* move onwards into visions of England that are both deeply affecting and shadowed by a sense of accumulating loss. The Dream Archipelago itself is an England half-submerged beneath the seas, a series of islands inhabited by survivors of the catastrophe that sank the satanic mills. The heart of the sequence lies in the palpable longing it generates in those who love England: it might be described as a longing for some convulsion that might save something of worth from the island's disintegrating culture.

Most of Christopher Priest's later work has moved away from SF. But his reluctance to play the games of the old SF does not mean that he will never again play on the fields of the new.

BIBLIOGRAPHY

NOVELS AND NOVELLAS

1970 **Indoctrinaire** Faber
1972 **Fugue for a Darkening Island** Faber,
      retitled **Darkening Island**
1974 **Inverted World** Faber
1976 **The Space Machine** Faber
1977 **A Dream of Wessex** Faber
1981 **The Affirmation** Faber
1984 **The Glamour** Cape
1990 **The Quiet Woman** Bloomsbury

SHORT STORY COLLECTIONS

1974 **Real-Time World** New English Library
1979 **An Infinite Summer** Faber

BOB SHAW

BORN **1931**

NATIONALITY **Northern Irish, resident in England**

KEY WORKS **Other Days, Other Eyes, the Orbitsville series, the Ragged Astronauts series**

S HAW tells jokes, a mug of beer in one hand, but his novels are mostly serious, and those meant to be funny are not very successful. He has a wry, watchful, European mind, but was first published in the United States. He is never quite where one expects him.

The first novels are impressive enough, mixing Space Opera venues with plots that lead one to the conclusion that interstellar space is not necessarily very happy. The best is probably *The Palace of Eternity*, an exceedingly grim tale for most of its length, during the course of which an astonishingly attractive planet is destroyed by opposing forces fighting an interstellar war; but at the end, as the dead and rescusitated hero becomes part of a transcendantal planetary consciousness, there is a sense of striven-for and earned victory.

But Shaw came full into his own voice with *Other Days, Other Eyes*, in which he unpacks the implications of Slow Glass – glass that "slows" light so much that to look into it is to look into the past. So long does it take for light to travel through Slow Glass that panes can be sent anywhere, for future viewing. In some cases, tragedies ensue.

Orbitsville and its sequels are back in space, with a vengeance. The novel represents the first effective SF use of the Dyson Sphere – a sphere that surrounds a sun, trapping all its energy.

Such a sphere must have an enormous diameter – equal to that of a planet's orbit – and Shaw is generally very successful at conveying a sense of such an astronomical scale.

Later years have seen good books and fairish, and one series – *The Ragged Astronauts*, *The Wooden Spaceships*, and *The Fugitive Worlds* – that is joyous with energy. Two planets are linked, like a barbell, by a band of atmosphere; the first volume of the series deals with an emigration from one planet, which has been cursed by a complex fatal plague, to the other, via wooden balloon; at mid-point, both planets are huge. As in all of Shaw's best work, the view can be breathtaking.

BIBLIOGRAPHY

NOVELS AND NOVELLAS
1967 **Night Walk** Banner
1968 **The Two-Timers** Ace
1969 **Shadow of Heaven** Avon, revised as **The Shadow of Heaven**
 The Palace of Eternity Ace
1970 **One Million Tomorrows** Ace
1971 **Ground Zero Man** Avon, revised as **The Peace Machine**
1972 **Other Days, Other Eyes** Gollancz
1975 **Orbitsville** Gollancz
1976 **A Wreath of Stars** Gollancz
1977 **Medusa's Children** Gollancz
 Who Goes Here? Gollancz
1978 **Vertigo** Gollancz, revised as **Terminal Velocity**
1979 **Dagger of the Mind** Gollancz
1981 **The Ceres Solution** Gollancz
1983 **Orbitsville Departure** Gollancz
1984 **Fire Pattern** Gollancz

1986 **The Ragged Astronauts** Gollancz
1987 **The Wooden Spaceships** Gollancz
1989 **Killer Planet** Gollancz
 The Fugitive Worlds Gollancz
1990 **Orbitsville Judgement** Gollancz
1993 **Warren Peace** Gollancz

SHORT STORY COLLECTIONS
1954 **The Enchanted Duplicator** privately printed, with Walt Willis
1973 **Tomorrow Lies in Ambush** Gollancz
1976 **Cosmic Kaleidoscope** Gollancz
1982 **A Better Mantrap** Gollancz
1986 **Messages Found in an Oxygen Bottle** NESFA Press
1989 **Dark Night in Toyland** Gollancz

NON-FICTION
1979 **The Best of the Bushel** Paranoid-Inca Press
 The Eastercon Speeches Paranoid-Inca Press

BARRY N. MALZBERG

BORN **1939**

NATIONALITY **American**

OTHER NAMES **Mike Barry, Mel Johnson, K.M. O'Donnell**

KEY WORKS **Beyond Apollo, Herovit's World, Chorale**

B ARRY Malzberg is a gloomy cuss. He believes that the world is rapidly going to the dogs, and that American SF , which had the self-declared task of telling us how to save ourselves from perdition, has utterly failed to save us. He has stopped writing five or six brilliant novels each year:

this is partly because he has now said much of what he wished to say, and partly because the market can no longer comfortably sustain so burning and negative a voice. In the 1990s, he contents himself with producing maybe 10 or 20 short stories a year: there are now well over 300 of them. Malzberg is a creative phenomenon: fast, gloomy, and compelling.

And *funny*. He appears at SF conventions with a long face, to make a speech so funny it is hard to believe what one has heard. He writes stories about defeated astronauts, compulsive gamblers, paranoids who are right about their grey enemies; but these stories are not depressing. They are painfully hilarious tales of the latter days. *Beyond Apollo* applies graveyard humour to the death of the American space programme. *Herovit's World* is the funniest novel ever to be written about SF. *Chorale* does Beethoven in. Malzberg is the voice in the wilderness, speaking in wisecracks.

BIBLIOGRAPHY

NOVELS AND NOVELLAS
1968 **Oracle of the Thousand Hands** Olympia
 Screen Olympia
1969 **The Empty People** Lancer, as K.M. O'Donnell
1970 **Dwellers of the Deep** Ace, as K.M. O'Donnell
1971 **The Falling Astronauts** Ace
 Universe Day Avon, as K.M. O'Donnell
 Gather in the Hall of the Planets Ace, as K.M. O'Donnell
1972 **Overlay** Lancer
 Beyond Apollo Random House
 Revelations Warner
1973 **The Men Inside** Lancer
 Phase IV Pocket Books .
 In the Enclosure Avon
1974 **Herovit's World** Random House
 Guernica Night Bobbs Merrill
 On a Planet Alien Pocket Books
 Tactics of Conquest Pyramid
 The Day of the Burning Ace
 The Sodom and Gomorrah Business Pocket Books
 Underlay Avon
 The Destruction of the Temple Pocket Books
1975 **The Gamesman** Pocket Books
 Conversations Bobbs Merrill
 Galaxies Pyramid
1976 **Scop** Pyramid
 The Running of Beasts Putnam, with Bill Pronzini
1977 **The Last Transaction** Pinnacle
 Acts of Mercy Putnam, with Bill Pronzini
1978 **Chorale** Doubleday

1979 **Night Screams** Playboy Press, with Bill Pronzini
1980 **Prose Bowl** St. Martin's Press, with Bill Pronzini
1982 **The Cross of Fire** Ace
1985 **The Remaking of Sigmund Freud** Ballantine

SHORT STORY COLLECTIONS
1969 **Final War** Ace, as K.M. O'Donnell
1971 **In the Pocket** Ace
1974 **Out from Ganymede** Warner
1975 **The Many Worlds of Barry Malzberg** Popular Library
1976 **Down Here in the Dream Quarter** Doubleday
 The Best of Barry N. Malzberg Pocket Books
1979 **Malzberg at Large** Ace
1980 **The Man Who Loved the Midnight Lady** Doubleday

NON-FICTION
1981 **The Engines of the Night: Science Fiction in the Eighties** Doubleday

SELECTED WORKS AS EDITOR
1974 **Final Stage** Charterhouse, with Edward L. Ferman
1976 **Arena: Sports SF** Doubleday, with Edward L. Ferman
1977 **Dark Sins, Dark Dreams: Crimes in SF** Doubleday, with Bill Pronzini
1979 **The End of Summer: Science Fiction in the Fifties** Ace, with Bill Pronzini
1980 **Neglected Visions** Doubleday, with Martin H. Greenberg and Joseph D. Olander

FREDERIK POHL

BORN **1919**

NATIONALITY **American**

OTHER NAMES **Paul Flehr, Warren Howard, S.D. Gottesman, Edson McCann, James MacCreigh, Scott Mariner, Ernst Mason, Charles Satterfield, Dirk Wylie**

KEY WORKS *The Space Merchants, Man Plus, Gateway, JEM, The Years of the City, The World at the End of Time, Outnumbering the Dead*

YOU do not usually praise writers by saying they do other things really well, but it is impossible not to praise Pohl for everything he has accomplished. And he has lived long enough to write his masterpiece. Had he died young, as did C.M. Kornbluth, who wrote several early novels with him, Pohl would be remembered for the other things.

He was precocious: by the mid-1930s he was already preparing to become part of the brand new SF world. By the end of the decade, under a dizzying plethora of pseudonyms, and often in collaboration with other young writers, he was publishing stories, some good, many pretty poor. At the same time, he was simultaneously editing *Astonishing Stories* and *Super Science Stories* by 1940. These were not important magazines, and they soon folded. At which point, just as World War II was ending, and writers were turning into civilians again, Pohl became a literary agent. He was influential, he was supportive, and he made friends.

By 1950 he was writing again, and within a few years – under his own name, finally – he was fully launched upon the first of his two careers as a writer. This lasted for about a decade, during which time he co-wrote the stunning social satires *The Space Merchants* (see page 219), *Gladiator-at-Law*, and *Wolfbane* with Kornbluth. For young readers of the 1950s, Pohl and Kornbluth were the cutting edge of social comment; even now, although their views are expressed with some moderation, they seem to have pierced to the heart of the consumerism and conformism that haunted the American soul during that decade. His solo stories at this time were also remarkable.

> **"** *In the 1950s, he was the cutting edge of social comment* **"**

Pohl also became one of the central anthologists of SF with his series of **Star Science Fiction** originals. Then he became editor of *Galaxy*: during his tenure, from 1961 to 1969, the magazine dominated the field, but he found less time to write, and what he wrote seemed desultory, although *A Plague of Pythons* remains effective. It was only in the 1970s that he began his second writing career, which has extended into the 1990s without letup, although he did serve from 1974 to 1976 as president of the SFWA, the American SF writers' professional body.

(see page 219)

NOTABLE WORK

ALTERNATING CURRENTS

There are a lot of Pohl stories from the 1950s, collected in *Alternating Currents* and in several later collections, including *The Man Who Ate the World*. Two of these stories stand out still: "The Midas Plague" is about a society so rich that only the wealthy can afford not to consume madly according to rigid quotas; and "The Tunnel Under the World" is a masterful exercise in paranoia, in which a man relives the same day again and again to test out various advertising slogans. These are stories that slip under the skin and stick in the mind forever.

His masterpiece is probably *Gateway*, an exuberant tale in which humanity has a chance to grab the stars and goes for it. *JEM* is a vivid utopia. *The Years of the City* is a fervent plea for urban life. *Chernobyl* applies a sharp SF mind to the Russian disaster. *The World at the End of Time* takes billions of years, and universes. *Outnumbering the Dead* is about a mortal in a land of the undying. His latest career is his biggest.

BIBLIOGRAPHY

NOVELS AND NOVELLAS
1953 *The Space Merchants* Ballantine, with C.M. Kornbluth
1954 *Search the Sky* Ballantine, with C.M. Kornbluth
  Undersea Quest Gnome Press, with Jack Williamson
1955 *Preferred Risk* Simon and Schuster, with Lester Del Rey, both as Edson McCann
  Gladiator-at-Law Ballantine, with C.M. Kornbluth
1956 *Undersea Fleet* Gnome Press, with Jack Williamson
1957 *Slave Ship* Ballantine
1958 *Undersea City* Gnome Press, with Jack Williamson
1959 *Wolfbane* Ballantine, with C.M. Kornbluth
1960 *Drunkard's Walk* Gnome Press
1964 *The Reefs of Space* Ballantine, with Jack Williamson
1965 *Starchild* Ballantine, with Jack Williamson

1965 *A Plague of Pythons* Ballantine, revised as *Demon in the Skull*
1969 *The Age of the Pussyfoot* Trident Press
1975 *Farthest Star* Ballantine, with Jack Williamson
1976 *Man Plus* Random House
1977 *Gateway* St. Martin's Press
1979 *JEM: The Making of a Utopia* St. Martin's Press
1980 *Beyond the Blue Event Horizon* Ballantine
1981 *The Cool War* Ballantine
1982 *Starburst* Ballantine
  Syzygy Bantam
1983 *Wall Around a Star* Ballantine, with Jack Williamson
  Midas World St. Martin's Press
1984 *Heechee Rendezvous* Ballantine
  The Years of the City Simon and Schuster
  The Merchants' War St. Martin's Press
1985 *Black Star Rising* Ballantine

1986 *Terror* Berkley
  The Coming of the Quantum Cats Bantam
1987 *The Annals of the Heechee* Ballantine
  Chernobyl Bantam
  Narabedia Ltd Ballantine
1988 *The Day the Martians Came* St. Martin's Press
  Land's End Tor, with Jack Williamson
1989 *Homegoing* Ballantine
1990 *The World at the End of Time* Ballantine
  Outnumbering the Dead Legend
1991 *The Singers of Time* Doubleday, with Jack Williamson
  Stopping at Slowyear Pulphouse
1992 *Mining the Oort* Ballantine
1994 *The Voices of Heaven* Tor

SHORT STORY COLLECTIONS
1956 *Alternating Currents* Ballantine
1957 *The Case Against Tomorrow* Ballantine

1959 *Tomorrow Times Seven* Ballantine
1960 *The Man Who Ate the World* Ballantine
1961 *Turn Left at Thursday* Ballantine
1962 *The Wonder Effect* Ballantine, with C.M. Kornbluth, revised as *Critical Mass*
1963 *The Abominable Earthman* Ballantine
1966 *The Frederik Pohl Omnibus* Gollancz, reprinted in part as *Survival Kit*
  Digits and Dastards Ballantine
1970 *Day Million* Ballantine
1972 *The Gold at Starbow's End* Ballantine
1975 *The Best of Frederik Pohl*
1976 *In the Problem Pit* Bantam
  The Early Pohl Doubleday
1980 *Before the Universe* Bantam, with C.M. Kornbluth
1982 *Planets Three* Berkley
1984 *Pohlstars* Ballantine
1987 *Our Best: The Best of Frederik Pohl and C.M. Kornbluth* Baen

1990 *The Gateway Trip: Tales and Vignettes of the Heechee* Ballantine

SELECTED NON-FICTION
1978 *The Way the Future Was: A Memoir* Ballantine
1991 *Our Angry Earth* Tor, with Isaac Asimov

SELECTED WORKS AS EDITOR
1952 *Beyond the End of Time* Permabooks
1953 *Star Science Fiction Stories* Ballantine, six volumes through 1959
1962 *The Expert Dreamers* Doubleday
1975 *The Science Fiction Roll of Honor* Random House
1986 *Tales from the Planet Earth* St. Martin's Press, with Elizabeth Anne Hull

JAMES TIPTREE JR.

BORN / DIED **1915-87**

NATIONALITY **American**

OTHER NAMES **born Alice Sheldon; Racoona Sheldon**

KEY WORKS **"The Last Flight of Doctor Ain", "And I Awoke and Found Me Here on the Cold Hill's Side", "The Women Men Don't See", "Love is the Plan the Plan is Death", "The Screwfly Solution", "Your Faces, O my Sisters! Your Faces Filled of Light!"**

JAMES Tiptree Jr. – the surname came from a brand of marmalade – burst onto the scene in 1968 with a rush of stories marking her (him) as a writer of maturity and energy. Given how many people still maintain that sex causes differences in style and content, it was not perhaps surprising that few people suspected that Tiptree was not a man.

He lived near Washington DC; he had a job in the Pentagon; and his letters were vigorous, direct, and humorous – qualities that (it is embarrassing to say) are still ascribed more to men than to women. And he did men well. The story that might have blown his cover was "The Women Men Don't See", a moving and witty portrayal of two women, made inconspicuous all their lives by the sheer noise men generate in the world, who choose in the end to leave the planet entirely aboard an alien spaceship that has paid a brief visit. The last line is famous: "Two of our opossums are missing." But the underlying cleverness is that the male protagonist is – although he utterly fails to understand the women – decent, gregarious, and generous. He sounds, in fact, just like Tiptree.

Alice Sheldon's parents travelled widely, and her mother was a prolific writer, fitting her daughter into more than one of her books. Alice's early life as an art critic, and her first marriage, remain obscure; it was after her second marriage, in 1945, that she began to become the figure her readers felt they knew. Her first story (not SF) appeared in *The New Yorker* in 1946; she took a PhD in psychology in 1967; she began to publish SF at the age of 52.

"Her stories are extrovert, joyous, and energetic; they are also astonishingly grave"

Her energy burned. Between 1968 and 1976 or so, she published about 20 tales of real greatness; it was one of the most significant spurts of creative energy the SF field – or any field – has seen. Even the titles spur the mind: "Faithful to thee, Terra, in our Fashion", "And I Awoke and Found me Here on the Cold Hill's Side", "The Last Flight of Doctor Ain" – a savage fable of a man who kills humanity to save the planet – "The Girl Who Was Plugged In", "Her Smoke Rose Up Forever", "Love is the Plan the Plan is Death" – encapsulating her philosophy in one terrifying axiom – "Your Faces, O my Sisters! Your Faces Filled of Light", and "The Color of Neanderthal Eyes". These stories are extrovert, joyous, energetic; they are also astonishingly grave. They seem, now that we know something of her, to combine Youth's lust for life with Age's more profound knowledge of the inevitable end of life. Almost every one of her stories ends, in other words, with a death. Their joys flicker in the night, and cease.

There are novels as well, written after a fan had worked out her identity. *Up the Walls of the World* is a complex and ambitious book – so complex and ambitious that it almost fails to work – in which a vast being, ignorant of tiny planet-bound life forms, comes close to wiping out the sentient species of our corner of the galaxy.

BIBLIOGRAPHY

NOVELS AND NOVELLAS

1978 *Up the Walls of the World* Berkley
1985 *Brightness Falls from the Air* Tor
1989 *The Girl Who Was Plugged In* Tor
     Houston, Houston, Do You Read? Tor
1990 *The Color of Neanderthal Eyes* Tor

SHORT STORY COLLECTIONS

1973 *Ten Thousand Light-Years from Home* Ace
1975 *Warm Worlds and Otherwise* Ballantine
1978 *Star Songs of an Old Primate* Ballantine
1981 *Out of the Everywhere, and Other Extraordinary Visions* Ballantine
1985 *Byte Beautiful* Doubleday
1986 *The Starry Rift* Tor
     Tales of the Quintana Roo Arkham House
1988 *Crown of Stars* Tor
1990 *Her Smoke Rose Up Forever: The Great Years of James Tiptree, Jr.* Arkham House

Brightness Falls from the Air is deeply savage, but again almost falls apart: on a distant planet, it is time for the natives to go through a death agony; the irony of the tale is that this vast experience of death psychically generates a nectar-like high for others.

Alice Sheldon's final stories are misshapen by out-of-control emotion – love and hate for the species and what we were capable of. She was famous and admired, but she feared for us. Her health was failing, and her husband had developed Alzheimer's Disease; in 1987 she shot him and herself.

NOTABLE WORK

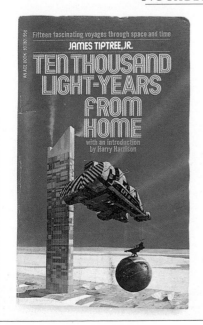

Terrible design, lousy proofreading, a general sense of disdain for the product: one of the worst publishing jobs ever. But the stories are the finest debut collection by a modern SF writer. Some of the earliest are just brightly competent, but stories like "The Snows are Melted, the Snows are Gone", "The Man Who Walked Home", and "Forever to a Hudson Bay Blanket" are full-blown *tours de force*. They are romantic, pell-mell, intriguing, and drenched with the knowledge that death is at the end. The best reappeared in *Her Smoke Rose Up Forever*, but this first book remains a collector's item.

TEN THOUSAND LIGHT-YEARS FROM HOME

Birth of an author
Tiptree's first work, "Birth of a Salesman", appeared in Astounding *in 1968.*

ROBERT SILVERBERG

BORN **1935**

NATIONALITY **American**

OTHER NAMES **T.D. Bethlen, Dirk Clinton, Ivar Jorgenson, Calvin M. Knox, Dan Malcolm, Webber Martin, Alex Merriman, David Osborne, George Osborne, Robert Randall, Eric Rodman, Hall Thornton, Richard F. Watson**

KEY WORKS **The 13th Immortal, Master of Life and Death, Collision Course, Hawksbill Station, The Masks of Time, Downward to the Earth, Tower of Glass, The World Inside, A Time of Changes, Son of Man, Dying Inside, The Book of Skulls**

ROBERT Silverberg's SF work takes up a fair chunk of this page. It looks pretty impressive: dozens of novels and collections over nearly 40 years of almost constant work. But this is just the tip of the iceberg. A full bibliography – including all the pseudonymous books in various genres he has never bothered to acknowledge – would run to hundreds more titles. He is a writing machine.

Or so it seems. The truth is rather different. Silverberg's career has been similar to that of the Belgian writer Georges Simenon. In their youth, both produced torrents of work, much of it pseudonymous. This was when Silverberg Space Operas like *The 13th Immortal* and *Collision Course* impressed and – just slightly – bored SF readers.

Then both writers slowed down, sometimes writing just two or three books a year, and produced work of stature. Simenon wrote the *Maigrets*; and between 1967 and 1976 Silverberg published 25 novels that are a feat of sustained and brilliant output. There is not a sequel in the lot: each is a new contribution to the world of story.

NIGHTWINGS
by ROBERT SILVERBERG

I spend my life in Watching for an enemy from beyond the stars — not seeing death here on Earth!

Awards
Silverberg has somewhat missed out on the major awards with regards to novels but has done better with his short fiction, beginning with a Hugo for "Nightwings" in 1969.

Hawksbill Station is a chamber opera set in a dissident prison camp at the dawn of time; *The Masks of Time* presents a man from the future's speculations on humanity; *Downward to the Earth* has a favourite theme, transcendence in the course of which a human moves to a better, higher, or more terminal state;

Tower of Glass examines egomania; *The World Inside* is a dystopia; *A Time of Changes* (see page 226) is an exobiology drama; *Son of Man* speculates about the future evolution of humanity; *Dying Inside* (see page 227) tells of a telepath with fading power; *The Book of Skulls* recounts a quest for immortality that becomes a dance of death; *Shadrach in the Furnace* is a moral tale of power and responsibility. The list seems endless; Silverberg, tireless.

Then, just as Simenon had a crisis, Silverberg gave up writing in the mid-1970s, disgruntled with what he saw as a lack of appreciation. Both writers began again, but from 1980 Silverberg's books, although broody and superbly professional, have tended to be yarns. His short stories, however, still catch the mind. He may not wish to do more, or he may erupt again.

BIBLIOGRAPHY

NOVELS AND NOVELLAS
1955 **Revolt on Alpha C** Crowell
1957 **The 13th Immortal** Ace
Master of Life and Death Ace
The Shrouded Planet Gnome Press, with Randall Garrett, as Robert Randall
1958 **Invaders from Earth** Ace
Lest We Forget Thee, Earth Ace, as Calvin M. Knox
Invisible Barriers Avalon, as David Osborne
Stepsons of Terra Ace
Aliens from Space Avalon, as David Osborne
Starhaven Avalon, as Ivar Jorgenson
1959 **Starman's Quest** Gnome Press
The Plot Against Earth Ace, as Calvin M. Knox
The Dawning Light Gnome Press, with Randall Garrett, together as Robert Randall
The Planet Killers Ace
1960 **Lost Race of Mars** Winston
1961 **Collision Course** Avalon
1962 **The Seed of Earth** Ace
Recalled to Life Lancer
1963 **The Silent Invaders** Ace
1964 **Regan's Planet** Pyramid
One of our Asteroids is Missing Ace, as Calvin M. Knox
Time of the Great Freeze Holt Rinehart
1965 **Conquerors from the Darkness** Holt Rinehart

1967 **The Gate of Worlds** Holt Rinehart
Those Who Watch Signet
To Open the Sky Ballantine
Thorns Ballantine
The Time-Hoppers Doubleday
Planet of Death Holt Rinehart
1968 **Hawksbill Station** Doubleday, retitled **The Anvil of Time**
The Masks of Time Ballantine, retitled **Vornan-19**
1969 **Up the Line** Ballantine
Nightwings Avon
Across a Billion Years Dial Press
The Man in the Maze Avon
Three Survived Holt Rinehart
To Live Again Doubleday
1970 **World's Fair 1992** Follett
Downward to the Earth Nelson Doubleday
Tower of Glass Scribners
1971 **The World Inside** Doubleday
A Time of Changes Nelson Doubleday
Son of Man Ballantine
The Book of Skulls Scribners
1972 **Dying Inside** Scribners
The Second Trip Nelson Doubleday
1975 **The Stochastic Man** Harper
1976 **Shadrach in the Furnace** Bobbs Merrill
1980 **Lord Valentine's Castle** Harper
1981 **The Desert of Stolen Dreams** Underwood-Miller
1982 **The Majipoor Chronicles** Arbor House
1983 **Valentine Pontifex** Arbor House

1983 **Lord of Darkness** Arbor House
Homefaring Phantasia Press
1984 **Gilgamesh the King** Arbor House
1985 **Tom O'Bedlam** Fine
Sailing to Byzantium
1986 **Star of the Gypsies** Fine
1987 **Project Pendulum** Walker
1988 **At Winter's End** Warner
The Secret Sharer Underwood-Miller
1989 **The Mutant Season** Doubleday, with Karen Haber
The Queen of Springtime Gollancz, retitled **The New Springtime**
To the Land of the Living Gollancz
1990 **Nightfall** Gollancz, with Isaac Asimov
Letters from Atlantis Atheneum
In Another Country Tor
Lion Time in Timbuctoo Axolotl
1991 **The Face of the Waters** Grafton
Thebes of the Hundred Gates Axolotl
Child of Time Gollancz, with Isaac Asimov
1992 **Kingdoms of the Wall** HarperCollins
The Positronic Man Gollancz, with Isaac Asimov
1994 **Hot Sky at Midnight** Bantam

SHORT STORY COLLECTIONS
1962 **Next Stop the Stars** Ace
1964 **Godling, Go Home!** Belmont

1965 **To Worlds Beyond** Chilton
1966 **Needle in a Timestack** Ballantine
1969 **The Calibrated Alligator** Holt Rinehart
Dimension Thirteen Ballantine
1970 **Parsecs and Parables** Doubleday
The Cube Root of Uncertainty Macmillan
1971 **Moonferns and Starsongs** Ballantine
1972 **The Reality Trip and Other Implausibilities** Ballantine
1973 **Valley Beyond Time** Dell
Unfamiliar Territory Scribners
Earth's Other Shadow Signet
1974 **Born With the Dead** Random House
Sundance Nelson
1975 **Sunrise on Mercury** Nelson
The Feast of St. Dionysus Scribners
1976 **The Shores of Tomorrow** Nelson
Capricorn Games Random House
The Best of Robert Silverberg Pocket Books
1979 **The Songs of Summer** Gollancz
1982 **World of a Thousand Colors** Arbor House
1984 **The Conglomeroid Cocktail Party** Arbor House
1986 **Beyond the Safe Zone** Fine
1992 **Pluto in the Morning Light: Collected Stories Vol. 1** Grafton, expanded as **The Collected Stories of Robert Silverberg Vol. 1: Secret Sharers**

SELECTED NON-FICTION
1961 **First American into Space** Monarch
1962 **Lost Cities and Vanished Civilizations** Chilton
1967 **The Morning of Mankind** Graphic Society
1969 **The World of Space** Meredith Press
1971 **Into Space** Harper, with Arthur C. Clarke
1972 **The Realm of Prester John** Doubleday
1974 **Drug Themes in Science Fiction** National Institute on Drug Abuse

SELECTED WORKS AS EDITOR
1966 **Earthmen and Strangers** Duell
1967 **Voyagers in Time** Meredith Press
1969 **Dark Stars** Ballantine
1970 **The Mirror of Infinity** Harper
Alpha 1 Ballantine, with eight further volumes to 1978
1971 **New Dimensions** Doubleday, with 11 further volumes to 1981
1975 **The New Atlantis** Hawthorn
1976 **The Crystal Ship** Nelson
1980 **The Arbor House Treasury of Modern Science Fiction** Arbor House, with Martin H. Greenberg, retitled **Great Science Fiction of the 20th Century**
1990 **Universe 1** Doubleday, a continuing series
1992 **Murasaki** Bantam

GENE WOLFE

BORN **1931**

NATIONALITY **American**

KEY WORKS **The Fifth Head of Cerberus, The Book of the New Sun series, Free Live Free, the Long Sun series**

THERE are more signficant writers of SF than Wolfe. Heinlein, Asimov, Dick, and Le Guin have all written large bodies of SF work that have had a defining and invigorating effect upon the genre; Wolfe has written very little pure SF, and his influence upon younger writers is only beginning to be felt in the 1990s. He is not deeply influential; but he is perhaps the best writer SF has produced.

He comes – some would argue – at the end. SF as a genre for young readers peaked in the early 1960s, just as he began. Since then, the old genre has faded as its readership aged, but it left a wealth of ideas and examples.

The childhood world of Future History may have melted into past history, but the best is yet to come – certainly if Wolfe's career shows how writers can use SF as an adult form of literature.

The Fifth Head of Cerberus – three stories that must be read as a tripartite novel – is Wolfe's most central SF text. Its portrayal of a colony world is muscular and atmospheric; its scrutiny of questions of identity where cloning is possible is savagely moving; and its narrative techniques test the reader's attention to text more thoroughly, and suavely, than anything before in the genre. *Peace* is a posthumous fantasy of astonishing (although indirect) cruelty.

In 1980 the four volumes of Wolfe's masterpiece began to appear. *The Shadow of the Torturer, The Claw of the Conciliator, The Sword of the Lictor,* and *The Citadel of the Autarch* are in fact one sustained novel, **The Book of the New Sun** (see page 231). It is set in a future so distant that Earth is now called Urth; throughout, echoes of Jack Vance's *The Dying Earth* can be detected. It is the story of Severian, an orphan brought up by the guild of Torturers at the Autarch's court, in the great southern city of Nessus. Severian is an avatar of a previous figure, known as the Conciliator. He becomes a torturer, betrays his calling for a woman, is sent into exile, has adventures, fights in a war, returns to Nessus, and becomes the new Autarch.

> *“Wolfe is not deeply influential; but he is perhaps the best writer SF has produced”*

BIBLIOGRAPHY

NOVELS AND NOVELLAS
1970 **Operation ARES** Berkley
1972 **The Fifth Head of Cerberus** Scribners
1975 **Peace** Harper
1976 **The Devil in a Forest** Follett
1980 **The Book of the New Sun: The Shadow of the Torturer** Timescape
1981 **The Book of the New Sun: The Claw of the Conciliator** Timescape
1982 **The Book of the New Sun: The Sword of the Lictor** Timescape
1983 **The Book of the New Sun: The Citadel of the Autarch** Timescape
1984 **Free Live Free** Mark V. Ziesing
1986 **Soldier of the Mist** Tor
1987 **The Urth of the New Sun** Gollancz
Empires of Foliage and Flower Cheap Street
1988 **There Are Doors** Tor
1989 **Soldier of Arete** Tor
Seven American Nights Tor
1990 **Castleview** Tor
Pandora by Holly Holander Tor

1990 **The Death of Doctor Island** Tor
1993 **Nightside the Long Sun** Tor
1994 **Lake of the Long Sun** Tor
Caldé of the Long Sun Tor

SHORT STORY COLLECTIONS
1980 **The Island of Doctor Death and Other Stories and Other Stories** Pocket Books
1981 **Gene Wolfe's Book of Days** Doubleday
1983 **The Wolfe Archipelago** Mark V. Ziesing
1984 **Bibliomen: Twenty Characters Waiting for a Book** Cheap Street
Plan[e]t Engineering NESFA Press
1988 **Storeys from the Old Hotel** Kerosina
1989 **Endangered Species** Tor
1992 **The Young Wolfe** New Mythologies Press
Castle of Days Tor

NON-FICTION
1982 **The Castle of the Otter** Mark V. Ziesing
1991 **Letters Home** United Mythologies Press

EMPIRES OF FOLIAGE AND FLOWER

One of the books Severian carries with him throughout **The Book of the New Sun** is a volume called *The Book of the Wonders of Urth and Sky*. It is a series of fables, some of which Wolfe's readers are allowed to sample. *Empires of Foliage and Flower* – which does not appear in **The Book of the New Sun** – is one of the tales. It tells of a girl who follows a sage called Thyme around the world and home again, where she becomes herself. This tale is also Severian's story.

It sounds simple enough, and rather like many other tales of the hero who becomes king. But Severian – who has a perfect memory, but who does not always tell the truth – is not only destined to be Autarch from the first. He is both Christ and Apollo. He raises the dead; he has half a dozen talismans of power, like any fantasy figure, but needs none of them; he works miracles of grace, although a torturer; he mediates between Urth and the aliens from a higher plane who work either to save humanity or to exploit us, or both. In *The Urth of the New Sun*, Severian finally brings the New Sun home. It is a white hole, which will give new life to the old, dying Sun; but will also drown most of humanity. Throughout the five volumes, miracles grow like weeds on Urth's holy ground.

> *“Wolfe has always been a parodist, but his parodies are accomplishments of loving craft”*

Dense, allusive, possessing and evasive and inescapable, **The Book of the New Sun** is overmasteringly a work in its own right. And because it sums up so much of what had gone before – everything from messiahs to robotics, from Space Opera to theatre of the absurd – it contributes very little that is new to the genre. In a sense, it merely is. This is, perhaps, enough. It was not an easy work to follow.

What Wolfe did was refuse to attempt, for many years, anything that could resemble **The Book of the New Sun**. *Free Live Free* is set in a hard-to-locate American city; its characters and plot replay L. Frank Baum's *The Wonderful Wizard of Oz* – Wolfe has always been a parodist, but his parodies are almost always accomplishments of loving craft. *Soldier of the Mist, Soldier of Arete, There Are Doors,* and *Castleview* are fantasies. Some of the stories assembled in *The Island of Doctor Death and Other Stories and Other Stories* have become classics. *Bibliomen* is a collection of imaginary characters who occupy or make themselves into various books.

Wolfe has begun another ambitious series. *Nightside the Long Sun, Lake of the Long Sun,* and *Caldé of the Long Sun* begin the story of Pater Silk, a man overwhelmed by a vast store of memory downloaded from a god. What he sorts out will, like all of Wolfe's work, almost certainly be a revelation.

PHILIPPE CURVAL

BORN **1929**

NATIONALITY **French**

OTHER NAME **born Philippe Tronche**

KEY WORKS *Le ressac de l'espace, L'homme à rebours, Cette chère humanité*

For many writers of SF whose original language is not English, or who have no instinctive predilection for the American genre, SF is often a closed shop. It is a bit, perhaps, the way that it used to be for women, and still is for most ethnic minorities: in order to be accepted as an equal, you have to accomplish far more than those who occupy, as if by right, the commanding heights of power and acclaim.

Philippe Curval, to take one instance, is a man of letters of quite signal accomplishments, as a journalist, novelist, short-story writer, and editor. He is recognized as such in France, where he has won awards including the Prix Apollo and the Prix Jules Verne.

But in a distinguished career that has spanned over three decades, only one of his many novels – the award-winning *Cette chère humanité* – has ever been published in English. The translation, *Brave Old World*, although it was moderately competent, did not really capture his fluent, poetic style.

Curval's work is deeply rooted in the models of European civilization and culture, and his treatment of the sacred icons of the dominant American mode of SF shows great ambivalence. It is an ambivalence that is only to be expected from a writer representing a culture that this dominant mode has always tended to treat as a beggar at the feast of the future.

BIBLIOGRAPHY

NOVELS AND NOVELLAS

1960 *Les fleurs de Vénus* Hachette, Rayon Fantastique **[The flowers of Venus]**

1962 *Le ressac de l'espace* Hachette, Rayon Fantastique **[The ebb tide of space]**

1967 *La forteresse de coton* Gallimard **[The cotton fortress]**

1973 *Attention les yeux* Éric Losfeld **[Watch out!]**

1974 *L'homme à rebours* Robert Laffont, Ailleurs et Demain **[The backwards man]**

1975 *Les sables de Falun* Jean Claude Lattès, Titres SF **[The sands of Falun]**

Un souvenir de Pierre Loti Robert Laffont, Ailleurs et Demain **[In remembrance of Pierre Loti]**

1976 *Cette chère humanité* Robert Laffont, Ailleurs et demain, translated as **Brave Old World**

1977 *Un soupçon de néant* Presses Pocket **[A hint of nothingness]**

1978 *La face cachée du desir* Calmann-Lévy, Dimensions SF **[The dark side of desire]**

1979 *Y a quelqu'un?* Calmann-Lévy, Dimensions SF **[Anybody home?]**

Le dormeur s'éveillera-t-il? Denoël, Présence du futur **[Will the sleeper awake?]**

Rut aux etoiles Presses Pocket **[The astral mating season]**

1981 *L'odeur de la bête* Denoël, Présence du futur **[The scent of the beast]**

Tous vers l'extase Jean Claude Lattès, Titres SF **[All together to ecstasy]**

1982 *En souvenir du futur* Robert Laffont, Ailleurs et Demain **[Remembrance of time to come]**

Ah! Que c'est beau New York! Denoël **[Ah! New York is so beautiful!]**

1986 *Comment jouer à l'homme invisible en trois leçons* Denoël, Présence du futur **[The invisible man in three lessons]**

1988 *Akilöe* Flammarion

SHORT STORY COLLECTIONS

1980 *Regarde, fiston, s'il y a un extra-terrestre derrière la bouteille de vin* Denoël, Présence du futur **[Take a look, boy, if there's an alien behind the bottle of wine]**

Le livre d'or de la science fiction: Philippe Curval Presses Pocket, Le Livre d'or **[The golden book of Science Fiction: Philippe Curval]**

1984 *Debout les morts, le train fantôme entre la gare* Denoël, Présence du futur **[On your feet, dead men, the phantom train is pulling in]**

1980 *Habite-t-on réellement quelque part?* Denoël, Présence du futur **[Do we really live somewhere?]**

AS EDITOR

1979 *Futurs au présent* Denoël, Présence du futur **[The future is now]**

1986 *Superfuturs* Denoël, Présence du futur **[Superfutures]**

JOHN SLADEK

BORN **1937**

NATIONALITY **American**

OTHER NAMES **Cassandra Knye, Thom Demijohn, James Vogh, Richard A. Tilms**

KEY WORKS **"Masterson and the Clerks"**, *The Reproductive System*, the *Roderick* diptych, *Tik-Tok*, *Bugs*

It is not only Europeans who feel like exiles in the future depicted by American SF in its assertive prime. John Sladek, born and raised in the American Midwest, wrote everything for which he is now honoured while living abroad, mostly in England. But he was formed in America, and it is a sign of the depth of his experience over the first few decades of his life that vanishingly little of his fiction is set anywhere but in the United States, however surrealistically distorted.

A comparison with Kurt Vonnegut is suggested almost every time Sladek is mentioned. It is worth recollecting here to emphasize that a profound alienation from the American way can be felt by men and women who remain profoundly American in every word they write; and also to emphasize the extraordinary funniness of Sladek's work. He may be the funniest writer – he is certainly the most devastatingly accurate parodist – ever to operate within genre SF.

The wit was evident from the very beginning. A scarring tale of the terminal effects of consumerism and office culture like "Masterson and the Clerks", from 1967, was almost the first thing Sladek ever wrote. It took years to reach print, even in England, and only ever reached book form in the obscurely published *Alien Accounts*, which is now out of print.

Most of his other works are out of print, too. The important novels are *The Reproductive System*, *The Müller-Fokker Effect*, the two volumes of *Roderick*, *Tik-Tok*, and *Bugs*. As with Vonnegut's work, they show a man helplessly in love with a native land whose flaws – and whose disastrous pellmell rush over the abyss into the horrors of the next century – he compulsively records, both for our merriment, and for our betterment. The recurring figures – robots, insane executives, manic AIs – tell recurring jokes, and teach a recurring lesson. They teach us that just being alive in these times is so hilarious that we could all die laughing.

BIBLIOGRAPHY

NOVELS AND NOVELLAS

1966 *The House That Fear Built* Paperback Library, with Thomas M. Disch, both as Cassandra Knye

1967 *The Castle and the Key* Paperback Library, as Cassandra Knye

1968 *The Reproductive System* Gollancz, retitled **Mechasm**

Black Alice Doubleday, with Thomas M. Disch, both as Thom Demijohn

1970 *The Müller-Fokker Effect* Hutchinson

1974 *Black Aura* Cape

1977 *Invisible Green: A Thackeray Phin Mystery* Gollancz

1980 *Roderick, or The Education of a Young Machine* Granada

1983 *Roderick at Random, or Further Education of a Young Machine* Granada

Tik-Tok Gollancz

1989 *Bugs* Macmillan

1990 *Blood and Gingerbread* Cheap Street

SHORT STORY COLLECTIONS

1973 *The Steam-Driven Boy and Other Strangers* Panther

1978 *Keep the Giraffe Burning* Panther

1981 *The Best of John Sladek* Pocket Books

1982 *Alien Accounts* Panther

1984 *The Lunatics of Terra* Gollancz

The Book of Clues Corgi

NON-FICTION

1973 *The New Apocrypha: a Guide to Strange Science and Occult Beliefs* Hart Davis MacGibbon

1977 *Arachne Rising: The Thirteenth Sign of the Zodiac* Hart Davis MacGibbon, as James Vogh, retitled **The Thirteenth Zodiac: The Sign of Arachne**

1978 *The Cosmic Factor* Hart Davis MacGibbon, as James Vogh

1980 *Judgement of Jupiter* New English Library, as Richard A. Tilms

C.J. CHERRYH

BORN **1942**

NATIONALITY **American**

OTHER NAME **born Carolyn Janice Cherry**

KEY WORKS **The *Alliance-Union* series**

THERE is no simple place to start with C.J. Cherryh. Almost all of her SF novels connect to each other, but they do so in no simple or linear fashion, and the vast Future History in which they nestle has proved – so far – too extensive and complex to allow any easy tracking. Some of her novels read like singletons, until – it is as if the floor suddenly disappears from beneath you – it becomes clear that a seemingly independent narrative dovetails into a dozen others. Other novels simply cannot be understood at all, until their context is known.

That context is the overarching *Alliance-Union* super-series, which embraces exceedingly diverse smaller sequences such as the **Merchanter** novels, the **Chanur** books, and the **Faded Sun** trilogy. Set within a radius of about 50 light-years from Earth, and taking place over the next 2,000 years or so, the series provides a convenient framework for the dozens of novels fitted into it so far. Earth has become gigantically powerful, and dominated by super-corporations; but its power is counterbalanced in space by the Union, an autocratic, manipulative, and expansionist array of like-minded planets, and by the Alliance, a much looser association of traders. Cherryh's galaxy is full of aliens, many of them protected by what is known as the Gehenna Doctrine: the principle, also familiar to much other recent SF, that prohibits any forced interaction between powerful, star-hopping races,

like humanity, and local cultures that they come across. Many of Cherryh's stories have little or nothing to do with the main Alliance-Union universe simply because the Gehenna Doctrine protects them from "contamination".

Perhaps the most remarkable thing to notice about Cherryh, however, is not the fact that she has written a great deal in a mere two decades of activity, but that many of her best novels seem about to burst at the seams with ideas, characters, and tales to tell. Not only does she write a great deal, and pack most of her stories with verisimilitude, energy, and pazzazz; at the same time she seems to be in a great hurry to continue. She strides fast and far.

Although many of Cherryh's tales exist right at the periphery of the main overarching series, the best of her early books – like *Downbelow Station* (see page 231), which won a Hugo, or *Merchanter's Luck*, or *Forty Thousand in Gehenna* – lie at the heart of the long epic. The first of these focuses on the long process by which Earth loses its control to the Alliance Merchanters, who dominate trade among the many thousands of active civilizations across the galaxy. *Gehenna*, an extremely complex and taxing tale, describes civilization on a planet that is seeded but then abandoned by a Union world, where profound conflicts take place between the artificially generated humans, or androids, and the "born men" who think themselves superior to

androids, both groups being outclassed, in the end, by the planet's original inhabitants, known as "calibans". Each strand of the tale awakens in the reader memories and anticipations of other tales, other tiles in the huge mosaic.

The culminating *Alliance-Union* novel is probably *Cyteen* (see page 233), set on the central Union planet, in a culture defined by its concentration upon the manufacture and breeding of androids, who co-exist uneasily with a human population. Cherryh controls the vast scope of the book – it was reprinted in three separate volumes –

(see page 231)
(see page 233)

NOTABLE WORK

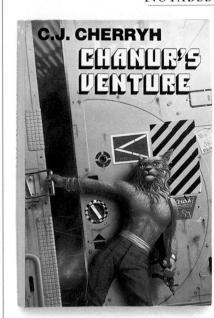

C.J. Cherryh's five-volume *Chanur* saga, part of the overall series of *Alliance-Union* novels, features aliens functioning in a highly complex, threatened interstellar venue. As in many of her books, most of the action takes place in space-based environments, such as spaceships and waystations. The series is characterized by fast-paced plots and realistically depicted alien cultures. The swaggering hani – cat-like aliens – are utterly believable, and in the final analysis it is the lone human who seems alien.

CHANUR'S VENTURE

by focusing on a complex relationship between a powerful human woman, the young male lover whom she abuses, the android attached to him, and the woman's distressed clone. Explosions of intrigue pull the reader along, while lighting up the world like fireworks.

There is no simple place to start: start anywhere. The only way to read Cherryh is to dive right in.

BIBLIOGRAPHY

NOVELS AND NOVELLAS
1976 *Gate of Ivrel* DAW Books
Brothers of Earth DAW Books
Hunter of Worlds Nelson Doubleday
1978 *Well of Shiuan* DAW Books
The Faded Sun: Kesrith Nelson Doubleday
The Faded Sun: Shon'Jir Nelson Doubleday
1979 *Fires of Azeroth* DAW Books
Hestia DAW Books
1980 *Serpent's Reach* DAW Books
The Faded Sun: Kutath Nelson Doubleday
1981 *Wave Without a Shore* DAW Books
Downbelow Station DAW Books
Ealdwood Donald M. Grant, expanded as
The Dreamstone
1982 *The Pride of Chanur* DAW Books
Merchanter's Luck DAW Books
Port Eternity DAW Books
1983 *The Tree of Swords and Jewels* DAW Books
Forty Thousand in Gehenna
Phantasia Press
1984 *Voyager in Night* DAW Books
Chanur's Venture Phantasia Press
1985 *Cuckoo's Egg* Phantasia Press

1985 *The Kif Strike Back* Phantasia Press
Angel with the Sword DAW Books
1986 *The Gates of Hell* Baen Books, with
Janet Morris
Chanur's Homecoming Phantasia Press
1987 *Kings in Hell* Baen Books, with Janet Morris
Legions of Hell Baen Books
1988 *The Paladin* Baen Books
Exile's Gate DAW Books
Cyteen Warner, republished in three volumes
as *The Betrayal, The Rebirth,* and
The Vindication
1989 *Rimrunners* Warner
Rusalka Ballantine
A Dirge for Sabis Baen Books, with
Leslie Fish
Wizard Spawn Baen Books, with Nancy Asire
Reap the Whirlwind Baen Books, with
Mercedes Lackey
1990 *Chernevog* Ballantine
1991 *Yvgenie* Ballantine
Heavy Time Warner
1992 *The Goblin Mirror* Ballantine
1992 *Chanur's Legacy* DAW Books

1992 *Hellburner* New English Library
1993 *Faery in Shadow* Legend
1994 *Foreigner: A Novel of First Contact*
DAW Books
Tripoint Warner

SHORT STORY COLLECTIONS
1981 *Sunfall* DAW Books
1986 *Visible Light* Phantasia Press
1987 *Glass and Amber* NESFA Press

AS EDITOR
1987 *Merovingen Nights: Festival Moon*
DAW Books
Merovingen Nights: Fever Season
DAW Books
1988 *Merovingen Nights: Troubled Waters*
DAW Books
Merovingen Nights: Smuggler's Gold
DAW Books
1989 *Merovingen Nights: Divine Right*
DAW Books
1990 *Merovingen Nights: Flood Tide* DAW Books
1991 *Merovingen Nights: Endgame* DAW Books

VONDA N. McINTYRE

BORN **1948**

NATIONALITY **American**

KEY WORKS **Dreamsnake, the Starfarers series**

IN the late afternoon of American SF, writer's workshops began to flourish. In the 1930s, budding authors might learn their trade, for good and for ill, on the cent-a-word pulps; by the 1970s, the pulps had gone, and SF had a history to learn, techniques to cherish (or to grow out of); and young writers needed somewhere to test their skills. Vonda McIntyre, one of the most successful graduates of the Clarion Workshop, tested out fine.

McIntyre's first prominent story, "Of Mist, and Grass, and Sand", appeared a couple of years after she left Clarion, and it won a Nebula Award for Best Novelette. Expanded in *Dreamsnake*, it recounts the experiences of a healer in a post-holocaust desert, whose craft suffers a blow when ignorant villagers kill her snake, with whom she had a complex empathetic link, and which interacted with her in her healing. But she recovers, and the rest of the novel version is her search for a new snake.

Her first novel, *The Exile Waiting*, makes use of the same desolate environment, although it is set in a city hidden in the midst of the waste.

Dreamsnake won McIntyre another Nebula, as well as a Hugo Award, but at this point in her career she decided to make a shift from stand-alone texts, and within a few years had written five **Star Trek** novels, two of them tied to the television series and three being novelizations of the films. In this, too, she followed a respectable route for writers of her generation, many of whom have enthusiastically involved themselves in the strange, compulsive, modern American legends of Kirk and Spock who – both military men – represent Earth to the galaxy at large. The series may be mocked for its naivety and for its cardboard sets, but it has penetrated more deeply into the modern consciousness than any other SF presentation. McIntyre's texts contribute to that penetration.

More recently, she has turned back to texts for which the responsibility is entirely hers. The **Starfarers** series –

> *" With the* **Starfarers** *series, McIntyre is travelling again "*

Starfarers, Transition, and *Metaphase,* so far – carries its protagonist, a black physicist, from an oppressed, and oppressive, Earth into interstellar space, after some very exciting moments in the first volume when it seems that she may not get free of the snares of an American government gone wrong. Once in space, there are moments when the story comes alive with thought. McIntyre is travelling again.

[signature: Vonda N. McIntyre]

BIBLIOGRAPHY

NOVELS AND NOVELLAS
1975 **The Exile Waiting** Doubleday
1978 **Dreamsnake** Houghton Mifflin
1981 **The Entropy Effect** Pocket Books
1982 **The Wrath of Khan** Pocket Books
1983 **Superluminal** Houghton Mifflin
1984 **Star Trek III: The Search for Spock** Pocket Books
1985 **The Bride** Dell
1986 **Enterprise: The First Adventure** Pocket Books
  Star Trek IV: The Voyage Home Pocket Books
1986 **Barbary** Houghton Mifflin
1989 **Starfarers** Bantam
  Screwtop Tor
1991 **Transition** Bantam
1992 **Metaphase** Bantam

SHORT STORY COLLECTION
1979 **Fireflood** Houghton Mifflin

AS EDITOR
1976 **Aurora: Beyond Equality** Fawcett Gold Medal, with Susan Janice Anderson

JOE HALDEMAN

BORN **1943**

NATIONALITY **American**

KEY WORKS **The Forever War, the Worlds series, The Hemingway Hoax**

THE literary establishment cliché about the American disaster in Vietnam that the experience was too painful, and too profoundly confusing, to generate good fiction. As long as one restricts one's reading to non-genre literature, the cliché does seem to have some truth. As long as one ignores Joe Haldeman – who served in Vietnam, and who began to write SF based on his experiences as early as 1972, with an ironic story called "Hero" – one can continue to disparage the American response to that trauma.

But the SF world has not ignored Haldeman. His first novel, *War Year*, was not SF, and got little genre press; but *The Forever War* was certainly SF, and although the span of the narrative exceeds a millennium, nobody in the SF world was fooled: *The Forever War* was about Vietnam. In the War between Earth and an unknowable foe, soldiers travel through space to the battle sites by a process of time dilation: a few months of subjective time on board the craft equals decades or more outside. After a thousand years, the soldiers are profoundly alienated and disenfranchised; they are caught up in a surreal conflict whose origins are totally obscure, and whose outcome will never be clear. As a metaphor for the experience of Vietnam, *The Forever War* is superlative. Its continuing obscurity outside the world of SF very sharply demonstrates the provinciality of the literary establishment.

BIBLIOGRAPHY

NOVELS AND NOVELLAS
1974 **The Forever War** St. Martin's Press
1975 **Attar's Revenge** Pocket Books, as Robert Graham
  War of Nerves Pocket Books, as Robert Graham
1976 **Mindbridge** St. Martin's Press
1977 **Planet of Judgment** Bantam
1979 **World Without End** Bantam
1981 **Worlds** Viking Press
1983 **There is no Darkness** Ace, with Jack C. Haldeman
  Worlds Apart Viking Press
1987 **Tool of the Trade** Morrow
1989 **Buying Time** Morrow, retitled **The Long Habit of Living**
1990 **The Hemingway Hoax** Morrow
1992 **Worlds Enough and Time** Morrow

SHORT STORY COLLECTIONS
1977 **All My Sins Remembered** St. Martin's Press
1978 **Infinite Dreams** St. Martin's Press
1985 **Dealing in Futures** Viking Press
1993 **Vietnam and Other Alien Worlds** NESFA Press

SELECTED WORKS AS EDITOR
1974 **Cosmic Laughter** Holt Rinehart
1977 **Study War No More: A Selection of Alternatives** St. Martin's Press

Haldeman's protagonists bear wounds. Readers reminded of Hemingway were pleased when Haldeman dealt with the anxiety of influence in *The Hemingway Hoax*: by becoming Hemingway, the protagonist beats the old man at last. *Worlds Enough and Time* climaxes the **Worlds** trilogy; it will be interesting to see what he does now. He has beaten War and the Father. What next?

[signature: Joe Haldeman]

First publication
Haldeman's first published story was SF. "Out of Phase" appeared in Galaxy *in 1969.*

OCTAVIA BUTLER

BORN **1947**

NATIONALITY **American**

KEY WORKS **The *Patternmaster* series, *Kindred*, the *Xenogenesis* series**

NOBODY should be surprised at how few black SF writers there are. Certainly no one who looks at the world depicted in SF writing before about 1960 could have any doubt that the genre was simply not designed to be written or read by the dispossessed. There is no secret here: American SF, the dominant form of the genre for many decades, was about the people who owned the world, or who were about to.

Here is a vision: a bright young inventor hero lands on a planet, dazzles the huddled, dark-skinned native villagers with his science and wisdom, and plants his flag on the world, now entitled to join the Galactic Confederacy. It is a vision, one can be certain, that was not aimed at black readers – not that there were many, for SF conspicuously lacked black readers for many decades; and they are still comparatively rare, if attendance at conventions is any sign. Nor was it a vision directed to readers – there have always been some – in the Third World. No. SF was not written for the underdogs; it was written for the inheritors of the Earth.

But (of course) the underdog is all of us and the inheritors of the Earth are all of us. By the 1960s it had become apparent that SF, if it wished to address the human race, was going to have to stop propagandizing for one small interest group: the affluent whites.

It is, perhaps, a sign of the inherent strength of the genre that writers like Samuel R. Delany and Octavia Butler were able, given all this background, to write SF that did not constantly refer to the fact that both were black, while at the same time composing work that radically subverted some of the old SF conventions. For the good of the story; and for the good of all of us.

The *Patternmaster* sequence, Butler's first series, begins with her first novel, *Patternmaster*. Against a genre conceit – two immortals wrestle with each other for centuries about how to shape the human race into a fitting pattern – gender and race issues surface subtly, and much of the conflict turns on a contrast between a rigid patriarchal conservatism and the more giving and communal pattern advocated by the strong women who dominate most of the sequence.

Kindred, which stands alone, is a timeslip fantasy: a black woman of the 20th century finds herself in 1820 Maryland. The horror of such a fate is alleviated by superb storytelling.

In the *Xenogenesis* series of the 1980s, the alien Onankali visit a devastated near-future Earth to try to salvage some useful genes. A black woman is chosen to liaise between the aliens and the frazzled remnants of humanity. Eventually, the Onankali create a transformed society. We would not be comfortable in that society: but it does not destroy the planet again.

> **«** *Butler radically subverted some of the old SF conventions, for the good of all of us* **»**

[signature: Octavia E. Butler]

BIBLIOGRAPHY

NOVELS AND NOVELLAS
1976 **Patternmaster** Doubleday
1977 **Mind of my Mind** Doubleday
1978 **Survivor** Doubleday
1979 **Kindred** Doubleday
1980 **Wild Seed** Doubleday
1984 **Clay's Ark** St. Martin's Press
1987 **Dawn** Warner
1988 **Adulthood Rites** Warner
1989 **Imago** Warner
1993 **Parable of the Sower** Four Walls Eight Windows

MICHAEL BISHOP

BORN **1945**

NATIONALITY **American**

KEY WORKS **A Funeral for the Eyes of Fire, And Strange at Ecbatan the Trees, Transfigurations, No Enemy But Time, Brittle Innings**

HE comes from Nebraska, but he has spent his life in the American South. He lives in a remote part of Georgia, and continues to sound like an anthropologist: alienated, alert, fascinated. He fills his novels, several of them set in the South, with the dispossessed of the Earth.

Even his first novels exhibit alienation and intensity. Most deal with complex alien societies: *A Funeral for the Eyes of Fire* focuses on a culture obsessed by the meaning of the eye. On the alien planet the protagonist must perform great wonders, or be sent back to a despotic Earth. *And Strange at Ecbatan the Trees* sets various cultures into conflict, while *Transfigurations* stars an anthropologist utterly obsessed by the rites of an alien culture that is considered less technologically advanced. His attempts to penetrate their mysteries constitute a voyage into the heart of darkness; and Joseph Conrad's influential novella, "The Heart of Darkness" (1902), with its underlying theme of the unknowableness of the Other, shapes the narrative.

A Little Knowledge and *Catacomb Years* make up a short Future History of 21st-century Atlanta. *No Enemy But Time* and *Ancient of Days*, although ostensibly linked, both have storylines

Eye worship
Hard SF and Gothicism combine in A Funeral for the Eyes of Fire.

that connect early prehistory with the present. In the first, a contemporary protagonist travels back in time to the Pleistocene epoch, marrying a habiline woman there. In the second, a habiline man is brought into contemporary Georgia, where he too marries. The ironies and melancholy of both tales remind one of stories by contemporary black SF writers, when they convey some sense of the nature of a world that allows so much of its heritage to be dismissed. There are many more novels, and the subjects vary, although most of them are set in Atlanta-like cities. The best of them, *Brittle Innings*, brilliantly recasts Bishop's whole career. It tells the story of the Frankenstein monster, in which he becomes a baseball player in the minor leagues in the American South.

[signature: Michael Bishop]

BIBLIOGRAPHY

NOVELS AND NOVELLAS
1975 **A Funeral for the Eyes of Fire** Ballantine, retitled **Eyes of Fire**
1976 **And Strange at Ecbatan the Trees** Harper, retitled **Beneath the Shattered Moons**
1977 **Stolen Faces** Harper
    A Little Knowledge Berkley
1979 **Catacomb Years** Berkley
    Transfigurations Berkley
1981 **Under Heaven's Bridge** Gollancz
1982 **No Enemy But Time** Timescape
1984 **Who Made Stevie Crye?** Arkham House
1985 **Ancient of Days** Arbor House
1987 **The Secret Ascension** Tor, retitled **Philip K. Dick Is Dead, Alas**
1988 **Unicorn Mountain** Arbor House
1989 **Apartheid, Superstrings, and Mordecai Thubana** Axolotl
1992 **Count Geiger's Blues** Tor
1994 **Brittle Innings** Bantam

SHORT STORY COLLECTIONS
1982 **Blooded on Arachne** Arkham House
1984 **One Winter in Eden** Arkham House
1986 **Close Encounters with the Deity** Peachtree
1991 **Emphatically Not SF, Almost** Pulphouse

SELECTED WORKS AS EDITOR
1983 **Changes** Ace, with Ian Watson
1984 **Light Years and Dark: Science Fiction and Fantasy Of and For our Time** Berkley

ANNE McCAFFREY

BORN 1926

NATIONALITY American, resident in Ireland

KEY WORKS Restoree, The Ship Who Sang, the Pern series

S HE always insisted that she writes SF, not fantasy, and it looks like her readers are beginning to believe her. There was no question about some of her early work. *Restoree* is pure SF, although baroque in its depiction of the flaying alive of a woman who – her skin restored – goes adventuring in space. *The Ship Who Sang*, also SF, is a central early vision of human/machine interface: a deformed young woman "becomes" a spaceship, and her life starts anew as a cyborg capable, at last, of getting along with young men.

These are messages of hope for forlorn children, and contrast tellingly with stories by James Tiptree Jr., whose take on the human/machine interface is very much less hopeful.

But the accessibility and intensity of these books is as nothing to the title published between them. *Dragonflight*, which is the first of a number of books set on the lost colony planet of Pern, made McCaffrey's name. Because the series revolves around the relationship between humans and a telepathic race of dragons, whom they ride like great ponies, it has long been assumed that *Pern* was fantasy. But McCaffrey always held – and in later volumes backed up her insistence by arguments showing a scientific rationale for large flying dragons – that she was writing SF, and that the critics should take her as seriously as her readers did.

While the adventures on Pern are romantic, they are based on a portrait of the planet that makes good sense. The dragons' capacity to breathe fire is an adaptation to the invasion of deadly spores called Threads; only dragon fire can destroy them. Other episodes, when the dragons go travelling through time, are perhaps less compulsive, but McCaffrey has touched a deep nerve. Some of her later books have been collaborations, and not really up to her best solo work. But *The Dolphins of Pern* is vintage McCaffrey.

BIBLIOGRAPHY

NOVELS AND NOVELLAS
1967 **Restoree** Ballantine
1968 **Dragonflight** Ballantine
1969 **Decision at Doona** Ballantine
1971 **Dragonquest** Ballantine
1976 **Dragonsong** Atheneum
1977 **Dragonsinger** Atheneum
1978 **Dinosaur Planet** Futura
  The White Dragon Ballantine
1979 **Dragondrums** Atheneum
1982 **The Crystal Singer** Ballantine
1983 **The Coelura** Underwood-Miller
  Moreta, Dragonlady of Pern
    Ballantine
1985 **The Girl Who Heard Dragons**
    Cheap Street
  Killashandra Ballantine
1986 **Nerilka's Story: a Pern Adventure** Ballantine
1988 **Dragonsdawn** Easton Press
1989 **The Renegades of Pern** Ballantine
1990 **Pegasus in Flight** Easton Press
  The Rowan Putnam
  Sassinak Baen, with Elizabeth Moon
  The Death of Sleep Baen, with Jody Lynn Nye
1991 **All the Weyrs of Pern** Bantam Press

Rescue Run Wildside Press
Generation Warriors Baen, with Elizabeth Moon
1992 **PartnerShip** Baen, with Margaret Ball
  The Ship Who Searched Baen, with Mercedes Lackey
  Crystal Line Ballantine
  Damia Putnam
1993 **The City Who Fought** Baen, with S.M. Stirling
  Damia's Children Putnam
  Powers That Be Ballantine, with Elizabeth Ann Scarborough
1994 **The Ship Who Won** Baen, with Jody Lynn Nye
  Treaty at Doona Ace, with Jody Lynn Nye
  The Dolphins of Pern Bantam

SHORT STORY COLLECTIONS
1969 **The Ship Who Sang** Walker
1973 **To Ride Pegasus** Ballantine
1977 **Get Off the Unicorn** Ballantine
1993 **The Chronicles of Pern: First Fall** Ballantine
1994 **The Girl Who Heard Dragons** Tor

GEORGE R.R. MARTIN

BORN 1948

NATIONALITY American

KEY WORKS Dying of the Light, Windhaven, the Wild Cards series, Tuf Voyaging

BIBLIOGRAPHY

NOVELS AND NOVELLAS
1977 **Dying of the Light** Simon and Schuster
1980 **Windhaven** Timescape, with Lisa Tuttle
1982 **Fevre Dream** Poseidon
1983 **The Armageddon Rag** Poseidon

SHORT STORY COLLECTIONS
1976 **A Song for Lya** Avon
1977 **Songs of Stars and Shadows** Pocket Books
1981 **The Sandkings** Pocket Books
1983 **Songs the Dead Men Sing** Dark Harvest
1985 **Nightflyers** Bluejay
1986 **Tuf Voyaging** Baen (linked stories)
1987 **Portraits of his Children** Dark Harvest

AS EDITOR
1977 **New Voices in Science Fiction** various publishers, four volumes through 1981
1987 **Wild Cards** Bantam, 11 volumes through 1992

H E makes it all look easy. His first novel, *Dying of the Light*, gives us, smoothly, with seeming effortlessness, a moony travelling world with a great city at the heart of it, and a great celebration held there as the world passes by a great sun and slowly into night again. The book is dreamy, but potent, and beneath the unflawed surface of the thing, fevers burn.

The stories in *A Song for Lya* and *Songs of Stars and Shadows* are similar, some of them set in the same universe as the novel, and most of them giving off a sense that copious energies are held in check. Martin is a little like Silverberg in this: both of the authors seem capable of pointing their pen at anything and then saying the right words to convey the realities back to us. The difference between them – and it is not entirely in Martin's favour – is that Martin has never overproduced. Indeed, the opposite is probably the case, as far as the SF world is concerned.

The reason for this is television. Since about 1980, Martin has written a lot of good scripts, made a lot of good money, and only occasionally opened his mind to SF or fantasy. *Windhaven*, which he co-wrote with Lisa Tuttle, describes an archipelago world that depends on messengers who fly between islands on artificial wings.

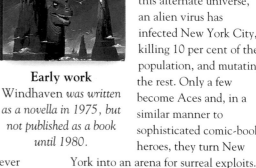

Early work
Windhaven *was written as a novella in 1975, but not published as a book until 1980.*

The Armageddon Rag is a superb horror novel, marrying the supernatural to a rock band, a trick done frequently since, but never as well. And *Fevre Dream* is an excellent vampire novel.

And then came the **Wild Cards** series, created and edited by Martin, who also contributes occasional stories to various volumes. If the the term "superhero" had not – incredibly – been copyrighted by a maker of action toys, the heroes of the series would be so designated. As it is, they are called Aces, and they are the lucky ones. In this alternate universe, an alien virus has infected New York City, killing 10 per cent of the population, and mutating the rest. Only a few become Aces and, in a similar manner to sophisticated comic-book heroes, they turn New York into an arena for surreal exploits. The linked stories of *Tuf Voyaging* are the last original work that Martin has done in the SF field. His management of **Wild Cards** is appreciated; but he is still missed.

JOHN CROWLEY

BORN **1942**

NATIONALITY **American**

KEY WORKS **The Deep, Engine Summer, Little, Big**

IT is not a long list of books for a writer this revered. And when one realizes that *Great Work of Time* is a very short novel – it also appears in *Novelty* – one begins to get a sense that there must be something very special indeed about John Crowley, if he has managed to achieve high status with six novels. But he has. He is one of the finest writers of English prose active in SF or fantasy. He has been since he began.

Crowley was already in his thirties when he published *The Deep,* one of the oddest SF novels ever to appear. In an obscure part of the universe, atop a vast pillar that extends downwards further than imagination can reach, is a kind of platform. On this platform – which is not nearly as large as Terry Pratchett's Discworld, but is large enough for lives to be led in relative safety, far from the edge – lives a warring society of human beings, brought there, according to rumour, by an omnipotent alien who wished to watch them. Their behaviour is complex, but readers with a knowledge of history soon begin to suspect the truth: they are replaying the War of Roses. And the novel ends. It is like a clenched fist in the utter void.

Crowley's third novel, *Engine Summer,* is even more impressive, perhaps because it concentrates on one lovingly developed protagonist, called Rush That Speaks. He lives in a pastoral, Indian summer culture, some time after high civilization has fallen.

His particular tribe is made up of people who long to speak the truth. His task in life is to become a "saint", a person whose truthfulness is so evident that he can – as it were – be seen through. What Rush That Speaks does not comprehend, however, is that he is a true engine summer: the freshness of his personality is, in fact, a recording. He is nothing but a crystal, activated again and again by a successor race of folk, whenever they wish to understand the truth about the time he lived in. So, in a way, he gets his wish. He is crystal; he can be seen through.

Soon after came *Little, Big,* which Crowley had been working on, intermittently, for a decade. Properly speaking, it is fantasy, not SF – Smoky Barnable leaves New York to marry Alice Drinkwater, who is known as Daily Alice, perhaps because she inhabits as marvellous a world as Alice's Wonderland; and lives there every day and makes Smoky happy for all his long life. In the meantime, however, a reborn Emperor Barbarossa has begun to rule a near-future America nearing the millennium; and Alice and her huge family are preparing to cross over from this world into Faerie. In the end, they must do so; and Smoky, who is entirely mortal, dies alone.

Crowley is a writer who uses whatever comes to hand, SF or fantasy. We are fortunate that he makes these worlds come together for us.

> **❝** *John Crowley is one of the finest writers of English prose active in SF or fantasy* **❞**

John Crowley [signature]

BIBLIOGRAPHY

NOVELS AND NOVELLAS
1975 **The Deep** Doubleday
1976 **Beasts** Doubleday
1979 **Engine Summer** Doubleday
1981 **Little, Big** Bantam
1987 **Aegypt** Bantam
1991 **Great Work of Time** Bantam
1994 **Love and Sleep** Bantam

SHORT STORY COLLECTIONS
1989 **Novelty** Doubleday
1993 **Antiquities** Incunabula

JOHN VARLEY

BORN **1947**

NATIONALITY **American**

KEY WORKS **The Ophiuchi Hotline, Steel Beach**

HE exploded onto the SF scene like a wild man, full of new ideas and pungent storylines featuring sexy, independent women. And he had a humbling sense of what it meant to be a member of the human race: to be human meant, in Varley's imaginative universe, to be a member of a junior species that was not doing a very good job of managing the Solar System. We were, to be blunt, making a slum of the Earth, and the Moon, and the planets. It was about time for a houseclean.

So, in his Future History, humanity is, without warning, simply evicted from Earth by aliens. In *The Ophiuchi Hotline,* which is set many years after that eviction, we have begun to evolve means of coping with our exile. We live in warrens in the Moon; we live in exorbitant habitats further out. We have learned to clone ourselves, to change our bodies, sexes, and volitions at will. We have become mobile and saucy, and teem everywhere but Earth, which is forbidden to us by aliens so powerful that we cannot dream of disobeying their Notice to Quit. Unfortunately, we are still making too much of a nuisance; and as the novel ends, it becomes clear that we are no longer welcome anywhere in the Solar System.

It is a grim message, but Varley passed it on with such joyful panache that he became, very quickly, the very model of a modern SF writer in the minds of many readers.

He was the kind of writer who would write the new SF, the kind of story that befitted a newly complex world. But he drifted off. *Titan* and its sequels are fine, but ordinary. *Millennium* is the same. Who knows why? It is only with *Steel Beach* (see page 235), a large and potent tale set in the Ophiuchi Future History, that he has returned to form: it is good to have him back.

[signature]

BIBLIOGRAPHY

NOVELS AND NOVELLAS
1977 **The Ophiuchi Hotline** Dial Press
1979 **Titan** Berkley
1980 **Wizard** Berkley
1983 **Millennium** Berkley
1984 **Demon** Putnam
1989 **Tango Charlie and Foxtrot Romeo** Tor
1990 **Press Enter** Tor
1991 **The Persistence of Vision** Tor
1992 **Steel Beach** Putnam

SHORT STORY COLLECTIONS
1978 **The Persistence of Vision** Dial Press, retitled **In the Hall of the Martian Kings**
1980 **The Barbie Murders** Berkley, retitled **Picnic on Nearside**
1986 **Blue Champagne** Dark Harvest

Bodysnatchers
The 1989 film of Millennium, *in which bodies mysteriously vanish from aircrashes, was scripted by Varley.*

1980-1984: A NEW AGE OF SF

TO UNDERSTAND WHAT IS now beginning to happen to SF, it is not enough to speak about the slow transformation of the dominant American genre SF from an essentially forward-looking tool of understanding and entertainment into an archive of futures past, into a vast library. It has become a place for writers to plunder old ideas, and for readers to revisit their childhoods – and the childhood of the century – by reading the texts made so available.

1980

NOTABLE WORKS

Timescape
GREGORY BENFORD

Songmaster
ORSON SCOTT CARD

Dragon's Egg
ROBERT L. FORWARD

Riddley Walker
RUSSELL HOBAN

King David's Spaceship
JERRY POURNELLE

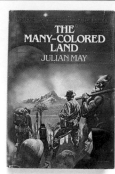

KING DAVID'S SPACESHIP

Molly Zero
KEITH ROBERTS

Lord Valentine's Castle
ROBERT SILVERBERG

Roderick
JOHN T. SLADEK

The Snow Queen
JOAN D. VINGE

The Book of the New Sun
GENE WOLFE

SONGMASTER

ICONS

As SF develops, its sense of the person capable of embodying a commanding role in a new world also becomes more complex. Thus we have monarchs like Vinge's Queen, Pournelle's King, Silverberg's Lord Valentine, and Wolfe's **Torturer**. The most striking is probably Severian the Torturer and Autarch, who encompasses all of SF in his tale.

DEBUTS

First SF books of interest include Jean M. Auel's *The Clan of the Cave Bear*, Jonathan Carroll's *The Land of Laughs*, David Brin's *Sundiver*, Christopher Evans's *Capella's Golden Eyes*, Barry Longyear's *City of Baraboo*, Rachel Pollack's *Golden Vanity*, Rudy Rucker's *White Light*, and Hilbert Schenck's *Wave Rider*. The first Michael Swanwick published, "The Feast of St. Janis", appears in the anthology *New Dimensions 11*.

1981

NOTABLE WORKS

Blood Sleep
SERGE BRUSSOLO

The Pride of Chanur
C.J. CHERRYH

Downbelow Station
C.J. CHERRYH

Little, Big
JOHN CROWLEY

VALIS
PHILIP K. DICK

BLOOD SLEEP

Lanark
ALASDAIR GRAY

Worlds
JOE HALDEMAN

Where Time Winds Blow
ROBERT HOLDSTOCK

Windhaven
GEORGE R.R. MARTIN AND LISA TUTTLE

The Many-Colored Land
JULIAN MAY

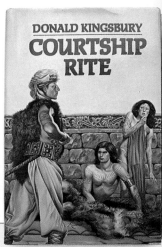

THE MANY-COLORED LAND

ICONS

Two of the most significant books of the decade, Crowley's *Little, Big* and Gray's *Lanark*, provide complex symbolic structures of understanding. Neither is – or is not – strictly SF, which is also a growing tendency. In both, the inner life of the protagonists and the outer world mirror and echo one another. The deeper one goes into either book, the bigger is the world revealed. More and more, SF broods about the meaning of existence.

DEBUTS

Julian May's *The Many-Colored Land* and Alasdair Gray's *Lanark* make a mark. Other first novels are Terry Bisson's *Wyrldmaker*, Jack Dann's *Junction*, A.A. Attanasio's *Radix*, James Morrow's *The Wine of Violence*, Nancy Kress's *The Prince of Morning Bells*, S.P. Sucharitkul's *Starship and Haiku*, and *Le silence de la cité* [The silence of the city] by **Elisabeth Vonarburg**.

19

NOTABLE WORKS

Helliconia Spring
BRIAN ALDISS

Foundation's Edge
ISAAC ASIMOV

No Enemy But Time
MICHAEL BISHOP

Friday
ROBERT A. HEINLEIN

COURTSHIP RITE

ICONS

SF does not stop at building worlds: it creates whole solar systems, and makes the universe anew. Brian Aldiss's **Helliconia** trilogy, with its detailed portrayal of an intricate, aeons-long year, begins this year. Isaac Asimov's resumption of the **Foundation** series hovers, as ever, around Trantor, and Donald Kingsbury's *Courtship Rite* has a vigorously interesting planetary venue.

DEBUTS

First SF novels this year include Lisa Goldstein's *The Red Magician*, Donald Kingsbury's *Courtship Rite*, Pat Murphy's *The Shadow Hunter*, Warren Norwood's *The Windhover Tapes*, L.E. Modesitt's *The Fires of Paratime*, Richard Bowker's *Forbidden Sanctuary*, and Haruki Murakami's *A Wild Sheep Chase*. First stories include Dan Simmons's "The River Styx Runs Upstream" in *Rod Serling's The Twilight Zone*.

The SF field, it is interesting to note, keeps more of its past works in print than any other fictional genre. What is happening is more than this. What we must understand is that the best SF books ever written are being written now.

Now that the finest writers working in the genre can see its arguments and its history more wholly, they can begin, far more consciously than they ever did before, to try to make great art out of the shape of things to come.

8 2

The White Plague
FRANK HERBERT

Courtship Rite
DONALD KINGSBURY

A Wild Sheep Race
HARUKI MURAKAMI

Software
RUDY RUCKER

Erasmus Magister
CHARLES SHEFFIELD

Light on the Sound
SOMTOW SUCHARITKUL

1 9 8 3

Orion Shall Rise
POUL ANDERSON

Nevèrÿona
SAMUEL R. DELANY

Golden Witchbreed
MARY GENTLE

Winter's Tale
MARK HELPRIN

Superluminal
VONDA N. MCINTYRE

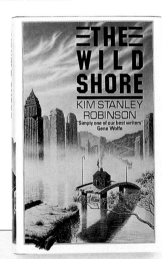

THE VOID CAPTAIN'S TALE

The Celestial Steam Locomotive
MICHAEL CONEY

The Armageddon Rag
GEORGE R.R. MARTIN

The Anubis Gates
TIM POWERS

The Void Captain's Tale
NORMAN SPINRAD

NEVÈRŸONA

1 9 8 4

Across the Sea of Suns
GREGORY BENFORD

The Practice Effect
DAVID BRIN

Neuromancer
WILLIAM GIBSON

West of Eden
HARRY HARRISON

Mythago Wood
ROBERT HOLDSTOCK

Divine Endurance
GWYNETH JONES

The Integral Trees
LARRY NIVEN

The Wild Shore
KIM STANLEY ROBINSON

Them Bones
HOWARD WALDROP

The Book of the River
IAN WATSON

Free Live Free
GENE WOLFE

THE WILD SHORE

Post-collapse cultures, an age-old theme in SF, feature this year. The civilization portrayed by Coney in **The Celestial Steam Locomotive** is far into the future; while Delany's Nevèrÿon is a barbarian culture that feels intrinsically post-collapse. A secondary theme this year is sex, particularly in the Delany and the Spinrad: sex is omnipresent, and taken for granted, in SF today in a way that, just a few decades ago, would have been unthinkable.

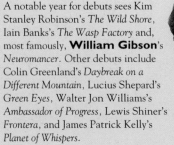

In the year that Cyberpunk becomes a buzzword, the icons are both numerous and nebulous: information, secrecy, control, complexity, artificiality, unreality, and new realities. In parallel with these is a seeking out of roots: the roots of California in the Robinson, the archaeological search for roots in the Waldrop, and the roots of the tree in the Niven.

Magazine, and in Australia, **Terry Dowling**'s "The Man who Walks Away behind the Eyes" in *Omega Science Digest*.

"The Taylorsville Reconstruction", Lucius Shepard's first published story, appears in *Universe 13*. Authors making their SF novel debuts include Stephen Barnes with *Streetlethal*, Sheri S. Tepper with *King's Blood Four*, and Timothy Zahn with *The Blackcollar*.

A notable year for debuts sees Kim Stanley Robinson's *The Wild Shore*, Iain Banks's *The Wasp Factory* and, most famously, **William Gibson**'s *Neuromancer*. Other debuts include Colin Greenland's *Daybreak on a Different Mountain*, Lucius Shepard's *Green Eyes*, Walter Jon Williams's *Ambassador of Progress*, Lewis Shiner's *Frontera*, and James Patrick Kelly's *Planet of Whispers*.

1985-1989: MERGING STREAMS

ALMOST AS SOON AS IT IS christened, Cyberpunk is a thing of the past. This is not to say that writers stop writing it, but that it is absorbed and modified, another part of SF's abundant and ever-growing heritage. Much SF in the latter part of this decade is still looking back, providing requiem for what went before or a reprise of it. In other ways, the genre is becoming broader – some would say diluted – and accepting new styles, new scenarios, and new approaches

1 9 8 5

NOTABLE WORKS

Blood Music
GREG BEAR

Eon
GREG BEAR

Ender's Game
ORSON SCOTT CARD

Dayworld
PHILIP JOSÉ FARMER

A Maggot
JOHN FOWLES

Saraband of Lost Time
RICHARD GRANT

Freedom Beach
JAMES PATRICK KELLY AND
JOHN KESSEL

Green Eyes
LUCIUS SHEPARD

Schizmatrix
BRUCE STERLING

Galápagos
KURT VONNEGUT

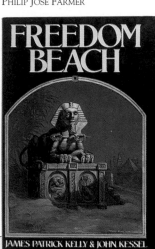

FREEDOM BEACH

1 9 8 6

The Handmaid's Tale
MARGARET ATWOOD

The Bridge
IAIN BANKS

Talking Man
TERRY BISSON

Homunculus
JAMES P. BLAYLOCK

Speaker for the Dead
ORSON SCOTT CARD

THE HANDMAID'S TALE

Fiasco
STANISŁAW LEM

The Falling Woman
PAT MURPHY

The Unconquered Country
GEOFF RYMAN

The Shore of Women
PAMELA SARGENT

The Ragged Astronauts
BOB SHAW

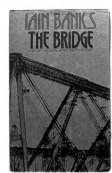

THE BRIDGE

1 9

Consider Phlebas
IAIN M. BANKS

Through Darkest America
NEAL BARRETT JR.

The Forge of God
GREG BEAR

The Uplift War
DAVID BRIN

Dawn
OCTAVIA E. BUTLER

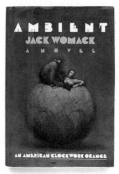

AMBIENT

ICONS

The century of SF advances: the future remains, but the past is bigger than before, full of old stories that have become nostalgic, fan folklore. SF has room for requiems. Bear's *Blood Music* imagines biochemical transcendence for humanity, while his *Eon* is a requiem for a Hard SF project that shifts stars and continua; both Grant's *Saraband of Lost Time* and Vonnegut's *Galápagos* are requiems for human culture at the end of time.

Just as often as they act as requiems, modern SF tales set themselves up as myths of origin: *The Handmaid's Tale*, *Speaker for the Dead*, and **The Unconquered Country** are all examples of this. And as the old stories of SF become part of the lore, they tend to be rewritten by their authors, hardened and heightened into myth: Asimov, throughout this decade, welds together his 1940s **Foundation** and **Robot** series into an edifice designed to withstand the sands of time. SF's past is increasingly becoming a set of myths to be retold.

Increasing complexity is the keynote of the year. Both *Ambient* and *Vacuum Flowers* present a future immensely, imponderably complex: Cyberpunk riffs only stir the surface. The offerings from Barrett, Bear, Butler, and Effinger all reflect this. On another level, the old and the new stories told by SF writers intermix more and more fruitfully.

DEBUTS

Lucius Shepard's *Green Eyes*, Richard Grant's *Saraband of Lost Time*, and *Freedom Beach*, by John Kessel and James Patrick Kelly, are notable debuts. Other first books of SF interest included Marc Laidlaw's *Dad's Nuke*, Roger MacBride Allen's *The Torch of Honor*, Dan Simmons's *Song of Kali*, Denis Johnson's *Fiskadoro*, **Michael Swanwick**'s *In the Drift*, Connie Willis's *Fire Watch*, Steve Erickson's *Days Between Stations*, and Geoff Ryman's *The Warrior Who Carried Life*.

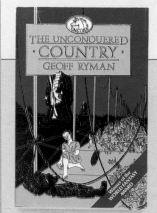

Debut SF novels this year include Karen Joy Fowler's *Artificial Things*, John Barnes's *The Man Who Pulled Down the Sky*, Lois McMaster Bujold's *Shards of Honor*, Bradley Denton's *Wrack and Roll*, Margaret Atwood's *The Handmaid's Tale*, Leigh Kennedy's *The Journal of Nicholas the American*, Julian Barnes's *Staring at the Sun*, Thomas T. Thomas's *The Doomsday Effect*, and Robert Charles Wilson's *A Hidden Place*.

Among the notable SF debuts of the year are Paul Park with *Soldiers of Paradise*, Judith Moffett with *Pennterra*, and Jack Womack with *Ambient*. Other writers who publish their first books of SF interest this year include Paul Auster with *In the Country of Last Things*, Storm Constantine with the first volume of her **Wraeththu** trilogy, *The Enchantments of Flesh and Spirit*, William T. Vollmann.

that would not have been recognized as SF a few decades or even just a few years before. Boundaries become blurred: non-SF writers write SF novels – this has always happened, but is becoming more widespread – and SF writers write novels that are not SF. As the decade closes, more SF titles are being published than ever before, but some say SF is disappearing. How so? Because everything else is looking more like SF, and SF is looking more like everything else.

87 · 1988 · 1989

WHEN GRAVITY FAILS

When Gravity Fails
GEORGE ALEC EFFINGER

Life During Wartime
LUCIUS SHEPARD

Vacuum Flowers
MICHAEL SWANWICK

Lincoln's Dreams
CONNIE WILLIS

Ambient
JACK WOMACK

Falling Free
LOIS MCMASTER BUJOLD

Cyteen
C.J. CHERRYH

An Alien Light
NANCY KRESS

Fire on the Mountain
TERRY BISSON

WORLDS IN THE ABYSS

The Empire of Fear
BRIAN STABLEFORD

Islands in the Net
BRUCE STERLING

The Gate to Women's Country
SHERI S. TEPPER

Worlds in the Abyss
JUAN MIGUEL AGUILERA

THE EMPIRE OF FEAR

The Boat of a Million Years
POUL ANDERSON

The Folk of the Fringe
ORSON SCOTT CARD

Look Into the Sun
JAMES PATRICK KELLY

Good News from Outer Space
JOHN KESSEL

Dream Baby
BRUCE MCALLISTER

The City, Not Long After
PAT MURPHY

The Child Garden
GEOFF RYMAN

Hyperion
DAN SIMMONS

NOTABLE WORK

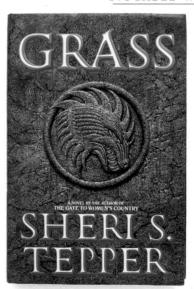

In recent years, Sheri S. Tepper, who lives in the ecologically fragile American West, has increasingly revealed her fear that the human race may wipe out all other forms of life. The villains of the trilogy comprising *Grass*, *Raising the Stones* and *Sideshow* tend to be men, tend to be religious, and tend to destroy worlds. Marjorie Westriding, who is instrumental in saving a planet in *Grass*, haunts subsequent volumes. She is Tepper's voice: an eloquent, unanswerable clarion call.

GRASS

If the world is too complex, make it anew: an Alternate World gives unlimited scope. Bisson rewrites the American Civil War to create a kind of paradise, Kress examines the reasons for doing so, Stableford writes an Alternate History, and Tepper, in **The Gate to Women's Country**, writes a dream of women's autonomy.

The planet is getting old, and this year, in books such as Poul Anderson's *The Boat of a Million Years*, or Dan Simmons's *Hyperion*, select pilgrims of the race have other goals than Earth. In other books, Card's protagonists leave a corrupt East, and Murphy's San Francisco is a goal of pilgrimages.

with *You Bright and Risen Angels*, and **Pat Cadigan** with *Mindplayers*.

First books of SF interest include Rebecca Ore's *Becoming Human*, Richard Kadrey's *Metrophage*, Scott Bradfield's *The Secret Life of Houses*, Ronald Anthony Cross's *Prisoners of Paradise*, Paul J. McAuley's *Four Hundred Billion Stars*, Pamela Zoline's *Busy About the Tree of Life*, Richard Paul Russo's *Inner Eclipse*, David Zindell's excellent *Neverness*, Ian McDonald's *Desolation Road*, and Michaela Roessner's *Walkabout Woman*.

Notable debuts of the year include Katherine Dunn's *Geek Love* and Gill Alderman's *The Archivist*. Other authors publishing their first novels of SF interest include Allen Steele with *Orbital Decay*,

Jack Butler with *Nightshade*, Michael Kandel with *Strange Invasion*, **Kim Newman** with *The Night Mayor*, Ben Elton with *Stark*, and Dave Wolverton with *On my Way to Paradise*.

GREG BEAR

BORN **1951**

NATIONALITY **American**

KEY WORKS **Blood Music, Eon, The Forge of God, Queen of Angels**

BEAR is a child of SF, he married into SF, and he was the chief carrier of SF through the challenging decade of the 1980s. He was an SF fan from an early age, an avid reader, and participant in every possible way in the subculture of fandom. His first story, "Destroyers", was published as early as 1967, when he was only 16 years old. His second marriage, to the daughter of Poul Anderson, signalled a continuing personal involvement in the world that he had embraced from his childhood; Poul Anderson is one of the most active and most revered of all living SF writers, and Bear's alliance with his daughter represents a dynastic and literary claim to occupy the living centre of the genre.

It took a while to get to the centre, however. Bear's earliest novels stand out only in retrospect. The first of them, *Hegira* and *Psychlone*, have reaches that considerably exceed their grasps. *Hegira*, especially, seemed almost comically overdrawn in 1979: it depicts a giant, hollow planet that is coursing through the universe in search of a route out of our current reality into the reality that will come into being after the end of time. Other early novels, like *Beyond Heaven's River*, similarly faltered in their attempts to mix complicated personal adventures and moral discussions of cosmology. Most of these early novels have, however, been revised in recent years, and the current versions of them are considerably smoother than those that were first published.

Not until the mid-1980s – and then with an impact similar to that made by Dan Simmons some five years later – did Bear come fully into his own as an SF author of stature, with the almost simultaneous release in 1985 of two quite different, and quite extraordinary, novels. The first of these, *Blood Music* (see page 232) is a tale of genetic engineering that combines a subtle mastery of the rigours and conventions of Hard SF with a soaring control of the language and dreams that belong to visionary SF, the sort of SF that writers like Olaf Stapledon and Arthur C. Clarke had written for decades from their British perspective. The best SF from British authors had always tended to view human life from very long evolutionary perspectives, and with some irony; on the other hand, American SF had, from the very start, generally avoided taking any point of view that might too-dizzyingly diminish the role of humanity in the long story of the universe. The triumph that Bear achieves in *Blood Music* is to tell part of that ages-long story in terms that grippingly take advantage of American SF's vivacity, narrative vibrancy, and creation of characters whom one can identify with.

> **"** *He has a soaring control of the language and dreams that belong to visionary SF* **"**

The story starts small: a resentful, small-time scientist takes advantage of bioengineering technologies to transform a colony of DNA molecules into living – and ultimately sentient – computers. The tale builds to an end that is inevitable: the DNA molecules join together into a single universe-encompassing consciousness, which gathers into itself those humans who are willing to forego their individuality, and sets off to climb great ladders of knowing into new and higher realities.

The plot of *Eon*, Bear's second great novel from 1985, is harder to describe than that of *Blood Music*, but it is an enormously exciting book to read. The scale of the story is hugely different: the central artefact of *Eon* is a vast asteroid, whose interior is hollowed out into a tunnel – but a tunnel that is without any end, a tunnel that seems to go on forever, forwards and upwards through time. Its human explorers encounter endless cornucopias of the unexpected along it, and a great deal happens all the time. The sequel, *Eternity*, is even more vast in scope than its precursor, although the gigantic perspective of the whole makes the tale itself perhaps rather less intoxicating to read.

BIBLIOGRAPHY

NOVELS AND NOVELLAS
1979 **Hegira** Dell
Psychlone Ace, retitled **Lost Souls**
1980 **Beyond Heaven's River** Dell
1981 **Strength of Stones** Ace
1984 **Corona** Pocket
The Infinity Concerto Berkley
1985 **Blood Music** Arbor House
Eon Bluejay Books
1986 **The Serpent Mage** Berkley
1987 **The Forge of God** Tor
1988 **Eternity** Warner
Sleepside Story Cheap Street
Hardfought Tor
1990 **Queen of Angels** Warner
Heads Century
1992 **Anvil of Stars** Century
1993 **Moving Mars** Tor

SHORT STORY COLLECTIONS
1984 **The Wind from a Burning Woman**
Arkham House, revised as **The Venging**
1988 **Early Harvest** NESFA Press
1989 **Tangents** Warner
1992 **Bear's Fantasies: Six Stories in Old Paradigms** Wildside Press

AS EDITOR
1994 **New Legends** Legend, with Martin H. Greenberg

The rest of Bear's career has been, in a sense, more of the same. Underlying the very considerable variety of his works one can always detect, as in the 1985 novels, an intense seriousness about the kinds of story SF can tell, a remarkable grasp of the relevant scientific knowledge, and an extremely coherently expressed sense of the huge transformations that the human race will necessarily experience if we are to continue to thrive.

The Forge of God and its sequel, *Anvil of Stars*, come about as close to Space Opera as Bear – or any other serious SF writer – can approach today. In the first volume, mechanical, autonomic weapons destroy Earth, simply because the planet contains life; in the second volume, the survivors of the holocaust take revenge, but suffer moral nausea from the terribleness of their act. *Queen of Angels* (see page 234) is a map of the transformations soon to confront us from nanotechnologies. Bear's books map the future: they are required reading.

NOTABLE WORK

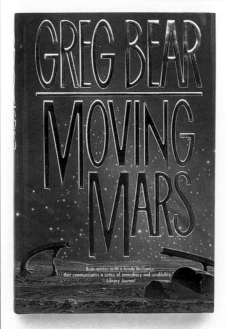

This is the most daring of all the several Mars novels that have appeared in the 1990s. Although it may not have the hard-earned authenticity of Kim Stanley Robinson's impassioned trilogy, it poses problems and solves them with an SF exuberance that lifts the heart. The story is told by a humourless, but lovable, Mars woman who becomes involved in opposition to Earth's crushing rule over the new colony. She becomes president of Mars, and helps to move it into orbit around a new star.

MOVING MARS

ORSON SCOTT CARD

BORN 1951

NATIONALITY **American**

KEY WORKS **The *Ender* series, the *Alvin Maker* series, the *Worthing Chronicle* series**

ORSON Scott Card and Greg Bear are exact contemporaries – born in the same year, publishing debut novels in the same year – but they are as different in their approach to SF as it is possible to be. It is a mark of the maturity of the genre that it is broad enough to contain the two of them. In contrast to a writer like Bear, to whom modern SF is a way of thought and a way of telling stories, and who can seem almost impersonal at times, because his works are so representative of the genre at its best, Orson Scott Card remains a maverick, almost an outsider, a writer who uses SF but does not represent it. He may have written some of the sharpest and most cunning SF novels of the past 15 years, he may have won most of the awards granted by the SF community, and he may have sold SF books in large quantities; but still he stands alone.

There are reasons for this. Card is a Mormon, and a profound concern for the values of Mormonism – whether or not that faith is directly mentioned or symbolized in a particular story – drives almost every word that he has written. One facet of this is that the central focus of concern in his stories is the family, and in this he differs radically from most SF writers who have been active in this century. The central focus of concern for genre SF has traditionally been either the individual or the community – in the latter case, generally a community whose fate is shaped by the actions of an individual, who is invariably charismatic, perhaps endowed with super powers, and almost always in possession of some central insight, some clue to the conceptual breakthrough that will transform the community and its world.

Card is not, in fact, very much interested in the whole matter of conceptual breakthrough, although he writes with such supple narrative skill that his readers can be forgiven the assumption that rite-of-passage novels like *Songmaster* or *Wyrms* will indeed carry them forwards into a new universe, where unheard-of marvels will occur. The concern that actually drives his best stories – like the famous *Ender's Game* (see page 232) and its two sequels, *Speaker for the Dead* and *Xenocide* – is a profound passion for reconciliation. All of Card's most memorable heroes, like Ender himself, are constantly moving backwards, towards reconciliation with families that they have somehow lost, or have never known.

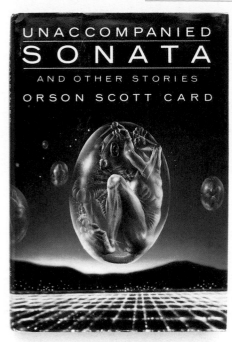
Ender, for instance, appears most like a traditional SF hero in the first of the three volumes that have appeared in his saga so far. He is a child with an abnormally acute sense of location (as though he has perfect pitch in space and time), and is taken from his family by the military, to be trained to become unbeatable in a series of wargames. Ender duly triumphs in these games, only to discover – after winning in the last and most difficult of them – that the puzzles he has been solving are real strategic problems in the real galaxy, and that by winning the games he has caused the genocide of an entire alien species. Subsequent volumes of the series – which are set many years after the conclusion of the first book – recount Ender's attempts, in the company of his sister, to make amends, and eventually implant him into a substitute family, where his tensions are resolved.

The *Alvin Maker* series – which is made up of *Seventh Son*, *Red Prophet*, and *Prentice Alvin* to date – describes Alvin himself very frequently in terms of the Alternate World, 18th-century American family he dominates.

> **" *The almost demonic skill of his writing is deliberately designed to sway our minds* "**

But Alvin's life is clearly modelled in some part on the life of Joseph Smith, the founder of Mormonism, and it appears that the America he is helping to create, in league with the dominant Native American Nations, will be a promised land on Mormon lines, and that the Indians will be seen – as they are in Mormon scripture – as something like the Lost Tribes of Israel.

None of this is usual SF fare. What makes Card so important, therefore, has little to do with the SF genre directly, except in as far as it demonstrates how excitingly broad-church SF has become – because his inward-looking religious parables are still very clearly modern SF, and nothing else. Card is important because what he says is important, although it is partisan. And Card is important because of the almost demonic skill of his writing, which seems to be clear and open, but which is deliberately designed to sway our minds – and does so astonishingly well.

BIBLIOGRAPHY

NOVELS AND NOVELLAS
1979 **Hot Sleep** Baronet
  A Planet Called Treason St. Martin's Press, revised as **Treason**
1980 **Songmaster** Dial Press
1983 **Hart's Hope** Berkley
  The Worthing Chronicle Ace
1984 **A Woman of Destiny** Berkley, expanded as **Saints**
1985 **Ender's Game** Tor
1986 **Speaker for the Dead** Tor
1987 **Wyrms** Arbor House
  Seventh Son Tor
1988 **Red Prophet** Tor
1989 **The Abyss** Pocket
  Prentice Alvin Tor
1990 **Eye for Eye** Tor
1991 **Xenocide** Tor
1992 **The Memory of Earth** Tor

1992 **Lost Boys** HarperCollins
1993 **The Call of Earth** Tor
  Lovelock Tor, with Kathryn H. Kidd
1994 **The Ships of Earth** Tor

SHORT STORY COLLECTIONS
1978 **Capitol** Baronet
1981 **Unaccompanied Sonata** Dial Press
1987 **Cardography** Hypatia Press
1989 **The Folk of the Fringe** Phantasia Press
1990 **Maps in a Mirror** Tor, reprinted in four volumes as **The Changed Man, Flux, Monkey Sonatas,** and **Cruel Miracles**

AS EDITOR
1980 **Dragons of Light** Ace
1981 **Dragons of Darkness** Ace
1991 **Future on Fire** Tor

VERNOR VINGE

BORN **1947**

NATIONALITY **American**

KEY WORKS **Grimm's World, True Names, The Peace War, Marooned in Realtime, A Fire Upon the Deep**

THERE is a lot of wisdom around, most of it false. One of the wise things said about SF is that it should be written either by scientists or those who thoroughly understand the workings of modern science. But the best SF work of the past half century has been written by men and women whose grasp of science is no greater than that of the enlightened reader. Another wise thing said, one that almost directly contradicts the first, is that SF should not be written by scientists because they simply do not know how to tell stories. But what about Greg Benford? What about Vernor Vinge?

Like Benford, Vinge is primarily a scientist, and only secondarily a fiction author. He has been a Professor of Mathematics in California since 1972; and he works at his job full time. It is perhaps because he is not a full-time author that his novels and stories seem to represent a rather more personal vision of the universe than that usually associated with writers of Hard SF – SF that takes some advantage of the arguments of science. Vinge's science is as competent as Benford's, or Niven's; and he incorporates many Hard SF devices (plausible psychic powers; cyberspace; stasis machines; intricate time-travel puzzles; genetic engineering; cosmological speculation).

But he does so within a framework of storylines that – though they have become less stringent over the years – convey a quite extraordinary grimness.

So it is not unfitting that his first novel is called *Grimm's World*, and that its protagonist – a gifted woman from a devastated colony planet, who is able to liaise with superior aliens – lives much of her life in frustrated isolation from the ignorant culture of her birth. The similar protagonist of *The Witling* only achieves a kind of happiness when she suffers brain damage, which reduces her to a more "normal" kind of person, one capable of making a good marriage.

There are emotional cripples and star-crossed lovers in *True Names*, too; but the thrill of this story lies in its early depiction of what would later be called cyberspace – a computer net that seems, from the perspective of those consciousnesses operating it, to be nothing short of magical. But the peak of Vinge's career – after a few further gloomy tales – is *A Fire Upon the Deep*, (see page 236) one of the finest Space Operas to have been written since the time of E.E. Smith, when the universe was simpler. In this novel, the galaxy proves to be a complex, lenticular trap for intelligence, and only as species escape its centre do they free themselves from its constraints. Out on the rim, where the action flies, and information highways connect millions of species, we are all free at last.

> **❝** He incorporates Hard SF devices within storylines that convey extraordinary grimness **❞**

BIBLIOGRAPHY

NOVELS AND NOVELLAS
1969 **Grimm's World** Berkley, expanded as **Tatja Grimm's World**
1976 **The Witling** DAW Books
1981 **True Names** Dell
1984 **The Peace War** Bluejay Books
1986 **Marooned in Realtime** Bluejay Books
1992 **A Fire Upon the Deep** Tor

SHORT STORY COLLECTIONS
1987 **True Names and Other Dangers** Baen
1988 **Threats and Other Promises** Baen

JOAN D. VINGE

BORN **1948**

NATIONALITY **American**

KEY WORKS **"Eyes of Amber", "Legacy", the Snow Queen series**

THE names are no coincidence. Vernor Vinge and Joan Vinge were married from 1972 to 1979. Their work has been dissimilar from the first, however, and they have both had their greatest successes since 1980. So we have entirely separate Vinges to thank.

Joan Vinge's first significant stories, like "Eyes of Amber" or "Legacy" and the linked *The Outcasts of Heaven Belt*, could be called women's fiction, but only if learning how to love and live and to understand oneself is not properly men's work as well. Underlying most of her stories is a sense of fable. Her best work returns to and enriches communal material and, as a result, tends to focus on coming to terms with the shape of life. Under their glittering surfaces, her stories are almost always about initiation, passage, and assumption of a fitting destiny. In "Eyes of Amber", a dispossessed, dislocated young woman recovers her selfhood and property, and rediscovers the forgotten relationship of her home world to the larger human enterprise throughout the Solar System. "Legacy", set in the asteroid belt, also tells the story of a disinherited young woman who finds meaning, love, and a good job. *Psion* is also a coming-of-age tale.

But these stories pale as fables when compared with the novel sequence that is her main work to date.

BIBLIOGRAPHY

NOVELS AND NOVELLAS
1978 **The Outcasts of Heaven Belt** New American Library, expanded as **Heaven Chronicles**
1980 **The Snow Queen** Dial Press
1982 **Psion** Delacorte Press
1983 **Return of the Jedi Storybook** Random House
Tarzan, King of the Apes Random House, with Edgar Rice Burroughs
1984 **The Dune Storybook** Putnam
World's End Bluejay Books
1985 **Ladyhawke** New American Library
Mad Max: Beyond Thunderdome Warner
Return to Oz Ballantine
Santa Claus, the Movie Berkley
1988 **Willow** Random House
Catspaw Warner
1990 **Tin Soldier** Tor
1991 **The Summer Queen** Warner

SHORT STORY COLLECTIONS
1978 **Fireship** Dell, retitled **Fireship, and Mother and Child**
1979 **Eyes of Amber** New American Library
1985 **Phoenix in the Ashes** Bluejay Books

The Snow Queen (see page 230) and *The Summer Queen*, with *World's End* as a pendant, represent one of the most ambitious attempts to combine the structures of fable, which shape fantasy, but are rarely thought to shape SF, with a surface plot consistent with SF. Vinge marries structures from the deep past to stories that point futurewards. In *The Snow Queen*, an elderly ruler attempts to maintain her wintery immortality by creating clones of herself. But, unexpectedly, one of these clones turns out to be a mirror of the old queen, rather than a continuation: everything that the old queen stands for is repudiated by the fresh successor, and the old queen has failed. The new queen subsequently brings spring to the world. In the sequel, *The Summer Queen*, the new queen attempts to control resurgent technologies, which are characteristic of her planet's winter phase and which are imported into the summer culture by imperialists from far stars, while realizing that these technologies are necessary for survival. In the end – well, fables, as one knows, unfailingly end happily.

Classic tale
The title and part of the plot of The Snow Queen *are from Hans Christian Anderson's fairy tale.*

WILLIAM GIBSON

BORN **1948**

NATIONALITY **American, resident in Canada**

KEY WORK **The *Neuromancer* series**

IF a little fame goes a long way, then Gibson's is due to hit Andromeda. As far as the media at large are concerned, he is the one contemporary SF writer of importance, the name to mention in programmes on "sci-fi" and the computer revolution. That he is not of such importance, and he would be the first to insist that he is not, means nothing to the outside world.

But within the SF field, it is vital to keep these things in perspective. William Gibson has written five novels since his debut in 1984, one of them in collaboration with Bruce Sterling, published a volume of short stories, and

done some work for Hollywood. He is influential, respected, clever, canny, rich, and (perhaps a bit unexpectedly) wise. And although the books he has published are certainly not the only worthwhile texts published in the field of SF since 1984, he has visibly had a profound effect.

But the importance of *Neuromancer* (see page 232) – already the target of dozens of scholarly essays – does not lie in the originality of its concepts. Cyberspace (or whatever name it was known by before Gibson came up with the perfect term) was familiar to SF readers long used to stories in which brains were neurally wired into or connected with living maps that can register the location and flow of information held within a computer network. This virtual reality "territory" can take almost any shape or form: the Mean Streets of Raymond Chandler's California; the Wild West; or any city centre. The important thing is that the maps stand for information. Gibson's importance lies in the fact that he recognizes the vital importance of information; and that he has worked out how to describe what it might feel like to hack into a world of data. So *Neuromancer* did not create

> **"** *Gibson's importance lies in the fact that he recognizes the vital importance of information* **"**

cyberspace; it created the way to feel it. The experience of cyberspace, and of the information-driven, polluted, corporation-controlled world that creates cyberspace – is what Cyberpunk is all about. Gibson did not invent that term, but *Neuromancer* soon became the Old Testament of Cyberpunk: the best place to taste its streetwise savvy, the cool-tongued sense of a world that has become a slum city under the control of powerful alien forces, the joy of surfing the data, and the underlying grim sense that surfing the surface is not the same as owning the ocean. Writers of Cyberpunk share some or all these concerns. But only Gibson had the literary knack to make it all flow. He is, in fact, a writer almost uncannily sensitive to the texture of the modern world as it changes. He puts his finger on the change. The two sequels to *Neuromancer* – *Count Zero* and *Mona Lisa Overdrive* – are more complex extrapolations from the same bases, but have had less effect on their readers, probably because the shock of recognition could no longer rattle the senses. And because it is always more fun to point to a change than to understand what happens the day after.

BIBLIOGRAPHY

NOVELS AND NOVELLAS
1984 *Neuromancer* Ace
1986 *Count Zero* Gollancz
1988 *Mona Lisa Overdrive* Gollancz
1990 *The Difference Engine* Gollancz, with Bruce Sterling
1993 *Virtual Light* Viking

SHORT STORY COLLECTIONS
1986 *Burning Chrome* Arbor House

Gibson did not shirk the task, but his readers, and the media, tend to stick to the simplicity of the earlier book.

The Difference Engine (see page 234) is an odd tale for Gibson, and although his input is clearly important throughout, the angular grimness of the text probably comes more from Sterling. *Virtual Light* is, once again, pure Gibson: Gibson on holiday. Set a few years into the future, in California, it features a glorious description of the Oakland Bay Bridge, after the cars have long disappeared, as a habitat for a complex niche society of human strays. But it does not pretend to take the pulse of the next world. *Neuromancer* is still the Gibson book.

[signature: WM. GIBSON]

NOTABLE WORK

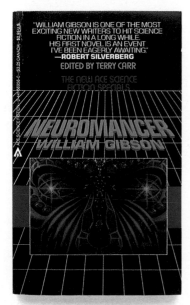

NEUROMANCER

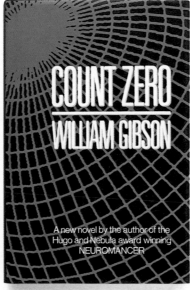

COUNT ZERO

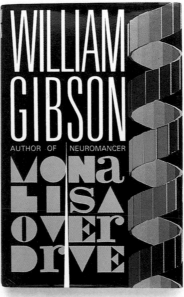

MONA LISA OVERDRIVE

Literary critics, especially those unfamiliar with SF, sometimes refer to "paperback originals" as though they were distasteful, unwholesome, pulpy, bad news. But *Neuromancer*, the most influential SF novel of the 1980s, first appeared as a paperback original. *Count Zero* and *Mona Lisa Overdrive* came out in hardback. The three make up Gibson's famous trilogy. The plots are complicated and interwoven: start at the beginning, memorize the routes in cyberspace, learn the names of the Voodoo Gods, get a sense of the geography, pick up something about Artificial Intelligence, big business, style, guns, sex, sorrow, and wisdom. Then take off into the map.

IAIN BANKS

BORN **1954**

NATIONALITY **Scottish**

OTHER NAME **Iain M. Banks**

KEY WORKS *Walking on Glass, The Bridge, the Culture series*

BIBLIOGRAPHY

NOVELS AND NOVELLAS
1984 **The Wasp Factory** Macmillan
1985 **Walking on Glass** Macmillan
1986 **The Bridge** Macmillan
1987 **Consider Phlebas** Macmillan, as Iain M. Banks
      Espedair Street Macmillan
1988 **The Player of Games** Macmillan, as Iain M. Banks
1989 **The State of the Art** Mark V. Ziesing, as Iain M. Banks
      Canal Dreams Macmillan
1990 **Use of Weapons** Orbit, as Iain M. Banks
1992 **The Crow Road** Macdonald
1993 **Against a Dark Background** Orbit, as Iain M. Banks
      Complicity Little Brown
1994 **Feersum Endjinn** Orbit, as Iain M. Banks

SHORT STORY COLLECTIONS
1991 **The State of the Art** Orbit, as Iain M. Banks, incorporating the novel of the same name.

IAIN Banks came out of the long, black nights of Scotland in 1984, with *The Wasp Factory*, and he has never stopped since. It is not just the number of books, or the two names: what is extraordinary is the turmoil, the huge, bleak, grinning energy of the work. Only about half of his tales are of genre interest, but he is the most important British writer in decades to do SF. That is remarkable, too: in a literary world of carefully separated sheep and goats, he is both literary writer and SF writer at the same time. He may be the first since H.G. Wells.

Of his Iain Banks novels, *Walking on Glass*, *The Bridge*, and *Canal Dreams* all incorporate strands of SF, usually parodies of bad genre adventure tales, or hints at a surrounding world that is not exactly the world of today.

The Iain M. Banks tales are explicitly and thrustingly SF. *Consider Phlebas* introduces readers to the Culture, a transgalactic civilization whose main homes are vast space artefacts, and which has long evolved past the capitalist-socialist quarrels of 20th-century Earth. Citizens of the Culture are, indeed, not too politely surprised when (in *The State of the Art*) they come across Earthlings, and begin to understand how punishingly cruel they can be to one another, especially when seeking a "legitimate profit". *Use of Weapons* is a darker parable about the moral costs of action. They all have bite, stamina, and heft.

Endless bridge
Banks's novel The Bridge *transforms the Forth Bridge into a nightmare environment that is reminiscent of Kafka.*

KIM STANLEY ROBINSON

BORN **1952**

NATIONALITY **American**

KEY WORKS **The *Orange County* series, the *Mars* series**

IT was one of those years. Like 1962, when Delany, Disch, Le Guin, and Zelazny all made their debuts, 1984 saw first books from Iain Banks, Clive Barker, William Gibson, James Patrick Kelly, Carter Scholz, Lewis Shiner, and Kim Stanley Robinson, who published three.

The three books of Robinson's debut year were a forecast of his work to date. *The Novels of Philip K. Dick* remains the best single introduction to this most influential SF writer. *Icehenge* introduces readers to the solidities and romance of Robinson's solar system, with physical textures almost tangible, so firmly are they grounded in hard scientific knowledge, and political structures of sweeping scope. And *The Wild Shore*, which was for years his best-known work, begins a demonstration of Robinson's genuine daring as a builder of imaginative societies.

The Wild Shore is his first book, and the trilogy that it begins – continued with *The Gold Coast* and *Pacific Edge* – is probably the only trilogy set in three Alternate Worlds. Intriguingly, each volume is set in the same location: Orange County, just south of Los Angeles. In *The Wild Shore*, America has lost a long war, and the inhabitants of Orange County have developed their own post-catastrophe culture; in *The Gold Coast*, all is as it is likely to be about 30 years hence: overbuilt, privatized, treeless, and full of the threat and promise of technology;

and in *Pacific Edge*, the United States has evolved into a nest of small, semi-independent entities, where sagacious environmental and population controls have generated a real-life utopia, but with some of the tragedies of life outside, too. The three constitute an argument about America, one whose implications cut deep.

There have been other books, and a lot of short stories, since. But the peak of Robinson's career is the **Mars** sequence, made up of *Red Mars*, *Green Mars*, and *Blue Mars*. A different kind of utopian thinking operates here. In accordance with his own theory about SF – that it can be defined as a speculative continuation of history into the future – the **Mars** books present the arrival of the human colonists on Mars, and their long, slow attempts to terraform the planet, as a story that is continuous with life on Earth, and as a logically arguable solution to our problems on this planet. Politics, personalities, science, economics, and culture are all conspicuously linked to what goes on.

"He is a daring builder of imaginative societies"

The result is enormously exciting. Together, the books are the first real attempt to make the planet Mars part of the human home.

BIBLIOGRAPHY

NOVELS AND NOVELLAS
1984 **The Wild Shore** Ace
      Icehenge Ace
1985 **The Memory of Whiteness: A Scientific Romance** Tor
1988 **The Gold Coast** St. Martin's Press
      Green Mars Tor (not the same as the 1993 novel)
1990 **Pacific Edge** Unwin Hyman
      A Short, Sharp Shock Mark V. Ziesing
1992 **Red Mars** HarperCollins
1993 **Green Mars** HarperCollins

SHORT STORY COLLECTIONS
1986 **The Planet on the Table** Tor
      The Blind Geometer Cheap Street
1987 **Escape from Kathmandu** Axolotl
1989 **The Blind Geometer/The Return from Rainbow Bridge** Tor
1991 **A Sensitive Dependence on Initial Conditions** Pulphouse
      Remaking History Tor

NON-FICTION
1984 **The Novels of Philip K. Dick** Ann Arbor

WILLIAM GIBSON

BORN **1948**

NATIONALITY **American, resident in Canada**

KEY WORK **The *Neuromancer* series**

IF a little fame goes a long way, then Gibson's is due to hit Andromeda. As far as the media at large are concerned, he is the one contemporary SF writer of importance, the name to mention in programmes on "sci-fi" and the computer revolution. That he is not of such importance, and he would be the first to insist that he is not, means nothing to the outside world.

But within the SF field, it is vital to keep these things in perspective. William Gibson has written five novels since his debut in 1984, one of them in collaboration with Bruce Sterling, published a volume of short stories, and

done some work for Hollywood. He is influential, respected, clever, canny, rich, and (perhaps a bit unexpectedly) wise. And although the books he has published are certainly not the only worthwhile texts published in the field of SF since 1984, he has visibly had a profound effect.

But the importance of *Neuromancer* (see page 232) – already the target of dozens of scholarly essays – does not lie in the originality of its concepts. Cyberspace (or whatever name it was known by before Gibson came up with the perfect term) was familiar to SF readers long used to stories in which brains were neurally wired into or connected with living maps that can register the location and flow of information held within a computer network. This virtual reality "territory" can take almost any shape or form: the Mean Streets of Raymond Chandler's California; the Wild West; or any city centre. The important thing is that the maps stand for information. Gibson's importance lies in the fact that he recognizes the vital importance of information; and that he has worked out how to describe what it might feel like to hack into a world of data. So *Neuromancer* did not create

> **"***Gibson's importance lies in the fact that he recognizes the vital importance of information***"**

cyberspace; it created the way to feel it. The experience of cyberspace, and of the information-driven, polluted, corporation-controlled world that creates cyberspace – is what Cyberpunk is all about. Gibson did not invent that term, but *Neuromancer* soon became the Old Testament of Cyberpunk: the best place to taste its streetwise savvy, the cool-tongued sense of a world that has become a slum city under the control of powerful alien forces, the joy of surfing the data, and the underlying grim sense that surfing the surface is not the same as owning the ocean. Writers of Cyberpunk share some or all these concerns. But only Gibson had the literary knack to make it all flow. He is, in fact, a writer almost uncannily sensitive to the texture of the modern world as it changes. He puts his finger on the change. The two sequels to *Neuromancer* – *Count Zero* and *Mona Lisa Overdrive* – are more complex extrapolations from the same bases, but have had less effect on their readers, probably because the shock of recognition could no longer rattle the senses. And because it is always more fun to point to a change than to understand what happens the day after.

BIBLIOGRAPHY

NOVELS AND NOVELLAS
1984 ***Neuromancer*** Ace
1986 ***Count Zero*** Gollancz
1988 ***Mona Lisa Overdrive*** Gollancz
1990 ***The Difference Engine*** Gollancz, with Bruce Sterling
1993 ***Virtual Light*** Viking

SHORT STORY COLLECTIONS
1986 ***Burning Chrome*** Arbor House

Gibson did not shirk the task, but his readers, and the media, tend to stick to the simplicity of the earlier book.

The Difference Engine (see page 234) is an odd tale for Gibson, and although his input is clearly important throughout, the angular grimness of the text probably comes more from Sterling. *Virtual Light* is, once again, pure Gibson: Gibson on holiday. Set a few years into the future, in California, it features a glorious description of the Oakland Bay Bridge, after the cars have long disappeared, as a habitat for a complex niche society of human strays. But it does not pretend to take the pulse of the next world. *Neuromancer* is still the Gibson book.

NOTABLE WORK

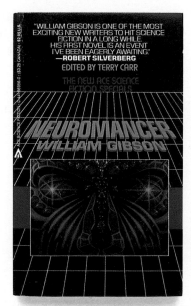

NEUROMANCER

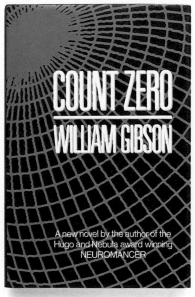

COUNT ZERO

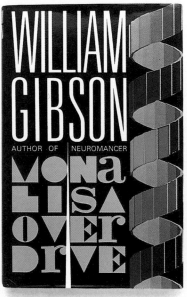

MONA LISA OVERDRIVE

Literary critics, especially those unfamiliar with SF, sometimes refer to "paperback originals" as though they were distasteful, unwholesome, pulpy, bad news. But *Neuromancer*, the most influential SF novel of the 1980s, first appeared as a paperback original. *Count Zero* and *Mona Lisa Overdrive* came out in hardback. The three make up Gibson's famous trilogy. The plots are complicated and interwoven: start at the beginning, memorize the routes in cyberspace, learn the names of the Voodoo Gods, get a sense of the geography, pick up something about Artificial Intelligence, big business, style, guns, sex, sorrow, and wisdom. Then take off into the map.

IAIN BANKS

BORN **1954**

NATIONALITY **Scottish**

OTHER NAME **Iain M. Banks**

KEY WORKS ***Walking on Glass, The Bridge,* the *Culture* series**

BIBLIOGRAPHY

NOVELS AND NOVELLAS
1984 *The Wasp Factory* Macmillan
1985 *Walking on Glass* Macmillan
1986 *The Bridge* Macmillan
1987 *Consider Phlebas* Macmillan, as
        Iain M. Banks
        Espedair Street Macmillan
1988 *The Player of Games* Macmillan, as
        Iain M. Banks
1989 *The State of the Art* Mark V. Ziesing, as
        Iain M. Banks
        Canal Dreams Macmillan
1990 *Use of Weapons* Orbit, as Iain M. Banks
1992 *The Crow Road* Macdonald
1993 *Against a Dark Background* Orbit, as
        Iain M. Banks
        Complicity Little Brown
1994 *Feersum Endjinn* Orbit, as Iain M. Banks

SHORT STORY COLLECTIONS
1991 *The State of the Art* Orbit, as
        Iain M. Banks, incorporating the novel
        of the same name.

IAIN Banks came out of the long, black nights of Scotland in 1984, with *The Wasp Factory,* and he has never stopped since. It is not just the number of books, or the two names: what is extraordinary is the turmoil, the huge, bleak, grinning energy of the work. Only about half of his tales are of genre interest, but he is the most important British writer in decades to do SF. That is remarkable, too: in a literary world of carefully separated sheep and goats, he is both literary writer and SF writer at the same time. He may be the first since H.G. Wells.

Of his Iain Banks novels, *Walking on Glass, The Bridge,* and *Canal Dreams* all incorporate strands of SF, usually parodies of bad genre adventure tales, or hints at a surrounding world that is not exactly the world of today.

The Iain M. Banks tales are explicitly and thrustingly SF. *Consider Phlebas* introduces readers to the Culture, a transgalactic civilization whose main homes are vast space artefacts, and which has long evolved past the capitalist-socialist quarrels of 20th-century Earth. Citizens of the Culture are, indeed, not too politely surprised when (in *The State of the Art*) they come across Earthlings, and begin to understand how punishingly cruel they can be to one another, especially when seeking a "legitimate profit". *Use of Weapons* is a darker parable about the moral costs of action. They all have bite, stamina, and heft.

Endless bridge
Banks's novel The Bridge *transforms the Forth Bridge into a nightmare environment that is reminiscent of Kafka.*

KIM STANLEY ROBINSON

BORN **1952**

NATIONALITY **American**

KEY WORKS **The *Orange County* series, the *Mars* series**

IT was one of those years. Like 1962, when Delany, Disch, Le Guin, and Zelazny all made their debuts, 1984 saw first books from Iain Banks, Clive Barker, William Gibson, James Patrick Kelly, Carter Scholz, Lewis Shiner, and Kim Stanley Robinson, who published three.

The three books of Robinson's debut year were a forecast of his work to date. *The Novels of Philip K. Dick* remains the best single introduction to this most influential SF writer. *Icehenge* introduces readers to the solidities and romance of Robinson's solar system, with physical textures almost tangible, so firmly are they grounded in hard scientific knowledge, and political structures of sweeping scope. And *The Wild Shore,* which was for years his best-known work, begins a demonstration of Robinson's genuine daring as a builder of imaginative societies.

The Wild Shore is his first book, and the trilogy that it begins – continued with *The Gold Coast* and *Pacific Edge* – is probably the only trilogy set in three Alternate Worlds. Intriguingly, each volume is set in the same location: Orange County, just south of Los Angeles. In *The Wild Shore,* America has lost a long war, and the inhabitants of Orange County have developed their own post-catastrophe culture; in *The Gold Coast,* all is as it is likely to be about 30 years hence: overbuilt, privatized, treeless, and full of the threat and promise of technology; and in *Pacific Edge,* the United States has evolved into a nest of small, semi-independent entities, where sagacious environmental and population controls have generated a real-life utopia, but with some of the tragedies of life outside, too. The three constitute an argument about America, one whose implications cut deep.

There have been other books, and a lot of short stories, since. But the peak of Robinson's career is the **Mars** sequence, made up of *Red Mars, Green Mars,* and *Blue Mars.* A different kind of utopian thinking operates here. In accordance with his own theory about SF – that it can be defined as a speculative continuation of history into the future – the **Mars** books present the arrival of the human colonists on Mars, and their long, slow attempts to terraform the planet, as a story that is continuous with life on Earth, and as a logically arguable solution to our problems on this planet. Politics, personalities, science, economics, and culture are all conspicuously linked to what goes on. The result is enormously exciting. Together, the books are the first real attempt to make the planet Mars part of the human home.

"He is a daring builder of imaginative societies"

BIBLIOGRAPHY

NOVELS AND NOVELLAS
1984 *The Wild Shore* Ace
        Icehenge Ace
1985 *The Memory of Whiteness: A Scientific
        Romance* Tor
1988 *The Gold Coast* St. Martin's Press
        Green Mars Tor (not the same as the
        1993 novel)
1990 *Pacific Edge* Unwin Hyman
        A Short, Sharp Shock Mark V. Ziesing
1992 *Red Mars* HarperCollins
1993 *Green Mars* HarperCollins

SHORT STORY COLLECTIONS
1986 *The Planet on the Table* Tor
        The Blind Geometer Cheap Street
1987 *Escape from Kathmandu* Axolotl
1989 *The Blind Geometer/The Return from
        Rainbow Bridge* Tor
1991 *A Sensitive Dependence on Initial
        Conditions* Pulphouse
        Remaking History Tor

NON-FICTION
1984 *The Novels of Philip K. Dick* Ann Arbor

SHERI S. TEPPER

BORN 1929

NATIONALITY American

OTHER NAMES Sheri S. Ebehart, E.E. Horlak, A.J. Orde, B.J. Oliphant

KEY WORKS *The Gate to Women's Country*, the *Marjorie Westriding* series, *Beauty*

BIBLIOGRAPHY

NOVELS AND NOVELLAS
1983 *King's Blood Four* Ace
     Necromancer Nine Ace
1984 *The Revenants* Ace
     Wizard's Eleven Ace
1985 *The Song of Mavin Manyshaped* Ace
     The Flight of Mavin Manyshaped Ace
     The Search of Mavin Manyshaped Ace
     Marianne, The Magus, and the Manticore Ace
     Jinian Footseer Tor
1986 *Blood Heritage* Tor
     Dervish Daughter Tor
     Jinian Star-eye Tor
1987 *After Long Silence* Bantam, retitled *The Enigma Score*
     The Awakeners: Northshore Tor
     The Awakeners: Southshore Tor
     The Bones Tor
1988 *The Gate to Women's Country* Doubleday
     Marianne, the Madame, and the Momentary Gods Ace
1989 *Grass* Doubleday
     Marianne, the Matchbox, and the Malachite Mouse Ace
     Still Life Bantam, as E.E. Horlak
1990 *Raising the Stones* Doubleday
1991 *Beauty* Doubleday
1992 *Sideshow* Bantam
1993 *A Plague of Angels* Bantam

SHERI Tepper sounds young. Her first book came out in 1983, most of her heroines are young women, much of her early work seemed to be written for a young audience, and she has the energy of a youth. But the date of birth above is not a mistake. She was in her mid-50s before she published a book. Today, she has published at least 30 (her detective tales under other names are not listed here), and is so much a part of the genre that she seems to have always been here.

Her latest books are her best. Most of the early tales are part of the *True Game* Planetary Romance sequence, with heroines who have psi powers and aliens to defend their homes from. It sounds not unlike Marion Zimmer Bradley's *Darkover* books, but never gained the wide readership of that series – perhaps because the connections between volumes were never very telling, so readers tended to pick them at random. *The Awakeners*, first (and unwisely) published in two volumes, is a metaphysical SF drama set in a world where one may not travel eastwards; *After Long Silence* is an SF puzzle set on a planet of mysterious aliens.

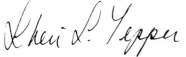

Setting the style
The Gate to Women's Country *sets a tone for Sheri S. Tepper's work.*

With *The Gate to Women's Country*, Tepper came into her full fame. The story is seemingly savage – in a harsh, post-holocaust world, men and women live almost entirely separate lives, with women apparently oppressed – but the revelations about the true state of affairs are surprisingly forgiving (although anger is never far). Anger drives her greatest works. The *Marjorie Westriding* trilogy – made up of *Grass, Raising the Stones*, and *Sideshow* – depicts a galaxy ransacked by human greed, self-delusion, fundamentalist beliefs, and arrogance. Anger also infuses Tepper's finest single tale, *Beauty*, the story of a Sleeping Beauty who escapes the 100-year sleep only to find herself transported, ageing rapidly, to a 21st-century dystopia; her ultimate destiny as a bearer of hope for ravaged Earth makes the tale a powerful fable.

JULIAN MAY

BORN 1931

NATIONALITY American

OTHER NAMES Ian Thorne, Lee N. Falconer

KEY WORKS The *Saga of the Exiles* series, the *Galactic Milieu* series

JULIAN May properly entered the SF field only after she had already lived a full life. She did publish an SF story as early as 1951 and, over the next 30 years, she published nearly 300 books under other names, mostly non-fiction for children; she also founded and ran a series of small presses, most notably Starmont House, with T.E. Dikty, her husband. So when she burst onto the stage she knew a few things about publishing.

"May's epic is complex, testing, adventurous, and fun"

Whether or not the *Saga of the Exiles* was calculated – it is in fact hard to see how so complex an enterprise could come from anywhere but the heart – its effect was very considerable. It is a fantasy epic in an SF frame; an opera told in prose; a family drama whose cast are avatars of profound human impulses. It is an exciting tale of humans versus aliens; it is intimate, taking place mostly in Pleistocene Europe, and immense, involving at least two alien races, aeons of time travel, and at least one galaxy. It is a Space Opera, for all these reasons, and an exercise in arcane philosophy, because much of the shape of the tale – including the World Mind and the Galactic Mind – reflects the work of the radical theologian and philosopher Pierre Teilhard de Chardin.

It is not simple, and *A Pliocene Companion*, which is a non-fiction guide to the main series, is very helpful.

The basic frame is a future Earth whose inhabitants have become mature enough to join the five races who monitor the galaxy, and who possess a freak time machine that only goes back in time, and only goes to one place and one time: France in the Pleistocene. The story follows, with opera-like flamboyance, the lives of a group of humans who opt for Pleistocene exile, and who find two warring sets of aliens already occupying the ground. The plot, inevitably, thickens.

Intervention returns to the near future of Earth and examines the historical course towards the year 2013, when galactic contact is made. It links the previous series to *Jack the Bodiless* and *Diamond Mask*, the **Galactic Milieu** series that, when it is complete, may well end up being even more ambitious than the first series. The theme of psychic evolution, which was evident early on, has become far more significant, and the resemblance of May's **Galactic Milieu** books to Doris Lessing's five-volume sequence *Canopus in Argos: Archives*, which is based on the philosophy of Sufism, may be more than superficial. The difference between May and Lessing is that May knows SF and fantasy backwards and forwards, and her epic is by far the more complex, testing, adventurous, and fun of the two.

BIBLIOGRAPHY

NOVELS AND NOVELLAS
1981 *The Many-Colored Land* Houghton Mifflin
1982 *The Golden Torc* Houghton Mifflin
1983 *The Nonborn King* Houghton Mifflin
1984 *The Adversary* Houghton Mifflin
1987 *Intervention* Houghton Mifflin, republished in two volumes as *The Surveillance* and *The Metaconcert*
1990 *Black Trillium* Doubleday, with Marion Zimmer Bradley and Andre Norton
1992 *Jack the Bodiless* Knopf
     Blood Trillium HarperCollins
1994 *Diamond Mask* Knopf

NON-FICTION
1977 *Gazeteer of the Hyborian World of Conan* Starmont, as Lee N. Falconer
1984 *A Pliocene Companion* Houghton Mifflin

DAVID BRIN

BORN **1950**

NATIONALITY **American**

KEY WORKS **The Uplift series, Earth, Glory Season**

THERE are exceptions to every rule, and David Brin is an exception to several of them. SF is supposed to have gone off the boil in about 1960, and the writers who have come into the field after that date are supposed to take something of a dim view of the old Space Opera universe, the old SF ladder that humanity could climb to the furthest stars, if we only had the gumption to do it.

And indeed, authors like Delany, Disch, Wolfe, or Zelazny do not tend to spend time conquering the galaxy. But Brin is as bright as any of them, and his central series – the *Uplift* books, beginning with *Startide Rising* and *The Practice Effect* and climaxing, for the moment, with *The Uplift War* (see page 233) – takes on the galaxy with all the exuberance of an E.E. Smith reborn. There is a ladder to the stars in these books, and humanity claws upwards into pole position in the Five Galaxies. The galaxies are seeded by a departed Progenitor race and supervised by five Patron Lines – one line per galaxy. Humans start off way down the pecking order, but discover that the local Patron Line has become corrupt, and that we will have to follow our own route to the great central Progenitor library of the wisdom of the ages. It is great fun, but it is not exactly science.

" Brin's writing is full of doubletalk, sweeping gestures, and lots of answers to hard questions "

And here is the second exception. Brin is a numerate man, with a doctorate in physics, and an occasional collaborator with the formidable Greg Benford, who is a professor of physics; but the Hard SF he writes is full of astonishingly breezy doubletalk, sweeping gestures, and lots of answers to hard questions.

The third exception is this: most Hard SF writers are conservative, and most of them take an (increasingly guarded) optimistic view of what technology and private enterprise can achieve. But Brin, in a novel like *Earth*, has no truck (until the last, when the Hard SF habit of big answers takes over) with the technophilia of writers like Jerry Pournelle. In *Earth*, Brin presents a planet at the verge of self-extinction, the immediate crisis being caused by an irresponsible entrepreneur. Oops.

With *Glory Season*, this Space Operatic, Hard SF, doomsayer-with-joy takes on a new world, and almost comes a cropper. An isolated and matriarchal planet is threatened by the rest of the male-dominated galaxy. In the sequel, we will see what Brin does with his likeable, independent women, after the ships land.

BIBLIOGRAPHY

NOVELS AND NOVELLAS
1980 *Sundiver* Bantam
1983 *Startide Rising* Bantam
1984 *The Practice Effect* Bantam
1985 *The Postman* Bantam
1986 *Heart of the Comet* Bantam, with Gregory Benford
1987 *The Uplift War* Phantasia Press
1989 *Dr. Pak's PreSchool* Cheap Street
1990 *Earth* Bantam
1993 *Glory Season* Bantam

SHORT STORY COLLECTIONS
1986 *The River of Time* Dark Harvest
1994 *Otherness* Orbit

AS EDITOR
1990 *Project Solar Sail* Roc, with Arthur C. Clarke

BRUCE STERLING

BORN **1954**

NATIONALITY **American**

KEY WORKS **Schismatrix, Islands in the Net, Heavy Weather**

HE never seems to stop improving. Of course, he had a way to go: *Involution Ocean* is a bit of a wallow, an overheated quest across a waterless planet; and *The Artificial Kid*, although it reeks of high-tech urban clatter, is too tied to its romantic Kid hero to make much sense of things. (One of Delany's less fortunate bequests has been the Kid, the streetwise, sexually alluring Childe figure who is the model for Sterling's artificial Kid.)

But then Cyberpunk came, and if Sterling did not invent it, he certainly soon became its definitive spokesman in articles, and through editing the best Cyberpunk anthology, *Mirrorshades*.

Cyberpunk was for Sterling a signal of a new SF – William Gibson being its most important writer – that would finally confront the new world we were coming into as the 1980s advanced: filthy, urban, unutterably complex, dominated supremely by the computer. It was a world in which human beings triumphed by adapting: mentally by learning to navigate cyberspace, where all the information power resided; and physically by becoming creatures who could live in any crevasse, climb any virtual reality mountain.

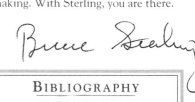

Steampunk
The Artificial Intelligence of The Difference Engine *is developed from Babbage's unlikely-looking computer.*

In *Schismatrix* and *Islands in the Net* (see page 233), Sterling postulated feverish new worlds, and strenuously advocated marriage to them. He talked evolution, system, adaptability, toughness, thrust, and transcendence. *Islands in the Net* creates real, oppressive paranoia in its near-future world of information nets under corporate control. *Schismatrix* is a kind of electronic-age Space Opera, with genetic engineering cohabiting with the more normal invading alien theme.

The Difference Engine translated this vision of the future into an alternate past, England in 1850 in a world transformed by the success of Babbage's computer. This is a daguerrotype of a machine gone insane, and the whole novel has – somehow – been generated by the computer itself.

Heavy Weather is back with a bump in the near future in the American West. The aquifer is drained dry, but global warming has increased rainfall – which cannot reach aquifer levels before new flora sop it up. And the weather is getting worse. The globe is in for a shaking. With Sterling, you are there.

BIBLIOGRAPHY

NOVELS AND NOVELLAS
1977 *Involution Ocean* Jove
1980 *The Artificial Kid* Harper
1985 *Schismatrix* Arbor House
1988 *Islands in the Net* Arbor House
1990 *The Difference Engine* Gollancz, with William Gibson
1994 *Heavy Weather* Bantam

SHORT STORY COLLECTIONS
1989 *Crystal Express* Arkham House
1992 *Globalhead* Mark V. Ziesing

NON-FICTION
1992 *The Hacker Crackdown: Law and Disorder on the Electronic Frontier* Bantam, and on the Internet

AS EDITOR
1986 *Mirrorshades: The Cyberpunk Anthology* Arbor House

JAMES P. BLAYLOCK

BIBLIOGRAPHY
NOVELS AND NOVELLAS
1982 *The Elfin Ship* Ballantine
1983 *The Disappearing Dwarf* Ballantine
1984 *The Digging Leviathan* Berkley
1986 *Homunculus* Berkley
1987 *Land of Dreams* Arbor House
1988 *The Last Coin* Mark V. Ziesing
1989 *The Stone Giant* Ace
1991 *The Paper Grail* Ace
     The Magic Spectacles Morrigan
1992 *Lord Kelvin's Machine* Arkham House
1994 *Night Relics* Ace

BORN **1950**

NATIONALITY **American**

OTHER NAME **William Ashbless**

KEY WORKS **Homunculus, Lord Kelvin's Machine, Land of Dreams, The Paper Grail**

SOME think Blaylock has only a remote connection with SF, and should be treated as a weaver of misty myths for New Age readers who like their truths soft, their music ethereal, and their sewage plants on the other side of the tracks. Others think he has a real SF understanding of the world.

The Elfin Ship and *The Disappearing Dwarf* are fantasy, although more sharp and problematical than most popular fantasy, but a novel like *Homunculus* is something else: a richly stewed trip into an alternate 19th-century London. There are echoes of Dickens and other less well-known writers, like Bulwer Lytton and Harrison Ainsworth, who wrote tales about the labyrinth of the 19th-century city that have come collectively to be known as novels of the Mysteries. Steampunk – in which Blaylock and his friend Tim Powers are central figures – makes use of similar dense plotting, dramatic vistas and incredibly complex conspiracies, to create an alternate-history vision of the modern world a-borning. As Blaylock writes in *Homunculus* and *Lord Kelvin's Machine,* steampunk is a genuine SF strategy for understanding, and making sense of, the industrial revolution. Which is to say, the roots of today.

California, however, remains Blaylock's actual and spiritual home, the setting for books like *Land of Dreams* and *The Paper Grail*. These tales attempt to capture a complex, new world through the creation of Alternate Worlds that expose rich veins of truth beneath the apparent surface of things. In Blaylock's hands, California is a magical-realist paradise of miraculous characters and events, but one whose very texture – whose soil and being – seems to be woven from the flamboyant scales of the Snake. His California is, in other words, at its very heart, both blessed and corrupt. An aged cripple on the Pacific coast may be a Fisher King hoping for a miracle to heal the land, or he may be a real-estate developer hoping to rape it, or both at once. In Blaylock's California, almost anything can happen.

TIM POWERS

BORN **1952**

NATIONALITY **American**

OTHER NAME **William Ashbless**

KEY WORKS **The Anubis Gates, Dinner at Deviant's Palace, On Stranger Tides**

UNLIKE his colleague Blaylock, Tim Powers began as a writer of routine Space Operas for Laser Books, which hoped to make SF as common as hospital romances. Laser folded, and Powers revised his titles; they should only be read in the revised versions.

Then came *The Drawing of the Dark*, a far-reaching fantasy, and then his breakthrough, *The Anubis Gates,* which won the Philip K. Dick Award for its year, and which is one of the finest steampunk novels yet, along with those by Blaylock. A contemporary man is sent back to early-19th-century England, ostensibly to attend an unrecorded lecture by Samuel Taylor Coleridge; but in fact he gets caught up in a plot involving Spring-Heeled Jack, Anubis, mages from ancient Egypt, the poet William Ashbless, and the subterranean Mysteries of London itself. The tale is haunting and intermittently grim; but, astonishingly, it is also full of geniality, a *joie de vivre* that pulls the reader through the darkness, smiling with delight.

Dinner at Deviant's Palace is SF, but in the richly textured mould that Powers and Blaylock have together developed in their mature fiction. It is set in a post-catastrophe San Francisco, and very competently presents the necessary sense of a desolated world. But, at the same time, the plot is riddled with magic, myth, and rich breakfasts in the ruins of America; its main characters re-enact, very movingly, the Orpheus and Eurydice story. *On Stranger Tides* is a pirate tale, which mixes supernatural elements with fantasy and SF, and demonstrates through the surreal intricacy of its plot how far he has come from the kind of fiction written by Rafael Sabatini, author of *Scaramouche*, whose influence upon Powers is well known.

The Stress of Her Regard and *Last Call* both continue along the rich seams uncovered in Powers's earlier work. Myths and high technology intersect, time-travel paradoxes darken the tale, and a fine, astonishingly complicated time is had by all.

BIBLIOGRAPHY
NOVELS AND NOVELLAS
1976 *Epitaph in Rust* Laser, revised as
     An Epitaph in Rust
     The Skies Discrowned Laser, revised as
     Forsake the Sky
1979 *The Drawing of the Dark* Ballantine
1983 *The Anubis Gates* Ace
1985 *Dinner at Deviant's Palace* Ace
1987 *On Stranger Tides* Ace
1989 *The Stress of her Regard* Ace
1992 *Last Call* Morrow

NOTABLE WORKS

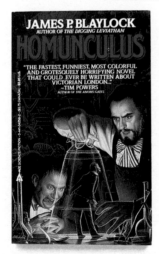

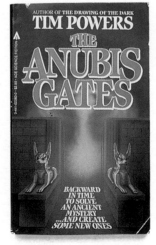

HOMUNCULUS   *THE ANUBIS GATES*

The great 19th-century poet William Ashbless links Blaylock and Powers. He is referred to in *Homunculus,* although he never appears. Nor can he be found in poetry guides. Not surprising: he is a complete fabrication by the authors, who have both written Ashbless poetry in novels and broadsheets. And it turns out – after a dizzy spiral of time paradoxes – that he is the protagonist of *The Anubis Gates.* His poetry is actually rather good.

CONNIE WILLIS

BIBLIOGRAPHY

NOVELS AND NOVELLAS
1982 **Water Witch** Ace, with Cynthia Felice
1987 **Lincoln's Dreams** Bantam
1989 **Light Raid** Ace, with Cynthia Felice
1992 **Doomsday Book** Bantam
1994 **Uncharted Territory** Bantam

SHORT STORY COLLECTIONS
1985 **Fire Watch** Bluejay
1994 **Impossible Things** Bantam
1994 **Uncharted Territory** New English Library
(the 1994 novel with stories added)

BORN **1945**

NATIONALITY **American**

KEY WORKS **"Fire Watch", "A Letter from the Clearys", "The Last of the Winnebagos", "At the Rialto", Lincoln's Dreams, Doomsday Book**

HAVING made a slow and careful start, writing intermittently for magazines in the 1970s, Connie Willis exploded into the SF world around 1980. Although she has only published two full-length novels over her 15 years in the limelight, she is rightly considered to be one of the central and mature voices of the genre. Her two novels with Cynthia Felice – *Water Witch* and *Light Raid* – are ebullient, but not very searching. The novels she wrote alone are something else entirely.

Lincoln's Dreams is one of the most deeply haunting time-travel stories ever, although there is no literal journey into the past. A richly drawn contemporary woman, who is engaged in research into the paranormal, finds herself caught into a psychic linkage across two centuries with General Robert E. Lee, entering into his dark imaginings about the outcome of the American Civil War, a conflict in which he cannot hope to triumph on behalf of the beleaguered, agricultural, slave-holding South. Simultaneously, the woman's male lover begins to reflect the partial, but vivid, awareness of events felt by

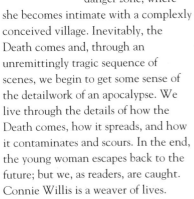

Historical figures
General Lee and his horse, Traveller, touch the present in Lincoln's Dreams.

General Lee's famous horse, Traveller. It sounds almost comic; but Willis – who knows how to tell a joke – knows exactly how to enter into, and present to us, the true nightside visions of the American psyche. *Lincoln's Dreams* relays to us the dreams of America.

Doomsday Book (see page 236) cannot do the same for Britain, and does not try. The frame story takes place in a near-future Oxford, and once again introduces us to a tale involving time travel; but in this case the journey is real. The Oxford historiographic unit, which is responsible for sending volunteers into the past – it also features in Willis's most famous single story, "Fire Watch", from 1984 – has been training a young woman to return to the mid-14th century, the time when the Black Death is about to ravage the country. A slight miscalculation sends her back to a danger zone, where she becomes intimate with a complexly conceived village. Inevitably, the Death comes and, through an unremittingly tragic sequence of scenes, we begin to get some sense of the detailwork of an apocalypse. We live through the details of how the Death comes, how it spreads, and how it contaminates and scours. In the end, the young woman escapes back to the future; but we, as readers, are caught. Connie Willis is a weaver of lives.

MICHAEL SWANWICK

BORN **1950**

NATIONALITY **American**

KEY WORKS **"Ginungagap", Vacuum Flowers, Stations of the Tide**

THERE are still fast and prolific writers in the world of SF, men and women who gift us with dozens of books in the course of careers that are both worthwhile and prolific. At the same time, however, the field has in recent years seen a distinct shift towards writers – such as Willis, Swanwick, and Cadigan – whose published stories appear with more deliberation than is usual in a genre literature. In earlier years, it should be remembered, writing SF paid very badly, and any man or woman who wished to write as a career was pretty well forced to generate a constant flow of huge amounts of copy. Recently, although most SF authors still remain pretty poor, the financial situation has changed just enough to allow the Michael Swanwicks of the world to settle slowly into each new enterprise.

Nod to Cyberpunk
Vacuum Flowers *comes close to Cyberpunk in its depiction of an intensely urban future life.*

Perhaps because of this, he has written no sequels, and not one of his books to date much resembles any of the others. *In the Drift*, his earliest and weakest text, is an Alternate World tale set in a Balkanized, post-castastrophe America that is much bedevilled by the radiation effects of a Three Mile Island that did explode. *Vacuum Flowers*, in contrast, depicts a humanity that is finally beginning to occupy space habitats throughout the Solar System, and exposes the Western-style heroics of the old Space Opera adventurers as something of an illusion, although a treasured one. Simultaneously, it is an acute analysis of the nature of human identity in a world – it is one we are fast approaching – where edited personalities can be inserted, in the form of medically implanted computer chips, into human minds, giving us new scope, new skills, new selves, and new imprisonments.

Griffin's Egg also describes a world that we may be rapidly approaching: it is set on a near-future Moon, which is dominated and ecologically threatened by multi-planet corporations, whose power far exceeds that of outmoded nation states.

Stations of the Tide (see page 235), Swanwick's best novel yet, leaves the near future for a setting several centuries hence, on a planet that has been quarantined by the human government that controls interstellar space. The protagonist of the tale, a "bureaucrat" sent onto the planet to trace a vital theft, is a most complex character. Seeming at first to be no more than a faceless bumbler, he turns out to be competent, wise, and dangerous, and a clear echo of the figure of Prospero in Shakespeare's *The Tempest*. The novel reads like a virtual-reality version of the Renaissance Theatre of Memory.

Then comes *The Iron Dragon's Daughter*, a stunning, acerbic fantasy. Swanwick never stays to repeat himself.

BIBLIOGRAPHY

NOVELS AND NOVELLAS
1985 **In the Drift** Ace
1987 **Vacuum Flowers** Arbor House
1990 **Griffin's Egg** Legend
1991 **Stations of the Tide** Morrow
1993 **The Iron Dragon's Daughter** Millennium

SHORT STORY COLLECTIONS
1991 **Gravity's Angels** Arkham House

LUCIUS SHEPARD

BIBLIOGRAPHY

NOVELS AND NOVELLAS
1984 **Green Eyes** Ace
1987 **Life During Wartime** Bantam
1988 **The Scalehunter's Beautiful Daughter**
 Mark V. Ziesing
1989 **The Father of Stones** Washington
 Science Fiction Association
1990 **Kalimantan** Legend
1993 **The Golden Mark** Mark V. Ziesing

SHORT STORY COLLECTIONS
1987 **The Jaguar Hunter** Arkham House
1989 **Nantucket Slayrides** Eel Grass Press, with
 Robert Frazier
1991 **The Ends of the Earth** Arkham House
1994 **Sports and Music** Mark V. Ziesing

BORN **1947**

NATIONALITY **American**

KEY WORKS **Green Eyes, "R & R",
Life During Wartime**

IF he were exclusively, or even primarily, an author of SF, Lucius Shepard would demand much space here; but he straddles several genres, and he must be regarded as a writer who ransacks genres – not only SF, but also horror and fantasy – for his material. It is not important to him as a writer whether a particular story obeys the rules of a particular genre; any rules will do, just as long as they allow him to examine the human situations that he chooses and extract lessons from those situations.

Despite his frequent iconoclasm, Shepard is, in other words, something of a moralist: his first two novels, which are those that are most easily described as SF, demonstrate this. *Green Eyes* examines medical ethics through the experiences of people raised from the dead, while the various stories that are combined in *Life During Wartime* punishingly translate the American experience of Vietnam into a South American nightmare, close to home and inescapable.

[signature: Lucius Shepard]

LOIS McMASTER BUJOLD

BIBLIOGRAPHY

NOVELS AND NOVELLAS
1986 **Shards of Honor** Baen
 The Warrior's Apprentice Baen
 Ethan of Athos Baen
1988 **Falling Free** Baen
1989 **Brothers in Arms** Baen
1990 **The Vor Game** Easton Press
1991 **Barrayar** Baen
1994 **Mirror Dance** Baen

SHORT STORY COLLECTIONS
1989 **Borders of Infinity** Baen

BORN **1949**

NATIONALITY **American**

KEY WORKS **"The Mountains of
Mourning", The Vor Game**

THE genre of SF is quite notoriously unfriendly to any kind of comedy: humour and wit seem terribly hard to convey in SF settings, and what we end up with instead is all too often the clumsiest of slapstick. Lois McMaster Bujold is not an overtly funny writer, nor does she ever indulge in slapstick. But her novels and stories always leave one with the feeling that one has been smiling while reading them. She is, in other words, a writer who takes joy in telling her stories, and who conveys that joy to the reader.

Almost all of these novels and stories concern a disabled, but extremely charismatic, good-natured, and astonishingly sharp young soldier-diplomat named Miles Vorkosigan, whose adventures traverse the feuding, human-dominated galaxy. He is a military genius, and a good man. *The Vor Game*, the best of the series, won a 1991 Hugo, and *Falling Free*, a separate novel set before the time of the **Vorkosigan** books, won a 1988 Nebula, while "The Mountans of Mourning", a short story about Miles Vorkosigan from 1989, collected both awards.

[signature: Lois Bujold]

PAT CADIGAN

BORN **1953**

NATIONALITY **American**

KEY WORKS **Patterns, Synners, Fools**

NO reader could finish even *Mindplayers*, Pat Cadigan's first and slightest novel, without knowing that the world she describes is both deadly and serious. Cadigan has often – perhaps rather too often – been described as the first woman to write truly effective Cyberpunk material.

Although there is an element of truth in the praise, her work is in fact far broader than that label. Cadigan's world is urban, complex, sultry, computer-ridden, dirty, and dangerous, but so is the reality of the 1990s: she writes novels, not labels.

The problem with *Mindplayers* – a tale that is, after all, built up from some of her very earliest published work – is that its protagonist has altogether too little difficulty confronting the fractures of the modern self, both in her own mind and in the minds of the patients whose dreams she enters on her therapeutic missions. Excessive simplicity is, however, no longer a problem with *Synners*, in which these psychic fractures are no longer contained within our heads,

Deadly friends
Synners *warns
against the dangers
of a computer-
dominated world.*

but have begun to colonize the urban mazes of the near future. AIs, which may in fact be computer viruses, are beginning to transmute, to deadly effect, the interfaces between threatened human selves and the infinite recesses of a world that has no firm base.

Cadigan's third novel, *Fools*, builds from the strengths of *Synners*, and is one of the most elegant – and difficult to parse – novels yet written by a contemporary SF author. In this novel, selves are no longer simply fractured; they have become tenements, whose inhabitants squabble over the one body they must share. Some strands of the heroine's overall personality squat within the main frame, some simply freeload on it.

The result is an exceedingly complex narrative, but one whose fame can only grow as we become accustomed to its techniques; and, perhaps, as we also begin to recognize, in our own mirrors, the multiple visages that Cadigan clearly thinks we will all soon be displaying to the world.

[signature: Pat Cadigan]

BIBLIOGRAPHY

NOVELS AND NOVELLAS
1987 **Mindplayers** Bantam
1991 **Synners** Bantam
1992 **Fools** Bantam

SHORT STORY COLLECTIONS
1989 **Patterns** Ursus Imprints
1991 **Letters from Home** The Women's Press,
 with Karen Joy Fowler and Pat Murphy
1992 **Home by the Sea** WSFA Press
1993 **Dirty Work** Mark V. Ziesing

1990-1994: FACING THE MILLENNIUM

AS THE MILLENNIUM LOOMS over the horizon, people start to ask what kind of a new age we face, and how we will face it. At the start of the 20th century, humanity was full of hopes and fears, and the SF of those long-gone days reflected the enormous changes that we sensed we were going to face. Now, we are at the other end of the century, and there are perhaps more enormous changes to come, over the hurdle of the Millennium. SF has gone from

1990	1991	19

NOTABLE WORKS

1990

The Ring of Charon
ROGER MACBRIDE ALLEN

Queen of Angels
GREG BEAR

Voyage to the Red Planet
TERRY BISSON

Earth
DAVID BRIN

The Vor Game
LOIS MCMASTER BUJOLD

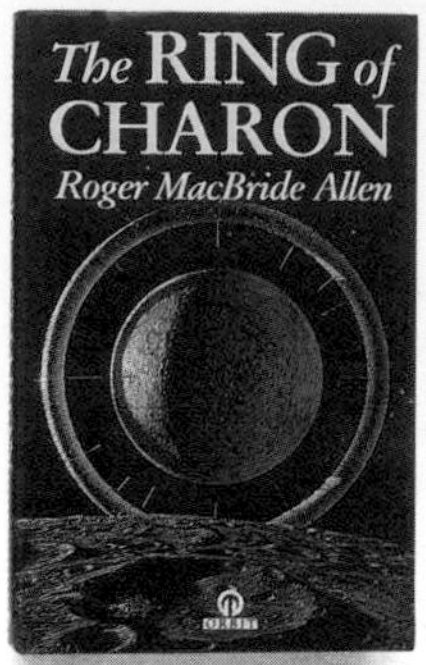

THE RING OF CHARON

The Gap into Conflict
STEPHEN DONALDSON

The Difference Engine
WILLIAM GIBSON AND
BRUCE STERLING

Take Back Plenty
COLIN GREENLAND

Brain Rose
NANCY KRESS

The Quiet Pools
MICHAEL P. KUBE-MCDOWELL

THE GAP INTO CONFLICT

1991

Synners
PAT CADIGAN

Sarah Canary
KAREN JOY FOWLER

White Queen
GWYNETH JONES

Lafferty in Orbit
R.A. LAFFERTY

Death Qualified
KATE WILHELM

Eternal Light
PAUL MCAULEY

The Ragged World
JUDITH MOFFETT

Jago
KIM NEWMAN

The Silicon Man
CHARLES PLATT

The Dark Beyond the Stars
FRANK M. ROBINSON

The Hollow Earth
RUDY RUCKER

The Face of the Waters
ROBERT SILVERBERG

Stations of the Tide
MICHAEL SWANWICK

DEATH QUALIFIED

19

A Million Open Doors
JOHN BARNES

Count Geiger's Blues
MICHAEL BISHOP

Lord Kelvin's Machine
JAMES P. BLAYLOCK

Fools
PAT CADIGAN

Destroying Angel
RICHARD PAUL RUSSO

FOOLS

ICONS

The more we learn about the human mind, the more it seems to be some kind of enormously complex land mine beneath the skin. Novel after novel now tells us, as does Nancy Kress's *Brain Rose*, that the landscapes within the head are both boobytrapped and infinitely alluring. Computers may be more powerful, but minds, like Houdini, escape our attempts to bind them.

Earlier in the century, SF writers had tended to assume – sometimes unthinkingly – that *Homo sapiens* would dominate the galaxy, just as we dominate our own planet. But it becomes less and less easy to think so. Much of the best current SF dramatizes a contrary vision: it is the humbling thought that perhaps we will be juniors in the universe, that perhaps we need to join rather than to conquer, and that, just possibly, we may need to ask the help of others in order to become fully mature citizens of our world, and of the greater worlds beyond.

The human race may be fast approaching an evolutionary crisis, a moment of truth. Like the first lungfish stuck on the dangerously exhilarating – but possibly fatal – sand beach, and breathing in the oxygen of the open air for the very first time,

DEBUTS

Authors publishing their first books of SF interest include Terry Dowling with *Rynosseros*, Michael Blumlein with *The Brains of Rats*, Gregory Feeley with *The Oxygen Barons*, Elizabeth Hand with *Winterlong*, Eric Brown with *The Time-Lapsed Man*, and Robert J. Sawyer with *Golden Fleece*.

Alexander Jablokov's *Carve the Sky*, Stephen Baxter's **Raft**, and Lawrence Norfolk's *Lempriere's Dictionary* stand out among debut SF novels this year. Other first books of SF interest include Janet Kagan's *Mirabile*, Tom Maddox's *Halo*, Iain Sinclair's *Downriver*, and Kristine Kathryn Rusch's *The White Mists of Power*.

Greg Egan publishes his long-awaited and well-received first SF novel, **Quarantine**. Other debuts include Richard Calder's *Dead Girls*, Lisa W. Cantrell's *Boneman*, Simon Ings's *Hot Head*, Sean McMullen's *Call to the Edge*, P.D. James's *The Children of Men*, Robert Harris's *Fatherland*, and

infancy through adolescent traumas to maturity in the course of the century, but it still faces the future with the same sense of challenge that it had at the beginning: face up to the future, or be left stranded. If anything, the situation is now more pressing: this century has brought us to the limits of our planet, and there is a sense in SF today that travel to other worlds is not a bold adventure, but a necessity. The Solar System is our next evolutionary step.

92

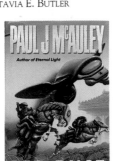

A MILLION OPEN DOORS

A Deeper Sea
ALEXANDER JABLOKOV

Red Mars
KIM STANLEY ROBINSON

Steel Beach
JOHN VARLEY

A Fire Upon the Deep
VERNOR VINGE

Doomsday Book
CONNIE WILLIS

we may all too soon find ourselves washed up on another new beach. Varley's *Steel Beach* describes this new environment: artificial, electronic, urban, intense, and demanding. And either we learn to breathe the new computer-monitored air of our habitat, or we will sink back into the poisoned mud of our landlocked childhood, and die there.

Daniel Quinn's *Ishmael*. Two more are Ken Kesey's *Sailor Song* and **Maureen F. McHugh**'s *China Mountain Zhang*.

1993

Harvest of Stars
POUL ANDERSON

Anti-Ice
STEPHEN BAXTER

Moving Mars
GREG BEAR

Glory Season
DAVID BRIN

Parable of the Sower
OCTAVIA E. BUTLER

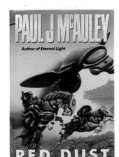

RED DUST

Beggars in Spain
NANCY KRESS

Kalifornia
MARC LAIDLAW

Red Dust
PAUL J. MCAULEY

Coelestis
PAUL PARK

The Broken God
DAVID ZINDELL

MOVING MARS

Mars may be the first steel beach: it is the next planet to Earth; it is geomorphically complex; and although it is now entirely inimical to unprotected human life, it is a genuine possibility that we may be able to terraform our neighbour and begin to settle there. Kim Stanley Robinson's *Mars* trilogy, begun in 1992, provides a most eloquent advocacy of Mars as the next New Frontier. This year, other novels, like Greg Bear's and Paul J. McAuley's, take that initial success for granted.

Authors publishing their first books of SF interest include Nicola Griffith with *Ammonite*, Will Baker with *Shadow Hunter*, Patricia Anthony with *Cold Allies*, and Tony Daniel with *Warpath*. Jeff Noon's debut novel, **Vurt**, wins the Arthur C. Clarke Award.

1994

Somewhere East of Life
BRIAN ALDISS

The Stars Are Also Fire
POUL ANDERSON

Feersum Endjin
IAIN M. BANKS

Mother of Storms
JOHN BARNES

Brittle Innings
MICHAEL BISHOP

Wildlife
JAMES PATRICK KELLY

Pasquale's Angel
PAUL J. MCAULEY

Necroville
IAN MCDONALD

Half the Day is Night
MAUREEN F. MCHUGH

Voices in the Light
SEAN MCMULLEN

Hot Sky at Midnight
ROBERT SILVERBERG

Heavy Weather
BRUCE STERLING

The Ultimate Egoist
THEODORE STURGEON

NECROVILLE

As the 1990s progress, we near a moment of huge symbolic importance to Western humanity – and to the rest of the human race as well, now that almost all of the world has accepted the same dating system. The year 2000 may be just another year for pretty much everything from planets to plants, but for humans it represents a point from which to cast runes, to assess the past and future, to settle our minds for glory, or Armageddon, or something somewhere in between. Dozens of SF novels from 1994 on will deal directly with this moment.

First books of SF interest published this year include *The Fermata* by Nicholson Baker, *Queen City Jazz* by Kathleen Ann Goonan, and *Gun, with Occasional Music* by **Jonathan Lethem**.

DAN SIMMONS

BORN **1948**

NATIONALITY **American**

KEY WORKS **The *Hyperion Cantos*, *The Hollow Man***

THE publication of *Hyperion* (see page 233) in 1989 was perhaps the most propitious emergence into the genre that the SF world had seen since Alfred Bester published *The Demolished Man* (see page 219) almost four decades earlier. Like Bester, Dan Simmons was not exactly unknown to the field when he published this first SF novel, but neither was he a figure of any very remarkable prominence: his work to date had been in the field of horror. Then suddenly, almost without notice, *Hyperion* appeared, with *The Fall of Hyperion*, its immediate sequel, in extremely close tow, and Space Opera became a new ball game.

Not that C.J. Cherryh and Vernor Vinge – to name the two of the best 1980s writers of galaxy-spanning tales – had been idle before *Hyperion* came along. Both of these writers have great energy and a sense of architecture, and their novels convey a sense of wonder; but they both gave plenty of signals in advance of what they were attempting, and presented their universes in stages. Only slowly has it become clear to us – certainly in Cherryh's case – just how remarkable and encompassing is the vision that is being presented to us. At the other extreme, Dan Simmons's universe comes across to the reader in one unstoppable, irresistible mass of words – nearly half a million of them in total, because the two titles make up, in reality, a single, sustained novel: they were published in one volume,

Hyperion Cantos, in 1990. Also, although both Cherryh and Vinge have written shapely books, neither of them attempts the bravura effects that make *Hyperion* so gripping and haunting. Simmons's subsequent novels mix SF and fantasy with horror; for now, *Hyperion* is his masterwork.

The tale is constructed on the model of Chaucer's *Canterbury Tales*: seven separate individuals have been selected to make a pilgrimage through interstellar space to the planet of Hyperion. This is the home of the mysterious Time Tombs, which move backwards through time, and of the Shrike, which guards them. The Shrike is a creature coated with scissoring blades with which it, in a kind of quasi-religious torture, plunges victims into an eternity of pain. Each of the seven pilgrims carries some secret inside themselves and, as they travel to Hyperion and tell each other their stories, the complexities begin to well. The plot is both as sharp and as mysterious as the Shrike itself.

> **❝ *His universe comes across to the reader in one unstoppable, irresistible mass of words* ❞**

John Keats comes into both volumes – which are named after his poems about the displacing of the old gods – and in the second book the plot thickens and explodes. The human-dominated galaxy – far too complex to describe – is in for profound upheaval: time travel, wormhole travel, AIs at war, and a great deal more. Maybe humans will be eliminated; maybe not. A sequel is promised.

BIBLIOGRAPHY

NOVELS AND NOVELLAS
1985 **The Song of Kali** Bluejay Books
1989 **Carrion Comfort** Dark Harvest
    Phases of Gravity Bantam
    Hyperion Doubleday
1990 **The Fall of Hyperion** Doubleday
1991 **Summer of Night** Putnam
1992 **Children of the Night** Putnam
    The Hollow Man Bantam
1994 **Fires of Eden** Headline

SHORT STORY COLLECTIONS
1991 **Prayers to Broken Stones** Dark Harvest
1993 **Lovedeath** Headline

NON-FICTION
1991 **Going After the Rubber Chicken** Roadkill Press
1992 **Summer Sketches** Lord John Press

STEPHEN BAXTER

BORN **1967**

NATIONALITY **English**

OTHER NAMES **Steve Baxter, S.M. Baxter**

KEY WORK **The *Xeelee* series**

ONCE upon a time, Hard SF was all very simple: it was SF that was written in obedience to – and in order to describe – the possible workings of the hard sciences. The hard sciences, according to the Hard SF writers, were those sciences whose outcomes were properly quantifiable, and could be understood in terms of real processes, operating in the real world. In contrast, the human sciences were deemed to be "soft" sciences. Perhaps for this reason, Hard SF has always tended to appeal most to male American writers, often of a distinctly conservative bent. British and other European writers have generally avoided the Hard SF

BIBLIOGRAPHY

NOVELS
1991 **Raft** Grafton
1993 **Timelike Eternity** HarperCollins
1993 **Flux** HarperCollins
    Anti-Ice HarperCollins
1994 **Ring** HarperCollins

route, and even when they do embark upon the kind of story that bases speculative arguments about human destiny upon a limited range of eligible sciences, they tend to avoid political arguments like those that shape the works of Larry Niven and Jerry Pournelle. Stephen Baxter is a case in point.

Readers familiar with Baxter's early short stories knew, when *Raft* appeared in 1991, that Baxter was not simply writing a single novel, although the Hard SF premise – which involved an erudite presentation of a universe with a gravitational field hugely stronger than our own – was intriguing on its own. No sequels seemed necessary. But *Raft* is part of a far larger storytelling game, and – along with *Timelike Eternity*, *Flux*, and *Ring* – fits neatly, and non-politically, into the universe-long tale of the Xeelees and their human successors.

NOTABLE WORK

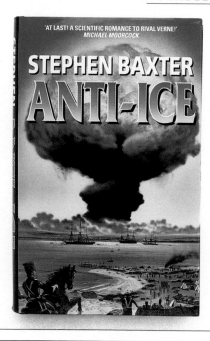

'AT LAST! A SCIENTIFIC ROMANCE TO RIVAL VERNE!'
MICHAEL MOORCOCK
STEPHEN BAXTER
ANTI-ICE

Perhaps the best place to start with Baxter is with his first non-Future History tale. *Anti-Ice* is a steampunk epic set in an Alternate World version of Earth, in which an extremely dangerous superconducting element is found in an African meteor. The element propels ships effortlessly, and the British government that controls it rules the world by the turn of the 20th century. The tale describes anti-ice's discoverer's wild trip to the Moon and back with lots of romance, glee, and sadness.

ANTI-ICE

NANCY KRESS

BORN **1948**

NATIONALITY **American**

KEY WORKS **An Alien Light, Brain Rose, Beggars in Spain**

SOME writers – like Poul Anderson or C.J. Cherryh – have migrated effortlessly from SF to fantasy and back again throughout their writing careers. Many others, such as Piers Anthony, Marion Zimmer Bradley, and Andre Norton, have gradually shifted from SF to fantasy over the years. Only a few have made the move in the other direction. Nancy Kress began her published career in the 1980s as a writer of ironic and somewhat subversive fantasies; but in 1988, with *An Alien Light*, she moved to SF.

She has never looked back since. *An Alien Light* is a slow, convincing, and melancholy examination of human nature. It portrays humanity as it is seen through the eyes of an alien race, which has captured various specimens of *Homo sapiens* in the course of a war and put them together in a camp in order to find out just what it is that makes them tick. The traditional, self-congratulatory assumption of SF – that our human quarrelsomeness is both inherently attractive, and ultimately adaptive in an evolutionary sense – is given very short shrift here. Kress is a writer working at the end of a long century, and a century that has not shown any evidence of a markedly positive side to our lethal incapacity to stop squabbling among ourselves. The message given in this book – that this incapacity is certainly governed by our genes – is not meant as praise for our species in any way.

Brain Rose, set in a devastated near future plagued by a memory-eating disease, deepens one's sense of Kress as a central end-of-century SF sensibility. She comes from a generation that can no longer assume that all will be well if us guys and gals are simply given our heads and allowed to invent our way out to the stars, and the devil take the hindmost. At the same time, however, her depictions of new worlds, and of what we can hope to accomplish on them, are couched in unmistakably SF terms. She sees that there are problems; and although, unlike the old Hard SF writers, she is unable to believe that we can continue to escape our problems through smart technological fixes alone, she is not, as so many writers of fantasy are, a Luddite. She tells us that if we are to come through the next decades at all, it will be through both our knowledge of the real world and our knowledge of ourselves. Both of these brands of knowledge are what the SF of the 1990s is all about.

It is, however, with her next novel, *Beggars in Spain* (see page 236), and its sequel, *Beggars and Choosers*, that Kress has taken off. She takes on another old SF cliché – that of genetically modified *Homo superior* children, who grow up in a secluded place and take over the world – and immensely complicates it. Genius is fine, but it must be used well in a world of infinite complexity – a world that is, of course, ours.

> **"** *Her message in* An Alien Light *is not meant as praise for our species* **"**

BIBLIOGRAPHY

NOVELS AND NOVELLAS
1981 **The Prince of Morning Bells** Pocket Books
1984 **The Golden Grove** Bluejay Books
1985 **The White Pipes** Bluejay Books
1988 **An Alien Light** Arbor House
1990 **Brain Rose** William Morrow
1991 **Beggars in Spain** Axolotl Press (novella publication)
1993 **Beggars in Spain** William Morrow (novel publication)
1994 **Beggars and Choosers** Tor

SHORT STORY COLLECTIONS
1985 **Trinity** Bluejay Books
1993 **The Aliens of Earth** Arkham House

PAUL J. MCAULEY

BORN **1955**

NATIONALITY **English**

KEY WORKS **Eternal Light, Red Dust, Pasquale's Angel**

THERE is no denying it: European SF writers, when compared with their transatlantic counterparts, can be a pretty glum lot. They seem drawn to entropy – the slow, but irreversible, flattening out of energy throughout the whole universe, which means that ultimately nothing will be able to happen because there will be no gradient for energy to flow down in order to make anything happen. Entropy is lurking everywhere, at least metaphorically, in European, and especially in British, SF. This is why most readers of SF, whether or not they are English speakers by birth, have always tended, and still tend, to turn to American-brand SF to find unfettered fun: because Yanks have never much cottoned on to entropy.

The earlier novels of Paul McAuley are certainly not immune to the lure of entropy. *Four Hundred Billion Stars* boasts, for example, a good, solid, Space Opera title; but the story itself takes a task force from a weary Earth out to a planet whose lifeforms negate and confuse any form of direct action. The problem with a scenario like this is not that SF readers want somehow to deny entropy, loss, and muddle, but that – especially when given a title such as this one – they expect a brief vacation from them.

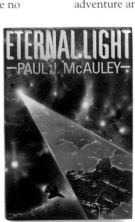

Eternal Light
McAuley's third novel is a Space Opera tale in the American mould.

BIBLIOGRAPHY

NOVELS AND NOVELLAS
1988 **Four Hundred Billion Stars** Gollancz
1989 **Secret Harmonies** Gollancz, retitled **Of the Fall**
1991 **Eternal Light** Gollancz
1993 **Red Dust** Gollancz
1994 **Pasquale's Angel** Gollancz

SHORT STORY COLLECTIONS
1991 **The King of the Hill** Gollancz

AS EDITOR
1992 **In Dreams** Gollancz, with Kim Newman

But McAuley soon began to shock – and to please – those critics and readers who thought he was just another tired adult slumming it in the fields of Space Opera. The story that was begun in *Four Hundred Billion Stars* was continued in *Secret Harmonies* and *Eternal Light*. The last book of this trilogy is a great, galumphing, energetic tale, involving life-or-death chases, huge dreadnoughts of space, wormholes to hide whole worlds in, and an impressively large cast. This is adventure and cosmogony combined.

Since then, McAuley has only got better. *Red Dust*, which is set on a Mars dominated by China several hundred years from now, is a tale that is simultaneously rambunctious and subtle; and it is also, in the classic American mould, the tale of a quest that changes a whole world. McAuley's most recent novel, *Pasquale's Angel*, demonstrating his increasingly adaptable fiction style, tells with hallucinated vividness the story of a painter in an Alternate World version of Italy dominated by an elderly Leonardo Da Vinci, whose paper dreams have been translated into a totalitarian reality.

On this present form, one which seems to be ever-improving, Paul McAuley has become both an author to read and an author to watch.

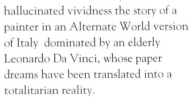

classic
TITLES

ANY GENRE IS THE sum of its works. Science Fiction encompasses cinema, television, and graphic media, all of which are important parts of its history. First and foremost, however, it is a literary genre. This chapter is a chronological showcase of SF titles from the very beginning of the genre to the most recent publications. These titles have gained the status of classics through awards, critical acclaim, or sheer long-term popularity. Details of first publication, publisher, and title are given for each work. The title may occasionally differ from the title on the book jacket shown, which may be from a later edition.

ABOVE: *DE LA TERRE À LA LUNE*
LEFT: DETAIL FROM RICHARD POWERS'S COVER ART FOR *CHILDHOOD'S END*

EARLY SCIENCE FICTION

IN THE 19TH CENTURY, works that we would recognize as SF were written, although the term Science Fiction had not yet been invented. The great SF books of this era were described as Gothics, or Fantastic Voyages, or Utopias, or Scientific Romances – the last a term that was utilized by H.G. Wells at the end of the century. These different categories had much in common: this was the first century in which people thought of history as the story of Progress, and the great speculative novels of the time all reflected a central sense that the world was transforming itself.

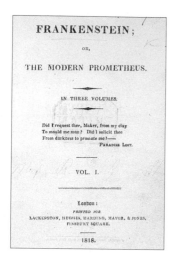

Frankenstein
MARY SHELLEY

Published 1818 **Publisher** Lackington, Hughes, Harding, Mavor and Jones

At the dawn of SF, the Monster begs for attention. Artificial, electrical, striving, he longs to become a self-made man. But, knowing he is manufactured, we loathe and fear him, and in the end he must flee.

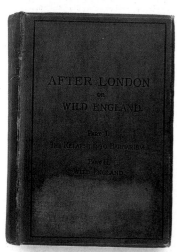

After London
RICHARD JEFFERIES

Published 1885 **Publisher** Cassell

By 1885, England had become an industrial nation. Some writers lamented the loss of the old Eden, and Jefferies dreamed a great dream: that foul, stinking London and the Satanic mills would drown in a vast new flood, and that, centuries hence, folk would thrive again in beloved Wild England.

From the Earth to the Moon
JULES VERNE

Published 1865 **Publisher** Hetzel

In the 60 works that are known as Extraordinary Voyages, Verne's imagination crossed and recrossed the Earth and the seas, the mountains and the abysses beneath the roots of the mountains. Only once did he convey a cast of explorers and savants into space, but *From the Earth to the Moon* – and its sequel, which carries the heroes back home – does so with enormous panache. In the heart of Florida, the great, volcano-like cannon Columbiad, its base sunk deep below the surface of the Earth, fires the intrepid crew into space, where astonishing phenomena dazzle them. After orbiting the Moon, they are returned safely – perhaps a little anticlimactically – to Earth. In SF, the Space Age begins here.

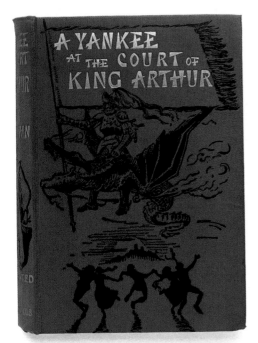

A Yankee at the Court of King Arthur
MARK TWAIN

Published 1889 **Publisher** Chatto and Windus

A hard-nosed Yankee bangs his head, wakes up riled in the England of King Arthur, makes himself boss, turns the world upside down, bangs his head, returns home. It is a time-hallowed time-travel tradition.

Two Planets
KURD LASSWITZ

Published 1897 **Publisher** Elischer Nachfolger

The most important German SF novel, *Two Planets* beats Wells to Mars, and treats the Martians as not only technologically superior, but better behaved, too. Finding them at the North Pole, we attempt in vain to evict them. Only centuries later, grown up at last, can we become partners in the Solar System.

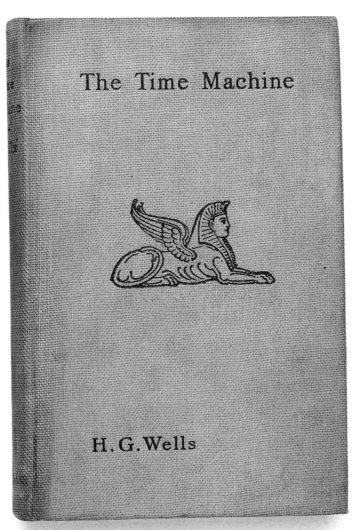

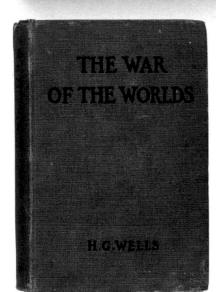

The War of the Worlds
H.G. WELLS

Published 1898 **Publisher** Heinemann

Aliens had visited Earth before, in our imaginations, but never before had they invaded. Wells's Martians land in huge projectiles that cut great grooves in the countryside. Their weapons are terrible, and the destruction is great. When in the end they are killed, it is our germs that save our skins, not human valour.

The Time Machine
H.G. WELLS

Published 1895
Publisher Heinemann

Twain's traveller goes back and rejigs the past; Wells's travels forwards, and witnesses not only the fate of human beings on Earth, but the last moments of the planet, from the final terminal beach, as the sun dies. The story is told in a calm, assured, plausible, and absolutely clear manner; it is a tone that many SF writers would later emulate. It is indeed hard to disbelieve the Time Traveller when he returns to 1895 to tell his friends about humanity's devolution into two species, the delicate but useless Eloi, and the deformed but competent Morlocks. When he describes the end of time itself, few readers could have failed to understand Wells's message: evolution is not always on our side.

A Princess of Mars
EDGAR RICE BURROUGHS

Published 1917 **Publisher** A.C. McClurg

Before Burroughs, other planets were almost always visited for purposes of education: writers created otherworldly societies to show readers by contrast what was wrong, or right, with the human world. But Burroughs's Mars is all escapist fun: a hero, a naked princess, swords, sorceries, battles, and wonders.

CLASSICS OF THE GOLDEN AGE

BEFORE THE GOLDEN AGE OF SF, in 1920, no book could be called SF, because the genre still had not been invented; by 1950, at the end of the Golden Age, we knew what to call a tale of marvels, inventions, and social speculation, set – almost invariably – in the future. As the genre was defined, it took on a very particular identity. In 1920, Russians, Czechs, Britains, Germans, Americans, and Canadians were all writing books about futures good and ill, but by 1950, American writers dominated, and visions of the American century shaped the dreams of the genre.

R.U.R. Rossum's Universal Robots
KAREL ČAPEK

Published 1923 **Publisher** Vydalo Aventinum

This play introduced the word "robot", suggested by Karel's brother Josef, to the world. It is Czech for "worker", and Čapek's robots are, in fact, what we would call androids, created as industrial slaves. They revolt, and the play ends in chaos and hope.

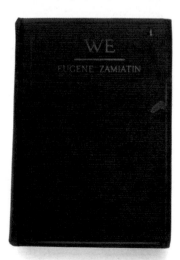

We
YEVGENY ZAMIATIN

Published 1924 **Publisher** Dutton

We is written in a searing, poetical style that defies translation. This great political dystopia paved the way for writers like Huxley and Orwell, Pohl and Dick, but because it revealed a "terrible truth" – that ideas, when triumphant, kill the human spirit – it was never published in the Soviet Union.

Ralph 124C 41+
HUGO GERNSBACK

Published 1925 **Publisher** Stratford & Co.

Nobody could pretend that Hugo Gernsback was a writer of elegance or subtlety, or that his characters were anything but ciphers. But, although it is almost unread now, *Ralph 124C 41+* remains the central text for anyone who wishes to know how SF became conscious of itself, as a genre, in the United States. Gernsback, a German who emigrated to the States, published the story in his magazine, *Modern Electrics*, in 1911. It fitted the magazine perfectly: set in the 27th century, it describes the marvels of technologies to come, and the triumph of Yankee know-how throughout the universe. By 1925, when *Ralph* appeared as a book, Gernsback was about to launch the first specialist SF magazine, *Amazing Stories*.

Brave New World
ALDOUS HUXLEY

Published 1932
Publisher Chatto and Windus

Brave New World is second only to *Nineteen Eighty-Four* as the most famous SF novel ever. Ironically, neither was published as SF: in 1932, the term was hardly known beyond pulp magazines. For Huxley, *Brave New World* was the culmination of a series of novels anatomizing the consequences of World War I. It reeks of aftermath, loss of faith, obeisance to new gods of technology, and the allure of raw pleasure. "Feelies" prefigure virtual reality by half a century, and "soma" predicts the use of drugs as a technique of social control: Huxley could not guess that, a few decades later, feelies and soma would be options, not controls.

Star Maker
OLAF STAPLEDON

Published 1937 **Publisher** Methuen & Co.

Aeons pile upon aeons, stars live and die in what seems an instant: Stapledon's last philosophical trek to the outermost boundaries of time and space – preceded by *Last and First Men* (1930) – still remains unparalleled in scope, ambition, and wondrousness.

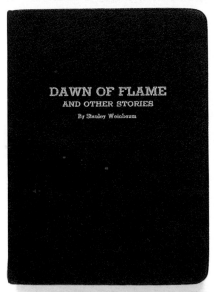

Dawn of Flame
STANLEY WEINBAUM

Published 1936 **Publisher** Milwaukee Fictioneers

Not many story collections are classic books in their own right, but *Dawn of Flame* stands out, collecting stories with which Weinbaum helped transform pulp SF into literature, like "A Martian Odyssey". It was published to commemorate Weinbaum's early death, and is the first SF book published for an SF audience.

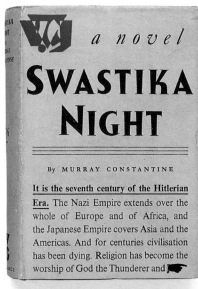

Swastika Night
MURRAY CONSTANTINE
(KATHARINE BURDEKIN)

Published 1937 **Publisher** Gollancz

Most SF classics have been famous in the genre since they first appeared, but *Swastika Night* is only now becoming well known. Set centuries into the future, and the first novel to predict a Nazi triumph, it is a scathing feminist anatomy of war, sexism, and power.

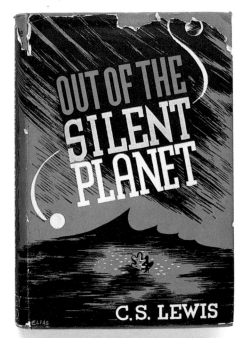

Out of the Silent Planet
C.S. LEWIS

Published 1938 **Publisher** Bodley Head

Much loved by many who dislike SF, the **Ransom Trilogy**, which also includes *Perelandra* (1943) and *That Hideous Strength* (1945), smoothly transforms the Solar System into a three-dimensional map of the will of God, and of Ransom's search for a means to save Earth, the fallen (hence silent) planet.

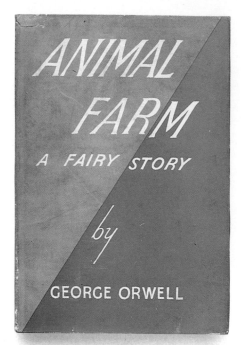

Animal Farm
GEORGE ORWELL

Published 1945 **Publisher** Secker and Warburg

Although it is a funny book, Orwell's satire is so savagely accurate that his publisher declined it for fear of offending Britain's Russian allies in the war against Hitler. This only increased the fame of the pig who becomes more equal than his brother pigs.

Slan
A.E. VAN VOGT

Published 1946 **Publisher** Arkham House

Slan is the tale of a young superman who must grow up in secret, because "slans" (read as "fans") are persecuted. Once grown, he becomes a super-scientist and saves the Solar System, and the World President reveals himself as his long-lost father. *Slan* shaped the dreams of young SF fans.

The Skylark of Space
E.E. SMITH

Published 1946 **Publisher** Buffalo Book Co.

Doc Smith's first Space Opera is a superbly well-named book, because we sense throughout a *joie de vivre* that lifts us into Wonderland. Not the first edisonade written, *The Skylark of Space* is certainly the most enjoyable. The young hero seems born to save humanity from dark-visaged villains, invent new weapons and drives by the shipload, tame alien races, and rescue the girl of his dreams from durance vile. More importantly, the Milky Way is established as a habitation for tales of human derring-do: *The Skylark of Space* gave us a platform for the launching of dreams.

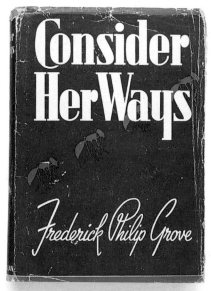

Consider Her Ways
FREDERICK GROVE

Published 1947 **Publisher** Macmillan Canada

Three ants from South America travel north, get into telepathic contact with a scientist, and muse deflatingly about humanity. Written decades before its publication, *Consider Her Ways* is its German-Canadian author's only SF work. Moral allegory, satire, and beast-fable, it deserves much wider fame.

Dark Carnival
RAY BRADBURY

Published 1947 **Publisher** Arkham House

There are no SF short story collections of any great note in the decade between Stanley Weinbaum's *Dawn of Flame* and *Dark Carnival*. Bradbury's first book, which rings in the post-war era, is magically exuberant in tone, but its tales are rich with hints about science's darker face.

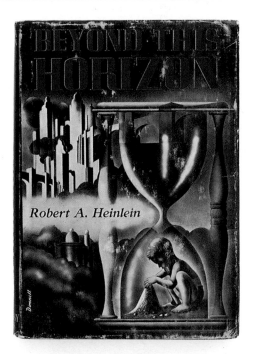

Beyond This Horizon
ROBERT A. HEINLEIN

Published 1948 **Publisher** Fantasy Press

Heinlein's first published novel is a grab-bag satire of a civilization shaped through genetic engineering that ensures fit children. The hero nearly revolts, before learning that the reactionary Survivor's Club is a dead end and marrying his preselected mate.

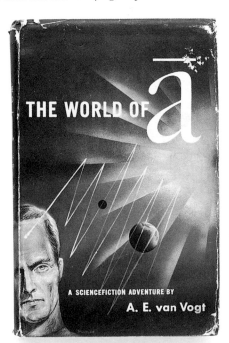

The World of Ā
A.E. VAN VOGT

Published 1948 **Publisher** Simon and Schuster

One of the delights of SF is the tale whose numerous complications beggar imagination. Almost the first of these, and perhaps the most intricate of them all, is *The World of Ā*, which mixes parallel universes, dark schemes, and a multi-bodied hero into a dream-like edifice of story that moves too fast to topple.

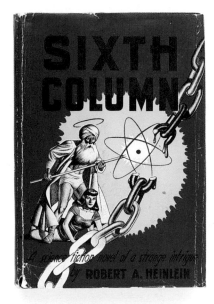

Sixth Column
ROBERT A. HEINLEIN

Published 1949 **Publisher** Gnome Press

Sixth Column was the first of three novels Heinlein published in *Astounding Science Fiction* magazine before he stopped writing to work for the military in 1942. A swift tale of pluck and trickery, it is set in an America occupied (briefly) by evil Asiatics, and the plot ensures that Justice and Valour soon triumph.

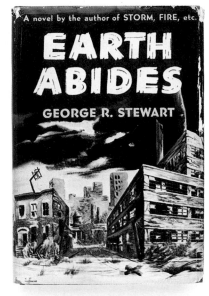

Earth Abides
GEORGE R. STEWART

Published 1949 **Publisher** Random House

American magazine SF toyed with catastrophe, but usually avoided depicting full-scale disasters. Stewart, a non-SF writer, felt no such compunction. *Earth Abides* gravely and calmly follows the lives of a small group who have survived world catastrophe as they slowly forget all about civilization.

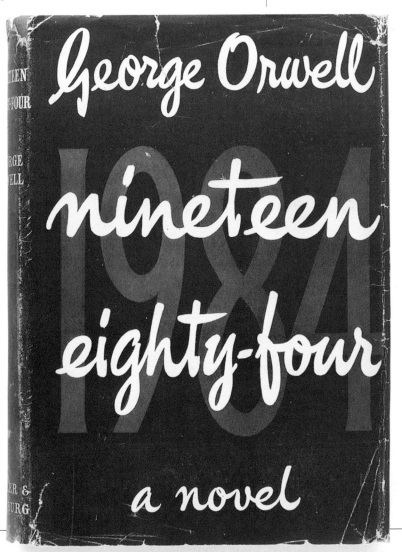

Nineteen Eighty-Four
GEORGE ORWELL

Published 1949 **Publisher** Secker and Warburg

It is one of literature's most famous openings: "It was a bright cold day in April, and the clocks were striking thirteen." Orwell never lets the pace slacken: *Nineteen Eighty-Four* is famous for its satire on both left and right, for doublethink, and for Big Brother, who is watching you; but almost more important than anything is the *feverishness* of the telling. The book is a nightmare: it *feels* like constant pressure, like a world mutilated by its political owners, like entrapment, despair, sudden brief joy. It may fail to describe contemporary politics, but for many it captures contemporary life.

CLASSICS OF THE 1950S

IT IS HIGH NOON IN THE worlds of SF and America, with everything to play for. The United States – where most SF is now written – has come triumphantly through World War II, has taken on Stalin's Soviet Union, houses the United Nations and the atom bomb, Coca-Cola and the utopian dream of Levittown, and is the most powerful country on the planet. This is as it had been foretold in hundreds of issues of SF magazines from 1926 on, and in dozens of books. In 1950, the future according to SF lies before us: it is within our grasp. Or is it?

I, Robot
ISAAC ASIMOV

Published 1950 **Publisher** Gnome Press

Asimov must be the most famous American SF writer to debut in book form as late as 1950. The stories that made up his **Foundation** and **Robot** series had been appearing for years in the pages of *Astounding* magazine, and "Nightfall" (1941) was already being acclaimed the best SF story ever written, but it was only with the appearance of *I, Robot* early in 1950 that he stepped into a larger limelight. The Three Laws of Robotics were – as Asimov hinted in later years – better at generating good stories than they were at describing the field of cybernetics. Certainly in this book, the laws that keep robots in the service of humans also help Asimov to construct a set of affectionate, gripping, argumentative tales.

The Day of the Triffids
JOHN WYNDHAM

Published 1951 **Publisher** Michael Joseph

British SF did not stand still in the 1950s. Mixing together technical savvy and storytelling fluency, Wyndham's tales of catastrophe – *The Day of the Triffids* is the best of them – carried a Battle of Britain spirit comfortably into the new age.

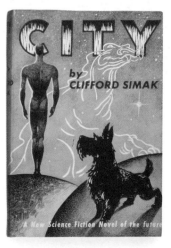

City
CLIFFORD D. SIMAK

Published 1952 **Publisher** Gnome Press

Simak had been writing the stories that make up *City* for years; woven into one narrative, their impact was, perhaps, unexpected. The compassionate robot Jenkins and the intelligent dogs he helps take over an Earth abandoned by its human masters are unforgettable. The tone is elegiac, twilit, wise.

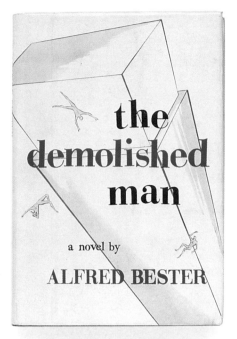

The Demolished Man
ALFRED BESTER

Published 1953 **Publisher** Shasta

SF had not been noted for style before Bester came along to explode the habit of writing novels in babytalk because adolescents read them. The tale of Ben Reich's attempts to escape just arrest in a world of telepath detectives is street-smart and fizzy.

Fahrenheit 451
RAY BRADBURY

Published 1953 **Publisher** Ballantine

The title *Fahrenheit 451* is a brilliant inspiration, being the temperature at which paper spontaneously ignites. The hero, who repents of his book-burning job as a "fireman" in a totalitarian America and begins instead to memorize great works of literature, remains an enduring image of the decade.

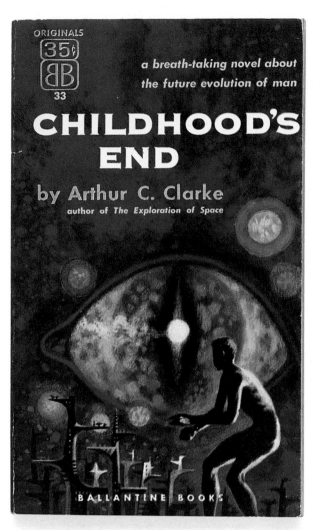

The Space Merchants
FREDERIK POHL AND C.M. KORNBLUTH

Published 1953 **Publisher** Ballantine

Pohl has long eclipsed Kornbluth, who died long ago and much too young, but it is arguable that the latter gave spine and bristle to his urbane partner. In any case, *The Space Merchants* is a classic piece of near-future satire: a demolition job on ad culture, on the selfish rich, and on monopoly capitalism.

Childhood's End
ARTHUR C. CLARKE

Published 1953
Publisher Ballantine

One topic disregarded in much American SF is evolution – evolution, that is, as a *process*. There is no lack of mutated monsters or hypertrophied super-brains "evolved" from "normal" human stock; what is lacking is any sense that evolutionary processes operate in a slow, incremental fashion, without huge visible leaps from "normality" – in Darwinian terms, of course, there is no such thing as normal. This most famous novel of the most dominant English SF writer of the century revives in genre SF a concern with the longer evolutionary perspectives common to both H.G. Wells and Olaf Stapledon. The plot is both dramatic and serene. The aliens who suddenly take over and govern Earth do so not, it turns out, for their own benefit, but as nursemaids while humans evolve to a point where they can migrate into union with a universal Oversoul.

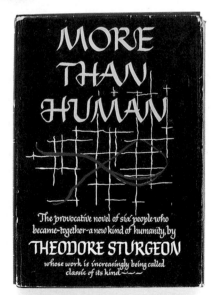

More Than Human
THEODORE STURGEON

Published 1953 **Publisher** Farrar Straus and Young

Sturgeon loved sex, romance, and all the dark (and sometimes soppy) corners of the human psyche; he was a misfit in the prim daylight world of classic SF. But these stunning tales, in which a paranormal gestalt defeats the cruel world, show him in full flight, speaking in his true, loving voice.

Brain Wave
POUL ANDERSON

Published 1954 **Publisher** Ballantine

One of the great wish-fulfilment tales. For aeons, our local galaxy has been wading through a radiation shower that retards electrochemical reactions. When we escape (about now), our brains speed up, we solve our problems, and we go adventuring in the universe.

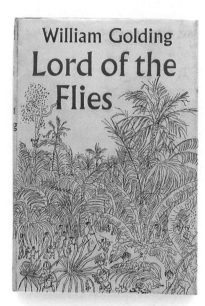

Lord of the Flies
WILLIAM GOLDING

Published 1954 **Publisher** Faber and Faber

In the manuscript version of this famous allegory, the cast of children is escaping a nuclear holocaust when their plane crashes, and they find themselves re-enacting all the old horrors of human behaviour on their Edenic island. The Lord of the Flies, Golding is saying, is the devil inherent in us all.

Double Star
ROBERT A. HEINLEIN

Published 1956 **Publisher** Doubleday

Heinlein in light mood is sometimes a bit of a menace, but in this swift, well-constructed tale he seems fully at ease. An actor who is seconded to impersonate a sick ruler finds that the role becomes permanent, and grows in stature. Any echoes of *The Prisoner of Zenda* are intentional.

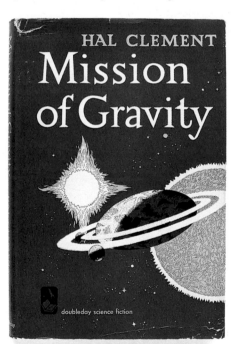

Mission of Gravity
HAL CLEMENT

Published 1954 **Publisher** Doubleday

Stories obedient to the laws of the hard sciences rarely count as literature, but Clement tells his story of Captain Barlennan's salvage mission with almost Vernean intensity. The knee-high captain inhabits a planet whose gravity is 700 times that of Earth, and we feel every ounce of his Extraordinary Voyage.

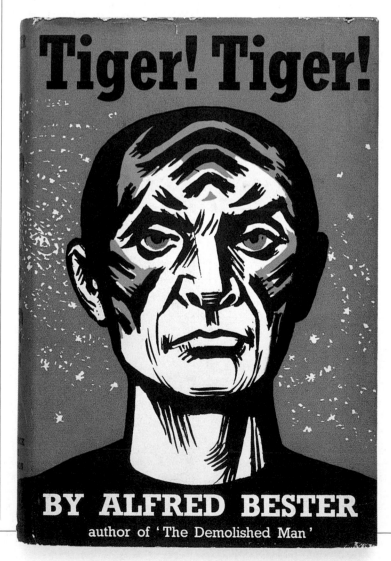

Tiger! Tiger!
ALFRED BESTER

Published 1956
Publisher Sidgwick and Jackson

Slightly revised as *The Stars My Destination*, and better known in America under that title, Bester's second SF novel retells Dumas's classic *The Count of Monte Cristo* for the Space Age. Gully Foyle is abandoned to certain death in a derelict spaceship by men who become rich and powerful through treachery, and escapes by teleporting across the Solar System. He suffers further imprisonment and torture before gaining his revenge; in the end, satiated, he passes on his paranormal gifts to the people of the planets. The raw bones of the story would be rich fare for most, but what makes some critics call *Tiger! Tiger!* the greatest SF novel ever is the richness of the language and the seamy veracity of its portrait of urban life, which points 25 years up ahead into the world of Cyberpunk.

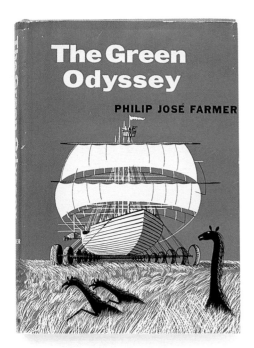

The Green Odyssey
PHILIP JOSÉ FARMER

Published 1957 **Publisher** Ballantine

After Edgar Rice Burroughs had created a medieval sword-and-sorcery Mars fit for heroes to cavort in, the Planetary Romance seemed to have reached its apogee. But here Farmer adds wit, science, irony, and a powerful SF imagination to the mix.

A Case of Conscience
JAMES BLISH

Published 1958 **Publisher** Ballantine

SF and religion do not usually make good literary bedfellows. But Blish (not himself a religious man) has contrived an excruciating case of conscience for his priest to resolve: if we come across an alien species without original sin, can we grant its members the existence of souls? If not, kill them.

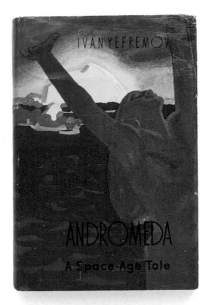

Andromeda
IVAN YEFREMOV

Published 1959 **Publisher** The Foreign Language Publishing House, Moscow

Andromeda was crafted from much the same generic background as, for instance, Doc Smith's Space Operas: technology and science build the highroad to the future, and humans ride that road to the stars. One main difference? The good guys are socialists.

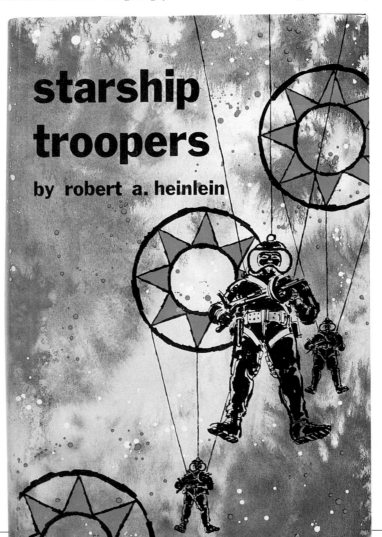

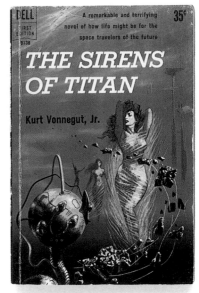

The Sirens of Titan
KURT VONNEGUT JR.

Published 1959 **Publisher** Dell

Kurt Vonnegut is too funny, too savage, and too melancholy to fit comfortably into the world of SF. In *The Sirens of Titan*, our history has been warped from the word go by aliens from Tralfamadore, who need parts to repair a robot spaceship carrying a message. The message is utterly banal.

Starship Troopers
ROBERT A. HEINLEIN

Published 1959 **Publisher** Putnam

The most astonishing fact about this remarkable text is that Heinlein wrote it as a juvenile and assumed that Scribners, who published his children's books, would happily publish it. Scribners balked at thrusting this savage tale into the library market, and Putnam took it as an adult book – which it is. *Starship Troopers* marks the start of its author's late period: Heinlein Unbound. It traces the coming of age of a cadet who learns to be a warrior ready for just the kind of conflict that many Americans were coming to abhor (Vietnam was just around the corner). But Heinlein set his face against liberal values: questioning Honour and Duty was poisonous, and sapped the manhood out of a lad.

CLASSICS OF THE 1960s

AFTER THE COMING OF AGE, after the first flush of success, after the Cold War has become an old nightmare that will not give way to dawn, it is time for SF to flourish, or to die. The previous decade had seen both consolidation and advance, with dozens of novels obedient to a future agenda that had been laid down in the years of the Golden Age. But now the time has come to question the validity of the assumptions that underlay the solid triumphalism of the preceding generations. It is time to query SF's easy dismissal of any doubts about the March of Progress.

A Canticle for Leibowitz
WALTER M. MILLER

Published 1960 **Publisher** Lippincott

Miller does two revolutionary things with this post-catastrophe masterpiece. Civilization is preserved by the Roman Catholic faith rather than by a cadre of scientists, and history is seen not as a linear pathway upwards to betterment, but as a cycle.

Solaris
STANISŁAW LEM

Published 1961 **Publisher** Państwowe Wydawnictwo

A central assumption of Golden Age SF was that aliens could be *understood*. Lem – a Pole whose views of the genre are scathing – thinks otherwise. The sentient ocean in *Solaris* is impenetrable to human probing, physical or metaphysical: it is totally Other.

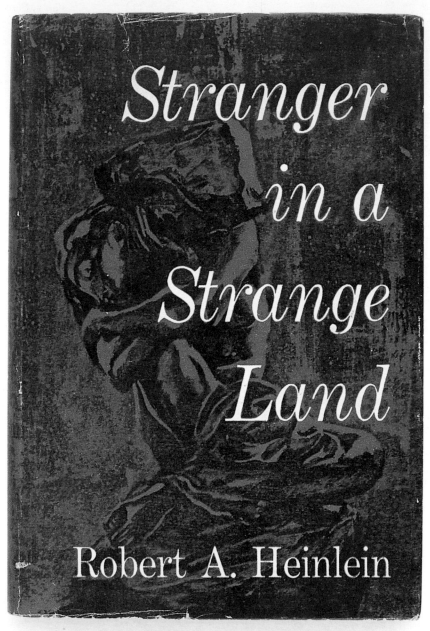

Stranger in a Strange Land
ROBERT A. HEINLEIN

Published 1961 **Publisher** Putnam

Heinlein Unbound, in spades. *Stranger in a Strange Land* was in 1961 by far the longest SF book ever published, and the first SF novel by a genre author to explode into bestsellerdom. It is cantankerous, talky, gripping, prolix, and very subversive indeed. When Valentine Michael Smith, raised by Martians, comes back to Earth as a stranger with paranormal powers, he finds human society incomprehensible. Jubal Harshaw, a Heinlein mouthpiece, sets him straight in radical libertarian terms. Experience everything with your magic touch, he says: cannibalism, free love, the painless killing of "grokking". One of the readers of the book, tellingly, was Charles Manson. Eventually, Valentine "discorporates" in a religious haze.

A Clockwork Orange
ANTHONY BURGESS

Published 1962
Publisher Heinemann

It often happens: the most famous book an author writes is the one book he dislikes most. Burgess was a very contrary, inflammatory personality, and did not take easily to Stanley Kubrick's icily violent film of his work, but it is still unfortunate that he so turned against his best SF – the rest tends to alternate unattractively between dyspepsia and tedium. Here, though, is the real thing: an Orwellian slum, whose inhabitants speak a pronged, barbarous argot, beautifully imagined by Burgess. The ironies of the young thug brainwashed by the state to ensure that the thought of violence will make him sick lash like snakes. The hopeful ending of the British edition was cut from the American edition.

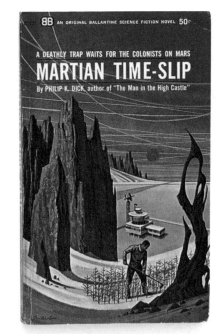

Martian Time-Slip
PHILIP K. DICK

Published 1964 **Publisher** Ballantine

Like William Faulkner, Dick is a teller of apocalyptic tall tales; and like Faulkner he can be astonishingly funny. *Martian Time-Slip* features slums, corrupt politicians, autistic children, desolation, strife, and hopelessness. It is one of the funniest SF novels ever.

The Man in the High Castle
PHILIP K. DICK

Published 1962 **Publisher** Putnam

Alternate History novels in which Hitler wins World War II have, over the years, become very common. One of the earliest – and still by far the best – is the book that first made Dick famous. In the Western States, occupied by Japan, people continue to live their small dry lives, as people must.

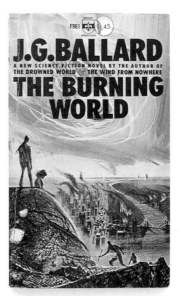

The Burning World
J.G. BALLARD

Published 1964 **Publisher** Berkley

The Burning World, *The Drowned World* (1962), and *The Crystal World* (1966) all follow the same course: a vast, transformative catastrophe embraces the protagonist, who undergoes epiphanies of entropy while migrating into the very heart of a surreal, inhuman, and transcendental new world.

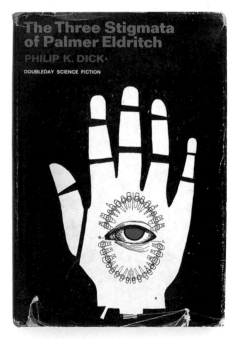

The Three Stigmata of Palmer Eldritch
PHILIP K. DICK

Published 1965 **Publisher** Doubleday

SF had little to say about drugs until the 1960s, failing to anticipate psychedelic trips, or (with the exception of *Brave New World*) the use of drugs to control populations. *Stigmata* is where things change: layers of reality cave in to the drug Chew-Z, and the terrible face of Eldritch rises to rule over the world.

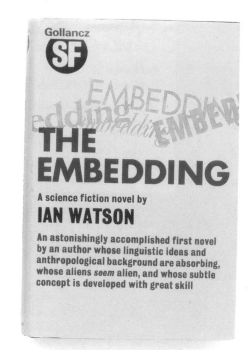

The Embedding
IAN WATSON

Published 1973 **Publisher** Gollancz

Ian Watson was not the first SF writer to speculate interestingly on the nature of language: Jack Vance started the ball rolling. But here the ways in which languages create the human world are brilliantly examined in an incandescently alert first novel.

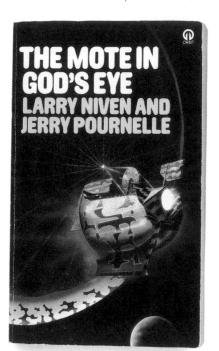

The Mote in God's Eye
LARRY NIVEN AND JERRY POURNELLE

Published 1974 **Publisher** Simon and Schuster

It is easy to cavil at the interstellar human empire depicted, its upper echelons stuffed with royalty and stiff-necked military duffers; but the alien Moties are ingeniously different from anything our own planet could have evolved, and the secret behind their life cycle is convincingly deadly.

The Dispossessed
URSULA K. LE GUIN

Published 1974
Publisher Harper

This may be Ursula Le Guin's most brilliant act of thought in fictional form, although it will never be either her most popular novel or a book that haunts its readers' dreams. It depicts a utopia, or rather a double utopia (as the subtitle puts it, *An Ambiguous Utopia*), set on a planet and its almost-barren moon. An emissary from the smaller, ecologically sound, small-is-beautiful culture on the impoverished moon visits the richer, larger, technology-dominated world. But, as the subtitle implies, the story is not as one-sided as it might sound. Each world suffers from its adherence to an ideal of society that undervalues some intrinsically important human needs. The book as a whole is complex, fruitful, and vibrant with thought.

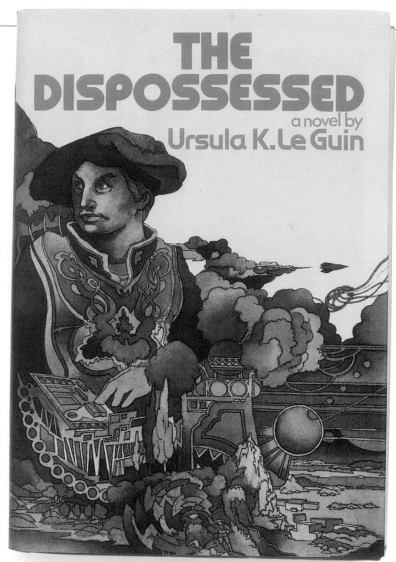

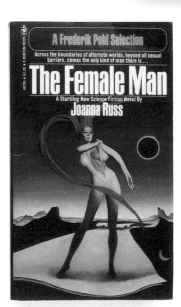

The Female Man
JOANNA RUSS

Published 1975 **Publisher** Bantam

This biting, complex, and beautifully constructed assault on our male-dominated world has become the classic feminist SF novel. Several versions of the same woman, in several Alternate Worlds, live out several versions of what it means to be a woman. One of these exhilarates; others are heartrending.

The Forever War
JOE HALDEMAN

Published 1974 **Publisher** St. Martin's Press

The trauma of Vietnam cut very deeply into the underlying story told by traditional SF: it proved that war could be endless, the "aliens" completely unconquerable, and the victory just a dead dream. Joe Haldeman's endless interstellar war, with its time-dilated soldiers forever lost, is Vietnam.

Man Plus
FREDERIK POHL

Published 1976 **Publisher** Random House

After many years of heavy-duty work as an editor, Pohl regained his central role as a writer with this intensely up-to-date tale. It tells of a human who is engineered into a body capable of living on Mars, and who welcomes the change.

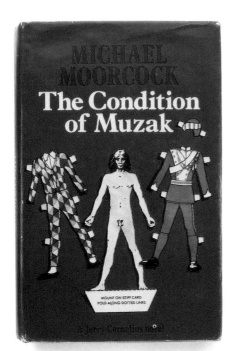

The Condition of Muzak
MICHAEL MOORCOCK

Published 1977 **Publisher** Allison and Busby

Jerry Cornelius embarked on his career, back in the mid-1960s, as a raffish counter-cultural icon: amoral, cruel, an aesthete of the multiverse, and forever free. By the time we get to this novel, in the mid-1970s, Jerry is revealed as a deluded faker, sleeping rough in the drama of the world city.

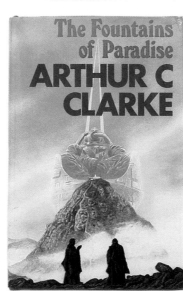

The Fountains of Paradise
ARTHUR C. CLARKE

Published 1979 **Publisher** Gollancz

In his last truly ground-breaking novel – which he announced at the time was to be his last novel altogether – Arthur C. Clarke vividly, and with his usual conviction, envisions a great space elevator: a space station tied to Earth, orbiting the planet like a yo-yo at the end of a string.

Gateway
FREDERIK POHL

Published 1977
Publisher St. Martin's Press

Gateway was an exhilirating start to Pohl's **Heechee** series. Following the success of his *Man Plus*, it both reasserts his dominant position in the field, and moves into new territory: the territory of the contemporary SF universe, a universe in which it is no longer simply assumed that *Homo sapiens* will necessarily take the leading role. Humanity has discovered a network of gateways that provide access to the riches of the galaxy, but the price of this cornucopia is that in accepting it, we must also simultaneously accept an extremely junior role in the universe, which we must be content with, forever.

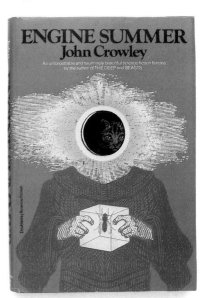

Engine Summer
JOHN CROWLEY

Published 1979 **Publisher** Doubleday

The title of this novel is complicated. It means an Indian summer, that time when an echo of summer returns in the autumn, making us nostalgic; it also means a period of mechanically maintained calm. The story, set in the dusk-time of Earth, tells us how the memory of its summer is preserved.

Helliconia Spring
Published 1982

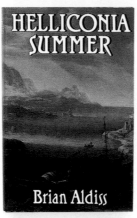

Helliconia Summer
Published 1983

Helliconia Winter
Published 1985

The Helliconia Trilogy
BRIAN ALDISS

Published 1982–85 **Publisher** Cape

It is a sure sign of the Englishness of Aldiss's *Helliconia* series that he begins in Spring and ends in Winter. The trilogy is set on a planet whose orbit around two stars results in a millennium-long Great Year: each Year, whole cultures thrive, and grow sere, and perish.

Neuromancer
WILLIAM GIBSON

Published 1984
Publisher Ace

Gibson never claimed to have invented Cyberpunk, or cyberspace, or even to know much about computers. Myths abound about the creator of *Neuromancer*, but the story goes that he wrote this first novel, the most famous and influential SF novel of the 1980s, on an old portable typewriter. The truth does not matter much, because Gibson did something other than describe viable computer routines. Through his potent imaginative grasp of things yet unseen, and some highly poetic writing, he manages to convey in *Neuromancer* so vivid a sense of the *texture* of virtual reality that, years later, we still seem to be feeling what he told us we would. More than that, he creates a myth for cyberspace: the myth of the mean-streets cowboy who hustles and rustles data from under the noses of the corporations who own us.

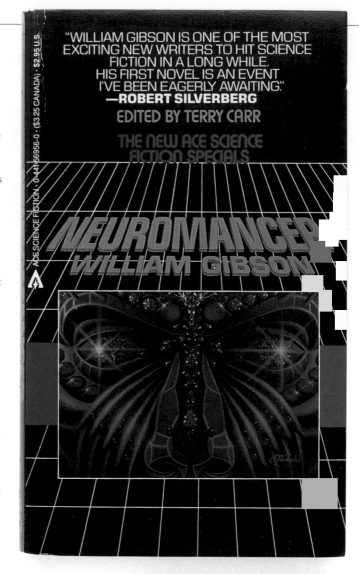

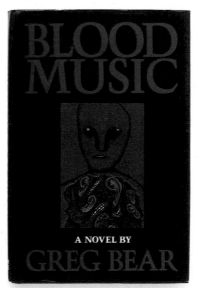

Blood Music
GREG BEAR

Published 1985 **Publisher** Arbor House

Earlier SF tended to ignore genetic engineering; Bear makes amends, in spades. Thinking microorganisms are tweaked into existence by a rogue scientist, and take over the world, transfiguring humanity in the process. By the novel's end, we have become a single organism, and leave Earth behind to go adventuring.

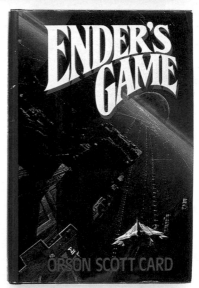

Ender's Game
ORSON SCOTT CARD

Published 1985 **Publisher** Tor

A brilliant story, told so fast we cannot stop to think. Ender is a child genius who is raised in secret by the military. They use his almost paranormal bump of direction in what he thinks are mindgames, but turn out to be real: all unwittingly, Ender oversees the genocide of the enemy.

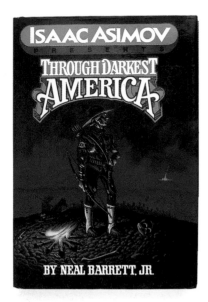

Through Darkest America
NEAL BARRETT JR.

Published 1987 **Publisher** Congdon and Weed

Barrett blew into the limelight with this searing epic of travel and quest through a bleak, dangerous, American landscape. It is Twain's *Huckleberry Finn* rewritten for a time of desperate troubles, when the Mississippi has turned to acid. The time is tomorrow.

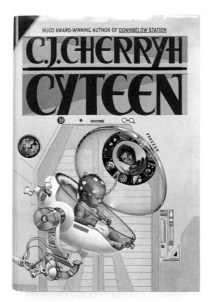

Cyteen
C.J. CHERRYH

Published 1988 **Publisher** Warner Books

At the heart of Cherryh's Alliance-Union, which encompasses some millennia and most of a galaxy, lies *Cyteen*, a vast book set on a vast planet. Cherryh makes sophisticated use of genetic engineering, and brings the ethics and urgency of politics to vivid life.

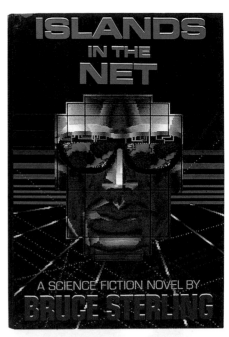

Islands in the Net
BRUCE STERLING

Published 1988 **Publisher** Arbor House

Most Cyberpunk novels star streetwise urchins with fabulous implants but nary a clue about the system whose slums they inhabit. Sterling's characters are, contrariwise, obsessed with the realities of power. They are brainy, and their ambitions are hard-wired.

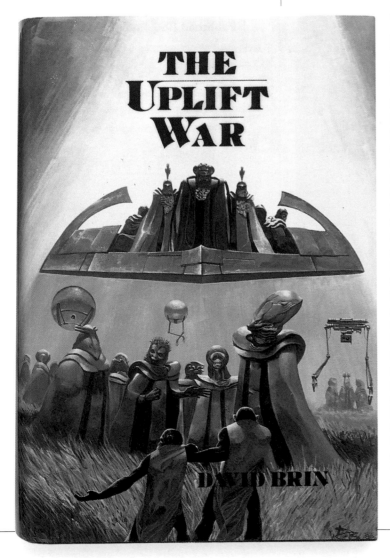

The Uplift War
DAVID BRIN

Published 1987
Publisher Phantasia Press

It is a scenario often found in SF: an ancient race seeds the galaxy with species and withdraws to observe the evolution of its multifarious children. Then, far out on a spiral wing of the galaxy, on the third planet of a minor sun, one of the experimental species suddenly advances at an unprecedented rate, alarming the mentors and stirring up trouble: that race is (surprise!) us. The best stories of this sort yet written are quite possibly the *Uplift War* series – this is the central tale so far. Long ago, the Progenitors set life going. But the human race is causing trouble, because we have sussed out the worm in the apple: the Progenitors' Galactic Library Institute, intended to feed us vital information, is corrupt. The legacy is being twisted out of true. All hell breaks loose.

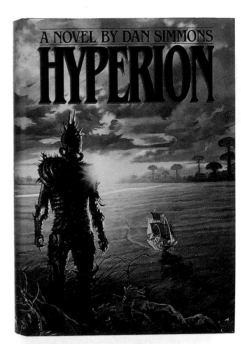

Hyperion
DAN SIMMONS

Published 1989 **Publisher** Doubleday

Splendidly intense, glitteringly complex, *Hyperion* is the ultimate tale about the origins of everything. Simmons tells a multifaceted tale about intelligence, life, the galaxy, alternate universes, and everything else, as Chaucer's *Canterbury Tales*: seven pilgrims plunge like lemmings into a sea of self-revelation.

graphic
WORKS

CHANGING FASHIONS IN art reflect the changing face of Science Fiction, and over the years certain illustrators have defined both their period and the genre. Over the years distinct traditions of graphics have grown up across the world. The American tradition has produced long-running stories and highly individual artists, such as Frank Miller, and is distinct from both the broader style of the European comics and the Japanese manga, such as Akira. In this chapter, the first publication date and original publisher are given for each work. In some cases, the jackets shown may be of subsequent publishers' editions.

ABOVE: MING THE MERCILESS FROM *FLASH GORDON*
LEFT: A DETAIL FROM FRANK MILLER'S *RONIN*

GREAT ILLUSTRATORS

THE JOB OF A COVER ARTIST – that is, an artist who creates the illustrations, almost always in colour, for the covers of magazines and books – is anything but an easy task. The primary task is not to illustrate the book, or provide any exposition of the story, but to attract a purchaser; hence the huge number of "generic" covers, which do no more than tell buyers whether a particular volume is SF, fantasy, horror, a thriller, a bodice-ripper, or a Western. Book jackets rarely illustrate the book. Almost always, they are hooks. But there have been some great hooks.

Frank R. Paul

Dates 1884–1963
Works include covers for *Amazing* magazine

Frank R. Paul's prime decades were the 1920s and 1930s, when he illustrated the covers of *Amazing* magazine, and the climax was his selection as a guest of honour at the first World Science Fiction Convention in 1939. He was not great at drawing people, but his work does show a builder's sense of the technology that his chief editor, Hugo Gernsback, wanted depicted.

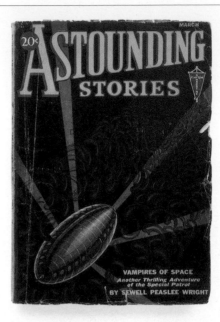

H.W. Wesso

Dates 1894–?
Works include covers for *Astounding* magazine

H.W. Wessolowski was born in Germany, and emigrated to America. He became dominant in SF illustration before the war, being responsible for all of the early *Astounding* covers. He was a perfect Space Opera artist: romantic, flamboyant, and tuned in to the icons and dreams of epic pulp. He fell out of favour when SF "grew up", slipping into obscurity, and the year of his death is not known.

Virgil Finlay

Dates 1914–71 **Works** include interiors for *Weird Tales* and *Startling Stories* magazines

The most astonishing thing about Finlay, given the prudish eye of his editors, was the very considerable erotic charge he managed to impart into almost every one of his thousands of images. He rarely illustrated in colour, or did covers. He was a superb craftsman, and his forte was detailed ink work.

Emsh

Dates 1925–90 **Works** include covers for *Galaxy, Amazing, Fantasy and Science Fiction,* and *Startling Stories* magazines, and for Ace books

Ed Emshwiller was not, perhaps, a particularly fine draftsman; he worked in great haste, and seems to have been happier as a maker of experimental films. But Emsh's numerous covers told their stories, and won awards. They were like good journalism.

Frank Kelly Freas

Dates 1922– **Works** include covers for *Astounding, Fantasy and Science Fiction,* and *If* magazines, and for Ace, Gnome, DAW, and Laser books

Unlike Emsh, Freas has always been immediately identifiable, both because of his technical skill, and because of his iconic imagination. His images – whether humorous or surreal – fix themselves in the mind. When we think of 1950s SF, we see Freas.

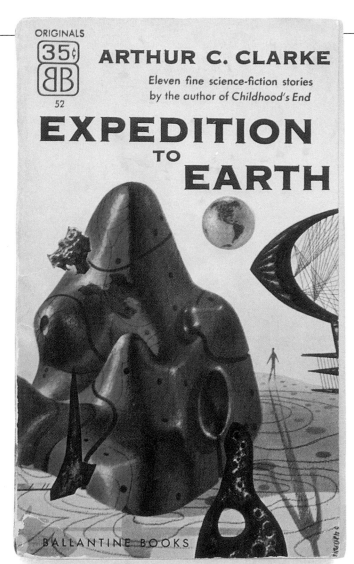

Richard Powers

Dates 1921–
Works include covers for Doubleday, Ballantine, and Berkley books

When we think of 1950s SF, we may see Kelly Freas; but when we dream, we dream Richard Powers. He began creating his style at the beginning of 1950, with the jacket of Isaac Asimov's first book, *Pebble in the Sky*, for Doubleday. By 1953, when he drew the covers for Ballantine's revolutionary list of paperback originals, he was the dominant shaper of the self-contained, abstract imagery of the SF field, and as a pure artist, he has never been supplanted. His modification of Surrealist art, making it evoke the sense of wonder of SF stories plunging over the edge of the known universe, was a stroke of genius. He never illustrated a story directly; his Ballantine covers – looked at end from end – are an autonomous suite of images. They tell the dream of SF, in their own terms, indelibly.

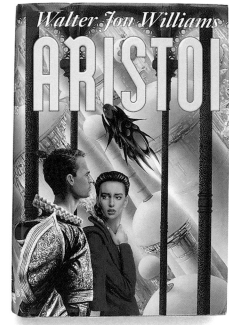

Jim Burns

Dates 1948– **Works** include covers for Sphere, Bantam, and Ace books

Jim Burns followed Chris Foss's example in the use of airbrush, but his covers soon excelled their model through their capacity to convey, simultaneously, generic images of SF and dramatic expositions of the story. It is apparent in his highly detailed work that he was inspired by the story he was illustrating.

Suidmak

Works include covers for *Fiction* magazine, and for Presses Pocket books

Suidmak's work is instantly identifiable from his very smooth, airbrushed technique and his penchant for abstract and rather surreal themes. Although some of his work from the 1970s can tend to look a little slick against today's harder, more gritty styles, he is still a venerated figure in France.

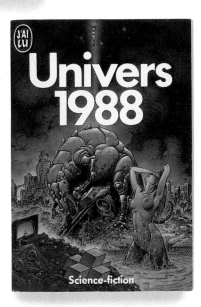

Caza

Works include covers for *Fiction* magazine, and for Flammarion and Kesselring books

Philippe Caza is another illustrator in the very distinct French mould of carefully executed, detailed illustration. His work tends to take SF towards the fantastic, and is frequently far more suggestive – even blatant – than would be acceptable on either American or English covers.

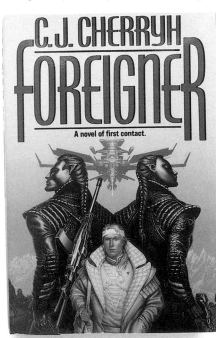

Michael Whelan

Dates 1950– **Works** include covers for DAW, Ace, and Del Rey books

The dominant figure in American SF cover art for nearly 15 years, Michael Whelan has an almost eerie capacity to hook the viewer into the world being depicted, exactly – like Burns – at the point the story bites. He is offered much prestigious work, and his original artworks can fetch a great deal of money.

AMERICAN COMICS

AMERICAN SF WRITERS HAVE gloried in the occasional superman in their books, and Philip Wylie's *Gladiator*, written in 1930, was a direct inspiration to the men who invented Superman, but it was the American comics that took the idea of the superhuman hero and ran with it.

Since Superman's conception, many hundreds of costumed heroes have used their powers to save the world. For years, little SF other than superheroes made it into comics, except for Flash Gordon, a Space Opera hero. Of late, the field has broadened, but the men in tights are still there.

Flash Gordon
ALEX RAYMOND

Dates 1934– **Publisher** King Features Syndicate, DC Comics

In 1934, Raymond introduced Flash as a full-colour Sunday page, and for a decade his flowing, rhapsodic style determined how we saw the world-renowned polo-player save the planet hundreds of times.

Weird Fantasy
VARIOUS ARTISTS

Dates 1950–53 **Publisher** EC Comics

In the early 1950s, EC Comics – which later concentrated on *Mad* magazine – put out *Weird Fantasy*, which took SF and fantasy stories that had already been published, written by established authors such as Ray Bradbury and Richard Matheson, and interpreted them in graphic form.

Action Comics: Superman
JERRY SIEGEL AND JOE SHUSTER

Dates 1938– **Publisher** DC Comics

Here is where Superman begins, if you listen to DC Comics, which bought the concept outright from writer Siegel and artist Shuster, who had in fact been hawking the idea around for years. Certainly, for his millions of fans 1938 marks the beginning of the story of the super-strong lad whose parents send him from the planet Krypton just before it explodes.

Disguised as mild-mannered Clark Kent, he becomes Superman, and saves us all from a thousand terrible fates. He got his own comic, *Superman Comics*, in 1939. Many writers – including Edmond Hamilton, Alfred Bester, and Henry Kuttner – and artists have contributed to the series. In recent years he has been updated and the series remains as popular as ever.

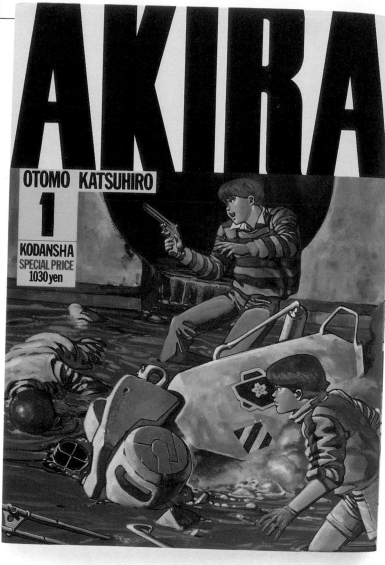

Akira
KATSUHIR...
OTOMO ...

Dates 1982–

Publisher K...

This Cyberpu...
in the frighte...
neon jungle o...
War III Neo-...
with all mann...
chaos – biker...
cults, rioters,...
organizations...
teenagers caug...
mysterious Ak...
military plan t...
people's psych...
(it emerges th...
devastating glo...
inadvertently...
paranormal po...
visionary futur...
scale, with the...
volume Japane...
the *manga* exc...
pages. Highly...
finely detailed...
hugely comple...
gained an adde...
the West wher...
spectacularly t...
an animated fi...

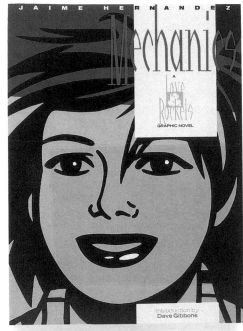

Mechanics
JAIME HERNANDEZ

Date 1981 **Publisher** Fantagraphics

First published in *Love and Rockets* comic, *Mechanics* describes attempts to salvage a spaceship. Drawn in Hernandez's distinctive style, the storyline includes a multimillionaire with horns, and encounters with superheroes, but the SF elements later vanished.

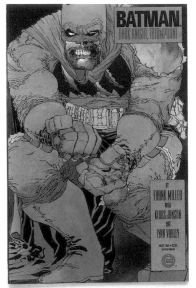

Batman: The Dark Knight Returns
FRANK MILLER

Dates 1985–86 **Publisher** DC Comics

Some critics feel Batman is not an SF character at all, just a man with a severe personality disorder. On the other hand, he occupies a Gotham so dark and dangerous it makes Metropolis look suburban. Miller gave the long-lived character a realistic grittiness.

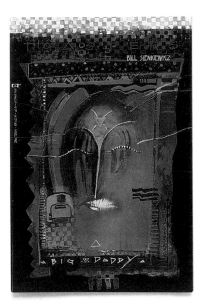

Stray Toasters
BILL SIENKIEWICZ

Date 1988 **Publisher** Marvel Comics

After a quarter of a century during which they dominated the superhero field, by 1988 Marvel Comics were being forced to innovate. *Stray Toasters* was Sienkiewicz to the extreme: a story influenced by David Lynch's films, and lurid, rapid artwork.

Lum – Urusei Yatsura
RUMIKO TAKAHASHI

Dates 1978–86 **Publisher** Shogakukan

One of Japan's best-loved artists, Takahashi found her first success with this zany social satire revolving around a love-struck, bikini-clad space girl's pursuit of a lecherous, hopelessly beleaguered high-school student. The bizarre comedic fantasy has as many characters as a soap opera, and is just as addictive.

Appleseed
MASAMUNE SHIROW

Dates 1985– **Publisher** Seish...

Shirow's 22nd-century utopian city of Ol...
artifical humanoids, is wonderfully realize...
"perfect" society disguising a sinister aim...
man's post-war development. Policewom...
and her cyborg sidekick battle with terror...
to destroy the central computer and resto...

Ronin
FRANK MILLER

Dates 1983–84 **Publisher** DC Comics

Frank Miller creates in this six-part graphic novel a decaying near-future American society, and an epic battle between an ancient demon and an austere warrior. Miller's unmistakable, cinematic style was next seen in *Batman: The Dark Knight Returns*, another apocalyptic drama from DC Comics.

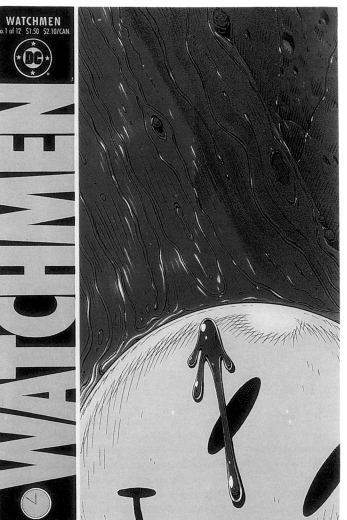

Watchmen
ALAN MOORE AND
DAVID GIBBONS

Dates 1986–87
Publisher DC Comics

For those readers who do not normally stretch to comics, this 12-part graphic novel is revelatory. It is a full-length, sustained, multi-level novel, and is simultaneously visual and literary. It incorporates an Alternate History vision of the United States, as a land in which costumed heroes do actually exist, and maintain law and order on a vigilante basis. *Watchmen* offers a satirical analysis of the human cost of being, or of needing, a superhero, and a portrait of a world in which one might exist. Alan Moore's vision is tough-minded and ironic.

JAPANESE COMICS

IN JAPAN TODAY, COMICS ARE as ubiquitous as television, with millions sold every week. Known as *manga* (literally, "irresponsible pictures"), they follow a long tradition of graphic storytelling, and are an established part of everyday life – covering virtually any subject imaginable, from sport

Tetsuwan Atomu
OSAMU TEZUKA

Dates 1952–68 **Publisher** Kodansha

The work of artist Osamu Tezuka was to prove as influential in Japan as that of Walt Disney in the United States. Tezuka lent new cinematic inspiration to his designs, revolutionizing the look of *manga*. "Mighty Atom" – better known in the West as Astroboy – relates the adventures of an atomic-powered robot boy who, with superhuman strength, a

computer mind, and rocket jets in
unending cast of villains in the yea
poignant overtones of *Pinocchio* as,
mad scientists, monsters, and super
yearns to be a "real" boy. The popu
an entire sub-genre of robot chara
made television history as Japan's f

genre CINEMA

SCIENCE FICTION FILMS WERE among the first films made: the early silents include fantastic trips to the Moon, Mars, and Jupiter, as well as screen interpretations of literary classics such as Frankenstein and Aelita. Although there have been long, dark stretches in which SF films were horror films in masquerade, the vastly improved special effects of recent decades seem to have assured SF of a place in the forefront of the film industry. This chapter gives chronological listings of SF films from the turn of the century to the present day, and examines the thematic trends that have defined each decade.

ABOVE: MÉLIÈS'S FAMOUS MOON
LEFT: STILL FROM THE FILM *UNIVERSAL SOLDIER*

VISUAL TRICKERY

IT SHOULD NOT BE forgotten that up to the moment when the first moving picture began to flicker on screens in front of awed (even frightened) audiences, cinema itself was SF. The idea of connecting a sequence of still photographs in such a manner that the eye was fooled into thinking it was observing a continuous motion was just as outlandish, and just as foolish – or just as wise – as any of those

The Mechanical Butcher
This Lumière film introduced an idea that was copied for years: feed a pig into a machine and take rashers and sausages out.

yet-unfamiliar inventions that the early film-makers mocked. But in this mockery, they began as they meant to continue. Even in the good decades – never mind the horrible periods like the 1940s – film-makers have been quite astonishingly conservative about anything that represents the new. For them, SF ideas represent danger, foreignness, radicalism. From the first days of the cinema, that which is different is almost invariably destroyed. Cute robots may survive the tender mercies of Hollywood, but not many scientists do – nor aliens, nor sassy women, nor monsters from the deep.

Early starter
The split-screen technique came into use in 1901, and made its début in an SF film, A la conquête de l'air (The Flying Machine). *First the bicycle was filmed with the lower half of the lens covered, and then Paris with the top half of the lens covered.*

The sky is no limit

For quite a few years, SF in the cinema stayed fun. The rising owners of the cinema industry might have been unwilling to finance films in which the future looked liveable, but none of this mattered hugely in the early days, when SF and cinema were one thing: a trick. It was all still a game. Film-makers revelled in their medium's capacity to fool the eye with double exposures, deceptive shooting angles, and anything else they could think of, and the SF themes of the day – mechanization of work, flight, rockets, robots – were also tricks, visual puns. You might think you were watching a cow, but – blink! – not a cow at all, but a cow-machine. There is nothing threatening in this, or not yet.

A film like *A Visit to the Spiritualist*, from 1899, makes it clear that magic and technology, within the context of the magical new medium, were really one thing.

Believable bottles
The alchemical Red Devil – usually attributed to Méliès – shrank people with a level of credibility that would shame many later film-makers.

Out of sight, men lifted the giant's hands on fine wires

Setting the stage
Much of Méliès's magic relied on elaborate sets, as in a theatre or music hall. By the time À la conquête du Pôle was made, this kind of approach was going out of favour, replaced by film trickery and editing. This was also among the last films made with this kind of story: incredible inventions, predictions of war, and the future were taking over.

The screen scene
While Méliès may have been old-fashioned in his approach, he undoubtedly achieved impressive results. Although far from realistic, this set has a fantastic atmosphere that might not have been achieved by slicker methods.

Flat panels could be used to hide people or machines

Winches and ropes were used to engineer movements in the giant's body and head

Stagehands off to the side of the set provided lateral movement

The slope gave an illusion of perspective from a low camera angle that kept tricks hidden

The marriage of the two in a short film, during the course of which a spiritualist hoodwinks a hick, was joyful in the extreme. Yesterday, it might have been a cheap conjuror's trick; today, it is true magic. A new century is dawning. Anything is possible, the new medium says, so let us tinker with the world.

The changing scene
This innocence did not survive indefinitely, and the audiences soon became bored with the simple sleight-of-hand that had satisfied them in the first days. From Georges Méliès's *La lune à un mètre* (*An Astronomer's Dream*) – a three-minute tale in which the Man in the Moon visits a dreaming astronomer – to his *Le voyage dans la lune* (*A Trip to the Moon*) may be only a few years by the calendar, but a whole new century has been

born. Almost 100 years later, cinema still entrances, and it still seems to thrust its way into the future. Look! it seems to say, No hands!

But of course the hands soon showed. Audiences soon tired of Méliès's joyful trickeries; although his *À la conquête du Pôle* (*The Conquest of the Pole*) features some elaborate

"real-life" sets that prefigure later epics, it is still nothing much more than a catalogue of wonders. What became necessary, for the sadder new world, was some kind of story, and tales like Mary Shelley's *Frankenstein* or Stevenson's *Strange Case of Dr. Jekyll and Mr. Hyde* provided exactly what cinema needed: exciting plots, conveniently twistable to confirm the industry's new owners' hatred of the new, and lots of chances to trick the eye with makeup. Only in the 1920s, with films like *Aelita* or Fritz Lang's great *Metropolis*, could the future be looked at, straight and full-frontal, once again.

All done with mirrors
Metropolis used clever camerawork, montage, set pieces, and the techniques of special-effects genius Eugene Schufftan, which made actors appear in miniature sets by means of mirrors.

INVENTORS AND ADVENTURERS

THE 1930S WERE A PATCHWORK decade for SF in the cinema. Sound brought its excitements; but it locked film-makers into constricted studios. Great novels were made into films; but were sequelized into triviality. War loomed, and some SF films brooded on the holocaust; but in general, the worse

The men who would be king

Where did they come from, these mad scientists? Who were their parents, where did they go to school, who funded their insane explorations into forbidden realms? These questions – which any reasonably intelligent child of ten might well have posed – are never answered in the numerous 1930s films that feature wild-eyed doctors who want to rule the world.

But they are good questions. In the United States, where most SF films were being made, scientists had a generally good press, although there was always an undercurrent of anti-intellectualism, and scientists had to be careful not to be laughed at as eggheads.

Meddling with nature
Hollywood was just waiting for Jekyll and Hyde. The transformation was the perfect combination of drama and horror, with a moral thrown in for good measure.

things looked up front, the more films looked backwards to the previous century, where most SF film plots originated. Over and above the conservatism of Hollywood's owners, the secret behind this failure of imagination may be simple: special effects, and makeup. SF had turned into gimmicks.

All the same, in the American popular consciousness, the perfect model of a major modern scientist was a figure like Thomas Alva Edison, the inventor of everyday miracles for everyone. Inventions had made America great. In the SF literature of the 1920s and 1930s, this is writ large. Gernsback had founded *Amazing* magazine in 1926 partly in order to advertise science and technology. Time and again, in dozens of magazines, cocky inventor-heroes in Edison's image conquered the cosmos, and the "edisonades" that described their exploits – like the **Skylark of Space** stories by Doc Smith – were among the most popular in the growing genre.

Looking to the future
In Things to Come, an age of chaos is followed by an age of sterile order. At the culmination of the film, a young man and woman are sent out into space to begin anew.

The city to come
Although less remembered than Metropolis, the sparkling white technological city of Wells's vision was effortlessly absorbed into the genre, and for a long time this was the shape of things to come.

Science fiction serials

The other feature of the 1930s was the serial, a ghetto into which SF was cast in the mid-1930s. Although they are barely watchable now, these serials are closer to the SF literature of the decade than their full-length contemporaries – perhaps because they were aimed at a younger audience. They concentrated on fast-moving tales of derring-do on new frontiers, and the villains were not just mad scientists, but also evil dictators and the denizens of lost civilizations.

They were usually accompanied by a range of gizmos to help them on their road to Galactic power: special-effects departments embarked on their decades-long love affair with the sparks of Van de Graaf generators, and death rays, disintegrating gas, artificial thunderbolts, rejuvenating drugs, invisibility, and robots were all put to bad use in attempts to either dominate or destroy Earth. All of them were, of course, foiled by heroes who had valour, ingenuity, and above all, right on their side.

Comic-book hero
Space Opera flamboyance hit the screen in 1936 in the blue-eyed-blonde personas of Flash Gordon and Dale Arden. They faced death – and worse – every week to save the Earth.

Monstrous creation
At first scripted with a romance that agreed with the original, Frankenstein was revised to appear more horrifying. The abandonment of Shelley's concerns set the pattern for Frankenstein films for several decades.

Lifting the veil

So why did SF films become a form of horror in the 1930s? Why were almost all discoveries blasphemous, why did all explorations discover monsters, and all speculations prove the speculator to be mad?

There are some practical answers, of course. Special effects are most effective when they tear the veil off the face of normality and uncover a nightmare – like Frankenstein, Hyde, Orlac, or the Golem. If cheap films have to be made on an assembly-line basis, there is every financial reason in the world to use and reuse the effects of the horrible.

More important, perhaps, were the memories of World War I, an apocalypse that some film-makers tried to purge through images of horror; but what interests us now are the unusual films, like *Things to Come*, which looked beyond the next abyss, instead of wallowing in the abyss of the past.

A DECADE OF STAGNATION

IT SOUNDS LIKE FUN. The 1940s had the lot: mad scientists, invisible men, invisible women, son of the Invisible Man, Frankensteins and Frankenstein monsters, Abbott and Costello, cousin of Frankenstein's niece, the Wolf Man, the Wolf Man's barber, Dr. Jekyll and Mr. Hyde, Flash Gordon and Buck Rogers, Batman, Superman, and Captain Marvel. Boris Karloff, Bela Lugosi, Lon Chaney Jr., and all the gang were there: it certainly *sounds* like fun. For Americans of a certain age with good memories, it sounds like Saturday mornings at the movie theatre. And it smells like popcorn. But what does any of it have to do with SF? Anything at all? The answer is a guarded yes.

Where is SF when you need it?

In the 1920s we saw how exciting SF could be for the adventurous intellectuals who plunged into film-making after the traumas of World War I. In the 1930s, we saw how much could be accomplished, on small budgets, by directors with passion and skill. And now we come to the 1940s, and it is as though all the advances that had been made have been abandoned, and all the lessons forgotten. There is almost no good SF at all in the films of this decade; indeed there is almost no SF of any sort. Beneath the extremely thin studio trappings that are supposed to show the scientists at work – amounting to little more than bunsen burners and soiled white dressing gowns – the so-called SF stories of the decade expose themselves as nothing but horror. When horror pretends to be SF, it betrays the world.

During the 1940s, the world finally became one vast theatre of action. World War II was the first genuine world-wide conflict: it was the first war whose dramatic turns were known to everyone across the globe almost immediately, because of the huge advances we had made in communications technology, and it was the first war the outcome of which would change everybody's lives. There were no civilians left in World War II, if by civilians one means non-combatants who would not be treated as a legitimate target for bombs, fire-storm raids, blitzkriegs, and nuclear warfare. So the world of the 1940s was a profoundly dramatic world, a changing world, and a world that we all had to understand, if we were not to run the risk of making fatal errors out of ignorance. We had to know exactly what was happening right now, and we had to have an idea of what might conceivably happen next.

The Perfect Woman
Plenty of silly comedies had loosely SF ideas, like this tale of a woman who impersonates a female robot. It was not a scriptwriters' decade.

But horror, as a dramatic genre, is not interested in investigating the unknown. The unknown – in any horror tale or film – is that which is forbidden; the unknown is that which, when investigated, punishes the impious investigator with a variety of fates worse than death. In the so-called SF films of the 1940s, while all the world outside participated in the great drama that would determine all our days, nothing happened that was not a slap in the face to science, to the men and women who were fighting, studying, and experimenting, test-driving the new land-weapons and test-flying the new planes.

The legacy

At a time when the world most needed images of the power of thought and the usefulness of action, we were not helped by the "SF" film industry turning its back on reality and spewing forth timid escapism. Moreover – less important perhaps, but significant for those interested in the genre – it may be the case that the bad press SF has suffered for decades now derives, at least in part, from the awfulness of the purported SF cinema that appeared during these years.

There are ironies here. It was just when SF films became most atrocious that written American SF was genuinely beginning to show signs of coming into its own as a genre.

House party
The awful House of Frankenstein *had the monster, the Wolf Man, and Dracula: the results verge on the surreal.*

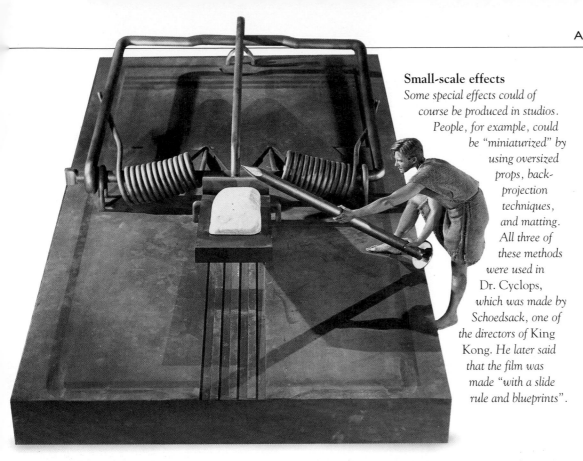

Small-scale effects
*Some special effects could of
course be produced in studios.
People, for example, could
be "miniaturized" by
using oversized
props, back-
projection
techniques,
and matting.
All three of
these methods
were used in
Dr. Cyclops,
which was made by
Schoedsack, one of
the directors of King
Kong. He later said
that the film was
made "with a slide
rule and blueprints".*

Not only were these stories old (therefore safe), almost every one was also a Dreadful Warning: "there are things we are not intended to know" was the message of almost every single film produced during the time when we most desperately needed to know everything possible about what might be happening to civilization. Even half a century later, it seems a melancholy indictment of an industry and a genre.

There are, of course, some extenuating circumstances. SF of any sophistication was extremely difficult to film in studio conditions (the outdoor freedom that was enjoyed by the silent film-makers had disappeared with the development of sound recording, which was to remain cumbersome for decades), and special effects were more or less restricted to ghoulish makeup and variations in size (giant apes, tiny men). Truly sophisticated special effects did not become a matter of course for another 20 years. But still: these are years of failure.

These are the years when writers like Asimov and Heinlein began to publish their best work, when John W. Campbell Jr.'s *Astounding* magazine created a Golden Age of SF. Campbell himself insisted upon plausible speculation, real arguments about the rapidly transforming world, and believable people earning a better future.

Not a hint of this, of course, penetrated Hollywood studios, whose owners had a distaste for anything that might upset any apple cart.

The age of the sequel
Intellectual foreigners, fresh from the killing fields of Europe, were shunned. Genuine 1940s SF literature was ignored. It was much safer to produce sequels to stories already old before they reached the screen: spin-offs or pallid remakes of *Frankenstein*, *The Invisible Man*, *Dr. Jekyll and Mr. Hyde*, et al., dominated the cinema screen.

Ceaseless sequels
Although he died in 1933, the Invisible Man returned, was revenged, and was joined by an invisible woman, boy, and agent. None of them were as invisible as one might wish.

FILMS OF THE 1950S

THIS DECADE BECAME FAMOUS in retrospect for the paranoia of its best-known films. But the 1950s really had everything: monsters, wise robots (or children), evil children (and robots), radioactive bugs, aliens from dying planets, mad scientists, feeble, frightened females, shapechangers, vampires, werewolves, and the end of the world.

★★★ OUTSTANDING ★★ RECOMMENDED ★ OF INTEREST

◻ Director   ◻ Screenplay   ◻ Time   ◻ Colour   ◻ Black and White

1 9 5 0

Rocketship XM
USA Lippert
★

◻ Kurt Neuman ◻ Neuman
◻ 78 mins ◻

This film slipped onto America's screens just before Destination Moon, and its cast slipped right past its destination, Moon. They land on Mars instead, and find relics of an ancient civilization, long since blown up by an atom bomb. Everybody dies, sooner or later.

Destination Moon
USA George Pal Production/Eagle-Lion
★★

◻ Irving Pichel ◻ Robert A. Heinlein, based on his own book *Rocket Ship Galileo* (1947)
◻ 92 mins ◻

For the first time in American film history, there was a film that tried to show what rockets would actually look like, and what spaceflight would actually accomplish. Robert A. Heinlein, who conveyed something of the dreams of SF readers for generations, was involved. The film itself was bland, but the ship fuelled the dreams of the children who would one day run NASA.

WHEN WORLDS COLLIDE

1 9 5 1

Five
USA Columbia
★

◻ Arch Oboler ◻ Oboler
◻ 93 mins cut to 89 mins ◻

Five guys and gals survive the Bomb, and reduce each other to an Adam-and-Eve couple looking towards the future. A pious parable of how positive thinking helps you live through the holocaust.

The Man from Planet X
USA United Artists
★

◻ Edgar G. Ulmer ◻ Aubrey Wisberg, Jack Pollexfen
◻ 70 mins ◻

Expressionist, shadowy, abrupt, and very black. The visiting alien is a decent sort, but the humans are not.

When Worlds Collide
USA Paramount
★

◻ Rudolph Mate ◻ Sydney Boehm, based on *When Worlds Collide* (1933), Philip Wylie and Edwin Balmer ◻ 83 mins ◻

The buildup to the crash of planets is slow and impressive; the escaping spaceship is cardboard; and the new planet is Eden.

THE DAY THE EARTH STOOD STILL

The Day the Earth Stood Still
USA 20th Century-Fox
★★★

◻ Robert Wise ◻ Edmund H. North, based on "Farewell to the Master" (1940), Harry Bates
◻ 92 mins ◻

Nobody who saw it in 1951 ever forgot it, and it is still a film one returns to with nostalgia and fright. A flying saucer lands in Washington DC, and a great robot and a human being emerge. The human tells Earth governments to behave, or they will be blown away. The human is duly murdered by us. The robot – who is, shockingly, the real boss – gives him rebirth. His disappointment in humankind is infectious.

The Thing
(The Thing from Another World)
USA Winchester Pictures/RKO
★

◻ Howard Hawks, uncredited, Christian Nyby, credited
◻ Charles Lederer, based on "Who Goes There?", John W. Campbell as Don A. Stuart
◻ 86 mins ◻

The secret behind this film is Howard Hawks (uncredited). The interaction of professionals, the flow of story, the grave smoothness: all are Hawks. The Thing itself is silly.

1 9 5 2

Red Planet Mars
USA Melaby Pictures/United Artists
★

◻ Harry Horner ◻ John L. Balderston, Anthony Veiller, based on Balderston's play *Red Planet* ◻ 87 mins ◻

A gross allegory: at a sign from Mars that Better Things are available, the Soviet government topples. The US president takes credit.

Four-sided Triangle
UK Hammer
★

◻ Terence Fisher ◻ Paul Tabori, Fisher, based on *The Four Sided Triangle* (1949), William Temple ◻ 81 mins cut to 71 mins ◻

Scientist plays dirty pool, creating a woman modelled on a woman who loves another man. The new model does, too. Oops.

1 9 5 3

It Came from Outer Space
USA Universal
★

◻ Jack Arnold ◻ Harry Essex, based on a screen treatment by Ray Bradbury ◻ 80 mins ◻ 3-D

Shapechanging aliens invade Earth, terrorize decent folk and are resisted (a common idea). But this time they only want to fix their ship. They manage to do so, restore everyone to their original shape, and leave. There is, thanks to Bradbury, some decent prose poetry.

Project Moonbase
USA Galaxy Pictures/Lippert
★

◻ Richard Talmadge ◻ Robert A. Heinlein ◻ 51 mins ◻

Heinlein's last attempt to script a film (SF writers rarely succeeded) has a silly story, silly spaceship, silly Moon, silly marriage in space. But it also has a few good moments, and the American president is a woman.

Donovan's Brain
USA Dowling Productions/United Artists
★★★

◻ Felix Feist ◻ Feist, based on *Donovan's Brain* (1943), Curt Siodmak ◻ 83 mins ◻

The second try at making a film of Siodmak's inexplicably attractive novel. Bottled brain of millionaire keeps on tax-dodging. Sensational.

The Twonky
USA Arch Oboler Productions/United Artists
★

◻ Arch Oboler ◻ Oboler, based on "The Twonky" (1942), Henry Kuttner as Lewis Padgett
◻ 72 mins ◻

Lame diatribe against TV, based on Kuttner's innocent tale. Twonky is a TV-shaped alien, and direly affects hero until turned off.

The War of the Worlds
USA Paramount
★★★

◻ Byron Haskin ◻ Barré Lydon, based on *The War of the Worlds* (1898), H.G. Wells ◻ 85 mins ◻

Being an American film, the hero has to protect a silly female, but other than that, this is a remarkably effective take on Wells's remarkably effective novel, cleverly updated to 1950s California, with flying saucers substituted for marching tripods. The invasion is thoroughly frightening, and the scenes of shattered cities are properly bleak; the death of the Martians at the end is a relief.

1 9 5 4

Gojira
(Godzilla/Godzilla, King of the Monsters)
Japan Toho/Embassy
★

◻ Inoshiro Honda ◻ Takeo Murato, Honda, based on a story by Shigeru Kamaya ◻ 98 mins cut to 81 mins in US ◻

While not a great film, it claws at dreams – certainly Japanese dreams. The monster Gojira, woken by A-bombs, stomps Tokyo. There were 15 sequels, all alike.

20,000 Leagues under the Sea
USA Walt Disney
★★

◻ Richard Fleischer ◻ Earl Felton, based on *Vingt mille lieues sous les mers* (1870), Jules Verne ◻ 127 mins ◻

It has a great cast, great action, huge squid, and catchy songs. But Verne was left on the cutting-room floor.

Them!
USA Warner
★★

◻ Gorden Douglas ◻ Ted Sherdemann ◻ 93 mins ◻

Radiation causes giant ants to breed in the New Mexico desert. Fabulous scenery adds to the air of menace.

1955

This Island Earth
USA Universal
★★★
🎬 Joseph Newman 📝 Franklin Coen and Edward G. O'Callahan, based on *This Island Earth* (1952), Raymond F. Jones ⏱ 86 mins 🎞
As usual, the aliens on Earth are emissaries from a planet at the point of death, but this film stands out from the herd in almost every way possible: complexity of story; pathos of aliens; usefulness of human science (rather than terror at its implications); quality of special effects; and a great title.

THIS ISLAND EARTH

Kiss Me Deadly
USA Parklane
★★
🎬 Aldrich 📝 A.I. Bezzerides, based on *Kiss Me Deadly* (1952), Mickey Spillane ⏱ 105 mins 🎞
It was not really supposed to be SF at all, and for most of the action the box with unknown contents seems no more than a McGuffin for Mike Hammer to pound heads in search of. When finally opened, however, it is an A-bomb.

The Quatermass Experiment
(The Creeping Unknown)
UK Hammer
★★
🎬 Val Guest 📝 Richard Landau, Guest, based on BBC television series *The Quatermass Experiment* (1953), Nigel Kneale ⏱ 82 mins cut to 78 mins 🎞
Not the greatest film in the world, but still hugely loved. Professor Quatermass is faced with an astronaut who is becoming a fungus, which is eating London. He stares it down in Westminster Abbey, and jolts it to death with electricity.

1956

1984
UK Holiday Film Productions
🎬 Michael Anderson 📝 William Templeton, Ralph Bettinson, based on *Nineteen Eighty-Four* (1949), George Orwell ⏱ 91 mins 🎞
There is no point in thinking that Orwell's nightmare novel does not quite mean what it says: it means every word. This film fatally smudges the anti-tyranny message, filling the foreground with love interest. Redgrave is a good villain.

Timeslip
(The Atomic Man)
UK Merton Park/Allied Artists
★
🎬 Ken Hughes 📝 Charles Eric Maine ⏱ 93 mins cut to 76 mins 🎞
A lesson in how hard it is to convey time paradoxes in film: here, the hero lives a few seconds in advance, but who can tell?

Forbidden Planet
USA MGM
★★★
🎬 Fred McLeod Wilcox 📝 Cyril Hume, based on a story by Irving Block, Allen Adler ⏱ 98 mins 🎞
Based on Shakespeare's Tempest, this is one of the great SF films: a rich, strange, brave, new world; Robbie the Robot; huge vistas; delights, and high talk are all there.

FORBIDDEN PLANET

Invasion of the Body Snatchers
USA Allied Artists
★★★
🎬 Don Siegel 📝 Daniel Mainwaring, Sam Peckinpah, (uncredited), based on *The Body Snatchers* (1955), Jack Finney ⏱ 80 mins 🎞
Despite the brilliance of the 1979 remake, this original has a black-and-white glow that defies imitation. The horror of the transformation – from human via cocoon into drone – is conveyed beautifully. Paranoia is justified, there are fates worse than death, America is invaded. The ending backs away, but not far.

1957

The Incredible Shrinking Man
USA Universal
★★
🎬 Jack Arnold 📝 Richard Matheson, based on his own *The Shrinking Man* (1956) ⏱ 81 mins 🎞
A profound metaphor of paranoia and loss: a man is irradiated, begins to shrink, and loses height, wife, manhood, home, job, meaning, country and, in the end, his life.

Chikyu Boiegun
(The Mysterians/Earth Defense Force)
Japan Toho/MGM
★
🎬 Inishiro Honda 📝 Takeshi Kimura, based on a story by Jojiro Okami ⏱ 89 mins 🎞
A film deeply haunting for 1950s Japan: aliens land (like Americans), and try to miscegenate with Japanese women (who resist). Underneath the story resentment glows, along with hints that tomorrow will be different.

Quatermass II
(Enemy from Space)
UK Hammer/UnitedArtists
★★
🎬 Val Guest 📝 Nigel Kneale, Guest, based on Kneale's BBC television serial *Quatermass II* ⏱ 85 mins 🎞
The best of the Quatermass films. This time he cleanses the temple of the British establishment, which has been infested by aliens.

The Amazing Colossal Man
USA Malibu/AIP
★
🎬 Bert I. Gordon 📝 Mark Hanna, Gordon, from a story by Gordon ⏱ 81 mins 🎞
The inverse of Shrinking Man, this is not a match. Radioactive man gets big and bad, kills, and is killed.

JOURNEY TO THE CENTRE OF THE EARTH

1958

I Married a Monster from Outer Space
USA Paramount
★
🎬 Gene Fowler Jr. 📝 Louis Vittes, from a story by Fowler and Vittes ⏱ 78 mins 🎞
Another dying planet and more shapechanging aliens, one of whom (played by novelist Thomas Tryon) marries a gal to mother its young, and confesses his alienness to her. She forms a vigilante posse, and drives the aliens out of America.

The Fly
USA 20th Century-Fox
★★
🎬 Kurt Neumann 📝 James Clavell, based on "The Fly" (1957), George Langelaan ⏱ 94 mins 🎞
What is astonishing is that such a stupid idea should be so effective: a scientist experimenting on himself gets materially confused with a fly. The resulting fly with a human head haunts us still.

The Space Children
USA Paramount
★
🎬 Jack Arnold 📝 Bernard C. Schoenfeld, from a story by Tom Filer ⏱ 69 mins 🎞
A real oddity for the 1950s, because its message is pacifist. An alien in space sabotages an H-bomb-bearing rocket before it reaches orbit.

It! The Terror from Beyond Space
USA Vogue/United Artists
★
🎬 Edward L. Cahn 📝 Jerome Bixby ⏱ 69 mins 🎞
This is an old SF plot, which van Vogt did best: the invincible alien that gets aboard a spaceship and eats the entire crew, one by one. In this film, however – unlike Alien – the actual alien is laughable.

1959

Journey to the Center of the Earth
USA 20th Century-Fox
★
🎬 Henry Levin 📝 Walter Reisch, Charles Brackett, based on *Voyage au centre da la terre* (1864), Jules Verne ⏱ 132 mins 🎞
It was not a good time for Verne: his sense of wonder tended to dissipate in the glare of Hollywood's juvenile leads and bad special effects. Here, the Earth's core is a bore.

On the Beach
USA Lomitas Productions/ United Artists
★
🎬 Stanley Kramer 📝 John Paxton, based on *On the Beach* (1957), Nevil Shute ⏱ 134 mins 🎞
Down under, it looks for a little time as if the Australians will survive the effects of the nuclear war that has wiped out the rest of us. But the winds bring death southwards, and a last-ditch rescue expedition to California ends in disillusion. The film is slacker than Shute's grim, workmanlike novel.

The World, The Flesh, and the Devil
USA Sol Siegel-Harbel/MGM
★★
🎬 Ranald MacDougall 📝 MacDougall, based on *The Purple Cloud* (1901), M.P. Shiel ⏱ 95 mins 🎞
One must wonder whether they knew what they were unleashing on an unsuspecting, philistine, racist West. Three people – a black man, a white man, and a white woman – are the only survivors of the holocaust. The black man and the woman get together; the white man resists, until the last moment, when all three join together in a mixed-race ménage a trois. Shocking.

OUTER SPACE, INNER FEAR

THE DECADE BEGAN WITH *Destination Moon* and ended with *On the Beach*, two extremely sober SF films. The first of them attempts to persuade us that visits to the Moon are easily within the grasp of a species that had perfected the V-2 rocket; the other tells us that global nuclear holocaust is also easily within the grasp of the very same species.

These two films, both of them genuine SF, represented attempts to make viewers envisage plausible worlds of the imagination: worlds whose potential existence we could argue about. Most SF films from the 1950s, however, took a very different view of things. They looked inwards, and they expressed the inner fears of a civilization at risk.

Perspective on paranoia

Now that we have survived the Cold War – which dominated world politics from 1945 to 1990 – it is easy for us to look back and mock the fears of the men and women who thought that unless they remained vigilant, a world-wide nuclear holocaust was more or less inevitable. It is also easy for us to make fun of the varieties of escapist art that tend to be popular during times of such unrelenting stress. By the time the 1960s came around, readers, and critics, and film-goers could be forgiven a certain amount of impatience with the themes and styles of the 1950s – a decade which could be designated the period during which Ostrich SF continued to triumph – but at the time the fears were real, and in our entertainments we needed to exorcise the ghosts of fear.

Pure SF, however, is not very good at exorcising ghosts. Its strengths lie in the exposure of ideas to discussion, and in telling action-filled stories that allow us to see how these ideas work out.

When it comes to putting our fears into some visceral shape, and then purging those fears by destroying the monsters that represent them, SF tends to flounder somewhat. Some films – like *Invasion of the Body Snatchers*, *Them!*, and *Forbidden Planet* – made stabs at the job, but the most explicitly argument-filled of these films, *Forbidden Planet*, has lasted least well. It attempts to represent the dark side of the psyche, the Id, in the form of a psychic monster that feeds on the fears and desires of its creator.

No welcome
The stature of The Day the Earth Stood Still *grows with the years. A robot and a humanoid arrive on Earth, and give us an ultimatum: stop our insane warlike ways, or be destroyed. Our answer? First we quarantine the flying saucer. Then we shoot the humanoid messenger.*

Unfortunately, this message is conveyed with comical awkwardness (although Walter Pidgeon is impressive as the Prospero figure who does not understand the darker side of his own mind). It also ends in the usual catastrophe: for decades, SF film-makers felt they had somehow failed in their duty if they did not manage, before the end of the last reel, to destroy any planet mentioned in any story, other than Earth itself.

Such men are dangerous

Forbidden Planet exposes one of the main preoccupations of 1950s American cinema: its dislike and fear of intellectuals. In Shakespeare's *The Tempest*, from which the film takes its plot, Prospero is a genuine intellectual: a scholar, a magician, a wise parent, and ruler of his domain. As the tale ends, he gives up power, but does not repudiate the world of knowledge. The Prospero of *Forbidden Planet*, on the other hand, does not know himself, dies in the end because he is a danger to others, and is revealed as an impostor.

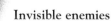

Invisible enemies
Although just a publicity photo set-up for Invasion of the Body Snatchers, *this scene summed up the film so well that it was filmed in the 1980s remake. We see the model small town, the panic, but not the foe. The foe is already within, invisible and parasitic.*

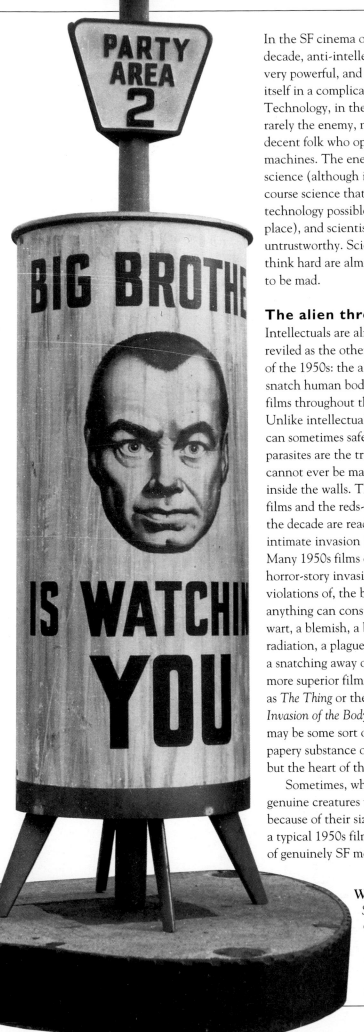

In the SF cinema of this decade, anti-intellectualism is very powerful, and it expresses itself in a complicated fashion. Technology, in these films, is rarely the enemy, nor are the decent folk who operate the machines. The enemy is science (although it was of course science that made the technology possible in the first place), and scientists are untrustworthy. Scientists who think hard are almost certain to be mad.

The alien threat

Intellectuals are almost as reviled as the other obsession of the 1950s: the aliens who snatch human bodies and souls in dozens of films throughout this decade of paranoia. Unlike intellectuals, who are highly visible, and can sometimes safely be made fun of, these alien parasites are the true menace, the one that cannot ever be made fun of, because they are inside the walls. The parallels between these films and the reds-under-the-beds paranoias of the decade are readily apparent, but this sense of intimate invasion is also an aspect of horror. Many 1950s films concentrate on just such horror-story invasions against, and violations of, the body. Almost anything can constitute an invasion: a wart, a blemish, a blast of nuclear radiation, a plague, a transformation, or a snatching away of the soul. In the more superior films of the decade, such as *The Thing* or the perennial classic *Invasion of the Body Snatchers*, there may be some sort of coating – like the papery substance over a wasps' nest – but the heart of the matter lies within.

Sometimes, when the monsters are genuine creatures who threaten us because of their size or their rage, even a typical 1950s film may make some use of genuinely SF modes of action.

The wrong box
As the box at the heart of Kiss Me Deadly *is a kind of Pandora's box, full of deadly radiation, it is fitting that a woman opens it.*

The series of Japanese *Gojira* or *Godzilla* films are based on the assumption that atomic bombs may have awakened a prehistoric monster from the sea bed; the destruction of Tokyo that ensues has a certain elemental grandeur. The American film *Them!* – although it reveals its roots by suggesting that radiation, like some ancient alchemical potion, is capable of creating giant ants over a period of a few months – does introduce into the mix a kindly scientist. His explanations, given in a fatherly tone of voice, at least try to make these events obey the laws of cause and effect.

Most films from the 1950s are only watched by the audiences of today in a mood of amused condescension. This may be a shame, and certainly there are a dozen or so superior films mixed in among all the dross, but it is still unmistakably the case. Putting the good films to one side, the most important accomplishment of this decade was the realization that gradually dawned on the film industry that real SF films – sometimes even lacking any monsters at all – could be marketable.

MONSTER MOVIES

They were everywhere in the 1950s. From the slime at the bottom of the black lagoon, from the hole at the bottom of the sink, from deep-frozen sleep under the Antarctic wastes, from 20,000 fathoms, or sometimes from other planets, the monsters came. They were scaly and cold-blooded, gilled, webbed, or otherwise, they were thick as two bricks and lustful after women in bikinis, and they did not have the gift of the gab. They were simply the 1950s' replacement for the sequelized horrors of the 1940s, but they are what many children – and even some adults – still think SF cinema is all about.

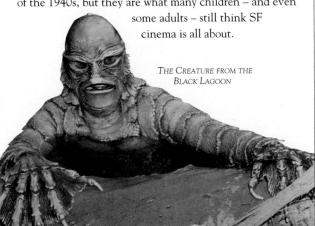

THE CREATURE FROM THE BLACK LAGOON

Watching you
Surveillance technology is virtually non-existent in 1984, *but an oppressive fear emanates from the screen. Big Brother lies in everyone's heart.*

FILMS OF THE 1960s

AFTER DECADES OF HORROR AND playing it safe, the major cinema factory, Hollywood, finally began to see the light. Until now, the SF film had been the premise of European cinema, or the exception to the rule. Here, we begin to see films that pose questions, post agendas, and direct our eyes outwards rather than inwards into our deeper fears.

★★★ OUTSTANDING   ★★ RECOMMENDED   ★ OF INTEREST

◁ Director   ⬚ Screenplay   ⬚ Time   ◉ Colour   ◖ Black and White

VOYAGE TO THE BOTTOM OF THE SEA

1960

Die Tausend Augen des Dr. Mabuse
(The Thousand Eyes of Dr. Mabuse/The Diabolical Dr. Mabuse)
Germany/Italy/France
CCC Filmkunst/CEI
Incom/Criterion
★★★
◁ Fritz Lang ⬚ Lang, Heinz Oscar Wuttig, based on characters created by Norbert Jacques ⬚ 103 mins ◖
Lang returns to Germany and the character that helped to make him famous. A reborn Mabuse sits in a hotel full of surveillance hardware, ruling a worldwide criminal empire. Seeing is never believing here. A powerful cinematic achievement, this complex and suspenseful film inspired another five sequels.

VILLAGE OF THE DAMNED

The Time Machine
USA Galaxy Films/MGM
★
◁ George Pal ⬚ David Duncan, based on *The Time Machine* (1895), H.G. Wells ⬚ 103 mins ◉
Hollywood delivers a romantic hero, ignoring the social parodies and implications of the novel. Still, the time-travel sequences are well done.

The Lost World
USA 20th Century-Fox
★
◁ Irwin Allen ⬚ Allen, Charles Bennett, based on *The Lost World* (1912), Arthur Conan Doyle ⬚ 97 mins ◉
This is a less happy adaptation than the 1925 attempt. The lizards are better, but everything else is worse.

Village of the Damned
UK MGM
★★
◁ Wolf Rilla ⬚ Sterling Silliphant, Rilla, George Barclay, based on *The Midwich Cuckoos* (1957), John Wyndham ⬚ 77 mins ◖
The treatment here is faithful, apart from the cuckoo alien children's glowing eyes. The children are genuinely chilling, the plot tense.

1961

Master of the World
USA AIP
★
◁ William Witney ⬚ Richard Matheson, based on *Robur le conquerant* (1886), *Maitre du monde* (1904), Jules Verne ⬚ 104 mins ◖
Neither the idealism of the first Verne novel nor the disenchantment of the second comes across: instead we have a big-budget, flying-machine adventure that owes more to the 1954 film of 20,000 Leagues Under the Sea.

The Day the Earth Caught Fire
UK British Lion/Pax/Allied Artists
★★
◁ Val Guest ⬚ Wolf Mankowitz, Guest ⬚ 99 mins ◖
Nuclear tests send the Earth crashing towards the Sun. More atomic explosions put it back in its proper orbit. This is fiction without science, but the effects are good.

Mysterious Island
USA American Films/Columbia
★
◁ Cy Endfield ⬚ John Prebble, Daniel Ullman, Crane Wilbur, based on *L'île mystérieuse* (1875), Jules Verne ⬚ 100 mins ◉
Here, Verne's novel is adapted to have Confederate prisoners escaping the American Civil War in a balloon, only to fetch up on the island with a couple of female castaways, several giant beasts, Captain Nemo, and all.

The Damned
(These Are the Damned)
UK Hammer/Swallow
★★★
◁ Joseph Losey ⬚ Evan Jones, based on *The Children of Light* (1960), Henry L. Lawrence ⬚ 96 mins ◖
Two lovers seek to free children who have been irradiated to enable them to live after a nuclear holocaust. The children, their keepers, and the doomed would-be rescuers are skilfully depicted, and the careful imagery impresses.

Voyage to the Bottom of the Sea
USA Windsor Productions/ 20th Century-Fox
★
◁ Irwin Allen ⬚ Allen, Charles Bennett ⬚ 105 mins ◉
The film that spawned the series (the cost of the submarine made a spin-off inevitable) is everything you would expect. An implausible fire in the Van Allen belts needs to be put out by implausible means. It is.

Mosura
(Mothra)
Japan Toho
★
◁ Inoshiro Honda ⬚ Shinichi Sekizawa, based on a story by Shinichiro Nakamura, Takehido Fukunaga, Yoshi Hotta ⬚ 100 mins ◉
Unlike the fierce Gojira or Rodan, this giant moth (a string-operated model) is not truly beastly – just a mother hell-bent on regaining her stolen offspring. Who can blame her if she clumsily destroys most of Japan in the process? Sequels cast the unwieldy female among fellow monster favourites.

1962

Dr. No
UK Eon/United Artists
★★
◁ Terence Young ⬚ Richard Maibaum, Johanna Harwood, Berkely Mather, based on *Dr. No* (1958), Ian Fleming ⬚ 105 mins ◉
The first of the Bond films has nuclear blackmail and plenty of gadgetry. It also has one of the nastier versions of the spy character, with bully-boy Sean Connery boiling the evil Doctor alive.

The Day Mars Invaded Earth
USA API/20th Century-Fox
★
◁ Maury Dexter ⬚ Harry Spalding ⬚ 70 mins ◖
This is a lacklustre imitation of Invasion of the Body Snatchers, but it did at least end with the Martians triumphant.

The Manchurian Candidate
USA MC/Essex/United Artists
★★★
◁ John Frankenheimer ⬚ George Axelrod, based on *The Manchurian Candidate* (1959), Richard Condon ⬚ 126 mins ◖
Captured American soldiers are subjected to elaborate brainwashing, as part of a plot to install a Chinese agent in the White House – as President. One man is programmed to become a killing machine when China gives the word. The first of Frankenheimer's political-paranoia films, this is stylish, sinister, and more timely than was intended.

THE MANCHURIAN CANDIDATE

Planeta Burg
(Planet of Storms/Storm Planet/Cosmonauts on Venus)
USSR Leningrad Studio of Popular Science Films
★★

Pavel Klushantsev Alexander Kazantsev, Klushantsev 85 mins cut to 74 mins

Cosmonauts on Venus encounter the local wildlife, but not the inhabitants, who may be just like us. They appear at the very end to watch the visitors leave. The sets are excellent, the script only slightly stodgy, and the robot with a liking for dance music is a nice touch. Fast paced, funny, and visually stunning, this is one of the best space-travel films made in the Soviet Union.

1963

La Jetée
(The Jetty/The Pier)
France Argos/Arcturus Films
★★★

Chris Marker Marker 29 mins

Released as a short on the same bill as Godard's Alphaville in 1965, this is very much a film of its time. Made up almost entirely of still shots, it explores a post-holocaust future where people are forced to live underground and time no longer has a coherent sequence. A man, in an attempt to reconnect with the past, investigates his memory of a face, which is eventually revealed as a witness to his death in the future.

THE BIRDS

The Day of the Triffids
UK Security Pictures/ Allied Artists
★

Steve Sekely (uncredited), Freddie Francis Philip Yordan, based on *The Day of the Triffids* (1951), John Wyndham 94 mins

With most of mankind blinded by a meteorite shower, our hero (whose bandaged eyes were saved) leads a motley gang of other sighted survivors against the giant vegetable enemy. The seven-foot-high, broccoli-like Triffids are terrible and the dialogue is even worse in this heavy-handed adaptation – a wasted cinematic effort. All of the atmosphere of Wyndham's novel has been excised in favour of love interest and adventure shenanigans.

The Birds
USA Universal
★★★

Alfred Hitchcock Evan Hunter, based on *The Birds* (1952), Daphne Du Maurier 119 mins

This is the film that launched a thousand (or it seemed that many) revenge-of-nature imitators. Most of the derivatives lacked the underlying power of the original, where the birds represent not just arbitrary vengeful force, but all the suppressed emotions and desires of the characters (and the director). While not strictly SF, this was closer to the genre than most of the monster film plots that had masqueraded as SF for years.

Children of the Damned
(Horror!)
UK MGM
★★

Anton Leader Jack Briley, based on *The Midwich Cuckoos* (1957), John Wyndham 90 mins

The plot is only very loosely based on Wyndham's novel: these superpowered alien children are not malevolent, and are scattered around the world. Brought together by UNESCO, and exploited by adults, they are destroyed accidentally.

X – The Man with the X-Ray Eyes
(The Man with the X-Ray Eyes)
USA Alta Vista/AIP
★★

Roger Corman Robert Dillon, Ray Russell, based on a story by Russell 88 mins

A surgeon experiments on himself and emerges with X-ray sight. This increases his skill, but brings terrible side effects. His vision into humanity utterly alienates him from it, and in the end he obeys the Biblical dictum and plucks out his eyes. Despite the rather simplistic special effects, this is one of Corman's best films.

Lord of the Flies
UK Allen Hodgson Productions/Two Arts
★★

Peter Brook Brook, based on *The Lord of the Flies* (1954), William Golding 91 mins

This is a faithful interpretation of Golding's novel, which was perhaps a mistake. The themes of original sin and the thin line between savagery and civilization are clear enough, but the tale of the schoolboys' descent into chaos is bogged down in literalism.

Ikarie XB-1
(Voyage to the End of the Universe/Icarus XB-1)
Czechoslovakia Filmové studio Barrandov
★

Jindrich Polák Pavel Jurácek, Polák 81 mins cut to 65 mins

A film oddly distanced from its subject, this has a giant spaceship on a long mission to find a white world – which became green and Earth in this year's absurdly altered Western version.

1964

The Time Travelers
USA AIP/Dobie
★★

Ib Melchior Melchior 84 mins

On post-holocaust Earth, survivors live in tunnels, protected from mutants on the surface by androids, who also assist in the building of an escape ship. They are joined by a group of scientists who, in 1964, ventured 107 years into the future and became locked in a time trap. Melchior's intriguing view of the future is enhanced by some inventive special effects. This lively film has a bleak ending, with the time travellers caught in a loop, endlessly flitting between 1964 and the future, unable to change the grim course of history.

From the Earth to the Moon
USA Waverley/RKO
★

Byron Haskin Robert Blees, James Leicester, based on *De la terre à la lune* (1865) and *Autour de la lune* (1870), Jules Verne 100 mins

This is possibly the most tedious film that has ever been made on the subject of space flight. Quite apart from the leaden dialogue and the unlikely events, there are no shots on the Moon.

The First Men in the Moon
UK/USA Columbia/Ameran
★

Nathan Juran Nigel Kneale, Jan Read, based on *The First Men in the Moon* (1901), H.G. Wells 107 mins cut to 103 mins

Wells survives a bit better than Verne in this year's adaptations, but not much. This film has the advantage of Ray Harryhausen's sets and effects, and is at least entertaining. But Wells it ain't.

Seven Days in May
USA Seven Arts/Joel/John Frankenheimer
★★

John Frankenheimer Rod Serling, based on *Seven Days in May* by Fletcher Knebel, Charles W. Bailey II 120 mins

In the second of Frankenheimer's political thrillers, made just after John F. Kennedy's assassination, it is the Hawks versus the Doves, with a star-studded cast on both sides. The scenario of this absorbing and intelligent drama has the American President negotiating a non-nuclear proliferation deal with the Russians, while White House generals plot to thwart this traitorous pacifism with a military takeover.

THE DAY OF THE TRIFFIDS

SEVEN DAYS IN MAY

Dr. Strangelove
(or: How I Learned to Stop Worrying and Love the Bomb)
USA Hawk/Columbia
★★★

 Stanley Kubrick Kubrick, Terry Southern, Peter George, based on *Two Hours to Doom/Red Alert (USA) (1958)*, Peter George as Peter Bryant 94 mins
Dr. Strangelove has seeped into our collective unconscious so thoroughly that one forgets how inventive its cinematic text of mad generals, out-of-touch world leaders, and bizarrely juxtaposed music and sequences was. Peter Sellers failed to win an Oscar for his three roles; the film, direction, and script were also nominated.

DR. STRANGELOVE

Fail Safe
USA Max E. Youngstein/ Sidney Lumet
★★★

Sidney Lumet Walter Bernstein, based on *Fail-Safe (1962)*, Eugene L. Burdick, Harvey Wheeler 111 mins
This film only suffers from comparison with Kubrick's *Dr. Strangelove*, which covers the same sort of ground in more style. Having initiated an accidental attack on Moscow, the American President has to bomb New York to prevent retaliation. In place of Kubrick's vigorous black farce, Lumet treats the horrors in bleak, matter-of-fact style. It works.

It Happened Here
UK Rath/Lopert
★★

Kevin Brownlow, Andrew Mollo Brownlow, Mollo 99 mins cut to 93 mins
Never widely shown, this unusual Alternate World film looks at the results of a successful invasion of Britain by Hitler. It is made in the kind of documentary style favoured by Peter Watkins, and most usually associated with British cinema of this period. Seven years in the making, the finely detailed and utterly convincing reconstruction outshines the somewhat muddled storyline.

DOCTOR WHO AND THE DALEKS

1965

Alphaville
(Une Étrange Aventure de Lemmy Caution)
France Pathé Contemporary/ Chaumiane-Film Studio
★★★

Jean-Luc Godard Godard 100 mins
The persona of Lemmy Caution had been around for years in other secret agent films: Godard's over-the-top version of the character is one of the most enjoyable ironies of this highly original and anarchic film. Caution, here an interplanetary agent, travels to the chillingly emotionless Alphaville to hunt down evil genius Dr. von Braun. He destroys the central computer by countering its logic with poetry, kills the villainous professor, and leaves the city with his beautiful daughter. Popular and high culture are mixed freely with philosophy, myth, and hard-boiled realism in this complex and fascinating SF film noir.

The War Game
UK BBC/Pathé Contemporary
★★

Peter Watkins Watkins 50 mins cut to 47 mins
This film speculating on the results of a nuclear attack on a small Kent town was made for the BBC, who then decided not to screen it. Their reasoning for this was that the work was too realistic – made in a format incorporating supposed documentary shots and simulated interviews with survivors – and might therefore upset its audience. The result of this facile judgment was instant cult status. While the film deserved this for its sharp images and style, its expectations of the aftermath of widespread nuclear attack were if anything almost too sanguine.

Doctor Who and the Daleks
UK AARU
★

Gordon Flemyng Milton Subotsky, based on the TV story "The Dead Planet" (1963–64), Terry Nation 85 mins
The Doctor, his granddaughters, and his incompetent assistant take off for war between the evil Daleks and good-guy Thals. Many people would like to see the television series back; few mourn the long-gone films.

La Decima Vittima
(The Tenth Victim)
France/Italy Champion/Concordia
★

Elio Petri Petri, Ennio Flaiano, Tonino Guerra, Giorgio Salvone, based on "The Seventh Victim" (1953), Robert Sheckley 92 mins
The game show where they give you liberty or give you death offers some SF in-jokes and a stunning secret weapon, but lacks Sheckley's wit.

Terrore Nello Spazio
(Planet of the Vampires)
Italy/Spain/USA
Italian International/Castilla Cinematografica/AIP
★

Mario Bava Callisto Cosulich, Antonio Roman, Alberto Bevilacqua, Bava, Rafael J. Salvia, Louis M. Hayward, Ib Melchior, based on a story by Melchior, based on a story by Renato Pestriniero 86 mins
Astronauts are forced to land on an alien planet, where they find an empty ship in a scene reminiscent of *Alien*. Inexplicable fighting leads to the deaths of three of the astronauts, who rise again, apparently taken over by the disembodied locals, who want a ticket out.

1966

Batman
USA 20th Century-Fox/ Greenlawn/National Periodical Publications
★

Leslie H. Martinson Lorenzo Semple Jr., based on characters created by Bob Kane and Bill Finger 105 mins
This film plays unashamedly off the success of the camp television series, with the entire cast transferring their roles onto the big screen. The plot is as thin as any of the TV episodes, with the quartet of villains stealing a machine that dehydrates people. This is somehow going to help them take over the world, and the dialogue is just as ridiculous. What gained a cult following in half-hour segments is unwatchable on a cinematic scale.

Cyborg 2087
USA Feature Film Corp.
★

Franklin Adreon Arthur C. Pierce 86 mins
A cyborg – in this case a man controlled by an implanted chip – gains momentary mental freedom and steals a time machine, returning from 2087 to the present to warn the professor whose invention made it all possible. The cyborg and his pursuers cease to exist when the professor destroys his experiments, along with everyone's memories of their visit.

Invasion
UK Merton Park/AIP
★★

Alan Bridges Roger Marshall, based on a story by Robert Holmes 82 mins
In this low-budget, low-key affair, a doctor at a country hospital refuses to hand over an alien to the pursuing extra-terrestrial police force, who promptly set up a force-field around the hospital. The determined doctor eventually outwits his adversaries. The film is highly atmospheric, the climax well-handled.

Daikaiju Gamera
(Gamera)
Japan Daei
★

Noriaki Yuasa Fumi Takahashi 88 mins
Gamera was Daei's rival to Toho's *Gojira*: a giant turtle, awakened by the inevitable atomic blast, sets out to eat its way to Tokyo. It gets blasted into space, but you know it will be back, and hungrier than ever.

BATMAN

FANTASTIC VOYAGE

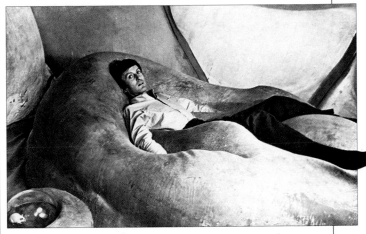

I LOVE YOU, I LOVE YOU

Fantastic Voyage
USA 20th Century-Fox
★

Richard Fleischer ☑ Harry Kleiner, based on a story by Otto Clement and J. Lewis [Jerome] Bixby ☑ 100 mins ☐

Long before fibre optics and keyhole surgery, Hollywood had the answer: miniaturize a bunch of doctors and send them into the body to sort it out. The sets are impressive, the effects are psychedelic, and there is of course a saboteur in the ranks (disposed of by the body's defence mechanisms), plus – not least – a race to get out of the body before reverting messily to full size. But in the end there is really nothing happening.

Daleks: Invasion Earth 2150 A.D.
(Invasion Earth 2150 A.D.)
UK AARU
★

Gordon Flemying ☑ Milton Subotsky, based on the TV serial story "The Dalek Invasion of Earth" (1964), Terry Nation ☑ 84 mins ☐

The Doctor and his granddaughters are off again, this time with a police escort. The Daleks have conquered Earth and incomprehensibly plan to hollow it out to use it as a spaceship. They are duly foiled and destroyed.

Island of Terror
(Night of the Silicates)
UK/USA Planet/Universal
★

Terence Fisher ☑ Alan Ramsen, Edward Andrew Mann ☑ 89 mins ☐

Research into a cure for cancer instead produces giant mutated viruses that suck the bones out of their victims' bodies. Some well-executed, if nasty, shocks are in store.

Around the World Under the Sea
USA Ivan Tors Productions/MGM
★

Andrew Marton ☑ Arthur Weiss, Art Arthur ☑ 120 mins ☐

A team of scientists is sent to place warning devices along fault lines under the sea. It is not a promising premise, and it does not deliver. The underwater sequences are the best of it, directed by Ricou Browning, last seen wearing green makeup as The Creature from the Black Lagoon.

One Million Years B.C.
UK/USA Hammer/ 20th Century-Fox
★

Don Haffey ☑ Michael Carreras, based on the screenplay of One Million B.C. (1940) ☑ 100 mins ☐

The chronology is absurd: humans and dinosaurs share the planet. The anthropology is questionable: Shell and Rock in tribal feud. The clothes are minimal: fur brassieres are de rigueur. The dialogue is, thankfully, incomprehensible, and at least this last is intentional.

ONE MILLION YEARS B.C.

Konec Sprna v Hotelu Ozón
(The End of August at the Hotel Ozone)
Czechoslovakia Československý armádní film
★

Jan Schmidt ☑ Pavel Juráček ☑ 87 mins ☐

In a post-holocaust world, women roam in gangs – scavenging, hunting, and killing. At the Hotel Ozone, they kill the aged owner for the sake of his record player – this may have something to do with the soundtrack.

Fahrenheit 451
UK/France Anglo-enterpris and Vineyard/Universal
★★

François Truffaut ☑ Truffaut, Jean-Louis Richard, based on Fahrenheit 451 (1953), Ray Bradbury ☑ 112 mins ☐

Where the novel was sharp, the film is fuzzy; where Bradbury is polemic, Truffaut is questioning; and where Bradbury believed, Truffaut doubts. The result is a film of ambiguities, in which the book learners seem not so very different from the book burners, and the spiritual (as opposed to the literal) survival of literature seems as much in the balance as ever. But the film is eloquently made, and Nicolas Roeg's camera work provides images that remain burned on the eye.

Seconds
USA Paramount/Joel/Gibraltar
★★

John Frankenheimer ☑ Lewis John Carlino, based on Seconds (1963), David Ely ☑ 106 mins ☐

A middle-aged businessman is surgically rejuvenated, and his death faked. Growing tired of his new life, he finds that he cannot return to his old one, and opts to die rather than go on, whereupon he is recycled for use by further customers. The film marks another step in Frankenheimer's growing distrust of technology.

1 9 6 7

You Only Live Twice
UK Eon/United Artists
★

Lewis Gilbert ☑ Roald Dahl, based on You Only Live Twice (1964), Ian Fleming ☑ 116 mins ☐

In this hardware-heavy Bond film, SPECTRE are snaffling space equipment from the Yanks and the Russkies to provoke international conflict. Agent 007 foils their plans.

The President's Analyst
USA Panpiper/Paramount
★★

Theodore J. Flicker ☑ Flicker ☑ 104 mins ☐

The President's psychoanalyst unsurprisingly cracks and, to escape government surveillance, takes refuge with a "militant liberal" family. The FBI are short, the CIA are pipe-smokers in tweeds, Canada's secret service is disguised as a Liverpudlian beat group, and they are all after him. Worst of all, the people really in charge, presciently, are the telephone company, run by robots with the goal of a phone implanted in every brain. The film is uneven, but rather witty.

Barbarella
France/Italy/USA De Laurentiis-Marianne/Paramount
★★

Roger Vadim ☑ Vadim, Terry Southern, Jean-Claude Forest, Vittorio Bonicelli, Brian Degas, Claude Brûle, Tudor Gates, Clement Biddle Wood, based on Forest's comic strip "Barbarella" (1962–64) ☑ 98 mins ☐

If you have seen the comic strip you know what you are in for: if not, you know pretty quick. The scantily clad Barbarella (Jane Fonda) is sent to capture an evil scientist and his weapon of destruction. The setting is Flash Gordon in the 40th century, and the filming is impressive, but the rest of it is not to be taken seriously.

Je T'Aime, Je T'Aime
(I Love You, I Love You)
France Parc/Fox Europa
★★

Alain Resnais ☑ Resnais, Jacques Sternberg ☑ 94 mins ☐

A man taking part in a time-travel experiment finds himself constantly oscillating back and forth around the doomed affair that led to his suicide attempt. The replaying of scenes and variations builds a haunting picture of his life. Sternberg's writing career has been SF via the fantastic; this is Sternberg through and through.

Perry Rhodan – SOS aus dem Weltall
(Perry Rhodan – SOS from Space)
Germany/Italy/Spain Tefi Film/PEA/Attor Film

Primo Zeglio ☑ K.H. Scheer, K.H. Vogelmann ☑ 79 mins ☐

The Perry Rhodan books are widely translated into other languages, but not so onto the screen. This try is nothing special: Rhodan and his pals sort out Earthbound baddies.

The Power
USA Galaxy Films/MGM
★

George Pal ☑ John Gay, based on The Power (1956), Frank M. Robinson ☑ 109 mins ☐

When there is an evil supermind on the loose, who better to take it on than another supermind? The twists are suspenseful, the effects alarming.

Privilege
UK Worldfilm Services and Memorial Enterprises/Universal
★

Peter Watkins ☑ Norman Bogner, based on a story by Johnny Speight ☑ 103 mins ☐

Brave New World had its popular songs, Nineteen Eighty-Four had prolefeed tunes. Here, Watkins's rock star is corrupted, then rebels, only to be murdered by his own fans.

Quatermass and the Pit
(Five Million Years to Earth)
UK Hammer/Seven Arts
★★

Roy Ward Baker Nigel Kneale, based on his BBC television serial 97 mins
Strange goings-on at a subway excavation turn out to be linked to an unearthed spaceship full of ancient Martians, who landed at the dawn of time looking for slaves, and kick-started our evolution. The plot cleverly blends SF with speculation on Jungian archetype, explaining how mankind's memories and behaviour patterns were implanted into our prehistoric consciousness by the alien visitors. When the spaceship's power source returns to life, it revives ancient nightmares through poltergeist phenomena, climaxing in an orgy of destruction by panicked Londoners as paranormal powers are unleashed.

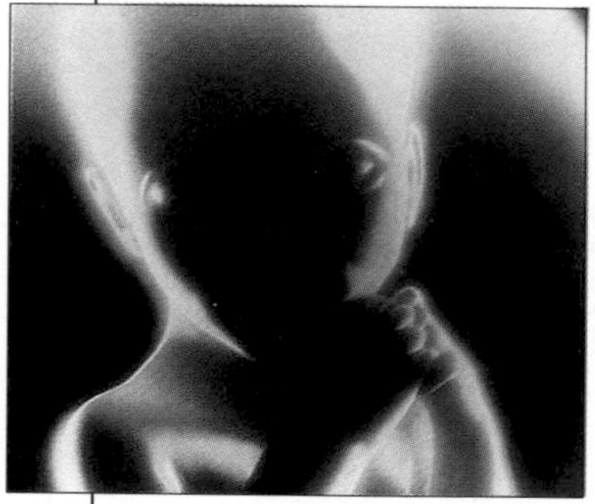

2001: A SPACE ODYSSEY

1968

2001: A Space Odyssey
UK MGM/Stanley Kubrick
★★★

Stanley Kubrick Kubrick, Arthur C. Clarke, based on Clarke's "The Sentinel" (1951) 160 mins cut to 141 mins (originally in Cinerama)
2001 *is a touchstone of the genre, so much so that today's producers of documentaries about SF seem to find their hands irresistibly drawn to tapes of* Also Sprach Zarathustra *for their background music. This was the film that changed how SF films looked, with its immensely detailed set, its intricate effects, and its post-rocket spaceships. It was also the film that updated the worlds of SF film, with its mysterious black monoliths, its meditations on humanity-as-property themes, and its computer nervous breakdowns. Although a great deal of the original wonder generated by the sheer visual effects of the Cinerama format is lost to today's audiences, the questions and the challenges that* 2001 *put to the cinematic genre remain. The intellectual audacity of the work earned it a Hugo award in 1969.*

Weekend
France/Italy Comacico/Copernic/Lira/Ascot Cineraid
★★

Jean Luc Godard Godard 103 mins
A drive to the end of the world: Godard's bickering bourgeois couple observe the descent from order into chaos, mainly through ever more horrific car crashes, before abandoning their own vehicle and joining the anarchistic future on foot. In the end, she eats him.

Planet of the Apes
USA Apjac/20th Century-Fox
★★

Franklin J. Schaffner Michael Wilson, Rod Serling, based on *La planète des singes* (1963), Pierre Boulle 112 mins
When three astronauts crash-land on a planet governed by apes, one is killed, one lobotomized, and one put in a zoo full of animalistic humans. The apes are seen as both more and less civilized than the human captive: they are ordered and sophisticated, but also casually cruel to what they see as animals. At the end of the film, the devastated astronaut makes the discovery that any audience must suspect all along: this is no alien planet, but a far-future Earth. The scene that tells him this is, of course, one of the most famous uses of the ruined Statue of Liberty as an icon. Sequels of the film were made in 1969, 1971, 1972, and 1973.

Charly
USA Selmur/Robertson Associates
★

Ralph Nelson Stirling Silliphant, based on *Flowers for Algernon* (1966), Daniel Keyes 106 mins
Keyes's classic depiction of Charly Gordon's journey from put-upon village idiot to genius, and horrifying regression back again, must seem like an actor's dream. Cliff Robertson – who put together his own production company to make the film – turns in a fine performance, which won him an Oscar. But the pathos of the book becomes bathos in the film, with sentimentality to the fore and platitudes in abundance.

Le Dernier Homme
(The Last Man)
France Anouchka Films
★

Charles Bitsch Bitsch 85 mins cut to 82 mins
A man and two women emerge from a caving expedition to find that they are the last people left alive on Earth after a nuclear holocaust.

Night of the Blood Beast
USA Balboa/AIP
★

Bernard Kowalski Martin Varno, based on a story by Gene Corman 65 mins
Cinema's first pregnant astronaut returns to Earth implanted with alien eggs. The results are pure Corman.

PLANET OF THE APES

THE ILLUSTRATED MAN

The Illustrated Man
USA SKM Productions/Warner-Seven Arts
★

Jack Smight Howard B. Kreitsek, based on *The Illustrated Man* (1951), Ray Bradbury 103 mins
Three Bradbury tales, linked by the device of being tattoos on the body of the illustrated man, are told, with the same actors playing the parts in each story. Astronauts are lost on Venus in "The Long Rains", *parents kill their child on* "The Last Night of the World" *(only to find that it was not), and children's fantasies come alive to destroy their parents in* "The Veldt". *(The last featured in another anthology film,* Vel'd, *in 1987.) Despite good performances, particularly from Rod Steiger in the title role, the format cannot sustain Bradbury's visions.*

Countdown
USA William Conrad Productions
★

Robert Altman Loren Mandel, based on *The Pilgrim Project* (1964), Hank Searls 101 mins cut to 73 mins
More soap opera than Space Opera, this fictionalization of the space race concentrates on the people involved – the bosses, the prospective astronauts, the stresses placed on their families – rather than the technological and gung-ho aspects. Coming early in Altman's career, the film was badly re-edited.

Mister Freedom
France Opéra/Les Films du Rondpoint
★

William Klein Klein 110 mins cut to 94 mins
A satire on America and its heroes, Mister Freedom finds that it becomes necessary to destroy the world in order to save it. Among the nice satirical touches are the transformation of the American Embassy in Paris into a hypermarket.

Tumannost Andromedy
(The Andromeda Nebula/Andromeda the Mysterious/The Cloud of Andromeda)
USSR Dovzhenko Studio
★

Eugene Sherstobytov Sherstobytov, Vladimir Dmitrievski, based on *Tumannost Andromedy* (1958), Ivan Yefremov 85 mins cut to 77 mins
Yefremov's classic suffers badly in this adaptation. The characters, on a spaceship bound for the Andromeda Nebula and alien contact, are too cheerful to be believed, the speeches are too wooden to be endured, and the adventure is too unadventurous to make any of it worth it.

Gladiatorerna
(The Peace Game/The Gladiators)
Sweden Sandrews/New Line
★

Peter Watkins Nicholas Gosling, Watkins 105 mins cut to 91 mins
Made in the director's usual pseudo-documentary style, this is set in a future where gladiators guided by computers have replaced the need for full-scale war. The whole thing lacks the immediacy of Watkins's other films: the nuclear threat was real, governments do manipulate, but nobody has, or is likely to, set up a system like the one depicted here.

Night of the Living Dead
USA Image 10 Productions/Walter Reade-Continental
★★

George A. Romero John A. Russo 96 mins cut to 90 mins
One of the great cinematic debuts, and an interesting turnaround: after all those horror films in the guise of SF, here is SF in the guise of horror. Made on a tiny budget over several weekends, it sets up all the usual expectations only to knock them down. The heroine remains in shock, the hero is killed, and the normals are every bit as savage as the zombies.

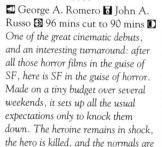

Shirley Thompson versus the Aliens
Australia Kolossal Films
★

Jim Sharman ▪ Sharman 104 mins
Aliens disguise themselves as a biker gang and use a waxwork Duke of Edinburgh as their spokesman (spot the difference). The story is told in flashback, unsurprisingly to a shrink. Sharman went on from this to his 1974 classic, The Rocky Horror Picture Show.

The Lost Continent
UK Hammer/20th Century-Fox
★

Michael Carreras ▪ Michael Nash, based on *Uncharted Seas* (1938), Dennis Wheatley 98 mins
A tramp steamer strays into killer seaweed in the Sargasso Sea. But its troubles are only just starting, as the balloon-borne descendants of Spanish conquistadores attack.

Wild in the Streets
USA AIP
★

Barry Shear ▪ Robert Thom 97 mins
Government exploitation of the young goes horribly wrong – or right. The rock star hired to catch the youth vote becomes President when the voting age is reduced to 14, and consigns all over-35s to camps where they are force-fed LSD. But the pre-teens are after power, too.

Popdown
UK Fremar Productions
★

Fred Marshall ▪ Marshall 98 mins cut to 54 mins
London circa 1968 is seen through the eyes of two alien visitors who, sent to observe Earth, end up obsessed with pop culture. They never came back.

1969

The Bed-Sitting Room
UK Oscar Lewenstein Productions/United Artists
★

Richard Lester ▪ John Antrobus, from the play by Antrobus, Spike Milligan 91 mins
Post-World War III mutations include characters who become parrots, wardrobes, and the bed-sitting room of the title. All takes place in a surreal, desert-like landscape, reminiscent of the no-man's-land of World War I. The film lacks drive, but events are amusing enough and worth watching.

The Monitors
USA Bell & Howell Productions/Commonwealth United/Second City
★

Jack Shea ▪ Myron J. Gold, based on *The Monitors* (1966), Keith Laumer 92 mins
The alien invaders of the 1950s wanted to turn us into food or slaves: those of the 1960s seem to want to turn us into hippies. The "monitors" arrive with pacifying gas and a doctrine of brotherly love, but they are no more successful than their predecessors: the inevitable resistance overthrows them.

Beneath the Planet of the Apes
USA Apjac/20th Century-Fox
★

Ted Post ▪ Paul Dehn, Mort Abrahams, based on characters created by Pierre Boulle 95 mins
In this sequel to Planet of the Apes (1968), another astronaut crash-lands on future Earth, and discovers a crazed Charlton Heston and mutant humans living under the surface of the planet in the ruins of New York. The mutants worship the Doomsday Bomb, which Heston eventually sets off, destroying the planet. Apparently the series was meant to end here, a decision unfortunately reversed when someone thought they could get a few more films out of the ape costumes.

Marooned
USA Columbia/Frankovitch-Sturges
★

John Sturges ▪ Mayo Simon, based on *Marooned* (1964), Martin Caidin 134 mins
A joint American/Soviet mission is mounted to rescue three astronauts stranded in orbit around the Earth. The quasi-documentary approach jars with various melodramatic sub-plots, and the sluggish suspense fails to engage. The high-powered cast struggles with an incredibly banal script, and the special effects, though technically deft, are unmemorable.

Manden der Taenkte Ting
(The Man who Thought Life)
Denmark Asa Film/Palladium
★

Jens Ravn ▪ Henrik Stangerup, based on the novel by Valdemar Holst (1938) 97 mins
A man has the mental power to create objects – even people. To increase the life span of his materializations, he seeks the help of a brain surgeon. When the doctor refuses, he "wills" a duplicate of him, who gradually takes over from the original, ultimately performing the requested operation and in doing so killing his creator.

Doppelgänger
(Journey to the Far Side of the Sun)
UK Century 21 Productions/Universal
★

Robert Parrish ▪ Gerry and Sylvia Anderson, Donald James 101 mins cut to 94 mins in USA
Astronauts on an expedition to reach a counter-Earth found on the far side of the Sun think the mission has gone wrong when they return home in half the time it should have taken, but of course it slowly becomes clear that they are on the other planet. Their doubles, we assume, are on Earth. It is hard, however, to care.

COLOSSUS, THE FORBIN PROJECT

Colossus, the Forbin Project
(The Forbin Project)
USA Universal
★★

Joseph Sargent ▪ James Bridges, based on *Colossus* (1966), D.F. Jones 100 mins
In the mould of many 1960s films that were paranoid about technology, this plot sees the national defence systems of both the United States and the Soviet Union turned over to supercomputers, Colossus and Guardian. The computers get chummy and together they take over the world. The film's release was delayed for over a year owing to the huge effect of 2001: A Space Odyssey with its own superpowerful computer. Unlike the neurotic Hal, however, Colossus is cold, arrogant, and ambitious. Shots of the omnipotent machine in vast caverns beneath the Rocky Mountains carry the message: better to entrust the world to foolish humans than to relinquish authority to an emotionless electronic entity.

The Mind of Mr. Soames
UK Amicus
★★

Alan Cooke ▪ John Hale, Edward Simpson, based on *The Mind of Mr. Soames* (1961), Charles Eric Maine 98 mins
A 30-year-old man is released from a life-long coma by a neurosurgeon. He is given a rudimentary education, but escapes to the harsh outside world. Greeted with hostility, the innocent turns violent himself. Despite its clichés, the film remains thoughtful.

Captain Nemo and the Underwater City
UK Omnia/MGM
★

James Hill ▪ Pip and Jane Baker, based on a character created by Jules Verne 106 mins
This has perhaps a little more to do with the 19th century than did Disney's 1954 interpretation of Verne, but lacks its sparkle. Nemo's city creates gold as a side effect of manufacturing air, and the tired plot revolves on some of the visitors wanting to steal the secret, others wanting to leave it be. All ends happily, thankfully.

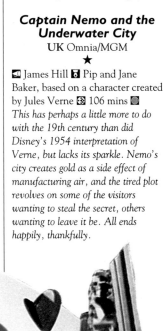

MAROONED

TOWARDS THE STARS

AT LAST, WITH THE 1960s, the long nightmare of horror masquerading as SF was ending. There were dark moments still to come – the long string of James Bond films, for instance, would continue to treat SF as a camp excuse to indulge in special effects – but there were glimmers of daylight.

The dawn of cinema SF

There are exceptions to every rule. There were, for example, some 1950s films, such as *This Island Earth*, that were real SF movies, set in genuine worlds, to which SF arguments applied. But these films stand out as real exceptions: most purported SF films of the 1950s were horror stories about external threats that had to be defeated.

When we speak of the 1960s as seeing the end of a nightmare, as portending the dawn of something new, we are remembering the huge relief felt, by those who knew what SF potentially had to say, when they noticed that studio-bound horror films were no longer dominating the screens with their easy answers, their profoundly irresponsible dodging of the requirements of plausibility, continuity of storyline, and of logic. The sheer numbing stupidity of the SF horror film had begun to fade, at last.

From now on, SF films would not just fill the screen with monsters, and yawning pits, and things that we humans should not know. The last significant SF horror film – before David Cronenberg and the makers of *Alien* rewrote the whole genre in the late 1970s – was Alfred Hitchcock's classic *The Birds*, released in 1963. This film shrugged off the tendency to indulge in fake "explanations" that had added insult to injury throughout the previous decade, and simply presented, without any rationale, a natural world that had suddenly turned alien and threatening. As viewers watched, SF premises welled easily into the mind, and shaped their responses. *The Birds* may have been "about" ecology – about nature repudiating humanity,

Triple bill
Peter Sellers in one of the three roles he played in Dr. Strangelove, *thinks dark thoughts.*

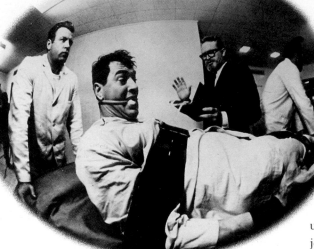

Second chance
In Seconds, *a businessman who is tired of life is technologically transformed into a handsomer, younger body, which he then cannot stand. The star, Rock Hudson, financed the film.*

as though it had become allergic to us – or it may not have been. The purpose of the film was not to make any particular argument, but simply to spark off a free flow of speculative response. By refusing to kowtow to the studios' demands for standard endings in which the menace of the unknown is defeated by the forces of good, it freed the world of cinema for SF.

Stanley Kubrick made *Dr. Strangelove*, which was perhaps the decade's best film in any genre. It was beginning to look as though the film-makers had finally realized that genuine SF films might not only be good for their creative souls but could also do well at the hallowed box office.

Fresh air

And just one year later came Kubrick's *Dr. Strangelove*. There is, of course, a great deal of hilarity in the film, a deep, sane, cynical black humour about human nature, the military mind, the excuses of politicians avid for self-advancement, and about the nature of the Cold War, which was still freezing human hearts in 1964. To an extent that may now, decades later, seem hard to understand, this film released huge energies of joyful, relieved laughter in its audiences. Over and above the jokes being good, and the targets being overdue for a puncture or two, there is another reason for this sense of release. Previous SF films that dealt at all with issues of war, science, and politics had tended to do so within that claustrophobic 1950s framework, and one of the main effects was that – because real problems were treated as though they came from evil outsiders, like monsters or aliens – no real issues could genuinely be brought into the air. *Dr. Strangelove*, on the other hand, gives the whole world an airing. Because the problems in Strangelove relate to our own circumstances on this planet, they can be faced and addressed.

In the underworld
In 1965, Jean-Luc Godard was at the peak of his fame, and films like Alphaville *were daring and sure of touch. Here, Eddie Constantine (who had played 1940s mean-streets private eye Lemmie Caution in several films) re-enacts that part in an SF context. Like Orpheus, he descends to Alphaville, a computer-run world, and returns with the girl.*

Psychological investigation
The mad computer may be a cliché, but it is entirely recast here, within the high-tech entrails of HAL, the computer who controls the Jupiter-bound spaceship of 2001, and who goes insane. He is unplugged, byte by byte, agonizingly.

Bleak view
*Very calmly and clearly,
The War Game exposes
the lunacy of civil defence.
The insanity lies in the assumption
that nuclear war is like an earthquake,
something to be survived, and then forgotten.*

This, after all, is one of the things that SF is supposed to be able to do for us. SF lays possibilities on the table. SF makes arguments that can be followed, and either accepted or rejected. It was high time for the cinema to allow some fresh air into its products, and it did happen. There was fresh air at last.

There were also some very stale draughts, but there always will be. Some literary-minded film-makers botch their attempts at SF tales. Jean-Luc Godard's *Alphaville* was racy, although stripped-down, but François Truffaut's *Fahrenheit 451*, based on Ray Bradbury's great SF fable, was fatally static and introverted. Most of the best SF films are open, rather than shut; argumentative, rather than settled in their minds. And because they are out in the open, emphasizing actions directed towards understandable goals, they can be fun.

New visions
But fun has to be seen to be believed; until the 1960s were almost over, the great problem with SF continued to be the problem of how to make visible that which did not yet exist, in venues that we could not, in fact, yet reach.

Cinematic special effects had remained quite astonishingly primitive for many decades: spaceships or underground cities built out of cardboard were the bane of any director who wanted the cast to behave normally; the plain fact was that SF sets were simply not solid enough to act in convincingly. Not until Kubrick's *2001* did special-effects technology begin to respond to film-makers' demands.

As an indication of the dominance of special effects in films over recent decades – and of the way that yesterday's special effect is about as impressive as yesterday's newspaper headlines –

it might be remembered that Kubrick's *2001* was originally made for the short-lived Cinerama format, and was only distributed through theatres able to mount the enormous, semi-wrap-around screen that was demanded by this process. A generation later, when most viewers acquaint themselves with this deeply influential film through video, it is easy to forget how its first audiences felt surrounded by space. New windows opened, and finally, from our cinema seats, we saw the stars.

The man in the maze
Charly is an extremely cruel film. We see a mentally handicapped person have his intelligence raised to genius level by drugs, and watch him delight in understanding the world. Then we have to watch his reactions as it starts to fade again.

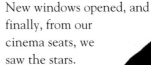

FILMS OF THE 1970s

FINALLY, SF FILM BEGAN TO grow up. There were still some cardboard sets and nonsensical plots, and scientists talking garbage, but finally studios began to understand that nobody wanted films about futures that looked like the insides of laundromats, with heroes in togas. It was time for guts, sex, dreadnoughts in space, and *dirt*.

★★★ OUTSTANDING   ★★ RECOMMENDED   ★ OF INTEREST

Director	Screenplay	Time	Colour	Black and White

1 9 7 0

City Beneath the Sea
(One Hour to Doomsday)
USA 20th Century-Fox TV Productions for NBC
★

Irwin Allen Ꮚ John Meredith Lucas, from a story by Allen 100 mins cut to 93 mins
An echo from the past: an asteroid threatens America; gold is stuck under the sea for safety; and villains try to steal same. Foiled again!

Hauser's Memory
USA Universal/NBC TV
★

Boris Sagal Ꮚ Adrian Spies, based on *Hauser's Memory*, Curt Siodmak 100 mins
Here comes Donovan's Brain, again: the sequel. A scientist injects himself with serum from a dead Nazi, and is haunted by Heils.

Brewster McCloud
USA MGM/Adler-Phillips/ Lion's Gate
★

Robert Altman Ꮚ Doran William Cannon 104 mins
SF becomes parable. A solitary boy builds wings under the protection of a murdering angel, and fails to fly. Society takes a beating.

The Love War
USA Paramount/ABC TV
★

George McCowan Ꮚ Gordon Trueblood, David Kidd 74 mins
Aliens use Earth as a duelling arena: the survivor falls for a woman, who turns out to be the opposing survivor. What banging is all about.

Punishment Park
UK Chartwell/Françoise
★

Peter Watkins Ꮚ Watkins 89 mins
The Vietnam War years were among the darkest in American history, and much of the trauma remains under the surface. A British director responded first, setting a mini-Vietnam in the heart of America.

No Blade of Grass
USA Symbol/MGM
★★

Cornel Wilde Ꮚ Sean Forestal, Jefferson Pascal, based on *The Death of Grass* (1956), John Christopher 96 mins cut to 80 mins
When grass vanishes from the world, strife and starvation strip humans of the pomps of civilized behaviour. Only a few – like those in this harsh, unrelenting film – gain safe haven.

Gas-s-s-s, or It Became Necessary to Destroy the World in Order to Save It
(Gas!, or It Became Necessary to Destroy the World in Order to Save It)
USA San Jacinto/AIP
★

Roger Corman Ꮚ Graham Armitage 79 mins cut to 77 mins
Dozens of targets in one ecological catastrophe film: everyone over 25 is killed by gas, everyone under 25 races to reproduce the idiocies of yore. The subtitle parodies an American explanation for destroying a Vietnamese village.

Der Grosse Verhau
(The Big Mess)
West Germany Kairos Film
★★

Alexander Kluge Ꮚ Kluge, Wolfgang Mai 86 mins
Here is the true story of the space race, seen from Germany: vicious company apparatchiks hack each other to bits in the space race for monopoly control. Americans had not the heart to make it.

Crimes of the Future
Canada Emergent Films
★★

David Cronenberg Ꮚ Cronenburg 70 mins
Quite astonishingly kinky – paedophilia necking with catastrophe in the cosmetics plant, and all adult females are kaput – but then so is life. Cronenberg treats scientists as control freaks out of control, and science as a loose cannon.

Trog
USA Herman Cohen Productions/Warner Bros.
★

Freddie Francis Ꮚ Aben Kandel, based on a story by John Gilling and Peter Bryan 93 mins cut to 91 mins
. . . or troglodyte. A caveman, spooked by rock'n'roll, bites the dust after going awol from a lab where his ancient mind was being plumbed.

A CLOCKWORK ORANGE

1 9 7 1

A Clockwork Orange
USA Polaris/Warner Bros.
★★

Stanley Kubrick Ꮚ Kubrick, based on *A Clockwork Orange* (1962), Anthony Burgess 137 mins
Anthony Burgess's view of the world is more akin to Kubrick's than Arthur C. Clarke's was in 2001. The result is a film that is almost too savage to be seen twice. In a stylish, Russified, supine, shrivelled-up England, a teenage gang member, after raping a woman, is given aversion therapy; forced to be good. Even the freedom to sin is lost.

The Andromeda Strain
USA Universal
★

Robert Wise Ꮚ Nelson Gidding, based on *The Andromeda Strain* (1969), Michael Crichton 130 mins
What one remembers are the extended opening sequences, during which spacesuited teams attempt to find out what has happened to an American desert community after being infected by an alien micro-organism. The rest is polish.

Quest for Love
UK Peter Rogers Productions
★

Ralph Thomas Ꮚ Terence Feely, based on "Random Quest", John Wyndham 91 mins
A man is shifted into a good-time parallel-world existence, and falls in love with his wife, who dies; back here, he looks for her again.

Escape from the Planet of the Apes
USA Apjac/20th Century-Fox
★

Don Taylor Ꮚ Paul Dehn, based on characters created by Pierre Boulle 97 mins See also *Planet of the Apes* (1968)
Round and round we go, in this second sequel to Planet of the Apes. Shot back in time to now, clever apes breed, and it looks like their child will inherit the future.

Glen and Randa
USA UMC
★

Jim McBride Ꮚ Lorenzo Mans, Rudolf Wurlitzer, McBride 94 mins
Strange, and rather beautiful: a happy couple leaves safe retreat and crosses post-catastrophe America looking for a magical Metropolis. She dies in childbirth; he continues across the sea, still searching.

BREWSTER McCLOUD

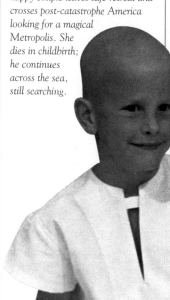

Silent Running
USA Universal
★★

◁ Douglas Trumbull ◨ Deric Wachburn, Mike Aimino, Steve Bocho, from a story by Trumbull ▣ 90 mins ▣
Everyone comments on the ending, because everyone remembers it. Nuclear war has shot Earth's ecological bolt. A spaceship stores samples of the cornucopia we have destroyed, but the army attempts to destroy this Eden, too. The ship escapes, the pilot dies: one last robot waters what is left of the green.

Z.P.G.
(Zero Population Growth)
USA Sagittarius/Paramount
★

◁ Michael Campus ◨ Max Ehrlich, Frank DeFelitta ▣ 97 mins ▣
A future government tries to enforce Zero Population Growth – in fact, zero birth rate. But the message of the film is that motherhood is all.

THX 1138
USA American Zoetrope/ Warner Bros.
★★

◁ George Lucas ◨ Lucas, Walter Murch, from a story by Lucas ▣ 88 mins restored to 95 mins ▣
Based on his own student film, this is George Lucas's first feature. In a stripped-down totalitarian future, after his mate has been sent off to bed by an evil computer technician, the hero tries to escape. Just in the nick of time, budget restrictions call off his hunters.

THX 1138

The Omega Man
USA Warner Bros.
★★

◁ Boris Sagal ◨ John William Corrington, Joyce H. Corrington, based on *I Am Legend* (1954), Richard Matheson ▣ 98 mins ▣
When the last real man on Earth, surrounded by zombies, is played by Charlton Heston, it is a good guess that the zombies will come a cropper, and that other folk (and a vital serum) will be found. Check.

1972

Conquest of the Planet of the Apes
USA Apjac/20th Century-Fox
★

◁ J. Lee Thompson ◨ Paul Dehn, based on characters created by Pierre Boulle ▣ 86 mins ▣ See also *Planet of the Apes* (1968)
This third sequel claws back through time towards the point when the original started, in the first place. It is a long trip.

Frogs
USA American International
★

◁ George McCowan ◨ Robert Hutchison, Robert Blees ▣ 90 mins ▣
Once again, humanity says sorry to the animal species that we have butchered. In this guilt-ridden tale it is the frogs that bite back.

Panico en el Transiberiano
(Horror Express)
Spain/UK Granada/Benmar
★

◁ Eugenio Martin ◨ Arnaud d'Usseau, Julian Halevy ▣ 90 mins cut to 88 mins ▣
Way back, a puppet-master alien goofed, possessing a missing link about to die. Reawakened, it goes on possessing.

Slaughterhouse-Five
USA Vanadas/Universal
★★

◁ George Roy Hill ◨ Stephen Geller, based on *Slaughterhouse-Five, or the Children's Crusade* (1969), Kurt Vonnegut Jr. ▣ 104 mins ▣
There is no newsreel footage of the firebombing of Dresden (because nothing much did survive the firestorm) so shots of Prague on fire are substituted here. In other ways, too, this film does not quite equal the original book, whose protagonist flees through time from memories of Dresden, ending up in an alien zoo. Here it sounds fun.

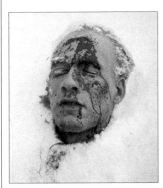

SLAUGHTERHOUSE-FIVE

Death Line
(Raw Meat)
UK K-L Productions
★★

◁ Gary Sherman ◨ Ceri Jones, from a story by Sherman ▣ 87 mins ▣
A cave-in during the building of an underground station in 1892 creates a society living in the deserted tunnels beneath London. A modern day police investigation into missing persons reveals the cannibalistic community, and the expected violence and scenes of rotting flesh ensue. Despite being full of the usual horror and gore, the film is surprisingly well constructed, containing a strong story line, pathos, and love. Sherman was highly praised for his directorial debut.

Everything You Always Wanted to Know about Sex, but Were Afraid to Ask
USA Jack Rollins and Charles H. Joffe Productions/United Artists
★

◁ Woody Allen ◨ Allen, suggested by *Everything You Always Wanted to Know about Sex, but Were Afraid to Ask*, David Reuben ▣ 88 mins ▣
A series of Woody Allen skits, most hilarious, two SF: a huge female breast runs amok; talking sperm prepare for action.

Pursuit
USA ABC Circle/ABC TV
★

◁ Michael Crichton ◨ Robert Dozier, based on *Binary* (1972), Crichton as John Lange ▣ 72 mins ▣
Crichton's directorial debut came with this made-for-television film. A psychopath who becomes obsessed with the machinations of politics, bears a particular resentment towards one Republican. In order to kill him, he plans the mass death of all the Republicans, conveniently gathered together to attend a convention.

Solaris
Russia Mosfilm
★★★

◁ Andrei Tarkovsky ◨ Friedrich Gorenstein, Tarkovsky, based on *Solaris* (1961), Stanisław Lem ▣ 165 mins cut to 132 mins for first US release ▣
Because the film medium is so good at making what it represents look like something, Solaris risks enchanting viewers with visible delights. A space station on the planet Solaris is in trouble; a psychologist goes to check things out, and finds that the planet itself is sentient and translates human dreams into bodily form. Why? For mere humans, there is no answer.

1973

Cold Night's Death
USA Spelling Goldberg/ABC
★

◁ Jerrold Freedman ◨ Christopher Knopf ▣ 73 mins ▣
In a desolate Arctic scientific station, two scientists experiment on apes. In the usual revenge-of-nature manner the apes rebel, reverse their roles, and experiment on the scientists.

Invasion of the Bee Girls
USA Centaur/Sequoia
★

◁ Dennis Sanders ◨ Nicholas Meyer ▣ 85 mins ▣
Queen-bee alien nympho madam suborns human gals to drive guys to death through repeated orgasms. The cops get suspicious.

Sleeper
USA Rollins-Joffe Productions/United Artists
★★

◁ Woody Allen ◨ Allen, Marshall Brickman ▣ 88 mins ▣
A Woody Allen vehicle, but strongly plotted. The Allen figure, who is cryogenically frozen after a failed ulcer operation, awakens in a world that nightmarishly – for him – gratifies his needs. He duly bites the world that feeds him.

The Final Programme
(The Last Days of Man on Earth)
UK Goodtimes Enterprises/ Gladiole Films/MGM-EMI
★

◁ Robert Fuest ◨ Fuest, based on *The Final Programme* (1968), Michael Moorcock ▣ 89 mins ▣
Moorcock's liquid-tongued epic of a world camping towards apocalypse becomes a fatally stiff SF tale. Jerry Cornelius meets Miss Brunner, they quarrel over an Earth-threatening computer programme, have sex, and give birth to a smirking ape creature that inherits the Earth. The film is glossily done, but the story is almost incomprehensible on screen.

Genesis II
USA CBS-TV
★

◁ John Llewellyn Moxey ◨ Gene Roddenberry ▣ 90 mins ▣
Yet another post-Star-Trek Roddenberry pilot. After a suspended animation experiment goes wrong, a scientist wakes in a future world which is suffering from the aftermath of a nuclear holocaust. Ordinary humans are ruled tyrannously by mutants. Aided by his newly found primitive vitality, the hero helps overcome the rulers.

Nippon Chinbotsu
(The Submersion of Japan/ Tidal Wave)
Japan Toho
★★

◁ Shiro Moritani ◨ Shinobu Hashimoto, based on *Nippon Chinbotsu* (1973), Sakyo Komatsu ▣ 140 mins cut to 110 mins cut to 81 mins ▣
A definitive Japanese nightmare is here exposed painfully on the screen, just as in the fine novel. The deep sea trench that runs beneath the islands is about to cave in, but no one heeds the scientists' warnings. When the Japanese authorities finally pay attention they turn to the Western world for help. The West is reluctant to offer any aid, and when Mount Fuji erupts, Japan sinks into the Pacific. Nobody wants the survivors.

The Crazies
(Code Name Trixie)
USA Cambist Films
★

◁ George A. Romero ◨ Romero ▣ 104 mins ▣
Romero's second film is almost a remake of his first, Night of the Living Dead. Villagers are infected by a warfare virus which makes them crazed, and the military are instructed to kill them. The military are portrayed as being as crazy as the villagers.

Soylent Green
USA MGM
★★

Richard Fleischer ▪ Stanley R. Greenberg, based on *Make Room! Make Room!* (1966), Harry Harrison ▪ 97 mins
Adding a touch of cannibalism to Harrison's overpopulation novel, the film defuses the grave impact of the original. But "Soylent" – food from corpses – is melodramatic stuff.

SOYLENT GREEN

Traumstadt
(Dream Town/City of Dreams)
West Germany Independent Film/ Maran Film Produktion
★

Johannes Schaaf ▪ Schaaf, based on *The Other Side* (1909), Alfred Kubin ▪ 124 mins
Made in the same year as Westworld, this film features a similar isolated city, where people live out their fantasies and dreams. The result, unsurprisingly, is chaos, and the city is eventually destroyed. Routine fantasies, dated set-pieces, and Schaaf's moralizing tone make for tedium, but the destruction scenes are magnificent.

Battle for the Planet of the Apes
USA Apjac/20th Century-Fox
★

J. Lee Thompson ▪ John William Corrington, Joyce Hooper Corrington, based on a story by Paul Dehn ▪ 88 mins
See also *Planet of the Apes* (1968)
In this, the final sequel, the mouth finally bites the tail of the story, going back up the hill of time to the very beginning.

Schlock
USA Gazotski Films
★★

John Landis ▪ Landis ▪ 77 mins
This is a hilarious spoof of the kind of film – 1950s monster films – that nobody dreamed could ever be outdone. Landis duly outdoes them.

Lost Horizon
USA Columbia
★

Charles Jarrott ▪ Larry Kramer, based on the film *Lost Horizon* (1937) ▪ 150 mins cut to 143 mins
The first version, made in 1937, is a great film. This one has song and dance, and Hollywood Big Thinks, and really not much else.

Mutations
UK Getty Picture Corp./ Columbia
★

Jack Cardiff ▪ Robert D. Weinbach, Edward Mann ▪ 92 mins
In 1973, it is good fun to see mad scientists still "mutating" folk into Venus Fly Traps. Tom Baker (later BBC's Doctor Who) takes part.

Phase IV
USA Alced/Paramount/PBR Productions
★

Saul Bass ▪ Mayo Simon ▪ 91 mins cut to 84 mins
Another revenge-of-nature film. This time the ants of Arizona decide to wipe us out. Weirdly, the human protagonists end up joining them.

Westworld
USA MGM
★★★

Michael Crichton ▪ Crichton ▪ 88 mins
Michael Crichton does not much like science (just see Jurassic Park if you doubt it), and his first feature film chillingly uses Yul Brynner as a robot who becomes a rogue killer in a Wild West theme park.

The Cars that Ate Paris
Australia Salt Pan/Australian Film Development Corporation/ Royce Smeal
★

Peter Weir ▪ Weir ▪ 88 mins
Not exactly Paris, France; in fact Paris, Australia. It is a terrifying sight: a posse of mutated autos, driven by demented teenagers.

Planet Earth
USA ABC
★

Marc Daniels ▪ Gene Roddenberry, Juanita Bartlett ▪ 75 mins
An example of what not to do when tired of Star Trek. Roddenberry's television pilot, on a post-holocaust Earth, is sanctimonious and leaden.

The Questor Tapes
USA Universal/NBC
★

Richard A. Colla ▪ Gene Roddenberry, Gene L. Coon ▪ 100 mins
Another failed television pilot, this one might have gone somewhere. Questor is an android who wants to know why he has been guarding Earth. We never find out.

Damnation Alley
USA Landers-Roberts/Zeitman/ 20th Century-Fox
★

Jack Smight ▪ Alan Sharp, Lukas Heller, based on *Damnation Alley* (1969), Roger Zelazny ▪ 95 mins cut to 91 mins
Not an improvement on Zelazny's apocalyptic run through America after the bomb, this is a disgruntled buddy flick. Cardboard backdrops stand in for the end of the world.

Chosen Survivors
USA/Mexico Alpine Churubusco/Metromedia
★

Sutton Roley ▪ H.B. Cross, Jeo Reb Moffly, based on a story by Cross ▪ 99 mins
Tricked into a pocket-universe-like bomb shelter as an experiment in induced paranoia, the cast soon finds itself fighting off vampire bats.

It's Alive
USA Larco/Warner Bros.
★★★

Larry Cohen ▪ Cohen ▪ 91 mins
Like so many successful SF films, it was made on a small budget. The monster baby – mostly just a flicker on the screen – is stunning.

Who?
(The Man in the Steel Mask)
UK/West Germany Hemisphere/ Maclean & Co.
★★

Jack Gold ▪ Gold as John Gould, based on *Who?* (1958), Algis Budrys ▪ 91 mins
In a classic intensification of 1950s films about paranoia (the era from which the novel dates), this film neatly and chillingly encapsulates the whole theme. An American scientist is captured by the Soviets after he is involved in a car crash, and transformed into a cyborg. When he is returned home after several months, the Americans must work out who he is. Martyr? Traitor? Himself? Somebody else?

Killdozer
USA Universal TV/ABC
★

Jerry London ▪ Theodore Sturgeon, based on his story "Killdozer" (1944) ▪ 74 mins
The World War II bulldozer of Sturgeon's original tale is possessed by an entity that was planted aeons earlier by aliens. Not much of this survives in the film.

Terminal Man
USA Warner Bros.
★

Mike Hodges ▪ Hodges, based on *The Terminal Man* (1972), Michael Crichton ▪ 107 mins cut to 104 mins
A contemporary variation on the Frankenstein story, in which scientists create a monster that they cannot control. The terminal of the film's title is a miniature computer that has been implanted into a psychotic man's brain in order to control his violence. Unexpectedly, he comes to enjoy the process of being controlled, and eventually goes on a murder spree solely to activate the implant.

Zardoz
UK John Boorman Productions/20th Century-Fox
★

John Boorman ▪ Boorman ▪ 105 min cut to 104 mins
The title refers to The Wizard of Oz, but the story is about a barren utopia and a harsh revolt. The post-holocaust world of 2293 is divided into two sections, the Outlands where the inhabitants live a brutal existence, and the Vortex where the "eternals" live, controlling the brutals through police exterminators. The film attempts to be both a revolt-of-the-masses film, and a disquisition on freedom. Unfortunately, the result is pompous and fatuous.

The Parasite Murders
(They Came from Within/Shivers)
Canada Cinepix/Canadian Film Development Corporation
★

David Cronenberg ▪ Cronenberg ▪ 87 mins cut to 77 mins
The parasite is implanted into patients by a research doctor, instead of the organ transplant they were expecting. It turns the victim into a sex maniac with venereal disease. Gore and horror follow as parasites can be seen emerging and leaping from one body to another. This was the first of Cronenberg's films to enter commercial cinema and was poorly received due to its graphic special effects, which were to be echoed later in the film Alien.

The Stranger Within
USA Lorimar/ABC TV
★

Lee Philips ▪ Richard Matheson, based on his story "Mother by Protest" (1953) ▪ 72 mins
Oddly enough, this weird little film, in which alien spores impregnate a panicked woman, ends happily, with newborn child levitating Marswards.

The Stepford Wives
USA Fadsin Cinema Associates/ Columbia
★★

Bryan Forbes ▪ William Goldman, based on *The Stepford Wives* (1972), Ira Levin ▪ 115 mins
Katharine Ross and Paula Prentiss play the wives who are newly arrived in the small town of Stepford in Connecticut where all the other women seem to be unusually passive and uncomplaining. It is eventually revealed that an ex-Disneyland employee is making robot replicas of the women for the husbands of Stepford. It is a feminist fable, but could have been much better with a lighter touch and a quicker pace.

Dark Star
USA Jack H. Harris Enterprises
★★★

John Carpenter ▪ Carpenter, Dan O'Bannon ▪ 83 mins
This is an absolute classic, and it was made on a tiny budget. John Carpenter went on to bigger things, as did Dan O'Bannon, but neither of them ever again made a film as blackly funny as this one. In the 22nd century, on a spaceship full of eccentric computers and a sentient, talking bomb, a crew of four with a deep-frozen captain cruise the universe, looking for unruly planets to terminate.

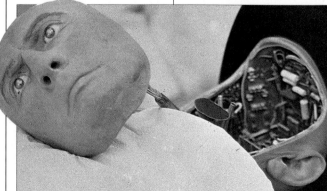

WESTWORLD

1975

A Boy and his Dog
USA LG Jaf Productions
★★

◨ L.Q. Jones ▣ Jones, based on "A Boy and his Dog" (1969), Harlan Ellison ▦ 89 mins ▣
This post-holocaust film savages human sentimentality about canines. Listen to the Dog's savage telepathic messages to the Boy; watch the Boy feed his Girl to the Dog; and go underground, to find a new world.

Rollerball
USA United Artists
★

◨ Norman Jewison ▣ William Harrison, based on his "Roller Ball Murders" (1973) ▦ 129 mins cut to 125 mins ▣
The story is wildly overcomplicated, and the game itself, dodgem mayhem on rollerskates, is sometimes hard to follow. The idea that corporations will soon be keeping us tame with bread and circuses is also not new.

ROLLERBALL

Death Race 2000
USA New World
★★

◨ Paul Bartel ▣ Robert Thom, Charles Griffith, based on a story by Ib Melchior ▦ 80 mins ▣
Like Rollerball, but zanier, wittier, more fun. The race across America by jumped-up stock cars is chock full of absurdities and futurisitic silliness, but a good time is had by all.

The Rocky Horror Picture Show
USA A Lou Adler-Michael White Production/20th Century-Fox
★★

◨ Jim Sharman ▣ Sharman, Richard O'Brien, based on O'Brien's The Rocky Horror Show (1973) ▦ 101 mins ▣
A cult-SF camp musical, with Dr. Frank-N-Furter and the gang. Very popular: singalongs in the aisles are still common.

Escape to Witch Mountain
USA Walt Disney
★

◨ John Hough ▣ Robert Malcolm Young, based on Escape to Witch Mountain (1968), Alexander Key ▦ 97 mins ▣
Amnesiac children with superpowers from another planet best the villains hoping to profit from their telepathy, and skedaddle back to space.

The Night that Panicked America
USA ABC TV
★

◨ Joseph Sargent ▣ Nicholas Meyer, based on the radio play of The War of the Worlds (1938), Howard Koch ▦ 100 mins cut to 78 mins ▣
The radio presentation of H.G. Wells's novel was clearly a play, but many thought it was for real. This mild film recreates the night.

Strange New World
USA Warner Bros. TV/ABC
★

◨ Robert Butler ▣ Walon Green, Ronald F. Graham, Al Ramrus ▦ 100 mins ▣
Astronauts return from deep sleep in space to a post-meteor-storm Earth split into hundreds of tiny countries, each different. A few are visited.

The Land that Time Forgot
UK Amicus
★★

◨ Kevin Connor ▣ Michael Moorcock, James Cawthorn, from The Land that Time Forgot, Edgar Rice Burroughs ▦ 95 mins ▣
Shenanigans in the Antarctic between Germans and Americans who discover the Lost World of Caprona, where dinosaurs roam, down a long tunnel.

The UFO Incident
USA Universal/NBC
★★

◨ Richard A. Colla ▣ S. Lee Pogostin, based on The Interrupted Journey (1966), John G. Fuller ▦ 100 mins ▣
SF and UFOs do not normally mix. SF readers see fiction, UFO buffs see real-life conspiracy. But this is good fiction about bad fact.

The Ultimate Warrior
USA Warner Bros.
★

◨ Robert Clouse ▣ Clouse ▦ 92 mins ▣
One of the first of the Kung-Fu, street-gangs-in-New-York flicks with kicks and stomps in the ruined air.

1976

God Told Me To
(Demon)
USA Larco
★★

◨ Larry Cohen ▣ Cohen ▦ 89 mins ▣
This is extremely weird, but as unforgettable as a childhood dream. God as alien; sons proclaiming Second Comings; gang warfare; and rampant but repressed sexuality everywhere, as a Catholic detective refuses the offer of a hermaphrodite offspring of "God" to bear his child.

The Food of the Gods
USA AIP
★

◨ Bert I. Gordon ▣ Gordon, based on part of The Food of the Gods, and How it Came to Earth (1904), H.G. Wells ▦ 88 mins ▣
H.G. Wells's novel was one thing. This silly ecology-exploitation flick, with lousy special effects purporting to demonstrate how big bugs eat muck, is another.

Embryo
USA Cine Artists
★

◨ Ralph Nelson ▣ Anita Doohan, Jack W. Thomas, based on a story by Thomas ▦ 105 mins ▣
A scientist grows a gal from a seed, and expects to shape her social life as femme fatale. Wrong move.

The Man Who Fell to Earth
UK British Lion/A Cinema V Release
★★

◨ Nicolas Roeg ▣ Paul Mayersberg, based on The Man Who Fell to Earth (1963), Walter Tevis ▦ 145 mins often cut to 138 mins ▣
A long, stiflingly claustrophobic tale of the gradual, forced transformation of a visiting alien into an entrapped human being. David Bowie is translucently splendid as the emissary from a desert planet who loses his mobility, sight, and family. In the end, chillingly, he is just one of us.

Carrie
USA Reg Bank/United Artists
★★

◨ Brian De Palma ▣ Lawrence D. Cohen, based on Carrie (1974), Stephen King ▦ 98 mins ▣
This is hardly SF at all, but cannot be ignored: it made Stephen King famous. It is a mythic vision of puberty, as Carrie gains her powers, and inflicts terrible revenge.

At the Earth's Core
USA Amicus/AIP
★

◨ Kevin Connor ▣ Milton Subotsky, based on At the Earth's Core (1922), Edgar Rice Burroughs ▦ 89 mins ▣
This is the inevitable sequel to The Land that Time Forgot (1975). This time what the guys find is Pellucidar, right inside the planet.

Futureworld
USA AIP
★

◨ Richard T. Heffron ▣ Mayo Simon, George Schenck ▦ 104 mins ▣
In this Westworld sequel, the robots begin to clank, the plot to boil, and the end comes none too soon.

Rabid
Canada Cinepix/Dibar Syndicate/Canadian Film Development Corp.
★

◨ David Cronenberg ▣ Cronenberg ▦ 91 mins ▣
She is mutilated, operated upon by a plastic surgeon with bats in his scalpel, and becomes a vampire who sucks blood through an underarm phallus. About none of these goings-on, we note, is David Cronenberg ever very serious.

THE MAN WHO FELL TO EARTH

KING KONG

King Kong
USA Dino De Laurentiis/Paramount
★

◨ John Guillermin ▣ Lorenzo Semple Jr., based on King Kong (1933) ▦ 134 mins ▣
In this, the second version of the film, the great-hearted ape topples from the World Trade Centre. Plus ça change.

Logan's Run
USA MGM/United Artists
★

◨ Michael Anderson ▣ David Zelag Goodman, based on Logan's Run (1967), William F. Nolan and George Clayton Johnson ▦ 118 mins ▣
A couple of years later, this sanitized future was no longer viable: cinema had learned about grit and gunge. But in 1975, clean-cut kids in fab togas could still revolt against saniseal elders and escape outdoors, where jolly avuncular Peter Ustinov shows them real life.

War Games
USA MGM-UA/Sherwood Productions
★★
John Badham Lawrence Lasker, Walter F. Parkes
113 mins
A computer-wise kid hacks into an army computer to play a war game. Unfortunately, the game is for real, and the world almost comes to an end before he can trick the army brass into letting him save it.

Strange Invaders
USA EMI Films/Orion/ Michael Laughlin
★
Michael Laughlin Laughlin, William Condon 93 mins
As our understanding of the universe grows more complex, alien invasions seem less and less likely, but alien visits are another matter. Here is a 1980s look at old fears and new kinds of trouble from the stars.

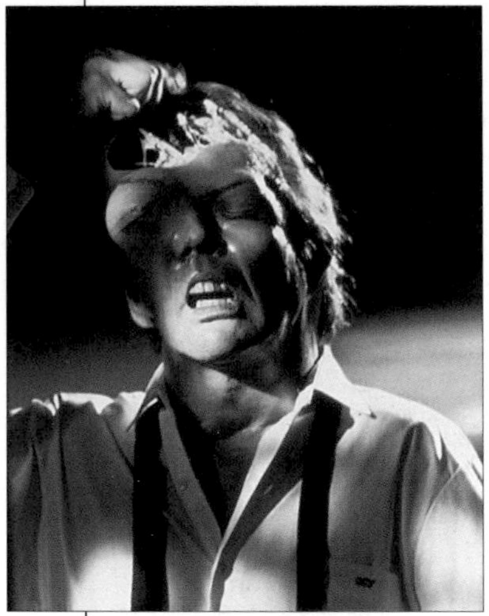

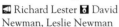

STRANGE INVADERS

Brainstorm
USA MGM/UA/JF
★
Douglas Trumbull Robert Stitzel, Philip Frank Messina, Bruce Joel Rubin, based on a story by Rubin 106 mins
Made just too soon to be plausible, this is a slowpoke look at electronic transfers of sensations from one brain to another.

Superman 3
UK Dovemead/Cantharus
★
Richard Lester David Newman, Leslie Newman
125 mins
Superman's character is warped by synthetic Kryptonite, causing him to use his power to wreak havoc. The problem with letting Richard Lester loose on Superman is that the Man of Steel is either myth or bad joke. In this film, laughter kills.

Testament
USA Entertainment Events/ American Playhouse
★★
Lynne Littman John Sacret Young, based on "The Last Testament", Carol Amen
90 mins
During the Cold War, few films dealt with the true consequences of nuclear war. By 1983, however, Testament *could look back at the fears, and show us the true ending.*

Born in Flames
USA Lizzie Borden/ Jerome Foundation/CAPS/ Young Filmmakers
★★
Lizzie Borden Borden
80 mins
Modern SF films tend to run to big money for special effects; but this feminist view of the downside of a socialist revolution in America is scathing, funny, complicated, and likeable. All on a tiny budget.

Return of the Jedi
USA 20th Century-Fox/Lucasfilm
★★★
Richard Marquand George Lucas, Lawrence Kasdan, based on a story by Lucas 132 mins
The set pieces continue, and the special effects are still magically evocative; but the dreamtime intensity of this conclusion to the Star Wars *trilogy is derived instead from the deepening of Luke's character as he reaches galaxy-spanning adulthood.*

Le Prix du Danger
(The Prize of Peril)
France/Yugoslavia Brent Walker/Swanie/TFI/ UGC/ Top 1/Avala
★★
Yves Boisset Boisset, Jan Curtelin, based on "The Prize of Peril" (1958), Robert Sheckley
98 mins, cut to 88 mins in English dubbed version
A bit of game-show paranoia. "The Prize of Peril" is a television game-show that pits contestants against killers, but rigs the outcome.

The Man with Two Brains
USA Warner/Aspen
★★
Carl Reiner Reiner, Steve Martin, George Gipe 93 mins cut to 86 mins
This is the fourth remake of Curt Siodmak's Donovan's Brain, *played this time for laughs, with Steve Martin as the dumb brain surgeon who mixes two women's brains up.*

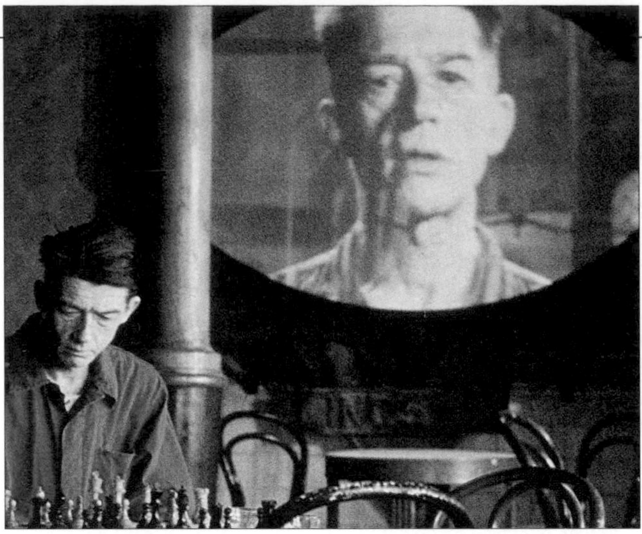

1984

1984

Dune
USA De Laurentiis/ Universal
★★
David Lynch Lynch, based on *Dune* (1965), Frank Herbert
137 mins
It is hard to know if this strange film should have been shorter, or much longer. Lynch tangles himself up in bits of plot, but might – given more time – have transformed Herbert's huge and ambitious novel into a great film: a sort of Twin Peaks *in the stars, with heroes.*

Threads
UK BBC TV
★★
Mick Jackson Barry Hines
115 mins
Once again – now that it seemed less imminent – the theme of nuclear holocaust is given the kind of soberly devastating examination that might have had a profound effect on an earlier Cold War generation. Civil defence is again no defence at all, and the film ends in barbarism.

City Limits
USA Sho Films/Video Form Pictures/Island Alive
★
Aaron Lipstadt Don Opper
85 mins
In the future, all the adults have died and young street gangs fight among themselves. The film is fast and full of humour, but the battle at the end is predictable and disappointing.

The Brother From Another Planet
USA A-Train Films
★★
John Sayles Sayles
108 mins
Made on a small budget, but with plenty of wit, this film demonstrates how familiar some SF themes – like alien visits – had become. This time the alien is black, mute, and cool.

1984
UK Umbrella/Rosenblum/ Virgin Cinema Films
★
Michael Radford Radford, Jonathan Gems, based on *Nineteen Eighty-Four* (1949), George Orwell 110 mins
Orwell did not write his classic novel to predict what gadgets we would have in 1984, but to warn us about totalitarianism and mind control. This film tries to replicate, in film terms, Orwell's 1948 guess at what 1984 would look like – which may be a nice idea, but has nothing to do with his message.

2010
USA MGM-UA
★
Peter Hyams Hyams, based on *2010: Odyssey Two* (1982), Arthur C. Clarke 116 mins
The trouble with sequels is that the original should be made to end with a question that needs answering. 2001 *ended with* Homo superior *gazing at us from beyond, and* 2010 *can do nothing with this.* Homo superior's *thoughts are not ours, Keir Dullea appears only to warn humans off, and the film becomes a routine adventure.*

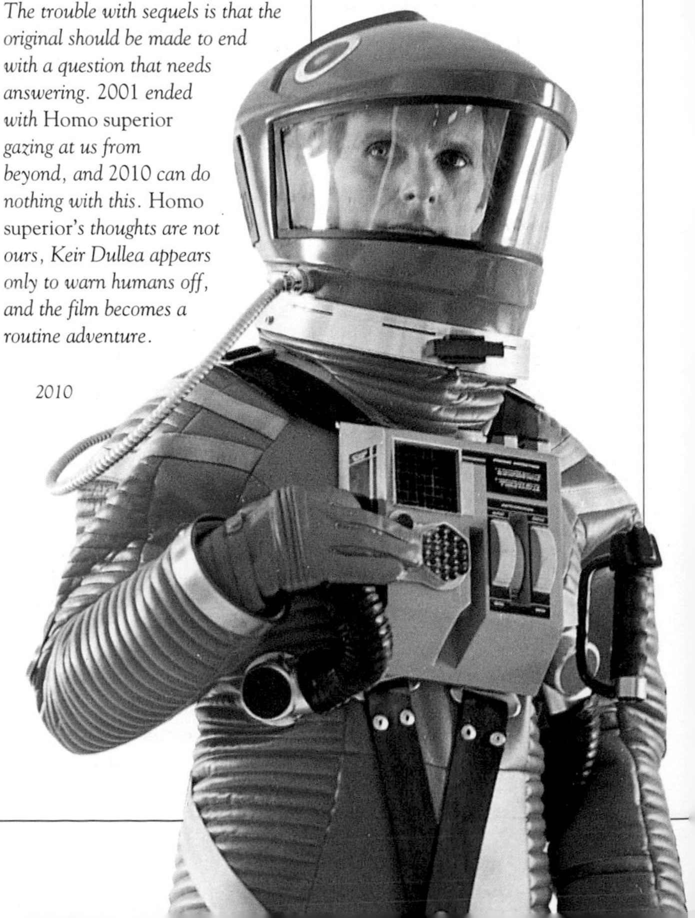

2010

The Philadelphia Experiment
USA New World/Cinema Group/ Douglas Curtis
★
Stewart Raffill William Gray, Michael Janover, based on a story by Wallace Bennett and Don Jakoby, based on *The Philadelphia Experiment* (1979), William I. Moore, Charles Berlitz
101 mins
A reversal of Final Countdown *of 1980. In this film sailors on a 1943 destroyer become trapped in today. They need comforting, and a contemporary girl is willing.*

Supergirl
UK Cantharus/Ilya Salkind
★
Jeannot Szwarc David Odell
124 mins
This is not exactly a feminist tract. Supergirl *is a total wimp, and the sorceress (who is superbly camped by Faye Dunaway) is a crone. There is some fearful flying, too.*

Trancers
(Future Cop)
USA Empire Pictures
★★
Charles Band Danny Bilson, Paul De Meo 76 mins
A cop called Jack Deth travels back from the future through time to 1985 Los Angeles, to kill a man who plans to take over the world with the aid of people under his psychic influence – Trancers. *Dizzy, but also occasionally delightful.*

Iceman
USA Universal
★

📽 Fred Schepisi 🎬 Chip Proser, John Drimmer, from a story by Drimmer ⏱ 99 mins 📀
A Stone Age man is revived, after 40,000 years of frozen sleep, to be experimented upon by two scientists, one good, one bad.

The Ice Pirates
USA MGM-United Artists
★★

📽 Stewart Raffill 🎬 Raffill, Stanford Sherman ⏱ 94 mins 📀
It does not much matter that space piracy is hard to imagine – the velocities being too great – because the film is a gas, chock-full of manic action.

Runaway
USA Tri-Star/Michael Crichton
★

📽 Michael Crichton 🎬 Crichton ⏱ 97 mins 📀
Crichton – the maker of Westworld and Coma and the man who inspired Jurassic Park – has never trusted machines. In this poor cousin to his other films, robots run amok.

STARMAN

Starman
USA Columbia/Delphi
★★

📽 John Carpenter 🎬 Bruce Evans, Raynold Gideon, Dean Reisner (uncredited) ⏱ 115 mins 📀
A stranded starman takes on the shape of Jeff Bridges, elopes with a human woman, fights off immoral government agents, and gains his goal. The love affair is convincing.

Star Trek III: The Search for Spock
USA Paramount/Cinema Group Venture
★

📽 Leonard Nimoy 🎬 Harve Bennett ⏱ 105 mins 📀
Psychoanalysis buffs love this one. Kirk is viciously treated in his search to redeem Spock from death – and the film was directed by Nimoy.

THE TERMINATOR

The Terminator
USA Orion/Hemdale/Pacific Western
★★★

📽 James Cameron 🎬 Cameron, Gale Anne Hurd, with Harlan Ellison acknowledged for idea ⏱ 107 mins 📀
Without a huge budget to clog the works, the makers of this film depend on the story; and it is a great one. Schwarzenegger plays a killer cyborg who is sent back from the 21st century to eliminate a young woman before she can conceive the child responsible for fighting the cyborg's machine masters. Also from the future comes a young man, who helps the intended victim to escape – and sleeps with her along the way, leaving her pregnant.

DefCon 4
Canada New World
★

📽 Paul Donovan 🎬 Donovan ⏱ 89 mins 📀
An attempt at post-holocaust realism. A spacecraft returns to Earth after World War III, to find it populated by survivors who have no hope of rebuilding their lives.

Repo Man
USA Universal/Edge City
★★★

📽 Alex Cox 🎬 Cox ⏱ 92 mins 📀
A repo man and his apprentice are hired to repossess cars whose owners have fallen behind on their payments. It is a mean streets job, and in this brilliant directorial debut it symbolizes a world that has sunk irretrievably into chaos and cod transcendentalism. The car they are chasing here is owned by a crazed scientist, and has something atomic in its trunk, and half the world seems to be after it, too – including some aliens, perhaps.

1 9 8 5

Cocoon
USA 20th Century-Fox/Zanuck/Brown
★

📽 Ron Howard 🎬 Tom Benedek, from a story by David Saperstein ⏱ 117 mins 📀
Aliens store cocooned fellow-aliens in a swimming pool that human oldsters are using. The water rejuvenates them, making them behave like juveniles.

Brazil
UK Embassy
★★★

📽 Terry Gilliam 🎬 Gilliam, Tom Stoppard, Charles McKeown ⏱ 142 mins 📀
This film about a dystopian world that oppresses individuals was criticized for gloom and lack of focus, but on examination the gloom proves to be shot through with affirmation, and the complexity is anything but foolish. Most films about the future simplify things; Brazil submerges us in its tomorrow.

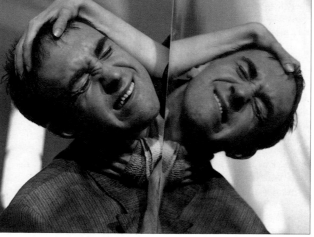

BRAZIL

Max Headroom
UK Chrysalis/Channel 4
★★

📽 various, including Annabel Jankel, Rocky Morton 🎬 Steve Roberts, George Stone, based on a story by Jankel, Morton ⏱ 70 mins 📀
The film is about a reporter trying to find out about blipverts – subliminal ads that make viewers explode – when he is killed, and his brain is turned into an electronic image. Max Headroom is born.

Mad Max beyond Thunderdome
Australia Warner/Kennedy Miller
★★

📽 George Miller, George Ogilvie 🎬 Terry Hayes, Miller ⏱ 107 mins 📀
It is long after the world collapsed. Max chases a thief to futuristic Bartertown where Tina Turner rules. The sky is the limit.

Real Genius
USA Tri-Star/Delphi III
★

📽 Martha Coolidge 🎬 Neal Israel, Pat Proft, Peter Torokvei, based on a story by Israel and Proft ⏱ 106 mins 📀
One of several mid-1980s films about real bright kids facing extremely stupid governments. This time the teenager builds a laser.

Life Force
UK Cannon
★

📽 Tobe Hooper 🎬 Dan O'Bannon, Don Jakoby, based on The Space Vampires (1976), Colin Wilson ⏱ 101 mins 📀
Deeply silly flick. Guys in space snaffle vampire space lady, who stalks naked through London, causing an understandable uproar.

Zone Trooper
USA Altar/Empire
★

📽 Danny Bilson 🎬 Bilson, Paul De Meo ⏱ 86 mins 📀
An alien crashes into World War II. A platoon of GIs befriends him. Adolf Hitler is punched in the nose. The fun continues.

Explorers
USA Paramount/Edward S. Feldman/Industrial Light and Magic
★

📽 Joe Dante 🎬 Eric Luke ⏱ 109 mins 📀
What might an alien think about its reception on Earth if it only had films from the 1950s to judge our world by? Here we find out.

Back to the Future
USA Universal/Stephen Spielberg
★★

📽 Robert Zemeckis 🎬 Zemeckis, Bob Gale ⏱ 116 mins 📀
For anyone who had the bad – or good – luck to grow up in 1950s America, Back to the Future is an extremely odd film. A contemporary teenager zips back to 1955 in a time machine, fends off his infatuated teenage mother, puts life right, and returns. 1955 is like – but also totally unlike – the reality: clean, decent, polished, simple, sweet.

Enemy Mine
USA Kings Road Entertainment/20th Century-Fox
★★

📽 Wolfgang Petersen 🎬 Edward Khmara, based on "Enemy Mine" (1989), Barry B. Longyear ⏱ 108 mins cut to 93 mins 📀
A standard theme of mature written Space Opera: individuals from opposing races find something to share in adversity. Here the planet is unfriendly, the alien dies giving birth, and the human adopts the infant, with tearjerks.

The Quiet Earth
New Zealand Cinepro/Pillsbury
★★

📽 Geoff Murphy 🎬 Bill Baer, Bruno Lawrence, Sam Pillsbury, based on The Quiet Earth (1981), Craig Harrison ⏱ 91 mins 📀
One thing about last-man-on-Earth films: you can save on casting. This is a typically modest example, and pleasingly lacks moral insistence – unlike, say, The World, the Flesh and the Devil. Here, everyone dies in a malfunction of the universe itself, except for those who were dying just when the glitch occurred. They get together.

NEW PREMISES

AFTER ALMOST A CENTURY, it seemed that in the 1980s, SF in the cinema might finally be catching up with the written article. For decades – hampered by budget constraints, conservative studio bosses who insisted on series, and by a tendency to translate every SF theme into a horror motif – SF cinema had tended to present us with impossibly naive, tinny, and antiquated visions of the future. But the 1970s showed the way, and now – although too many action-figure heroes still strutted their stuff – it looked as though we were about to experience some exhilarating visions of new worlds rushing pellmell upon us. We were not disappointed.

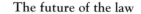

The future of the law
Blade Runner *gave the 1980s the mean streets. And down these mean streets a man – or a robocop – must go, to save us from the evils of city life. Although the hero of Robocop is in fact a cyborg – a human head grafted onto a mechanical body – he has all the ambiguous allure of the robot, guarding us but haunting our dreams. And like so many robots, he wants to know who he is.*

New monsters
The replicant – Blade Runner-speak for android – is a kind of haunting pun on humanity. He is stronger and cleverer than we are, but his lifespan is tiny. He is dying right now, and not even his maker can do anything for him.

Genuine SF takes over

There was no great conversion in Hollywood. SF film-makers still tended to suffer from sequelitis, and as a result many of the most prominent films from the 1980s followed on from stories first told in the 1970s. *Superman, Star Wars*, and *Alien*, for example, all gave birth to strapping offspring; although none of the sequels had the fresh-minted impact of the originals, it was certainly the case that by the *Return of the Jedi* the implications of the Star Wars universe had deepened; *Aliens* was an intensely visceral experience.

The fact that some of the many 1980s sequels were decent films is dependent on a basic shift in the industry: these 1980s sequels are genuine SF films. It had not always been thus. For much of the century, most so-called SF films were thinly disguised horror. Horror tends to lose its effect when repeated, so the remakes and sons-of into which the industry insisted on putting money were almost all significantly worse than the original films.

The literature of SF, on the other hand, has never been averse to sequels or to shared-world adventures, at least in part because a universe is an elaborate thing to create, and single stories almost certainly fail to exhaust its implications. SF stories – unlike tales of horror – frequently tend towards the epic, and anything epic, such as *Star Wars*, will tend to go on (and on).

Future fighter
There is no ambivalence here. The Terminator is a cyborg: humanity on the outside, coating a computer-controlled weapon. He is here to destroy our future.

Split Second
UK Entertainment/
Challenge/Muse
★

🎬 Tony Maylam 📝 Gary Scott
Thompson ⏱ 90 mins 📀
*London in the next century, after
decades of rising damp, is nearly
underwater. Old crimes continue,
but with new villains: in this case, the
perpetrator is a very nasty alien.*

Star Trek VI: The
Undiscovered Country
USA UIP/Paramount
★

🎬 Nicholas Meyer 📝 Meyer,
Denny Martin Flynn, based on a
story by Leonard Nimoy,
Lawrence Konner, Mark
Rosenthal ⏱ 110 mins 📀
*Trekkies might have a good word to
say for this tepid and overblown sixth
film instalment, but its makers had
clearly tired of the enterprise.*

Bill and Ted's Bogus
Journey
USA Columbia/Tri-Star/Orion/
Nelson Entertainment
★

🎬 Peter Hewitt 📝 Ed Solomon,
Chris Matheson ⏱ 93 mins 📀
*This rather lame sequel sees the dim
Californian dudes Bill and Ted visit
Hell, and hornswaggle the guy in
charge. There are some laughs along
the way, but the joke is as thin
as these boys are thick.*

BILL AND TED'S BOGUS JOURNEY

The setting of the decade
When Metropolis *was made in 1926, even architects hardly dreamed of
cities so monolithic, so complex, so all-embracing, as* Blade Runner's *vision
of Los Angeles. This may not be progress, but it is certainly movement.*

So there are lots of sequels in the literature of SF, and
lots of precedents available, therefore, to guide the
film industry when it does what it has always done
and looks for ways to do remakes.

Dark and light
Two of the most successful 1980s films, however,
failed to generate sequels, and for very good reasons.
Blade Runner is set early in the 21st century, after the
owners of the planet have
more or less abandoned it to
slum dwellers, criminals, and
entrepreneurs. It is a vision of
the Millennium, and it is a
terminal vision. It tells us that
we have exhausted the planet
and ourselves, and that the
new story is somewhere else –
in the stars, perhaps, where
happier tales are told. The
story on Earth has a finality
that forbids sequels. But in a
sense, several 1980s films were
the offspring of *Blade Runner*:
its grim city and its questions
about real and artificial life
surfaced everywhere.

Surreal vision
*In Gilliam's nightmare
vision of* Brazil, *the city
resembles the entrails of
some mad, world-
devouring dragon.*

The other major singleton,
E.T.: the Extraterrestrial, is an
extremely clever tale of
healing. E.T., wounded and adrift in a foreign world,
dies but is restored to life by the arrival of his home
ship. The human family that befriends him shifts from
dysfunctional single-parenthood to a point where it
looks as if a kindly scientist will fall in love with the
protagonist's mother. E.T. speaks of transcendence,
an outcome that does not call for sequels.

All in all, with SF epics and their sequels, with
terminal woes, with transcendence and reunions,
the 1980s was a busy decade.

Gotham's hero
*It has often been said that people who live in
cities are actors in a great costume drama, and
that it is sometimes hard to separate reality
from mask. Batman has always had that
trouble, from the moment he was born as a
comic-book figure back in the 1930s. Rescued
in Tim Burton's 1989 film from the clean and
colourful camp of the television series, he is
grim, dangerous, confused, neurotic, and
obsessed. He is the perfect product of
Gotham's dark streets: safely encased in
his high-tech black armour, he
glares at the light at the end
of the tunnel like an
angry bat.*

FILMS (

AFTER A DECADE OR
that had grown incr
film-makers would e
happened. The 1990
reruns, but relativel

★★★ Outstanding

| Director | Screen |

1 9 9 0

Robocop 2
USA Rank/Orion
★

Irvin Kershner Frank Mil
Walon Green 118 mins
*This has lots of effects, and Detro
clearly no paradise as the next
century begins to bite; but nothing
new. Paul Verhoeven, who direct
the 1987 original, is badly missed*

Flatliners
USA Columbia-Tri-Star/
Stonebridge
★

Joel Schumacher Peter
Filardi 114 mins
*The odd-sounding title refers to a
electroencephalogram reading wh
indicates no brain activity; the sto
sees medical students experimenti
at being dead and finding it is no*

Prayer of the Rollerbo
USA First Independent/Gaga
Lorber/Academy/JVC/TV To
★

Rick King W. Peter Iliff
94 mins
*In an America racked with violen
the streetwise Rollerboys, led by a
possible descendant of Hitler, go*

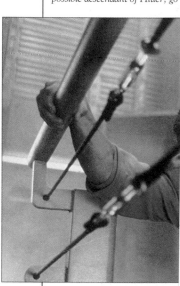

CHAPTER EIGHT

international TELEVISION

THERE HAVE BEEN SOME very successful Science Fiction series produced on television. They were usually made on shoestring budgets, strong scripts, and faith, but all the same have turned out to be hugely popular. So much so, that some have subsequently graduated to the big screen. This chapter looks at the range of programmes produced around the world, and at the characteristics of American and British television SF: to examine the traditions of television SF across the rest of the world in detail is the remit of a specialized book, but a summary of the most significant works is included here.

ABOVE: A DALEK FROM *DOCTOR WHO*
LEFT: THE USS *ENTERPRISE*, WHICH GRADUATED INTO CINEMA

AMERICAN TELEVISION

IN THE UNITED STATES PARTICULARLY, past and present television intermingles, almost indistinguishably. With a burgeoning number of cable channels, most running syndicated series (some of these half a century old), we can now nostalgically re-view almost all our SF heritage.

◀ Producer/Director   🖊 Screenplay   ⏱ Time   ⬤ Colour   ◑ Black and White

1 9 5 0 s

Captain Video
1949–53, 1955–56
◀ Larry Menkin 🖊 various, including Maurice Brockhauser, Damon Knight, C.M. Kornbluth, Robert Sheckley ⏱ 5 episodes per week of 30 mins ◑
The Captain is a genius inventor whose Cosmic Vibrator terrifies all villains except Dr. Pauli, whose "sound barrier" allows him to sneak up on the hero – for seven years.

Tales of Tomorrow
1951–56
◀ George Foley, Dick Gordon 🖊 various ⏱ weekly episodes of 25 mins ◑
Despite prejudice and a low budget, this anthology series featured some vigorous adaptations – like a version of 20,000 Leagues Under the Sea.

Science Fiction Theater
1955–57
◀ Ivan Tors 🖊 various ⏱ 78 episodes of 25 mins ◑ last season ⬤
Something of a sleeper, this anthology series presented its SF material soberly, without silliness, but was cancelled after two short years.

THE TWILIGHT ZONE

The Twilight Zone
1959–64
◀ various, including Rod Serling 🖊 various, including Serling, Ray Bradbury, Richard Matheson ⏱ 138 episodes of 25 mins, 18 cf 50 mins ◑
This anthology series, the most famous ever crafted, covered a lot more than SF, exploring – sometimes in depth – every possible region of the Fantastic.

LOST IN SPACE

1 9 6 0 s

The Outer Limits
1963–66
◀ various, including Leslie Stevens 🖊 various, including Joseph Stefano, Clifford D. Simak ⏱ 49 episodes of 50 mins ◑
One of the creators of this fine anthology series had worked with Orson Welles, and it shows in the risk-taking and flamboyance. But network programming stupidity soon killed it.

Voyage to the Bottom of the Sea
1964–68
◀ Irwin Allen 🖊 various, including William Welch, Harlan Ellison ⏱ 110 episodes of 50 mins ◑ after first season ⬤
Almost all voyages of the submarine Seaview were fraught with dangers from spies, monsters, women, and natural and unnatural disasters. But the world is saved, dozens of times.

The Man from U.N.C.L.E.
1964–68
◀ Norman Felton 🖊 various, including Harlan Ellison, Henry Slesar ⏱ 105 episodes of 50 mins ◑ after first season ⬤
It was hardly SF at all, though some of the James Bond-like spy devices were extremely implausible. The cast seems to have considerable fun spoofing genre conventions.

Lost in Space
1965–68
◀ Irwin Allen 🖊 various, including Peter Packer ⏱ 83 episodes of 50 mins ◑ after first season ⬤
Producer Irwin Allen had released a version of Swiss Family Robinson, which flopped. But when he moved the tale to space, circa 1997, he scored a modest winner. The cast of characters includes the indomitable but decidedly unsmart Professor Robinson, his wife and children, the villainous spy who has knocked them out of orbit, and a very popular robot.

The Wild, Wild West
1965–69
◀ various, including Michael Garrison 🖊 various, including Henry Sharp ⏱ 104 episodes of 50 mins ◑ after first season ⬤
Like The Man from U.N.C.L.E., this broad-gauge spoof series uses SF devices without thought and to little consequence, although some of the villains bring a whiff of Steampunk ingenuity to the 19th-century setting.

The Time Tunnel
1966–67
◀ Irwin Allen 🖊 various, including William Welch ⏱ 30 episodes of 50 mins ◑
In one of the worst 1960s series, time travellers – trapped in a vortex created by experimenting scientists – carom through cardboard sets, overturn whole societies, and escape again and again.

Star Trek
1966–69
◀ Gene Roddenberry 🖊 various, including Jerome Bixby, Robert Bloch, Harlan Ellison, Norman Spinrad, Richard Matheson, David Gerrold, Theodore Sturgeon ⏱ 79 episodes of 50 mins ⬤
Nothing can be said about this immortal programme that has not been said before, frequently. It is the most-discussed SF series ever aired. Captain Kirk and his crew are the most famous figures yet to inhabit the future, as the crew of a starship monitoring the hinterlands of human-dominated space, keeping the peace by defeating aliens, traitors, and godlings. Now and then, a genuine SF idea is given room to breathe.

STAR TREK

The Invaders
1967–68
◀ Alan Armer 🖊 various, including Don Brinkley, Jerry Sohl ⏱ 43 episodes of 50 mins ⬤
Perhaps a little late (paranoia about Communism had already peaked), this series, in which aliens who look like us have infiltrated everywhere, echoes 1950s films like Invasion of the Body Snatchers, and soon died.

THE INVADERS

Land of the Giants
1968–70
◀ Irwin Allen 🖊 various, including Bob and Esther Mitchell ⏱ 51 episodes of 50 mins ⬤
An aeroplane passes through a portal into another world, the land of the giants. Its passengers spend the next few years dodging huge children and other menaces – the special effects are good. The series ended without managing to extricate the cast.

1 9 7 0 s

Rod Serling's Night Gallery
1970–72
◀ Rod Serling 🖊 various, including Serling, based on original stories ⏱ 29 episodes of 50 mins, 16 of 25 mins ⬤
Serling's name is prominent, but his influence is less evident here than in the great Twilight Zone years. Most of the stories are horror or occult; little SF has survived.

The Six Million Dollar Man
1973–78
◀ various, including Glen A. Larson, Harve Bennett, Allan Balter 🖊 various ⏱ 100 episodes of usually 50 mins ⬤
A normal guy is more or less killed, but is resurrected by scientists into a superhero cyborg with a wide range of enhancements for saving the day.

WONDER WOMAN

Wonder Woman
1974–79

Wilfred Baumes, Mark Rodgers, Charles B. Fitzsimons various, including Jimmy Sangster, Stephen Kandel, Alan Brennert 58 episodes of 50 mins plus specials
Cathy Lee Crosby starred in the pilot, but Lynda Carter (and good action sequences) made the eventual series into a five-year success story.

Planet of the Apes
1974

Stan Hough various 14 episodes of 50 mins
As a one-year spin-off from the extremely popular film series, and starring much of the original cast, this TV outing was surprisingly successful when aired in Britain, but CBS cancelled it within the first season.

Mork and Mindy
1978–82

Garry K. Marshall various, including Dale McRaven 92 episodes of 25 mins plus pilot of 50 mins
Mork, played brilliantly by Robin Williams before he became famous, is an alien sent to Earth to study our emotional ways. He lands in Boulder, Colorado, and gradually falls in love with Mindy, a human girl. Wacky, improvisational-seeming, profound, the show proved that real SF could work on TV.

Battlestar Galactica
1978

various, including Glen A. Larson, Don Bellisario, John Dykstra various 19 episodes of 50 mins, 1 of 100 mins, pilot
It cost a lot, and it flopped. A vast fleet of spaceships, filled with humanoids like Lorne Greene, nears Earth in its attempts to escape the dread Cylons, a mechanical race inimical to biological life. Some of the special effects – created by John Dykstra, who did the tricks in Star Wars – are great.

Project UFO
1978–79

Jack Webb, Col. William T. Coleman various, including Harold Jack Bloom, Donald L. Gold 26 episodes of 50 mins
If an SF UFO story is fiction, then UFOs are imaginary; if UFOs are real, where is the fiction? Here, the perennial dilemma is half-solved by a documentary tone.

1 9 8 0 s

The Martian Chronicles
1980

Michael Anderson Richard Matheson 3 episodes of 110 mins
This adaptation of Ray Bradbury's famous stories from the 1940s is very faithful to the style of the original author. But Bradbury's highly poetic prose does not come across well when recited in front of the TV camera.

"V"
1983–85

Kenneth Johnson, Richard T. Heffron, Dean O'Brien, Garner Simmons various, including Johnson, Brian Taggert, Peggy Goldman. David Braff 2 mini-series plus 19 episodes of 50 mins
Here, the aliens are not secret invaders. In "V", it is perfectly obvious that the Visitors from elsewhere, who make themselves look human to hide the fact that they are really lizards, are up to no good. After lots of soap opera and violence, peace is declared.

"V"

The Twilight Zone
1985–87

Philip DeGuere, James Crocker, Harvey Frand various, including Ray Bradbury, Alan Brennert, George R.R. Martin 36 episodes of 50 mins or 25 mins
Amid constant feuding between CBS and the creators of individual episodes, some good stories did get aired.

Steven Spielberg's Amazing Stories
1985–87

Steven Spielberg, Joshua Brand, John Falsey various, including Spielberg, Richard Matheson 43 episodes of 25 mins, 2 of 50 mins
Despite lots of money, plus Steven Spielberg overseeing (and directing some episodes), this anthology series never really got off the ground.

Star Trek: The Next Generation
1987–94

various, including Gene Roddenberry, Rick Berman, Michael Piller various 174 episodes of 50 mins, 2 of 90 mins
After nearly two decades in TV limbo, Star Trek finally returned. Set a generation later, with a new cast, and a much more modern-looking Enterprise, The Next Generation ran twice as long as its parent, excelling it in maturity, plausibility, subtlety, and dramatic strength. If the old series still enjoys a greater allegiance, the reason may be simply mythology.

Something is Out There
1988–89

Frank Lupo, Richard Colla, John Ashley Lupo, Burt Pearl, Paul Bernbaum, Christian Darren mini-series plus 8 episodes of 50 mins
It did not last, but might have gone somewhere. A friendly, mind-reading alien helps human cops track an evil alien who – surprise – is an insidious shape-changer, and looks human.

Alien Nation
1989–90

Kenneth Johnson various 21 episodes of 50 mins plus pilot
This is another buddy series, again involving an alien and a cop. But the background is complex – half a million humanoid aliens have recently landed on Earth, and are seeking refugee status here – and the story is a rather obvious but not too preachy commentary on racial intolerance.

Quantum Leap
1989–94

Donald P. Bellisario various, including Bellisario 95 episodes of 50 mins plus pilot of 90 mins
In its complexity and its subversion of old genre expectations, Quantum Leap is a pure late-century example of SF at its best – a time-travel series that sounds superficially like the awful Time Tunnel, but which quickly transcends its roots. The hero is trapped into a one-way voyage backwards through history, occupying different bodies as he plummets downwards. This is more like it.

1 9 9 0 s

Prisoners of Gravity
1990–94

Gregg Thurlbeck Rick Green weekly episodes of 25 mins
This imaginative Canadian magazine show, featuring dozens of interviews with SF figures, was occasionally flippant, but always knowledgeable. There was nothing like it elsewhere in the English-speaking world.

Star Trek: Deep Space Nine
1993–

Rick Berman, Michael Piller various weekly episodes of 50 mins plus pilot of 100 mins
A logical development of the Star Trek universe, this series is set in a vast space habitat, where an unending succession of enterpreneurs – human and alien – intersect, quarrel, fall in love, run foul of the law… By the third season, the DS9ers resume Trekkie tradition as they set off on adventures beyond their intergalactic outpost.

Babylon 5
1993–

J. Michael Straczynski, Douglas Netter various, including Straczynski weekly episodes of 50 mins plus pilot of 90 mins
SF is a genre that prides itself on its common language, themes, icons, and plots. This did not stop criticism of Straczynski's new series, which does rather resemble Deep Space Nine.

Lois and Clark: The New Adventures of Superman
1993–

Deborah Joy LeVine various, including LeVine, Dan Levine weekly episodes of 50 mins
The joke title refers to the 19th-century Lewis and Clark Expedition, which expanded America westwards. The show itself emphasizes Superman's relationship with Lois Lane, and is ironic, matter-of-fact, and quite funny.

THE NEW ADVENTURES OF SUPERMAN

The X-Files
1993–

Chris Carter various, including Carter, Glen Morgan, James Wong, Howard Gordon, Alex Gansa weekly episodes of 50 mins
A maverick FBI agent driven by a belief in all things strange teams up with a coolly logical female sceptic to solve crimes involving the paranormal or unexplained. The atmospheric tone, low-key scares, and wittily played sexual tension have earned this creepy yet sophisticated series a cult following.

SeaQuest DSV
1993–

Steven Spielberg, Tommy Thompson, David J. Burke, Rockne S. O'Bannon, Patrick Hasburgh various weekly episodes of 50 mins, plus pilot of 90 mins
This high-budget return to the watery world of Voyage to the Bottom of the Sea is simply more of the same, with a seasoning of ecological concern.

DEFENDING THE PRESENT

AMERICAN TELEVISION PRODUCERS first became interested in SF almost half a century ago and, except for a few empty years, they have never stopped trying to make a go of it. The task has not been easy. Good SF television requires intelligent scripting and sometimes expensive sets, both of which may be hard to come by. But, far more important than either of these, good SF television requires a readiness to accept change. Much SF only pretends to explore the new, but it is important at least to pretend. American producers have found this astonishingly difficult to do.

The American series

The story of SF on American television begins with *Captain Video*, which ran from 1949 to 1956. In its prime (1950–52, more or less) it was broadcast four nights a week. It was set in the 22nd century, and the Captain was chief of the Video Rangers. Through his scientific acumen, he managed to invent a huge number of weapons and gadgets just in time to defeat various extraterrestrial villains and invaders.

There are two things to note about this programme and its long-term implications for American SF television. The first is obvious: *Captain Video* was a children's show, and the dozens of children's SF programmes that followed were all the offspring of this one show. The second thing is clear too and, although seemingly insignificant, even more important: it was a series. In the early years, television in America tended to emphasize the sponsored series,

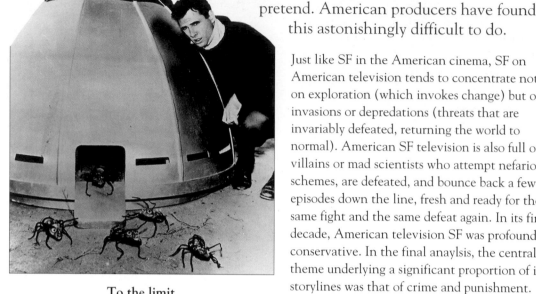

To the limit
Not quite as successful as The Twilight Zone, *and scuppered by foolish scheduling (long before videos dethroned schedules),* The Outer Limits *was, for some viewers, even better than its bigger rival.*

It's a mystery
The Twilight Zone *was known for its sting-in-the-tail plots.*

in direct contrast to British television, which tended to go for either one-off dramas or serials. The main difference between a serial and a series is that a serial is a single story, designed to begin and to end, whereas a series is basically a collection of episodes, designed not to end. And when we remember that SF purports to explore change, which implies both beginnings and endings, it comes clear that there is a problem here. Perhaps we can now explain why so many American SF stories on television seem to go, boldly or otherwise, into the unknown, but only until the half-time commercial break. After which point, they spend the second half returning things to the *status quo ante* – ready to start all over again, exactly where they began, when the next episode comes around. The themes that most easily fit the requirements of a television series are sometimes, therefore, hard to identify as genuine SF at all.

Just like SF in the American cinema, SF on American television tends to concentrate not on exploration (which invokes change) but on invasions or depredations (threats that are invariably defeated, returning the world to normal). American SF television is also full of villains or mad scientists who attempt nefarious schemes, are defeated, and bounce back a few episodes down the line, fresh and ready for the same fight and the same defeat again. In its first decade, American television SF was profoundly conservative. In the final anaylsis, the central theme underlying a significant proportion of its storylines was that of crime and punishment.

ROD SERLING

Rod Serling (1924–75) was something of a miracle worker. He created *The Twilight Zone*, by far the most commercially successful of any SF anthology series on television, and also the best of them all. For some episodes, he wrote and produced the story, as well as introducing it to the audience. Other writers included Ray Bradbury and Richard Matheson. Some episodes were fantasy, others were pure SF, but the central impulse behind them all was clever storytelling: many ended in surprise twists, and some even generated a genuine SF sense of wonder in their closing moments. Nothing

ROD SERLING AND ONE OF THE EXTRAS

Science Fictional was forbidden in the show: rockets, aliens, robots, invasions, plagues, ghosts, new worlds, strange dimensions, time travel, and delusions. The quality varied, and at times veteran SF readers found themselves guessing plots before the end, but the thrill of the new seemed always just around the corner. In 1985, a new series appeared, and did not disgrace its father. Harlan Ellison was creative consultant, and many SF writers contributed.

Beyond the twilight zone

The main exceptions to this prevailing pattern were *The Twilight Zone*, which ran from 1959 to 1964, and *The Outer Limits*, which ran from 1963 to 1965. These were both anthology series, a particularly American phenomenon, and each week's story was entirely self-contained. *The Twilight Zone* lasted several seasons, though with breaks due to network doubts about its viability; *The Outer Limits* was chopped before the end of its second season.

Then there were series like *The Man from U.N.C.L.E.* and *Voyage to the Bottom of the Sea*, in which the genuine SF tended to disappear in plots that emphasized super-criminals and other threats to the *status quo*: written SF has never been much interested in criminals, nor in the heroes who defeat them. It came, then, as something of a relief to turn to *The Time Tunnel*, which did have a few ideas.

Mork and Mindy
The alien-on-Earth has been a rich vein for comedy: this was not really SF, but it was fun.

And then came *Star Trek*. There are a lot of criminals here, and at least one threatening alien species, but there are also hints of new sciences; new wisdoms; and new civilizations. And in *The Next Generation*, a sense of change is sometimes almost dominant. But the picture in recent decades is not thrilling. In the 1970s, we saw a retreat to series in which more superheroes defeat more criminals, again with minimal SF content, and comedies of variable quality and dubious SF content. In the 1980s, except for the long overdue revival of the *Star Trek* format, old material was yet again reworked, with the exception of a couple of genuine serials – *World War III* (1982) and *The Day After* (1983) – in which the world does change radically. In the 1990s, *Steven Spielberg's Amazing Stories* almost clicked, but faded; and *SeaQuest DSV* was an underwater dud. By now, the real action was in films.

U.N.C.L.E.
Not much SF content penetrated into these dizzy, camp storylines, but once again it was the fun that counted.

STAR TREK

The genius of Gene Roddenberry (1921–91), *Star Trek's* creator, took years to be revealed. The initial launch, in September 1966, was only moderately successful, and after 78 episodes the series died, never – or so the network, NBC, thought – to be reborn. But Captain James T. Kirk, Mr. Spock, and the rest of the crew did not fade. The series soon went into syndication, and within a few short years Kirk and Spock had become

contemporary myths. Phrases from the show, including the classic split infinitive, have become famous worldwide. The budget restrictions ensured that the series was set almost entirely on the starship *Enterprise*, which toured the galaxy in defence of our home planet's interests, with short excursions to briefly sketched planets – Scottie's beam cost nothing to film. But we believed with all our hearts; and still do.

Next Generation
A child more sophisticated than its parent: Picard never took the personal risks that Kirk constantly strode into, and the new starship Enterprise *was very high-tech. Some found it marginally less fun, but this was because Star Trek had grown up.*

Original cast
A determinedly multiracial crew comprised American Captain Kirk, Vulcan Mr. Spock, the incomprehensible Scotty, Bones McCoy, black – and female – Lieutenant Uhura, oriental Mr. Sulu, and Russian Ensign Chekov.

BRITISH TELEVISION

SF ON BRITISH TELEVISION HAS always suffered from an inadequate budget. Yet despite this – and the manifest hostility of many programme controllers – the genre has seen a number of distinguished contributions, some proving exceptionally popular and long-lived.

THUNDERBIRDS

◀ Producer/Director   ▣ Screenplay   ▣ Time   ◑ Colour   ◐ Black and White

1 9 5 0 s

The Quatermass Experiment
1953

◀ Rudolph Cartier ▣ Nigel Kneale ▣ 6 episodes of 30 mins ◐
The first man back from outer space has been infected by an unknown virus that turns him progressively less human and more alien – although never unsympathetic. Troubleshooting space scientist Quatermass stops the mayhem by persuading the human within the vegetable-like monster to destroy himself – and hence the beast.

Nineteen Eighty-Four
1954

◀ Rudolph Cartier ▣ Nigel Kneale ▣ 120 mins ◐
Astonishingly, this play was filmed live – twice! The repeat performance, despite public outcry (presumably based on the misapprehension that this was prescription, not warning), had the biggest British television audience to date aside from the Coronation. Starring Peter Cushing and André Morell, the film is bleakly faithful to Orwell's novel.

The Lost Planet
1954

◀ Kevin Sheldon ▣ Angus MacVicar ▣ 6 episodes of 25 mins ◐
This children's serial, based on MacVicar's own radio play, follows the adventures of a party of humans transported to the planet Hesikos. A lesser sequel, Return to the Lost Planet, sees our heroes back on Hesikos. Neither broadcast – with their crude special effects – can really compare with the radio original.

Quatermass II
1955

◀ Rudolph Cartier ▣ Nigel Kneale ▣ 6 episodes of 35 mins ◐
A top-secret establishment proves to be a centre from which militaristic alien invaders are "possessing" human beings, en route to world takeover. This small-screen version is vastly superior to the 1957 film.

Quatermass and the Pit
1958–59

◀ Rudolph Cartier ▣ Nigel Kneale ▣ 6 episodes of 35 mins ◐
A Martian spaceship is unearthed beneath a London Underground station, and emanations from it give some individuals horrific visions. Using a new device, Quatermass projects these onto a TV screen, and so discovers that familiar legends such as the Devil are actually Martian in origin. Again, the series surpasses the subsequent film.

QUATERMASS AND THE PIT

1 9 6 0 s

A for Andromeda
1961

◀ Michael Hayes, Norman James ▣ John Elliot, Fred Hoyle ▣ 7 episodes of 45 or 50 mins ◐
Radio signals from the Andromeda Galaxy help scientists build an advanced computer, which teaches itself enough of mankind to enable the construction of a human. Official paranoia leads to the destruction of the alien knowledge and a tragic end.

Supercar
1961–62

◀ Gerry Anderson ▣ Gerry and Sylvia Anderson, Hugh and Martin Woodhouse ▣ 39 episodes of 25 mins ◐
At the time, Anderson's new "SuperMarionation" puppetry seemed tremendously sophisticated; now the process, and the scripts, seem banal.

The Avengers
1961–69

◀ John Bryce, Brian Clemens, Albert Fennell, Leonard White, Julian Wintle ▣ numerous, including Brian Clemens and Terry Nation ▣ 161 episodes of 50 mins ◐ for last 2 seasons ◑
In perhaps the archetypal 1960s TV series, secret agent John Steed, aided by a succession of female sidekicks, tackles various villains. Three phases can be distinguished, corresponding approximately – and doubtless coincidentally – to the reigns of the sidekicks: the Cathy Gale phase presented relatively orthodox, although very stylish, thrillers; the Emma Peel phase (the series' golden age) consisted of wilder, often almost surrealist, plots and productions. Finally, in the short-lived Tara King phase, everything got a bit silly.

THE AVENGERS

Doctor Who
1963–92

◀ various ▣ various, notably Terry Nation ▣ 679 episodes of 25 mins, 15 of 50 mins, and 1 of 90 mins ◐ after 6th season ◑
Less a television character than a phenomenon, the Doctor is one of several ever-regenerating Time Lords who battle for good or evil. He flits through time and space in the TARDIS, which outwardly resembles a British police telephone box. After the introduction of the Daleks in the second episode, the series never looked back. The Doctor's handy ability to periodically renew his entire body neatly explained the programme's succession of leading men as it wended its way to becoming the most successful Space Opera in television history, topping even Star Trek.

Stingray
1964–65

◀ Gerry Anderson ▣ Gerry and Sylvia Anderson, Alan Fennell, Dennis Spooner ▣ 39 episodes of 25 mins ◑
Troy Tempest, pilot of the atomic mini-submarine Stingray, battles underwater baddies while trying to decide if he loves his commander's daughter or a mermaid.

Thunderbirds
1965–66

◀ Gerry Anderson, Reg Hill ▣ various ▣ 32 episodes of 50 mins ◑
The Thunderbirds are the versatile vehicles run by a privately owned recovery operation, International Rescue, whose self-imposed task is the forestalling or minimizing of disasters in space, in the air, on land, or underwater. Their aristocratic London agent, Lady Penelope – complete with pink Rolls-Royce – is the undisputed star of the show, probably the most popular of all the SuperMarionation children's series.

Out of the Unknown
1965–71

◀ Irene Shubik Alan Bromly ▣ various ▣ 49 episodes of 50 or 60 mins ◐ last 2 seasons ◑
The first three seasons of this fine, ambitious continuation of Out of This World consist of one-shot dramatizations of well-known SF stories and novels. The fourth is rather different, comprising original ghostly/eerie teleplays.

The Prisoner
1967–68

◀ David Tomblin ▣ various, including Terence Feely, Patrick McGoohan (series creator), George Markstein, Roger Woddis ▣ 17 episodes of 50 mins ◑
This bizarre series is perhaps British SF television's flagship, despite being itself only fringe SF. A spy abruptly resigns. He is whisked to confinement in the absurdist Village (in fact, Portmeirion in Wales) and robbed of his name: he is now Number 6. In each episode he tries to escape, while a new Number 2 (Number 1, the head controller, is not identified until the end, and then enigmatically) tries – through quasi-hallucinatory means – to persuade him to explain why he resigned.

Captain Scarlet and the Mysterons
1968

◩ Reg Hill ◧ various
▣ 32 episodes of 25 mins ▣
In this further SuperMarionation series, the inhabitants of Mars – the Mysterons – misinterpret Earth's first landing there as an invasion. They attempt to infiltrate and eventually destroy the threat by converting two top Earth agents into Mysteron Fifth Columnists. In the case of Captain Black they succeed, and he becomes the series' villain – opposed by the Mysterons' failed conversion, the now immortal Captain Scarlet.

1970s

Timeslip
1970–71

◩ John Cooper ◧ Victor Pemberton, Bruce Stewart ▣ 26 episodes of 30 mins ▣
Two children fall through a hole in the Time Barrier, becoming able to explore their own past and future. This set of four serials, intended for children and with some educational content, has become highly regarded.

Doomwatch
1970–72

◩ Terence Dudley ◧ various, including Gerry Davis and Kit Pedler (series creators) ▣ 38 episodes of 50 mins ▣
The Department of Measurement of Science Work – an idiosyncratic, semi-covert government agency – confronts a new technology-sparked catastrophe in each episode. Hugely influential (and popular) in its time, the series now seems simple-minded.

UFO
1970–71

◩ Reg Hill ◧ various, including Gerry and Sylvia Anderson ▣ 26 episodes of 50 mins ▣
Here Anderson ditches puppets for live action, but keeps the actors no less wooden. In 1980, aliens in flying saucers invade Earth, and are resisted by the Supreme Headquarters Alien Defence Organization (SHADO).

The Tomorrow People
1973–79

◩ Ruth Boswell, Vic Hughes, Roger Price ◧ Brian Finch, Price, Jon Watkins ▣ 68 episodes of 25 mins ▣
A group of children have evolved into Homo superior, with psychic powers enabling them to time travel, teleport, and act at a distance. From a hideout in the London Underground, they and their talking computer use these powers, and high-tech inventions, to battle evil on Earth and elsewhere.

MOONBASE 3

Moonbase 3
1973

◩ Barry Letts ◧ various
▣ 6 episodes of 50 mins ▣
This deliberately non-fanciful series set in 2003 concerns the setting-up of a lunar base; the series even had a scientific adviser, in the shape of popular-science TV presenter James Burke. Unfortunately, the accent on "realism" made the series pretty tedious, and it was short-lived.

SPACE: 1999

Space: 1999
1975–78

◩ Sylvia Anderson, Fred Freiberger ◧ various ▣ 48 episodes of 50 mins ▣
The Andersons' second venture into live-action SF was visually splendid but flopped owing to mediocre acting and, most of all, rotten scripts. The Moon, including a manned base, is blasted out of Earth's orbit by a nuclear accident. Cruising through the galaxy, the colonists meet and kill implacably hostile aliens.

Survivors
1975–77

◩ Terence Dudley ◧ various, notably Terry Nation (series creator) ▣ 38 episodes of 50 mins ▣
A virus kills most of the world's population; in Britain only a few thousand are left. The series follows small groups of (mainly middle-class) survivors as they struggle to unite and recreate some semblance of civilization. Restrained, almost sombre, the first season was among the finest televised SF; thereafter the series descended towards post-holocaust soap opera.

The New Avengers
1976–77

◩ Brian Clemens, Albert Fennell ◧ various ▣ 26 episodes of 50 mins ▣
France and Canada so loved The Avengers that they co-funded a further series, with the action now shared between France, Canada, and Britain. An elderly Steed is assisted by Purdy (Joanna Lumley) and Mike Gambit (Gareth Hunt). This was a doomed attempt to revive something whose time had passed.

1990
1977–78

◩ Prudence Fitzgerald ◧ various, mainly Wilfred Greatorex ▣ 16 episodes of 55 mins ▣
In 1990s totalitarian Britain the welfare state is all-powerful. A maverick journalist helps infiltrators from the freedom-loving United States, and assists British rebels in fleeing there. Intended as a dire warning of the consequences of trade-unionist socialism, the series' caricatures in fact make the venture risible.

Blake's Seven
1978–81

◩ Vere Lorrimer, David Maloney ◧ various, including James Follett, Trevor Hoyle, Tanith Lee, Terry Nation (series creator) ▣ 52 episodes of 50 mins ▣
Far in the future, a small group of rebels against the all-powerful Federation escapes incarceration, and thereafter battles the forces of totalitarianism over the galaxy. This series differed – very successfully – from most other TV Space Operas in eschewing black-and-white character portrayals, in being unafraid to let its major figures die (Blake himself disappears early on, returning only in the final episode, when he is killed by the now-megalomaniac flawed hero Avon), and in enabling the heroes only to irritate the oppressor. It acquired a huge audience, and has remained a cult. Its deliberately seedy, pessimistic ambience was enhanced by legendarily cheap sets.

Sapphire and Steel
1979–82

◩ Shaun O'Riordan ◧ P.J. Hammond (series creator), with 1 story by Don Houghton, Anthony Read ▣ 34 episodes of 25 mins ▣
This baffling series can be viewed as either a high-point of SF TV or self-indulgent nonsense. Sapphire and Steel (Joanna Lumley and David McCallum), ostensibly beings from the far future, police the corridors of time to prevent any untoward leakage between past, present, and future (such leakages causing phenomena like ghosts and doppelgängers).

1980s

The Hitchhiker's Guide to the Galaxy
1981

◩ Alan J.W. Bell ◧ Douglas Adams ▣ 6 episodes of 35 mins ▣
An Englishman is rescued by a humanoid alien just as the Earth is demolished by Vogon constructional engineers. Together they hitchhike around the galaxy, encountering various grotesqueries, assisted by the eponymous talking guidebook. The radio original is generally preferable, but the computer graphics here are exceptional. Extraordinarily inventive and often very funny, the two series, and complementary novels, made the number 42 universally famous.

The Tripods
1984–85

◩ Richard Bates ◧ Christopher Penfold, Alick Rowe ▣ 25 episodes of 30 mins ▣
Adapted from John Christopher's **The Tripods** trilogy (1967–68), this excellent serial was cut short by the accountants. Towards the end of the 21st century the Earth is enslaved by aliens, with humans controlled through skull implants. Those who have escaped the treatment struggle to form a resistance movement.

Max Headroom
1985, 1985–87, 1987–88

◩ Peter Wagg, Brian Frankish, Steve Roberts ◧ Roberts ▣ 1 film of 65 mins, various rock promotional programmes, 14 episodes of 50 mins ▣
A computer-generated head was devised as a linkman for a rock series, The Max Headroom Show, and a television film giving him fictional origins was created as a sort of prequel. Max is the survival, in electronic form, of a journalist investigating a murderous conspiracy. American television, however, forsook the rock show and commissioned a series of SF dramas.

Star Cops
1987

◩ Evgeny Gridneff ◧ various, notably Chris Boucher (series creator) ▣ 9 episodes of 55 mins ▣
Midway through the first half of the 21st century the International Space Police Force, charged with maintaining order in near space, sorts out various crimes.

Red Dwarf
1988–

◩ Hilary Bevan Jones, Ed Bye, Rob Grant, Doug Naylor ◧ Grant, Naylor ▣ weekly episodes of 30 mins ▣
Millions of years in the future, a crewman awakens from suspended animation aboard a large spaceship to find that humankind is long extinct. His sole companions are a sentient hologram, a neurotic computer, and a cat that has evolved to become humanoid. Later they are joined by an android. Red Dwarf began as an attempt to place the then-fresh anarchic New Wave of British comedy in an unexpected locale. Gradually it came to transcend that aim, and imaginatively to explore SF scenarios and concepts while retaining its wit and satirical edge.

RED DWARF

IRREVERENCE AND INSURRECTION

ONE OF THE FIRST QUESTIONS that springs to mind when watching SF television is why is everything done in slow motion? There are two answers. The first is that the makeup worn by actors playing aliens tends to be awkward, and often allows only limited vision, so that the actor risks falling over.

The second is that the sets are often extremely cheap, and any excessive activity on the part of actors could make the walls shake more than they do anyway, or even cave in. Experienced viewers of SF on television know this: almost everything happens slowly in order to protect the sets.

The British approach

In the world of American television, the sheer physical fragility of the illusion created by the setting has sometimes been disastrous, because SF series on American television have, on the whole, tended to take themselves pretty seriously. But there is quite a different attitude – and consequently a different picture – on British television. On first encountering television productions from Britain, American viewers are often surprised, and sometimes even a bit disconcerted, at these shows' apparently casual acceptance of the awfulness of their production values: sets, props, costumes, and creatures are all quite often transparently cheap; what it sometimes takes them a little while to work out is that British television SF is not, and has never been, really serious about creating the future.

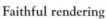

Faithful rendering
The BBC's Nineteen Eighty-Four remains the most faithful screen adaptation yet made. Its audiences rivalled the Queen's coronation of the previous year.

Rebellious beginnings

Right from the start, no British television production of any note has ever presented an image of a Future History even remotely resembling the visions that were proclaimed by classic 1960s American shows like *The Time Tunnel* or *Star Trek*, whose protagonists have a mission to make the future work in the way that it should. The heroes of the best American series are loyal soldiers, oath-bound to serve their governments (and to put the needs of Earth above the needs of the "foreign" planets they invade). In contrast to this, the greatest early success that SF had on British television was a live performance of George Orwell's *Nineteen Eighty-Four* in 1955, starring the late Peter Cushing, and scripted by Nigel Kneale. *Nineteen Eighty-Four* is a classic political dystopia, scathing about all forms of coercive government, and very far from being an attempt to map out the future.

Kneale went on from this to write the *Quatermass* stories: *Quatermass* itself is unusual in the history of British television because it deals with alien invasions, more generally thought to be an American theme;

and although the second instalment of the trilogy, *Quatermass II*, even features the classic invasion threat of bodysnatcher aliens, in Kneale's tale they are in cahoots with a corrupt British government. Even here, in other words, British television skews away from allegiance to the powers that be; even here, British television is cynical about the world, rather than loyal about those who serve its masters.

The closest that British SF ever came to presenting a Future History with a mission was *Doctor Who;* and that was not really very close. The Doctor was almost always at odds with any establishment going – from the very start he was a renegade, out of favour and on the run from the other Time Lords. This might go some way towards explaining the cult following that this purported children's programme has among adults. It is true that British productions have been aimed more at adults than their American counterparts, but even serials clearly made for children, like *Time Trap,* could subvert their adult heroes into authoritarian villains.

Who is number one?
Set in the surrealist model village of Portmeirion in Wales, The Prisoner mixes Kafka and spy thriller. The Prisoner's constant escape attempts may be only a test, because he himself may be the true boss.

As we come closer to the end of the century, this questioning attitude becomes more and more overt. *The Prisoner* was corrosively contemptuous about those who wield power; *Blake's Seven* quite subtly undercut Blake's own straight-arrow virtues with compelling anti-hero characters, and ended in pessimism and chaos.

The art of self mockery

In the 1980s, *The Hitchhiker's Guide to the Galaxy* hilariously spoofed all government, all authority, all wisdom, and all high-toned visions of the road to the future. It is hard to think of a cliché that did not turn up in these scripts. Perhaps less successful, but in the same vein, is the most recent offering, *Red Dwarf*. While America sent a new generation of *Star Trek* out into the populous beyond, Britain sent three no-hopers cruising vast reaches of empty space in a decaying ship, meeting failed versions of great SF standards.

   British television SF is much closer in tone and subject matter to British written SF than it is to American television or American written SF.

This, of course, might seem perfectly natural, but in fact, the extraordinary dominance of the American genre sometimes makes it hard to see what is going on elsewhere. British television SF has always been low-budget, camp, derisive, depressive, argumentative, and fun. So what if it wobbles? The glory of the Doctor and Ford Prefect is that they are on our side.

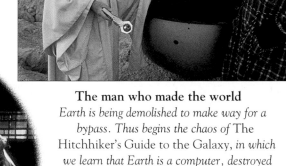

The man who made the world
Earth is being demolished to make way for a bypass. Thus begins the chaos of The Hitchhiker's Guide to the Galaxy, *in which we learn that Earth is a computer, destroyed just before revealing the meaning of life.*

Heroes and villains
In Blake's Seven, Blake *and his gang, on the run from a totalitarian Federation, stir up trouble, run amok, steal and cheat, are hounded by wicked Servalan, and are wiped out.*

DOCTOR WHO

It began in 1963, and millions felt betrayed when the BBC, after 695 episodes, called a halt in 1989. The Doctor was a Time Lord – and a less pretentious Lord it would be hard to find – who scooted back and forth through time and space, sometimes because he was on the run, sometimes because he was lost, sometimes because he wanted to, and sometimes because he felt a need to protect

Earth from Daleks, Cybermen, or some other menace. The Doctor could metamorphose into a new body when it was necessary. Each of the seven actors was, therefore, the same Doctor, with the same memories, rejuvenated, and the Doctor had three more of these transformations left up his sleeve when the series was dropped. Each of the incarnations was accompanied by a young woman who, being mortal, grew up, left,

and was replaced with another young woman, usually remarkably similar. In the early years, the companion usually got herself, with "female" irrationality, into hot water, from which she had to be extricated by the Doctor; in later, more politically correct times, she was no longer required to be a certifiable idiot, and the plots of the four- or six-part stories were more involving.

Rubber aliens
The Doctor is constantly on the move through time and space, in his time machine, the TARDIS. Sometimes he is saving Earth, but usually he is in trouble.

WILLIAM HARTNELL
1963–66

PATRICK TROUGHTON
1966–69

JOHN PERTWEE
1970–74

TOM BAKER
1974–81

PETER DAVISON
1982–84

COLIN BAKER
1984–86

SYLVESTER MCCOY
1987–89

EUROPEAN AND JAPANESE TELEVISION

THERE IS FAR MORE TO SF television than the cult American and British programmes we know so well. Europe and Japan have spawned many fascinating productions worthy of wider recognition and which reflect the strength and diversity of the genre worldwide.

◄ Producer/Director   ◈ Screenplay   ◈ Time   ◉ Colour   ◉ Black and White

1 9 6 0 s

Operazione Vega
(Operation Vega)
Italy 1962
◄ Vittorio Cottafavi ◈ Friedrich Durrenmatt ◈ approx. 120 mins ◉
Exiles on Venus choose to be bombed by Earth authorities rather than assist in military action against the Mars colony, fighting for its independence.

Przyjaciel
(Friend)
Poland 1965
◄ Marek Nowicki, Jerzy Stawicki ◈ Nowicki, Stawicki, based on a Stanisław Lem story ◈ 20 mins ◉
In this adaptation of a classic Lem story, an oversized computer tries to take over the world – as oversized computers usually do.

Raumschiff Orion
(Spaceship Orion)
Germany 1966
◄ Michael Braun, Theo Mezger ◈ Rolf Honold, W.G. Larsen ◈ 7 episodes of approx. 60 mins ◉
Germany's classic Space Opera series – set in the year 3000 – was launched just before Star Trek, and has similar cult status. Produced as serious fodder then (starring famous actor Dietmar Schönherr), and axed after one season as too costly, reruns are today viewed as high comedy.

Ultraman
Japan 1966–67
◄ Eiji Tsuburaya ◈ Tetsuo Kinjo ◈ 39 episodes of 25 mins ◉
Each week, rubber-suited Ultraman (a union of man and alien) single-handedly saves Japanese society from a rampaging monster, using traditional martial arts and high-tech wizardry. These reassuring morality plays with Gojira-style action inspired numerous spin-off programmes.

La Fantarca
(The Fantarca)
Italy 1968
◄ Vittorio Cottafavi ◈ Giuseppe Berto, Pier Benedetto Bertoli, Roman Vlad ◈ 65 mins ◉
In a future Italy ruled by techno-efficiency, "unproductive" southerners are exiled to Saturn. This "grotesque" satirical opera traces their bizarre journey in a Noah's Ark-type ship.

Przekładaniec
(Pie)
Poland 1968
◄ Andrzej Wajda ◈ Stanisław Lem ◈ 36 mins ◉
A famous sportscar driver survives numerous accidents, thanks to equally numerous transplants. Now the courts must decide who exactly this man is – a complicated issue, as he now wears female clothing, since a woman was one of his organ donors.

Les Shadoks
(The Shadoks)
France 1968
◄ Jacques Rouxel ◈ 416 episodes of approx. 5 mins ◉
In the wake of the 1968 civil uprisings, this controversial daily cartoon series split French public opinion in two. The surreal and outrageous adventures of the Shadoks and the Gibis, two rival alien races – including their discovery of Earth in a distant past and their struggle against the entity "Gegene" – remain among the most disconcerting phenomena in television history.

1 9 7 0 s

Die Delegation
(The Delegation)
Germany 1970
◄ Rainer Erler ◈ Erler ◈ 110 mins ◉
When a TV newsman investigating an alleged UFO near a Latin American village uncovers the truth about local alien encounters, certain interested parties try to silence him.

Hydrozagadka
(Hydro-enigma)
Poland 1970
◄ Andrzej Kondratiuk ◈ Andrzej Borowski, Kondratiuk ◈ 70 mins ◉
In this hilarious parody of "superhero" films, a mad scientist plots to steal a lake and sell it to an Arab country. Our protagonist tries to foil the evil plan, whereby a nuclear reactor boils the water, the ensuing cloud travels to the desert, and is then turned into rain by balloon-borne refrigerators.

Le Voyageur des Siècles, Julesvernerie Moderne
(The Traveller of Centuries, Modern JulesVernerie)
France 1971
◄ Jean Dréville ◈ based on an original idea by Noël-Noël ◈ 4 episodes of 90 mins ◉
Time travellers journey into the past, with inevitable consequences. Their risky attempts to modify history see them trying to prevent the Revolution in one episode, then in the next meeting not Louis XVI as expected, but Bonaparte, a modest hosier…

WORLD ON A WIRE

L'Amor Glaciale
(Cold Love)
Italy 1971
◄ Dino Partesano ◈ Giuseppe Cassieri ◈ 58 mins ◉
A depressed accountant is prescribed seven years of hibernation as a cure. When he returns to life, full of energy and health, can he so easily rejoin the society he has temporarily left?

L'Alphoméga
(The Alphomega)
France 1972
◄ Lazare Iglésias ◈ 6 episodes ◉
Tonton and Biceps run the shop "The Key to the Galaxies", in this pastiche of the spy novel – notable as a rare French attempt at comedic SF.

Toki wo Kakeru Shojo
(Time Traveller)
Japan 1972
◈ Toru Ishiyama, based on a novel by Yasutaka Tsutsui ◈ 6 episodes of 25 mins ◉
Based on a famous Japanese SF novel, this series (later adapted into a film) about a female alien's encounters on Earth was both a critical and popular success. Junko Shimada's role as the heroine made her a national star.

Mazinger Z
Japan 1972–74
◄ Yugo Serikawa, Nobuo Oogai, Takafumi Hisaoka ◈ Go Nagai, Dynamic Production ◈ 92 episodes of 25 mins ◉
This ground-breaking animated series was a huge hit in France as well as Japan, and launched the "giant robot" craze. The cartoon follows the adventures of robot warrior Mazinger Z – controlled by its inventor's young grandson – in the ongoing fight against mad scientist Dr. Hell.

Welt am Draht
(World on a Wire)
Germany 1973
◄ Rainer Werner Fassbinder ◈ Fritz Muller-Scherz, Fassbinder, based on Counterfeit World (1964), Daniel F. Galouye ◈ 210 mins ◉
A computer holds the artificial personalities of thousands of "identity units" – perfect imitations of human beings, who exist believing they are real, rather than electronic entities manipulated by uncaring scientists.

Das Blaue Palais
(The Blue Palace)
Germany 1973–75
◄ Rainer Erler ◈ Erler ◈ series of 5 films of 90 mins ◉
Set in an advanced research institute, this intelligent series of thrillers speculates on the implications of scientific discoveries falling into the wrong hands. Topics explored include synthetic matter, parapsychology, artificial intelligence, and immortality.

Operation Ganymed
Germany 1976
◄ Rainer Erler ◈ Erler ◈ 125 mins ◉
A spaceship returns unexpectedly from Jupiter, with the survivors of an abandoned project, in this critical look at the space programme.

Le Uova Fatali
(Fatal Eggs)
Italy 1977
◄ Ugo Gregoretti ◈ Gregoretti ◈ 2 episodes of 60 mins ◉
A ray that speeds the growth of eggs is used by the government to boost production, but a bureaucratic error results in the hatching of huge reptilian monsters, in this political satire inspired by a work by Mikhail Bulgakov.

SPACESHIP ORION

Blindpassasjer
(Stowaway)
Norway 1978
Stein-Roger Bull Jon Bing, Tor Age Bringsvaerd 3 episodes of 37 mins

Aboard a starship returning from a recently discovered planet, an alien has assumed the body and identity of one of the crew – but who? Investigation uncovers the shocking truth about the strange planet's robot population. Norway's most successful SF series to date owes much to its co-authors, founders of the modern Norwegian genre.

Etot Fantastichesky Mir
(This Fantastic World)
USSR 1978
Viktor Spiridonov Ludmilla Ermilina, Andrei Kostenetzky 15 episodes of 60 mins

Allowed onto Soviet screens as ostensibly "for children", this series evolved from SF quiz, to discussions with famous writers, to a TV play slot featuring low-budget dramatizations of Western and Russian works. SF fan and cosmonaut Georgi Gretchko presented many episodes, with author Arkady Strugatski as consultant. Since repeats ended in 1991, no similar Hard SF show has been seen in Russia.

Kido Senshi Gundam
(Mobile Suit Gundam)
Japan 1979–80
Yoshikazu Yasuhiko Yoshiyuki Tomino 43 episodes of 25 mins

The first Japanese animated series to have a Hard SF feel, Gundam tells the story of a huge war between Earth and colonies established along the lunar orbit, now seeking independence. Close combat in mobile battle suits is mixed with an intricate web of sub-plots among a vast array of characters, including our young hero aboard a roving warship. The saga has been continued in numerous sequels, and the massive marketing surrounding the series reflects its enduring popularity.

1 9 8 0 s

Ta Den Ring
(Take This Ring)
Norway 1982
Stein-Roger Bull Jon Bing, Tor Age Bringsvaerd 3 episodes of 46, 52, and 68 mins

An academic who has traced the origins of an ancient sun symbol to a supernova explosion 5,000 years ago becomes embroiled in a secret brotherhood of ring-bearers which is eventually revealed as a weird circle of descendants from a spaceship crew who fled a planet near the doomed star. The ship, still hidden on Earth, is at last discovered.

THE MYSTERIOUS DOCTOR CORNELIUS

Chojiku Yosai Macross
(Super Dimensional Fortress Macross)
Japan 1982–83
Noboru Ishiguro Kenichi Matsuzaki 36 episodes of 25 mins

When an alien battleship crash-lands, the warring Earth is united in defence. The aliens duly return, and after much fighting (and soap opera) mankind is virtually wiped out. The story formed part of the complex American cartoon series Robotech.

SUPER DIMENSIONAL CENTURY ORGUSS

Chojiku Seiki Orguss
(Super Dimensional Century Orguss)
Japan 1983–84
Noboru Ishiguro, Yasuyoshi Mikamoto Kenichi Matsuzaki 35 episodes of 25 mins

A new bomb has fractured dimensions on Earth, creating a surreal world of mixed realities, with random storms throwing people into the past or future. If not restabilized, the planet will perish.

Návštěvníci
(The Visitors)
Czechoslovakia 1983–84
Jindřich Polák Ota Hofman 13 episodes of 30 mins

To avert Earth's destruction in a cosmic catastrophe, scientists return to the 20th century to recover vital calculations left by a child genius.

Le Mystérieux Docteur Cornélius
(The Mysterious Doctor Cornelius)
France 1984
Maurice Frydland Jean-Pierre Petrolacci, Jean Daniel Simon, Pierre Nivollet, based on a series of novels by Gustave Le Rouge 6 episodes

In this excellent adaptation of Le Rouge's classic 18-volume SF serial, dating from 1912, two brothers at the head of a secret society of evil-doers plot to control the world, and become engaged in a titanic battle with a pair of equally determined multi-millionaires.

Bambinot
Czechoslovakia 1984
Jaroslav Dudek Miloš Macourek, Josef Nesvadba 6 episodes of 58 mins

The most "serious" Czech SF series to date deals with the issues of gene manipulation and selective breeding, via an invention enabling parents to "design" a child to order.

Kosmiczny Test
(Space Test)
Poland 1984–87
Romuald Szoka monthly episodes

In this spirited quiz show, teams tackle questions on subjects including writers (both Eastern and Western), films, and fandom. SF clubs and "normal" contestants alike test their knowledge for prizes and honours as genre masters.

Un Pianeta Ritrovato
(A Planet Rediscovered)
Italy 1986
Mario Chiari Massimo Bucchi, Chiari, Aldo Zapallà 80 mins

In pseudo-documentary style, "experts" from the year 2222 attempt to interpret our present-day culture. The programme provides a forum for a semi-serious discussion of SF in cinema and literature.

Sommarens Tolv Månader
(The Twelve Months of Summer)
Sweden 1988
Richard Hobert Hobert 130 mins

Workers at an isolated building site are made the unwilling subjects of a bizarre mind experiment. This tense, scary film ends with the men back home, speaking a language no one understands.

Zucker
(Sugar)
Germany 1989
Rainer Erler Erler 95 mins

This satire on genetic engineering – inspired by real-life experimentation in waste disposal using cellulose-eating bacteria – sees newly constructed micro-organisms spread like a plague, turning every scrap of paper into sugar.

Kido Keisatsu Patlabor
(Mobile Police Patlabor)
Japan 1989–91
Mamoru Oshii Kazunori Ito 48 episodes of 25 mins

Japan's hugely successful animated SF cop show follows, with great detail and realism, the exploits of a small mobile police team on its patrols against the misuse of giant piloted robot labourers for crime and other mayhem.

1 9 9 0 s

Gagarin – en Romfartsopera
(Gagarin – a Spaceflight Opera)
Norway 1991
Morten Thomte Jon Bing, Tor Age Bringsvaerd 64 mins

A grand-style homage to the world's first space traveller, this sophisticated and beautiful production incorporates models, special effects, and film-stock shots from NASA and the Russian Space Agency. The libretto describes the life and tragedy of Yuri Gagarin, and a chapter in Russian history.

Toinen Todellisuus
(Another Reality)
Finland 1991
Jussi-Pekka Koskiranta Marko Ahonen, Johanna Sinisalo, Kari Öhman 3 episodes of 30 mins

This mini-series for young adults uses familiar SF scenarios to address topical issues such as pollution and the exploitation of television.

Ålder Okänd
(Age Unknown)
Sweden 1991
Richard Hobert Hobert 3 episodes of 50 mins

An anti-ageing drug is being secretly tested on clients at a health farm. When it yields extreme and deforming effects, an antidote proves tricky. A fine cast distinguishes the familiar plot.

Les Hordes
(The Hordes)
France 1991
Nguyen Thi Lan, Jean-Claude Missiaen Jacques Zelde, Joël Houssin, Jean-Luc Fromental, Daniel Riche, Missiaen 4 episodes of 90 mins

The near-future vision here is of an urban fascist state on the outskirts of Paris. As wild gangs fight it out in Mad Max style, the protagonist struggles for a saner world.

Yötuuli
(Nightwind)
Finland 1992
Olli Soinio Soinio 84 mins

This grimly realistic drama, set in a bleak future society under military rule after some undefined catastrophe, traces a family's struggle to survive in harsh, isolated conditions, having fled to the country from a violent town. The understated tone makes the pessimistic, anti-utopian story all the more convincing.

GAGARIN – A SPACEFLIGHT OPERA

GLOSSARY

Alien A non-human being from somewhere other than Earth.
Alternate Worlds Different versions of reality substituted for our own. *See also* **Parallel Worlds**.
Android. A robot that is built to look like a human being.
AI or Artificial Intelligence Computer with human-like intelligence. Common in SF.

Black hole A region of space of such gravity that not even light can escape it, which is the reason why it appears black. In SF, black holes can be weapons, navigation hazards, or gateways. *See also* **Wormhole**.

Clone An individual bred from another individual, usually by growing a parental cell into a duplicate of that parent.
Colonization Colonization of other planets normally involves a small settlement, which flourishes or not. *See also* **Lost Colony**.
Corpsicle A body frozen at death, awaiting revival. *See also* **Cryonics**.
Cosmology Studying the origin and the end of the universe.
Cryonics The preservation of bodies by supercooling at the point of death. *See also* **Corpsicle**.
Cyberpunk Stories set in a computer-dominated environment (cyber) with a streetwise, anti-Establishment culture (punk).
Cyberspace The virtual reality experienced when a user plugs into the computer nets.
Cyborg A partly artificial human or a partly human robot.

Dianetics *See* **Scientology**.
Dreadful Warning tales Stories that warn of the dire consequences of certain action. Early examples often involve **Future Wars**.
Dying Earth tales Stories set on an ancient Earth, in a universe displaying extreme age, where nothing remains new or untested. *See also* **Far future**.
Dystopia A negative model of an ideal society. *See also* **Utopia**.

Edisonade A tale in which an inventor-hero goes adventuring, meets and defeats enemies, and conquers new territories.
ESP or Extra Sensory Perception The ability to perceive things beyond the range of normal senses. *See also* **Psi powers**.
Extraterrestrial Anything not on or from Earth. *See also* **Alien**.

Fantastic Voyage A voyage in which unknown territories are visited, and strange creatures are discovered. *See also* **Proto SF**.
Fanzine A magazine in which SF fans communicate with each other. Contents vary from literary criticism to gossip.
Far future Near the end of time, when all resources are spent. *See also* **Dying Earth**.
Future History A framework of future events, within which a writer constructs stories.
Future War tales Stories predicting war in the near future. *See also* **Dreadful Warning**.

Gaia theory The concept that Earth is a living organism with a purpose. *See also* **Living worlds**.
Galactic empires States that rule more than one solar system.
Gaslight Romance Nostalgic fantasy, in which, for example, H.G. Wells meets Jack the Ripper. *See also* **Steampunk**.
Generation starship A spaceship designed to support a human community until the nearest habitable planet is reached.
Genre SF Adventure-driven, optimistic SF created in 1920s' American pulp magazines.
Golden Age of SF The period between about 1938 and 1943, when *Astounding Science Fiction* published dozens of stories by central figures in the genre.

Hard SF Fiction that often features scientists, and appears to be scientifically plausible.
Hive mind A being that is not a single body, but the totality of a group and, in SF, communicates telepathically with the group.
Hollow Earth An Earth either hollow, or honeycombed with tunnels and chambers, or having an inner Earth whose sky is the bottom of the planetary crust. *See also* **Lost Worlds**.
Homo superior Humans with superior senses or abilities. *See also* **Psi powers**.
Hugo Award Named after Hugo Gernsback, the premier award in SF since 1953.
Hyperdrive A drive that moves a ship faster than the **speed of light**, or through **hyperspace**.
Hyperspace A fictional kind of space where the usual constraints on speed do not apply, and which therefore permits rapid interstellar travel. *See also* **Space warp**, **Speed of light**.

Invasion paranoia A fear of the unknown, symbolized by an invading force such as aliens.

Jonbar Point The point where realities diverge in an **Alternate World** tale.

Living worlds In traditional SF, a living world may be a vast **hive mind** or even an organic planet. More recently, the **Gaia theory** has tended to dominate.
Lost colony A colony, usually settled during some past wave of human expansion, in which new cultures have developed, and old secrets have been retained.
Lost Race A long-forgotten or never-known race that inhabits a **Lost World**.
Lost World A hidden part of the world, sometimes inside it, often inhabited by a **Lost Race**. *See also* **Hollow Earth**.

Machine cultures Cultures of machine intelligences, or cultures created to imitate mechanical predictability.
Marrying out Aliens are seen as potential partners, rather than threats. By marrying out – sometimes literally – to other species, we may counteract some of our worse qualities. *See also* **Invasion paranoia**.
Matter transmission The instantaneous shifting of either an object or person from one place to another. *See also* **Teleportation**.
Mutant Any being whose genes differ from its ancestors' – in fact, we are all mutants. *See also* **Homo Superior**.

Near future Any future that is not more than a generation or so away, and recognizably continuous with the present.
Nebula Award A prestigious award granted by the Science Fiction Writers of America annually since 1966.

Parallel Worlds Worlds existing simultaneously, separated from each other by some sort of barrier. *See also* **Alternate Worlds**.
Parasitism The dependency of one species on another for its existence. *See also* **Symbiosis**.
Planetary Romance Archaic, sword-and-sorcery plots, usually set on a planet other than Earth.
Pocket universe Environment regarded by its inhabitants as the whole of reality.

Post-holocaust tales Stories set after a disaster has terminated our known history.
Precognition Ability to foresee the future. *See also* **Psi powers**.
Proto SF Stories written before SF became a recognized genre.
Psi powers Various kinds of paranormal senses or abilities. *See also* **ESP**, *Homo superior*, **Precognition**, **Telekinesis**, **Telepathy**, and **Teleportation**.

Ramjet or ramscoop A drive that sucks in matter in front and pushes it out the back for propulsion. *See also* **Rocket**.
Robot A machine, usually mobile, generally controlled by a built-in **AI**. *See also* **Android**.
Rocket An engine propelled by burning fuel contained within its structure – a self-contained, controlled explosion – or a vehicle with such an engine.

Scientology A form of religion founded by SF writer L. Ron Hubbard, and based on his "mental science" of **Dianetics**.
Sense of Wonder The sense of awe that is experienced in a story, usually when a sudden vast enlargement of perspective brings home the true scale of events or of the universe itself.
Sharecrop Trademarked universes, often associated with TV or films, with writers engaged to produce stories in them.
Shared Worlds Storylines or environments created by an author, into which other authors set characters in cooperative ventures. *See also* **Sharecrop**.
Sleeper Awakes The hero awakes, from either suspended animation, or other time-killing devices, in a future world.
Space habitat A construct designed to sustain life in orbit. *See also* **Space station**.
Space Opera Action tales set in interplanetary or interstellar space, concentrating on warfare between **galactic empires**.
Spaceship In SF, a spaceship may be either a method of transport, or the venue for the story.
Space station A construct, usually in orbit, designed to be a transfer point rather than for habitation. *See also* **Space habitat**.
Space warp A fictional fold in space allowing travel across the points where the sides of the fold join. *See also* **Hyperspace**, **Speed of light**, **Wormhole**.

Speed of light 186,000 miles per second, a speed impossible to exceed, according to Einstein's theories of relativity. In SF, this is a constraint on interstellar travel. *See also* **Hyperdrive**, **Space warp** **Hyperspace**, **Wormhole**
Steampunk Versions of 19th-century **Alternate Worlds** describing variant outcomes of the Industrial Revolution. *See also* **Gaslight Romance**.
Symbiosis The mutual dependency of species on each other. *See also* **Parasitism**.

Telekinesis The ability to move objects from one place to another, at a distance. *See also* **Psi powers**.
Telepathy The ability to read minds. *See also* **Psi powers**.
Teleportation The ability to transport matter through space and/or time. *See also* **Matter transmission**, **Psi powers**.
Terraforming Tinkering with another planet to make it habitable for human life.
The Three Laws of Robotics Created by Isaac Asimov and John W. Campbell Jr. in the early 1940s, they were a code of ethics to control robot behaviour in SF. They are: first, that a robot may not injure a human being or, through inaction, allow a human being to come to harm; second, that a robot must obey the orders given it by human beings except where such orders would conflict with the First Law; and third, that a robot must protect its own existence as long as such protection does not conflict with the First or Second Law.
Time paradox An impossible situation created by travelling back through time, for example when a man travels back and kills his father, so that he himself could never have existed.

UFO or Unidentified Flying Object The SF world tends to keep as far away as possible from ufology: the essential difference between an SF alien and a "ufology" alien is that the first is understood to be a fiction, and the second is an article of faith.
Utopia A fictional text in which a positive ideal society is described. *See also* **Dystopia**.

Wormhole A route from one part of the galaxy to another through a **black hole**. *See also* **Speed of light**.

INDEX

ACKNOWLEDGMENTS

AUTHOR'S ACKNOWLEDGMENTS

I could thank by name several dozen friends and colleagues who answered questions, and in other ways tolerated me, but there's only room to mention a few: Eric Arthur, Ted Ball, Judith Clute, Giles Gordon, Robert Kirby, Rob Reginald, Roger Robinson, Anna Russell, and John Urling-Clark. Paul Barnett, at a very late moment, supplied some necessary text by return post and saved our bacon. The editors at Dorling Kindersley – Krystyna Mayer and Candida Frith-Macdonald – and the designer Lee Griffiths, were true co-creators of this book, and I obeyed their every command with true reverence.

PUBLISHER'S ACKNOWLEDGMENTS

The publisher would like to thank the following for their assistance in the preparation of this volume:

Ivan Adamovic, Prague, Czech Republic; Eric Arthur, Fantasy Centre, London, England; Chizuru Asaoka-Wright, Tokyo Broadcasting System, London, England; Mihai Badescu, Bucarest, Romania; Miquel Barcelo, Ediciones B, Barcelona, Spain; Andreas Björklind, Linköping, Sweden; Piotr W. Cholewa, Katowice, Poland; Bess Cornelia, ARD, Munich, Germany; Sylvie Denis, Cognac, France; Andrea Druschba, Bavaria Film GmbH, Geiselgasteig, Germany; Rainer Erler, Perth, Australia; Nigel Fisher, Bangor, Wales; Mayumi Fujikawa, NHK, Tokyo, Japan; Einar Gjaerevold, Oslo, Norway; Neyir Cenk Gökçe, Sincan-Ankara, Turkey; Eva Hauser and Syril Semsa, Prague, Czech Republic; Ellen Herzfeld and Dominique Martell, Paris, France; Jyrki Ijäs, Helsinki, Finland; Tony Jerrman, Helsinki, Finland; Wolfgang Jeschke, Heyne Verlag, Germany; Solange Khaled, INA (Institut National de l'Audiovisuel), Bry-sur-Marne Cedex, France; T. Kobayashi, London, England; Werner Küchler, Munich, Germany; Shizue Kumano, Fuji Television, Tokyo, Japan; David Lally, London, England; Heidi Lyshol, Woking, England; Helen McCarthy, London, England; Jürgen Marzi, Koblenz, Germany; Franz H. Miklis, Nussdorf, Austria; Hiroshi Miyagi, Osaka, Japan; Sam Moskowitz, New Jersey, USA; Alison Packman, Revelation Film Group, London, England; Larry van der Putte, Amstelveen, Holland; Eugenio Ragone, Bari, Italy; Roger Robinson, London, England; Yuri Savchenko, Moscow, Russia; Andy Sawyer, Science Fiction Institute, Cheshire, England; John Spencer, Surrey, England; Junko Takao, London, England; Amanda Tolworthy, Manga Entertainment Limited, London, England; Francis Valéry, Bordeaux, France; Bruno Valle, Rapallo, Italy; Bradley S. Warner, Tsuburaya Productions Co. Ltd., Tokyo, Japan; Bridget Wilkinson, London, England; Pawel Ziemkiewicz, Katowice, Poland.

Jill Fornary for editorial assistance and invaluable research into European and Japanese television, and Japanese comics; Cangy Venables for editorial assistance; Nick Goodall for specialist photography; Leigh Priest for compiling the index; Daniel McCarthy for artwork on page 66 and DTP design assistance; and Lorna Ainger for picture assistance.